From Civil Rights to Human Rights

POLITICS AND CULTURE
IN MODERN AMERICA

Series Editors

Glenda Gilmore, Michael Kazin, Thomas J. Sugrue

Books in the series narrate and analyze political and social change in the broadest dimensions from 1865 to the present, including ideas about the ways people have sought and wielded power in the public sphere and the language and institutions of politics at all levels—national, regional, and local. The series is motivated by a desire to reverse the fragmentation of modern U.S. history and to encourage synthetic perspectives on social movements and the state, on gender, race, and labor, on consumption, and on intellectual history and popular culture.

From Civil Rights to Human Rights

Martin Luther King, Jr., and the Struggle for Economic Justice

Thomas F. Jackson

PENN

University of Pennsylvania Press
Philadelphia

10   9   8   7   6   5   4   3   2

Published by
University of Pennsylvania Press
Philadelphia, Pennsylvania 19104-4112

Library of Congress Cataloging-in-Publication Data

Jackson, Thomas F.
    From civil rights to human rights : Martin Luther King, Jr., and
    the struggle for economic justice / Thomas F. Jackson.
        p.   cm. — (Politics and culture in modern America)
    Includes bibliographical references (p.   ) and index.
    ISBN-13: 978-0-8122-3969-0
    ISBN-10: 0-8122-3969-5 (cloth : alk paper)
    1. King, Martin Luther, Jr., 1929–1968.   2. Human rights—United
    States.   3. African Americans—Civil rights.
    E185.97.K5 J34   2007

                                              2006050930

In memory of

my mother, Dorothy R. Jackson,

and a dedicated mentor, Michael F. Foley

The essence of being human is that one does not seek perfection, that one is sometimes willing to commit sins for the sake of loyalty . . . and that one is prepared in the end to be defeated and broken up by life, which is the inevitable price of fastening one's love upon other human individuals.

George Orwell

I won't have any money to leave behind. I won't have the fine and luxurious things of life to leave behind. But I just want to leave a committed life behind.

Martin Luther King, Jr.

Contents

Introduction

Over the course of his public ministry, between the Montgomery bus boycott of 1956 and the Memphis sanitation workers' strike of 1968, Martin Luther King, Jr., wove together African American dreams of freedom with global dreams of political and economic equality. King opposed racism, imperialism, poverty, and political disfranchisement in increasingly radical terms. Often he referred to the American civil rights movement as simply one expression of an international human rights revolution that demanded economic rights to work, income, housing, and security. For most Americans, however, King's freedom dreams have become a sound bite recorded in August 1963 on the steps of the Lincoln Memorial, when he envisioned a world where all men sit down together at the table of brotherhood and children are judged "not by the color of their skin, but by the content of their character." King overshadows the mass movement that made him famous, his sharp, dissident critique compressed into simple messages of nonviolence and American democracy celebrated as an accomplished fact rather than thwarted as a deferred dream.

Few Americans recall the discordant notes with which King began his legendary speech at the March on Washington for Jobs and Freedom. One hundred years after Lincoln's Emancipation Proclamation, Negroes still wore shackles of segregation, discrimination, and impoverishment. They existed "on a lonely island of poverty," banished to "the corners of American society." The nation's founders had issued a "promissory note" guaranteeing life, liberty, and the pursuit of happiness to all Americans. But the check bounced when black Americans tried to collect. "We refuse to believe that the bank of justice is bankrupt. We refuse to believe that there are insufficient funds in the great vaults of opportunity of this nation," King's voice boomed from his electronic pulpit. Negroes were demanding "the riches of freedom and the security of justice."[1] The March on Washington pushed to the foreground economic needs and demands that reflected the movement's broadening social base and ongoing northern struggles for jobs and justice. Dreams of economic justice had long been central to the black freedom struggle and to King's social gospel vision. Though activists could speak of winning civil, political, and economic rights in sequence, many also considered these human rights as mutually reinforcing and international in scope.

By 1965, King's radical voice rang more clearly when he confessed that his dream had turned into "a nightmare." The dream shattered when whites murdered voting rights workers in Alabama, when police battled blacks in Los Angeles, when he met jobless and "hopeless" blacks on desperate Chicago streets, and when he saw hunger and poverty in rural Mississippi and Appalachia. But King picked up the shards of his shattered dreams and reassembled them into more radical visions of emancipation for all poor people. As he preached on July 4, 1965, "I still have a dream that one day all of God's children will have food and clothing and material well-being for their bodies, culture and education for their minds, and freedom for their spirits." Later that year he dared to dream: "One day men will no longer walk the streets in search for jobs that did not exist . . . one day the rat-infested slums of our nation will be plowed into the junk heaps of history."[2] Dreams of decent jobs, affordable integrated housing, and adequate family incomes remained central to King's public ministry until his death.

As the first half of this book makes clear, King's vision of economic freedom was rooted in his intellectual development and early experiences in the southern black freedom movement. Since the 1956 Montgomery bus boycott, King had repeatedly urged blacks to dream of a world free of racism, militarism, and "materialism." For King, materialism encompassed the irrational inequalities of wealth under the American system, the "tragic exploitation" of a racially divided working class, and the morally corrosive and socially isolating obsession with individual success. As early as 1956, King publicly described his dream of a world in which "privilege and property [are] widely distributed, a world in which men will no longer take necessities from the masses to give luxuries to the classes," a "world in which men will throw down the sword" and learn to love and serve others.[3]

Movement veterans never forgot King's radicalism. In the accurate, sardonic words of Vincent Harding, King's legacy has been compressed into "safe categories of 'civil rights leader,' 'great orator,' harmless dreamer of black and white children on the hillside." Documenting King's radicalism but overstating the degree to which the events of the 1960s radicalized him, David Garrow argued in his seminal books that King transformed himself from a "reassuring reformer" into "a radical threat" to America's class system and dominant institutions. By November 1966, King concluded that the movement's most stubborn obstacles "were economic rather than legal, and tied much more closely to questions of class than to issues of race," Garrow argues. It is true that in 1968, King affirmed publicly what he had denied ten years earlier: that blacks were engaged in "a class struggle." But since the 1940s, King consistently had understood race *and* class as mutually reinforcing structures of unequal power. As a young man, King recognized racism's "malignant kinship" with the nation's class-based power structures; over time, his understanding of their deeply intertwined roots only became more sophisticated.[4] In 1956 he committed himself to winning "political and economic power for our race." Later he advocated liberation from the coercive control of the "slum colony" that had been constructed by public agencies and private interests to isolate and exploit poor and working-class blacks. King's early critiques of the southern "oligarchy" and of "business control" over the state became more thorough indictments of state capitalism as it reinforced middle-class and corporate privilege and consigned jobless and poorly paid workers to reserve armies of "cheap surplus labor."[5]

Even in the 1950s, King was never simply a "civil rights" leader unconcerned with the national political economy. Many authors echo Adam Fairclough's notion that King was a "non-ideological pragmatist" before he was radicalized in 1965, that he regarded racism as a southern problem and was only vaguely concerned with capitalism. Like his father, King advocated thrift, hard work, "economic individualism," and self-help, Fairclough argues.[6] Again it is true that King in 1965 stopped preaching that the Negro should lift himself up by his "bootstraps."[7] But King was much more radical, earlier and more consistently, than he is credited for being. He always conceived of self-help to include collective mutual aid and black political assertion as much as individual self-improvement. Self-help was perfectly consistent with broad social and governmental "action programs." King also denounced the more "subtle" but equally insidious forms northern racism assumed, especially segregated and unequal housing. He criticized "class systems" that segmented black America, even when he did not openly call for an American class struggle. Historians have rediscovered the underlying continuity of "individualist" civil rights goals and "collectivist" social welfare goals in the freedom movement since the 1930s, while others document consistent white resistance to black assertions of basic constitutional and economic rights in the North and South before the 1960s. Those who argue that a dramatically radicalizing freedom movement precipitated its own decline in the mid-1960s overlook the continuity and ferocity of both black assertion and white resistance.[8]

King's opposition to racism, war, and poverty did grow more overtly radical in the 1960s as the nation became polarized over these issues. He advocated increasingly militant protest tactics, from boycotting and marching to civil disobedience and mass urban disruption. He hoped the national government would move from guaranteeing legal protections for civil and voting rights to spending billions of dollars for full employment, income guarantees, and massive reconstruction of urban communities. Yet King was already radical by 1964, even as he tailored his messages to liberal or moderate audiences.

King did not rise up suddenly against poverty and war when American cities burned and Vietnamese villagers fled American napalm. His lifelong convictions grew from deep roots in the black freedom movement and the democratic left. He sought to win equality and political power for African Americans and to further economic justice for all Americans. As early as 1958, he called for world disarmament and a global war on poverty. His opposition to the Vietnam War in 1965 emerged from his lifelong internationalism.

King's ideology and leadership emerged from and fed back into the political culture of the democratic left. Throughout the 1950s, the non-communist interracial democratic socialist left opposed cold war militarism, white supremacy, and class power. In black churches and progressive seminaries, on college campuses and in many trade unions, a tradition of often religiously inspired democratic socialism that had been vibrant during the 1930s and 1940s endured through the Red Scare of the 1950s. Historical studies of northern movements, women activists, and national civil rights organizations reveal that a locally diverse nationwide black freedom movement gained momentum much earlier than the 1950s. Many activists believed that racial and economic justice were indissoluble. Appreciating the movement's most immediate roots in the New Deal and the Popular Front of the late 1930s and 1940s, we no longer speak of it in narrowly southern terms or entertain the fiction that the movement "moved north" after 1964. Since the 1930s, national civil rights organizations continuously pursued a "dual agenda" of civil rights and economic justice, Charles and Dona Hamilton show. Race "has always been fused with class in the political struggle to obtain equitable policies" for black people.[9]

King absorbed and popularized this radical interracial American tradition. But radicals of the 1960s tended to dismiss King's ideas, for he and his social democratic circle stood outside the student-led New Left and offered alternatives to revolutionary Marxism and revolutionary nationalism.[10] King criticized Marxism for its materialism and for its subordination of the person to the state. He opposed revolutionary black nationalism for espousing political violence, failing to develop solutions to metropolitan inequality, and denying that African Americans' destiny is bound up with that of whites and other racial-ethnic groups. King and his circle offered radical alternatives in response to disillusioning setbacks in civil rights, economic policy, and foreign policy in the mid-1960s. They criticized the insufficient funding and undemocratic structures of Lyndon Johnson's War on Poverty. Though critical of nationalist economic strategies, King nevertheless used nationalist terms of analysis to oppose institutional racism in employment, housing and the local administration of education, welfare, and criminal justice. He struggled to find nonviolent alternatives to the uprisings that convulsed the nation's ghettos between 1964 and 1968. His synthesis of nonviolence, integration, black power, and social democratic planning for full employment was a powerful challenge to the centrist liberalism of Kennedy and Johnson.

To trace the development of King's radicalism therefore requires careful attention to change, continuity, and above all, context. King indeed spoke of phases in the movement's strategic objectives. Early movement protests asserting African American "dignity" on buses and at lunch counters cost the nation little, but by 1964 the movement demanded costly programs to guarantee "opportunity" for everyone. "It is not a constitutional right that men have jobs, but it is a human right," he asserted in 1965.[11] Just as often King spoke of deeper continuities in the movement's commitments to winning civil and economic rights. King's activism, sermonizing, rhetoric, writings, correspondence, and interviews reveal a continuous evolution in his thinking through changing contexts, rather than a radical departure at a specific juncture. Almost every radical "set piece" historians cite from King's final years can be found in some form much earlier. King has been variously interpreted because he varied his rhetorical repertoire in relation to diverse audiences. Like Walt Whitman, he could contradict himself because he sought to contain democratic multitudes. King kept basic terms of liberalism and radicalism constantly in play, and the continuities are remarkable. His dialectic of prophetic vision and political strategy transcended any singular tradition or influence, religious or secular, black or white, American or international. Already on the left as a result of his upbringing, his education, and his immersion in traditions of black and interracial activism, King by 1965 was further radicalized by the movement's praxis, its dynamic interplay of theory and practice, and especially the tension between high expectations and painful disillusionment that the 1960s presented. Rooted in Christian social gospel traditions, King drew on the legacy of civil rights unionism and democratic socialism, on the inspiration of anticolonial movements, and on the intellectual ferment on the democratic left as it confronted cold war liberalism. After 1965, the "social learning" and the "emergent ideas" of the movement itself radicalized King and many others.[12]

Contexts of Influence and Persuasion

Veteran organizer Robert Parris (Bob) Moses once compared King to a single wave in the vast ocean of the movement, inviting scholars to turn from the study of King to collective and grassroots movements. Historian Nathan Huggins responded that "the person in history is important" and that King's enormous wave can teach us much about the ocean.[13] This study examines the wave and the ocean and their relationship. As an interracial ambassador, mobilizer, mediator, prophetic dreamer, and politician, King remains exciting today as a lens through which to view the social, ideological, and political crosscurrents of his time and the traditions of thought and action that shaped him.

To understand King fully, we must understand who inspired him and whom he sought to persuade: early influences, advisors, fractious colleagues, media interpreters, critics, competitors, and vilifiers, national leaders and local activists, humble people he sought to empower and powerful people he sought to bend. King appealed to the broad white middle class, whose idealism and political energies were essential to dreams of a renewed liberalism. He depended on and needed the cooperation of militant black activists in mobilizing people at the grassroots. He increasingly believed that poor black folk were his primary constituency in any successful war on racism and poverty. King played multiple roles, even when they threatened to tear him apart. The tension between his media celebrity and his identity as an indigenous mass leader was especially agonizing. The publicity he received as a result of the Montgomery bus boycott anointed him interpreter of the civil rights movement to whites. But King was also a mobilizer, seeking to empower black people through politics and protest, not just make their goals acceptable to whites.[14]

King often described himself as a mediator between moderates and militants, avoiding two ineffective extremes: on the one hand traditional Negro leaders bargained with whites and won concessions, but became beholden to white patronage and unresponsive to black communities; on the other hand revolutionary hotheads inspired the masses to action, but provoked repression and wrecked chances for interracial reconciliation. King's solution was to remain un-bought and nonviolent, which he achieved with the help of 50,000 Montgomery blacks in 1956. In 1963, King embraced a more coercive nonviolent strategy that orchestrated local confrontation to dramatize southern racism to the world and force federal government intervention to protect equal rights and dismantle the most egregious forms of white supremacy. Though the Southern Christian Leadership Conference (SCLC) did not engage in sustained local community organizing, the Birmingham crisis of 1963 and passage of the 1964 Civil Rights Act confirmed for many the power of this strategy of "nonviolent theater." Until his assassination, King continued to pursue this strategy in the hope of shaping national policies involving voting rights, poverty, urban power, and international peace.

King also faced the challenge of assembling and holding together a progressive coalition that could build power locally and orchestrate pressure for change nationally. Although local organizers saw the world differently from social democrats concerned with national economic planning, King knew that social change came when grassroots movements and national initiatives converged. King conceded in his last book that he had not been an effective local "organizer" of people in an ongoing struggle. Ella Baker and the Student Nonviolent Coordinating Committee (SNCC, pronounced "snick") criticized him for flying into communities with ongoing movements, drawing media attention to dramatic confrontations, and then leaving others to pick up the pieces. But, whether blacks faced police dogs or "slum colonialism," King countered that such problems could not be resolved locally when black people faced intractable elites and structures of metropolitan inequality. King therefore developed powerful strategies to arouse larger constituencies and move the federal government to protect civil rights and end poverty. King underestimated the resistance of elites, the ferocity of white working-class racism, and the shallowness of white middle-class supporters out in their suburban refuges of racial innocence and complacent individualism. He expected too much from the federal government and the strategy of protest. Arguably his failings were also America's. King appealed to the central tenets of liberalism—equality, justice, freedom, community participation, a belief in positive government. He never abandoned these terms, but he concluded that radical means and radical new constituencies would have to mobilize power against compromised liberalism and resurgent conservatism.

King himself, journalists, and ordinary people all shaped and contested his symbolism as "the American Gandhi." Although political celebrity is properly the subject of another study, it structured many of the dilemmas King faced. White journalists and news consumers proved overwhelmingly concerned with the possibilities of violence inherent in nonviolent protests. They placed King in dualistic opposition to militants such as Malcolm X and asked who would win the loyalties of the black urban masses. Reporters confined King to narrow "frames" of "civil rights" leadership that minimized his demands for more costly changes in public policies on jobs, housing, and welfare. Invariably, King was cast as "the general" and local leaders his "lieutenants" in a way that obscured the array of community issues and roles that local leaders, especially women, played in the grassroots organizations that did not make the headlines but certainly made history.

King's concern with forging coalitions across lines of race and class helps explain the diversity and eclecticism of his evolving ideas. He hoped to energize and coordinate three broad political constituencies. First, African Ameri-

cans needed to unify across class lines, joining the resources and leadership of
the black middle class to the protest energies of "the masses." Accordingly,
King criticized middle-class black individualism and consumerism by insisting
that Christian service mattered more than worldly success. Second, reaching
across racial lines to white leaders and the white middle class, King mixed religious idealism and secular American traditions of equal rights. Liberals, especially in the North, had to be galvanized to support equality in schools,
neighborhoods, and corridors of government, to look beyond their suburbs of
sovereign privilege and act in the interest of the metropolis as a whole. King
was adept at stretching the terms of civic nationalism toward ideals of social
democracy. Equal rights to integrated education and political participation
depended on fulfillment of human rights to economic security and dignified,
well-paid work. King stretched the meaning of integration beyond desegregation and colorblind fairness to demand structural changes in the geography of
homeownership, the relations and compensations of work, and shared political power. In his third and most difficult mobilizing challenge, King hoped to
revive the insurgent populism of the 1930s and the civil rights unionism of the
1940s. Dreaming of a powerful Negro-labor alliance for "democratic socialism" that was committed to organizing workers, especially in the anti-union
South, King eventually sought to mobilize a "legion of the deprived." He
dreamed of uniting organized and unorganized workers, the unemployed,
welfare-reliant mothers, and the poor of all racial-ethnic groups. Only the
most progressive interracial unions—the meatpackers, the hospital workers,
and the public employee unions—stood by him to the end. The mainstream
of the labor movement chose to defend its racial privileges in jobs and housing
and maintain its loyalties to the Democratic Party and Lyndon Johnson over
the risky alliance King offered.

Despite the prominence of women as grassroots leaders in community-
based organizing for civil rights, King's discourse, models of leadership, and
policy solutions all showed gender biases common to many of his contemporary male civil rights leaders and ministers. Though dedicated to the racial
struggle, movement women wanted respect for their contributions, for their
grassroots-oriented organizing styles, and for the issues that concerned them.
Recent scholars criticize King's "sexism" without examining his complex relationships or the concepts of black "manhood" (which black women often
shared) that structured black resistance. Though King made it clear he wanted
a wife and homemaker, he married a strong, independent woman in Coretta
Scott and did not narrowly circumscribe her public role. Yet, for most of
King's career, the "Negro" in his rhetoric was gendered male, seeking to be
the family breadwinner and asserting himself in politics as a courageous free-

dom fighter. "The Negro does not want to languish on welfare rolls anymore than the next man," King wrote in 1964.[15] Black men deserved a "family wage" sufficient to support their wives and children, he believed, even though black married women had a long history in the paid labor force. A few black women activists challenged this norm, but black feminism did not fully develop as an independent theory until the 1970s. Most African American men and women shared aspirations for white recognition of black "manhood," and many black women's definitions of freedom involved not being compelled by poverty to slave in white kitchens. Arguably, King never fully abandoned the ministerial tendency to speak "for" the poor rather than acting as a catalyst for their own self-emancipation. But in his later years King displayed a growing appreciation of women's difficulties and contributions as mother workers, wage workers, culture carriers, and community leaders. Septima P. Clark criticized King's sexism but came to appreciate his support for her grassroots citizen education efforts. She also admired the fact that he incorporated women's welfare rights agenda into his own in 1968. King demanded adequate incomes for women whose primary labor remained child rearing, as well as guaranteed jobs and decent wages for both men and women.

Dilemmas and Dreams

King's dilemmas were those of the postwar black freedom movement and American left. With his keen dialectical habit of mind, King struggled to resolve tensions between race and class, political and economic empowerment, moderate and militant nonviolence, American constitutional rights and international human rights, equal opportunity and compensatory justice, cold war freedom and anticolonial liberation, self-help and government activism, integration and black power. King suggested syntheses that could help forge effective progressive coalitions in diverse movement contexts. Usually we hear King echoing the values and languages of specific audiences, yet challenging them with antithetical truths, stretching their terms of understanding and prodding them to think and act in new directions. King offered syntheses that transcended false dichotomies of theory and action.[16] For example, for black militants and the whites they frightened, King redefined black power to mean full integration into America's political and economic institutions. For those disappointed with the limitations of Lyndon Johnson's War on Poverty, King offered a synthesis of local empowerment, affirmative action, urban reconstruction, and full employment to benefit all workers.

At its most basic level, King's nonviolence aimed to transcend the destructive alternatives of passive acquiescence to oppression and revolutionary violence, both of which perpetuated hierarchies of power and engendered lasting resentments. Before 1956, King was already steeped in an African American Gandhian tradition that called for close identification between leaders and masses in the struggle. During the Montgomery bus boycott, King embraced the requirements of national and international Gandhian symbolism; as northern Gandhians pressed him to rid his home of guns and bodyguards, King adopted a philosophical as well as tactical commitment to nonviolence shared by few southern activists. The moderate side of the Gandhian symbol called for restraint, responsibility, and reassurance. But King's nonviolence was not an ideology of containment or a denial of militancy. He continually defied others' definitions of proper Gandhian action and often asserted the radically egalitarian implications of Gandhian nonviolence. Nonviolence demanded genuine equality among the oppressed as well as equality with and independence from oppressors. Most important, King had to pragmatically confront entrenched white assumptions that almost any political assembly of black people might initiate mass violence and must be forcibly suppressed. Even liberal politicians and journalists saw nonviolent street protests as unjustifiable provocations to violence. Protesters exercising their First Amendment rights were held responsible for "unrest" and "racial tensions" unless it was absolutely clear that brutal violence had been forced upon them. King and SCLC found ways to dramatize to the nation the inherent violence of white supremacy. But, as Pat Watters and Reese Cleghorn have argued, mainstream news coverage amplified the national obsession with violence. Reporters tallied up "box scores of broken heads" without substantially explaining the creative and potentially redemptive power of nonviolence. And in covering the action, they typically downplayed the constitutional and economic grievances motivating black protest.[17] King's political commitment to nonviolence was informed by a realistic appreciation of the history and possibility of lethal white repression, a fear borne out tragically in the late 1960s.

In seeking to forge progressive coalitions, King confronted complex dilemmas of race and class. Unprecedented postwar prosperity and the growth of the middle class coincided with persistent poverty and racial exclusion. Most poor people were white, but higher proportions of blacks and other minorities were poor, unemployed, and ill served by often discriminatory public institutions, such as welfare and police departments and schools. Widening class stratification increasingly strained the idea of a black "community," although an increasingly prosperous black middle class could supply leadership and resources for the racial struggle. Could the black freedom movement unify across lines of class and forge enduring alliances with members of all races disadvantaged by class? The racist oligarchy of the South, the chief obstacle to national reform, seemed unconquerable without a revival of the left-led, class-based Negro-labor alliance of the 1930s and 1940s. That required a creative approach to anticommunism as well as white supremacy. The movement also needed a strategy to transform white class ideology and political alignments across metropolitan landscapes of relative racial and class privilege. Blacks' most immediate competitors for jobs, housing, schooling, and services were working-class whites, who King and the movement challenged in many sites. Their fierce resistance corroded the possibilities for an interracial working-class alliance, as had been the case since the 1940s at least. Middle-class whites in suburban refuges beyond the reach of black protest could afford to disdain working-class racism and support Dr. King—up to a point. King tried to persuade them that the homes and neighborhoods they regarded as individual class achievements were in fact massively subsidized collective spaces of racial and class privilege. Business elites, politicians, and middle-class whites needed to be persuaded or coerced into redistributing political and economic power, easing the burdens of integration on the black and white working class by creating jobs, housing, and secure family incomes for all. King and his circle tried, but never resolved these dilemmas of class coalitions and power. For example, their campaign to challenge metropolitan inequality by marching on homogenous white working-class neighborhoods in Chicago's inner suburbs in 1966 did little to galvanize ghetto blacks, strengthen the working-class coalition, or awaken the conscience of the middle class to press Congress to pass open housing legislation. King then looked to mobilize poor people of all ethnicities to dramatically march in Washington, D.C., in 1968, hoping to pressure government and the middle class to wage a real war on poverty.

America's crusade against international communism existed in some tension with the American left's allegiances with movements of national liberation in Asia and Africa. King frequently spoke as a cold war liberal, hoping that U.S. competition with the Soviets and Chinese Communists for the loyalties of the world's "uncommitted peoples" would compel the United States to end homegrown apartheid, which became dramatically visible on the world stage with the spread of new media of mass communication. But King's principal loyalties were with emerging nations shucking off colonial rule. The southern black freedom struggle and anticolonial movements were both expressions of a global human rights revolution against "political domination and economic exploitation." New nations had to overcome economic underdevelopment and poverty, which were the legacies of colonialism. So too was African American poverty the legacy of slavery and segregation; political empowerment and civic equality necessarily pointed to economic emancipation as a precondition for full freedom. King consistently argued that rich Western nations had moral and political responsibilities to redress global poverty, something they would never do without world disarmament. In the 1950s, he began a lifelong commitment to ending the South African apartheid regime through nonviolent resistance and international trade sanctions. Ultimately, King completely abandoned liberal cold war nationalism in favor of an anti-imperialist critique of U.S. intervention in Southeast Asia and Latin America. Because of the Vietnam War, King denied that American military power was anything other than an instrument of economic imperialism. America could still become a beacon of multiracial democracy, but not as an empire imposing its will on other peoples, and not when it remained riven by class and racial inequalities.

King looked beyond the false choices of self-help, mutual aid, and government economic activism. American Negroes confronted great challenges derived from serious dilemmas, he often said in the 1950s. Southern modernization was eroding white supremacist folkways and opening opportunities to blacks. Competing with whites in a "new age" of widening opportunities, while still afflicted by manifold disadvantages of segregation, the Negro must strive even harder than the white man, he preached.[18] And yet, insisting there was nothing automatic about progress, King increasingly denounced persistent and "murderous" job discrimination all over the nation, which only vigorous government enforcement of fair employment laws could remedy. By the early 1960s many activists—King among them—concluded that "fair employment practices" legislation at the state level had not addressed the group effects of discrimination or the structural roots of mass unemployment affecting all workers, especially low-skilled black workers earning the lowest wages. Should African Americans regard themselves as individuals entitled to equal opportunity, or as members of a group entitled to "special treatment" in compensation for historic and ongoing racism? King's trip to India in 1959 taught him about the Indian government's array of special programs to assist the untouchable caste, and by 1961 he began arguing vigorously for group compensation. By the election of 1964, King transcended both equal opportunity and affirmative action strategies, demanding full employment and family income supports that would benefit all Americans. Public-sector programs to guarantee economic security constituted the fertile soil in which self-help efforts could flourish, he argued, not the sterile ground of permanent dependency. King sought black inclusion in the political economy in alliance with poor whites, but he recognized that the process would transform the architecture of American power and opportunity in fundamental ways.

In the 1950s, King envisioned a synthesis of mass direct action protest and voter registration as powerful alternatives to cumbersome and elitist NAACP legal strategies. SCLC failed to make significant breakthroughs until students forged their own protest movement in 1960, however, after which the whole movement discovered that voter registration and direct action could powerfully work in tandem. But King concluded by 1962 that the dangerous dialectic of black assertion and white repression was irresolvable locally. The South and therefore the nation could only achieve equality through crises that forced the national government to make good on its promises of support for desegregation, and protection for civil liberties and political participation.

One of the movement's greatest challenges stemmed from a dilemma of political and economic disempowerment. Whether confronting southern oligarchies or northern power structures, black activists risked devastating economic reprisals. When politicians and business elites mobilized massive resistance to southern desegregation and voter registration campaigns, thousands of rights activists faced job loss, eviction, coordinated denial of public assistance, and loss of credit and supplies crucial to their farms and businesses. Southern voter education and registration campaigns especially were crucibles where the pursuit of black political rights led activists to confront poverty, dependency, and white economic power. White dominated urban political machines in the North also wielded enormous economic power and used reprisals to suppress independent political challenges. African Americans found ways creatively to wield economic power at the point of consumption through community boycotts. They organized to relieve economic dislocation and achieve economic independence through black-owned businesses and cooperatives. These became essential bases for political assertion. Blacks also fought for rights within white-dominated institutions: they sought equal educational and employment opportunity and equal access to welfare state benefits as a fundamental right and precondition of their political citizenship. Blacks needed economic power and autonomy to protect their movement from devastating reprisals. They also needed political power at every level to secure access to public services and job opportunities, equal protection of the law against violence and reprisals, and effective nondiscriminatory educational and social policies.

Class, gender, and racial inequities had been woven into the decentralized New Deal state, which promised security for everyone but in many ways favored middle-class and working-class white men and their dependents. For example, domestic and agricultural workers—disproportionately women and minorities—fell outside of minimum wage, Social Security, and collective bargaining protections created in the 1930s and 1940s. Blacks faced inordinate discrimination in welfare, the administration of the GI Bill, and the distribution of benefits from federal housing policies. King fought to bring African American workers and the unemployed into the safety net, hoping to cleanse the American welfare state of its racism and provide universal full employment and income security on the model of Scandinavian social democratic states.

The black struggle for power intersected in complex ways with Lyndon Johnson's new War on Poverty, begun in 1964, which promised more power and economic benefits than it could deliver. King supported the efforts of activists to expand the resources and democratize the administration of the poverty war. He wanted blacks to benefit because they were disproportionately poor, and because the disadvantages of discrimination and concentrated poverty affected them most severely. King insisted on attention to race and institutional power in the context of a poverty war Johnson wanted to remain free of racial conflict or costly economic redistribution that the middle class might reject. But King did not want the programs to be publicly perceived as disproportionately benefiting blacks, lest they be attacked as "preferential treatment" or "welfare" for the undeserving. Unfortunately, the War on Poverty was conducted on a scale so limited and so identified with pacifying urban upheaval that this outcome became almost foreordained. King's challenge then became one of reconciling necessarily race-specific programs with full employment and income support policies that would benefit all Americans. The War on Poverty also created new dilemmas by bringing activists off the streets into bureaucracies and separating them from the people King knew must be mobilized politically if any effective war on poverty and racism was not to wither on the vine for lack of constituent support. King's central insight was that the problem of poverty was the problem of power, and that poor people needed to be mobilized politically to realize the nation's promises of economic opportunity and emancipation.

Economic Freedom Movements and King's Pilgrimage to Democratic Socialism

Many traditions of thought and sites of social learning informed King's expanding human rights vision. The theological and social perspectives he absorbed in his youth were foundational (Chapter 1). In the Great Depression, King's father and grandfather were social gospel preachers committed to this-worldly service to the poor and to black people's political enfranchisement. King was influenced by his father's left–New Deal concepts of social and economic rights and his Baptist social mission to "preach the gospel to the poor."

By his teens, through experience King had become aware of the "malignant kinship" between poverty and racism. King embraced an egalitarian Christianity critical of both capitalist and communist materialism from his many academic mentors and popular black and white Protestant preachers. His Christian socialism was also clearly influenced by the many books he read during his ten years of higher education. King's own writings reveal he was a committed socialist and Gandhian by 1950. He found ample grounds for opposing the corruptions of wealth and the exploitation of the poor in the Old Testament prophets, the Gospel of Jesus, and in social and religious thinkers and activists such as Walter Rauschenbusch, Mordecai Johnson, and Howard Thurman. For King, Gandhi was not merely a practitioner of nonviolence and anticolonial struggle but an exemplary leader who took a vow of poverty and adopted an untouchable daughter, proclaiming his personal identity with the poor and the importance of equality within the struggle. King also found in the works of American theologian Reinhold Niebuhr an evolutionary socialist schema for sanctioning social struggle to redistribute political and economic power.

Paradoxically, the Montgomery bus boycott vaulted King to an unprecedented celebrity and simultaneous identification with poor black folk (Chapter 2). King shed some of his ministerial elitism as he plunged into the daily struggles of thousands of working-class people asserting their dignity and coping with the economic warfare that lay at the core of the protest. King's Gandhian and Christian identification with "the least of these" gained substance and commitment as he faced the personal risks of mass leadership. As whites coordinated massive economic retaliation, King grew to appreciate both the economic power of the independent black middle class and the economic resilience of working-class blacks. Increasingly, however, King had to develop viable strategies to counteract economic reprisals which threatened to throw politically active blacks into poverty.

As an emerging national leader in the black freedom movement, King played his many roles skillfully, sharpening a rhetorical repertoire he carried into the 1960s. He preached about nonviolent restraint and constructive self-help to local people and national supporters who were nervous about communism and uncontrolled mass action. Along more radical lines, proclaiming his allegiances to anticolonial struggles, King challenged black religious leaders to forsake materialism and dedicate themselves to moving the masses and challenging capitalism. King's role as chief spokesman and fundraiser for the boycott brought him in touch with trade unionists, especially leaders of the interracial United Packinghouse Workers and A. Philip Randolph, who led the all-black Brotherhood of Sleeping Car Porters. They raised King's sights to the potential of a powerful working-class alliance against southern white supremacy. After a year of struggle, a dramatic victory over Montgomery's segregated buses inspired King to dream of a regional movement challenging the entire system of segregation and inequality. Blacks had a right to level off the high mountains of privilege and raise up those trapped in dark valleys of oppression, King concluded.

A mass nonviolent movement did not follow the formation of the SCLC in 1957, as massive white resistance repressed efforts to spread direct action and expand the black southern vote (Chapters 3 and 4). As SCLC acting executive director, Ella Baker criticized King's disappointing lack of commitment to direct action and ideals of shared leadership that might make room for women and youth. King's celebrity and role as chief SCLC fundraiser kept him away from local fields of struggle. But fame also brought widening ideological horizons and closer contacts with New York leftists, interracial trade unionists, and a national network of Gandhians committed to pacifist internationalism and left-liberalism. During King's two trips to India and Ghana, he discussed political economy with Ghana's president, Kwame Nkrumah, leader and spokesman for the Pan-African movement, and India's prime minister, Jawaharlal Nehru, whose nonaligned socialism and advocacy of "atonement" for centuries of untouchability inspired King. King kept his socialism relatively private in a place and time where red baiting and race baiting suppressed movements for basic constitutional rights. But he also openly supported leftist causes in the United States. And King's support for anticolonial struggles included searing indictments of militarism, war, and global economic inequality.

Influenced by his new contacts in the democratic left, King's first book, *Stride Toward Freedom*, outlined the dream of a Negro-labor alliance to overthrow the southern oligarchy and bring social democracy to the nation. King interweaved cultural and structural explanations for black poverty. He would not shy away from group self-criticism in talking about black crime, "illegitimacy," or political apathy. But he repeatedly made clear that all of these "pathologies" constituted social and psychological adaptations to historic and ongoing oppression. A national effort to wipe out poverty, ignorance, and disease, together with political mobilization on the scale experienced in Montgomery, was the only way to eliminate black poverty and "improve the Negro's personal standards" through constructive social action, he wrote.[19]

When dramatic student sit-ins at whites-only lunch counters spread in 1960, King sought to support them and guide them toward wider struggles against segregation and economic injustice. King in turn was radicalized by the students' courage, willingness to fill the jails without posting bail, and commitment to emancipating poor black folk in isolated rural communities. Organizing for southern voting rights also had radical implications. King incorporated into SCLC's programs Septima Clark's Citizenship Education Program, which trained southern activists to teach literacy and promote voter registration. Often coping with local economic reprisals, the voting rights field workers increasingly addressed issues of governance and community life, equal access to welfare and disability benefits, and better housing, jobs, and public services for black communities. In myriad ways, black southerners discovered for themselves the links between civil and political rights and their aspirations for economic citizenship.

After the 1960 election, King shared many black activists' growing disillusionment with Kennedy's cautious liberalism, especially his refusal to fulfill his campaign promise to desegregate federally subsidized housing developments (Chapter 5). Cross-fertilizing southern and northern movements raised the political salience of jobs, housing, police brutality, welfare, anti-unionism in state policy, and racism in conservative trade unions. In the Kennedy years, King analyzed the alliances of public authority, private interests, and racial privilege that lay behind the spreading "second ghettoes." King also called upon the U.S. to imitate the Indian government's policies of "atonement" for the untouchable caste, in order to compensate blacks for their accumulated disadvantages and help them overcome their ongoing oppression. King further strengthened his ties to progressive labor unions, supporting New York's hospital workers in their drive to unionize and A. Philip Randolph's challenge to discrimination within the AFL-CIO. Randolph raised alarms about a looming crisis of mass black unemployment, while National Urban League executive director Whitney Young openly feared that a growing northern urban "underclass" would soon explode in revolt. Socialist Michael Harrington articulated widespread belief among northern activists that poverty derived not only from unemployment and inadequate welfare policies but also from institutional disempowerment in relation to the police, urban renewal authorities, educational bureaucracies, and city hall. King shared all of these concerns. Additionally, in 1962 SCLC inaugurated Operation Breadbasket, its first effort to address the crisis of joblessness that became King's principal preoccupation as he pursued desegregation and voting rights at mid-decade.

Southern voting rights struggles and direct action campaigns raised consciousness about southern poverty and drew King back into contact with masses in motion. In Southwest Georgia, the Albany Movement of 1961–62 radicalized King's public discourse, highlighting his appreciation of how poverty suppressed citizenship and how southern modernization would not benefit African Americans unless they joined with powerful government allies and compelled southern elites to extend equal opportunity. By 1962–63, working-class and poor people's issues reoriented what has conventionally been characterized as a movement with "middle-class values and leadership." "What good is a hamburger in a desegregated restaurant if you cannot afford to pay the check?" was widely asked in the movement by 1963. The growing chasm between liberal promise and performance pushed King in a radical direction. How could the movement achieve equal access to public accommodations for blacks and translate those gains into equal opportunity? How could they turn voting rights into shared power? These became the dilemmas of the mid-1960s.

The Birmingham protests and the 1963 March on Washington for Jobs and Freedom (Chapter 6) illustrate the many intersections between civil and economic rights both locally and nationally. The Birmingham protests began narrowly focused on pressuring downtown merchants to desegregate their stores and hire black clerks. King hoped the "economic power structure" could be forced to lend its support for broader municipal desegregation and employment. Soon, confrontations between nonviolent protesters, brutal police, and "bystanders" escalated into an international media event. King and Fred Shuttlesworth of the Alabama Christian Movement for Human Rights (ACMHR) decisively won the desegregation demands but were unable to overcome stronger white resistance to hiring blacks downtown and throughout the city. Nevertheless, as members of the white business establishment hid their faces, the SCLC leaders proclaimed victory in both jobs and desegregation, affirming their coequal importance in the evolving movement.

After Birmingham, King joined A. Philip Randolph in calling for a March on Washington demanding labor market reforms that would address the youth unemployment crisis of the 1960s. Seeking to limit civil disobedience and avert violence that might embarrass the United States, the Kennedy administration and moderate civil rights leaders successfully quashed plans for anything more than a one-day rally. King was not a major force in moderating the march's tactics or goals, and he joined the march's leaders in vigorously pressing the case for economic reforms upon a reluctant Kennedy administration. Kennedy favored desegregation of public spaces, but black leaders and activists insisted on job creation programs in the context of an economy battered by unemployment due to technological advances and five years of sluggish growth. Decent wages, desegregated housing, federal protection for civil rights workers, federal enforcement of nondiscrimination in employment, and guaranteed jobs were at the center of the "dual agenda" by 1963. Between the summer of 1963 and the summer of 1964, Presidents Kennedy and Johnson turned away from a promising opportunity to bring civil rights and economic policy into coordination, to implement employment and wage policies that might have addressed the root causes of a crisis of joblessness that persisted for the rest of the century.

When Lyndon Johnson declared war on poverty in January 1964, King had developed a sophisticated indictment of economic racism (Chapter 7). The spring protests in St. Augustine, Florida, confirmed that desegregation would not emancipate most black people from poverty or dependency on white employers. The passage of the Civil Rights Act and the War on Poverty in the summer, coupled with a looming white backlash, caused King and his associates to broaden their attack on economic racism to accommodate the needs and fears of the white poor. They advanced proposals going far beyond "special treatment" for Negroes or simple job training and education for the unskilled and the jobless. For the first time King advocated a guaranteed annual income and speculated that a real war on poverty might require mobilizing an interracial movement of the poor, a coalition much broader and more radical than the liberal-religious-labor-civil rights coalition the 1963 March on Washington had pulled together.

From 1964 on, King confronted urban rioting, an accelerating white backlash, rising black nationalism within the movement, and the contradictions of cold war liberalism itself. Nowhere were these contradictions more evident than in black people's struggles for power and purpose in the War on Poverty, which King insisted must marshal adequate resources, fight racism, and democratically enfranchise poor citizens in local governance. King's support for the Mississippi Freedom Democratic Party that summer brought to the fore his criticism of the ostensibly color-blind but deeply racist conservative politics of opposition to welfare, crime, and government activism. King responded to race riots in Harlem and Rochester, New York, by blaming socioeconomic deprivations and proposing employment and housing programs to address the needs of urban blacks. Locally, King recognized that police brutality and urban institutional "powerlessness" contributed to the violence. But it would be two years before he would fully and openly incorporate police brutality and political poverty into his explanations of the urban revolts. After accepting his Nobel Prize in Norway, King began pointing to Scandinavian democratic socialist states as models for what the United States could achieve in fighting poverty and slums.

King struggled to translate black voting into shared power in the South, as he imagined direct action protests in the urban North against the racial ghettos (Chapter 8). His rhetorical commitment to the dream of an interracial Negro-labor alliance never became a priority for action, principally because he became preoccupied with the mounting urban crisis, the failings of the War on Poverty, and the diversion of national resources to war in Southeast Asia. White economic reprisals actually accelerated in the wake of the Selma protests and the passage of the Voting Rights Act in 1965, underscoring for King the need for simultaneous political and economic empowerment. SCLC helped local southern activists in their struggles to win a measure of control over anti-poverty programs and resources, which to a degree promoted literacy, education, and the organization of small black producers' cooperatives. By and large, however, the War on Poverty disillusioned those who hoped federal money would support political and economic emancipation. King fruitlessly tried to intervene in a bitter dispute in Los Angeles between city hall and neighborhood groups seeking representation in the poverty program. Weeks later, blacks in Watts came into violent conflict with police, and King returned to the smoldering city to mediate its divisions and challenge Mayor Sam Yorty, President Johnson, and the nation to meet the crisis of urban violence with genuine democracy and economic opportunity.

The limited scope, elite control, and paternalism of many local wars on poverty stimulated black militancy, as did the rapid shift in funding and policy priorities to the Vietnam War in 1965 (Chapter 9). King was not centrally involved in the controversy over the Moynihan Report on the Negro family or the White House conferences of 1965 and 1966. But he criticized Lyndon Johnson's apparent abandonment of his vaunted promises of African American "equality as a fact and a result." King disagreed with the paternalistic assumptions behind Moynihan's policy perspectives and the War on Poverty itself. Again he acknowledged that "pathology" and self-destructive behavior afflicted black poor people. But he insisted that ongoing racial exclusion and class exploitation in the modern metropolis principally accounted for these problems. A grassroots democratic movement for urban renewal involving poor people as partners rather than clients of government would be the key to reconstructing the urban ghettos and giving poor people a sense of optimism and constructive purpose, King and many others argued.

By 1966, King was a relentless critic of the broken promises of the War on Poverty, as he increasingly sought to integrate local mobilization and national policy reform. King had explicitly rejected metaphors describing poverty as a cycle or culture in which parents purportedly transferred deviant norms to their children from generation to generation. Now he insisted that poverty was a structural pillar sustaining low-wage urban labor markets and that poverty derived from changing but relentless forms of oppression imposed upon poor people, generation *after* generation.

In his most thorough set of policy recommendations before Congress in late 1966, King advocated guaranteed work for the unemployed, a raise in the minimum wage for the working poor, and a federally guaranteed minimum income for those outside of the labor market. A society built on abundance could no longer distribute its rewards only on the basis of traditional forms of work. Service, self-fulfillment, and citizenship were public goods worthy of remuneration, King argued. To break down ghetto walls, King called for a long-range program of urban desegregation and open housing that could integrate the metropolis across wide racial and class lines. Over the short term, he called for more resources to strengthen core institutions in the ghetto: schools, housing, and community centers offering recreation and health services. To remedy black powerlessness, King called for a shift in power from bureaucracies and city halls to more responsive neighborhood agencies in accordance with federal promises of "participation" for the poor in planning their own war on poverty. King called for voter registration drives and legal recognition for tenant and welfare unions. His policy alternatives synthesized an array of critiques on the democratic left.

King's radicalization accelerated as Mayor Richard Daley's control over the War on Poverty in Chicago helped thwart political mobilization in 1966 (Chapter 10). His experience in the Chicago Freedom Movement provided King with a new analysis of urban political economy. From the "color tax" that black renters paid absentee landlords in segregated housing markets, to the coercive control exercised by local welfare caseworkers and police, to the high ghetto walls erected by suburban realtors, banks, and white homeowners, King analyzed the architecture of what he called the ghetto "prison." He promised to dismantle "domestic colonialism" and end "slum exploitation." Initially putting resources and organizational talent into neighborhood and tenant unions, SCLC found in the summer of 1966 an issue, housing discrimination, around which to stage dramatic confrontations in working-class white suburban neighborhoods. The limits of the resulting agreement with Mayor Daley and the real estate industry led King to explore a range of possibilities for local economic development and political empowerment: welfare and tenant unions, community organization, voter registration, neighborhood adult literacy programs, and Operation Breadbasket, which coordinated community boycotts to pressure employers to hire disadvantaged workers. The limitations of these strategies and the failure of black power proponents to develop economic programs on a scale adequate to the challenges of concentrated urban poverty led King and his circle of advisors back to the drawing board. Congressional legislation mandating open housing had failed in 1966, but again King looked to the federal government to develop policies that might resolve the dilemmas of unequal metropolitan space and power by pouring federal resources into democratically directed urban reconstruction, designed to provide decent housing and create millions of jobs for dislocated workers. How to tap into the largest resources of white class power without provoking massive white resistance remained King's most difficult dilemma.

King struggled to find nonviolent alternatives to the ghetto uprisings that convulsed the nation between 1964 and 1968. When Chicago police clashed with black youth in 1966 and Newark and Detroit were aflame in 1967, King now described them as revolts not just against socioeconomic "conditions" but against "powerlessness," joblessness, police brutality, and institutional racism (among other factors). "Powerlessness" he conceived not as a psychological state, as did many liberals and social scientists, but as a relational condition of unjust disempowerment. Nonviolent grassroots struggles and violent rebellions profoundly shaped King's emergent understanding of political poverty.

King made the lonely Gandhian decision to oppose the war in Vietnam in light of its corrosive effect on civil liberties, the War on Poverty, and the left-liberal coalition (Chapter 11). By the spring of 1967 King dramatically advanced a radical critique of U.S. economic imperialism, transposing the terms of his earlier critiques of British imperialism. King's most radical public statements indicted the U.S. government for using military force to secure multinational corporate interests in foreign markets. More frequently, King denounced the deadly U.S. air and ground war, questioning President Johnson's self-appointed roles as world policeman and democratic redeemer of a country he failed to understand. The convergence of domestic and international crises underscored for King the importance of racial justice and economic redistribution in America and around the world. The developing world needed a new Marshall Plan, and to outgrow its nationalism and economic individualism United States needed to undergo a "revolution of values."

By the summer of 1967, with the lethal cycle of urban violence and white backlash propelling Congress and the administration rightward, King decided that the way to end the Vietnam War and revive the war on poverty was to amass a coalition of poor people capable of escalating civil disobedience to the point of dislocating the functioning of a city (Chapter 12). With his sights set on Washington, D.C., King attempted to forge this new, bottom-up, multiracial coalition of the jobless, the working poor, and welfare-reliant women. From women's welfare rights activism, King had recently learned a great deal about gender inequities in the welfare state. Poor people from urban ghettos, the Mississippi Delta, and Appalachia—African Americans, European Americans, Native Americans, and Latinos—would all join this crusade. King's detour to Memphis in March 1968 was meant in part to dramatize the plight of the working poor and the importance of unionism to the interracial struggle for economic justice. He died supporting sanitation workers on strike against the city, supported by a remarkable community–trade union alliance for economic justice.

As evidenced by the demands of his final campaign, the Poor People's

March on Washington, King confronted governmental power more than corporate control of the means of production. Selectively reading opinion polls, King overestimated the strength of liberalism and underestimated the power of resurgent conservatism. His solutions usually looked to the federal treasury and to an expanded public sector to reconstruct the metropolis and guarantee jobs and income. King was sure that the government had acted to privilege the middle class and white suburbanites at the expense of minorities and the poor. A publicized march to the center of America's civic culture, the Lincoln Memorial, might nonviolently mobilize the poor, pressure Congress, and awaken the conscience of the individualistic and racially innocent suburban middle class. King died believing in the possibility of democratizing the state and the economy through "a bottom-up coalition," exposing himself to what seemed like an inevitable assassin's bullet in the service of that dream.

After King's death, the egalitarian nonviolent dream he shared with many on the democratic left impelled the organizers of the Poor People's March forward. "Resurrection City," the shantytown they built on the Washington Mall, sank in a sea of mud and bad publicity. The campaign lost the focus on dramatic militant civil disobedience that King envisioned. But the appeals and actions of multiracial activists testified to years of social learning in the struggle. King was part of a much broader movement, participating in and contributing to a tradition of thinking about race and poverty that outlived him. Despite efforts to canonize King and consign pieces of him to elaborate political reliquaries, fuller and more accurate pictures of his mature radicalism survived, especially among grassroots organizations working for international justice, peace, minority rights, union rights, and the empowerment of poor communities.

Martin Luther King confronted but never resolved tensions between Gandhian symbolism, political power, and his own humanity. King colluded in his own construction as the American Gandhi by the celebrity culture, but he could not control the inevitable contradictions between his private and public selves, between his self-awareness as a flawed human being and his outsized mythic persona. Called to leadership by the masses, almost as an accident of history, repeatedly affirming that he must reflect popular militancy or be cast aside, King was also expected by whites to guide the masses with near unlimited charismatic power. He often confessed to a sense that he did not deserve his honors, and lived most of his life with relentless defamations and harassment from people no less powerful than FBI Director J. Edgar Hoover. On tape and film, the fearless voice often could not hide the anguished face. Accepting responsibilities far beyond anyone's capacities, knowing full well celebrity was not power, he counted on the enduring power and resilience of his charismatic leadership. Showered with tributes, relentlessly accused of corruption, he accepted his honors and defended his integrity and humility. Accepting the Nobel Peace Prize in 1964 on behalf of the movement and donating all of the $54,000 prize money to civil rights organizations, he caught hell at home for neglecting his children's educational needs. "I am conscious of two Martin Luther Kings," he once told his mentor Rev. J. Pious Barbour. "The Martin Luther King that the people talk about seems to me somebody foreign to me." Pulled in every direction by his advisors with little time to reflect, King suffered from relentless and intensifying vilification by reactionary whites and a growing judgment among militant blacks that he was both grandiose and irrelevant. But in opinion polls he was always black people's favorite leader, with 88 percent approval ratings in 1963 and 1966. He could joke in 1957 about how long he would be expected to pull rabbits out of his hat. By 1967, nonviolent miracles became imperative, as urban violence fueled reactionary and repressive political forces. By all accounts, it was a miracle in the last year of his life that he could sustain his sharply dissident voice between bouts of almost incapacitating depression. But he had strong spiritual medicine: his ancestors had overcome shattered dreams by struggling together and clinging to hope.[20]

Chapter 1
Pilgrimage to Christian Socialism

Martin Luther King's family and mentors immersed him in a river of collective memory stretching back to slave times. His father escaped the exploitative sharecropping system in 1918, becoming a prosperous minister in Atlanta by the time Martin was born in 1929. But poverty was still a near neighbor. Why were so many people "standing in bread lines," King, Jr. asked in 1934 in the midst of the Great Depression. By his teen years he knew that the "inseparable twin of racial injustice was economic injustice." It was the source of his "anti-capitalistic feelings," he recounted in a 1950 autobiographical essay. The family's security could not hide "tragic poverty" all around him, evident in the hunger and tattered clothing of his playmates. His grandfather's Ebenezer Baptist Church was also a community center providing food, clothing, medicine, and childcare for wage-earning mothers. "Whosoever carries the word must make the word flesh," its pastor, A. D. Williams, preached.[1]

King scaled heights of achievement in both black and white society. But he remained acutely aware of his roots in the collective strivings of ordinary African Americans. King met Howard Thurman in 1953 during his final year studying for a Ph.D. at the School of Theology at Boston University (BU). Thurman had traveled far from his own poor rural roots, graduating from Morehouse College and Rochester Theological Seminary and becoming dean of BU's Marsh Chapel that year. King had read Thurman's book, *Jesus and the Disinherited,* in which Jesus is portrayed as a "poor Jew" and a social revolutionary. In chapel King sat shaking "his head in amazement at Thurman's deep wisdom," his roommate Philip Lenud recalled. King adopted Thurman's description of slavery as a "low, dirty and inhuman business." How had slaves built spiritual defenses against fear, humiliation, and violence? Thurman recalled his grandmother tell of an open-air gathering of slaves who had assembled to hear a sermon. In a "triumphant climax," the slave minister exhorted them, they were neither "niggers" nor "slaves" but "*God's children!*" "Something welled up within them," King later preached, as they sang, "I got shoes, you got shoes, all of God's children got shoes." It was not simply a ser-

mon of Reassurance. The social gospel promised shoes on earth, not just freedom in the hereafter.[2]

King described his "pilgrimage to nonviolence" in 1958, surveying his
nonviolent inspirations and theological development. King never wrote of his
parallel pilgrimage to democratic socialism, which is understandable given the
repressive anticommunist climate of the 1950s.[3] But the seeds of his mature
socialism are clearly visible in his youth and education. King emulated his
father and grandfather's social gospel ministries. As King learned Baptist
preaching, important mentors—Benjamin Mays, Walter Chivers, George
Davis, and Howard Thurman—fostered King's commitment to racial and economic equality. King read nineteenth-century critics of capitalism—Walter
Rauschenbusch, Edward Bellamy, and Karl Marx—at the same time that he
developed a repertoire of sermonic set pieces borrowing from now obscure
Protestant preachers, such as Harry Emerson Fosdick, Eugene Austin, and
Robert McCracken. In ways not fully appreciated, Reinhold Niebuhr's socialist
writings guided King's understanding of political and economic power, class
conflict, and class alliances, as much as Niebuhr shaped King's theology.

History and Heritage

King, Jr. inherited a determination to fight economic and racial injustice from
his family and community. We should not identify his or his father's values
too closely with their "bourgeois" class positions. They both witnessed poverty
firsthand, envisioned collective political action to overcome it, and disdained
acquisitiveness and class pretensions among Atlanta's black "bourgeoisie."
King, Sr.'s memoir, *Daddy King,* vividly recalls the dilemmas of resistance and
repression, despair and endurance that poor rural black folk faced after Reconstruction. Toiling in a rock quarry as a young man, his father, James King,
lost part of his right hand in an explosion. His employer fired him without
compensation. He returned to sharecropping, but landowners regularly
cheated him when they "settled up" the cotton crop. James King was treated
as "an object instead of a man," Daddy King (called "Mike") recalled. He
respected his father's hard work and occasional defiance of white authority.
But ultimately he judged him harshly for growing "old on somebody else's
land," a broken, bitter, alcoholic man. In contrast, King, Jr. later wrote, Daddy
King resisted segregation's "brutalities at first hand." Compelled to work the
fields, Mike attended school only three months a year. Whites saw him "first
as a worker" and only then as a child. As a naïve twelve-year-old, Mike protested when a landlord defrauded his father of money due him from the sale

of some cottonseed. The landlord publicly branded James King a trouble-maker and evicted the family. One breach of Jim Crow economic subordina-tion elicited harsh reprisals. King, Jr. learned from the history of his family and people. Emancipation freed blacks from "physical slavery," he later testi-fied, but they gained no "land to make that freedom meaningful."[4]

Survival, dignity, and resistance were grounded in communal life and in "the redeeming value of sharing," King, Sr. learned. His mother Delia King worked in cotton fields and kitchens to keep her family together, drawing Mike into church as a place of refuge and renewal. Delia taught Mike that making money carried an unacceptable price if it threatened personal safety, kin or family. He got a job heaving coal into locomotive engines at age four-teen—perilous work that nevertheless stoked his dreams of rescuing his family from poverty. The racially segmented southern labor market was harsh and unforgiving. Mike observed how bosses favored white workers in assigning extra work, as they in turn pandered to the bosses and denounced each other as labor agitators. It was the end of his childhood, he wrote. Delia King tracked down Mike and rebuked his boss for hiring her underage son. She also refused $500 in wages owed Mike, protesting that she would accept nothing that would allow anybody to exploit her child. Mike could not even reap the bitter fruit of his own exploitation.[5]

Mike King moved to Atlanta in 1918 with little money or education. Established middle-class blacks scorned his "rough, country" roots as he trained as a young preacher in the 1920s. He considered the elitism of Atlanta's black bourgeoisie to be as bad as white racism. But the turn-of-the-century Negro and mulatto upper class, whose status derived from serving elite whites, had to accommodate a new class of professionals and entrepreneurs who rose with the expanding Negro market—insurance men, realtors, businessmen, professors, and, of course, ministers. Mindful of their origins, many genuinely aspired to become "race men." They admired both Booker T. Washington *and* W.E.B. Du Bois, mixing strategies of race uplift through business enterprise and protest for equal citizenship rights. One of these, Reverend Adam Daniel Williams, the father of Mike's future wife, Alberta, took Mike King under his wing. "Change is coming whether the white man can handle it or not," he told Mike in 1920. Williams had arrived in 1893 from rural Georgia, filling Ebenezer Baptist Church with migrants swelling the Auburn Avenue neighborhood. Ministering to the poor and working class, he preached that every minister should be "an advocate for justice" all week long, not just on Sunday. Presi-dent of the Atlanta NAACP from 1917 to 1920, Williams agitated for voting rights and equal educational funding; he helped found Booker T. Washington High School, Martin Luther King, Jr.'s alma mater. King, Jr. grew up comfortably among ambitious people whose class consciousness was leavened by humble origins and a strong sense of racial solidarity and determination to fight the injustices of caste.[6]

King, Sr. rose quickly in black Atlanta, graduating from Morehouse College in 1930, marrying Alberta Williams, and inheriting the Ebenezer pulpit in 1931. Martin admired his father's political fight to equalize teachers' salaries and his protests of Jim Crow elevators in the courthouse. Ministers, unlike teachers, were comparatively immune from white reprisals, King, Sr. recognized, and had special obligations. In 1935, he led several hundred protesters downtown, demanding the ballot. Whites looked on dumbfounded; white newspapers never covered black protests. King, Jr. grew critical of his father's success ethic but admired his politics. He also seems to have picked up Daddy King's disdain for "slick businessmen" who profited from housing segregation and the low wages they paid black workers. "The poor, black and white, were taught to hate each other," King, Sr. recalled. "Businessmen made money from both." Martin clearly carried forward his father's conviction that "the masses had to take part in social change." Daddy King organized consumer boycotts targeting a "vital part of our city's life—its economy."[7]

Auburn Avenue gave King, Jr. a "deeply religious" identity, and both parents actively discouraged feelings of class superiority in their children. King recalled growing up in neither a crime-ridden "slum district" nor a refuge of the "upper class." This picture of frugal, middle-class solidity is at some variance with Daddy King's own claim to have been "the best paid Negro minister in Atlanta." But the black class structure was overpopulated at the bottom and fluid at the top, and nowhere near as stratified as white society. The Kings were not so far from humble origins to consider assuming aristocratic airs. King, Jr. wrote with pride of his father's scrupulous "saving and budgeting." Daddy King did not "live beyond his means" or show off his wealth. Early in their marriage, Martin cooked pigs' ears for Coretta Scott King. Being his "father's son," she recalled, he liked them because they were "good" and "cheap."[8]

"Before Black people in Atlanta had access to City Hall—much less occupied it," Martin's sister Christine King Farris recalled, "Dad was a voice for the voiceless . . . above all else, a man." Daddy King once rebuked a policeman for calling him "boy" as Martin watched in awe. "Manhood" meant confronting racism in the public sphere, demanding equal respect, treatment, and representation, speaking truth where others might fear or be unable to speak for themselves. Provisioning and protecting the private sphere created an intertwined meaning of manhood. Within the home, King, Sr. considered his authority paramount. But like her mother, Jennie Celeste Williams, Alberta Williams King was not caged in the private sphere: active in Ebenezer Baptist

Church, she directed the choir, frequently taking it on the road. Martin later mentioned only his mother's domestic roles, but in the context of racial oppression, black norms of middle-class motherhood differed from whites'. Strong men's characters contained "antitheses strongly marked," King often said. He acquired "the sweet gentleness of my mother and the strong, hard, rough, courage of my father." Alberta King in her "natural" sphere lavished "motherly cares" central to children's secure character development. When her children faced racism, she explained its history "as a social condition rather than a natural order," bolstering their sense of dignity and desert. When as young adults they showed off their fancy cars in the front of the house, she commanded them to move the cars out back, admonishing that "this is a sin because we're supposed to be serving the people." In this context, Martin learned to respect women first as mothers and culture carriers, and then as activists. King, Sr. exercised final authority over family decisions; Martin could not remember one family argument. His father's model of unquestioned authority surely influenced his leadership style. Many in SCLC recalled that King avoided heated debate, delegating strong antithetical positions to staff and reserving final decisions for himself. King's limits in appreciating women's leadership and issues must be understood against this background.[9]

King's father and grandfather shared commitments to economic reform and religious as well as secular ideals of social obligation to the poorest Americans. King, Sr. preached in 1940 to a Baptist association, quoting Jesus as he had quoted the prophet Isaiah in Luke 4:18: "The spirit of the Lord is upon me, because he hath anointed me to preach the Gospel to the poor; he hath sent me to heal the broken-hearted, to preach deliverance to the captives, and the recovering of sight to the blind, to set at liberty them that are bruised." Blacks facing severe discrimination and disproportionate unemployment had not yet begun to benefit substantially from the economic recovery driven by World War II defense production. Ministers must speak for the "broken-hearted, poor, unemployed, the captive, the blind, and the bruised," King, Sr. preached. "How can people be happy without jobs, food, shelter and clothes?" His son's last sermon at Ebenezer Baptist Church demanded he be eulogized as a servant of the bruised and captive poor, not as a Nobel Prize winner. Deciding on the ministry in 1947, King credited his father's example and an "inescapable urge to serve humanity" that seized him in 1944. In January of that year, Franklin Roosevelt promised an "economic bill of rights" that would extend rights to life, liberty, and the pursuit of happiness to include human rights to jobs, decent homes, medical care, old age security, collective bargaining, and living family wages.[10] In the age of radio and fireside chats (and soon television), how would the ministerial imperative to preach to and "speak for the poor" translate into mass politics? Would the voiceless poor recognize their own aspirations in King's words?

King, Jr. adopted this expansive notion of rights appropriate to a high-consumption society and a nation at war with racist "warfare states." As a high school senior in 1944, Martin won his way to the state finals of a speech competition sponsored by the Black Elks. His oration, "The Negro and the Constitution," pushed the limits of New Deal liberalism, weaving a powerful criticism of racial inequality into King's own evocation of social and economic rights. How could America achieve an "enlightened democracy" when Negroes remained uneducated and "ill-nourished," suffering from diseases that spread across all "color lines"? How could the nation remain whole while forcing people "into unsocial attitudes and crime"? How could America prosper with a whole people "so ill-paid that it cannot buy goods"? Victory over fascism abroad demanded "free opportunity" and victory over racism at home, King argued, echoing discourse of the wartime black Double V campaign. Invidious walls of caste blocked African American class and status achievement. The "finest Negro" lived at the mercy of the "meanest" white. Whites exalted a few Negroes and slapped down the rest "to keep us in 'our places.'" Tokenism was the norm. "Even winners of our highest honors face the class color bar," he stated. King spoke from experience. He had grown up acutely conscious of his exclusion from white schools, downtown stores, and theaters; he recalled seeing episodes of police and Ku Klux Klan violence on Atlanta's streets. And Jim Crow tainted even his teenage triumph. After tasting honor at the all-black competition, King rode home in his "place," forced to yield his bus seat to a white passenger. "It was the angriest I have ever been in my life," he recalled.[11]

Morehouse Mentors

King, Jr. entered Morehouse College in the fall of 1944, when his commitment to "racial and economic justice was already substantial." He immediately felt the magnetism of President Benjamin Mays, whom he acknowledged as one of his "great influences." The son of sharecroppers, Mays preached the ethics of political agitation and success through education, admonishing students to perform their work, however humble, "so well that no man living [or] unborn could do it better." King repeated these phrases verbatim in his sermons on black achievement in the face of adversity. Mays also preached the social gospel, writing in 1940 that "a religion which ignores social problems will in time be doomed." Religion must transcend all secular faiths, Mays argued, including communism, fascism, and "capitalistic individualism." King had other activist social gospel models, but Mays clearly stood out as a towering exemplar.[12]

As postwar cold war tensions intensified, Daddy King worried that Martin was "drifting away" from his own belief in "capitalism and Western democracy." The specifics of King, Jr.'s anticapitalism remain obscure until 1950, but he clearly thought that democracy was incompatible with capitalism built on exploitation and white supremacy. In 1946, a rash of racial murders swept the South as soldiers returned from World War II. King wrote to white readers of the *Atlanta Constitution* in conventional terms of postwar racial liberalism. Blacks merited full citizenship rights: the right "to earn a living at work for which we are fitted by training and ability; equal opportunities in education, health, recreation and public services; the right to vote; [and] equality before the law." Sounding more radical in a critique of black class power, King wrote to his "'brethren'" in the Morehouse newspaper in 1947. "The purpose of education," he wrote, was to expose repressive propaganda and sharpen social action. Yet most of his classmates thought education would help them forge "instruments of exploitation so that they can forever trample over the masses."[13]

A. Philip Randolph, president of the Brotherhood of Sleeping Car Porters, the nation's largest all-black labor union, addressed Morehouse in June 1945. Benjamin Mays welcomed to Morehouse radical race men who were committed to mobilizing, not just uplifting, the masses. Well before King met "the dean of Negro leaders" in June 1956, he was surely exposed to the "socialist thinking" that shaped his mature political philosophy. Under Randolph's threat of a massive march on Washington, Franklin Roosevelt had agreed to create the Fair Employment Practices Committee to ensure nondiscrimination in defense industries. At Morehouse, Randolph issued a Popular Front call to arms against global and American capitalism, fascism, and racism. The "purpose of education" was to equip people both to live within society and to change it. But Negroes were "devastatingly individualistic," he said. They were all witnessing "the breakup of a great civilization . . . the civilization of capitalism." Capitalism was turning into fascism to survive because "white and black, brown and yellow peoples" were revolting globally against "property relations" based on empire and coercion. "World financial materialism" generated rampant militarism to protect the "economic spheres of influence, trade routes, and political suzerainty" of imperial capitalist nations. The only alternative was socialism, he proclaimed. Racial "demagogues" would no longer manipulate the anxieties of white and black workers, who must together "climb up out of the ditch of economic, political and social backwardness."

What then could Morehouse men do? Serve the masses, said Randolph. "Establish organic contact with the people in the shacks and the hovels. There resides the power . . . They, the masses may be poor in property but they are rich in spirit."[14]

King's education continued on the shop floor. During summers off from college, he worked in factories, wanting to learn about workers' "problems and feel their feelings," classmate Lerone Bennett, Jr., heard him say. King hauled furniture at a mattress company and worked at Railway Express until he quit when the foreman called him a "nigger." King thought it outrageous that black men at the same jobs earned much less than whites. But King later stressed that "the poor white was exploited just as much as the Negro." His speeches consistently alternated between an appreciation of class exploitation crossing racial lines and the racial economic oppression specific to blacks, who worked for comparatively low wages in the South's "mean and dirty" jobs reserved exclusively for them.[15]

King chose the secular discipline of sociology as his major, graduating from Morehouse in 1948 at age nineteen. His advisor, Walter Chivers, exposed him to secular critiques of social inequality. A graduate of the New York School of Social Work, Chivers held no Ph.D. and had published no books, but his students revered him as a "cosmopolitan sociologist." Chivers had investigated rural lynchings and conducted field research on urban black poverty. King saved none of his writings for Chivers, but Bennett vividly recalled Chivers's argument that "money was the root not only of evil but of race." Chivers's own writings suggest a more complex bequest; his "situationist" sociology bears close resemblance to King's later views of race, culture, and poverty. Chivers surely supported King's challenges to Baptist propriety as he sorted out whether he wanted to pursue law, medicine, or the ministry. Chivers lambasted Morehouse's "puritanical Baptist Missionary heritage," describing how parents frowned on dancing, smoking, birth control, and Darwinian theory. Yet Chivers was awed by Negro ministers' "power over Negro masses," a potentially "destructive force" but also an untapped well of popular mobilization. Dynamic leadership developed in churches serving "common people," where ministers created new "avenues of public service" and free African American spaces. Nevertheless, Negro ills were "almost insoluble" in segregated locales and could only be healed through "conflicts and crises" that directly challenged the color line.[16] How could leaders isolated in segregated enclaves lead socially transforming confrontations with white power? How could segregated churches challenge segregation? Chivers hardly suspected his teenage student would grab both horns of this dilemma, mastering black and white vernacular speech and using churches as inspirational bases for nonviolent protests.

Chivers shaped King's developing understanding of culture and poverty. In Chivers's view, black poverty produced infant mortality, crime, and family instability, matters not of "race" but of "environment." Unemployment, job discrimination, poor housing, inadequate recreation, and lack of medical care severely stressed black people's physical and mental health. The Chicago School of Sociology had viewed crime and "social disorganization" as temporary obstacles in new migrants' progress toward assimilation and social and geographic mobility. Its critics saw caste and class as serious barriers to mobility, and "situationist" sociologists like Chivers suspected that a coherent lower-class culture compounded the problem. Harlem's poor people developed an "antisocial life-routine," he wrote, engaging in vice, numbers rackets, and petty crime. These were compensations for joblessness, tenant exploitation, and "economic despair," self-destructive, perhaps, but essentially "adaptations" to poverty and racism. When police disrupted Harlem's routines in 1935, suppressing the rackets and enforcing evictions of penniless people, "these abnormal people 'blew up,'" Chivers explained. The Harlem riot of 1935 was an uprising of people "emotionally unbalanced and neurotic from hunger and other deprivations." Grounded in an analysis of economic racism, Chivers's emphasis on psychopathology reflected what Alice O'Connor identifies as an "increasingly psychological" analysis of lower-class culture characteristic of the 1940s.[17] Situationists reemerged in the 1960s as the cities burned, and experts again debated culture and structure, economic stress and police provocation, the psychology of despair and the politics of violent protest.

Crozer and the Social Gospel Tradition

King attended the interracial but predominantly white Crozer Theological Seminary in Pennsylvania between 1948 and 1951. Founded by a Baptist industrialist, Crozer had become a bastion of the social gospel. King's liberal and progressive instructors nurtured his sense of a loving, suffering, personal God, creative in history and manifest in human service to those whom Jesus called "the least of these." King's exposure to liberal Protestantism and the social gospel presaged his later indictment of the intertwined "triple evils" of racism, economic exploitation, and militarism. Scholars have shown that King's "borrowing" of sermonic language from liberal Protestant preachers was a common practice among seminarians, more like musical homage than scholarship. In graduate essays, King usually quoted, rearranged, and commented on others' words, listing his sources in bibliographies. King chose material that reflected his core values and emerging social mission. One essay praised the Hebrew prophet Jeremiah for rejecting hierarchical religion as "organized hypocrisy" and offering a democratic, dissenting religion of the heart. An essay on late Judaism praised the patriarch Issachar, who practiced simplicity of living, joyful work for spiritual rewards, and service to God and the poor. The patriarch Zebulun modestly provisioned his household, then gave to "the sick, the aged and the needy [to] be blessed by God for his compassion." King agreed: "all wealth belongs to God," who sees no distinction between rich and poor. In an essay on Buddhism, King rejected the "narrow and selfish" Hinayana tradition in favor of Mahayana Buddhism, whose compassionate Bodhisattvas delay their Enlightenment to return to the cycle of life, death, and rebirth to serve "all suffering beings." King's lone history paper admired George Whitefield's ecumenical, learned, charismatic, and populist evangelical preaching. Whitefield's 1740 tour of the colonies ignited the Great Awakening, which touched "all classes," gave rise to abolitionism, and spread popular "concern for Indians and Negroes and underprivileged people."[18]

Of the all-white Crozer faculty, King felt closest to George Washington Davis, the working-class son of a Pittsburgh labor activist. King took seven classes with Davis, bathing in "warm evangelical liberalism." King peppered his religious analyses with observations of social contradictions and historical crosscurrents. One paper sought to synthesize liberal theological optimism with a neo-orthodox attention to sin: the South had a "vicious race problem," but the "noble possibilities of human nature" revealed themselves in the region's racial improvements. Davis introduced King to the concept of agape, which saturated his many sermons on nonviolence. Agape was the unconditional "sacrificial" love Jesus practiced, a counterweight to cold "commercial transactions" of modernity. Interdependence defined human life. We prosper not by our selfish efforts, King wrote, but by other people's sacrificial gifts "beyond our merit and deserving." Another essay exuded postmillennial optimism. The Kingdom of God would arrive not after apocalypse but gradually through people practicing "trust, love, mercy and altruism." King always preferred the social ministry of Jesus to the sufferings of Christ on the cross, though toward the end of his life he spoke increasingly of the cross he had to bear.[19]

King dreamed of a world at peace waging a global war on poverty. Breezily reconciling Darwinism and Christianity, King wrote of a God imminent in nature who guided humanity's "creative evolution." When Davis asked King to explain the problem of evil in a world created by a good and all-powerful God, King addressed the political and economic sins of militarism, poverty, and slavery. If knowledge were the only obstacle, humanity would "conquer poverty, for there is 'enough and to spare' for all," King claimed. If only we could substitute a crusade against poverty for the ceaseless "preparation of war." But God-given free will leads inevitably to human "selfishness, pride, greed, [and] lust for power."[20]

George Davis influenced King's understanding of the class system, and the moral and global costs of acquisitive individualism. With Davis, King read the writings of Walter Rauschenbusch, whose 1907 book *Christianity and the Social Crisis* indelibly marked King's evolving "social concern." Harry Emerson Fosdick's paraphrase of Rauschenbusch was good enough for King to use in later writings and sermons: "Any religion which professes to be concerned about the souls of men and is not concerned about the social and economic conditions that scar the soul, is a spiritually moribund religion." Rauschenbusch did not discuss racism, but King felt his horizons broaden precisely because of Rauschenbusch's analysis of class and poverty. King shared Rauschenbusch's love of the Hebrew prophets and the parables of Jesus recorded in Luke regarding the corruptions of the wealthy and the dignity of the poor. He often used the parables to decry the spiritual snares of individualism. The "rich fool" hoarded his property without thinking about his dependence on God or other people. "A victim of the cancerous disease of egotism, the fool failed to realize that wealth always comes as a result of the commonwealth," King preached. "Men no longer love the Commonwealth, because it does not stand for the common wealth," Rauschenbusch wrote. "Exploitation creates poverty." And Rauschenbusch linked capitalism and militarism in ways King openly professed by 1958. Rauschenbusch wrote,

When we comprehend how few wars have ever been fought for the sake of justice or the people; how personal spite, the ambition of military professionals, and the protection of capitalistic ventures are the real moving powers . . . then the mythology of war will no longer bring us to our knees. . . . In the same way we shall have to see through the fictions of capitalism. We are assured that the poor are poor through their own fault; that rent and profits are the just dues of foresight and ability . . . that we cannot compete with foreign countries unless our working class will descend to the wages paid abroad. These are all very plausible assertions, but they are lies dressed up in truth.[21]

King began his public ministry demystifying the moral fictions of capitalism and individualism. He ended it explicitly denouncing his own country's practice of imperial war in the service of profit.

Recent scholars rightly view King's "religious identity" in relation to his indigenous black roots. Yet King spent six years in predominantly white theological institutions, where his political identity, social vision, rhetoric, and language developed in ways appropriate to diverse audiences. How else could he have merged so well the languages of Baptist folk preachers, liberal Protestantism, and the democratic left? To ask who shaped King most decisively poses a false choice, an either/or King would have rejected.[22]

While King tasted a new freedom in the North, he discovered its hidden, two-faced racism. He had worked on a tobacco farm in Connecticut in 1944 and 1947, traveling "anywhere" he wanted, he wrote home. Crozer was a progressive interracial institution, and King was elected president of the senior class. But when King and three black friends insisted on service in a New Jersey tavern in June 1950, the proprietor fired a gun, later testifying he feared hoodlums would rob him. King dropped charges when whites refused to testify. King transcended his earlier "antiwhite" feelings, he wrote. But he did not shy away from confronting whites blind to any difference between black seminarians and criminals.[23]

American Gandhism

King had often discussed the Indian independence leader, Mohandas K. Gandhi, at Morehouse, friends recalled. But not until attending Crozer did he study Gandhi in depth. In the spring of 1950, Howard University president Mordecai Johnson lectured on Gandhi in Philadelphia. King found Johnson "profound and electrifying," and quickly bought a half dozen books on Gandhi. Johnson had followed Benjamin Mays and Howard Thurman to India to meet Gandhi during the 1930s. Gandhi led the nonviolent movement that freed India from British control, Johnson lectured, and then embraced India's "Untouchables as children of God." The Howard University Gandhians did not reduce Gandhi to a one-dimensional prophet of civil disobedience simply confirming black Christian beliefs. Black leaders had long appreciated Gandhi's vow of poverty, repudiation of Indian caste, the Indian economic boycott of British goods that Gandhi initiated and Gandhi's consequent efforts to develop home manufacturing. "We are all one—we the Despised and Oppressed, the 'niggers' of England and America," W.E.B. Du Bois had declared in 1919. In 1928, Mary Church Terrell praised Gujarati farmers who resisted British taxation and showed how the oppressed could resist "the rich and powerful." Gandhi's simple loincloth inspired Mordecai Johnson, who told Howard University graduates in 1930 to don the "cheapest variety of homemade overalls to let the Negro farthest down know that they are one." In 1936, Thurman heard Gandhi simultaneously blame India's poverty on colonialism and call on all Indians to assume responsibility for the indigenous depredations of class and caste. Gandhi adopted an untouchable daughter and changed the term "from outcaste to 'Harijan', meaning 'Child of God,' " Thurman wrote. These symbolic acts of solidarity reconciled and united Indians who remained demoralized and divided by inequality, thereby releasing "energy needed to sustain a commitment to nonviolent direct action." All of these themes resonate in King's later Gandhism.[24]

Johnson also resisted the ideological alignments of the cold war. The "free world," he told delegates to the 1950 Congress of Industrial Organizations (CIO) convention, had perpetuated its freedom for two hundred years "by the political domination, economic exploitation and social humiliation of over half the human race." No other single phrase so persistently rings through King's sermons on colonialism and domestic racism. Johnson's dissident anti-imperialism was remarkable in light of the CIO's mass expulsion of communists the year before, although it resonated with a deeply rooted black tradition of anti-imperialism. The United States could live in peace with Russia only if it initiated disarmament, Johnson told Howard University's 1951 graduating class. Then both nations could help unravel the West's "imperialistic habits." Anticipating King's call for a world war on poverty, Johnson urged the United States to sponsor a United Nations program of "economic reconstruction . . . to bring about adequate subsistence in food, clothing, housing and health for every human family of every race, color, nationality and culture on the earth."[25]

King's favorite book on Gandhi was British cleric Frederick Fisher's *That Strange Little Brown Man Gandhi,* according to Crozer professor Kenneth Smith. King would have learned from Fisher that Gandhi made his vow of poverty while aiding striking Indian miners in South Africa. Through their "poverty and struggle," the miners inspired Gandhi to put service above "personal gain." Gandhi was a high-caste Hindu and a British university graduate, but South African whites treated him as "simply a 'coolie.' " He went on to challenge attitudes of superiority among "the ruling classes in India, both brown and white, English and Brahman," Fisher writes. Gandhi linked militarism and capitalism, discerning in "the system of war the seeds of its own destruction," perceiving "in private capital the destruction or subversion of spiritual values." He was a "master dramatist" on the world media stage, Fisher argues, describing the highly publicized Salt March of 1930 in defiance of Britain's monopoly on salt production. King found the Salt March especially compelling. Beginning with one man's defiant symbolic act—"the simple act of holding aloft a pinch of free, untaxed sea salt"—it led to a protest involving millions. Finally, Gandhi wrestled with the dilemma of political independence and economic underdevelopment. "Britain's destruction of

India's handloom industries" retarded Indian economic progress long after nationhood came in 1947, Fisher reports. Gandhi's spinning wheel became a symbol of resistance and a source of work "for the largest body of unemployed in the world."[26]

Radicalism, Anticommunism, and Cold War Liberalism

Over the 1949 Christmas break, King preached at Ebenezer and read Karl Marx's *Das Kapital* and *The Communist Manifesto*. This deeply unsettled his father, who made few distinctions between Marxian socialism, atheism, and totalitarian communist regimes. J. Pious Barbour, a Baptist preacher, socialist, and family friend who welcomed King into his home for many conversations, recalled King's growing conviction that "the capitalistic system was predicated on exploitation prejudice, [and] poverty." Marx got the economics of capitalism right and it was time for "a new social order," King told Barbour. "Capitalism carries the seeds of its own destruction," King wrote in his notes in the spring of 1951. All systems carried such seeds, but capitalism failed "to meet the needs of the masses." Postwar waves of trade union strikes and popular support for socialized medicine signaled "a definite revolt" by the American proletariat, part of a global "move away from capitalism." Organized labor would eventually force the "nationalization of industry." What was "more socialistic than the income tax [or] the T.V.A. [Tennessee Valley Authority]?" King asked. President Truman's 1948 reelection had proved labor would soon be powerful enough to elect a president. True, capitalism was "trying all types of tactics to survive."[27] But King believed socialism was coming.

King's sunny optimism blinded him to the dark clouds already lowering upon the left. Congressional conservatives and the American Medical Association had fatally weakened the drive for socialized medicine by 1949. The income tax and the TVA proved perfectly consistent with corporate capitalism. The Popular Front of the 1930s and 1940s had sought to link domestic civil rights to a powerful labor movement, an expanded welfare state, and an anti-imperialist movement for democracy at home and abroad. Anticommunism broke many of those links and eviscerated the core institutions of the left, especially the unions. After the largest strike wave in American history in 1946, the Republican Congress passed the Taft-Hartley Act of 1947, overriding Truman's veto. Corporations and conservatives stalled union organizing by hampering basic tactics of labor solidarity and permitting states to pass "right-to-work laws" banning union shops (union shops required all new workers to join a union if the majority of workers chose to unionize). In the 1950s and

1960s, failure to repeal this provision (section 14b) was the greatest blow to the Negro-labor alliance that King dreamed might draw unorganized workers into a powerful progressive movement. Under Taft-Hartley, unionists also had to purge their "Communist" leadership or risk loss of legal protections for collective bargaining. The CIO expelled eleven left-led industrial unions with a million members in 1949—unions that supported civil rights, social welfare, and aggressive drives to organize unorganized workers. In the South, white supremacists manipulated fears of communism to stall Operation Dixie, the AFL and CIO's major drive to unionize southern industries. By 1950, the civil rights unionism that joined left-led unions to grassroots African American voters' leagues and robust NAACP chapters was seriously weakened. Mainstream unions withdrew from social democratic politics and organizing drives to focus on collective bargaining. Simultaneously, the NAACP made pariahs out of "fellow travelers" like W.E.B. Du Bois and Paul Robeson and helped shut down the Council on African Affairs, the main institutional vehicle for African American internationalism.[28]

King dreamed of socialism when even social democratic liberalism was on the ropes. Despite the promises of the New Deal and the Fair Deal, economic liberalism had been in retreat since the 1938 elections. Congressional conservatives abolished New Deal agencies responsible for public employment and economic planning during World War II. The 1945 Full Employment Bill would have targeted public investments on places and persons vulnerable to economic dislocation. The Employment Act of 1946 promised only maximum employment through fiscal and tax policies affecting aggregate economic growth. This moderate fiscal Keynesian orthodoxy in economic policy took root and lasted through the 1960s, despite continued social democratic challenges from the interracial left, including King's. Even Truman's attempt to revive the wartime Fair Employment Practices Commission (FEPC), an instrument for enforcing equity in federal contracting, was defeated. Truman's Fair Deal also proposed to abolish the poll tax, provide federal direct aid to education, and raise the minimum wage and broaden its coverage. But only veterans, the elderly, upwardly mobile white homeowners, and some public housing tenants saw gains by the time congressional conservatives roared back to power in 1950. The Korean War and McCarthyism stalled reform until the mid–1960s.[29]

As liberals increasingly severed civil rights from economic justice, race took on heightened urgency. Theologian Reinhold Niebuhr saw in the new racial liberalism a challenge to the New Deal faith that economic progress alone could further black "assimilation" into the mainstream. Prosperity and modernity were entirely compatible with persistent, even newer forms of racism, he argued. The powerful engine of postwar economic growth left millions behind. The economy surged ahead, stimulated by military spending and pent-up consumer demand. But federally sponsored southern industrialization did not equalize wages between whites and blacks or open opportunities in skilled jobs and technical professions. Moreover, the structural foundations for the urban crisis were already being laid. Black migrants poured out of the declining agricultural South into urban centers already beginning to lose manufacturing jobs, where walls of segregation had been reinforced by federal policy, banks, builders, corporations, and white working-class homeowners who used the language of New Deal rights to defend their "decent" homes and turf against black "invasion." Still, the cold war gave domestic freedom fighters new leverage; racism now became an international embarrassment to a U.S. government upholding the mantle of "free world" leadership. This advantage was severely blunted by the marriage between racial liberalism and anticommunism, however, which cut a wide destructive swath through the left.[30] How could minority rights and workers' rights be secured if racial liberalism separated the fight against class power and inequality from the antiracist agenda?

The cold war intellectual climate shaped King's public discourse, but he also resisted a liberalism that reduced racism to prejudice and separated racial and class inequality. Liberal social scientists and intellectuals studied the social psychology of race as they turned away from the political economy of race and class and lost faith in labor unions as the vanguard of social change. The Swedish economist Gunnar Myrdal had published his monumental *American Dilemma* in 1944, which had been a moral summons to America's egalitarian "conscience" and a broad social democratic program for intervening in the economy and providing opportunity for people Myrdal feared might become trapped in a permanent "underclass." The weakening of progressive forces in the late 1940s led social scientists to downplay his analysis of structural racism and focus almost exclusively on white prejudice. King eloquently appealed to white America's conscience in terms of this racial "moralistic liberalism," Walter Jackson argues. King believed liberal promises and used the cold war rhetoric of American freedom. Yet he never forgot that racism and class power were coequal and powerful forces shaping social structure. And though he often criticized racist union locals and conservative labor hierarchies, he retained a faith in the revitalization of progressive interracial and social democratic unions.[31]

After his exposure to the religious and academic left, King learned much about socialism from survivors of the carnage on the political left. Anticommunist socialists and social democrats continued to advocate civil rights, social democracy, and détente with the Soviets. King entered a circle whose key figures were A. Philip Randolph of the Brotherhood of Sleeping Car Porters, socialist and pacifist Bayard Rustin of the War Resisters League, New York lawyer and former Communist Party fund-raiser Stanley Levison, NAACP activist Ella Baker, Ralph Helstein of the United Packinghouse Workers of America (UPWA), and Walter Reuther, the powerful president of the United Auto Workers (UAW) and the CIO. The auto workers and the meatpackers became King's most generous financial backers in the 1960s. As Kevin Boyle has shown, Reuther envisioned not class struggle but "corporatist" cooperation among government, business, labor, and consumers. Like King, Reuther arrived at a dialectical "middle way" between communist statism and unfettered free market capitalism. America must steer a course between the "ideological nonsense which holds that the profit motive is the exclusive incentive for progress" and the "regimentation and dictatorship that characterizes total state ownership of economic resources." The CIO and the NAACP joined the liberal anticommunist bandwagon but did not renounce social democracy or economic justice. At the NAACP's forty-fifth convention in June 1954, CIO treasurer James Carey condemned the antiliberal, antilabor, anticommunist demagogues of the right. Free the South from "its obsession with race" and mobilize black and white workers against the racial and regional shackles on the New Deal, he exhorted. He dreamed of an America "where there is no endless chain of poverty from generation to generation—where monopoly does not make you a beggar for a job." After the merger of the AFL and CIO in 1955, progressives challenged union hierarchies to be more responsive to black aspirations for representation. The greatest challenge involved persuading white workers that in an era of recession and manufacturing job shrinkage, black workers were not the ones threatening them with beggary.[32]

Marx and McCarthyism

King's contacts with the labor left lay in the future. In the early 1950s, teachers, preachers, theologians, and Gandhians enlarged King's vision of racial and economic justice. He deplored McCarthyism, but his approach was very cautious. He frequently sermonized on the dangers of individual conformity and "adjustment" to a repressive social order. King's sermon "Transformed Nonconformist" drew language directly from the liberal Baptist Eugene Austin, who condemned anticommunism at King's 1951 Crozer graduation. America might travel the road "toward thought-control, business-control [and] freedom-control, until we land in totalitarianism," Austin warned. Federal workers were fired simply for advocating "peace and civil liberties" and "equal rights for all races and classes." Austin called on men of conscience to oppose "the anaesthetizing security of identification with mass movements," as did many anticommunist liberals in the 1950s who thought Joseph McCarthy was a "populist" threat to the republic. King, in sharp contrast, never abandoned the radical left's faith in mass action.[33]

King moved to Boston in the summer of 1951 to earn a Ph.D. in systematic theology at Boston University. He told his new girlfriend, Coretta Scott, that he was not pro-capitalist like his father and had no ambitions to wealth. "A society based on making all the money you can and ignoring people's needs is wrong," she recalled him saying. A small elite should not "control all of the wealth." King's frequent claim that capitalism took "necessities from the masses to give luxuries to the classes" has the ring of the late nineteenth-century Protestant critique of capitalism. After reading Edward Bellamy's 1888 utopian novel, *Looking Backward,* Martin wrote Coretta that he was "much more socialistic in my economic theory than capitalistic." In Bellamy's fictionalized America of 2000, state ownership replaced competitive capitalism, shared abundance replaced poverty, and industrial peace replaced class war. Private property led to "poverty with servitude," argued Reverend Barton, a voice for Bellamy in the novel. Bellamy synthesized prophecy and social science, and properly believed in peaceful evolution toward socialism, not violent revolution, King wrote.[34]

In criticizing capitalism and developing his own defense against charges of communism, King drew eclectically from Christian thinkers. After reading the writings of the Catholic theologian Jacques Maritain in 1951, King wrote that communism arose in response to "a Christian world unfaithful to its own principles." The popular Protestant preacher Robert McCracken supplied most of the wording for King's 1952 sermon titled "The Challenge of Communism to Christianity." Communism propounded "metaphysical materialism," "ethical relativism," and "strangulating totalitarianism." It lacked "moral absolutes" and quashed civil liberties. Under communism, "Man is made for the state and not the state for man." But King also praised *The Communist Manifesto* as a work "aflame with a passionate concern for social justice." Marx's devotion to a classless society made him almost Christian, said King. Marx championed "the poor, the exploited, and the disinherited," dreaming of "a world society transcending the superficialities of race and color, class and caste." But tragically, communist regimes created "new classes and a new lexicon of injustice."[35]

Marx also voiced King's lifelong anger at "the gulf between superfluous wealth and abject poverty," King preached and wrote in 1950s. The "profit motive" should not be the cornerstone of the economy. Morally, capitalism inspired men to be "more concerned about making a living than making a life." Money and status especially corrupted the middle class. We judge success by "our salaries or the size of our automobiles, rather than the quality of our service and relationship to humanity," King repeatedly stressed. Capitalist nations had already reduced inequality, though not nearly enough. King envisioned a synthesis of the two opposing moral philosophies. Capitalists could not see the truth in collectivism: "life is social." Marxists failed to see the truth in individualism: "life is individual and personal."[36] Marx exerted considerable influence over King's view of capitalism, but King remained circumspect and more deeply influenced by the American social gospel.

King did not praise the Soviet Union's racial policy or openly criticize private control of the means of production. When Melvin Watson, dean of the Morehouse School of Religion, heard King's sermon in August 1952, he alleged that King misunderstood Marxian materialism, the "disturbing" but irrefutable claim that human life was conditioned "*by the means of production.*" Watson charged King with ignoring the Soviet constitution's clear denunciation of racism, which grounded socialism's strong appeal in third world nations. McCracken had praised Soviet advances in literacy, workers' rights, women's rights, and the fight against "racialism." In 1952, both Benjamin Mays and Mordecai Johnson hailed Stalin's achievements in overcoming racism and poverty.[37] King rejected this line. Publicly, he denounced "the profit motive" but not corporate control of the means of production. Until 1963, and even thereafter, King generally attributed poverty to the unequal distribution of wealth and the government's failure to fulfill its responsibilities, without specifically indicting the corporate "captains of industry."

Niebuhr, Tillich, and Wieman

Black Christianity, Chivers's situationist sociology, the social gospel, Gandhism, and Marxism all informed King's opposition to racism, exploitation, poverty, and militarism. Reinhold Niebuhr helped him think through strategies of social change and specific dilemmas of political and economic power. By 1952, Niebuhr had abandoned the pacifism and socialism of his early career to embrace liberal anticommunism. Yet the socialist Niebuhr of the 1930s most profoundly influenced King. Scholars have long focused on Niebuhr's importance to King's theology and nonviolence, but not his influence on King's political economy. In the spring of 1952, King recalled, he devoured Niebuhr, almost "uncritically" swallowing all his "social ethics." King praised Niebuhr's early ministry to the Detroit working class in a paper on Niebuhr's ethics writ-

ten for his Ph.D. advisor, L. Howard DeWolf. King agreed that injustice
resulted from "the concentration of power and resources in the hands of a
relatively small wealthy class." Free markets could not create housing for the
poor, and squads of social workers could not address systemic injustices, Niebuhr argued, and King copied. Only Christian "'equalitarianism'" could
redress the inequality and "economic chaos" endemic to capitalism. Change
would come only by setting "the power of the exploited against the exploiters," King quoted with approval. King deemed Niebuhr's social analysis "profound."[38]

King's political economy and his understanding of the dilemmas of social
change were influenced by Niebuhr's *Moral Man and Immoral Society*, published in 1932. Niebuhr also helps us conceptualize the central dilemmas of
political and economic power preoccupying King at mid-century. Several times
King praised the book, lauding Niebuhr's insights into coercive power. Prac-
titioners of nonviolence must be responsibly coercive, Niebuhr argued. White
individuals might support black freedom, but "the white race in America will
not admit the Negro to equal rights if it is not forced to do so." Neither white
goodwill nor black violence could free Negroes from their "menial social and
economic position." Philanthropy, education, improvements in sanitation, and
police protection would never dismantle the foundations of black oppression,
which lay in the Negro's "political disfranchisement" and "economic disinher-
itance." What caused that? For Niebuhr, disproportionate economic power
over the means of production was the "root of social injustice." "The combination of political and economic power which the dominant classes set against
the worker in the modern state must be met by a combination of political and
economic power."[39] The words "political and economic power" ring powerfully
and persistently throughout King's discourse and gained radical force over the
years.

Given the strength of capitalist power, could the state democratize a class
society? Would oligarchies bend to the political and economic power of the
masses? Niebuhr was ambivalent; so was King. The only counterweight to concentrated economic power was "a vigilant and potent state." But proletarian
revolutions dedicated to classless societies generated their own oppressive class
systems and totalitarian states. As a graduate student, King approved of Niebuhr's call for democratic power "to resist the inordinate ambition of rulers."[40] He increasingly recognized the state as a central site of struggle, where
power was already stacked in favor of the privileged but where the powerless
could, with imaginative leadership and creative tactics, force concessions from
their oppressors.

King shared Niebuhr's threefold approach to democratizing the state:

moral appeals to the white majority; interracial working-class mobilization; and consolidated black economic and political power. Despite employers' power, industrial workers had forged new rights to organize and bargain collectively, exerting power on legislatures to pass income and inheritance taxes and welfare state protections. And nowhere had the "economically and politically weaker classes" reached their full strength. Furthermore, workers could mobilize middle-class allies. Welfare states had also emerged in countries where strong labor movements did not exist and exploited workers appealed to the "conscience of the community." Dominant classes might "recognize minimum social needs" as extensions of "previously accepted political and social principles." Traditional consensus symbols and rights declarations—the Declaration of Independence and the Constitution—grounded King's later claims for human rights to employment, decent housing, political participation, and guaranteed income. Finally, Niebuhr speculated that a farmer-labor coalition might bring about "melioristic socialism" in America. King held similar hopes for a labor–civil rights coalition and, later, a radical multiracial coalition of the "deprived" and the "powerless."[41]

Niebuhr touched on a dilemma all activists confront: how to sustain activist faith in the face of inevitably shattered dreams. "No one will suffer the perils and pains involved in the process of radical social change, if he cannot believe in the possibility of a purer and fairer society than will ever be established," he wrote. The dreams of imagined societies could be "dangerous because they justify fanaticism." But to abandon utopias was equally perilous, a capitulation to the "inertia" of the status quo. King frequently preached about how to sustain faith in the face of shattered dreams, which are "a hallmark of our mortal life." King David dreamed of building a Hebrew temple that he never finished. Saint Paul dreamed of preaching in Spain, but mourned his last days in a Roman prison. The only viable response was that of King's slave forebears: accept "inexpressible cruelties" and cling "tenaciously to the hope of freedom."[42]

Niebuhr showed King a way to mobilize Christian faith against the horrors of war and technological fanaticism. A paper King wrote for DeWolf in June 1954 grappled with several texts, including Niebuhr's *Nature and Destiny of Man*, written after the September 1939 Nazi invasion of Poland. Liberal Christianity, mystified by "optimistic charms of modernity," could no longer stand up to the "calculated cruelty" of trench warfare, death camps, and urban firebombing. To expect redemption through science or technology only fed "pride of power," which was itself the source of totalitarian repression. Niebuhr's line of reasoning left King purged of pride but grasping for hope. Niebuhr extended a frail lifeline: a chastened heart open to empowering grace could climb "heights of *Agape* normally impossible," King appropriated. Niebuhr offered sparse biblical theology, but Christ promised guidance as the "the everlasting mind of God" breaking through into human history.[43]

King moved to Montgomery, Alabama, on October 10, 1954, to pastor Dexter Avenue Baptist Church, where until April 1955 he balanced his pastoral duties with long early morning hours writing his dissertation. "A Comparison of the Conceptions of God in the Thinking of Paul Tillich and Henry Nelson Wieman" plagiarized material from a previous BU dissertation and various secondary and primary sources. King was moving quickly out of academia toward his ministerial calling and cobbled together note cards that lacked proper documentation. The dissertation made few social or biblical references, but King's selection of material does reveal ideals and ambivalences central to his emergent political ministry. King's Afro-Baptist heritage informed his acceptance of theological Personalism, the basis for his criticisms of Tillich and Wieman, both of whom rejected the idea of a God limited by personhood. Tillich described God as a powerful "ground of being," while Wieman thought of God as a "creative event" continuously infusing meaning and value into the world. Neither theologian provided a God whom King could worship. But King clearly liked Tillich's dialectical claim that justice depended on love, which could not countenance retribution (a theme echoed in King's later critique of capital punishment).[44]

King clearly preferred the naturalistic theology of the relatively apolitical American-born Wieman to the systematic theology of the German-born Christian socialist Tillich. As a chaplain in the German trenches during World War I and a refugee from Nazi persecution of the left, Tillich made no secret of his affinities with Marxist humanism. But King mostly attended to Tillich's highly abstract 1951 tome, *Systematic Theology*. Wieman comes through as more socially and politically grounded. History's greatest "creative event" was when the early Christians embraced forgiveness in the context of "intermingling races" in the Roman Empire. Divinely inspired creative human "interchange" could move history. Wieman also grappled with class hierarchy in a way King found compelling enough to copy at length. The "richest fulfillment" of human culture emerged from cosmopolitan elites freed from toil. But exploited majorities thereby suffered unnecessary pain and "hard labor," while most elites exalted their own desires over what was noble, beautiful or just. King came to believe that fulfillment and creativity lay within reach of the masses through democratic distribution of the common wealth.[45]

King's own Christian socialism structured much of his thinking regarding class and race, political and economic power. The need to appeal for black unity across class lines and for white majority support, together with the weakening of civil rights unionism, worked against King's overtly embracing a socialist program. But the terms on which King rejected Kennedy–Johnson liberalism were close to Niebuhr's early socialism. King embraced the faith that democratic socialism would be possible if black people could consolidate power, the poor could emancipate themselves, and the majority could see the justice of their cause.

"Lost Values" and Radical Dreams

Daddy King married Martin and Coretta Scott on June 18, 1953. Coretta insisted that her duty to "obey" be stricken from the marriage vows. She was a pacifist and a graduate of progressive Antioch College. Though she gave up her ambition to be a professional singer to be a preacher's wife, the couple accepted an ideology of companionate marriage that accorded her authority and gave her scope for public activism. Martin was not "self-conscious" about sharing housework, she remembered, for "he was too sure of his manhood." He thought women were as intelligent as men and capable of holding "positions of authority and influence." But for himself, he wanted a wife, "a homemaker, and a mother." Coretta King took seriously the job of raising children in a society that devalued them, and confronted her husband when she seriously differed with his judgments about the family's financial needs. Her father, Obie Scott, was "a poor but self-respecting land owner." When he became the first Negro in town to buy a truck, armed men threatened him and police arrested him on traffic charges. He bought a sawmill, and whites burned it and his house down. "Any assertion of black manhood was regarded by the ruling class as dangerous and was quickly put down," she commented in 1968. It was difficult "for black men to take their natural place as the head of the household and the protector of their families." Mrs. King spoke at prayer pilgrimages, peace rallies, and college commencements, performed concerts, and marched at Selma and in welfare rights demonstrations. Though, like Alberta Williams King, she did not work for wages, neither did she accept a narrowly circumscribed public role or a rigidly traditional marriage of "separate spheres." King was no feminist forerunner, but his views on gender were more liberal than the male norms of his day. And like many black women, Coretta prized an ideal of masculinity central to black traditions of resistance.[46]

If King's egalitarianism remained bounded by gender, he continually elaborated upon a critique of economic inequality evident in his earliest sermons. King drafted many of his major sermons before he became a public figure and published them in *Strength to Love* in 1963. The texts draw widely on liberal Protestant preachers and will soon be published for scholars interested in the performative, communal dimensions of King's preaching. King first preached "Three Dimensions of a Complete Life" in 1953, a critique of individualism that drew upon the parable of the good Samaritan to make the case for practicing "dangerous altruism." Individuals and nations limited to the self-developing "length" of life too often pursued "nationalistic concerns and economic ends," King preached in 1958. Living out of the "breadth" of Christian service, the Good Samaritan stopped on the dangerous Jericho Road to care for a victim of robbery. Perhaps the priest and Levite hurried by in haste to reach a meeting of the "Jericho Road Improvement Association," King quipped in a 1960 version. But the Good Samaritan asked, "If I do not help this man, what will happen to *him?*" In 1963, determined to change the "conditions that make robbery possible," King's Samaritan had transcended loyalty to "tribe, race, class or nation." He rejected patronizing charity in favor of compassion and respect for poor people's capacity for social action. By 1965, King demanded more than "Good Samaritan approaches" for the Jericho Road's individual victims. Now he demanded "massive action . . . to get rid of the Jericho Road which brought the victims into being." By 1966, African American history itself was one long Jericho Road, robbing blacks of dignity and decent work. The road stretched from slave plantations to "the triple ghetto" of poverty, race, and "human misery." By 1968, King's own dangerous road detoured to Memphis, where he preached, "If I do not stop to help the sanitation workers, what will happen to them?"[47]

King contrasted Christian communalism with rampant consumerism in a Detroit sermon in February 1954. Man's "better world" would come through rediscovery of "precious values," not economic growth. Moral relativism was an "atomic bomb" in men's souls, leading to "damaging selfishness." Humankind's "moral genius lags behind" its technological and scientific progress, he asserted in perhaps his most common set piece. "Automobiles and subways, televisions and radios, dollars and cents, can *never* be substitutes for God," King exhorted. Technology itself had become a false god, an expression of the lust for power whose end could well be nuclear Armageddon. King preached his sermon "Dives and Lazarus" weeks before the Montgomery bus boycott began in December 1955. There was an "impassible gulf" between the wealthy and the invisible poor. On earth, wealthy Dives spurned Lazarus who appeared at his door begging for crumbs. Later roasting in hell, Dives fruitlessly implored Abraham to send Lazarus from heaven with water to cool his tongue. Dives was "a conscientious objector in the war against poverty," King explained in his last Sunday sermon at the National Cathedral in 1968.[48]

King developed his famous sermon "A Knock at Midnight" in 1955. He drew on the parable of Jesus in Luke 11:5–6, in which a householder, safely in bed at midnight, resists an importunate neighbor who bangs on his door asking for three loaves of bread to feed a hungry traveler. The mid-twentieth century had brought midnight to the social order, King preached. How long would churches withhold "the bread of hope" from a world dominated by power-hungry leaders proliferating the nuclear means for global annihilation? How long would white churches slam their doors in the faces of Negroes seeking "the bread of freedom" and turn their back on impoverished African nations seeking "the bread of social justice"? How long would sheltered ministers give benedictions to naked nationalistic aggression, denying "the bread of peace" to a world "gone mad with arms buildups, chauvinistic passions, and imperialistic exploitation"? How long would clergymen align themselves with "privileged classes" against the disinherited of the world seeking "the bread of economic justice"? And how long would elite Negro churches continue to serve up bread "hardened by the winter of morbid class consciousness?"[49]

Experience, education, and compelling role models all had led King to an eclectic but coherent Christian radicalism by 1954. King determined to follow in his father's and grandfather's footsteps, practicing an egalitarian social ministry and "manfully" challenging racial segregation. King's personal witness to racial and economic inequality gained analytical substance by exposure to academic mentors Walter Chivers and George Davis, by his reading of Marx and the ministers who interpreted him, and by his mature identification with the "meliorist socialism" of Reinhold Niebuhr. King had been exposed to a Gandhism more nuanced and radically egalitarian than most Americans would ever recognize. He was still developing a ministerial identity that could balance his elite learning with his commitment to minister to common people. One observer of a King sermon criticized King's aura of "disdain and possible snobbishness" toward ordinary people. Others noticed King's humility and accessibility, despite his "bourgeois" origins.[50]

King's initial solution was to mobilize the privileged to serve the disinherited. Dexter Avenue Baptist Church was known as "the big folks' church," serving professionals, professors, and businessmen. King gave his first sermon in May 1955, firmly setting the tone for a socially engaged ministry politically activating the black middle class. "I have felt with Jesus that the spirit of the Lord is upon me, because he hath anointed me to preach the gospel to the poor, to heal the brokenhearted, to preach deliverance to the captives and set at liberty those that are bruised." King's first "Recommendations" sounded authoritarian, demanding his congregation unconditionally accept God-given authority descending from "the pulpit to the pew." But King democratized some church functions and fostered leadership among the parishioners, including women. King followed his predecessor Vernon Johns in pressing for a more authentically religious, egalitarian, and politically active congregation. He did not want to pastor an exclusive "social club with a thin veneer of religiosity." The "gospel of Jesus is a social gospel," King preached. Everyone should register to vote and recruit for the NAACP. He set up a new committee focusing on "social, political, and economic" improvement, appointing as cochairs Mary Fair Burks and Jo Ann Robinson, leaders of Montgomery's Women's Political Council (WPC). A new Social Service Committee he charged with "visiting the sick and needy." A year later, the Social and Political Action Committee had excelled in registering voters. Dexter led the city in contributions to the NAACP, King boasted. This was hardly mass militancy, but neither was it bourgeois complacency. J. Pious Barbour tried to lure King away from what he considered an anti-intellectual backwater. "This is the day of Mass preachers except in certain spots. Hurry and get one," Barbour counseled. The allures of status tested King's commitment to the poor, but events outside his control and the ideal of an egalitarian ministry compelled more democratic choices.[51]

Chapter 2

The Least of These

"Could the militant and the moderate be combined in a single speech?" King asked himself on Monday, December 5, 1955, preparing to address Montgomery's Holt Street Baptist Church as the newly elected president of the Montgomery Improvement Association (MIA). Fifty thousand Negroes refused to ride city buses that morning. Twenty-four hours earlier, King had no inkling he would be thrust into leadership, but his hastily composed speech pulled in social and ideological crosswinds central to his whole career. Could he be "militant enough to keep my people aroused to positive action," yet "moderate enough to keep this fervor within controllable and Christian bounds"? It was hardly a formal philosophical dilemma. Black Montgomery was lifted up with gales of exhilaration and uncertainty. Could Montgomery's contentious black leaders unite behind King's leadership in a movement comprising college professors, ministers, maids, cooks, and day laborers? Abusive white bus drivers and unfair seating rules brought them to Holt Street. But the buses were lightning rods for grievances against the entire system of segregation codified at the turn of the century to control aspiring, politically restive blacks and to suppress populist alliances at society's bottom. Would white leaders negotiate or repress the movement? That morning, police cars tailed buses, looking in vain for "goon squads" that were presumably intimidating black riders. Could blacks sustain militancy and absorb white retaliation without resorting to violence, which would divide the movement and provide whites a rationale for bare-fisted repression? Thousands listening in and around the church had discovered an "unplumbed passion for justice," King recalled. Reporters were there "to record my words and send them across the nation."[1]

King gathered and focused black grievances at Holt Street, describing collective memories of a people "tired" and "trampled over by the iron feet of oppression." He struck chords of global and historical theme and variation, playing to antinomies of love and justice, persuasion and coercion, black unity and class solidarity. Negroes themselves must transform democracy "from thin paper to thick action." The "right to protest for right" was foundational, a right denied to people "incarcerated behind the iron curtains of a Communistic nation." From this safe cold war rhetoric, King immediately turned to inspiring domestic traditions. "Disinherited" Negroes should emulate American workers "trampled over by capitalistic power," whose powerful trade unions faced down massive repression in the 1930s and 1940s. Then King struck black keys to rhythms of call and response, certain that a "race of people, a *black* people," would inject "new meaning" into democracy. Though he never rode a bus with Montgomery's working people, he would lead them without fear or thought of expense, he promised. He had heard the voice of Jesus, "'If you do it unto the least of these, my brother, you do it unto me.'" The mass meeting broke into thunderous applause and shouts of "*All right!*" and "*Yes, Sir!*"[2]

King leapt nimbly from elite to vernacular speech across racial and class divides. Sudden and unexpected leadership plunged him into Montgomery's democratic trenches. Sharing the struggle with domestic workers and manual laborers, he shed some of his elitism. A powerful celebrity culture made him the "Alabama Moses," an "American Gandhi." National black elites from the NAACP to the National Baptist Convention (NBC), the nation's largest African American denominational organization, blended rivalry and support for the star of the biggest movement in a decade. Pacifists, socialists, trade unionists, and self-styled Gandhians offered strategic advice, public relations expertise, and dollars. King faced a dilemma of democratic leadership in a mass-media age. Could he be one of the people, identified with their strivings and sufferings in local communities, and yet lead the Negro people and the nation toward nonviolence, integration, reconciliation, and justice?

The yearlong Montgomery boycott, the first mass protest rooted in churches, marked a turning point in the black freedom struggle. Buses had long been rolling "theaters" of racially contested working-class space. There had been bus boycotts before, like the one in Baton Rouge in 1953. But Montgomery sustained an unprecedented community solidarity and attracted undreamed-of outside support. Media attention stimulated contributions, publicized the regional and national possibilities for nonviolent direct action, and elevated King as a symbol of black political aspirations. Black and white American Gandhians persuaded King to embrace philosophical nonviolence. Equally significant, economic war broke out between black and white Montgomery. King learned important lessons about black economic power, economic dependency, and poverty. Though advisors counseled moderation and the mainstream press framed his message in moral terms, King's evolving rhetoric richly documents his growing sense of the linkages between civil rights and economic justice.[3]

The course of events in Montgomery exemplifies the dynamic relationship between mass mobilization and charismatic leadership, local and national power. Rosa Parks was arrested on December 1 for refusing to give up her seat to a white passenger. Local leaders initiated a successful one-day boycott on December 5. Ready to undertake a concerted campaign, the MIA, made up mostly of ministers, elected King president. The group's goals were remarkably moderate: to modify segregated seating, win courtesy from whites, and get jobs for black bus drivers. Weeks of official stonewalling culminated in mid-January with the city's "get tough" policy of reprisal against black protesters. After white terrorists bombed King's house on January 30, the MIA challenged segregation in federal court, joining the NAACP in *Browder v. Gayle*. In February, a state grand jury indicted 115 black leaders for violating an antiboycott law designed to hamper labor organization. King went to trial on March 19 and then appealed his conviction. A U.S. district court ruled bus segregation unconstitutional in *Browder v. Gayle* on June 5. Segregationists appealed to the Supreme Court. Through the long months of the summer and fall, blacks walked or carpooled to work, sustaining remarkable racial unity and nonviolent discipline. A court upheld a city injunction against the car pools on November 13. But that very day, the Supreme Court upheld the *Browder* decision. On December 20, federal marshals finally delivered writs of injunction, ending bus segregation in Montgomery forever. Direct action, litigation, publicity, and a tide of community and external support delivered the MIA a historic victory. "King's greatest genius" was translating into words "the aspirations of masses of people," Anne Braden later wrote. King transformed "a battle for a seat on a bus [into] a war against an entire system of segregation and degradation." But in Montgomery and the fields of Alabama, the broader battle was already raging. King's genius also grew from soils of social learning.[4]

Ground of Protest

Montgomery's political and economic crosscurrents decisively shaped King's leadership and learning. The Alabama State College historian Lawrence Dunbar Reddick described Montgomery as "maddeningly Janus faced," the capital of a vanishing cotton empire, "part agricultural, part commercial, part government-business and only slightly industrial." Modernizers had recently built a coliseum free of Jim Crow, but segregationists still honored Montgomery's statue of Jefferson Davis. Rural whites flocked to the city, upsetting the elite's political control and swelling a constituency ripe for exploitation by race-baiting segregationists. An independent black middle class led by ministers and

Alabama State College teachers was gaining political confidence with the slow growth of the black electorate and the relentless accretion of grievances. Montgomery's blacks suffered "severe economic deprivation" and job discrimination, King realized. Barred from city and state jobs, they worked as unskilled domestics or day laborers. Demeaning face-to-face contacts while blacks were cleaning whites' houses, hemming their skirts, and carrying their groceries sharpened racial and class grievances. Whites called blacks "boy," "girl," or worse. Bus drivers exercised police powers arbitrarily.[5] After a day serving whites, black workers riding the buses often had to stand next to empty seats reserved for whites. In "unreserved" sections between the front and back, drivers often bullied blacks out of their seats. King reported several bus drivers' insults during his trial. "Get back, you ugly black apes," was typical. The city's history of white physical and sexual violence was long and horrific. Though intimidated, blacks, including women, were not passive. When a driver called one maid a "motherfucker," she went for her razor, ready to "cut his head slamp off." The terrified driver said nothing.[6] If King were to preach nonviolence—and his commitment as yet was unclear—he faced a real challenge.

Blacks had not passively suffered the "iron feet of oppression" in Montgomery. Local leaders pressed ongoing political agendas. Black Montgomery had fifty-two churches and fifty associations devoted to mutual aid, such as the Women's Federated Clubs, which aided poor students and elderly people needing medicine. Alabama State College was Montgomery's main cultural center, but it was risky soil for movement organizing because of its financial dependence on the state. Independent mortician and Dexter parishioner Rufus Lewis organized voting rights drives with black professionals and World War II veterans. Jo Ann Robinson, president of the WPC, laid most of the groundwork for the bus boycott, keeping a low profile because she might easily have been fired from her position as an English professor at Alabama State, where the WPC was founded. With three hundred members by 1954, the WPC was a determined group of "educators, supervisors, principals, teachers, social workers, and nurses," according to Robinson, "woman power" organized against manifold injustices. Robinson wrote Mayor W. A. Gayle in May 1954 requesting what became the MIA's early blueprint for bus seating: Negroes should "sit from back toward front, and whites from front toward back until all the seats are taken." Blacks were 75 percent of all bus riders and were well organized. But of course there was no need for "forceful measures," she smoothly threatened.[7]

Local ministers shared King's commitment to the social gospel and political activism. Ralph Abernathy, a World War II veteran, became King's lifelong aide and friend. Born on a poor Alabama farm, he graduated from Alabama

State in 1950 and pastored First Baptist Church, the largest and oldest of Montgomery's "mass" black churches. His flock grew dramatically in response to his earthy and dramatic preaching. Abernathy pushed voter registration and organized the community for improved housing and recreation. King saw his predecessor at Dexter, Vernon Johns, as a pioneer of Montgomery's "social revolution," one of two Montgomery heroes he identified in *Stride Toward Freedom*. Johns urged blacks to "pool their economic resources" in producers' cooperatives like his own Farm and City Enterprises. Skeptical that whites would welcome blacks into an equal opportunity society, Johns believed blacks first needed economic power. He preached folksy sermons about agricultural self-sufficiency, like "Mud Is Basic," to his well-heeled parishioners.[8]

King's other acknowledged hero was labor leader Edgar Daniels Nixon, a Montgomery link to the civil rights unionism of the 1930s and 1940s. Head of the Alabama division of the Brotherhood of Sleeping Car Porters, E. D. Nixon shared Randolph's faith in working-class mass action. His out-of-state employer and union contract ensured his job security and political independence. A leader of the state and local NAACP, Nixon had organized the Welfare League in the 1930s, which provided housing, food, cash, medicine, and job referrals for the poor. Nixon frequently attended Highlander Folk School in Tennessee, which trained labor organizers. Head of the Montgomery Voter's League in 1941, he marched with 750 blacks to register at the courthouse. In 1952, he was president of Alabama's all-black Progressive Democrats. Gandhian activist Harris Wofford called him "Gandhi with a gun."[9]

Progressive Democrats aimed to translate electoral power into concrete benefits, especially in public employment. At a public meeting in March 1955, Nixon asked candidates for city commissioner: Would the commission support the WPC's bus seating proposal? What about the deplorable lack of fireplugs, sewers, decent parks, and paved streets in Negro neighborhoods? Would Negroes, who paid taxes, sit on city boards? Would white candidates approve a new subdivision of decent homes for Negroes? Would Negroes ever work for the city? Segregationist candidate Clyde C. Sellers frightened whites by publicizing Nixon's demands and posturing as their defender against "a block of Negro votes." Sellers insisted the Negro already had equal opportunity to find work "for which he is qualified"—somewhere else than Montgomery. In other words, submit to municipal neglect and work under the mudsill, or leave town.[10]

Militant segregationists increasingly dominated Montgomery's politics. Sellers was carried to victory by the wave of "massive resistance" to desegregation that followed the *Brown v. Board of Education* decision. Southern blacks petitioned to integrate schools, exposing themselves to political, physical, and economic retaliation. The first White Citizens' Council in Mississippi denounced the Supreme Court and NAACP as "socialistic," warned of racial "AMALGAMATION," and denounced "Pinkos in the Pulpit." Such radical black ministers allegedly undermined the Christian principles of "racial preference" (for whites), "private enterprise, rugged individualism and conservatism." The group expanded to Alabama in late 1954, promising integrationists they would make it impossible "to find and hold a job, get credit or renew a mortgage." Over half of the twenty-nine blacks who petitioned officials to integrate schools in Selma lost their jobs. Whites torched the business of a black grocer who boycotted the dairy of a white councilman.[11] How southern blacks overcame this economic warfare is one of the most fascinating dimensions of the civil rights era. Stories of reprisal and relief illustrate how community-based civil rights struggles remained struggles for economic autonomy and justice. King helped fight these poorly publicized battles in numerous local movements that captured his attention.

Chains of Democratic "Mutuality"

When King went on trial for conspiracy, legal strategy dictated he deny the boycott had any one leader, which was true. "Wasn't no one started it. We all started it over night," Gladys Moore testified on March 22. Many leaders described a mutual transformation of leaders and masses in the democratic struggle. Mass militancy pushed leaders into confrontations they might not otherwise have sought. Leaders sought to guide the masses toward victories they believed only nonviolence could ensure. Before the boycott, King thought only a miracle would cure black Montgomery's "crippling factionalism." For Montgomery's middle- and working-class blacks, fear of losing "economic security" paralyzed resistance, he mistakenly thought.[12]

When Rosa Parks refused a bus driver's order to give up her seat to a white man, black leaders had the test case they had sought for months. Parks was educated and respectable, youth secretary to the NAACP, and Nixon's assistant. Born into rural poverty, she found that her high school education earned her no respect from white employers, so she labored for low wages in a hospital and as a seamstress. On Thursday, December 1, she spent a full day altering clothing for whites at Montgomery Fair Department Store. Black labor made daily life "easy and convenient for white people," but their rights on buses were limited to paying and being pushed around. When would blacks win their "rights as human beings?" she wondered while awaiting arrest. Immediately, Jo Ann Robinson secretly printed 52,500 leaflets at Alabama

State. Robinson recognized that if the boycott became a sustained, mass protest, neither she nor the WPC had the resources or independence to guide it. Thelma Glass remembered that within several months, under the threat of firings, the WPC dwindled to three members.[13]

Over the weekend, ministers, professionals, and teachers canvassed black neighborhoods and immediately felt a democratic leavening. King and Abernathy roved through Montgomery's "clubs and dives," where Abernathy recalled the enthusiasm of working-class "sinners." Upper-crust "saints" met them with cautious respect. Canvassers found "poorly clad and undernourished children, alcoholics [and] human deprivation they hardly realized existed," Rev. Edgar French recalled. Almost no blacks rode the buses on Monday morning. King was awed by the "majestic" bravery of working-class folk. Men rode mules to work, and the sidewalks were thick with "laborers and domestic workers . . . trudging patiently to their jobs."[14]

The successful one-day boycott led sixteen leaders to form the MIA on December 5. Nixon and Lewis vied for the presidency, but, sensing his vulnerability, Lewis nominated his pastor and they all acclaimed King. King later speculated that as a newcomer, he had "no known enemies." King owed no debts to "city fathers" who would purchase any minister's soul with a handout, Nixon believed. Calling the ministers "scared boys" for even thinking they might hide their names and rebuking them for living off of "poor washwomen" and never returning the favor, Nixon admired King when he shouted he was no coward.[15] King soon preached about the leadership's utter dependency on the poor washwomen of Montgomery.

Indeed, it was the people who "picked up and swept along their leaders," Reddick recalled. Militancy moved from pew to pulpit. Leaders had "to catch up with the masses," Robinson remembered. Yet Ministers and independent businessmen, those most secure from reprisals, lent resources and social spaces to the protest and dominated the MIA board. Robinson endorsed the view that ministers must "give Christian guidance to a rebellious people." Rev. B. J. Simms thought a "blood bath" would have been inevitable had not "educated and civic minded" leaders joined militant "lower economic blacks." Few followed King into philosophical nonviolence, but together they remained nonviolent for a year.[16]

Late in December the MIA pursued negotiations to modify segregated bus seating and win jobs for blacks. Nixon was confident that a black consumer "strike" would compel negotiations. The MIA adopted the WPC's plan for bus seating: blacks starting at the back, whites at the front, taking seats as available with none "reserved for any race." Their first request was "courtesy," which company representatives quickly promised. The third goal spoke to broader aspirations: "employment of Negro bus operators in predominantly Negro residential sections." This demand was more radical than it seemed, because bus drivers wielded police powers and white supremacy demanded no black ever hold authority over any white. African Americans appealed to whites mainly as aggrieved consumers, however. An ad in the *Montgomery Advertiser* in January protested, "DEMOCRACY gives to each Citizen equal opportunities and privileges to enjoy the benefits of what ever service he is able to pay for."[17]

Official intransigence and escalating white violence in December and January led the MIA to seek complete integration on the buses. On January 30, the MIA voted to join with the NAACP in filing *Browder v. Gayle,* which challenged the constitutionality of Montgomery's segregation ordinance in federal court. King had pushed the jobs goal, but bus company negotiators stonewalled the proposal, fearing white hate strikes if blacks received any job assignments. On December 17, King had asked the company simply to accept applications, but they refused. MIA board member Ronald Young argued that jobs should be their highest priority. Black bus drivers with police powers could implement both courtesy and desegregation. They never put it to a vote. The NAACP's refusal to take any case that stopped shy of a full challenge to segregation led the MIA to drop the jobs demand. There was nothing unconstitutional or illegal in Montgomery about job discrimination—yet.[18]

The official "get tough" policy began on January 23 when Mayor Gayle announced that he and the city commissioners had joined the White Citizens' Council. Just as much as Negro radical outsiders, the "cooks and maids who boycott the buses 'are fighting to destroy our social fabric,'" he had announced. Whites should fire them. Dozens of businessmen pledged to do so. Then on January 26, King was arrested for speeding and thrown in jail. King recalled concluding from the severe repression that segregation was designed not just to separate but to "oppress and exploit" people. The privileged did not "give up their privileges on request."[19]

Official repression paved the way for death threats and violence. A telephone caller threatened King's life the night after his release. Sleepless, King prayed into his coffee cup, fearing the people would lose heart if he lost his "strength and courage." A quiet "inner voice" told him, "Stand up for righteousness, and God will be at your side forever," he recalled. It became a pivotal moment in his private and public autobiography. More than just the discovery of a personal relationship with God, the "kitchen conversion" marked King's shift from pastoral to mass leadership: exemplary, humble, identified with the sufferings and struggles of ordinary blacks. "I came to feel that, *as we struggle together,* we have cosmic companionship," he later told an interviewer. King later hitched his story to the parable of the rich fool, the "self-made man" who ate, drank, and was merry, heedless of others until God revealed he would soon lose his life and all his wealth. Daddy King had wrapped up King, Jr.'s life "in a Christmas package." But the democratic "struggle" and the death threats put him on a road more dangerous than any path circling family or congregation. "The choice leaves your hands," he often said. People would be demoralized if they saw him falter; they depended on him, as he did on them and on God. In other versions, the "voice of Jesus" had assured him. Know his name, King insisted, and don't try to find it in the "principle of concretion," or the "architectonic good," theological abstractions useless to anyone in distress. Their slave ancestors knew Jesus "as a rock in a weary land . . . my bread in a starving land . . . my sister and my brother . . . my mother and my father." King's new relationship with God emerged from and reaffirmed his commitment to the common struggles of humanity, the gospel of Luke, and his ministry to the poor, bruised, and imprisoned.[20]

Even as he rose in the celebrity culture, King achieved new intimacy with the masses, who responded with love and adulation. False rumors of a settlement in January 1956 compelled the MIA to delegate all official statements to Nixon and King, boosting King's media prominence and symbolic power. On January 30, city officials offered the MIA a compromise that would have barely altered the humiliating seating rules. It was tempting to return to safe obscurity, but King warned the leaders they be "would be ostracized" if they even mentioned the compromise to a mass meeting. People would reject his leadership if he failed to mirror their militancy. "If M. L. King had never been born this movement would have taken place," he told the people that evening. Pew and pulpit had been joined in a democratic "mutuality." "We are a chain. We are linked together, and I cannot be what I ought to unless you are what you ought to be." King tried to feign "strength and courage." But Mother Pollard, the revered stalwart of Montgomery's "walking city," was not fooled. "Poverty-stricken and uneducated" yet "amazingly intelligent," she saw King's distress and reassured him of popular and divine support. Just then he learned that whites had bombed his house.[21]

King's toughest test of nonviolence made him famous before any outside Gandhians arrived to counsel him. Rushing home to find his family fortuitously unharmed, he calmed an angry crowd on the edge of "race war," he later wrote. Several people reportedly had weapons, and one challenged a policeman to a shootout. "He who lives by the sword will perish by the sword," King cautioned. Calming the crowd won him praise even from segregationists, but black Montgomery's nonviolent commitment remained uncertain. "Colored folks ain't like they use[d] to be. Guns don't scare us," a maid told one researcher. If whites started a war, she was ready to "kill 'em all 'cause if they hurt Rev. King, I don't mind dying." King had armed guards and loaded revolvers in his home when he called for restraint. King acknowledged that in many places there was no nonviolent space for a protest like Montgomery's. In brutal Mississippi, "a couple of those white men [need] to lose some blood," King told an interviewer shortly after the bombing; "then the Federal Government will step in." King knew any move in Montgomery from self-defense to retaliation could provide whites with an excuse for massive repression. Headlines would sensationalize "racial unrest" or state simply that violence had "flared" in Montgomery, leaving whites to fill in the blanks with stereotypes of insurrectionary Negroes. "Bullet Clips Bus" was the *Advertiser* headline the day after Holt Street.[22]

King was exploring the public and private requirements of his own Gandhian convictions. "I never heard of Attila drinking the Hemlock or Stalin going to the cross," J. Pious Barbour had written. "Don't believe that mess about the Pen is mightier than the sword. Give me the Sword!" Now, Barbour was thrilled with King's publicized statement that protesters should not morally stoop "so low as to allow our enemies to make us hate." Barbour recalled King's all-night arguments with him in the 1940s "about Gandhi and his methods, against my thesis of coercion." Barbour was amazed: "YOU REALLY MEANT IT!" Black America was aflame with the news. The Chicago sociologist St. Clair Drake wrote that he and Reinhold Niebuhr had dreamed in the 1930s of an indigenous black Gandhi. Now he was here. Drake "burned up the wires" raising money.[23]

Activists as well as academics were convinced they had found the American Gandhi. Strategist, spokesman, orator, administrator, fund-raiser, negotiator—King played many roles at the center of a local struggle that became a national and international cause célèbre. King felt called to speak for those at the bottom of society, to elicit support from black religious elites and professionals, and to explain the "New Negro" to the national and international press. Thereafter, his monumental celebrity and the brevity of his presence in local movement struggles made sustained contact with local people difficult, though he never stopped learning from them and preaching service to their needs for bread and dignity. National publicity highlighted exceptional personalities and obscured collective leadership. The media spotlight also cast into the shadows women's roles in initiating and sustaining the boycott and obscured the movement's economic methods, challenges, and goals. Admired by most national reporters, King emerged in these accounts as a more central figure in initiating and sustaining the protest than he or anyone in Montgomery ever claimed.[24]

In late February 1956, an all-white grand jury indicted 115 leaders of the bus boycott and police arrested 75 of them under a 1921 anti-union statute prohibiting boycotts. King voluntarily submitted to arrest, advised to do so by pacifist Bayard Rustin. "Television cameras ground away" as 100 leaders joined 5,000 cheering men, women, and children at a rally on February 23, Rustin remembered. Though militant local people ensured that King remained identified with the masses, they, too, shared with the MIA leaders a mixture of adulation, pride, and protectiveness toward him. Robinson observed that King "knew how to deal with angry people, poor people, frightened people, uneducated people," and they never doubted him in Montgomery. Popular adoration reached its zenith at a mass meeting following King's March 22 conviction. "He's next to Jesus himself," said a woman. Rev. Moses Jones introduced King: "We all know him. He is a part of us. . . . Whatever happens to him, happens to us. Today he was crucified in the courts."[25]

Self-styled Gandhian advisors cautioned King about outside "interference" but offered themselves as mentors. The southern novelist Lillian Smith doubted nonviolence had any "experts" but suggested consulting Howard Thurman and Bayard Rustin. Stick to "indigenous" roots, interracialism, "love and quiet courage," Smith wrote, informing King about how left sectarian struggles in Arkansas sharecroppers' unions during the 1930s completely alienated the people. "Northern do-gooders" should raise money and cultivate a "sympathetic and honest press." Meanwhile, Harris Wofford counseled massive Gandhian "jail going" on the buses; he was the only true radical Gandhian around, King joked in response. Wofford also warned King about Rustin, who treated King like "a precious puppet." But "King was a symbol we were all manipulating," he later admitted.[26]

Bayard Rustin of the War Resisters League and Rev. Glenn Smiley of the Fellowship of Reconciliation (FOR) earned King's greatest trust. Rustin traveled to Montgomery with the blessings of pacifist A. J. Muste, Socialist Party leader Norman Thomas, John Swomley of FOR, and A. Philip Randolph himself. Rustin had been a Communist during the 1930s, joined Randolph's March on Washington Movement, and served prison time as a World War II draft resister. He helped found the Congress of Racial Equality (CORE) and led its southern freedom rides in 1947; he was sentenced to a chain gang for the offense. Rustin later claimed he and the Montgomery struggle itself, not King's earlier "professors who had read Gandhi," taught King nonviolence. But Rustin and Smiley's tutelage has been overstated. J. Pious Barbour knew that King's engagement with Gandhian thought was not shallow or derivative. For three months, King sorted out the balance between preaching nonviolence and protecting himself. King recalled deciding to disarm just after his house was bombed in heated discussions with his father and with Coretta. Actually, it took a bit longer. By the end of February, King was "decidedly Gandhi-like," Rustin reported with considerable satisfaction.[27]

Arriving in Montgomery in late February, Smiley confirmed King had "Gandhi in mind when this thing started." But Smiley worried about King's ambivalence and "violent" associates. The "deadly" news was "the place is [still] an arsenal," Smiley confided on February 29 in a letter to Swomley. King was a national "symbol of growing magnitude." But could he control the movement through the "sheer force" of symbolism? Only if he practiced and preached pure philosophical nonviolence, Smiley concluded. "King can be a Negro Gandhi, or he can be made into an unfortunate demagogue destined to swing from a lynch mob's tree," Smiley advised two dozen clergy. "*Hold Martin Luther King in the light.*" Who would make King into a demagogue? Smiley's assumption that King was safer without armed protection spoke mainly to the public requirements of Gandhian symbolism. King embraced and preached nonviolence, but his high profile put him in constant jeopardy. "Go where the Mahatma goes. He might get killed," Pat Watters remembers his *Atlanta Journal* editor telling him. King lived the rest of his life with an agonizing sense of personal responsibility for averting collective violence. Ralph Abernathy seems to have agonized less, expressing a more practical nonviolence: "The white folks have more guns."[28]

King finally got rid of his armed guards and guns. By June, he was teaching "non-violence as a way of life and as a technique," he wrote Rustin. Armed MIA leaders now saw retaliation or even self-defense as futile, King reported in September. Evoking shared hopes in revolutionary change, King noted that mass meetings embraced a vision of struggle "much larger than a bus situation . . . just one aspect of the total question of integration."[29]

The Political Economy of the Boycott

Montgomery represented more than the victory for nonviolence that King, journalists, and scholars proclaimed it to be, and more than the constitutional victory the NAACP celebrated. Montgomery's predominantly working-class black population won an economic battle with a wealthier adversary wielding a formidable arsenal. Black Montgomery needed a leadership protected against reprisals. Shifting the terms of economic struggle to a moral high ground, they won vital outside financial support. They banked on King's national image of nonviolence and incorruptibility. They appealed to conservative black churches, left-led interracial unions, and everyone in between. They needed to protect themselves from economic reprisals and to support protesters who lost their jobs or homes. In doing all these things, black Montgomery challenged white supremacist assumptions that blacks produced nothing and remained parasitically dependent on whites.

Montgomery taught King profound lessons about the importance of economically independent activists, powerful black consumers, and the resourcefulness and economic vulnerability of black workers. King knew that integrated buses were temporary vehicles for black freedom dreams. The boycott revealed both the need and the potential for broad changes in the region's politics and political economy. Supporting the boycott, local pockets were deep, but not deep enough, and the scramble for external support taught King how to speak multiple languages of social struggle. The national press framed the boycott as a moral and constitutional conflict with King as its inspiration and guiding light, a northern-educated new Negro bringing nonviolent wisdom to uneducated, emotional southern Negroes locked in titanic struggle with white bigotry and ignorance. A rare exception was black reporter Ted Poston of the *New York Post*, who described a struggle for economic power. Poston's main characters were working-class women and economically independent blacks using humor and their wits to spiritually and economically overcome white economic power. "We've got to get political and economic power for our race," Poston heard King preach in May 1956.[30]

The night riding and whipping of the 1920s had become an "abomination," the *Montgomery Advertiser*'s editor, Grover Hall, wrote in February. But the bigots now practiced "a more decorous, tidy and less conspicuous method—economic thuggery." Hall had warned blacks in December 1955 about white artillery and skill in waging "economic warfare." But Hall's also printed open threats on his editorial page. "Where is your appreciation, your sense of duty?" one white man asked blacks. The white race provided black people with food, medical care, housing, electricity, clothing, automobiles, and every other amenity, including "95 percent of your education." "Now what have you done for yourself?" And where would they go if they found themselves sacked or evicted, he asked. Negroes accepted white privileges and made "no contribution to civilization," an attorney told Fisk University researchers. He regarded segregation as white people's only defense against Negro crime, Negro rape, and the mounting Negro burden on public school and welfare agencies. At a White Citizens' Council rally of over 12,000 people on February 10, 1956, a flyer warned whites to stop supporting "African flesh eaters," lest everyone "wake up to find Reverend King in the White House." Removing even one stone from the political and economic pillars of white supremacy risked demolishing the whole edifice.[31] In *U.S. News & World Report*, Grover

Hall insisted Negroes must "work their passage" from poverty to wealth, just like earlier immigrants. Blacks could not prosper by idly dreaming of handouts or "40 acres" and a mule. Their weak work ethic was their problem, not his bigotry, Hall argued, as any glance at "welfare rolls and crime statistics" in northern cities could attest. King's "adverse" mail between 1956 and 1968 was filled with attacks on liberalism for coddling blacks dependent on welfare. Blacks must earn citizenship first and only then expect to be accepted as equals, many whites argued.[32] African Americans knew about their dependency on white employers, but equally about their contributions, self-reliance, and economic weapons.

King joined the war of words and principles, seeking to place the black boycott on a higher moral plane than the economic thuggery of the White Citizens' Councils. Whites wielded "terror, brutal intimidation and threats of starvation to Negro men, women and children," he protested. White integrationists also suffered devastating reprisals. By contrast, white economic suffering was "incidental" to the Negro strategy of noncooperation with evil. The point was not to "to put the bus company out of business," he repeatedly insisted, "but to put justice in business."[33] Rustin ghostwrote King's first published article in the pacifist *Liberation* magazine, announcing that "economics is part of our struggle." King hoped whites would see they were losing business to black merchants and then talk sense to the bus company and politicians. The MIA was attacking "the basis of injustice," not capitalistic power but "man's hostility to man." Rustin wrote King that their attention to the "moral aspects" of the boycott would appeal to religious leaders "intensely interested in non-violence." Elsewhere, King showed himself a shrewd tactician of economic power, telling *Redbook* magazine that boycotts were useless in poor communities where white "counter boycotts can upset the total economic structure of the Negro." In Montgomery, on the other hand, "the Negro wields a great deal of economic influence and power."[34]

Evidence of black economic resourcefulness abounded. Independent institutions and businesses serving a black clientele provided the movement's protected meeting spaces. The MIA was evicted from its offices several times, finally settling in a building owned by Montgomery's predominantly black bricklayer's union. The city ended "cheap taxi service" by ordering cab companies to charge a minimum fare of forty-five cents, King recalled. Rufus Lewis improvised a car pool, and drivers paid uncounted bogus traffic tickets. Lewis established fifty transfer stations, mainly at churches. Eddie Posey's privately owned parking lot became the car pool's central downtown hub. Across the street, pharmacist Richard Harris dispatched the cars and doled out emergency cash. Whites couldn't touch him: his clientele was 90 percent black and relatives owned the building. Beauticians Hazel Gregory and Bertha Smith publicized and donated to the boycott. The bus company and downtown merchants were deep in the red. "We buy all of our gas from eight Negro filling stations," Lewis boasted. White business moderates, afraid bad publicity would scare away outside investors, called for negotiations. Politicians were trashing Montgomery's image as "a city of 'good will, pleasant living, and cordial relations between the races,'" a white woman publicly complained.[35] One merchant asked Ted Poston in frustration, "Don't King and that bunch realize that people are losing their jobs over this foolishness?" Were they Negro people, Poston asked. Obviously not. Sure, protesters were "beefing about having Negroes hired in sales jobs," the merchant complained, but if "they wreck the stores, there won't be no jobs for anybody." Lewis saw the white merchants suffering, correctly pointing out it was the politicians who were the hard-liners. Despite a 50 percent fare increase, the bus company was pulling in only half of what it cost to keep the buses running. They laid off thirty-five white bus drivers, their union now permanently hostile. Poor whites also lost out when the company cut back on service. But they did not support the boycott.[36]

Crosswinds of race, class, and gender could blow in the boycotters' favor. For all Mayor Gayle's haranguing, white women would not live "without their maids," King noted. Domestic workers knew they occupied subordinate but strategic positions in white families that relied on wives' earnings to keep up middle-class appearances. One maid earned $12 a week working for a white woman who earned $52 a week. "Without that $40 a week she makes on me," she told Poston, they couldn't make payments on their nice house and new Buick. When "the Mister" fired her for supporting "all this Communist foolishness," his wife kicked him out the door to get her cheap labor back. No way would she return without a $3 raise, the maid insisted, because half of the wife's recent $6 raise "belonged to me." The Mister relented—for the kids' sake. For other African Americans threatened with job loss, kin and community also provided security. A white woman overheard talk of "starving the maids for a month" and asked her own to come secretly. "Well, Mrs., I just won't come at all and I sure won't starve," she replied. Her husband and children had jobs, and her father's farm produced "plenty of food." She couldn't wait to see Negroes driving buses downtown.[37]

During the first weeks of the boycott, fund-raising was entirely local. "Wealthy or poor," King wrote, Negroes "gave what they could." The MIA paid four women to run the office, the mass meetings, the car pools, and finances. A women's "Club from Nowhere" competed with another "Friendly Club," raising funds through bake sales that catered to both whites and blacks. Thousands of dollars poured in from mass meetings, special church funds, club dues, and hat passing in pool rooms and bars. Montgomery's working class rose up to challenge "the racial status quo at its weakest link, white economic dependence on black consumers," Lizabeth Cohen writes. It was a mass movement, not just a "middle-class" movement.[38]

Blacks' economic resourcefulness may have initially prevented King from appreciating the costs Montgomery's working people were paying. But he soon learned from national and local relief efforts and from struggling to help Montgomery's poor people. Drawing up the list of plaintiffs for *Browder v. Gayle* on January 30, all of whom were women, King insisted on brave people who were "not susceptible to losing their jobs."[39] A "lot of people lost their jobs," recalled Rosa Parks, head of the MIA Welfare Committee, who sought employment for laid-off workers. Financial secretary Erna Dungee Allen bought food and paid people's rent, gas, water, and doctor bills. "We even buried somebody," she said. Usually the poorest people needing help went to King, who was "real sympathetic" to their needs, Allen remembered. King realized the impossibility of sorting out deserving from undeserving cases. Rosa Parks suffered greatly. After she was fired, her rent was raised and her mother and husband became ill. Virginia Durr appealed for support to Highlander Folk School director Myles Horton, commenting, "It is fine to be a heroine but the price is high." The Parks moved to Detroit after failing to find work in Montgomery. "Some people never knew the sufferings that she was facing," King later lamented.[40] "So far the economic conditions of Montgomery are holding up very well," King wrote in June to a northerner curious about reprisals. He was thrilled with all the outside financial support. "We have had only minor cases of Negroes losing jobs."[41] His view would quickly change.

King's growing national support network helped him comprehend the widespread havoc the White Citizens' Councils wrought. In February 1956, radical NAACP activist Ella Baker joined A. Philip Randolph, New York lawyer Stanley Levison, and several northern clergy to found In Friendship, an organization devoted to providing financial relief to southern activists suffering reprisal, including those in the MIA. In Friendship organized two New York City benefits for the MIA and supported voting rights and school desegregation activists like Mississippi's Amzie Moore, struggling under reprisals to keep his service station in business. In Mississippi, Baker learned the difficulties involved in discerning who was suffering from political reprisals and who were victims of economic deprivation. They were two sides of the same counterfeit coin.[42]

By the time King testified in August before the Democratic National Convention, he had learned much more about violence and reprisals. "Many noble citizens are losing jobs" for supporting the Constitution, he testified, demand-ing federal protection. Whites boycotted then bombed a roadside market operated by Koinonia Farm, an interracial Christian cooperative devoted to nonviolent integration and "common ownership," a group with whom King had several ties. By November, King was publicizing the Montgomery problem with supporters of In Friendship. All two hundred drivers in the Montgomery car pool were "marked men and women" whose long-term job prospects were bleak.[43] In December, King addressed the National Committee for Rural Schools, a relief organization sponsored by the Brotherhood of Sleeping Car Porters. King denounced region-wide "economic reprisals and boycotts and threats." King listened to labor leader Jack Stetson tell of arson and terror directed against integrationist farmers and businessmen in South Carolina. When family farms failed because white suppliers denied them fertilizer or seed, it was silly for northerners to send schoolbooks to black kids. Schools were "a part of a total economic problem." King then listened to businessman Billy Fleming dream of building a cooperative store "to beat the white man at his own game" by furnishing rural victims of reprisals with "fertilizer, seeds, feed, groceries, clothes, gas," and the spiritual balm of "self-support."[44]

From the outset King knew the MIA needed all the material support it could get from anyone who might donate a few dollars or a station wagon. With legal fees and the cost of the car pool mounting, the MIA turned to out-side sources. Publicity after the February arrests ensured a steady flow of con-tributions. King knew he had to maintain an image of incorruptibility. One Quaker woman advised him that since "the greatest are the humblest," celeb-rity should not lead him to "put on airs" or buy a Cadillac. His "old Pontiac" was just fine, King wrote back; he sought to lead with "humility and staggering simplicity." King's hate mail is filled with ugly allegations of King as a corrupt huckster, using his celebrity to bilk poor dupes and ride in fancy cars while the people walked. Public allegations of corruption could wreck the MIA's rep-utation and destroy internal morale. When MIA official Uriah Fields charged in June that "egotistical" leaders were profiting at the masses' expense, King dashed home from California to deal with a major crisis. The leaders quickly persuaded Fields to recant.[45]

King sought major contributions from NAACP chapters, northern black churches, and labor unions. He wrote Revs. J. H. Jackson and James A. Carey of the NBC in late December 1955 asking for help. But they apparently did not respond. On February 13, he met in Chicago with officials of the UPWA, whose president, Ralph Helstein, had skillfully avoided anticommunist purges and maintained the meatpackers union's interracial progressivism. Many UPWA locals defied the race baiters and red baiters, organizing workplaces and communities to agitate for equality in wages, jobs, housing, schools, and recreation. Two Montgomery locals supported the MIA, and northern locals donated thousands of dollars. But King's overture to the meatpackers may have irked the NBC ministers. In late February, after the mass arrests, Carey offered support but warned King against encouraging any perceptions that the MIA was "financed by northern money or directed by outside influence."[46] By mid-February, the MIA had raised over $25,000. Publicity around King's court conviction in March boosted contributions dramatically. In mid-March, E. D. Nixon addressed a convention of the UAW, stunned by their pledge of $35,000. Even generous unions with radical pasts donated money under banners of broad social unionism harkening back to nineteenth-century "producerist" appeals. San Francisco Longshoremen sent $500, predicting victory when "untold numbers of men like longshoremen, miners, doctors, painters, ministers, teamsters and lawyers are willing to lend a hand."[47]

Polarities and Constituencies

King balanced militancy and moderation as he spoke to diverse audiences, transposing Montgomery's struggle into a national and international epic. Novelist Robert Penn Warren heard in the rhythms of King's antiphonal speech an intense intellectual effort to "deal with and include antitheses, to affirm and absorb the polarities of life." Warren thought it a matter of temperament, but King's leadership demanded it. King dealt with many overlapping social and ideological polarities. King appealed to middle-class, working-class, and poor blacks across economic lines, to middle-class whites across racial lines, and to working-class and poor whites along class and across racial lines. He preached racial unity, integration, and economic justice, varying his language and emphases according to his audiences. Setting local and national struggles in international context, he envisioned a world of peace and of racial and economic equality.[48]

King was careful not to offend cold war sensibilities. The NAACP promoted domestic civil rights as necessary to America's credible leadership of the "free world," but segregationists still red baited it as a Communist front organization. King wrapped the Montgomery movement in the flag whenever possible. Nonviolent protest had no kinship with "'damaging revolution' as set forth by 'Karl Marx and communism,'" King told a February mass meeting. Hegel was right, "growth comes through struggle," he told L. D. Reddick, "but not when Marx makes it necessarily a class struggle." Correspondents warned King to beware of "the trained Red agitator" manipulating "mob psychology" and subverting democracy with "strife, violence, and disorder." The movement must be ever vigilant against "exploitation by Communistic forces," King responded.[49]

The cold war card was also potentially powerful with American elites. The world's colored "uncommitted peoples" smelled hypocrisy in U.S. claims to defend freedom. To compete with "evil communistic ideology," America had better put its house in order, King told the June NAACP convention. "To Asia and Africa—let the world know—that we are standing up for justice," King preached to 2,500 people packed into Brooklyn's Concord Baptist Church in late March. God was threatening to break the "backbone" of American power by destroying its "international prestige," King told a Montgomery rally. Liberal Democratic congressman Chester Bowles wrote King from New Delhi agreeing that nothing "undermines America's prestige more than our lingering racial discriminations" in Asia and Africa. Presidents Eisenhower and Kennedy found this logic compelling when racial crises embarrassed the United States on the world stage.[50]

King's addresses also reached beyond cold war rhetoric to proclaim solidarity with independence movements in Asia and Africa. "We are God's children," he preached to an MIA mass meeting in early March, "tired of being suppressed politically [and] economically; tired of being segregated and discriminated." For King, the triple oppressions that Mordecai Johnson identified in his 1950 Philadelphia speech characterized Asian, African, and American inequality. "Every true Christian is a fighting pacifist," King told his Dexter congregation. If "peace" meant enduring exploitation, domination, and humiliation, he wanted none of it. At New York's Cathedral of St. John the Divine on May 17, King equated America's civil rights movement, the world's anticolonial struggles, and the Israelite Exodus. The biblical Egypt was the symbol of "humiliating oppression, ungodly exploitation and crushing domination." He often praised Gandhi's anticolonial movement in the same terms. Before a Wisconsin Baptist assembly in July, King described the billion and a half Asians and Africans who had lived "under the pressing yoke of some foreign power" and were resisting domination, humiliation, and exploitation. "The struggle of the Negro" was part of this great global struggle, he announced.[51]

Racial unity was King's most common clarion call. He flattered and shamed a newly prosperous and confident black middle class into lending their wealth and skills to organized protest. King joined a chorus of Montgomery leaders claiming the boycott had leveled occupational and status distinctions and fostered social intimacy and solidarity. "Preachers, lawyers, doctors, businessmen, and ordinary folks picked up people walking," treating them all "as brothers," Jo Ann Robinson remembered. Fisk University researchers noted that "college professors, maids, ministers, and drunkards" mixed intimately in mass meetings and car pools. Coretta King later credited Martin with single-handedly forging this unity, but King credited the people. "The Ph.D.'s and the no 'D's' were bound together in a common venture," he wrote. "People separated from each other by false standards of class were now singing and praying together in a common struggle." "False standards of class" was a telling choice of words, in which class seemed more an illusory status to be overcome than a system to be transformed. King evangelized middle-class churches, fraternities, and civic organizations to take up a life of "service" and guide social change. In August, he demanded that his Alpha Phi Alpha fraternity brethren reject selfishness and serve the masses rather than trample upon and exploit them. They were wealthy and esteemed "because the masses have helped you get there." Playing to traditional ideas of racial uplift and leadership, he described the masses wandering "in the wilderness," unable "to speak for themselves," waiting for educated leadership. But he pointed them toward equality, not paternalism, demanding a "new world in which men will live together as brothers." Ordinary folk mattered. "Teamwork and unity are necessary for the winning of any game," he told the June NAACP convention. "The backfield must recognize that it needs the men on the line. . . . *So away with our class systems.*"[52]

King left abundant evidence of a moderate repertoire, as he appealed to ideals of self-help and mutual aid, black unity and racial reconciliation. He often assured northern financial contributors that they could count on Negro "discipline, wise restraint and dignity." Blacks must prepare themselves to compete in newly desegregated schools and workplaces, King preached to the Dexter congregation on Mother's Day. Black mothers should teach their children hard work and self-respect, because Negroes "must run a little harder or forever remain behind." If one's lot was to be a street sweeper, he exhorted, echoing Benjamin Mays, "sweep streets like Michelangelo painted pictures." King added an egalitarian twist, stressing the dignity of all work, even mother-work among the poorest of the working class. "There have always been mothers . . . who didn't know the difference between 'you does' and 'you don't,' but who wanted their offspring to 'get it all.'" King's persistent call for self-help invariably pointed toward political agitation. "Integration will not be some lavish dish that will be passed out by the white man on a silver platter, while the Negro merely furnishes the appetite," King declared, sounding like Vernon Johns.[53] Freedom would not simply be handed to Negroes; they must seize it with economic grappling hooks of self-sufficiency.

King simultaneously voiced more radical themes drawn from the social gospel, America's equal rights tradition, and international anticolonial movements. Throughout 1956, he indicted monopoly capitalism in terms similar to those he used in 1966, linking capitalist materialism, militarism, and racism. When whites insisted King stay out of politics, he preached the social gospel. King asked a January MIA mass meeting: how could he preach about honesty to poor folk without condemning the "economic conditions" pressuring them into theft and trickery? With black audiences, King explicitly criticized capitalism. Twice before the NAACP, King attacked the unequal distribution of American wealth. On May 17, he called for "creative maladjustment" against the status quo of "segregation and discrimination . . . the tragic inequalities of an economic system which takes necessities from the masses to give luxuries to the classes . . . [and] the madness of militarism and the self-defeating method of physical violence." He later printed the speech in the Socialist Party newspaper. At the June NAACP convention, King linked American white supremacy with the world colonial system. His enslaved forebears had to accept "injustice, insult and exploitation," toiling as "depersonalized cogs" of plantation machines. Southern segregation was "glaring and conspicuous," but northern segregation was equally menacing, if "subtle and hidden," he added.[54]

King's radical visions over time gained historic depth and programmatic concreteness through A. Philip Randolph's influence. Addressing the same NAACP convention, Randolph presented a radical history lesson and a road map for political revolution through interracial unionism. After Reconstruction, when class power shifted from planter oligarchs to industrial capitalists, New South Negroes confronted "prejudiced and illiterate white worker-competitors," people "drugged with the opium of white supremacy by political demagogues." The "color caste" system reserved jobs for whites and paid Negroes the lowest wages, inviting "lily-white unions" to protect their material caste interests. Whites in the 1950s still monopolized jobs as railroad engineers, train conductors, skilled textile workers, and skilled construction workers, Randolph explained. Black workers had long believed capital a better friend than labor, accepting business propaganda and philanthropy and willingly serving as strikebreakers. The racial split in the working class helped only union-busting bosses, depressing wages for everyone and retarding southern growth and purchasing power. White and black workers alike needed "decent wages, improved working conditions and shorter hours of work." Poor whites were also disfranchised by poll taxes and literacy tests. They shared blacks' interest in unionizing and raising their wages by repealing Taft-Hartley and the "sinister right-to-work laws" proliferating in the states. While the Democrats and Republicans wrestled in the swamp of 1950s corporate centrism, Randolph demanded that the newly merged AFL-CIO organize unorganized southern workers. Union locals would have to fight discrimination in their own ranks and in company hiring. The whole AFL-CIO leadership needed integration, he said. Praising AFL-CIO vice president Walter Reuther, chief of the new Industrial Union Department, Randolph insisted they fight racism as vigorously as they had fought communism. Only then could they forge a social-democratic coalition of students, teachers, unionized workers, preachers, and journalists against a "decadent racist oligarchy" that controlled Congress and southern state governments. Though you can search in vain in King's speeches for further references in 1956 to labor "trampled over by capitalistic power," by 1958 King trumpeted Randolph's themes as he grew closer to the organized socialist left.[55]

King issued his most scathing indictment of capitalism at the NBC annual convention in September 1956. Over 10,000 black clergy listened to him read his fictional letter from Saint Paul to American Christians. Avoiding specific references to class struggle or corporate control of the means of production, King criticized capitalism's moral and economic consequences. Capitalism, technology, and science dramatically advanced wealth and productivity, he argued, but America's "moral and spiritual progress" failed to keep pace. The country was a tightly wired "neighborhood" and not a real "brotherhood." Americans made idols of skyscrapers and big cars. "Money can be the root of all evil," he preached, producing "gross materialism" and "tragic exploitation." The unequal distribution and control of wealth particularly troubled him. Just one-tenth of 1 percent of the population controlled 40 percent of the nation's wealth. Americans could democratically redistribute this wealth, ending the "abuses" of capitalism. The United States could use its "powerful economic resources to wipe poverty from the face of the earth."[56]

King's critique was controversial in the black world, but it did not make mainstream news. Alabama Baptist minister Charles Kelly praised King's critique of "capital's misuse of capitalism." J. Pious Barbour praised King for upstaging NBC president J. H. Jackson: "the center of attraction was THE KING," he wrote. A Philadelphia lawyer protested King's reference to "the exploitation of the masses." "Gaps in the economic system" challenged the whole nation, King replied; the nation did not need "a socialistic economy" to equalize wealth or provide "economic security" for Negroes. The attorney advised King to stay within safe boundaries of racial liberalism and not harm his powerful celebrity by thoughtlessly impairing "the prestige of 'our economic system.'" King stood his ground and later published the sermon.[57]

As the boycott approached its dramatic conclusion, King increasingly insisted that overcoming immoral racism also required social and economic leveling. The social psychologist Kenneth B. Clark introduced King at the December meeting of the National Committee for Rural Schools, and King praised Clark's analysis that had informed Chief Justice Earl Warren's opinion in the *Brown* decision: "segregation generates a sense and feeling of inferiority within children that distorts their personality." Clark followed sociologists and psychologists such as E. Franklin Frazier in concluding that slavery and white racism produced black "pathology," "family disorganization," and religious "emotionalism." King shifted his audience's attention back to the source. Segregation still reduced the Negro to "a depersonalized cog in a vast economic machine." And whites internalized a "false sense of superiority" that was equally damaging. Segregation scarred both oppressed and oppressor.[58]

For King, the end of segregation demanded not an aggressive assertion of individual rights but communal reconciliation and a mandate for extending equality. On November 13, the Supreme Court ruled that segregation on the buses was unconstitutional. The same day, Montgomery's city attorney won an injunction against the car pool as a "public nuisance and private enterprise." Montgomery's African American citizens continued to walk for five weeks before the court order reached Montgomery. King preached restraint in asserting black "rights." Freedom could never mean black supremacy, he insisted. Blacks must respect everyone's rights, even those of whites who wished to deny their freedom. But exercising freedom's duties required equal respect and real social equality. They had to keep "the whole of humanity level" and to discourage spiritually deadening, community-killing delusions of superiority and inferiority. The ancient god Nemesis raised the lowly and lowered the mighty, King preached. Negroes had "a right to level this thing off."[59]

The costs of struggle could not diminish the sweetness of victory. On December 20, the Supreme Court's desegregation order reached Montgomery. The next day, King rode a desegregated bus with Glenn Smiley. "We started out to get modified segregation," he boasted, "but we got total integration." For now, King endorsed Smiley's commitment to interracial reconciliation more fully than Rustin's belief in mass black mobilization. Negroes must move "from protest to reconciliation," seeking "integration based on mutual respect," he told mass meetings of over 2,500 ecstatic and victorious boycotters. Desegregated buses were merely the first step toward real integration, "genuine intergroup, interpersonal living."[60]

For Rustin, Montgomery's extraordinary unity and mass nonviolent discipline showed the way to a regional direct action movement. "People who had a *daily* task of action and dedication" could move mountains, he wrote King. "The movement must now widen to political areas," Rustin advised. But the community had been involved in politics for years. King was receptive to the idea of a wider regional movement, but his immediate action was to reaffirm Montgomery's longstanding political agenda. On Christmas Eve, King presented the MIA program: desegregation of parks and schools and a voter registration drive to challenge Montgomery's segregationist coalition of power. Envisioning a Gandhian "constructive program," King recommended community self-help campaigns "to raise economic, health and intellectual standings."[61]

The *New York Times* did not report the new MIA agenda. The headline news of December 23 was that King's front door had been shattered by a shotgun blast. "Some of us may have to die," King reportedly said, but he vowed the struggle would continue. The next day, King cautioned the bus riders to remain calm in the face of possible violence. If local police did not act to protect citizens in their new constitutional right, "there is always the FBI." That, too, was a leap of faith, as future waves of white violence would show. "Dear Mike; Can you overthrow a social system without violence?" J. Pious Barbour later asked. King gave his life to find an answer.[62]

Chapter 3
Seed Time in the Winter of Reaction

The three years following the Montgomery bus boycott have been called "fallow years" for King and the Southern Christian Leadership Conference (SCLC), the regional organization that King and sixty affiliated ministers formed in 1957. During these difficult years, King widened his ideological horizons and extended his networks of support, raising money from outside the region for local leaders who otherwise would have worked in isolation. King projected reformist and moderate messages to middle-class white and black audiences, but when he spoke to local groups or took inspiration from newly independent nations, he could be quite radical. King developed increasingly sophisticated analyses of racism and of the national and international political economy. He consistently looked to voting as the key to a democratic political revolution in the South with far-reaching economic implications, including rights to equal education, trade unionism, fair and full employment, and decent social welfare protections for all working-class southerners, especially blacks, who remained disproportionately poor. Ella Baker, SCLC's acting executive director, thought King traveled too much, flaunted his charismatic authority, neglected grassroots leadership, and devalued women's contributions. King did cultivate his own celebrity more than local indigenous leadership; he accepted honors and speaking invitations mainly to raise money for the organization. But he was not stuck in the "middle-class outlook" of the "traditional Negro leadership class," seeking to contain "the awakened black masses," as Glen Eskew argues. Certainly, SCLC failed to develop direct action or massive voter registration during this period. Its decentralized structure relied mainly on local initiative, and it fielded few organizers. Above all, a harsh winter of repression almost immobilized the grassroots and left half the southern NAACP frozen on the vine. White repression and reprisals are principally to blame for SCLC's lack of momentum. Mass protest did not spread across the South until the student sit-in movement inspired broader community action in 1960. Only when the masses were already in motion did King involve himself again in direct action.[1]

King took political risks by supporting known leftists and exposing himself to charges of communism in the late 1950s. He developed close ties with left trade unionists and New York socialists, not only Bayard Rustin, A. Philip Randolph, and the UPWA, but the militant interracial locals, District 65 of the Retail, Wholesale and Department Store Union (RWDSU), and the Drug and Hospital Employees Local 1199, affiliated with the same international. King also began a fruitful lifelong collaboration with the left-wing New York lawyer Stanley Levison. King supported such controversial critics of U.S. foreign policy as the American Committee on Africa and the Committee for a Sane Nuclear Policy (SANE). After he spoke at the red-baited Highlander Folk School in Tennessee, posters across the South pictured King in a "Communist Training School." When the Tennessee legislature investigated Highlander for subversive activities, prosecutors cited its relationship with both King and folk singer Pete Seeger "as proof of Highlander's Communist connections," Highlander director Myles Horton informed King. Responding to an appeal from Communist Party leader Benjamin Davis, King supported the release of Davis's comrade Henry Winston, whose health had rapidly deteriorated in prison. King endorsed leftist causes in an anticommunist climate that smeared even liberal organizations. In January 1957, the FBI noted King was honorary chairman of "Enroll for Freedom," a "campaign to provide economic relief for victims of racist terror in the South sponsored by the Young Socialist League."[2]

Orator, movement strategist, and fund-raiser, King lacked administrative experience to cope with his expanding responsibilities. President of SCLC while still heading the MIA and pastoring at Dexter, he traveled to Africa and Asia, wrote a book on the Montgomery bus boycott, and spoke constantly to radio, television, and newspaper reporters. King was pressured from every political angle, "almost pulled apart," L. D. Reddick remembered. What goals should the movement pursue after Montgomery? How should the new organization relate to the more cautious, legalistic NAACP? School integration was the NAACP's turf, so SCLC concentrated its modest forces on voting rights.[3]

To Redeem the Soul of America

SCLC brought together a unique convergence of northern and southern, religious and secular talent. Revs. Joseph Lowery of Mobile, Fred Shuttlesworth of Birmingham, Ralph Abernathy of Montgomery, Kelly Miller Smith of Nashville, and C. K. Steele, who led the successful 1952 Tallahassee bus boycott, were determined to change the South. Their priorities and models of social change benefited from, but stood in some tension with, those of the northerners, who brought resources, ambitious strategies, and a holistic understanding of civil rights, national political realignment, and economic justice. Baker, Levison, and Rustin dreamed of a mass, indigenous, all-black organization, continually energized by the wisdom people gained "in the course of the struggles," as Rustin wrote. Rustin prepared a flurry of ambitious "working papers" in advance of the ministers' Southern Negro Leaders Conference on Transportation and Non-violent Integration in January 1957, sketching a remarkable road map of the coming struggles. Southern activists' "refusal to accept jim crow in specific areas challenged the entire social, political and economic order" that had oppressed blacks since Reconstruction, he asserted. Montgomery showed that a united black "mass protest" could attract "all social strata." Negroes should look for guidance to labor unions, who had shown in the 1930s that strong leadership and spontaneous protest could be revolutionary. The struggle for integration and equality was part of the "fight of the common man" against poverty and ignorance. Civil and economic rights would merge in collective struggle. Understanding the radical threat, whites inflicted vicious violence and economic reprisals on protesters, and SCLC had to develop means to support them economically. Industrialism and economic development were already opening new possibilities for racial progress, Rustin argued, but the South's "political structure" resisted democratization. Nothing came without agitation and organization. How could black leaders "identify with the people at every stage of the struggle"? Voter registration would challenge the white supremacist Democratic Party and expose the roots of black people's "enforced economic and social" oppression. A dynamic "congress of organizations" could move into politics and officeholding. In the interim, "mass direct action" was their best "political weapon." Montgomery had shifted the movement from legal action to community action, which could awaken the masses through new goals "basic to the welfare of the community," Rustin concluded.[4]

The assembled ministers moderated Rustin's more revolutionary ideas and did not endorse militant direct action. Their founding statement argued that America would never reach "its vast economic, social and political potential" without equal rights. Racism "stunted and frustrated" national institutional development, especially when a racist minority in Congress repeatedly defeated federal aid to education and the expansion of Social Security coverage to all workers (agricultural workers and domestics, disproportionately black, continued to be excluded). King left the conference early to investigate a rash of bombings in Montgomery, but his absence was probably inconsequential rather than a missed opportunity to implement Rustin's radical political mandate. Black voting was one thing the ministers could all agree on, and they faced severe political constraints pursuing even that strategy. Their statement struck both internationalist and anticommunist chords when they expressed solidarity with "revolts against European imperialism" and with "Hungary's death struggle against communism."[5]

The successful conference drew sixty-seven people from twenty-nine communities in ten states, mainly Baptists who had "the masses of the people," Rev. S. S. Seay remembered. Three members of the United Packinghouse Workers of America (UPWA) attended. On February 14, ninety-seven ministers met again to elect King president and Abernathy treasurer of the Southern Negro Leadership Conference. They drafted the first of many telegrams to President Eisenhower inviting him south to witness white brutality. Again in August, they met to plan voter registration drives and put "Christian" in their name to deflect charges of communism. An all-black regional coordinating body for local affiliates, SCLC would not recruit individual members or compete with the NAACP. Ministers dominated, but the group attracted diverse activists, including many unskilled workers. SCLC's organizational structure facilitated swift, flexible, spontaneous action, but not sustained organizing. Local leaders looked to King, who periodically brought inspiration, money, publicity, and talent into their communities. The Baptist ministers regarded him as their undisputed leader, the man who made decisions after their contentious and heated debates. After the UPWA donated $11,000 in SCLC's first year, most of its money came from King's speaking engagements and from contributions he solicited. He was constantly in motion, giving 208 speeches in one year spanning 1957-1958, Coretta King recalled. Before 1961, they raised about $50,000 annually, mostly from individuals, black religious and fraternal organizations, and trade unions with black membership. On and off, Ella Baker was acting assistant director, returning after the Baltimore minister John Tilley failed to fulfill the duties of his position. The organization could afford to hire only two clerical workers.[6]

Stanley Levison offered his considerable talents gratis, drawing on long experience with the Communist Party in fund-raising, ghostwriting, and political and legal strategizing. Independently wealthy from real estate ventures and car dealerships, he had managed the finances of the Communist Party until 1955, whereupon he embraced the southern racial struggle as a more vibrant grassroots movement. King soon found Levison's political savvy, public relations advice, and loyal, if occasionally patronizing, friendship indispensable. Reams of FBI surveillance documents from 1962 to 1968 betray no attempts to make King toe the party line. In fact, after 1964 Levison often urged King to moderate his radical dreams. Several times Levison suggested that controlled violence could compel concessions from politicians, but King never agreed.

Levison advised King on taxes, investments, and his "public image" as an "intellectual and moral leader." Rejecting the values of the "commercial jungle" and refusing payment from King, Levison explained that serving the "liberation struggle" was his way of atoning for white racial privilege. As Rustin later summarized their collaboration, he and Levison put on paper "ideals we knew [King] had or would quickly accept," the FBI recorded. King refused a lucrative lecture tour in 1958 after Levison insisted that the people King should be proselytizing for nonviolence were too poor to pay for lectures. Levison especially helped King balance his celebrity and SCLC's need for contributions with his responsibilities to the movement and poor people.[7]

As Montgomery's black leadership descended again into factionalism, King helped shape the MIA's political and economic agenda, but concluded that strategies of constructive self-help bore the ripest fruit. At a meeting in March 1957, the MIA Future Planning Committee outlined programs for political education, slum clearance, relief for the indigent, and development of businesses and credit unions. The MIA intended to challenge racial barriers to employment, home ownership, and education. King declared that Montgomery still faced "tragic inequalities" in education, recreation, voting rights, and poverty, but he admitted in April that they did not know where to go next. King's fragmented duties paralleled the MIA's growing organizational disarray. As people returned to more private concerns, the MIA turned to voter registration and internal community development. Gandhians wrote to King recommending "constructive programs" of self-help. In December 1957, Abel Plenn of the *New York Times* quoted King's advice that blacks "lift themselves up by their own bootstraps." The black community in Montgomery succeeded in raising "moral and social standards," King claimed, citing "a decline in heavy drinking, once prevalent among the poorest people." Crime also declined as MIA leaders developed programs of "health education, youth recreation and adult education and employment aid." "Level-headed businessmen" sought biracial local progress "across the table of common economic needs," Plenn noted.[8]

Challenged to think about grander strategy, King was sure racism and economic exploitation should be fought together, especially in urban housing markets. On December 5, 1956, Dr. Francis Townshend had written to King, asking him to endorse his plan to "abolish poverty in the United States [and] throughout the world." Townshend had organized millions of elderly Americans during the Great Depression around the radically redistributive Old Age Revolving Pension Plan. By the 1950s, his constituency shrunken, Townshend had devised a new plan to end poverty by redistributing income, lecturing King that two-thirds of the Negro's troubles "would be eliminated if poverty were wiped out." It was a radical extension of New Deal faith in economic growth as the best solvent of racism. King promised to study the plan and write back, but he never did. King was not going to downplay antiracism in hopes that economic growth or redistribution alone would solve the problem. In 1957, a minister sent him an article titled "Racism in Suburbia," and King responded, "the housing problem is the crux of the race problem in the North and the West." Open housing and income redistribution became two central keys to King's later solutions to poverty and the racialized ghettos.[9]

King took his Baptist ministry to middle-class audiences between 1957 and 1959, preaching widely and syndicating a column in *Ebony* magazine. Bits of this ministerial rhetoric could support the thesis that King promoted individual striving more than he advocated fighting poverty in these years. But King nearly always couched his rhetoric in a critique of middle-class consumerism and a call for material sacrifice and the coercive use of black dollars in the collective racial struggle. Often he sounded more like Benjamin Mays than Karl Marx, praising Booker T. Washington and Marian Anderson for overcoming poverty and winning wide acclaim. King praised Jews who overcame anti-Semitism, citing Albert Einstein, Sigmund Freud, and Marx, whom King guardedly described as a controversial man who contributed to the "accumulated knowledge of political science." Material prosperity had changed black people's estimate of their own personal and collective capacities. With a total income comparable to that of Canada ($18 billion), Negroes could make the difference between "profit and loss" in white businesses. The Negro had no excuse not to support organized protest and would suffer in God's eyes if "he spent more for frivolities than for the cause of freedom," King repeatedly insisted.[10]

King's advice to *Ebony* readers ranged widely, from opposing the death penalty and advocating birth control to defending interracial marriage as an individual choice. Personal responsibility and honest talk were his most frequent pieces of advice. He lambasted the cultural forces contributing to "the breakdown of the family" and communities: gambling, rock-and-roll music, premarital sex, men's domination of women as "breeding machines," and, most frequently, shallow consumerism. Don't "keep up with the Joneses," King wrote. "Much of the blame for unhappy or broken homes King places on the strains that arise out of our struggle for material possessions and prestige," Reddick wrote in *Crusader Without Violence*, citing interviews with King in 1957. None of King's *Ebony* articles mentions poverty as a strain on cohesive families. Women should receive "equal pay for equal work" but were most biologically suited to be mothers, he wrote.[11]

King showed little public concern for poor mothers' dilemmas. A woman who wrote to King told him she had had a child out of wedlock, the father had left, and she was now a "black sheep" in her community. Black voting rights and women's suffrage were empty victories when men routinely ruined women's reputations, "leaving them to rear children the best way they can and alone," she protested. King was no longer writing for *Ebony*, his secretary curtly replied. Another unwed mother wrote that social workers had judged her "unfit," denying her assistance from the Aid to Dependent Children program. Day care costs ate up half of her earnings of $25 a week. How could SCLC help? King was "deeply sympathetic," but SCLC had no "welfare program," King's aide James Wood replied. They both agreed she should appeal to the social workers who cut her off. King shared the 1957 award of the National Conference on Social Welfare with reformer Wilbur Cohen, who stood next to King decrying recent cuts in child welfare services. Yet until the mid-1960s, nowhere did King echo Cohen's calls for more generous family and child welfare appropriations.[12] Jobs for men remained the cornerstone of his agenda for economic justice.

Internationalism and U.S. Racism

Traveling outside the United States for the first time, King stretched his rhetoric beyond cold war liberalism to embrace a nonaligned internationalism that demanded a democratic equalization of wealth among races, classes, and nations. The Kings attended Ghana's independence ceremonies in March 1957 with A. Philip Randolph, Mordecai Johnson, Vice President Nixon, and others as guests of Prime Minister Kwame Nkrumah. King watched in awe as they lowered the Union Jack and raised the Ghanaian flag, an event fraught "with eternal meaning" for the world's colored masses, he told a Chicago radio station and his church: "There is no basic difference between colonialism and racial segregation." Nkrumah confirmed Gandhi's lesson; "colonialism was made for domination" and exploitation of subject peoples. Poverty, low wages, and the "servile attitudes" of Ghana's workers troubled the Kings, but Accra's luxury hotels impressed them, Mrs. King recalled. They had believed "the propaganda that all Africa was primitive and dirty." King spoke reverently of Nkrumah as an unprivileged Gandhian who had worked himself out of poverty, spent years in America washing dishes and studying, embraced Pan-Africanism, and returned to Ghana to agitate against British domination and exploitation. Having been elected prime minister while imprisoned for sedition, Nkrumah and his comrades donned their "prison caps and coats" for the independence ceremonies, King wrote in admiration.[13]

King and Nkrumah discussed the challenges of economic underdevelopment for newly independent nations. King concluded the world's poor had a right to level off the hills and valleys of privilege and deprivation. He took home Nkrumah's last speech to the Gold Coast Assembly calling for nonalignment in the cold war and stressing the economic "interdependence" between Ghana, Africa, and the world. With per capita income one-sixth that of Britain, Ghana's sluggish economy and low productivity resulted from "chronic ill health" and malnutrition, problems not "of race but of environment," Nkrumah argued. His solutions lay in modern medicine, education, and foreign investment controlled by and benefiting Africans. In Africa, twenty-eight cents a day was "a good wage," King told his church. Ghanaians had crossed the political Red Sea but faced an economic wilderness: a one-crop economy (cocoa), underdeveloped industries, and widespread illiteracy. King urged African Americans to lend technical assistance. Quoting Isaiah 40:4, he promised that "every valley shall be exalted, and every hill shall be made low"— from Ghana to New York, from Britain's imperial "pinnacles" to Africa's "dark deserts," from America's mansions of "inordinate superfluous wealth" to its slum dungeons of "abject, deadening poverty." To accent the imperative of democratic leveling, King frequently deployed this biblical metaphor derived from the building of roads for ancient kings. Everyone had marching orders from God "to break down the bondage and the walls of colonialism, exploitation and imperialism."[14]

The trip reinforced King's socialist commitment to redistribute political and economic power. He met with the Marxist historian C.L.R. James in London en route home. James later wrote to friends that Gandhian movements like Montgomery and Ghana's revolution showed "unsuspected power." Marxists should heed the "boldness," "strategic grasp," and "tactical inventiveness" of nonviolent struggles. His book *Nkrumah and the Ghana Revolution* celebrated the two revolutionary world historical events. King understood and agreed with James's "fundamentally Marxist-Leninist" ideas, James later claimed, but King said his ministerial "reserve" dictated he "not say such things from the pulpit." Randolph later told Levison that Nkrumah and "most of the representatives from the new Asian and African nations were socialist thinking men." Levison quoted Randolph: "only a socialist philosophy possesses the humanitarian essence" necessary to inspire the black masses to revolution. Randolph didn't broadcast his "partisan viewpoint," Levison noted, but he knew King admired Randolph.[15]

After this journey abroad, King increasingly used the rhetoric of cold war freedom not to reinforce nationalist ideals but to criticize U.S. politics and foreign policy. Racial oppression within the United States emerged from the history of Western imperialism, he emphasized. Ghana's finance minister told King that "beautiful words and extensive handouts" from the United States would never muffle Ghanaians' support for their oppressed American "colored brothers." Ghana's sympathies were with the "free world," King told an audience of 8,000 in April 1957 at a St. Louis freedom rally. But time was running out for America to prevent "uncommitted" peoples from shifting international and ideological loyalties. As vice chairman of the American Committee on Africa, King called for an international day of protest on December 10. White rule in South Africa survived only through "totalitarian control" and "organized inhumanity," he said.[16] American segregationists were the same as white South Africans, King told activists gathered at Highlander Folk School in September. King delivered an even more radical message to 3,000 delegates to the National Conference on Christian Education of the United Church of Christ (UCC) the next summer. Western racism, militarism, and nationalism sustained an international system of racial and economic oppression, King preached: "we leave the battlefields of the world painted with blood [in] wars that burden us with national debts higher than mountains of gold, filling our nations with orphans and widows." European empires oppressed 1.6 billion "colored brothers in Asia and Africa." America betrayed its founding heritage by treating 16 million Negroes as "things rather than persons." The richest nation on earth had become "spiritually and morally poverty-stricken, unable to speak to the conscience of this world." When the UCC later published the sermon, they did not laud King's militancy. The editor praised King as an exemplar of Negro efforts to win "acceptance as citizens and neighbors."[17]

Visiting Ghana emboldened King back in the United States. At the April rally in St. Louis, he denounced American economic inequality more militantly and concretely than ever before. Negro poverty was "appalling" and persistent. Seventeen percent of white Americans and 43 percent of Negroes scraped by on less than $2,000 a year; 7 percent of whites and 21 percent of Negroes subsisted on less than $1,000. At the other end of the spectrum, 40 percent of whites but only 12 percent of Negroes made more than $5,000. Americans were afflicted with "dangerous optimism" about their so-called "affluent" society, he warned. Addressing black and white southern ministers in April, King decried America's "startling" economic inequalities, systemic racial job exclusion, and "appallingly low" wages. Employers were committing "murder in the first degree," he thundered. Such statements belie any claim King thought of race in "narrow terms of 'civil rights'" and legal equality, or that he overlooked African Americans' "mass poverty" in the 1950s.[18]

On June 23, 1958, King joined Randolph, the NAACP's Roy Wilkins, and

Lester Granger of the National Urban League to meet President Eisenhower, insisting he withdraw funds from all federally subsidized projects in "education, hospitals [and] housing" that discriminated on the basis of race. These leaders outlined the rights agenda that came to partial fruition in 1964. The federal government must combat growing unemployment among Negroes, which was caused by "widespread discrimination . . . in industry, business and government."[19] Eisenhower did little while the economy plunged into recession in 1957 and again in 1960. After that, civil rights and labor leaders increasingly argued that "automation" and a politically hostile national antilabor coalition, not simply discrimination, left unskilled black workers behind even as it undercut white economic security.

King wore his ministerial mien on national television, balancing activist antiracism and faith in economic growth. Optimism about southern modernization and liberalization was in some tension with King's stress on the need for mass activism and vigorous federal civil rights enforcement. On NBC in February 1957, he explained that industrialization was a powerful agent of equality, though he also argued that "privileged classes do not give up their privileges voluntarily." Again on NBC in October, King did not mention income distribution, murderous discrimination, mass poverty, the labor movement, or the power of "*black* people" to reshape civilization. He dreamed of a society where men could live as "brothers and forget about distinctions." American democracy, southern economic development, and interracial alliances would make segregation nonexistent by the year 2000, he predicted. Industry and cities "inevitably undermine the folkways of white supremacy," he said, echoing Rustin and Reddick. "Good businessmen" learned the costs of bigotry when racial conflict put a city's progressive image with new investors at risk. King's messages to white middle-class audiences could therefore support a racially optimistic view of capitalist modernization. But Gavin Wright argues that before popular and governmental activism forced integration on the southern economy in the 1960s, southern development resembled that of South Africa. Native-born and in-migrating whites monopolized higher-paid technical and skilled positions in a new economy that overlay, more than it replaced, the segregated and poor old South. Segmented labor remained the norm, as huge racial wage differentials persisted. By 1962, King explicitly reflected this realism, and his cold war rhetoric celebrating progress had all but disappeared. Already King appreciated the power of mass communication technology, concluding that the Little Rock school desegregation crisis exposed *mass* white brutality to the international press. King was sure "the rolling tide of world opinion will force the federal government" to throw its power behind justice.[20]

The Cornerstone of Rights

On May 17, 1957, 20,000 protesters gathered in Washington, D.C., at the Prayer Pilgrimage for Freedom, an event Rustin, Baker, and Randolph organized after Eisenhower refused to travel south to combat "organized terror." King joined Randolph and Wilkins in the call to march against "oppression and inequality." Unequal justice, lynching, disfranchisement, and Jim Crow in the military were the first grievances. Education, jobs, and housing, issues that defined the next decade, were already urgent. Widespread white reprisals against black workers, merchants, and farmers compelled them to march on Washington. Rustin lined up generous contributions from the auto, steel, and garment workers' unions. He and Randolph urged King to tout the Negro-labor alliance against "economic injustice." Rustin sent King ghostwritten text for King's speech, claiming "that economic and social change for the uplift of all poor people is part of the struggle of Negroes for justice."[21] But after UPI charged that communists had infiltrated the march, King, Wilkins, and Randolph narrowed the focus to publicizing white violence, demonstrating unity, and supporting the 1957 civil rights bill protecting voting rights. Speaking on the steps of the Lincoln Memorial, King demanded, "Give us the ballot." Voting would win equal justice, school desegregation, and protection from violence and "crippling economic reprisals." Both parties harbored reactionaries, and northern liberals must become fully committed to civil rights, he implored. A militant call was followed by a moderate speech. Rustin seems not to have minded, proudly writing King that the national "press was excellent."[22]

Focusing on voting rights seemed the most pragmatic course. Direct action was being effectively suppressed or deflected with concessions. Fred Shuttlesworth could not sustain the struggle in Birmingham, though the Alabama Christian Movement for Human Rights (ACMHR) staged sit-ins on buses and attracted thousands to mass meetings. Police harassment, arrests, beatings, Klan bombings, and a news blackout nearly suppressed the movement. One activist was sentenced to six months in jail for passing out leaflets. Voting rights legislation promised a new climate for organizing. Senate passage of the civil rights bill would boost American prestige more "than all of the billions of dollars we spend on defense," King told the NAACP in June. In September, Congress passed the bill, approving a new Commission on Civil Rights and empowering individuals or the attorney general to seek injunctive relief in voting rights cases (although the proposed Title III, which would have given the attorney general broad authority to bring school and other desegregation suits, did not pass). Playing the cards of calculated nonpartisanship, King reminded Vice President Nixon that black voters held "the balance of

Figure 1. Unity and voting rights in a repressive time. A. Philip Randolph's themes of Negro-labor insurgency took second seat to voting rights as he cooperated with the NAACP and SCLC in organizing the Prayer Pilgrimage in 1957. King's admiration for Randolph is evident. Left to right: Roy Wilkins, King, and Randolph. Library of Congress (LC-USZ62-126523).

power in so many important big states," such as Pennsylvania, Ohio, and New York. He put Nixon on notice that he was organizing a "sustained mass movement" to achieve voting rights and electoral power.[23]

King unveiled plans for the Crusade for Citizenship in August, envisioning a $200,000 annual budget, a broad regional "mass organization," and ample publicity to "arouse the conscience of the nation." King promised to increase the southern black vote from 1.2 million to 5 million by 1960. Rustin and Levison volunteered Baker to coordinate kickoff rallies and publicize the campaign, but she had no staff and little time. King again tried to enlist National Baptist Convention president J. H. Jackson's support. Jackson favored institutional development within the black community over protests for integration, so King assured him mass voting would not lead to "social mixing." But voting was key to "all other rights, school integration, adequate housing, job opportunities, [and] integrated public transportation." King's appeal to Jackson flopped. On October 3, he appealed again to the UPWA. As hundreds of black, white, and Mexican American meatpackers cheered, Ralph Helstein gave King $11,000 to fund the crusade. Addie Wyatt, a black Chicago UPWA leader, had successfully canvassed white locals throughout the Midwest for donations, arguing that integration and black voting were in the best interests of white workers.[24]

The crusade took on the political and class rhetoric of Helstein, Rustin, and Randolph. Kicking off the campaign in Miami on Lincoln's birthday, King promised to crush the reactionary anti–civil rights and antiwelfare southern oligarchy. Americans had "the duty to remove from political domination a small minority that cripples the economic and social institutions of our nation and thereby degrades and impoverishes everyone." Southern reactionaries condemned poor whites and blacks to "ignorance, deprivation and poverty." Once conservative politicians were voted out of office, regional wages would rise, while police brutality and racist courtrooms would disappear. King sharpened the militant edge on his cold war rhetoric: America amplified its international dishonor when it denied free elections at home and conscripted Negroes into wars defending "the right to vote abroad."[25] King already connected oligarchic rule, reactionary politics, militarism, and persistent poverty, themes that defined his later radicalism.

King's rhetorical vision exceeded any organization's capacities. The Crusade for Citizenship did not double the black vote. Explanations for its failure usually cite SCLC's administrative chaos, King's inexperience, and a running feud with the NAACP over fund-raising, organizational turf, and the legitimacy of direct action protest. Thurgood Marshall even called King an "opportunist" and a "first-rate rabble rouser." But white resistance more than anything else stymied both organizations. NAACP activists reeled under the force of Citizens' Council and state repression. Operations in Alabama were shut down completely. Thousands lost their jobs. From 1955 to 1957, the NAACP lost 226 southern branches and membership shrank by 38 percent to under 80,000. SCLC faced the same severe repression. Meeting in Clarksdale, Mississippi, in May 1958, they prayed for Rev. George Lee of Belzoni, murdered for his voter registration activities in 1955. NAACP leader Aaron Henry praised King's inspiration to "working-class people," and King proclaimed it SCLC's "finest meeting." But they all acknowledged that reprisals and violence had completely deterred any "prospective Negro voters" in thirty-three counties.[26] Baker complained that SCLC was stuck in "routine procedures" for organizing voter registration, neglecting "our major weapon—mass resistance." But she, too, soon encountered the severe chill of white resistance and reprisals. SCLC leaders in Shreveport and Baton Rouge reported that several dozen "registration committees" and "social and civic clubs" were organizing voters "house to house." A year later, Baker found almost no progress in Louisiana. Though 250 people marched in Shreveport, only 15 registered. Those who dared to try were denied a market for their crops or cut from local "welfare rolls," S. O. Simpkins recalled. Mississippi was even worse. In August 1957, white officials blocked shipments of clothing bound for Cleveland, where Amzie Moore coordinated voting rights and poor relief under relentless economic harassment. "Mississippi is still in dire need," with the worst record of economic reprisals, King wrote a northern supporter. In the face of such repression, SCLC failed to build a lasting organization among the state's ministers.[27]

People seeking other explanations for the failure of the voting rights campaign cited "apathy" and skepticism among people long deprived of political power. King repeatedly criticized middle-class blacks' unwillingness to take the "short walk" to the voting booth. Thousands of teachers should step forward every "time one school teacher is fired for standing up courageously for justice," King told the NAACP in June 1957. A year later, his explanation to television reporter Mike Wallace was more nuanced: economically vulnerable teachers would not risk "sacrifices" by fighting for voting rights. Black businessmen, especially realtors and morticians, profited from segregation; lacking confidence that they could compete in an integrated society, they refused to rock the boat. Many black poor adjusted to "the system" that had disempowered blacks for centuries. But King distinguished their "exhaustion" from "internal apathy." He had great faith in the unlettered and unorganized "masses" who were ready to move. SCLC maintained in February 1959 that southern blacks were not apathetic but harbored "a strong fear and a deep antipathy toward anything having to do with politics." King argued that the same phenomenon occurred in the North, where too few blacks exercised their rights.[28] But they lacked allies and dramatic appeal. In sharp contrast to Montgomery's dramatic bus boycott, grassroots organizing for voting rights was not newsworthy. The *New York Times* never mentioned the Crusade for Citizenship.

King's manifold responsibilities and grueling speaking schedule prevented him from fostering local organizing. To Baker, King and Levison's cultivation of a charismatic "public image" far from the fields of grassroots direct action and leadership development, especially among women and youth, seemed just plain wrong. A veteran of socialist, CIO, and NAACP organizing in the 1930s and 1940s, Baker inspired students and feminists in the 1960s with her group-centered, radically democratic approach to organizing. She criticized SCLC's strategy of mobilizing people for headline-catching but episodic protests and the authoritarian "leader-centered" model of social change she thought King embodied. As a child in rural North Carolina, Baker was deeply impressed with how local people shared their labor, their food, and "*their lives*," thereby discovering "their own value, and their strengths." In 1930s Harlem, she learned from a wide "spectrum of radical thinking," working in consumer education and job training. The dense, impersonal, and obscenely unequal city desperately needed community institutions dedicated to "the *wider* brotherhood," she concluded. Traveling throughout the South in the 1940s as NAACP director of branches, Baker sought out leaders like Harry T. Moore, a Florida high school principal who fought for black-white teacher salary equalization and was murdered in 1946. Local people knew little theory, but Moore "was a *man* who served *their* interests and who *identified* with them." Perhaps King was such a man, Baker surely thought. Middle-class status was no obstacle to organizing if leaders started "where the *people* are." People knew their needs and would respond when organizers spoke of police brutality or discriminatory wages. Baker also valued interracial class alliances. Organizing for the CIO in Alabama's shipyards in the 1940s, she recalled with pride the time when a white worker denounced the "ditch" of exploitation he shared with black workers.[29]

Baker exceeded King in disdaining individualism, materialism, and class pretensions. Southern masses were "flocking" to King as the symbol of militant protest, she realized, hoping King's charisma might radicalize southern black leaders. But after two years, she concluded that SCLC was steeped in favoritism, sexism, and unquestioning deference to King's "personality." Baker had been an activist for thirty-six years, King for just three, but he was her boss. Baker challenged King's comfortable, familial definitions of femininity, and she chafed at what she saw as a Baptist minister's tendency to defend the "exclusive rightness of his position." Moreover, celebrity warped leaders, Baker concluded, sealed them off in narcissistic cocoons, and did little to empower local people or build community. People's own capacities wilted when they depended "upon a charismatic leader" prominent in "the public media," whose celebrity could be made and quickly undone.[30]

"Whoever falls in love with publicity is not fit to have it," King declared in 1956. King later admitted that SCLC relied excessively on mobilization for "crises" and national publicity. But King was also hugely popular at the grassroots, orchestrating dramatic confrontations and moving public opinion and political elites to support national legislation. This legislation helped local people uproot entrenched forms of white supremacy. Despite King's continuous efforts to "guide" the masses and "speak for the poor" from his many pulpits, King never lost his countervailing commitment to identify and speak *with* as well as *to* ordinary people.

Dilemmas and Dialectics in *Stride Toward Freedom*

Supporters had urged King to write a book on the "miracle of Montgomery." In early 1958, King toiled over the manuscript, shuffling through material sent by Harris Wofford, Rustin, Reddick, and Levison. *Stride Toward Freedom* was published in September. Editors and advisors pulled at him from every direction as he revised and excised passages from his handwritten drafts. Capitalism produced materialism "far more pernicious" than communism, he wrote. Change it to "as pernicious," wrote Melvin Arnold, a Harper editor experienced at protecting liberal authors from red baiting. Socialism and capitalism each embodied a half-truth, King wrote. Make it "a partial truth," Arnold advised; don't exalt "equality" over "liberty"; and avoid the word "collectivism," with its connotations of "Soviet slave-labor camps." King changed it all. For unknown reasons, his clearest paragraph advocating a black-white alliance for economic justice ended up on the cutting room floor. The "economic power structure usually supports and controls the political power structure," King had written. Economic elites used racist politicians to "arouse the fears" of poor whites, who traded real opportunities for decent wages through interracial solidarity for cheap myths of racial superiority. Sharing "grinding poverty" with blacks, they must join the "quest for economic justice," King urged. Perhaps someone deemed it too radical to include in a book intended for Harper's Protestant liberal readership. King also cut other set pieces about the "murder" inherent in Negro unemployment and the obscene racial gaps in relative incomes and rates of poverty.[31]

The book balanced numerous antinomies. King argued in dialectical fashion that education to change racist attitudes and legislation to control violence simply represented two lanes on the "road to racial justice." Nonviolence avoided the untenable extremes of acquiescence to oppression and destructive violence. Nonviolent persuasion, the moral conversion of the southern oppressor, complemented nonviolent coercion, the national dramatization of southern white violence to win federal intervention. Harris Wofford suggested King endorse gradual desegregation and interracial ministerial committees. King called for the committees but advocated militant religious "social action" in "housing, education, police protection," criminal justice, and "economic justice."[32]

King's final chapter attempted a grand synthesis of programs in black self-help and politics, direct action protest, and church, labor, and government action. In drafts, King and Levison locked horns over how to balance structural critiques of race and poverty with cultural critiques that held Negroes responsible for their behavioral standards and political future. King drew language from a previous Montgomery sermon criticizing low Negro "personal standards." New York City's blacks committed crimes at rates three times their share of the population, he argued. Negroes too often victimized their own people. They had "eight times more illegitimacy" in St. Louis than whites, and composed 76 percent of the welfare caseload. These self-destructive behaviors had structural roots. When King spotted a reporter in the audience during his sermon, he made sure everyone understood that honest black self-criticism did not leave white racists off the hook. "Internal" efforts to rehabilitate people and social action to abolish the "external" system of segregation complemented each other. Oppression's tragic results should never rationalize its perpetuation. But Levison regarded King's draft text a callous invitation to white enemies determined to seize on "damaging facts" to smear the movement. Segregation and poverty, not innate inferiority, caused "illegitimacy" and "broken homes," Levison wrote—as if King had not said exactly that. Levison did have a point, however; segregationists liked King's self–help sermons. Several wrote to King insisting that liberalism and welfare dependency, not segregation or poverty, produced "Negro shortcomings." In this view, "Roosevelt-type 'emancipation'" and "equalitarian Marxist-liberalism" had mutated blacks into "shiftless" and "irresponsible" paupers, criminals, and "sociological fiascoes."[33] Negroes should strive for respectability rather than stride toward freedom.

King repeatedly insisted that even malicious half-truths could help Negroes with "creative reconstruction." But after Levison's critique, he deleted all the statistics, simply stating that Negro crime rates were "too high." Not mentioning "illegitimacy," King advised parents to give children "the love, attention, and sense of belonging" that racist America denied them. King still sharply criticized "loud and boisterous" Negroes and young "deviants" in trouble with the law. But crime, delinquency, and school dropouts resulted from "environmental problems"—"urban dislocation . . . poverty, and ignorance"—rather than "racial inferiority." Antisocial behavior was an adaptation to "economic deprivation, emotional frustration, and social isolation," just as Walter Chivers had described it. Levison had urged King to write that "broken" Negro families emerged from slavery, but King cited more recent history. "Lagging standards" bespoke scarred souls and degraded personalities, products of "slavery and segregation, inferior schools, slums and second–class citizenship." The analysis reflected widespread sociological, historical, and literary ideas about "damaged" black psyches, families, and communities. But King's prescription was not merely liberal or rehabilitative: the movement itself could be the greatest healer. Uneducated blacks, often self-destructive and passively inured to segregation, had gained self-respect from Montgomery's protest, reducing rates of crime and alcoholism. "A sense of social mission and human brotherhood" transformed them, King told a group of socialist students. Activists and academics such as Kenneth B. Clark and Michael Harrington later looked to Montgomery and suggested that social action was the best cure for ghetto "pathology" and the "culture of poverty."[34]

An anticommunist fanatic stabbed King in Harlem in October 1958, nearly killing him. Mrs. Izola Curry was surely mentally ill, but she was also an angry anticommunist who tried to report King to the FBI. King described her as the victim of a societal disease, tracing her disorder to "racial tensions and a lack of brotherhood." After she was sentenced to a hospital for the criminally insane, King hoped she might become "a constructive citizen in an integrated society where a disorganized personality" need not menace anyone.[35]

King's approach to self-help in *Stride Toward Freedom*, was neither individualistic nor myopically "bourgeois," and he thought it perfectly consistent with collective and governmental activism. Acknowledging the influence of E. Franklin Frazier's recently published *Black Bourgeoisie*, King criticized the "middle-class struggle for status and prestige," which made "conspicuous consumption" more important than fighting injustice. In his book King praised "habits of thrift and techniques of wise investment." The Negro could not wait for "the end of the segregation that lies at the basis of his economic deprivation"; he must act to strengthen his own community institutions. Like Vernon Johns, King called for Negro "cooperative enterprises" and credit unions. Blacks must ready themselves to compete in a desegregated society, simultaneously working for their own political redemption, rather than worshiping "the white man's Cadillac." Negroes had "primary responsibility" for achieving first-class citizenship, since whites rarely accepted responsibility for remedying the effects of racism. The "uneducated or poverty-stricken" Negro could take "direct action against injustice without waiting for the government to act or a majority to agree with him or a court to rule in his favor." At the same time, local protest would hardly be enough, King made clear. Nonviolent resistance would be incomplete without "imaginative, bold, constructive action" to end deeply rooted community "demoralization."[36] What did he have in mind?

Stride Toward Freedom called for a "new frontal assault on the poverty, disease, and ignorance of a people too long ignored by America's conscience," but it contained few specific demands for national government action other than school desegregation. King chastised government, churches, the media, and welfare and civic institutions for failing to develop "action programs" for integrated schools. Eisenhower was "appallingly silent" when blacks needed strong leadership and vigorous enforcement. The president had argued that laws could not change the mores of the South. King countered that "morals cannot be legislated, but behavior can be regulated." In the book's only mention of fair employment legislation, King added that the "law cannot make an employer love me, but it can keep him from refusing to hire me because of the color of my skin." The government's greatest failure was Reconstruction, a lost opportunity to "guarantee economic resources to a previously enslaved people—as much entitled to the land as their former owners."[37]

Elements of class analysis remained in King's book, but he betrayed his lifelong ambivalence toward poor whites. Southern elites' underinvestment in education and their congressional veto of federal aid to education meant that poor white and black children alike bore "scars of ignorance, deprivation and poverty." The segregated South lagged behind the nation as a whole, "socially, educationally, and economically." Implicit in the analysis was a great dilemma: poor whites might choose their psychological or marginal material privileges over socialist pie in the sky. In fact their privileges were not so marginal. Melba Pattillo Beals wanted to integrate Little Rock's Central High School in 1957 because whites had "more privileges, more equipment and five floors of opportunities." King invoked the principle of "harm to one is injury to all," echoing the interracial unionist slogan of the Industrial Workers of the World (IWW). But he charted no concrete path to an interracial alliance.[38] Understanding and overcoming the complex economic predicament and racial consciousness of working-class whites never became a successful theoretical or political project for King.

Stride Toward Freedom included King's harshest words yet for southern white workers, whose "acts of meanness and violence" reflected "abnormal fears and morbid antipathies" toward blacks. The reactionary behavior of Montgomery's white workers may have confirmed a lifelong skepticism that coexisted in tension with his dreams of reviving civil rights unionism. King drew portraits of southern poor whites that resembled those of journalists who focused on fear and prejudice as the key ingredients of white reaction. Having excised his references to political and economic power structures, he did not explicitly analyze white upper-class interests or the construction of white supremacist alliances that accorded racial privileges to working-class whites. Levison vigorously protested in response to King's first draft: "Uneducated masses" had no monopoly on "meanness." Little Rock mobs included educated whites, "businessmen, and idle, middle-class housewives." King incorporated Levison's critiques, but he kept the harsh language about poor whites' morbid antipathies. But he also conceded the Klan attracted poor whites who saw "in the Negro's rising status a political and economic threat." Southern demagogues defied the Supreme Court and inflamed popular resentments with shouts of "interposition" and "nullification." And the White Citizens' Councils' public vitriol created "the atmosphere in which violence thrives."[39] One thing was clear in his appeal to northern readers: his faith in southern whites and southern modernization was slipping.

King still regarded white massive resistance as a fruitless effort to preserve "a feudalistic plantation system" that was destined for extinction with "growing urbanization and industrial expansion." But now he stressed that progress was neither "automatic nor inevitable." A range of groups and institutions, not least black people themselves, would make history.

King's book was curiously tougher on labor unions than on either government or business. The novelist Lillian Smith chided King for being far "too easy" on southern business moderates. Labor now seemed to have both the most progressive and reactionary forces in play. King hoped to bolster antiracism in existing unions, stimulate labor support for civil rights, and renew the 1940s dream of an expansive interracial and political labor alliance. But King lamented that the "organized labor oligarchy," many of whom were active in the Citizens' Councils, had caused the AFL-CIO to virtually abandon southern organizing. King did not discuss the earlier failure of Operation Dixie in the late 1940s, when state law and aggressive red-baiting corporations beat back AFL and CIO organizers, who weakened their own drive by purging leftists from their ranks. The white "labor oligarchy" was indeed now obsessed with protecting its contracts, benefits, and racial privileges. As southern workers increasingly joined reactionary movements, King's dreams of a Negro-labor alliance were sorely tested. Of the complex coalitions King tried to hold in play, King's class-based and transracial coalition was the most promising— and disappointing.[40]

King, Levison, and Rustin joined in a militant critique of discriminatory AFL-CIO affiliate unions after the initial hopes of the labor merger of 1955 were undermined by reactionary unions and locals. Randolph, then vice president of the AFL-CIO, and Herbert Hill, labor secretary of the NAACP, became their most articulate critics. Despite "clear policies of nondiscrimination" at the top, King wrote, "unions, governed by the racist ethos, have contributed to the degraded economic status of the Negroes." King criticized color bars in union locals, apprenticeship programs, and vocational schools, as well as segregated job ladders controlled by white unionists. Since one-tenth of the

13.5 million AFL-CIO members were black, King hoped that labor would contribute generously to civil rights organizations. Negroes helped build the unions; trade unionists must help assure black people's "place in American society." Democratic antiracist unions needed to aggressively expand, organize new industries, and promote progressive policies. White and black workers needed a fair share of the nation's wealth, "job security, old-age security, health and welfare protection," King wrote. "The organized labor movement, which has contributed so much to the economic security and well-being of millions, must concentrate its powerful forces on bringing economic emancipation to white and Negro by organizing them together in social equality."[41]

Why did King excise his most biting critique of the southern business oligarchy, in which the "economic power structure" was the crucial agent manipulating politicians and dividing the working class? Why did he expound at such length on the failures of labor? Why since Holt Street had he omitted militant references to "labor trampled over by capitalistic power"? King may have wanted to shame his labor audiences while not offending his northern middle-class readership by seeming anticorporate. Public esteem for labor unions had dramatically declined in 1957, when red-baiting and racketeering investigations led by Senator John McClellan and his chief counsel, Robert F. Kennedy, exposed rampant corruption within the Teamsters union. As important, by the late 1950s few organizations in the South could organize poor black and white people in a common struggle for economic justice. The Highlander Folk School kept the dream alive, as did Carl and Anne Braden in Louisville, who sustained the Southern Conference Educational Fund through years of anticommunist prosecution. Neither organization had a fraction of the resources of the AFL-CIO, whose unions had marginalized them both during Operation Dixie. The black freedom struggle remained largely outside the workplace: in streets where direct action pressured local business and civic elites; and in the halls of government, where concern for America's international image and domestic order provided new levers of social change.[42]

Stride Toward Freedom did not mention the progressive unions that stood by him in Montgomery and remained his staunchest allies. The UPWA continued to stress the benefits of collective bargaining and desegregation to all workers, northern and southern, black and white. Although some white UPWA locals resisted civil rights, the Chicago meatpackers' local was majority black; in many locals whites and blacks collaborated to open jobs and equalize the wages of whites, minorities, and women. They strove to win the allegiance of southern whites. A 1953 union pamphlet explained that discrimination lowered the wages "not only of all Negro and all women workers, but . . . all white men too." Between 1941 and 1953, southern meatpacking wages more than tripled, as the union nearly eliminated the North-South differential. Northern majority-black locals made it possible for southern whites to catch up to their levels, they explained. There was no clearer evidence that black and white southern workers both suffered from racism and anti-unionism.[43]

King continued to forge links with progressive northern unions. In the fall of 1958, he won the lifelong support of New York's District 65 of the Retail, Wholesale and Department Store Union, led by Jamaican-born black trade unionist Cleveland Robinson. "I am sure that your union can be of tremendous assistance to us," King wrote. "For as we well recognize: The forces that are anti-Negro are anti-labor and vice-versa." King told Robinson he was "thrilled" by the defeat of "the Right-to-Work Law" in recent state referenda. Robinson later joined King's advisory "research committee" and supported his antiwar activism, pressing him to integrate the civil rights and trade union movements in 1965, just at the moment King's energies turned to organizing ghetto communities. In 1958, appealing to ethnic and class identities, King sought support from the International Ladies Garment Workers Union. The South elected "viciously reactionary" congressmen who spouted propaganda that was "anti-labor, anti-Semitic, indeed, anti-democratic," King wrote David Dubinsky. In the North, despite the inroads made by civil rights unions, whites protected segregated job categories and neighborhoods. *Stride Toward Freedom* called for a "committed" liberalism "that firmly believes in integration in its own community as well as in the Deep South."[44]

Many readers recognized in King's book their own convictions, hopes, and preconceptions. Randolph praised it as "a deep source of inspiration." Reinhold Niebuhr thanked his "dear friend" for a "splendid example" of nonviolence. Chief Justice Earl Warren, praising King's "quiet patience," revealingly misnamed it "A Step Toward Freedom." Wofford called it "deeply moving," but told Levison it was a bit too "dignified" to capture the movement's true militancy. Robert Carter, a black Detroit autoworker, took King's summons to mass action as "a guide and reference." Fed up with discrimination at General Motors and within the United Auto Workers, disgusted with the "complacency" of Detroit's middle-class black ministers and NAACP leaders, Carter applauded King's critique of inequality. Negroes and Mexicans remained stuck in "the hardest and dirtiest" jobs at GM. King was right to blame the white labor oligarchy for the degraded economic position of Negroes, he wrote. All UAW leaders wanted was "that $3.00 monthly dues" payment. Black businessmen profited by segregation, exploiting "poor uneducated working-class Negroes as the whites do." Middle-class Negroes were "too busy getting their own pockets lined" to help others. If only the "harmony and cooperation" of Montgomery could be imported to Detroit, Carter dreamed. King tried in Chicago in 1966, the year before Detroit burned.[45]

Rustin and Randolph spent the summer of 1958 organizing a mass Youth March on Washington for school integration, scheduled for October 25. One skeptic pleaded with King not to incite violence in Washington. "Reconstruction was made more difficult by ill advised and unrestrained exhibitions of newly freed slaves," he wrote. King enthusiastically agreed to speak, but his slow recovery from the September assassination attempt required that Coretta King deliver his speech. An interracial team of student democratic socialists gathered around Rustin to organize the event, but the crowd was overwhelmingly black. Coretta King's speech was decidedly more militant than Martin King's Prayer Pilgrimage speech of 1957. Gone was the admonition that Negroes must behave with quiet dignity and wise restraint. She cited the Indian and Chinese revolutions and the Israelite Exodus as inspirations for black freedom fighters. Rather than criticize overzealous freedmen during Reconstruction, she praised the subversives of the Underground Railroad. Mrs. King applauded the emerging militant student consciousness: "the 'silent generation' is not so silent . . . the so-called 'beat generation' . . . is definitely not 'beat.'" The NAACP boycotted the event, but many NAACP youth councils and college chapters joined the nearly 10,000 protesters at the Lincoln Memorial. Levison wrote King that the publicity was excellent. He hoped that finally "youth and labor" were overcoming their "lethargy" and might join together in a cross-class movement as they had in the 1930s. Already he saw an emerging "student movement for civil rights on major campuses."[46] They, not the unions, spearheaded the new 1960s social insurgency.

Chapter 4
The American Gandhi and Direct Action

When a mass direct action movement burst forth from the historically black colleges and universities in 1960, no national organization plotted strategy. The sit-in movement mixed spontaneous action from the grassroots and reliance on preexisting local organizations. King learned many lessons from Mahatma Gandhi, but black students prodded him to action. Not until Birmingham in 1963 did SCLC get it right: bringing their resources and King's powerful celebrity to a local movement, demanding desegregation and jobs, and orchestrating a publicized confrontation in such a way as to move national policy elites to pass the strongest civil rights legislation since Reconstruction. That process is better known than an underlying, yet equally important, process of social learning about economic and political power that emerged from hundreds of local sites of organization and action. As King cultivated national constituencies, he and thousands of southern blacks learned that voter registration and direct action were intimately connected. They also realized that basic civil rights, the vote, and economic security against poverty and white coercion were inseparable goals.

India, Gandhi's Legacy, and Nehru

King's Gandhian supporters had long recommended that he visit India. His month-long trip in February 1959 deepened his understanding of poverty, imperialism, mass leadership, socialism, affirmative action, and cold war nonalignment. King did not address India's most difficult postcolonial dilemmas: persistent religious and ethnic conflict, the entrenched power of landowners, and the intractable caste system. But, in sharp contact to American leaders, India's leaders spoke out and acted against the economic legacy of colonialism and the sinful inheritance of caste. King did not find the Mahatma, but instead found factions of Gandhians at odds with each other over issues such as national economic planning and military armament. He nevertheless returned preaching about a more profoundly radical Gandhi than the simple saint of nonviolence. This Gandhi was courageously opposed to economic imperialism, completely identified in symbol and spirit with the poor, willing to name and overcome shortcomings of self and community, and able to make lonely, principled decisions.

When King stepped off the plane in Bombay with Coretta and L. D. Reddick, he announced to reporters that he had come to learn about the Gandhian Christian synthesis of love in action. Indian reporters were more interested in political questions, especially whether Negroes were "leftists" or believers in "free enterprise." What did King think of the red-baited black leftist Paul Robeson, they asked. Only a few Negroes held "extreme leftist views," King replied; most dreamed of equalizing wealth and winning their "economic and political rights under democracy." As for Robeson, King had no comment.[1]

Indian leaders wrote to King about Indian underdevelopment, but King was still shocked by the wretched poverty he saw. Seeing and smelling masses of "emaciated human beings" in dirty loincloths "picking through garbage cans" left Martin "angered and depressed," Coretta recalled. He blamed colonialism for a level of "abject, despairing poverty" that exceeded what he had seen in Africa. Bombay's half a million homeless people subsisted on less than $20 a year, King told his Dexter congregation on his return. British economic exploitation and extortionate taxation meant that all but one-tenth of India's 400 million people earned less than $25 a year. King and Reddick described India's unemployment and deprivation in *Ebony:* Indians were "poor, jammed together and half starved" but did not victimize each other (in contrast to America's poor). Wealthy Indian elites, overfed and lavishly dressed, languished on "landed estates." "The bourgeoisie—white, black or brown—behaves about the same the world over," they wrote. When the party toured the magnificent Taj Mahal, King saw a symbol of gross opulence amid squalid poverty.[2]

Following an exhausting schedule laid out by Bayard Rustin and their Quaker sponsors, the Kings met several Indian leaders who practiced Gandhi's "constructive program" of village self-sufficiency. Jayaprakash Narayan's ashram practiced *sarvodaya* (nonviolent socialism), where villagers ran their own cooperatives. They visited Gandhigram (Gandhi village), where people produced handicrafts and shared their work and income equally (though King doubted any village could achieve complete self-sufficiency). Vinoba Bhave's controversial *boodhan* (land gift) villages, cooperative farms organized on millions of acres donated by rich landlords, fascinated and impressed them. But King echoed growing skepticism of the "sainted" Vinoba's idealistic plans for land redistribution. He remained unconvinced that the rich would voluntarily give up enough of their privileges or that the Indians had enough "organization and drive" to diminish "the magnitude" of India's poverty. In India, King finally realized "'Love' alone will not cure poverty and degradation," Reddick told Virginia Durr.[3] Reddick saw India as pivotal to King's emerging identity as a Gandhian leader. Indians celebrated King as "the real thing," not an "imposter." They visited the communist state of Kerala, and a school principal introduced King as "a fellow untouchable." Initially affronted, King vividly recalled realizing that he and millions of poor blacks "housed in rat infested, unendurable slums" were indeed untouchables.[4]

Prime Minister Pandit Jawaharlal Nehru met with the party for four hours, convincing King that ameliorating mass poverty required national industrial policy and affirmative action for the untouchables. National economic planning and decentralized village cooperatives could be complementary strategies, attractive alternatives to Western "materialism, cutthroat competition and rugged individualism," Nehru told King. King immediately warmed to Nehru's idea of "atonement" for the historic and ongoing sin of untouchability. Reddick, however, was skeptical: did not all the special grants, scholarships, and employment opportunities in fact constitute reverse discrimination? No, Nehru replied; atoning for past "injustices and indignities" was simply fair compensation. Not yet ready to publicly endorse affirmative action, King announced on his return that India was "integrating its untouchables faster than the United States is integrating its Negro minority." Coretta King would have spoken more in conversation with Nehru, she recalled, had she known earlier what she learned in India: women had shared in the struggle, gone to jail, and shared political leadership to a much greater extent than they did in America. Gandhi had "worked to liberate women from the bondage of Hindu and Muslim traditions."[5]

In India, as in Ghana, King moved from "free world" loyalties toward nonaligned internationalism. First he endorsed Vinoba's Gandhian call for unilateral disarmament as an example to the world. But Nehru opposed disbanding the Indian army, so King called for world disarmament. The superpowers in particular lacked the "moral courage" to disarm, King said. Later, he praised Nehru's earnest will to achieve peace and his vision of India's role as a buffer between the "raging antagonisms" of East and West. King called for "generous economic and technical aid" from the West, with no paternalistic strings attached, to help India democratically solve its problems of "unemployment, food shortages, housing," and other social ills. This simple humanitarianism might "save one of the great nations of the World for democracy."[6]

King's Palm Sunday sermon to the Dexter congregation in 1959 richly evokes his deepening identification with Gandhi and his faith in the transfornational power of mass marching. Gandhi was a "prized and prominent lawyer" in England, but in South Africa he took his vow of poverty alongside Indian miners and raised the fundamental question of capitalist power, "Who's got the properties?" Donning the common loincloth, Gandhi identified completely with the "disinherited masses." He adopted an untouchable girl and fasted until Indians publicly repudiated the caste system. King also admired and idealized Gandhi's charismatic power. When Gandhi waged a hunger strike against untouchability, millions who had not "touched each other for two thousand years were now singing and praising God together." Gandhi set a high standard of self-criticism and transparent leadership, the key to his mass identification, King thought. King also admired Gandhi's willingness to make principled, solitary decisions. In 1922, when an Indian mob killed twenty-eight British officials, Gandhi angered many fellow leaders and his followers by calling off the protest in order to preserve the principle of nonviolence. Gandhi's skill at mass mobilization shaped King's freedom dreams until the end. Starting with just eighty people in Ahmadabad, Gandhi gathered a nonviolent army of millions who followed his march to the sea, where he broke the British tax on Indian salt. It was a powerful symbolic act of noncooperation "with an evil law," the beginning of a movement that broke "the backbone of the British Empire," King believed.[7]

Coretta King and Stanley Levison recalled King's struggle to embrace the Gandhian ascetic ideal. A popular leader did not need a house, property, or a family, Martin once told Coretta. India confirmed that most social corruption came from materialism, but King believed his family obligations prohibited him from taking a vow of poverty. "Even so, he did not want those possessions which would separate him from the masses," Coretta remembered. She speculated that perhaps poor black people needed a "President of the Negroes" upon whom they could shower "pomp and tribute." But King repeatedly expressed guilt, insisting "he had not earned" his class inheritance, swearing that his honors and awards were "not his alone," Levison recalled.[8]

Visiting Jerusalem on the way home in March 1959, King walked the Stations of the Cross, felt the loneliness of Gethsemane, and shed tears at Calvary. His moving Easter sermon at Dexter melded Christian, Gandhian, and internationalist commitments. Jesus bore the cross "to restore broken communities." When he stumbled under the weight of the cross, "a black man" carried it for him, a potent symbol of redemptive interracialism and personal sacrifice. Jesus would rain justice down on the earth's peoples who are dominated, exploited, "trampled over and humiliated." Easter offered hope to people crucified and "buried in numerous graves—the grave of economic insecurity, the grave of exploitation, the grave of oppression."[9]

King's internationalism swelled in his speech at the Morehouse College commencement a few months after he returned from India. Addressing the graduates of his alma mater, he called for a world war on poverty and a world democratic revolution against the legacies of foreign "exploitation and oppression." Even a billionaire could never be truly rich as "long as there is poverty in the world." The United States spent millions of dollars annually to store its agricultural surplus instead of using it to fill the "wrinkled stomachs" of the world's hungry millions. America was blinded to its shared humanity by scientific and technological hubris. The United States had become a nation of "guided missiles and misguided men," spending billions on global military bases instead of establishing international "bases of genuine concern and understanding." Harris and Clare Wofford probably inspired King's example, having sent King their 1951 book, *India Afire*, an unabashed defense of noncommunist, nonaligned socialism. Western liberals committed to "individual freedom and civil liberties will find their most wholehearted Asian allies under the banner of democratic socialism," the Woffords wrote. The Red Scare had blinded Americans to their true allies. But America must first share its rotting agricultural surpluses with the world. "We cannot stock-pile wheat like atom bombs," they wrote. Two-thirds of the world's people went to bed hungry, ripening to "the destructive rage of Communist revolution. . . . Indian Socialists are already calling for some of America's wheat to be stored in Calcutta." But the United States preferred "sending 10,000 tanks to the French in Indo-China."[10]

Liberals and Radicals

In 1959, King spoke widely in support of nonviolence, racial equality, and economic justice, stressing economic rights with one audience and constitutional rights with another, mirroring and stretching his listeners' values and viewpoints. Invited by Vice President Nixon to address a conference of four hundred religious leaders convened by the President's Committee on Government Contracts, King powerfully affirmed social democracy. King sharply rebutted Nixon's claim that discrimination was principally a "moral problem" that religious leaders should combat from the pulpit. Of course "morality is influenced by poverty," King argued, referring to the "appalling" income gap between blacks and whites. How could hungry children respect private property? Denial of "honest work and fair pay is not only immoral, it is almost murderous," he argued, "a deliberate strangulation of its victims." It was not up to religious leaders to combat workplace discrimination. Only the government could cancel federal contracts and make examples of offending corporations. King also directed attention to the North. Discrimination was rampant in northern "liberal and progressive" cities, not just the rural South. King rolled out his shocking statistics on income inequality, ending the speech with his dream of equal opportunity, "privilege and property widely distributed," and a nation where the privileged "few" no longer robbed necessities from disinherited masses. The *New York Times* quoted King's economic indictment at length right after quoting Nixon, the newspaper's first suggestion that King might be more than simply a civil rights leader.[11]

While he pushed his social democratic agenda in Washington, King reinforced his democratic socialist credentials with the left. King appealed to the Young People's Socialist League (YPSL) in an interview, affirming their democratic socialism but implicitly challenging the dangers of left sectarianism. Affiliated with the Socialist Party, YPSL had recently merged with the Young Socialist League, which included Rustin's protégés, Tom Kahn and Rachelle Horowitz. They had helped organize In Friendship and had spearheaded both Youth Marches for Integrated Schools in 1958 and 1959. These radical youth were followers of the influential ex-Trotskyite Max Schactman, who argued for a socialist "third way" rejecting both state capitalism and totalitarian "bureaucratic collectivism." YPSL had charged that King functioned to keep the black revolt "respectable." King responded that integration was no moderate goal; he wanted "complete political, economic and social equality." Socialists and workers of all races wanted decent working conditions, "adequate housing and medicine," and the repeal of "right-to-work" laws. King also reminded the leftists of the broadly humanistic values underlying the Youth Marches, which moved "the conscience of millions" by championing "values of brotherhood."[12]

King's emphasis on economic justice reflected a growing assertiveness among liberals and democratic socialists in the wake of the 1958 elections, when it seemed that the Republican-Dixiecrat alliance might finally lose its hammerlock on reform. Eisenhower's anti-inflationary economic policies had done nothing to alleviate the 1957–58 recession. After a brief recovery, another deep recession in 1959–60 froze unemployment at over 6 percent for the next five years. Black unemployment rates soared to twice those of whites, where they remained for the rest of the century. The political reaction to economic hard times was a stunning defeat for Republican candidates for Congress. Democrats now controlled the Senate, 64 to 34, and the House, 282 to 154. The UAW's Walter Reuther led a liberal-labor insurgency to pass long-delayed extensions in unemployment benefits, public works programs, investment in "depressed areas," and health insurance for the elderly. But the insurgency stalled, and King blamed the persistent power of the Dixiecrat "minority veto" exerted through the Senate filibuster. With technological change and the decline of heavy industries in the old industrial cities, unions were losing power locally and hemorrhaging national membership. At the 1959 AFL-CIO convention in Puerto Rico, Reuther called for a mass march on Washington of the unemployed to shake the government "out of its complacency." AFL-CIO president George Meany blocked it, and President Eisenhower ridiculed it, accusing labor leaders of plotting a bonus march from the beach resorts of Puerto Rico. King had already supported three smaller marches on Washington, for the vote and school integration. The March on Washington for Jobs and Freedom was four years away.[13]

Crusaders in Search of a Crusade

While King pushed creatively for policies to address economic inequality, SCLC's voting rights struggle stagnated. Through 1958 and 1959, Ella Baker, Levison, Fred Shuttlesworth, and Reddick all criticized SCLC's programmatic sluggishness and King's distance from the masses. King was a better orator than democratic crusader, they concluded. Levison warned in November 1958 that King was a "star," but SCLC needed an action program to stave off demoralizing and "discrediting" bankruptcy. On January 24, 1959, seventy-five Alabama SCLC black leaders again resolved to organize voter registration drives. Looking to Washington more than to the grassroots, King dashed off another telegram to Eisenhower demanding protection from violence and reprisals. Baker persuaded blacks in Louisiana and Alabama to press voting rights complaints in February but increasingly complained that SCLC's voting rights resolve lay dormant in Atlanta.[14] At the annual meeting in May, Shuttlesworth insisted that "flowery speeches" were no substitute for the "hard job of getting down and helping people." Reddick wondered to himself whether King was becoming "a crusader in a gray flannel suit." King continued to call for federal action. After SCLC voting rights activist Asbury Howard was savagely beaten, jailed, and placed on a chain gang in Alabama, King denounced the Ku Klux Klan, the White Citizens' Councils, and lawless southern politicians who incited such "atrocities." King demanded legislation to send federal marshals into the Deep South to guarantee voting rights. Otherwise, he threatened to take the case to the United Nations Commission on Human Rights.[15]

King remained preoccupied with national demonstrations, public relations, and fund-raising. His most concrete action proposal was to protest segregated airport waiting rooms before the Civil Aeronautics Board, a move unlikely to fire up the grassroots. In September, he recommended that SCLC hire Rustin for his valuable press contacts and writing skills. SCLC's leaders supported hiring Rustin, but Baker did not. She insisted that the organization needed a "field secretary" rather than a public relations person to polish King's image. Admitting to the SCLC board they had not "scratched the surface" of voting rights, King called for "intensified voting drives" in several cities where they were unlikely to meet strong official "resistance." King publicly defended SCLC's programs but readily admitted his own limitations when a Mennonite volunteer coordinator asked about rural opportunities for service. The rural South had the gravest "economic injustices," King replied, but he had been campaigning in cities and knew very little about it.[16]

King was moved by examples of creative mass protest at the grassroots. Virginia's militant activists particularly inspired him. In June 1959, Rev. Wyatt T. Walker broke away from the NAACP and formed the Petersburg Improvement Association to push for direct action against segregated libraries and schools. Walker drew from his experience as a radical activist. In the late 1930s Walker had joined the Young Communist League, listening to radical speeches in New York's Union Square. "The question nobody wants to say, or has not said, or doesn't *know* to say, is that the people around Dr. King, and Dr. King himself—we were all left-wingers," he later recalled. In January 1959, Walker led a march on Richmond, protesting the governor's decision to close public schools rather than desegregate them. Despite the cold rain, 1,500 protesters marched on the capitol, singing spirituals. King sent a supportive audiotape. For a dozen blocks they marched, "men, women, and children; the halt and the lame; the young and the aged," Walker wrote King. A month later, 13,000 Virginia schoolchildren returned to desegregated classrooms. The "defeat of massive resistance in Virginia is the Gettysburg of today," King told the War Resisters League. Litigation was fine, but impatient masses in the streets won real battles, he boasted to George Meany.[17] Inspired by Walker's success in the Virginia campaign, King hired him as SCLC executive director in May 1960.

Under pressure to take charge, King decided to move to Atlanta. He promised a "broad, bold advance" against segregation in all its forms, including a "huge and dramatic demonstration on a national scale" for the vote. At the December SCLC meeting, he called for "open civil disobedience" and mass jailings to awaken the nation's conscience. "Uncle Toms who will sell their souls for a mess of economic pottage do not speak for the Negro," he preached. Whites could no longer divide blacks by buying off and silencing token leaders with "measly handouts." Freedom was "worth losing a job for." Though King's rhetorical militancy increased, an action program still had not crystallized. Black students, who did not fear losing their jobs, soon emerged as the movement's vanguard.[18]

An international symbol of nonviolence, King joined an ideologically charged national controversy within the NAACP over how to respond to the rising wave of white terrorism in mid-1959. What one journalist called the "biggest civil rights story of 1959" played into simplistic dichotomies of violence versus nonviolence. Robert Williams, president of the Monroe, North Carolina, NAACP chapter, had organized a self-defense gun club that effectively chased the Klan from black neighborhoods. When two white men who had assaulted black women escaped justice at trial, Williams urged blacks to "meet violence with violence" and "lynching with lynching." News stories sensationalized Williams's words as a call to insurrection and ignored King's calls for federal protection from terror. Doubts about nonviolence were spreading even within SCLC. Affiliate member Sam Williams promised that anyone attacking his home risked being shot to pieces. Shuttlesworth confided to Reddick, "we need to get non-violence into our preachers because most of them don't really understand it."[19] As the story spun out of control, NAACP leaders suspended Williams, and delegates to the July convention supported them, 764 to 14. At the convention, King did not mention Williams but praised NAACP youth chapters who nonviolently desegregated lunch counters through sit-ins in Oklahoma and Kansas. Strategic "retaliatory violence" was immoral and impractical, he argued. Sensationalized calls to "violence" would provide ready cover for whites to rationalize massacring "innocent Negroes under the pretense that they were inciting a riot." Williams defended a grassroots tradition of self-defense. King countered with collective memories of deadly racial pogroms.[20]

The simple dichotomy between "nonviolence" and "self-defense" obscured more than it revealed. During Reconstruction and again during the 1950s and 1960s, armed protection repeatedly created space for black voting and nonviolent protest. Williams and King shared more than they admitted or the media recognized, then or later. King conceded the common ground of self-defense they shared when they took the debate to *Liberation* magazine in the fall. Even Gandhi preferred "weapons and bloodshed" to abject submission. But King argued that Williams chose the wrong side of the false dichotomy King rejected as a divinity student: the oppressed must either be "submissive or take up arms." King alleged Williams advocated organized violence "as in warfare." Small, desperate, armed bands could never involve masses in a "real collective struggle." Anne Braden corrected King's distortion, pointing out that Williams did *not* advocate "aggressive violence," only deterrence. But Braden shared King's worries that gun clubs might initiate violence, provoke repression, and discredit the movement.[21]

King and Williams wrestled with the same dilemmas of race and class. But just as journalists overlooked King's radical call for nonviolent revolution against a southern oligarchy dividing the impoverished working class, so too the black and white media paid little heed to Williams's views on political economy. Williams filled his newsletter, *The Crusader*, with appeals to start and patronize black businesses. Like King, he endorsed the need for "black-union solidarity . . . dedicated to the mission of a higher standard of living for all working people." Unlike King, Williams attended to stories of abandoned and hungry mothers and children abused and denied by racist welfare departments. He mixed militant calls for self-defense against the Klan with prayers from St. Francis: "Lord, make me an instrument of Thy Peace."[22]

Citizenship Education

"The word CRUSADE connotes for me a vigorous movement," Ella Baker wrote on October 23, still pressing SCLC's leadership toward grassroots organizing and nonviolent protest. She recommended that 1,000 ministers go into black communities and register voters person to person. She wanted to set up a parallel literacy crusade galvanizing "religious bodies, civic and fraternal organizations (composed of women, especially)." Literacy schools could provide "a 'respectable' channel" at a safe distance from the struggle. For militants, SCLC should organize "teams in nonviolent direct action," joining forces with action-oriented Gandhians like James Lawson of Nashville. It was a veritable road map for the 1960s. By September, Baker thought she had found a solution to SCLC's inertia in an adult education program administered by Septima P. Clark at Highlander Folk School in Tennessee. Baker recommended that the SCLC board make a huge investment in "leadership training" to supplement voter registration.[23] Within a year and a half, Clark was running the dynamic Citizenship Education Program out of an office across the hall from King's.

Born in 1898, Clark was a transitional figure between the voluntarism of turn-of-the-century black club women and the militant rights-conscious organizers of the 1960s, women dedicated to fostering self-activity among the oppressed and demanding economic and welfare rights from the state. Clark had taught in South Carolina's schools from 1916 to 1956. Starting on impoverished and isolated Johns Island south of Charleston, she forged links between adult literacy and democratic community organizing responsive to ordinary people's aspirations. Poverty, malnutrition, illiteracy, and the harsh demands of the plantation system on Johns Island all radicalized Clark as a young teacher. Later, in Charleston and Columbia, she fought to open public school teaching jobs to blacks and to equalize teachers' salaries. Her voluntarism ranged widely, from adult literacy for black soldiers to child immunization back on Johns Island. In Charleston in 1955, she agitated for retirement benefits and lighter teaching loads for overburdened black teachers. A referendum on inclusion of state workers in the federal Social Security system requiring a three-fourths majority made a black-white coalition necessary. Clark enjoyed the rare sight of whites politically courting blacks to get it passed. She expected the referendum would lead to "widespread Federal aid in South Carolina," she wrote Myles Horton at Highlander, including "the minimum wage law, which is 75c an hour, for domestics." But in 1956, with the rise of massive resistance, as vice president of the Charleston NAACP, Clark lost her job and her retirement benefits. She invited 726 teachers to join her in protest, but only 5 showed up. People chose their own livelihoods over her concept of how they should fight for their rights, she concluded. She could not count on teachers and ministers to risk losing their jobs for freedom. "The people in the masses . . . do better than the teachers. They come out. They're willing to fight," Clark later wrote.[24]

Back on Johns Island, seeds of a quiet but powerful political revolution were germinating. Clark's former high school student Esau Jenkins, a bus driver, restaurant owner, and community leader, packed three hundred people into a small church to discuss education and voting. To pass South Carolina's voter registration test, Jenkins's neighbors had to read and interpret the state constitution to the satisfaction of white registrars. Two dozen people had recently passed, but illiteracy and discrimination barred most from registering. Driving a bus every day filled with domestics and factory workers, Jenkins tried to teach them the rudiments of literacy. In 1954, Clark won a scholarship to Highlander Folk School and within a year was leading her own workshops. Esau Jenkins and Clark's cousin Bernice Robinson, a self-employed beautician, attended Clark's two-week workshop on the United Nations in September 1955. Asked what they would do to promote the UN, they both insisted "the people at home [come] first, the little people, the poor and underprivileged folk, Negro and white . . . and then the United Nations." Jenkins ran for school board, the first black since Reconstruction to do so. He lost, but the race educated people about the possibilities of literacy and voting.[25]

Highlander's director, Myles Horton, hired Clark full-time in the spring of 1956. Horton, Jenkins, and Clark planned the Johns Island school in late 1956. They hired Bernice Robinson because she was economically independent and could meet poor folk on their own terms. Highlander loaned them $1,500 to buy a building, where they set up a grocery store in the front "to fool white people." The profits went to pay back the loan and to aid the sick. The school opened in January 1957 with fourteen students. Robinson started with people's practical needs, listening to stories about "plowing the land," writing them down, and using them as texts. She helped with public speaking, the tax laws, and traffic safety for young people, then moved on to the election laws and the state constitution. She even posted the UN's Declaration of Human Rights on the wall, she informed Horton, and required students to "read and understand the entire thing." One can imagine callused hands slowly copying, "Everyone has the right to take part in the government of his country . . . to protection against unemployment . . . to join trade unions . . . to a standard of living adequate for the health and well-being of himself and of his family." But the declaration does not seem to have caught on as a standard text. "Better take it to the people first. Find out what *they* see the problem as being," Horton counseled Robinson. As the movement spread, teachers and local people forged their own connections between civil, political, and economic rights, by the mid-1960s voicing far-reaching claims to economic rights of employment and income support.[26]

Citizenship schools spread rapidly throughout the Low Country. By 1958, six were in operation. Blacks on Edisto Island became literate and realized that as "voting citizens they might be able to assert some power," Clark wrote. Clark trained teacher activists at Highlander, discussing school desegregation, economic reprisals and relief, the social roots of juvenile delinquency, and techniques of mass boycotting. In August 1956, black contractor L. A. Blackman of Elloree, South Carolina, told of widespread reprisals after his community circulated a school desegregation petition. Many teachers in Elloree resigned under fire, Clark wrote Horton: "Negro preachers' wives will lose their jobs if the church is used by the N.A.A.C.P. or the Voters League." In 1963, when King invited northern blacks to march on Washington for jobs and freedom, he cited the brave teachers of Elloree. If they could lose their jobs for freedom, surely his *New York Amsterdam News* readers could march for jobs and freedom.[27]

Increasingly the schools and workshops moved from voter registration to the uses of political power and the rights of economic citizenship. Local people worked for equitable public services in neglected black neighborhoods. They sought equal access to county-administered welfare, Social Security and disability benefits, and job training programs. Clark invited King to the second of two workshops titled "Social Needs and Social Resources" in January 1959. Previously, four beauticians, several teachers, and ministers had discussed social stresses on poor families and the tendency of ministers to harshly judge

Figure 2. Citizenship Education class, 1956. Septima Clark, center, Alice Wine, second from left, Bernice Robinson, standing. Wine's photographic memory of the South Carolina Constitution helped her pass the literacy test for voter registration, but she pressed Esau Jenkins to teach local people "their letters." Wine minded the store out front "to fool white folks" while they held literacy classes in the back. Photo by Ida Berman, courtesy of the Highlander Research and Education Center.

youth ensnared in the criminal justice system. "Juvenile delinquency is greatly involved with housing, job opportunities, education, religion and recreation," they agreed. Though King did not come to the workshop, Clark's growing reputation piqued his interest. By the spring of 1961, eighty-three activists trained at Highlander were teaching in Alabama, Georgia, South Carolina, and Tennessee. Clark organized workshops until the state of Tennessee red-baited and closed the school. Clark and Robinson then moved to SCLC in Atlanta in 1961.[28]

Sit-ins, Leadership, and Economic Power

The direct action crusade King, Levison, and Baker envisioned came out of historically black colleges and universities, far from the national offices of any civil rights organization. In early 1960, thousands of students sat in at lunch counters in scores of cities from Baltimore to Miami. Student activists convened in April and October 1960 to form the Student Nonviolent Coordinating Committee (SNCC). They pushed King and SCLC into renewed direct action. Baker sponsored their organization, became their mentor, and encouraged and protected their independence. King publicly lauded the students' courageous methods and uncompromising militancy. He defended them against charges of communism, lent financial support, and reaped publicity and contributions from their activism (thereby inflaming their resentment). After the 1961 Freedom Rides, students fanned out to the poor rural corners of the South, practicing a radically democratic style of organizing that focused on the everyday needs of poor southern blacks. Working from varied social, regional, and ideological bases, SNCC challenged intertwined structures of disfranchisement, violence, and impoverishment. Rooting egalitarian ideals in the rich soil of southern black culture, organizers learned alongside participants through the process of struggle itself. Most became persuaded that poor folk were the best experts on their own life circumstances. SNCC militancy, their willingness to go to jail and risk death, and their work in isolated rural communities organizing poor people provided an impetus for King to push direct action and voter registration deeper into the heart of the segregated South.

When four North Carolina A&T University freshmen sat down at Woolworth's lunch counter in Greensboro on February 1, 1960, they confronted a glaring affront to black dignity. They were permitted to buy toothpaste at one cash register but could not eat at the lunch counter. "If this is a private club . . . you ought to sell membership cards," Franklin McCain politely suggested to a bewildered waitress. State and federal courts upheld the property rights of business owners to refuse service to anyone. Blacks asserted that businesses had no moral right to discriminate on the basis of color. Four years later, in the Civil Rights Act of 1964, the federal government redrew the boundary between property rights and human rights, as much in the interests of domestic tranquility and international image as morality. In 1960, lunch counters and retail stores became the lightning rods for mass grievances. Stores refused blacks not only seats but also jobs. Blacks paid taxes, but received inferior public services (schools, sewers, streetlights and sidewalks, hospital beds, parks, and libraries). They paid higher rents for inferior housing. They were paid low wages, crowded under the "mudsill" of the southern labor market. Millions of whites thought most of them were happy in their places. Students dispelled those illusions with a new language whites could not ignore, inserting their respectably dressed bodies into the cogs of commerce. Greensboro business owners claimed they could not act unless the entire community reached consensus in the context of "civility." Local managers told McCain that corporate headquarters set policy. Corporate heads said they would not interfere with local "customs." An elderly white woman cheered them on, while a black dishwasher called them rabble-rousers. Later on, McCain learned how much she had feared for their safety and for her own job. "I might have been fired and that's my livelihood," she told him.[29]

The Greensboro protests mushroomed into a full-scale confrontation between a united black community and Greensboro's business and political establishment. Negotiations broke down after the principal white mediator called the sit-ins a "direct violation of the owners' legal rights." On March 31, 1960, 1,200 students, whose status made them relatively immune from white reprisals, resumed picketing. Adults organized a boycott. High school students joined the picketing through the summer. Merchants lost 20 percent in sales and 50 percent in profits. Greensboro's black community hailed a victory on July 25 after Woolworth's, Kress, and Meyer's Cafeteria all agreed to desegregate. Meanwhile, student protest had inundated the South. By the end of March, eighty cities from Xenia, Ohio, to Sarasota, Florida, saw sit–ins, the largest wave of mass protest since the 1930s. White crowds attacked nonviolent students with ketchup, lit cigarettes, and bottles of ammonia. Police arrested students for trespassing. Often, students managed to shut down the stores themselves, and black communities organized pickets and boycotts. Northern activists staged sympathy sit-ins and pickets. Local elites, especially in the upper South, negotiated desegregation; in the Deep South, they often brutally suppressed protests.[30]

The sit–in tactic had been practiced by Gandhians seeking desegregation before Greensboro, and the protests quickly spilled beyond lunch counters. SCLC board member Rev. Douglas Moore had led student sit-ins at an ice cream parlor in Durham in 1957. Ezell Blair, Sr., the father of one of the Greensboro four, had led a 1959 campaign to open sales jobs to blacks in a local shopping center. Nashville students had tested the sit–in tactic at lunch counters in late 1959. Gandhian seminarian James Lawson of Fisk University and Rev. Kelly Miller Smith, SCLC's affiliate director in Nashville, had conducted nonviolence workshops since 1958. They were joined by Rev. C. T. Vivian, who had led successful sit-ins at restaurants in Peoria, Illinois, between 1945 and 1947. In early February 1960, Moore phoned Lawson, and forty-five Nashville students immediately staged sympathy sit-ins. Dramatic confrontations led to negotiations and a breakthrough with the merchants and the mayor. In Nashville, Smith and Vivian made the small step from the right to sit at a lunch counter to the right to work, asking several merchants, "How many Negro clerks do you have?"[31]

SCLC leaders tried to catch up with the masses, raise the stakes of struggle, and publicly defend black economic coercion. "Watch out, my daughter will put you and me off the front page," Philadelphia minister William Gray warned King after her arrest. In reply, King hoped the students would "knock some of the oldsters out of their state of apathy." He urged SCLC affiliates to join in, congratulating Rev. C. K. Steele when Tallahassee demonstrators chose jail instead of paying $300 fines. Acting on King's advice "to fill the jails," Tallahassee students transformed a mark of criminality into a "badge of honor," King proudly announced. On February 16, touring lunch counters in Durham, King announced that American students were out in front of "the world-wide struggle." Foreign freedom fighters were closely examining America's creeds and deeds, and naturally the student movement would "go beyond eating places," he promised *U.S. News & World Report* in March. Relatively poor blacks had to shop at inexpensive five-and-dimes, which forced "appalling" conditions upon them but depended on their money, King explained. Although blacks had not "achieved economic justice," they made enough money to pressure economic elites. *Newsweek* erroneously presented King as the brains behind the protest. King wanted to support and help lead the student movement; indeed, journalists assumed he was already in charge.[32]

Few reporters captured the political and cultural audacity of student non-violence, especially their belief in redemptive brotherhood, the *Atlanta Journal*'s Pat Watters remembered. Looking everywhere for violence and headlining the rare "fistfight," journalists labeled protests "racial disturbances," obscuring the fact that blacks almost invariably absorbed white violence. In a national NBC television debate with Richmond newspaper editor James J. Kilpatrick, King denied Kilpatrick's charge that every sit-in produced "riot and disorder." Disciplined nonviolent protesters nearly always absorbed white "extremist" violence, despite reports to the contrary. James Lawson scolded the media and its white consumers in April for believing polite citizen protesters were "disorderly [mobs] breaking the peace [and] inciting riots."[33]

King took on President Harry Truman when the former haberdasher red baited the students in early April, telling reporters he would have physically ejected any communist agitator who invaded *his* store. Truman abetted the "violent forces in the South," King told a national television audience. Businessmen's "legal right" to exclude Negroes violated "moral justice" and the spirit of the Fourteenth Amendment. Negroes were assailing "the whole system of segregation." Only sit-ins, not just consumer boycotts, amassed sufficient economic pressure to move power structures. Harris Wofford tried to mediate the dispute, explaining to Truman that the SCLC ministers and their student protégés were all Gandhians practicing "love and redemption." But

King had already condemned Truman's "McCarthy-like accusations," demanding an apology. None came.[34]

King could only protest as state officials crushed the Montgomery sit-in movement. When thirty-five Alabama State College students tried to integrate the courthouse cafeteria on February 25, Governor Patterson ordered President H. Councill Trenholm to expel them all and anyone who followed. Montgomery's fire department, using water hoses and aided by 5,000 angry whites, pushed black protesters back into Ralph Abernathy's church on March 6. After students boycotted classes, heavily armed police invaded the campus and arrested thirty-six students. Montgomery's "Gestapo" police were "trying to incite a riot," King telegraphed President Eisenhower, who called the sit-ins "constitutional and proper" but refused to intervene. King again feared "violence" would be blamed on nonviolent Negroes. Sheriff's "race-riot" posses were forming in response to "racial disturbances," the *New York Times* reported. Protests stalled under the relentless repression and the refusal of the MIA to support the students. The governor pressured Trenholm to fire eleven faculty members potentially sympathetic to the students, including L. D. Reddick. King appealed to liberal organizations on behalf of "academic freedom . . . free speech and free assembly." But now in Montgomery, all he had was rhetoric. Neither was he any longer so optimistic about self-help, telling an interviewer that blacks still depended on white employers and extortionate white creditors who routinely intimidated them into silence.[35]

In Atlanta, the student movement moved haltingly toward direct action, confronting both white repression and an established Negro leadership that believed in good-faith negotiations with whites in the "City Too Busy to Hate." Student leaders Lonnie King and Julian Bond recruited 150 students to sit in at Kresge's and Woolworth's in February. President Rufus Clement of the Atlanta University Center persuaded them to delay protests until mid-March and shift their focus to "public" facilities. King mediated and supported this compromise on March 10. The students agreed first to publish "An Appeal for Human Rights" in the *Atlanta Constitution*. Bond saw it as a delaying tactic, but it worked only briefly. On March 15, two hundred students marched downtown to sit in at cafeterias in the state capitol, county courthouse, city hall, and interstate bus and train stations. A few days later, facing internal divisions over strategy and severe repression from the city, the students ended their sit-ins. On March 18, eighty-six students faced charges carrying maximum sentences of forty years in prison and $27,000 fines. The movement conducted sporadic protests throughout the summer but did not regain momentum until October. Only then did King answer SNCC's inevitable question, "Where is your body?"[36]

Student governments of all five of Atlanta's black colleges and universities signed the "Appeal," written by Julian Bond and Atlanta University's dean of social work, Whitney M. Young, Jr., a student strategic advisor who soon became executive director of the National Urban League. The document casts doubt on Bond's claim that students had not considered "much more than a hamburger" until Ella Baker opened their eyes to the larger implications of the struggle in April. Political exclusion from "city, county and state government," not retail commerce, was their largest concern in the "Appeal." Widespread "inequalities and injustices" violated human rights and retarded "social, economic, and political progress." Their first grievance was separate and unequal education: Georgia spent fifteen times more on higher education for whites than blacks. Negroes could not rise above "menial" jobs in city offices. One-third of Atlanta's population was crammed onto one-sixth of its land, in segregated and poor housing. Black citizens were denied equal access to the vote. Segregation in theaters and restaurants was their *sixth* grievance, which might explain why students outside Atlanta did not flock to its banner. Their final grievance was police brutality and the city's failure to hire or promote Negro police.[37] It was a comprehensive indictment of black political and economic exclusion.

King dreamed of a broad attack on the southern system, exhorting students with his most radical rhetoric of international human rights. King's April 10 speech at Spelman College inveighed against materialism, world poverty, and the arms race. Too many striving and succeeding African Americans believed in the eleventh commandment: "Thou shalt not get caught. . . . It's all right to exploit, but be a dignified exploiter." He praised student protesters who instead identified with the people and demanded changes more radical than "a cup of coffee and a hamburger." Karl Marx had faced exploitation and dreamed of "a classless society" based on the principle, "from each according to his ability to each according to his need," King preached. Edward Bellamy had condemned "the inequalities of monopoly capitalism." Students should not just demand equality for consumer-citizens, but aim to bridge the gap between inordinate wealth and abject poverty in the United States and the world. Poverty pervaded the Middle East, India, and Africa because imperial nations dominated and exploited the masses. "Violence is the inseparable twin of western materialism, the hallmark of its grandeur," King preached. World leaders must "bring an end to the armament race." King made no cold war appeal to the loyalties of "uncommitted" peoples.[38] He encouraged a black internationalism that students were already making their own, long before they met Malcolm X or traveled to Africa.

Supportive wealthy or middle-class whites expected a different kind of talk, and King gave it to them. Raising money in New York for the students, King denied the Negro student was "soft, pliable and conformist—a mechanical organization man or an uncreative status seeker." Elsewhere he had praised the "majestic and sublime" women arrested in the Atlanta sit-ins. But with white donors, King described the galling frustrations of professional Negro men, applauding activist "pioneers" who forged "priceless qualities of character" on wild frontiers of protest. Thomas Patton of the Committee to Assist Sit-In Demonstrators wrote from Sausalito, California, proposing an art auction for the students. This Marin County progressive dreamed that if southern Negroes stayed nonviolent in the "struggle against racial exploitation," eventually whites would join "the ultimate struggle against all exploitation." It was a widely shared dream, but to many whites, King *was* the southern Negro.[39]

SNCC

King's rhetorical flights did not satisfy Baker, who worked to foster the students' commitment to local democratic organizing and independence from established civil rights groups. With $800 of SCLC's money, she called a founding conference at Shaw University in Raleigh, North Carolina, on April 15–17, 1960. Claude Sitton of the *New York Times* expected that "students would lean heavily on Dr. King." Baker informed King that both Glenn Smiley and Doug Moore agreed the meeting should "be youth centered," and adults would speak "only when asked." Over two hundred student activists showed up. Reporters looking for information about the students turned to King, who advocated a "continuing organization" carrying the struggle into "every nook and cranny" across the South. King advocated massive community boycotts and urged upon the students uncompromising "jail—no bail" tactics. Maybe they could compel federal enforcement of civil and voting rights, he speculated. At the conference, King praised the students' "revolt" against middle-class aspirations for "big cars and ranch-style homes." He criticized protracted NAACP-style litigation that only fed into white "delaying tactics." King alone attacked the segregationists' defense based on property rights. Any store open to the public was "not private property in the sense that it may deny accommodations," he argued.[40]

James Lawson and Baker made bigger splashes than did King. Recently expelled from Vanderbilt University, Lawson had been a student of Gandhism in India. Was all this "just a lot of nonsense over a hamburger?" Obviously not. The students adopted Lawson's words in their statement of purpose, affirming "the philosophical or religious ideal of nonviolence" as the basis of their faith and action. The beloved community would overcome "systems of gross social immorality." Lawson outdid King in criticizing the NAACP as a "black bourgeois club" devoted only to fund-raising and legalism. NAACP executive director Roy Wilkins, who had not been invited to the conference, hit the roof. King tried to patch things up, but the students were a new, independent force challenging all established organizations.[41]

Baker's influence far exceeded Lawson's or King's. All that survives of her speech is her own report, exuding pride in students who already knew that human rights demanded "something much bigger than a hamburger": the total defeat of "racial segregation and discrimination." They were determined to avoid "struggles for personal leadership," and she was thrilled they resisted adult attempts to "capture" their movement. Transparently challenging King, she praised student plans to rotate leadership within groups, so that movements would not stagnate "when the prophetic leader turns out to have heavy feet of clay." Julian Bond remembered Baker's speech as pure pedagogy, "an eye-opener" and "a big leap" for him and many others who had not looked beyond lunch counters. Baker was profound and catalytic, but she was surely right about the participants' sense of the monumental task before them. Claude Sitton had surveyed many student activists in early February 1960, concluding "the Negro's right to sit at a lunch counter" was the entering wedge of a broad insurgency.[42]

Student protesters had diverse class backgrounds and aspirations for social change and inclusion. Clayborne Carson argues that most students embraced "conventional American values" of assimilation and economic mobility. They were affronted by segregated lunch counters, exhilarated by nonviolence, and inspired by militant African students. Only "in struggle," as they confronted violence, racism, poverty, and the failure of the federal government to protect lives and liberties, did they embrace political radicalism. Many students came from poor and working-class backgrounds with raw grievances against poverty, power, and racism, however. Jane Stembridge, Ella Baker's first protégée in Atlanta, noted that many of their "parents were still farming, sharecropping and barely able to keep [their] kids in college." Students put their parents' dreams of individual success at risk by seeking their education and collective liberation in dank jails next to disreputable criminals. John Lewis grew up poor in rural Alabama, his father deeply in debt. Lewis knew by the age of six that the "grinding, monotonous rhythm of cotton" was an economic "bottomless pit." He remembered King on the radio in 1955 preaching "Paul's Letter to American Christians," with its castigations of capitalist abuses. King's "social-political" teaching articulated what Lewis was "feeling and fighting to figure out for years." Lewis and James Bevel were sem-

inarians at American Baptist Seminary, where communal poverty was less a
Christian ideal than a fact of daily life. Bevel, who later joined SCLC, "hated
greed, and he hated selfishness at the most personal level," reporter David
Halberstam remembered.[43]

Charles Sherrod was the first of six children born to a single mother who
relied on welfare; as a child, he shined shoes to help support the family. While
training for the Baptist ministry, Sherrod joined sit-ins in Rock Hill, South
Carolina, energizing the movement by opting for "jail, no bail." James
Forman, who joined SNCC in 1961, was an educated northerner and already a
committed Marxist. Raised "dirt poor" by his grandmother in rural Mississippi—he literally ate dirt as a child, a sign of severe nutritional deficiency—
Forman revered the communalism of poor black folk. As a Chicago high
school student, he came to see the "theory of surplus value [as] a down-to-
earth matter of slave owners and racist employers." In the 1950s, Forman
dreamed of a revolutionary organization of southern blacks, "broadly socialistic" and dedicated to changing America's "political, economic, and social
structure" from the ground up. His radicalism was exceptional, but his leadership suggests that many in SNCC were primed to challenge, rather than simply
join, the American Dream.[44]

If King meant to capture the student movement, the state of Alabama
posed greater obstacles than Ella Baker. Two weeks after the sit-ins began, King
faced felony charges of tax fraud in Alabama that threatened to smear him as
a corrupt movement profiteer. King denied he owned anything other than his
old 1954 Pontiac; his arrest was part of a pattern of legal and economic
"harassment" that included Tennessee's recent successful closing of Highlander Folk School. Yet Coretta never saw "Martin affected so deeply." He
agonized to the point of feeling "a sense of guilt." To defend himself , King
hitched his fund-raising effort to that of the students, opening himself to the
very charges of financial opportunism he sought to combat. The Committee
to Defend Martin Luther King and the Struggle for Freedom in the South,
organized by Rustin, Levison, Randolph, and Harry Belafonte, took out a *New
York Times* ad attacking "Southern violators of the constitution" for suppressing "peaceful protests." Wofford thought the strategy disgraceful, because the
students' legal needs far exceeded King's and the New Yorkers made King look
like a helpless "kind of Scottsboro boy," the "puppet" of a northern cabal.
King was elated when in May 1960 he was acquitted of all charges by an all-
white jury. But criticism of his fund-raising continued to dog him. King
assured baseball legend and NAACP activist Jackie Robinson that he had
no wish to divert donations from the NAACP and that he had no "messiah
complex."[45]

Liberal whites did in fact send King thousands of dollars for himself and the students. After his acquittal, King continued to appeal for funds for himself and student activists reliant upon "our organization for aid and guidance." SNCC increasingly resented King's command over publicity and contributions. "They'd piggyback on everything we did," Bond later alleged. Aware of SNCC criticism, King and Harry Belafonte arranged a fund-raiser for SNCC in May 1962. King mingled with the students and wealthy New Yorkers, gave a laudatory speech, and left without mentioning SCLC.[46]

King could no longer preach "jail—no bail" and refuse to join the pioneers. Students held their second conference in Atlanta on October 14–16, 1960. King's outline for his speech expressed hopes they would avoid sloppy planning, seductions of "publicity," and destructive "ego struggles." Now formally calling themselves the Student Nonviolent Coordinating Committee, they created a national structure and determined to remain an "action organization." About 140 delegates from 46 protest centers attended, with 80 observers from northern colleges.[47]

Atlanta students decided to protest segregation by sitting in at Rich's department store, setting in motion events that landed King in prison and helped elect John Kennedy president. King broke with his father and Atlanta's elite, joining student protesters on October 19. King and fourteen others who were arrested refused bail. The mayor and sixty black leaders agreed to release the prisoners in exchange for a thirty-day pause in demonstrations and negotiations with store owners. But a Georgia judge sentenced King to Reidsville state penitentiary for violating his probation from a minor traffic conviction. The ensuing media frenzy confirmed that King was never more newsworthy than when threatened or imprisoned. John Kennedy placed a consoling phone call to Mrs. King, and Robert Kennedy interceded to win King's release. Daddy King promised "a suitcase of votes" for Kennedy. King, Jr. praised Kennedy's "courage" on the radio, reminding everyone that Negro votes in key northern states could swing the election, which is exactly what happened. A less publicized drama reported only locally unfolded in Reidsville prison itself, where King read notes slipped to him by prisoners describing horrid conditions. Upon release King declared prison officials treated inmates like "animals rather than persons." Several days later, half of the 1,100 black prisoners staged a two-day hunger strike to protest their treatment. King managed to help Kennedy, demonstrate his solidarity with the students, and publicize separate and unequal prison conditions.[48]

In Atlanta, a community boycott and negotiations continued throughout the winter. King successfully brokered a compromise in March 1961 between the young people and established black leaders. Whites agreed to desegregate restaurants and stores after school desegregation in the fall. The students cried foul at the delay but relented after King passionately defended his father's courage and appealed for "unity." The differences between student militants and their elders were not over goals but tactics and timing. Adults and students alike gave first priority to "equal job opportunities, pay and promotion," a contemporary researcher discovered. Desegregation of schools and public accommodations came second.[49]

Political Power and Radical Dreams

In June 1960 King and Randolph announced the March on the Conventions Movement to pressure Democrats and Republicans to adopt strong civil and voting rights planks by protesting against "double disfranchisement"—at registrars' offices and in party organizations. Rustin, who was now running SCLC's New York City office, drew together a talented interracial team of fellow socialists: Michael Harrington, Tom Kahn, Rachelle Horowitz, and Norman Hill, the black executive secretary of the Socialist Party. Hill had written to King in January 1960 celebrating the bonds between the party of Eugene Debs and "Negroes, who are exploited politically and socially as well as economically." Just as this coterie of talent came together, Harlem's congressman Adam Clayton Powell, Jr. threatened to expose King and Rustin as gay lovers if Rustin continued. Rustin resigned, furious and disappointed when King did not defend him. The Socialists drifted to other organizations. King now depended on Levison and his protégé Jack O'Dell at the Harlem office. Both men's past affiliations with the Communist Party provided all the pretext J. Edgar Hoover needed for a campaign of surveillance and harassment against King beginning in 1961.[50]

King and Randolph's joint proposals to the Democratic National Committee (DNC) were more far-reaching than the plank drafted by Wofford and liberal Congressman Chester Bowles. But King and Randolph kept their democratic socialism under wraps. They advanced a comprehensive civil rights agenda, but did not mention the workplace organizing rights essential to the success of the Negro-labor coalition. They demanded the federal government set up voter registration offices, which Negroes would help administer. The plank as passed called for enforcement of existing laws. They demanded action banning "discrimination in government employment" and federally subsidized housing. The Democrats promised executive orders, litigation, and legislation.[51] King called the platform unprecedented, "positive, dynamic, and meaningful." It was the first Democratic Party platform ever to mention the

Fair Employment Practices Commission, yet it drew few linkages between economic policy and civil rights. The Democrats advocated "economic justice for all Americans," but they located civil rights explicitly in a realm beyond "material goals," involving "the spiritual meaning of American society." Kennedy promised policy initiatives to alleviate "poverty in an affluent society." But in the West Virginia coal-mining region where he campaigned, the face of poverty was overwhelmingly white. King and Randolph failed to mention the central demand of the AFL-CIO: repeal of section 14b of the 1947 Taft-Hartley Act allowing states to hamper unionization by banning the union shop. Their omission is puzzling, but it portended larger weakness of labor liberalism. As Nelson Lichtenstein argues, minority and women's rights to equal employment in individual hiring dramatically expanded through new laws and administrative agencies in the 1960s. But the collective rights and political clout of unions and workers declined, adversely affecting wages, working conditions, and job security. The postwar legal framework so disadvantageous to union expansion remained unreformed.[52]

Privately at the convention King spoke freely with Michael Harrington about his democratic socialism. Reaping the benefits of Harrington's advance work in the Los Angeles black community, King and Roy Wilkins led a march of 6,000 to the Shrine Auditorium. Moderation was "a tragic vice" if it meant delaying "human rights" by accepting "states rights" defenses for school segregation, King said. In the face of a bipartisan "conspiracy of apathy and hypocrisy," King was ready to "*federalize* the schools." Harrington organized a round-the-clock vigil at the convention, amazed that everyone seemed to accept that a white man led "a picket line for black freedom." He and King enjoyed long private conversations in their hotel about civil rights and economic justice. King was "a conscious Randolphite" and "a democratic socialist . . . dedicated to the program of an integrated class struggle against both exploitation and racism," Harrington concluded. They both agreed that "full civil rights for an exploited and hungry mass of black Americans constituted only a first step in the transformation of the intolerable conditions under which they lived." But Harrington appreciated how King had to muffle his socialism in the absence of a "mass socialist movement that could have given his immediate struggles real support."[53] To the extent that the movement was assuming mass dimensions, it remained a black struggle for equality, broadly inclusive of socialists, reformists, integrationists, and incipient nationalists. King remained a minister, an interracial mediator, a crusader against southern segregation and disfranchisement, and a dreamer for economic justice.

While Harrington and King dreamed of democratic socialism, southern white business and governmental elites organized reprisals against activists on an unprecedented scale. Two campaigns of economic reprisal highlighted the connections between economic power, community welfare, and political freedom. In both cases, coalitions of black activists fought to protect the economic rights of people fighting for their civil rights. These dramas of reprisal, relief, and resistance foreshadowed much of the conflict in the 1960s.

In New Orleans, public officials purged thousands of blacks from the welfare rolls in the wake of school desegregation and voter registration drives. State welfare officials judged 98 percent of black children "illegitimate," and 23,000 black children lost public assistance. On December 10, 1960, King denounced Louisiana's leaders, who sought to maintain their power and "preferred economic position" by frightening whites with nightmarish visions of slippery slides from desegregation to miscegenation and mass Negro welfare dependency. To supporters amazed that the governor would take such risks with federal funding, King explained that denial of welfare was indeed a new form of "retaliation" against constitutionally protected citizenship rights.[54] In Fayette and Haywood counties in eastern Tennessee, whites reacted to black voter registration drives with boycotts against black businesses and threats to evict nearly seven hundred families from their homes. The NAACP, SCLC, Congress of Racial Equality (CORE), UPWA, J. H. Jackson, and student groups all joined the relief effort and counterboycotts against whites. On December 22, 1960, King sent $800 to help "stem the tide of segregationist retaliation." His aide James Wood denounced a white conspiracy to deprive blacks of food, "freedom, and the right to vote." Legal victories in March and April 1961 provided relief, and the white boycott collapsed in July. It was a tremendous flexing of movement muscle, and it raised hopes that the Kennedy administration might further support black freedom.[55]

For King, the lessons of 1959 and 1960 were manifold. Visiting India solidified his anger at poverty and imperialism, along with his Gandhian leadership identity. As King sought to widen students' appreciation of the political and economic dimensions of their struggle, they forced him to act on his preachments. He had learned about a democratic form of grassroots citizenship education that he would soon incorporate into SCLC. As King subsequently turned from the vote to direct action and an array of national issues, he advocated federal and social action to aggressively protect activists' rights and African Americans' interests in decent jobs, housing, international peace, and economic justice for all.

Chapter 5
The Dreams of the Masses

John Kennedy won the presidency in 1960 by a narrow margin with black votes in key states, boosting Martin Luther King's hopes for vigorous federal action to secure civil and economic rights. But the same political arithmetic that made the black vote so important worked to minimize its impact. Despite Democratic majorities in both the House and Senate, Congress remained locked down by conservative Democrats whose southern power base was disproportionately white and rural. So King looked to the president to take executive action to equalize opportunity and redress long-standing oppressions.

Kennedy's inaugural address was filled with soaring rhetoric: "If a free society cannot help the many who are poor, it cannot save the few who are rich." He did not mention desegregation or civil rights. "A rising tide lifts all boats," Kennedy promised, but he embraced a moderate Keynesian "New Economics" only in 1962, when the economy lurched into its sixth year of high unemployment. To the dismay of liberals and civil rights advocates, the president was consumed by foreign affairs and neglected domestic policy. In response to congressional concern about "depressed areas" spearheaded by Senator Paul Douglas, he supported the Area Redevelopment Act. Congress passed his Manpower Development and Training Act, as economists raised concerns about a glut of unskilled workers and a deficit of skilled workers. But these measures had limited reach and little punch.[1]

Ira Katznelson has ably summarized a growing scholarly consensus that white men and their dependents benefited disproportionately from the New Deal state, and that 1960s liberalism had a limited effect on the fragmented and multi-tiered structure of social insurance and public assistance that took shape in the 1940s. The conflicted and sclerotic alliance between southern conservatives and urban liberals that was the mid-century Democratic Party spoke a rhetoric of universal rights. But through a series of fatal compromises in which the southerners held inordinate power, the New Deal and the Fair Deal reinforced unequal social and economic contours of race, gender, and class. North and South, the dominant interests in the coalition willingly accepted

federal benefits but denied blacks their fair share. The GI Bill disproportionately benefited white men, and black beneficiaries faced restricted opportunities in vocational education and higher learning. The Social Security Act
rewarded male retirees and their dependents through formulas reflecting their
stable work histories and higher lifetime earnings. Centrally, agricultural and
domestic workers did not enjoy Social Security, minimum wage, or labor
union protections; this was a huge disadvantage to lower paid blacks and
women who disproportionately worked in these job categories. With federal
money, states and localities administered the Aid to Dependent Children program in highly variable, racially discriminatory, and often coercive ways. Public housing was segregated and underfunded. Blacks and poor whites did not
benefit from the federally subsidized Federal Housing Administration (FHA)
and Veterans Administration (VA) loans that underwrote the suburban boom
in new home construction. Federally subsidized urban renewal and redevelopment projects commonly benefited downtown corporate or large institutional
interests, often leaving poor and black people without homes or relocation
assistance. Could the limitations of the New Deal racial state ever be sur-
mounted? This was the largest challenge of the 1960s. Not without a political
revolution in the South, many liberals and the labor–civil rights coalition concluded.

   In the civil rights arena, Kennedy acted only during crises that threatened
lives, jeopardized domestic tranquility, or caused international embarrassment, such as when white mobs battled federal marshals at the University of
Mississippi in 1962. Kennedy preferred to keep civil rights issues within the
safe, orderly bounds of elite negotiations and executive orders timed to provoke the least controversy. The president's two-year delay in fulfilling a campaign promise to equalize opportunity in federally assisted housing left
activists wondering if the federal government could possibly head off a racial
explosion in the nation's cities.[2]

   King publicly dedicated himself to extending New Deal liberalism within
the Democratic Party, but he had to confront cleavages in the party's coalition.
King did not want a "socialistic economy" to solve the dilemma of wealth
and poverty, he again told an interviewer in March 1961. The New Deal tradition—and coalition—offered the best possibilities for "a broader distribution
of wealth." The Democratic Party was "schizophrenic," he explained, split
between Dixiecrats and liberals, but it deserved the electoral loyalty of the
"Negro masses" because it was simply better on economics and social welfare.
But in addition to the Dixiecrats, liberals faced a growing northern movement
of working-class whites increasingly resistant to any threat to their ostensible
"rights" to decent homes in exclusively white neighborhoods or to the privi-

leges of union-protected job niches. In a sluggish economy and with cities hemorrhaging manufacturing jobs, they feared for their own and their children's economic futures. Homeowners' movements became decisive political forces blocking public housing, electing mayors, and policing the color line with violence. Ordinary northern blacks implored King for help. A poor single mother in Chicago wrote in April 1961 that the NAACP did little more than "fund raising to help King or for sit in down South . . . Write or do something to let us know some one still mean some good. We poor people feel very very bad here."[3]

"Equality Now": Dreams of Executive Action

In the early 1960s, King developed a metropolitan economic and spatial analysis that implicated government, businesses, institutions, and homeowners in the reengineering of big-city segregation and inequality. "Equality Now—The President Has the Power" was his first annual report on civil rights for the *Nation,* published in February 1961. King demanded that Kennedy issue executive orders against discrimination in housing and employment. Among prominent liberals he widely circulated his "amazing" discoveries about presidential power gleaned from a report published by the Southern Regional Council. King's text argued the president must issue another Emancipation Proclamation and appoint a secretary of integration. For the first time, King called on the federal government to follow India's example of "atonement" by providing "special treatment" for America's untouchables. He called for "scholarships, financial grants and special employment opportunities" to help poor blacks "leap the gap from backwardness to competence."[4]

Over the next two years, as the New Frontier increasingly seemed neither new nor pioneering, King produced a flurry of speeches, articles, and interviews, becoming more critical by the month. He cobbled everything together in a detailed "Appeal" to President Kennedy in May 1962, a document that reflects widespread political and academic hopes for executive policymaking characteristic of the early 1960s. King cited abundant examples of vigorous presidential assertion, especially Lincoln's Emancipation Proclamation and Franklin Roosevelt's expansion of the regulatory state to protect and provide collective bargaining, wages, relief, and public works. Roosevelt secured permanent mass consent for activist government, King thought (consistently overlooking evidence of local and congressional brakes on progressive reform). Kennedy should propose legislation with "crusading zeal," especially in voting rights. The president could directly appeal to Americans, issuing executive orders in education, health, federal hiring, agriculture, and federally subsidized housing. He could withhold subsidies from segregated hospitals and schools. He could prevent white landowners from using agricultural subsidies to evict their black tenants, and aid thousands of black farmers denied credit in retaliation for seeking their "citizenship rights."[5]

King's call for "special treatment" put him to the left of most civil rights leaders. On March 6, Kennedy issued an executive order mandating fair employment by the federal government and contractors, creating the President's Committee on Equal Employment Opportunity (PCEEO). Kennedy's order borrowed the phrase "affirmative action" from labor law, but at the time it simply meant affirmative enforcement of fair hiring. In the liberal establishment, "classic nondiscrimination was itself a radical proposition in 1961," Hugh Davis Graham argues. With no powers of enforcement, the PCEEO relied on voluntary business compliance and held a series of relatively ineffective conferences under the rubric "Plans for Progress." L. D. Reddick advised King to praise Kennedy's action and demand immediate implementation. But not until the following February, in a negative assessment of the administration's progress, did King call for vigorous enforcement.[6]

King was clearly more concerned with housing and ghettos than jobs, despite local white political resistance to residential desegregation. In 1957 he had called housing "the crux of the race problem" in the cities. Now it was "the most tragic expression of discrimination." Federal agencies, banks, and construction companies colluded in preventing blacks from securing loans for new homes, forcing blacks into "ghettos and overcrowded conditions." King clearly learned from the National Committee Against Discrimination in Housing (NCADH), whose advisory committee he joined in 1960. Inviting King to join, Oscar Hammerstein II explained that housing held the key to equal education and job opportunities. The NCADH informed King of its defense of an integrated housing development against a reactionary white homeowners' movement in Deerfield, Illinois. Modern Community Developers had reserved a minority of the fifty-one homes for Negroes. King publicly endorsed their attempt to "prove that integration can work." But Deerfield whites passed a referendum blocking the project in late 1959. King was unwittingly dragged into a local debate when veteran community organizer Saul Alinsky cited King's endorsement of the "quota system" on Chicago television. A Lutheran cleric protested King's support for "quota integration," and King replied that Alinsky had "misinterpreted" him. Alinsky had no problem lecturing the American Gandhi. King knew well "the cool comfortable climate on the mountain-top where one can indulge in self-satisfied, safe, militant denunciations of the evils of segregation," Alinsky wrote. Only when Alinsky and his

Industrial Areas Foundation "descended into the valleys of implementation" in housing did he feel the "full violence and anger of every racist Negro-hating group in Chicago." Progressive housing developments everywhere employed a "quota as the opening wedge" to stabilize integration, Alinsky instructed, enclosing copies of his hate mail. In truth, King knew less about local politics and grassroots white resistance than he did about the federal government's role in making the "second ghetto" after World War II.[7] Popular white defense of racially exclusive suburban turf was a third rail of postwar liberal politics, he eventually learned.

King criticized government more harshly than he did corporations or homeowners. In a March 1961 television interview with Mike Wallace, King indicted the multibillion-dollar federal investment in the new urban apartheid. Since 1934, the Federal Housing Administration (FHA) had insured more than $30 billion in home mortgages in subdivisions that explicitly excluded minorities, King explained. By the time the FHA stopped honoring racially restrictive private housing covenants, two years after the Supreme Court declared them illegal in 1948, millions of Negroes had been denied decent homes. The Housing Acts of 1949 and 1954 promised "a decent home" and "adequate housing for all." But the Public Housing Administration financed the segregation of over two million people, and Kennedy would not use judicial precedent to crack down on racist local housing authorities. The Urban Renewal Administration tore down so-called blighted black housing without providing the relocation assistance required by law. The practice "served to accentuate, even to initiate, segregated neighborhoods." King pointed out that most of the Veterans Administration's loan guarantees still went to whites. By implication, the federal government must be held responsible for cleaning up the mess it helped make. King again called on Kennedy to honor his promise to eliminate discrimination in federally assisted housing "with the stroke of a pen." "Residential discrimination" was the key to the ghetto and de facto segregated schools, recreational facilities, and churches, he told a Dartmouth College audience in May 1962. In fact, little was "de facto" in urban apartheid.[8]

Moderate blacks urged caution and realism. *Pittsburgh Courier* editor P. L. Prattis insisted that Kennedy could not remedy northern housing segregation until "a new power structure in the South" buried the reactionary Congress. And whether motivated by "prejudice or snobbery," whites simply did not "WANT TO LIVE NEXT DOOR TO NEGROES." King agreed with him about the southern political revolution, but dilemmas of federalism did not excuse Kennedy, he responded. Whitney Young at the National Urban League asked for King's patience in realizing Kennedy's promises of growth. Blacks were "hardest hit" by the Eisenhower recession, and Kennedy was right in "getting the economy moving before antagonizing the southern element." Young is often credited with developing the civil rights community's first case for affirmative action, a massive Marshall Plan for the Negro, but his first mention of "special compensation" does not appear until November 1962 in a speech to the Negro American Labor Council, a year and a half after King's public embrace of the concept. By 1964, both men were trying to broaden their concepts of "special treatment" for the disadvantaged to include white poor people in social democratic programs neither Kennedy nor Johnson was willing to entertain.[9]

"Fumbling on the New Frontier" was the title of King's second *Nation* article of March 1962. Kennedy's "cautious and defensive" civil rights policy was a shambles, though King acknowledged Kennedy's fair employment order and an increase in Justice Department voter registration suits. But Kennedy had recently called for a national "consensus" in advance of any executive order prohibiting housing discrimination, an impossible standard for any civil rights measure to meet. Kennedy's trade negotiations with the Common Market on behalf of U.S. corporations were apparently more important than opening southern labor markets to African Americans, King angrily charged. Thomas Jefferson's devotion to equal, inalienable rights was giving way to Calvin Coolidge's axiom, "The business of America is business." Gradualism, "tokenism," deference to powerful private interests, and "piecemeal" remedies were all unacceptable. If Kennedy could persuade the nation to put a man on the moon, why not help "put a Negro in the State Legislature of Alabama"?[10]

Kennedy finally signed the housing order on Thanksgiving Day 1962, prohibiting the FHA from insuring any mortgages benefiting discriminatory home builders. But the FHA insured only 20 percent of newly constructed homes, so black FHA director Robert Weaver urged Kennedy to extend the prohibition to all financial institutions. Pressured by big-city Democratic congressmen, Kennedy exempted banks, savings and loans, and two million federally insured housing units already under construction. The order was a good-faith gesture, King conceded in the *Amsterdam News*. But it was two years late and weakened by Kennedy's failure to secure a "retroactive clause" affecting these FHA loans. African Americans would continue to find it difficult to secure private loans. "The dreams of the masses lay in tatters" as a result of executive timidity, King later wrote. Soon even moderates grew tired of waiting. "Negroes are getting very weary of tokenism hailed as victories," P. L. Prattis wrote in the *Courier*.[11]

Internationalism and Anticommunism

King became increasingly critical of U.S. foreign policies and the chilling effect of militarism on domestic freedom. King still used cold war anticommunist logic to press the case for domestic civil rights, but he consistently advocated disarmament and reallocation of the world's resources from the affluent North to the impoverished South. Florence Luscomb, a suffragist, pacifist, and labor organizer, wrote King urging him to stop using liberal anticommunist rhetoric. It was a heavy hammer forged by reactionaries to smash progressive movements in civil liberties, civil rights, labor, and peace, she wrote. Popular anticommunism fattened useless "armaments programs," and peace lovers should not "add a whisper's weight to this hate." King used the argument less and less. When Soviet premier Nikita Khrushchev demanded that the United Nations be moved to a less racist country, King contended that America's international prestige had reached "its lowest ebb." How could the United States invest $20 billion in the inter-American Alliance for Progress without making an equal investment in the "turbulent South"? Whites might want peace, but "Negroes *need* an international *détente*," King argued. The government forgot black needs during international crises, when "political rigidity grips the nation and sharply inhibits social change."[12]

King supported the South African struggle against apartheid, even after the African National Congress (ANC) took up armed struggle in response to the police massacre of sixty-nine nonviolent protesters at Sharpeville in 1960. King and L. Howard DeWolf hoped the nonviolent defiance campaign against South African pass laws led by Chief Albert Lithuli might succeed, even after Lithuli was imprisoned in 1960. International economic sanctions seemed to be working without U.S. participation, King and DeWolf agreed. King repeatedly insisted civil disobedience could work inside South Africa, exaggerating the degree to which the defiance campaign had brought the South African "government to its knees" in 1957. In late November 1962, King joined with the American Negro Leadership Conference on Africa, again calling for stiff sanctions against South Africa and generous foreign aid to Africa. U.S. trade policies could not continue supporting the "political, economic domination of native Africans." Change policy or face an inevitable sub-Saharan "bloodbath," he commanded. After a long struggle, international sanctions and indigenous South African resistance overturned apartheid in the 1990s.[13]

King also decried the hypocrisy of American senators and congressmen who voted to invest Peace Corps dollars in Asia and Africa while they continued to exclude African ambassadors from their diplomatic clubs and neighborhoods. Echoing left critiques of domestic housing and welfare policy, King predicted that "the Peace Corps will fail if it seeks to do something *for* the underprivileged peoples of the world; it will succeed if it seeks creatively to do something *with* them." "It will fail as a negative gesture to defeat Communism," he continued; "it will succeed only as a positive effort to wipe poverty, ignorance and disease from the earth."[14]

Kennedy's botched invasion of Cuba at the Bay of Pigs in April 1961 infuriated King, as he poured out his moral outrage in a letter to a supporter. "We just don't understand the meaning of the revolution taking place in the world . . . against colonialism, reactionary dictatorship, and systems of exploitation," he wrote. Unless the United States returned to the "revolutionary spirit" of 1776, King feared the nation would become "a second class power" bereft of any internationally respected "moral voice." In seeking to overthrow Fidel Castro, the United States was on the wrong side of the world revolution. Later, King opposed U.S. intervention in Vietnam in identical terms.[15]

King engaged in a curious, indirect debate about communism and political economy with W.E.B. Du Bois, who joined the Communist Party (CP) shortly before emigrating to Ghana. In 1961 on Cleveland television, King noted how remarkable it was that given their multiple oppressions more blacks had not become communists. A Nashville *Tennessean* editorial charged King with endorsing communism, and King responded with his boilerplate critique of "crippling totalitarianism." Nevertheless, "a major Negro intellectual" had become so disillusioned with American "democracy" that he joined the Communist Party, King wrote. Du Bois sent King his defense of joining the CP, anticipating key elements of King's alternative to the War on Poverty: the "abolition of poverty," "no exploitation of labor," "training for jobs and jobs for all," and appreciation for Swedish social democracy as a model for what the U.S. could achieve.[16]

King's anticommunism did him little good. FBI director J. Edgar Hoover spun a web of surveillance, public slander, and personal intimidation that unsettled King and severely damaged his lines of communication with the Kennedy and Johnson administrations. The FBI had noted King's contacts with black CP leader Benjamin Davis and his support for Carl Braden of the Southern Conference Educational Fund, who went to prison for refusing to tell the House Un-American Activities Committee (HUAC) whether he was a communist. King denounced the covert racist purpose of HUAC "to thwart integration." Yet, as late as September 1961, the FBI field office in Memphis found "no Communist Party (CP) influence" in SCLC's activities. That all changed in January 1962, when Hoover learned that Stanley Levison had ghostwritten King's speech to the AFL-CIO in December 1961 (which King publicly denied). Hoover wrote Attorney General Robert Kennedy that Levison was a CP apparatchik manipulating King. The FBI added King's name to the "Reserve Index" of individuals to be detained in the event of a national emergency. King defied repeated entreaties from the Kennedy administration to break with Levison. His criticism of FBI field agents in Albany, Georgia, for their apparent collusion with segregationists and local police further stoked Hoover's vendetta.[17]

Defending Ralph Helstein and the UPWA against red baiters in HUAC and the AFL-CIO, King refined his argument that interracial democracy was the best defense against communist "disloyalty." Addressing HUAC hearings in Chicago in June 1959, King called it "a dark day" when unionists could not work for "brotherhood without being labeled communist." King served on the AFL-CIO Pubic Review Advisory Commission that investigated and cleared the union. King's self-defense against red baiting resembles a May 1959 letter from Helstein contained in the final report. Helstein argued that the strongest bulwark of democracy was the redress of "grievances and frustrations on which Communist ideology can otherwise flourish."[18]

Dreams of a Negro-Labor Alliance

Black churches, wealthy white liberals, and interracial labor unions, especially the UAW and UPWA, had most reliably supported the southern movement. In turn, King lent his support to progressive unions. In the spring of 1959, over 3,000 white, black, and Puerto Rican workers in Local 1199 struck seven private New York hospitals. Industrial unions were losing members, but labor was making inroads into the rapidly expanding, low-paid service sector. Hospital laundry workers, maids, janitors, and orderlies were barred by New York law from bargaining collectively. They were excluded from minimum wage protections and denied even the medical insurance that might give them access to the hospitals in which they worked. Harlem's black community rallied to their defense. Bayard Rustin worked tirelessly to coordinate the Citizens Committee for a Just Settlement of the Hospital Strike, chaired by A. Philip Randolph and Reinhold Niebuhr. They warned that low wages and "shameful working conditions threaten the health of the infants and children of these workers." Overworked and underpaid parents could not prevent children from falling into "juvenile delinquency, crime and violence." King cheered a struggle that transcended "a fight for union rights" and became a "fight for human rights." In the end, Local 1199 failed to win recognition, gaining only wage concessions and grievance procedures, but the unionists proclaimed victory. King frequently visited their headquarters and rallies as they became a district, then a national union. The union finally won the right to represent hospital workers throughout the state in 1975.[19]

Levison and King plotted strategy for the new stage of the struggle, but fund-raising remained central to SCLC's labor strategy. In speeches and written appeals in 1961 and 1962, King spoke of the common problems, common interests, and common needs of black and white workers, seeking support from organized labor in exchange for promises of a mobilized black electorate. He sought to mediate racial conflict within the AFL-CIO and galvanize progressive forces against a looming economic crisis. The glory days of the expansive political CIO remained King's touchstones. At the UAW convention in April 1961, King honored labor's historic interethnic and interracial battles against employers, conservative politicians, red baiters, and communists. Students owed the sit-in tactic to striking workers who sat down in the auto factories to secure unions and higher wages in 1937, he said. They would never "collectivize a single lunch counter" or nationalize coffee drinking, he promised.[20]

Any Negro-labor alliance would have to confront racism within the house of labor, King believed. International unions included lofty antidiscrimination clauses in their constitutions, but labor bureaucrats were unwilling or unable to integrate their own ranks or challenge the decentralized network of locals maintaining rigid color bars, especially in the building trades and the southern steel and railroad unions. In May 1960, Randolph helped found the Negro American Labor Council (NALC), hoping to bring "trade union consciousness" to unorganized blacks (and civil rights consciousness to unionists). Randolph's loyalty to the AFL-CIO never wavered, but some NALC activists threatened to bolt from the very beginning. King endorsed their goals at a NALC workshop, "Race Bias in Trade Unions, Industry and Government," in February 1961.[21] Randolph soon locked horns with George Meany over discrimination by affiliate unions. In June 1961, Randolph issued a "fair union practices code" to compel locals to desegregate and open leadership and apprenticeship programs to blacks. He demanded specific timetables. The AFL-CIO executive council censured Randolph for the widening "gap" between labor and blacks. Calling the action "shocking and deplorable," King defended Randolph at the AFL-CIO convention in December. As he had in *Stride Toward Freedom,* King attributed Negro workers' "degraded economic status" to racist unions. Unions colluded with business to bar blacks from entire industries, denying them apprenticeship training and public vocational education. Where was labor's national tradition of asserting its "great power, its vision and resources"? District 65's Cleveland Robinson wept as the laborites cheered the "American Gandhi." Meany thanked King profusely, but King knew his real support came from the progressive, interracial unions.[22]

By 1962 many liberals and leftists recognized a looming national crisis of structural unemployment and ghetto poverty that might wipe out progress for a whole generation of black Americans, just as mass militancy was winning civil and voting rights. Standard remedies of growth economics and equal opportunity legislation no longer seemed adequate to the challenge. New technologies in auto manufacturing, meatpacking, steel production, and the entire goods-producing economy were making old skills obsolete and requiring fewer workers. To King, workers' security and black equality were imperiled by the relentless "catastrophe" of automation eliminating jobs in basic manufacturing. "Progress" for the wealthy meant "destruction" for the unskilled working class. Industry was more than technology and assembly lines, King told the UAW. Industry included "people who must live in decency, with security for children, for old age, for health and a cultural life." Blacks knew through their historic bondage that "when human values are subordinated to blind economic forces, human beings can become human scrap." U.S. industry exalted corporate over human values, profits over people. In the 1950s King had muted his references to "labor trampled over by capitalistic power." Now, revising his sermons for religious and middle-class readers, King wrote, "Our unswerving devotion to monopolistic capitalism makes us more concerned about the economic security of the captains of industry than for the laboring men whose sweat and skills keep industry functioning."[23]

The employment crisis occupied the left for the rest of the decade and beyond. Mechanization of the cotton harvest, accelerated by New Deal crop allotment policies, had cut total agricultural employment in the South in half between 1940 and 1960. Millions of black economic refugees spilled into industrial cities where blue-collar manufacturing employment was stagnant or declining after 1953. King later wrote that "no national planning was done to provide remedies," despite precedents like the Homestead Act of 1862 and the GI Bill of 1944, and despite the fact that agricultural and industrial policies had subsidized these massive sectoral shifts in the economy. Technological change worked against blacks' interests, but so did aggressive corporate union-busting strategies and plant relocation, King might have more clearly explained. In the steel, auto, meatpacking, and tobacco industries, electrical and paper manufacturing, and mining, new technologies wiped out millions of jobs. Technology was color-blind, but blacks were restricted to the dangerous and dirty unskilled and semi-skilled jobs most at risk. Corporations shipped "runaway jobs" to new plants in small, nonunion cities in the South and West, away from the older industrial cities where blacks were concentrated. Detroit hem-

Figure 3. Architects of the Negro-labor alliance, 1963. Bayard Rustin, deputy director, March on Washington Committee, and Cleveland Robinson, District 65, chairman of the Administrative Committee, at headquarters, 170 West 130 Street, Harlem. Though they compromised on tactics in the interest of a broad coalition, they repeatedly insisted that the "the blight of black second-class economic citizenship" could only be remedied by "a broad and fundamental program of economic justice." Photo by O. Fernandez. NYWT & S Collection. Library of Congress (LC-USZ62-133369).

orrhaged half of its manufacturing jobs in the 1950s, and blacks bled the most. The UPWA was devastated. Armour alone closed twenty-one plants employing 14,000 workers between 1956 and 1965. Chicago's facilities, with majority-black locals, were hit hardest. The union became whiter and more rural but still resisted wage concessions and insisted that "progress should not mean enrichment for a few and misery for many."[24]

In the shift from a goods-producing to a service-based economy, the labor market split between low–wage, insecure jobs and good jobs requiring highly skilled and formally educated workers. Between 1950 and 1962, unemployment rates for workers with less than a high school education rose. Both the unemployment gap and the income gap between black and white workers increased, along with inequality in the overall distribution of wealth. As economic growth picked up after 1962, King continued to insist on the importance of race and place: young black men's employment prospects in communities suffering from deindustrialization remained gloomier than their fathers' had been.[25]

For King, the only solution to black economic subordination would be political coalitions that pushed a social democratic agenda of economic planning. Blacks were mainly working people with the same needs as those of white workers, King explained to the AFL-CIO. Only a liberal Congress could provide "decent wages, fair working conditions, livable housing, old age security, health and welfare measures." Negroes and labor had the same insidious political enemies: the right-wing John Birch Society, the military-industrial complex, and the conservative coalition in Congress. The left would have to uncork "Negro political power," which would invariably "vote liberal and labor" out of self-interest. Blacks and labor together must coalesce behind policies that distributed "abundance to all instead of concentrating it among a few." King offered no concrete strategies for limiting corporate decision making. But in an August 1962 appeal to the United Electrical Workers, King called for "fearless, creative, social planning" at the highest levels of government to ensure "national security and national welfare."[26]

Democratic gains in both houses of Congress in 1960 had not overthrown the anti-union, anti–civil rights coalition, but liberal and labor hopes were rising. Labor's political history gave King hope in the coalition that Rustin had urged on King in 1957 and he had endorsed in *Stride Toward Freedom*. In the era of "economic democracy," organized labor had achieved "equality" with management, raising "the living standards of millions," King told the AFL-CIO, with more inspiring hyperbole than accurate history. But black direct action could revive "labor's historic tradition of moving forward to create vital people as consumers and citizens." Public employee unions were growing, but labor was no stronger and was less popular than when King dreamed of labor's triumph over capital in 1950. In a May 1962 appeal to ten industrial unions, King wrote that the recent Supreme Court reapportionment decision in *Baker v. Carr* could tip the balance of congressional power, redressing the rural bias in southern voting. When a fully enfranchised southern working-class coalition sent true liberals to Congress, "segregation will breathe its last—the South as a haven for run-away shops will end—and labor's right to organize in the South will become a reality." SCLC needed union money now to realign the South. But King in his many appeals did not explicitly mention repealing Taft-Hartley. Nor did he promise any SCLC commitment to organizing drives at southern workplaces.[27] Would urban business elites and middle-class suburbanites in fact replace the southern oligarchs in defense of more polite forms of segregation? King did not yet speculate.

King asked for more than money. The unions must not shrink from a bold liberalism that challenged key white privileges in housing and employment that the New Deal had stabilized. Speaking to the Transport Workers Union led by Mike Quill, King cheered a multiethnic union of "Irish, Italians, Negroes and Jews" who had struggled against prejudice and discrimination and should therefore support the Negro "struggle for equality." A person of "genuine good will" would righteously protest a KKK lynching or torching of a freedom riders' bus, King told the transport workers. But he must also "rise up to righteous indignation when a Negro cannot live in his neighborhood" or work for his company. King was an American Jeremiah, castigating sins among the believers and calling them to a higher plane of action in line with their principles. But by the 1960s, the New Deal state had deeply etched white property entitlement across the steep hills and low valleys of America's metropolitan landscapes.[28]

Cross-Fertilization: North and South

Northern and southern protests cross-pollinated in the early 1960s in ways that profoundly shaped King's thinking about racial and economic justice. Northern blacks mobilized to fight for equal employment, education, fair housing, and the integrity of their communities in the face of highway construction and massive urban renewal projects benefiting middle-class and commercial interests. By 1961, while supporting lunch counter sit-ins and freedom rides, they confronted northern racism with new boldness. In May 1961, for example, 2,500 blacks belonging to South Chicago's Woodlawn Organization jammed into forty-six buses in their own "freedom ride" to city hall, flying banners that read "Better Housing," "Jobs," and "Vote." FEPC laws had been on the books in many northern states for fifteen years, but blacks found themselves either excluded from employment or still relegated to lower-paid, less-skilled jobs. Northerners in CORE and the NAACP increasingly embraced direct action to secure actual jobs, not just formal nondiscrimination policies. From Philadelphia to Oakland, California, grassroots activists despaired of the fair employment approach based on case-by-case adjudication, embracing instead the logic of atonement, reparations, and militant economic action.[29]

Whitney Young became the executive director of the National Urban League in 1961, mediating between the black freedom movement and business and political elites. Young's "moderate" image concealed his increasingly fierce critique of the limits of equal opportunity liberalism. At the September 1962 SCLC convention, Young warned of an impending urban crisis that only vigorous government action could forestall. Blacks just might end up with "a mouthful of rights and an empty stomach," he warned. They were losing ground economically because of industrial restructuring and the Eisenhower recession. Detailing the racial gaps in employment, income, housing, educa-tion, and health, Young described the Jim Crow welfare state: blacks were denied their equal share of federal expenditures, social services, and welfare benefits. What Gunnar Myrdal had called the "underclass" would only grow; it was already "social dynamite." Young's political solution lay beyond equal opportunity and fair employment, as he now echoed King's argument for spe-cial measures to uplift America's untouchables. Erasing black people's "scars of historical abuse and deprivation" required "better schools and retraining programs, better social agencies and health clinics, better housing, recreation and cultural outlets." Blacks faced sharper political dilemmas as civil rights dreams came within reach. "Gentle people of prejudice" who had supported legislation and "equal opportunity" would now blame blacks for a structural crisis with historical roots invisible to them. Whites would counsel "patience" and self-help, blind to the fact that they had enjoyed affirmative discrimina-tion for centuries. They would honor Dr. King, Young declared, as long as he stayed in the South. Northern white homeowners and employers especially would retreat from racial equality when confronted with their own practices of discrimination in jobs, housing, and education. They would deflect respon-sibility and murmur about housing "depreciation" or the prejudice of their customers. Blacks needed multiple strategies to counteract this "colorblind" racism, including direct action, civil disobedience, litigation, research, "com-munity organization, and policy negotiations." And, Young later added, "a single Messianic leader" could never produce enough loaves and fishes for the restive urban masses.[30]

By 1962, "Don't Buy Where You Can't Work" was a slogan not yet forgotten from Harlem in the 1930s, signifying a way to rally black community boycotts of businesses guilty of job discrimination. Leon Sullivan, pastor of Philadelphia's Zion Baptist Church, carried it to a militant new level of mass effectiveness, recruiting four hundred local ministers to threaten boycotts and win jobs for African Americans in 1959. An organizer of the 1941 March on Washington Movement, Sullivan had organized Philadelphia's Youth Employment Service in the late 1950s, promoting Negro hiring on an individual basis in a city suffering from rapid manufacturing job loss and black youth unemployment double that of whites. First hit management with the loss of a quarter of a million customers, he preached, then "let management take care of unions" that excluded blacks from membership. By 1963, Sullivan estimated that the campaign won over 2,000 "breakthrough" jobs for blacks in the service sector as bakers, clerical workers, and deliverymen. It was all "self-help," but, like citizenship education, the term carried more militant implications. More than simple individual merit hiring, Sullivan's principle of "discrimination in reverse" measured success by numerical outcomes and countenanced hiring blacks ahead of whites with seniority. "Black men have been waiting for 100 years," he said, so "white men can wait for a few months" for the good jobs.[31]

"Selective patronage" fired King's imagination. SCLC held a luncheon for Sullivan in Atlanta on October 29, 1962, inviting him to help plan what King announced would be "a massive attack on job discrimination" called Operation Breadbasket. Sullivan graciously credited King and Montgomery's citizens with the idea. John Middleton of Atlanta's SCLC targeted flagrant violators in the baking industry. Ralph Abernathy was the "call man," informing each employer that if negotiations failed word would pass rapidly through the city's pulpits to boycott discriminatory companies. Hunts Foods flew in its industrial relations manager from California to negotiate a compliance settlement that would open jobs to Negroes and ban reprisals against workers who had filed complaints. With a little coercion, corporate voluntarism could be compelled to work.[32]

King continued to cultivate and challenge the black middle class. Searching for allies in his own church, King faced a bitter defeat in 1960 and 1961 when progressive Baptists failed to replace National Baptist Convention president J. H. Jackson with King's friend Gardner Taylor. A sharp critic of sit-ins and civil disobedience, Jackson charged that the black pulpit was full of "hoodlums and crooks" preaching "disrespect for law." For the rest of King's life, America's most powerful black minister remained the enemy of its most famous civil rights leader. They profoundly differed in strategy. In 1961, Jackson argued that blacks must move "beyond protest to production." Black capital accumulation and self-help comprised the truly "revolutionary movement," capable of building "self-respect, stronger character, and a more wholesome family and community life." Progressives called Jackson's address "a masterpiece of Tomism." At the 1962 NBC annual convention, Jackson argued that black business development would end "the oppression of the many by the few." Protest, legal action, and legislation would not emancipate Negroes: "the liberated who seek to ride another's train without paying the just fare will become hobos and tramps," Jackson preached.[33]

King got more help from ambitious black entrepreneurs who combined the ideals of Booker T. Washington and Frederick Douglass. Alfred Duckett had written flattering news articles about King, but in 1959 Levison had prevented his becoming King's public relations agent. Duckett nevertheless organized several fund-raising events for King during his trips to New York in 1962. "I make no apologies for seeking to combine such service with substantial profits," he wrote Wyatt Walker, SCLC's new executive director. According to Duckett, the black struggle sought "economic growth and security, not the either/or of Dr. J. H. Jackson's self-defeating philosophy, but the also/and theory of expanding the fight" for justice with powerful "economic weapons." King valued the rhetorical talents of this articulate black capitalist. In August, he hired Duckett as a ghostwriter for his book *Why We Can't Wait*.[34]

White Socialist Michael Harrington supplied King with insights about racialized poverty he had gained in the northern black freedom movement. Harrington's popular and influential 1962 book, *The Other America*, "belonged to the movement" that taught him much more than he gave back to it, he recalled. The influence was circular. "We never knew we were poor until we read your book," King once joked. Harrington mixed a tradition of Catholic social action with a socialist structural analysis of race, power, and poverty. *The Other America* sketched poverty's many forms: black, white, and Latino; urban and rural; generational and gendered; poverty stemming from corporate disinvestment and state-sanctioned inequality. To give the phenomenon coherence and make a case for massive national action, Harrington borrowed anthropologist Oscar Lewis's concept of the "culture of poverty." Harrington did not mean to implicate poor people morally or behaviorally in perpetuating their poverty but to demonstrate the tight linkages between structural inequality and psychological hopelessness. Poverty was an "institution, a way of life," "a culture, an interdependent system" in which a "web of disabilities" intensified each separate affliction. Any solution must be part of a "comprehensive" national "war on poverty." Automation eliminated jobs and rendered skills useless, disproportionately harming Negroes but producing "interracial misery." Low wages trapped people in marginal, nonunion jobs as farm workers, restaurant workers, laundry workers, and hospital workers. "All of them are poor," Harrington wrote; "regardless of race, creed, or color, all of them are victims." In part through Harrington's influence, a holistic attention to the unemployed and the working poor informed King's radicalism.[35]

America's "new poor" faced unprecedented racial, spatial, political, and cultural obstacles to social mobility that did not immobilize earlier immigrants, Harrington argued. The other America was "populated by the failures, by those driven from the land and bewildered by the city . . . and by minorities facing a wall of prejudice." For many stuck in poverty, "the crucial problem is color," because "ghetto walls" had risen to historic heights through public-private partnerships of suburban privilege. Harrington did not discuss urban black poverty in safe nonracial codes, as did the Ford Foundation in funding efforts to rehabilitate "grey areas" of deterioration and disinvestment between central cities and suburbs. For Harrington, racial poverty was "the most institutionalized poverty in the United States, the most vicious of the vicious circles," he wrote. This was not the "cycle of poverty" liberals used to describe the black family's purported failure to transmit the dominant culture's norms, though Harrington noted, without judgment, that black families were increasingly "female based." Harrington's cycle metaphor linked political structures to racial and economic systems. Bereft of unions, political parties, or fraternal societies, the ghetto poor had no lobbyists or "legislative program." They were "politically invisible," he wrote, coining a metaphor that King later used extensively. Safely ignored by city hall, the poor were isolated by the suburbanizing middle class. Urban renewal projects, which Harrington called "bureaucratically enforced rootlessness," robbed them of community. Fear of the police infused their daily lives with unparalleled "psychological depth and torment." Blacks were second-class citizens even in Harlem, he argued. "Harlem's economy is white. Practically all the stores are presided over by white men. . . . The welfare state is for the middle class and the rich." No wonder poor people lost "aspiration [and] hope."[36]

For Harrington, as for Randolph, Rustin, and King, African Americans would never rise out of poverty without the economic emancipation of all poor people through a mix of mobilization from below and reform from above. Black freedom required more than civil rights or political equality; Harrington prescribed "a massive assault on the entire culture of poverty in American society: upon slums, inferior education, inadequate medical care, and all the rest." King copied these exact words in 1964 when he called for a grand alliance between civil rights, labor, and church forces to mount a "massive assault" on poverty. As a corollary, King argued, human rights for all would be delayed until the Negro's "institutionalized position in the American economy is radically changed." Conquering structural unemployment would disproportionately benefit Negroes, Harrington argued. They would also gain through the redistribution of public benefits from the rich and the middle class to the poor, many of whom scavenged for their subsistence "beneath the welfare state." Curiously missing from Harrington's analysis was any mention that labor unions could be the vanguard of social transformation. The civil rights movement had shown how to make change from below and inspire hopeless people to hope. The Montgomery bus boycott, by reducing crime, pointed to how a movement-based "esprit" could transform the other America. "Thousands of people had been given a sense of purpose, of their own worth and dignity," he wrote, echoing King. The same could happen with poor whites, Latinos, and others. A team of social scientists tested this thesis in the early 1960s, finding that cross-class protest movements generally reduced crime, in one city as much as 50 percent. Democratic social action was effective in fighting poverty *and* crime, they confirmed.[37]

Southern Radicalization: Direct Action and Voter Registration

In May 1961, CORE sent interracial teams of "Freedom Riders" through the Deep South, testing the Supreme Court's ruling on the unconstitutionality of segregation in interstate transportation. Whites firebombed a bus in Anniston, Alabama, and in Birmingham, Klansmen mercilessly beat freedom riders with the tacit support of T. Eugene "Bull" Connor's police. Reinforced by Nashville SNCC activists, freedom riders continued to Montgomery. When a mob threatened to burn down Ralph Abernathy's First Baptist Church, King demanded federal protection and promised to lead thousands of activists in voter registration and direct action. "We will present our physical bodies as instruments to defeat the unjust system," he vowed. Students expected King to present his own body on the freedom ride to Jackson, Mississippi. King declined, declaring only he could "choose the time and place of my Golgotha." For the first time Nashville SNCC activist John Lewis heard students call King "De Lawd," a mocking reference to "the Lord." But King credited journalists as much as the students for desegregating interstate buses. "Without the presence of the press, there might have been untold massacre in the South," he wrote a supporter. "The world seldom believes the horror stories of history until they are documented via mass media." The Freedom Rides alone could not have moved the Interstate Commerce Commission (ICC) to enforce the

Supreme Court decision later that year, he believed. Federal action only followed international publicity.[38]

Desperate to avoid any more publicized southern "crises," Robert Kennedy tried to entice activists into what he mistakenly thought would be a less
confrontational form of activism: voter registration. Several SNCC members
recalled Kennedy's verbal guarantees of protection from the Department of
Justice and the FBI. The government's failure to deliver that protection profoundly disillusioned them. Many activists became radicalized as they discovered close links between political and economic coercion and poverty in the
Deep South, and stood by poor people taking enormous risks to act for their
own emancipation .

With money raised from the Field and Taconic Foundations, the Voter
Education Project (VEP) spread nearly $1 million among the civil rights orga-
nizations between April 1962 and November 1964. The VEP helped fill the sails
of a voter registration movement that had been immobilized by white reaction. The percentage of registered eligible black voters in eleven southern states
had hardly risen at all in 1960 and 1961; in the Deep South, registration actually
declined. By 1964, however, scores of local drives added an estimated 668,000
blacks to the rolls. In his December 1964 Nobel Lecture at the University of
Oslo, King declared that "we have the left the dusty soils of Egypt and crossed
a Red Sea whose waters had for years been hardened by a long and piercing
winter of massive resistance." In some states, almost half of the eligible black
citizens registered; in others, especially Mississippi, less than one in ten could
surmount the violence, reprisals, and administrative obstacles. Voter registration relied on black-controlled institutions and touched many more ordinary
people than did direct action. Black bar owners refused to sell drinks to unreg-
istered patrons, and black businessmen would hire only registered workers. In
Roanoke, the tobacco workers union paid poor people's poll taxes. Most gains
came in the cities. Hosea Williams's Chatham County Crusade for Voters in
Georgia set an impressive example, and SCLC later hired Williams as voter
registration director. The crusade pulled in Savannah's black businesses,
schools, PTAs, churches, and youth groups to register 5,000 voters in less than
a year.[39]

In the summer of 1961, SNCC heatedly debated whether to pursue direct
action or voter registration. King counseled voter registration, but Ella Baker
persuaded them to develop parallel efforts. Each strategy proved to be equally
dangerous. People attempting registration endured beatings, arrests, firings,
evictions, and the loss of public assistance. Black communities countered
repression with mass protests or economic boycotts. In other places, lunch
counter sit-ins, department store pickets, and community boycotts boosted

voter registration. Having initially opposed registration as a Kennedy ploy, SNCC's Lawrence Guyot concluded that it actually posed a greater threat to the status quo. "If you sit at a lunch counter, you're either served or you're not served, and that's it. But when you get control over the electorate, everything else happens."[40]

Voter registration workers fanned out into rural Mississippi and southwest Georgia, arriving penniless and living with local people, and discovering forms of poverty, economic vulnerability, and resiliency invisible to most Americans. Many came to realize that poverty could be both an enormous deterrent and a powerful incentive to political action. "There is a relationship between your not being able to feed your children and your not registering to vote," Guyot told Mississippi blacks. Many responded with courage and faith in the power of voting to improve their quality of life. Mrs. Mattie Pilcher believed that voting would "give us all our equal rights and equal payments when we work." They would win better schools and more jobs, and "a job would be more of a job for colored people." Could such optimism be sustained given the inevitable gaps between winning the ballot, officeholding, and exercising economic power? Many families lacked basic food, clothing, shelter, and medical care, and poverty could be the greatest obstacle to political courage. Student canvassers "told of the ragged children . . . the people caught in nightmare mazes of credit and installment buying, of charcoal in a bucket used to light and heat the house where the electricity had been cut off for nonpayment of the bill." Legal and extralegal obstacles to voting ranged from costly poll taxes and white-administered literacy tests to police harassment, actual terrorism, and economic reprisals. A standard VEP form included a question regarding why a potential voter had not registered: the number one reason was "fear of economic pressure." SCLC's one full-time field organizer in Mississippi, Annell Ponder, informed Atlanta about reprisals against eight women after she recruited them for citizenship education: "One teacher had two sons arrested and put on a penal farm because of participation in a protest march." Local blacks were fed up with "shootings, beatings, jailings and economic reprisals such as job loss, withholding of welfare checks and surplus commodities," she wrote.[41]

Challenging authority, coping with reprisals, and distributing relief were central acts in local dramas of political radicalization. Sharecropping had entrapped blacks in webs of debt. Mechanization of the cotton harvest and government subsidies to planters to reduce their acreage eroded any remaining black economic power. Many blacks became virtual squatters on plantations that no longer required their work. In 1959, the Mississippi Delta had 17,563 sharecroppers; over the next five years nearly half joined the exodus from the land. Charles McLaurin of SNCC reported from Ruleville in 1962 that whites evicted tenants who even talked about registering to vote. Banks refused loans to anyone who tried, as well as their relatives. Planters had traditionally welcomed county administration of federal surplus commodities, feeding their workers over the winter and cutting them off at planting time, but that now ended. Several Mississippi counties stopped administering the commodities program in the fall of 1962. Donations of food and clothing poured in from the North, and activists used limited relief to entice poor blacks to register. SNCC's Bob Moses concluded, "When 1000 people stand in line for a few cans of food, then it is possible to tell 1000 people they are poor, that they are trapped in poverty, that they *must* move if they are to escape." Where and how to move and escape raised difficult dilemmas. Mrs. Fannie Lou Hamer was fired from her job as a plantation timekeeper and evicted for trying to register. SCLC wired $100 to James Bevel, who rented a truck and paid rent on a house for her in Ruleville. It violated their foundation grant's rules, Andrew Young recalled, but relief gave many activists a bridge to new vocations as civil rights workers.[42]

SNCC increasingly looked to poor blacks themselves as the only truly reliable constituency that could change the poverty that was itself a principal obstacle to political citizenship. Years of registering voters in southwest Georgia taught Charles Sherrod that the poor were the best experts on their own economic deprivations: "A man may be so ignorant to make a pair of shoes, but not so ignorant that he doesn't know when a pair of shoes pinches him . . . or that white folks have power over [whether] his belly is empty." Sherrod demanded that "the new society of Democracy for which we strive be based on the wisdom of the pinched toe and the empty belly." James Forman and white student activist Tom Hayden had reached broader revolutionary conclusions. They met while doing relief work in Fayette County, Tennessee. Forman pointed Hayden to McComb, Mississippi, where white supremacists dragged Hayden from his car and beat him with a club. An AP photo of the incident made Hayden famous among an emerging New Left. Hayden told his friend Al Haber, who was president of Students for a Democratic Society (SDS), in September 1961 that SNCC was not leading a bourgeois "movement but a revolution" inspired by liberation movements around the world: "Beyond lunch counter desegregation there are more serious evils which must be ripped out by any means: exploitation, socially destructive capital, evil political and legal structures, and myopic liberalism."[43]

King exposed himself to the wisdom of the pinched toe and came to appreciate that oppression, more than apathy, deterred black voting. "The white ruling class in the South has always recognized the power of the Negro vote," he told the NAACP convention in July 1962. That was why resistance and reprisals were so cruel. Blacks now had to organize "block-to-block, door-to-door," in "every segment of the community." In February 1962, King had embarked on his People to People tour through the Mississippi Delta, South Carolina, and Virginia's black belt. In Clarksdale, Mississippi, rural folk in "overalls, ginghams and worn shoes" stared at King "in awe and unbelief," the *SCLC Newsletter* reported. In Sherard, only one man showed up, reporting that his neighbors were "afraid they would be put off the land if they met with Dr. King." King toured Mound Bayou, an all-black town of 1,200 and a bastion of independent black political organizing.[44] Virginia's fourth congressional district was similar to Mississippi. "Economic suppression is the rule rather than the exception," King wrote in the *Amsterdam News*. He happily reported that 2,500 supporters packed the high school and 118 Freedom Corps volunteers were recruited in Petersburg. The effect of the trip on King's thinking is evident in a speech he gave at Dartmouth College in May. King had long urged blacks to awaken "from their apathetic slumbers." Now King argued that "external resistance," "economic reprisals," and "conniving" literacy tests were principally responsible for black nonvoting. Even black Ph.D.s were judged illiterate in Alabama. King still saw apathy in the cities, but he appreciated more fully the iron feet of oppression in the rural South.[45]

In February 1961, King and SCLC's executive director, Wyatt Walker, eagerly welcomed the citizenship educators from Highlander, who brought their own foundation funding and innovative ideas for mobilizing voters. "Here is an open door to the grassroots," James Wood told King after traveling to Highlander. SCLC could foster working-class groups "led by their natural leaders" like Esau Jenkins. SCLC could prove it was more than "a middle-class movement" by involving itself in emerging issues of "economic development." SCLC could dwarf the NAACP, creating in every location a long-lasting "voter machine" involving young people who might otherwise be attracted to black nationalism. King hardly needed persuading.[46]

In August, Andrew Young became director of the new Citizenship Education Program (CEP). He left his office job with the National Council of Churches in New York to join his "people" in their struggle, he wrote King. Young, Septima Clark, Bernice Robinson, and Dorothy Cotton, an aide to Walker from Petersburg, started workshops at Dorchester Community Center near Savannah. Young appreciated Clark's experience and organizing philosophy. The son of a dentist and a schoolteacher, and a graduate of Howard University, Young had pastored poor farmers in Thomasville, Georgia, in 1955. Helping them work their farms, Young revered rural traditions of mutual aid, as did Clark and Baker. He railed against farm subsidy programs that paid owners to withdraw land from cultivation that was worked by their tenants: "When the big farmers went on 'welfare', eventually their former workers were driven to welfare too." But only the poor were stigmatized. Young shared Clark's conviction that freedom would emerge "from the struggle of the masses," not "the materialistic middle class." He agreed to a "nonhierarchical staff structure" and accorded women authority, as did his Congregationalist church tradition. By 1964, the CEP claimed to have trained over 1,000 literacy teachers in three years, who taught over 10,000 adults and registered 27,993 voters.[47]

King heralded Clark's citizenship education model as a valuable Gandhian "constructive program." But in the *Amsterdam News,* King praised unsung brave heroes of voter registration—all of whom were male. He praised Esau Jenkins for establishing the CEP, failing to give Clark and Robinson the credit they deserved. In coming years, King alternately patronized Clark, praised her work, and defended her against anyone who questioned her right as a woman to serve on the SCLC executive staff. Clark bristled when they laughed at her suggestion to put leaders other than King forward in local movements. It often seemed to Clark "as if Citizenship Education is all mine, except when it comes time to pick up the checks." Direct action was too glamorous by comparison, she complained: "most young people prefer demonstrations to genuine education." "I was on the Executive Staff of SCLC, but the men on it didn't listen to me too well," Clark recalled. In the beginning, male SCLC leaders regarded women as "sex symbols" with "no contribution to make." King eventually overcame this, she said, because women proved their skills at organizing. For the most part in 1961, Clark brushed off the SCLC leadership's devaluation of women and its bias toward mass mobilizing, focusing on her fieldwork in citizenship education.[48]

The CEP tried to show concrete links between literacy, education, voting, public employment, shared power, and fair access to public services and welfare. Clark listened to local people's needs, providing food and clothing in addition to education. In south Georgia, she recruited a black banker to teach personal finance to local people. She asked them whether the town had an employment office, opening discussion of discrimination in the agency and how white-elected officials controlled all the local agencies with power over the black community. Clark's students traveled home from Dorchester to start their own classes, asking questions like "How come the pavement stops when the black section begins?" Dorothy Cotton recalled looking for "natural black leaders," people with "Ph.D. minds, but third-grade educations." Their texts were daily newspapers, "IRS forms, Social Security forms, job or driver's license application forms." People saw the courthouse as a place where police "beat up" black folk and registrars denied them voting rights, Cotton recalled. "We started to ask questions like, 'Why aren't you that clerk?' It blew their minds." In February 1962, Clark reported that the CEP was confronting the Jim Crow welfare state everywhere: "Ignorance of welfare benefits and Social Security laws are but two of the great mill stones around the neck of much of the Negro community." She regularly boasted of students' achievements. Through a citizenship school a parent successfully pushed a state special education school to admit her mentally retarded daughter. An illiterate worker who had been permanently disabled in an industrial accident successfully applied for disability benefits through a citizenship school, receiving $4,000 after two years with no income.[49]

Black poverty was in part the product of discriminatory welfare state institutions concerned with alleviating symptoms, not attacking deep economic causes, Clark concluded in her 1962 autobiography, *Echo in My Soul*. "Social and welfare institutions conform with local custom and habit," she wrote. Dramatic protests had not served impoverished Negroes lacking "education, jobs, housing, safety and participation in governmental processes affecting citizenship." She called for new creative programs to include the poorest people and enlist a leadership that identified with them. CEP workshops were addressing diverse quality of life issues: "safe driving, social security, cooperatives, the income tax, and an understanding of tax supported resources such as water testing for wells and aid for handicapped children." Clark taught hundreds of southern activists much about the dynamics of power and poverty. King praised Clark "as a community teacher, intuitive fighter for human rights and leader of her unlettered and disillusioned people." Clark wrote Myles Horton in September 1963 that they were educating around issues of "taxes, social welfare programs, labor management relations, schools, and old age pensions," issues that touched people's "daily lives and are definitely tied to the vote." "Getting jobs, eliminating drop-outs, [and] seeing that children share in the dream of the founding fathers" all reached beyond desegregation and required that blacks vote and share power. This kind of democracy could definitely not work through "one man planning and telling."[50] Not only were constitutional and economic rights intertwined, but on the contested terrain of America's semi-welfare state, political empowerment was more important than ever to economic survival.

In 1962, Andrew Young and the CEP drew King into a local labor struggle. On March 15, King informed reporters he had asked the Department of Labor to investigate minimum wage law violations by Sea Pak Shrimp Factories on the Georgia coast. Several hundred black workers were threatened with firing if they refused to sign affidavits that they were "handicapped workers," a ruse whereby Sea Pak could pay them fifty cents an hour, less than half the federal minimum wage. Violations of the Fair Labor Standards Act seriously threatened "the security of the entire southern Negro population," Young had written. "Our only hope of economic survival is through such Federal aids to our economic well being." Depressed wages gave employers inordinate economic power over the southern black working class, they realized, and enforcement of existing economic rights might be half the battle.[51]

The Lessons of the Albany Movement

On December 14, 1961, King answered a call from William Anderson, the leader of a dynamic mass direct action movement in Albany, Georgia. Student-led protests against segregated interstate bus and train terminals had landed over four hundred people in jail, galvanizing adults and making national news. King agreed to give a speech and return home the same day, but he walked into a house of cards that collapsed around him. The Albany Movement was internally divided, King's staff was overbearing, and SNCC's suspicions of a takeover by SCLC were overblown. Intransigent city authorities and the noncommittal Kennedy administration handed the movement what most outside observers deemed a "defeat." The mayor and city commission gave Police Chief Laurie Pritchett wide discretion to enforce segregation, and he arrested hundreds for violating everything except segregation, including parading without a permit, loitering, and blocking traffic. Having read King's words on "filling the jails," Pritchett sent prisoners to jails in surrounding counties. He kept his police nonviolent, at least while they were within view of national reporters. Without any violent "crisis" to compel intervention, the Kennedy administration congratulated Pritchett on his policing and offered rhetorical and token legal support to the demonstrators. But Albany was no simple defeat. Local participants felt transformed by the experience of collective nonviolent commitment. SCLC and SNCC learned lessons about direct action, voter registration, and political and economic power they carried forward in the struggle.

Albany was an agricultural distribution center with a stubborn white oligarchy, a poor black working class, and a small black middle class. African Americans saw little benefit from the pharmaceutical plants and textile and furniture factories that sprang up after World War II. Among the independent middle class who were "free to speak out" was William Anderson, an osteopathic physician who led an unsuccessful campaign in the 1950s to secure paved streets and sewers in his neighborhood. Anderson was joined in formal

leadership by a realtor, Slater King, his brother C. B. King, the only black lawyer in southwest Georgia, and Marion Page, a retired railroad worker. Ministers stepped into a leadership vacuum left by a cautious NAACP chapter and
the economically vulnerable educators and administrators of Albany State
College. Rev. Samuel B. Wells explained that Albany's whites kept blacks under
their thumbs, dispensing favors to handpicked "leaders." "That's the way racist America has kept us crawling on our bellies and quiet," he told journalist
Fred Powledge, "by keeping us poor . . . living from hand to mouth."[52]

SNCC organizers lit the tinder. Charles Sherrod and Cordell Reagon
came in October 1961, intending to register voters but instead triggered the
largest direct action campaign since Montgomery. They turned first to the 650
Albany State College students and the high schools, assuming adults would be
drawn into a movement if white people "messed with their baby," as Sherrod
put it. On November 1, when the ICC's desegregation order took effect, nine
students sat in at the bus station, cheered on by a local crowd. Sherrod saw in
the eyes of those working-class people "years of resentment—for police brutality, for poor housing, for disenfranchisement, for inferior education, for the
whole damnable system." As protests snowballed, Anderson and the King
brothers organized the Albany Movement. Reflecting the priorities of the
SNCC and community militants, they adopted a broad set of targets: integrated interstate bus and train stations, libraries, parks, city buses, and hospitals, as well as an end to police brutality and job discrimination in local
government and private businesses. By December 13, 471 people were in jail.
The community boycotted downtown stores that catered to black customers
but hired no black employees. James Forman was thrilled: people "of all ages
and class backgrounds" were willing to go beyond boycotting or donating food
and money "to march in the streets, confront the police, [and] go to jail." It
was a "people's movement," not a second coming of the "Messiah."[53]

Unwittingly, Martin King walked into a storm of acrimonious rivalries
and irresolvable dilemmas that left him looking responsible for a colossal
movement failure. Anderson later admitted that King was attractive as "a
media event," bringing attention and resources to Albany. "Racism and colonialism must go," King preached on the evening of December 15: "They can
put you in a dungeon and transform you to glory." King expected to go home,
but the crowd inspired him, and Anderson announced he would march with
them. King led an unprecedented 265 protesters to jail the next day. With 737
people in jail and Albany on the front pages, victory was in sight. SNCC's Bill
Hansen conceded that, whatever their differences in organizing philosophy,
King could raise more hell "by being in jail one night than anyone else could
if they bombed city hall." Then everything started to unravel. In the city jail

Anderson became manic and delusional, calling King "Jesus" and keeping everyone up all night. King had publicly announced he would stay in jail until Christmas if necessary. But Anderson had to be bailed out, and he refused to leave without King. King could not explain why they suddenly emerged from jail without exposing Anderson's breakdown, so Forman judged him a betrayer with feet of clay. By then SCLC and SNCC were at war and the Albany Movement had clumsily forfeited its advantage. Walker and Abernathy fed SNCC's suspicions with postures of command recorded in the press. Reporters heard Ella Baker disparaging SCLC's tendency to move in and out of a community with a big publicity show, leaving locals to pick up the pieces. Secretary Marion Page called a press conference to ask, "Why can't these national organizations understand that this is a local movement?" He wanted protesters released and was willing to accept the city's verbal promises in place of enforceable guarantees. On December 18, the city agreed to release prisoners but not to drop charges. They promised a biracial committee in thirty days—but only if no protests intervened. King grudgingly accepted the compromise. The NAACP's Ruby Hurley saw no choice: blacks had no "political power." Thinking they had won something, King "discovered it was all a hoax," he admitted. The *New York Herald Tribune* deemed it one of King's "most stunning defeats."[54]

In fact, the movement had become as much a captive of the national media as its collaborator in publicizing southern racism. Journalistic obsession with violence obscured the spirit and goals of the movement. Pat Watters later argued that his colleagues simply could not see black Albany's mass commitment to nonviolence. Claude Sitton of the *New York Times* was one of the most discerning white civil rights reporters, but he shared many journalistic "frames" of reference, including the habit of relying on official sources. Police faced an "explosive situation" that could "erupt into violence at any minute," Sitton quoted Pritchett as the chief malignly reframed nonviolence to look like violent provocation. Sitton simply listed charges against protesters—congregating on a sidewalk, threatening public safety—without explaining the First Amendment rights Pritchett systematically violated. Headlines and stories citing "racial tension" and "Negro unrest" captured none of the movement's nonviolent enthusiasm and discipline. According to Watters, such reporting fed whites' convictions that "nigger rioting" was latent in any gathering of black people. Blacks retaliated exactly twice in one year. And as Richard Lentz has shown, the news magazines all but ignored Albany because it lacked the "bloodied demonstrations, burning buses, and mobs coursing through the streets" that defined civil rights "news" since the Freedom Rides.[55]

Albany faded from the news as the city commission refused to create a biracial commission to negotiate desegregation. The Albany Movement's eloquent statement of philosophy and goals received no national coverage. On January 23, 1962, they requested that the city honor its verbal promises and outlined their agenda: "Equal opportunity to work and advance economically," and interracial cooperation in fostering "a climate in which the talents and abilities of the entire community may be used for the good of all, unfettered by considerations of race or class." The city should stop discriminating "in public facilities, both in employment and in use." Private employers must treat all citizens equally, as workers or consumers. They asked for paved streets and sewers whites had enjoyed for sixty years, and protested segregated polling places. Pritchett's arrest of over seven hundred protesters on charges of "parading without a permit" and "breach of peace" were transparent pretexts for repression of free speech and assembly, they contended. But where was the federal government? And where was the media?[56]

The movement shifted from direct action to boycotting, although sporadic protests continued. Avoiding publicity, the court delayed judgment and then sentenced King to jail. When he promised to serve time, Pritchett had him bailed out. By July 20, enthusiastic crowds poured back to the mass meetings, fed up with the city's intransigence. But city attorneys obtained an injunction against protest from segregationist Judge J. Robert Elliott, a Kennedy appointee. Elliott denounced "picketing, demonstrations, parades, boycotts, and riotous conduct which threatens the good order, public peace, and tranquility of the city." Nonviolence "threatened mob violence," endangering *white* people's Fourteenth Amendment rights. King chose to obey a federal court order, but another federal judge soon struck it down. On July 23, while forty protesters marched into paddy wagons, two thousand angry black onlookers gathered. Some threw rocks at police. "Marchers Hurl Rocks at Police After Protest Ban Is Voided," screamed the *Atlanta Constitution*, blaming the nonviolent protesters. Police had brutally beaten protesters in jail. But Albany's second incident of black retaliation won the headlines. King declared a day of penance, assuming, like Gandhi, "responsibility" for his people. Forman thought the rocks legitimate democratic responses to white violence and denounced King's attempt to protect his own "reputation." But King had to keep the line sharp between protest and violence. "Did you see them nonviolent rocks?" Pritchett yelled at reporters. John Kennedy had begun urging negotiations, and King knew the majority would never sanction federal intervention on behalf of "riotous" Negroes. He went into the pool halls and bars, explaining that the power of nonviolence lay in its ability to confuse and disarm oppressors. African Americans in Albany never retaliated violently again that year.[57]

The frustrations of the summer put a radical edge on King's public discourse. His *Amsterdam News* column castigated Albany's "political, economic, and educational suppression." Almost nowhere could blacks earn the minimum wage. Domestic workers earned barely $15 per week, and local teachers were fired for teaching democracy. King now doubted that southern modernization would erode white supremacist folkways. If industry shifted from "unskilled, cheap Negro labor into semi-skilled unionized labor," new jobs might—and actually did—go to whites. In August, King tried to revive flagging spirits, telling a mass meeting that their movement had achieved historic unity across class lines. He affirmed, in a new rhetorical set piece, "We are bound up with the destiny of America. For centuries we worked here without wages. We made cotton king. We built our homes and homes for our masters, enduring injustice and humiliation at every point. And yet, out of a boundless vitality, we continued to live and grow. If the inexpressible cruelties of slavery could not stop us, certainly the opposition that we now face cannot stop us." In a few words, King dismantled the white supremacist image of lazy and dependent blacks, as well as the liberal assumption that blacks were so damaged by their oppression that they could not be full partners in their own emancipation. "Pandemonium" was the crowd's response, Watters recorded.[58]

Despite ongoing boycotts and voter registration, direct action petered out, and King pulled out of Albany. Downtown merchants lost perhaps half of their business, but they backed Pritchett. The city shut down three parks and two libraries "in the interests of public safety," Pritchett said. King predicted Albany could become "the most explosive racial situation in the United States today." But the fire had almost gone out, and SCLC would not return. Instead, the world's attention fixed on the deadly white riot at the University of Mississippi in Oxford in September. King gave no credit to the Kennedys for sending federal marshals when a "screaming mob propelled by bottled-up venom" rioted against the admission of African American James Meredith to the university. King blamed the North, the South, and both political parties for burying Reconstruction and tolerating decades of "executive inaction" that produced this "ugly harvest of lawlessness and violence." He also blamed Governor Ross Barnett, sundry "political demagogues" at the university, and the whole Mississippi "aristocracy," who worshiped gods of bigotry every Sunday in "sprawling brick monuments dedicated to the Glory of God."[59]

In southwest Georgia, locals turned to the slow work of voter registration. Whites burned three rural churches in August and September. But Albany's black community was permanently transformed. Fifty volunteers came out to help, something that would have been impossible six months earlier, Charles Sherrod thought. Unprecedented numbers of blacks met in tents next to the

Figure 4. Charles Sherrod (standing at right) and Randy Battle (seated) canvassing potential voters, southwest Georgia, 1963. "We explained to them that we had stopped school because we felt compelled to do so since so many of us were in chains. . . . I saw in their eyes years of resentment . . . for the whole damnable system," Sherrod recalled. Sherrod stayed on and became a member of the Albany City Council. Photo by Danny Lyon, courtesy of Magnum Photos.

charred remains of the churches. "These are the people on whose backs, in the heat of the day, the South was built . . . through them again . . . the South as it exists today will be destroyed," Sherrod prophesied. King spent a day in Lee County, publicizing the bombings. There were no lunch counters or interstate buses, King wrote, "only a handful of the plain and simple people of the land" pursuing voting rights, aided by SNCC workers on subsistence pay of $40 a week.[60]

Disputes over the reasons for the "failure" of the Albany Movement recapitulated the divisions and dilemmas that weakened the movement at the time. King and Walker blamed southern repression and the Kennedys' failure to deliver on promises of federal protection. "No president can be great, or even fit for office, if he attempts to accommodate injustice to maintain his political balance," King told SCLC's convention in September 1962. Walker argued that Albany was a failure of "the segregationist white South." The movement found America's "Congo" and tasted the "bitter fruit of the white man's seed." SNCC activist Bernice Reagon remembered that the mass meetings and the

unifying songs were what mattered, opening new spaces for protest and burying decades of ingrained fear. King echoed this view. How could Albany be a
failure when thousands of blacks finally straightened their backs? Fully one in
twenty of the city's blacks submitted to arrest, overcoming fears of violence
and the jails. Looking back in 1990 as a member of the Albany City Council,
Sherrod took the long-range view: "How can we have failed when we're no
longer segregated? How can we have failed when we are sharing the power?"
Pat Watters argued that the whole country failed to recognize a historic lost
opportunity, when an entire black community affirmed the spiritual promise
of nonviolence and offered reconciliation to whites on a higher plane of equality. Henceforth the movement was more secular, coercive, provocative, and
bitter. Watters argued that both SCLC and SNCC failed to turn organizational
conflict into productive strategic syntheses. SNCC's faith in people might have
tempered SCLC's growing "tendency to manipulate and use" them in dramatic protests. SCLC's "grasp of American socio-political reality" might have
broadened what Watters thought was an unrealistic idealization of local powerless people.[61]

King tried to salvage some strategic lessons. Though merchants had not
persuaded the city commission to negotiate, Negroes again discovered that
black dollars were a "dormant power on the economic front." For King, Negro
voting also opened possibilities for power sharing. "Albany will serve as a
guide post for other communities," King promised at the time, having tested
all the major techniques of social change. Direct mass action, boycotts, legal
action, and voter registration, if well orchestrated, might just defeat segregation and economic deprivation. Most of SCLC's leaders agreed that the Albany
Movement's diffuse goals prevented concerted pressure that might have won
tangible, limited victories. King criticized their "scattergun approach," targeting segregated transportation, public accommodations, jobs, and voting rights
simultaneously. Walker agreed that they erred in "assaulting too many things."
King stated shortly after Albany they should have targeted the merchants more
intensively: "if you can pull them around, you pull the power structure
because really the power structure listens to the economic power structure."[62]
Birmingham in 1963 tested that theory.

Chapter 6
Jobs and Freedom

In the "Negro Revolution" of 1963, job opportunities, decent wages, and political power sharing were central to King's public definitions of freedom. But national and local white elites more readily conceded to movement demands for equal access to public accommodations than for jobs and power. Before any protests began in downtown Birmingham, King wrote in the *Amsterdam News* that desegregation would mean little if Negroes lacked money to "buy the goods and pay the fees" that regulated access to middle-class spaces of consumption and leisure. Negroes were victims of "political and economic exploitation," so voting remained "the key that opens the door to economic opportunity." Politics in the Deep South already proved as dangerous as direct action, as whites mobilized to defend their privileges.[1] King's annual report on black America for the *Nation* in March also emphasized employment and political power. King appealed to liberal hopes in a coalition for economic progress. Businessmen knew that new investors and skilled workers avoided cities "where dying customs create social tensions" and impoverished schools and cultural institutions. The government sent missiles into deep space. Why could it not "make the Constitution function for human rights" in southern luncheonettes?[2]

The Birmingham protests of April and May 1963 began with segregated luncheonettes, but their goals radiated outward to include jobs and power throughout the city. King initially hoped to win concessions on desegregation and hiring from downtown merchants, who might then pressure the "political power structure" on schools, parks, and city jobs. But the confrontation attracted media attention when Commissioner of Public Safety "Bull" Connor brutally suppressed demonstrations. SCLC filled the jails with high school students, and the media captured unforgettable images of children being attacked by police dogs and bowled over by fire hoses. As black bystanders retaliated violently against police brutality, the Kennedy administration intervened directly to broker negotiations. With its hold over popular violence rapidly slipping, SCLC succeeded in pushing the city's business elite into negotiations. On May 10, SCLC and Fred Shuttlesworth's Alabama Christian Movement for

Human Rights (ACMHR) boldly announced a local victory over segregation and employment discrimination. Birmingham accelerated a mass protest movement already under way across the nation, forcing the Kennedy administration to commit itself to major civil rights legislation in June. But Shuttlesworth criticized King for halting demonstrations and compromising on demands for "immediate" desegregation and desperately needed jobs.

"If lunch-counter sit-ins appeared central to press reports," King wrote in 1965, "they were but a part of our broader aims. In Birmingham, employment opportunities was a demand pressed as forcefully as desegregation of public facilities." Was this true, or were King's priorities of 1965 distorting his memories of 1963?[3] The students who started the downtown protests in 1962 put jobs first. Employment was important to King, but white resistance to job demands, the moderate composition of the negotiating teams, the need to secure bail money for jailed protesters, and the Kennedy administration's promises of national legislation all led SCLC to compromise. In the vacuum created by timid white negotiators who would not reveal their names or the terms of the settlement, SCLC announced their version of a victorious agreement on desegregation and jobs. In Birmingham SCLC found the formula for bringing King's celebrity, mass protest, publicity, and national power to bear on southern dilemmas of segregation and disempowerment. When a horrific bombing led again in September to confrontation, hiring police and clerks in downtown stores became the movement's principal demands.

Birmingham

King was unaware of the deep divisions within Birmingham's black and white communities in 1963 but well aware of the city's reputation for "violence and brutality." Stanley Levison reminded King that before Bull Connor's election as Birmingham's commissioner of public safety in 1937, Connor and his corporate police had successfully red baited and suppressed interracial unions in the steel industry, beating, detaining, and even murdering organizers. Connor and Birmingham's industrial elite granted white workers a stake in racial apartheid, forging a white supremacist coalition. The black share of jobs in the coal mines and steel mills declined substantially. "If you wanted a job in this city, one of the greatest iron- and steel-producing centers in the nation," King later wrote, "you had better settle on doing menial work as a porter or laborer." The city was losing population and manufacturing jobs, trailing the industrial South in new investment because of its reputation for violence.[4]

Any organized expression of black politics had been dangerous in the

1950s. Moderates made small progress, building a black day care center and a new black hospital. Ousted in a sex scandal in 1953, Connor roared back to power in 1957 on the crest of massive resistance, driving moderates into abject silence. Into the vacuum stepped Shuttlesworth and the ACMHR, demanding the city hire black policemen. Born in 1922 to a single farmwoman reliant on "the welfare," Shuttlesworth arrived to pastor Bethel Baptist Church in 1955. He survived a bombing on Christmas Day 1956 that destroyed his home. Whites bombed seventeen churches and homes in Birmingham between 1957 and 1963. In 1958, whites beat him with chains and stabbed his wife when he tried to enroll his children in a white school. The ACMHR filed costly lawsuits against segregated schools, bus terminals, libraries, parks, and all-white juries. Many of the organization's one thousand or so brave middle- and working-class members suffered job losses and vicious beatings. When the ACMHR won a suit to desegregate the parks, Connor closed all sixty-seven of them. Connor won reelection in May 1962 with Klan support; all three city commissioners were now hard-line segregationists. White business moderates grew increasingly distressed. "We've become known as a city of reaction, rebellion and riot, and because of that we're not gaining industry," a corporate leader told the *Wall Street Journal*.[5]

In Birmingham as elsewhere, college students initiated mass action against downtown merchants and city government. In January 1962, seven hundred out of eight hundred Miles College students began a boycott of downtown stores. Asserting their rights foremost as workers and then as consumers, they demanded the following: "I. Hiring of Negro clerks, salesmen, and upgrading Negro employees. II. Equal Opportunity. Hiring of Negro policemen. III. Desegregation of all rest rooms and all drinking facilities in stores." Students marched with sandwich boards: "Don't buy where you can't be a salesman." Their boycott collapsed in April under the weight of city reprisals. The city commission voted to block federal surplus commodity distribution to 20,000 poor families, almost all of them black. "A boycott can work both ways," Connor stated. Connor targeted the wrong people, Shuttlesworth shot back, "the poor Negro rather than those who are a buying force in the city." Shuttlesworth, King, and the black moderates concluded that only massive direct action would force concessions. When the SCLC convention was in town, the ACMHR threatened businessmen with demonstrations and pickets and reversed the priority students had given to jobs over consumer desegregation. Businessmen promised to desegregate restrooms, fitting rooms, and water fountains and to talk about opening sales and clerical jobs to Negroes. After SCLC left, they resisted the employment demands, complaining that black sales personnel drove away white customers. The ACMHR went public, and the deal was off. "The Jim Crow signs reappeared in the stores," King later wrote.[6]

SCLC did not begin with a clear plan to provoke and publicize racist violence and compel intervention by the national government, though oral histories and memoirs can read these outcomes back into diverse intentions. Only after police brutality in mid-April attracted wide publicity did Wyatt Walker start calling the campaign "Project C," for confrontation. SCLC prepared for "Project X" in January, agreeing that boycotting, sit-ins, and picketing must focus on specific targets: segregated lunch counters and Birmingham's business elite. SCLC could not expect Birmingham officials to violently suppress protests for the television cameras, because the structure of government itself was in question and Connor had only a tenuous hold on power. Spurred by Connor's abuses, white business moderates successfully placed a referendum on the November 1962 ballot to replace the three-member city commission with an eleven-member mayor–city council government. The reform passed by a slim margin, but Connor challenged it in court, and the commissioners were not ousted until May 23, 1963. Hedging his bets, Connor also ran for mayor. SCLC and ACMHR delayed demonstrations, lest Connor benefit from a backlash. Albert Boutwell, a moderate segregationist, defeated Connor with a margin of black votes. SCLC began demonstrations the next day, in the middle of the Easter shopping season. Throughout the protests, Connor remained in legal limbo but in firm control of the police and fire departments.[7]

In April, King managed a complex effort to recruit middle-class black supporters and volunteers willing to risk jailing and reprisals. He struggled for agreement on clear, compelling goals, and he raised money for bail and legal defense of the right to protest. Almost none of the black moderates supported Shuttlesworth. King's conversion of men like J. L. Ware of the Interdenominational Alliance and businessman A. G. Gaston, who were more eager to negotiate with Boutwell than to protest, was crucial. "I'm tired of preachers riding around in big cars, living in fine homes," King exhorted 150 ministers. "If you can't stand with your people, you are not fit to be a leader!" Ralph Abernathy told working-class blacks that the doctors, lawyers, and insurance men of the black "Bourgeoisie" must join the movement or lose their patronage: "Year before last they lived like us, across the railroad tracks, took baths in a tin tub, and went to an outhouse. Now they are strutting around proper. How did they get rich? We made them rich." On April 12, over sixty moderates signed an ad in the *Birmingham News*, blaming the failure of negotiations on timid businessmen and hostile city commissioners. Protest expressed the "deep yearnings" of every Birmingham Negro, they said. King paid a price, however, conceding to the moderates substantial control over negotiations.[8]

It proved impossible to keep the protests focused on specific targets. Lunch counter demonstrations began against private businesses on April 3, but Shuttlesworth also demanded the city repeal all segregation ordinances and begin "merit hiring." SCLC and ACMHR demanded complete store desegregation, the immediate opening of "white-collar jobs" to qualified blacks, the reopening of city parks, and a biracial committee to plan school desegregation.[9] Andrew Young, who had experience in television news production, advised King to craft concise visual messages dramatizing varied injustices "before the court of world opinion." Praying in front of a bank that refused to hire Negro tellers would illustrate the need for national fair employment legislation, he thought. Young coordinated arrests at voter registration offices with the announced intention to "get the Justice Department in on this." But the Kennedys had just retreated from defending the civil liberties of voting rights activists in Greenwood, Mississippi, a decisive moment of missed opportunity that was lost on the press when attention turned to Birmingham. King was able to get civil liberties back in the papers only by suing in federal court to prevent city officials from arresting peaceful protestors for "breach of peace" and "parading without a permit."[10]

It would take a crisis compelling to the national press and the federal government to galvanize the country and salvage the local movement, SCLC strategists realized, and Connor was still in power. Connor released his police dogs on April 7, and pictures of them attacking Leroy Allen poured out of Birmingham. Wyatt Walker was delighted to see reporters conflate scores of protesters with hundreds, then thousands of "bystanders." Successful "dramatization," he later admitted, required shrewd manipulation of perceptions and careful planning to "precipitate crises." But when bystanders responded by heaving rocks and paving stones, the line between nonviolent protesters and crowds in a more retaliatory mood proved nearly impossible to redraw. King's Good Friday arrest with sixty other marchers made front-page news. The *New York Times* called it King's "most spectacular" march, and television crews and *Jet* magazine arrived to cover the arrest. But on Easter Sunday, when Young tried to dramatize attempts to integrate white churches, reporters covered a clash between the police and a crowd of up to 2,000 "onlookers" hurling rocks and bottles. Police waded into the crowd wielding nightsticks. Journalists praised Connor for his "restraint" and blamed the "violence" on "protesters." Ignoring the long history of police brutality and Connor's flagrant violations of civil liberties, reporters echoed moderates who called for negotiations. Orderly processes would "ease racial tensions," allowing for progress. The papers reported a plea from local white clergy for "law and order" and an end to "unwise and untimely" demonstrations. King composed his famous "Letter from a Birmingham City Jail" in response, though it only became celebrated later. Protesters were not responsible for the violent repression visited on them, King argued. But clearly, media coverage of repression was becoming central to SCLC expectations of effective nonviolence.[11]

Money and volunteers evaporated quickly after Connor put the movement's main bail-bond agent out of business. SCLC was broke on Good Friday when King chose arrest and was saved only when Harry Belafonte came through with $50,000 in cash. Moderates wanted to bail out all four hundred people in jail, as they were already feeling the whip of economic retaliation from white suppliers, landlords, and banks. Liberal and labor supporters came through with demonstrations and donations. District 65 organized a national coalition of unions and civil rights groups to boycott and picket four retail chains with Birmingham stores. CORE, the NAACP, the National Urban League, the Teamsters, the UAW, Local 1199, and the electrical, packinghouse, and transport workers turned out to picket all across the country. The International Union of Mine, Mill and Smelter Workers, which had been red baited out of Birmingham in the 1940s, joined in sending tens of thousands of dollars to SCLC. Attorney General Robert Kennedy started climbing off the fence before his brother did, announcing on April 21 that there would be racial violence for years to come and America's international image would be soiled unless and until blacks enjoyed full equality.[12]

As the movement captured national attention, however, King feared it might be Albany all over again. "The press is leaving, we've got to get going," he told the ACMHR in late April. SCLC field secretary James Bevel arrived to work with Birmingham youth. Bevel explained to students the four pillars of segregation: disfranchisement, economic denial, alienation from God, and inferior education. Students were great assets, Bevel and Shuttlesworth agreed, because they were relatively immune from economic reprisals. On April 29, SCLC recruiters canvassed the black high schools, announcing mass protests for May 2, which Bevel called "D-Day." Officials locked students in school and threatened to expel them, but over 1,000 young people broke free and marched to jail. Parents faced felony prosecutions for contributing to the delinquency of minors. UPI dubbed King the "mastermind" of the protest, but he remained deeply ambivalent until the students' mass arrests proved the strategy viable. The mass marchers made up the mastermind's mind.[13]

May 3, "Double D-Day," transformed the strategy of confrontation into international spectacle. Connor faced over 2,000 students in Kelly Ingram Park who were ready to march downtown. Firemen blasted children back toward the church with their hoses. "Negroes retaliated by hurling bottles, stones and chunks of concrete at the officers," UPI reported. Connor loosed the dogs. AP photographer Bill Hudson photographed a police dog attacking the tender midsection of "bystander" Walter Gadsen. Police swung their clubs indiscriminately at protesters, onlookers, and newsmen. Charles Moore captured shocking images: firemen blasting children at short range, a police dog ripping the trousers off Henry Lee Shambry. Millions of Americans saw the savagery in their papers or on the evening news, and "the moral conscience of the nation was stirred," King wrote. Leaders called off demonstrations in mid-afternoon as the crowd continued to heave projectiles. Congress of Racial Equality (CORE) national director James Farmer compared Alabama to "the racist police state of South Africa." Robert Kennedy declared that "primary responsibility for peaceful solutions is with the leaders of business, labor and the bar, as well as the city officials themselves," but he sent the director of the civil rights division, Burke Marshall, to mediate negotiations. President Kennedy said the pictures made him "sick," and he was "dismayed" whites could not settle the dispute.[14]

Public opinion tilted toward the protesters, but the rapidly blurring line between protesters and retaliating bystanders threatened to undermine the image of black nonviolence King deemed so essential to success. On May 4, as smaller groups of protesters invaded the downtown area, a crowd of 3,000 gathered in Kelly Ingram Park, taunting police and firemen, ducking behind trees, dancing in the park, and daring the dogs. Some hurled rocks at the agents of their oppression. Bevel again called off the marches, having seen "several pistols and knives." Total arrests from the three days amounted to 1,100. King announced the rocks came from "outsiders." Sights raised, he now said, "If we can crack Birmingham . . . we can crack the South." National publicity was crucial. "We had Huntley and Brinkley every night," Walker remembered. Bayard Rustin later called Birmingham "television's finest hour." Police beatings and children felled by "water hoses, that's news, that's spectacularism," Shuttlesworth later commented.[15] Money poured in from trade unions, Jewish groups, churches, and people around the world.

But Americans consumed the news on their own terms. Almost half of King's mail, which doubled in one month, decried the protests. "Thank God for television!" wrote a Louisiana woman on May 6. "The whole world got a glimpse of what a 'Congo jungle' is like when they saw the howling, screeching, frenzied mob of Negroes in Birmingham, even small children!" Another commanded King to "clean up the mess amongst your race first before you agitate race riots." None of the supporters mentioned the demands, which is understandable given the sparse press coverage of constitutional or economic issues.

A San Francisco woman wrote to King, describing her shock at pictures of Birmingham's riotous "white trash." A New York fireman deplored the use of his Birmingham comrades to repress "American Negro citizens."[16]

By May 8, 3,200 protestors were in custody, filling the jails and the Birmingham fairgrounds. On May 7, merchant resistance gave way to serious negotiations. James Forman and CEP organizer Dorothy Cotton coordinated "Operation Confusion" in the morning. Three thousand black youths in small groups bypassed police lines into downtown, staging "guerilla" sit-ins and protests in stores, in restaurants, and on the streets. But the afternoon convinced most SCLC leaders (except Shuttlesworth) that they could no longer prevent bloodshed. Two thousand students wanting to join Operation Confusion were bottled up in Kelly Ingram Park by police, dogs, and firemen. Again the crowd pelted Connor's forces with rocks. Bevel and Walker took police bullhorns and tried to herd them back into the church. Connor turned on the hoses and sent out his white armored car to intimidate the crowd. Governor George Wallace sent six hundred state troopers armed with submachine guns, carbines, sawed-off shotguns, and tear gas to the city, commanded by Alabama's "paranoid," pill-popping state police chief Al Lingo. "Rioting Negroes Routed by Police at Birmingham," read the *New York Times* headline. Though he later corrected himself, Claude Sitton conflated the morning's jubilant nonviolence with the afternoon's near riot. Birmingham's blacks were protesting on their own terms with weapons of their choosing, unwilling to "fill the jails" and outraged by police brutality and murder that had been occurring for decades. But King, Walker, and Young began to smell the smoke of discrediting defeat for the intertwined local and national movements. Nonviolent mobilization was meant to coerce whites while denying them their historical justification for repression: the public specter of riotous Negro mobs. Young admitted to Sitton, "It's too hot. We couldn't have controlled this crowd." "We wanted to get out of it, as bad as Birmingham was," Walker later acknowledged.[17]

The dramatic confrontations between police and young people had already compelled whites to rescue their city's image. On May 3, the Senior Citizens Committee, eighty-nine of Birmingham's most prominent businessmen, authorized real estate magnate Sidney Smyer and attorney David Vann to start talks strictly limited to "privately owned store facilities and employment upgrading." The black coalition presented its "Points for Progress": immediate desegregation of downtown stores; hiring of black clerks; and a nondiscriminatory hiring policy throughout the city's private sector. They asked merchants to try to persuade politicians to drop criminal charges and establish a biracial committee, which would discuss hiring black police, opening voter rolls, and desegregating schools, movie theaters, hotels, and parks. Business-men refused to acknowledge that they wielded any political influence, contra-dicting King's assumptions about the political leverage inherent in economic power. On May 7 in the middle of Operation Confusion, the Senior Citizens Committee considered asking for martial law, then broke for lunch and walked into streets dominated by 3,000 jubilant protesters. President Kennedy had already instructed his cabinet to call CEOs of corporations with Bir-mingham offices. So the committee made a "dollar-and-cents" decision to avoid risking the "black eye" of federal intervention, Smyer recalled. Mer-chants were reporting that business was off by 30 percent. They came to the bargaining table, determined to concede as little as possible.[18]

Did King and SCLC end demonstrations under pressure from the Ken-nedy administration, accommodating "empty biracial negotiations" and giv-ing up the victory King had promised Shuttlesworth? Although King's and Shuttlesworth's priorities were different, and the black moderates compro-mised on every demand, Shuttlesworth accepted the outcome and saw the value of a national victory.[19] The crucial but widely overlooked fact about the Birmingham campaign is that there was no clear "agreement": blacks and whites had different interpretations of what they had agreed to, especially with regard to employment. SCLC took advantage of the merchants' anonymity and secrecy to score a public relations coup, announcing its own version of the settlement and declaring victory.

White negotiators' records of the settlement they hammered out in the small hours of the morning on May 8 reflected their desire for a "timetable for delay" of all desegregation and employment demands until at least thirty days after the Alabama Supreme Court settled the question of Connor's tenure. Andrew Young, who joined A. G. Gaston and others from the Inter-Citizens Committee to hash out the final agreement, proposed gradual deseg-regation of the stores and then opening of job opportunities, implemented "quietly, and without fanfare." They agreed to begin with the removal of "whites only" signs from stores within thirty days and lunch counter desegre-gation within sixty days. Whites composed an absurdly worded statement maintaining the fiction they were already redressing job discrimination, and promised to hire "at least 1 salesperson or cashier" in the downtown stores. They promised to form a "committee on Racial Problems in Employment" to begin negotiating "a program of upgrading and improving employment opportunities" throughout the city (which they never did). Young and King recalled the agreement differently the next week, but Smyer denied promising to hire one clerk in *every* store.[20]

SCLC was unable to push jobs as vigorously as desegregation because merchants stubbornly resisted the demands and more pressing issues intruded. King was desperate for money to bail protestors out of jail. Merchants refused to pressure the city or lend the movement bail money. King prevailed upon Robert Kennedy to lean on Walter Reuther, who raised the cash. Young recalled that King received "private assurances" the Kennedys would introduce a strong civil rights bill soon. For King, of course, both bail money and national legislation seemed more important than hiring clerks in downtown stores. King, Young, and Marshall all wanted to avoid a bloodbath they feared was imminent. Shuttlesworth was furious that King neither consulted him nor visited him in the hospital, and he threatened to lead thousands of children in continued protests. Though he later denied having substantive disagreements with King other than on the timing of demonstrations, Shuttlesworth disparaged the "timetable of delay" and the weakness of the jobs agreement. "When four thousand folk go to jail for you, many of them lose their jobs; homes, that's sacred," he recalled. "I told them Burke Marshall didn't live in Birmingham and I lived there and I had to care for these people after they left." His greatest regret, after months of pursuing the issue, was the sacrifice of concrete employment gains. "We would never have agreed to the hiring of just one Negro after 2,800 people have gone to jail," he later said. If he could do it again, he said, he would "fight until a certain percentage of the clerical [workers] both in the local city and the State Capital were black." In the end, however, Shuttlesworth deferred to King, because the "man with the marbles dominates the game."[21]

On May 10, SCLC released a substantially different version of the agreement, claiming that in addition to desegregating the downtown stores, the city's business leaders promised to offer "equal job opportunities, equal access to public facilities, and equal rights and responsibilities for all of its people." They did not mention waiting for the Alabama Supreme Court's pending decision on Bull Connor's tenure. Businessmen agreed to upgrade and employ blacks "throughout the industrial community of Birmingham," promising to hire "Negroes as clerks and salesmen within the next 60 days." A biracial committee would immediately implement "an area-wide program" to upgrade job opportunities. Without these moves, which more closely approximated the May 3 Points for Progress, they threatened more demonstrations. Recriminations and accusations of bad faith flew furiously during the next few weeks, but they never were enough to compel King or Shuttlesworth to resume demonstrations. Reading the New York papers, Levison sent an urgent message to King telling him to "highlight the job opportunity potential of the Negro because the issue hasn't reached the press." There were both skillful public relations and potential leverage in the SCLC-ACMHR version. Whites were furious over the announced agreement. In the absence of any clear civic leadership or news coverage, Birmingham's whites saw only an invasion by outsiders and multiple capitulations by a bunch of anonymous businessmen. White politicians' denials and denunciations created a dangerous climate of bitterness and betrayal. That evening, the KKK held a huge rally outside Birmingham; its leaders goaded the crowd to "turn Alabama upside down for God" and prevent their children from being "mongrelized."[22]

On May 11, bombers targeted King's hotel room and the house of his brother, A. D.. Neither man was injured, but hundreds of furious black people poured into the streets, throwing rocks at police, smashing windows, looting, and setting fires in stores. Rioting raged for three hours, subsided, and flared again after state troopers continued indiscriminately clubbing people on their porches and in the street. King waded into the melee counseling nonviolence. Celebrating the courage of nonviolent black civil defense workers and ministers, Claude Sitton detailed the full extent of Al Lingo's provocation both in the *New York Times* and to Robert Kennedy. Irregulars accompanied by state troopers armed with double-barreled shotguns had rushed into the Gaston Motel parking lot and beat people with gun butts and nightsticks, including Wyatt Walker's wife, Anne. Sitton blamed the anonymous Senior Citizens Committee, cowardly men who "turned their backs on police brutality [and] allowed white supremacists to speak for their communities, thus encouraging the lawless fringe element."[23]

The Kennedy administration sent troops to a military base just outside Birmingham. Robert Kennedy wanted to denounce the bombings, convinced by Sitton's accounts that the credit for averting a race war in Birmingham belonged to King. The president wanted Negroes "off the street" and insisted on "law and order" and peaceful negotiations. He denounced "extremists" on both sides. FBI snoops heard Levison tell Jack O'Dell that "a little violence is good" in order to wake Kennedy up to the danger to his "image around the world." King did not share Levison's assessment of violence, fearing more bloodshed and a demolished agreement. He drew a crowd of fifty into a pool hall, explaining that bombers were trying to "sabotage" all their achievements by provoking violence and looting. Preventing "further retaliatory violence was one of the finest accomplishments of our campaign," Andrew Young recalled.[24]

Birmingham revealed that "organization, together with nonviolent direct action, was explosively, powerfully and socially transforming," King later wrote. Victory came when Birmingham's Negroes marched in "democratic phalanx," doctors and window cleaners, lawyers and laundresses, "Ph.D.'s and no-D's," all risking injury and arrest in "perfect equality." But Birmingham was neither Montgomery nor Albany. Class, generational, and ideological chasms separated working-class crowds from nonviolent demonstrators and the middle-class members of the Inter-Citizens Committee. King did not exaggerate Birmingham's larger significance, however: the movement thereafter acted "on a thousand brightly lighted stages" across the nation.[25]

Mass Activism and the Civil Rights Bill

"In city after city where the spirit of Birmingham has spread, the Negroes are demanding fundamental social, political and economic changes," Bayard Rustin wrote in June. Birmingham's drama accelerated a wave of demonstrations across the country, many of which had already begun. To obtain decent jobs, good wages, and opportunities to advance, Rustin urged "nonviolent resistance . . . against local and federal governments, the labor unions, against the AFL-CIO hierarchy and any construction plant or industry that refuses to grant jobs." A truly mass movement had emerged nationwide, incorporating thousands of working-class African Americans pursuing a broad agenda. Activists staged over eight hundred boycotts, sit-ins, and marches in two hundred cities and towns across the South that summer. Hundreds of actions in northern and western cities supported desegregation and focused attention on the national problems of unemployment and urban disempowerment.[26]

At a huge Los Angeles rally in May 1963, King thanked western SCLC affiliates for supporting Birmingham's protestors. More important for them, King declared, was ridding Los Angeles of discrimination in housing and jobs. Dr. Christopher Taylor, president of the local NAACP, agreed, breathlessly urging the crowd to act on its own grievances: "police brutality, unequal administration of justice, ghettoization of Negroes in Los Angeles, de facto segregation of schools, lack of adequate housing, great numbers of unemployed, lack of job opportunities and discrimination in employment not only in private industry but in city, county, state and federal levels, despite a state FEPC law and a presidential executive order." After leading a march in Detroit of 150,000 people on June 23 organized by Reverend C. L. Franklin and the Detroit Human Rights Commission, King listed three sites of segregation in the North that were "just as injurious" as Jim Crow: jobs, housing, and schools. These remained Rustin's principal issues, but soon King's list also included Taylor's concerns with police, justice, and urban power.[27]

SCLC and King looked for the next "big push" in several cities battling segregation. Nowhere could they invest the resources they had in Birmingham. In Savannah, Georgia, Hosea Williams and the Chatham County Crusade for

Voters pioneered the effective but dangerous tactic of night marching. On July 11, the police and National Guard used tear gas to battle a crowd that was increasingly willing to fight back. Young and Bevel suspended protests and negotiated desegregation of hotels, motels, and theaters with a committee of one hundred businessmen. In Danville, Virginia, marchers demanded desegregation of the downtown stores and jobs in municipal agencies, including the police and fire departments. On June 10, police bloodily suppressed peaceful prayer marches. After withering legal and financial reprisals from the city, activists turned to voter registration. In Louisiana and Alabama, SCLC affiliates met even more severe repression. The lesson: reactionaries could maintain segregation in the face of determined black protest, but segregation could not survive except by relentless repression. Local elites might grant concessions, but black people would suffer immense reprisals. The case for federal legislation grew more urgent.[28]

Cambridge, Maryland, a working-class city on the Eastern Shore, set the template for broader protests and a more systemic analysis linking civic and economic grievances. Gloria Richardson led a movement that pressed for desegregation in schools and public accommodations and demanded low-rent public housing, job-training, public and private jobs, and an end to police brutality. On June 14, local authorities declared martial law, and the Justice Department intervened. "Desegregated schools are irrelevant to families who cannot afford to buy their children school books," Richardson declared. Social welfare policy was piecemeal, discriminatory, and abstracted from the interlocking needs of poor communities. "Federal housing projects are irrelevant if the rest of the ghetto conditions—faulty education and lack of employment—remain," she said. Explicitly including poor whites and poor blacks in a revolutionary coalition, she argued that middle- and upper-class whites must share power with more than a few middle-class blacks. They must accept the democratic principle "that the people as a whole really do have more intelligence than a few of their leaders."[29]

Working-class blacks poured into CORE chapters, pushing the jobs agenda from the grassroots across the nation. In New York, police battled demonstrators demanding jobs at a Harlem Hospital construction site where only 10 percent of the workers were black. A broad cross-section of blacks and Puerto Ricans forced the mayor to address "cronyism and nepotism" in the building trades. In Philadelphia, protestors marched on city hall and picketed construction sites to oppose "discrimination by unions and contractors on public building projects." White workers' hostility was rising, with fistfights breaking out at construction sites and the American Nazis organizing counter-demonstrations. "The pie of decent jobs, good low-income housing, and good education is too small in this city to be shared with the Negro community, which now demands a proportionate slice," Martin Oppenheimer commented in *New America*. "Only an increase in the employment pie for everyone combined with a major effort by labor to end discrimination within its ranks" could solve the problem.[30]

The fight against economic racism directly challenged the material wages of whiteness in the workplace and community, even as it raised difficult class dilemmas within black society. NAACP labor secretary Herbert Hill testified before the House Labor Subcommittee in support of a bill to create a federal fair employment practices commission. Equal employment would be the key to the entire "civil rights record of this Congress and the Kennedy administration." While economic restructuring forced upon whites a "crisis of unemployment," it forced blacks into "a major depression," he said. Negroes suffered at least double the white unemployment rate, and the income gap between black and white workers was growing. Mainstream journalists noticed a rising tide of racial consciousness and militancy that was reshaping the existing civil rights organizations and swelling the appeal of black nationalism, especially in the urban ghettos. M. S. Handler of the *New York Times* concluded, "The widening gulf between the dominant white majority and the Negro minority in the United States is paralleled by a growing gulf separating the educated Negroes from the Negro masses."[31] Responding to this mass disaffection and channeling it in directions likely to strengthen progressive coalitions rather than white reaction became the central challenge of the decade.

The Kennedy administration unveiled its legislative initiative on civil rights on June 11. Civil rights, Kennedy began on television, was a "moral issue" as "old as the scriptures" and "clear as the American Constitution." A full century after emancipation, Negroes still struggled against "bonds of injustice" and "social and economic oppression." He endorsed their rights to "equal service" and to vote without "fear of reprisal." King hailed Kennedy's televised speech as "eloquent, profound and unequivocal," a beacon to "millions of disinherited people." Morally compelling, the speech also revealed Kennedy's overriding political imperatives to preserve domestic tranquility and international prestige. Demonstrations "threaten disorder, and threaten lives," he said. His rhetorical improvisations also reveal the limits of the cold war liberal imagination. Preaching freedom to the world and cherishing it at home, "are we to say to the world—and much more importantly to each other—that this is the land of the free, except for the Negroes; that we have no class or caste system, no ghettos, no master race, except with respect to Negroes?" The implication was that racial equality would make America a classless society. Kennedy abandoned racial innocence but maintained a sanguine view of class, a myopic biracialism, and an unwarranted optimism about the equal opportunity society.[32]

The administration proposed much less than what civil rights activists sought. The Kennedys decided to defer the issue of voting rights, downplay jobs, and put desegregated public accommodations at the top of their legislative agenda. Title II on public accommodations would crown the Kennedy bill, the Kennedy brothers and Burke Marshall agreed on May 20 and June 1. It was a way to get activists "into the courts and out of the streets," Robert Kennedy insisted. Demonstrations were "bad for the country" at home and abroad. The president feared that "Negroes are going to push this thing too far." Northern Negroes grew militant watching police brutality on television, Marshall explained. But the lunch counters made southern Negroes "maddest." Marshall had concluded Negroes "didn't know what they wanted," he told the Kennedys, but King explained to him the goals of desegregation and hiring in the downtown stores. And they knew the civil rights leadership wanted much more. Black leaders hoped to revive Title III of the 1957 bill, authorizing the attorney general to sue on behalf of anyone deprived of the rights routinely trampled in the South, including assembly, speech, petitioning, and voting. Fearful that clearing the field for nonviolent protest would precipitate violence, Marshall and the president agreed that anything strengthening "the right to demonstrate" would backfire politically. Protection for civil rights workers did not pass Congress until 1968, after disillusioned activists had retreated from organizing and lost faith in the government.[33]

Georgia's Democratic senator Richard Russell attacked Title II on the Senate floor, charging Jack Kennedy with threatening "mass violence" so he could trample on "property rights" and create a "special right for Negroes." For Russell, "demonstrations, law defiance and civil disobedience" were indistinguishable from insurrection and communism. The government could just as well compel whites to admit Negroes to the "bedroom of any citizen." Kennedy told Congress on June 19 that in regulating private business practices, he saw no conflict between "human rights and property rights." The public interest often trumped private property, as when the government limited "the property rights of slaveholders" and intervened in the market in cases of "zoning, collective bargaining [and] minimum wages." Beneath their differences both Kennedy and Russell agreed that street demonstrations led to bloodshed. Kennedy could not understand southern white resistance to Title II. "Public accommodations is *nothing*," he later implored Birmingham businessmen. Negroes would not be seeking access to Birmingham's expensive hotels. "They will have the right to, but they won't have the money," he insisted, spinning the movement's cruelest dilemma into smooth reassurance for segregationists. Class could segregate just as effectively as race.[34]

Blacks wanted jobs more than they wanted hotel rooms or hamburgers, a July Harris-*Newsweek* poll revealed. From a list of sixteen gripes about "discrimination," three times as many Negroes chose "Prevents my getting a job and wages I want" than "Could not eat and be served." Since the end of World War II, civil rights activists had lobbied for reestablishing a Fair Employment Practices Commission (FEPC) with authority over all private employment. But Title VII called for the creation of the Equal Employment Opportunity Commission (EEOC) with jurisdiction only over government hiring and contracting. Speaking to Congress, Kennedy conceded how small an achievement it was to admit the Negro to "hotels and restaurants if he has no cash in his pocket and no job." Economic growth was the key to shrinking black unemployment, he said, and Congress should pass his $11 billion tax cut, expanded manpower training, youth employment, vocational education, area redevelopment, basic adult education, and work relief programs. But aside from the tax cut, these were all piecemeal measures. The economic weaknesses of the Kennedy bill were the black leaders' most common grievances that summer. The civil rights lobby and House Judiciary Committee chairman Emanuel Cellers extended the jurisdiction of the EEOC to private business in September, and Lyndon Johnson shepherded the whole bill past the Senate filibuster in the spring. Nowhere in the original 1963 bill was there an equal employment agency with enforcement authority or jurisdiction over major employers.[35]

In retrospect, 1963 and 1964 presented the last, best opportunity of the postwar era to institutionalize social democratic policies that could have addressed the growing crisis of joblessness at the heart of the racial and urban crises that endure to this day. Fair and equal employment opportunity might have been more firmly ensconced in a policy of full employment. By 1965, when the unusually liberal 89th Congress joined Lyndon Johnson in Washington, Kennedy-Johnson policy priorities had become relatively entrenched, black disillusionment and the white backlash relatively advanced. Like Kennedy, Johnson counted on "commercial Keynesian" fiscal restraint to spur economic growth. He looked to education and training rather than targeted spending for job creation to solve unemployment. And he solidified the nation's commitment to defend South Vietnam. The democratic left continued to agitate vigorously for social democratic and "social Keynesian" labor policies, with King carrying the torch. Beginning in May 1963, Senator Joseph Clark's yearlong Senate Subcommittee on Labor and Public Welfare hearings on the "Manpower Revolution" uncovered widespread doubts that Kennedy's economic and civil rights policies would address the structural roots of mass unemployment. Clark's report proposed investing $5 billion a year in public works jobs for the most disadvantaged unemployed workers. Senator Hubert Humphrey incorporated most of Clark's recommendations into S. 1937. But in the fall, to overcome the objections of Senate minority leader Everett Dirksen, Democrats dropped the Humphrey bill and stripped Title VII and the EEOC of powers to issue cease and desist orders against discriminating companies.[36]

In 1963 civil rights leaders signed on to the House Judiciary Committee's EEOC and did not seize on S. 1937 as a more powerful alternative. Blacks were not even invited to Clark's manpower revolution hearings. Only Roy Wilkins, Andrew Young, and A. Philip Randolph attended separate hearings on equal employment opportunity in July. Randolph and Senator Clark briefly agreed that "fair employment and full employment" could not be achieved without each other. Wilkins was mainly concerned with "fair employment," especially affecting unions, though he did recommend synthesizing the Kennedy and Humphrey bills. And Young voiced concern that even if full employment were interpreted to mean 3 percent aggregate unemployment, that would still bear disproportionately upon blacks. Stressing affirmative action, Young did not think full employment was "possible in the immediate future, before the program of Negro unemployment is resolved." Without support from the administration, or fuller black inclusion in the policy process, the government again failed to integrate economic policy and civil rights policy.[37]

Moderating the March on Washington

Collective memories and historical interpretations of the 1963 March on Washington for Jobs and Freedom run the spectrum from liberal triumphalism to radical disillusionment. Both views distort the multiple meanings of the march. The March on Washington emerged from long-range planning by Randolph and the NALC and was energized by the direct actionists of CORE, SNCC, and SCLC. The introduction of Kennedy's civil rights bill altered activists' agendas, as the coalition widened to include mainstream civil rights groups, white churches, and progressive labor unions. Many who dreamed of militant civil disobedience or a dramatic demonstration of the economic crisis of black America saw only fatal compromises of the march's methods and goals. King has been unfairly blamed for moderating both tactics and goals, allegedly handing the Kennedy administration the staged spectacle of freedom it demanded, rather than the militant confrontation it deserved. Though in the end King stole the show, he was never powerful enough to direct the march's agenda or as inclined to moderate its methods as were the Kennedys,

Whitney Young and Roy Wilkins. Organizers rejected calls for massive civil disobedience in favor of an interracial rally at the Lincoln Memorial. But the march had no single "original" plan; it represented a convergence of several streams of expectation and hope. Especially in the media and the moderate organizations, the freedom goals did loom larger than the economic demands for jobs, higher wages, and decent housing,. But the march still loudly affirmed economic demands that went beyond the Kennedy bill. The entire March on Washington leadership wanted Kennedy to extend his promises to combat employment discrimination, unemployment, and disfranchisement.[38]

King remembered a "radiant day" that both demanded interracial democracy and enacted it for the world to see. People of every faith, class, profession, and party united with masses of "ordinary people," firmly determined "to achieve democracy." The militants were more furious at the march's tactical moderation than any diminution of its economic demands. Malcolm X charged the Kennedys with coordinating liberals to integrate, "infiltrate," and tame the "black revolution" by expanding the coalition, pouring the cool cream of ersatz brotherhood into hot, angry, black coffee. Thrilled with the revolutionary potential of Birmingham, Danville, Cambridge, and Greenwood, SNCC and CORE militants found in Washington only a feel-good rally rather than a militant protest. James Forman argued that it became an integrated public relations advertisement for "American Democracy," not a demonstration of the need for democracy in America.[39]

In his bitter 1968 "Reminiscences," Rustin lamented that "pass the bill" became the march's central focus, instead of jobs. His fellow coordinator, socialist Norman Hill, agreed that many in the "Big Ten" organizations planning the march did not see the "relationship between race and poverty." But Hill gave Rustin the credit he deserved for keeping key constituencies focused on demands for economic justice. The march served as a bridge between "the old civil rights struggle and the struggle for black people for economic justice and racial equality."[40] If Rustin, Randolph, King, and the march leadership made any error, it was not in giving up economic goals. Rather, it was in failing to make clear and necessary connections between fair employment and full employment, between job training and job creation, so that if the nation bothered to listen, they could join the debate about how to integrate civil rights and economic policy.

The March on Washington was a long-deferred dream for Randolph. In May 1962 the Kennedys had ignored Randolph's request to bring "Negro trade unionists and workers" to the White House to discuss the deepening unemployment crisis. The following December, Randolph had asked Rustin, Hill, and Tom Kahn to sketch plans for protests. They returned in January with a

Figure 5. "There go my people." The March on Washington leadership scrambled to get ahead of the March, held August 28 on Constitution Avenue. Printed signs reflect the agenda of the coalition that reached beyond the Kennedy bill: "Full Employment," "Jobs for All Now!" "Voting Rights Now!" "An FEPC Law Now!" "UAW Says: End Segregated Rules in Public Schools," and "Decent Housing Now!" Front line, right to left: Rabbi Joachim Prinz, Cleveland Robinson, Martin Luther King, Jr., Floyd McKissick, Matthew Ahmann, John Lewis. Copyright Bettmann/CORBIS.

document outlining the democratic socialist agenda for the next five years. The government had done nothing since abolishing slavery to end black "economic subordination," they wrote. Automation, unemployment, and persistent income inequality would severely limit any benefits accruing to blacks from integrated housing, schools, or public accommodations. A century of discrimination and joblessness had made black people's "cumulative handicaps" so serious that the nation needed to go beyond equal opportunity. But the democratic socialists subordinated affirmative action to the more politically feasible universal goal of creating "more jobs for all Americans." The black struggle might catalyze "all workers behind demands for a broad and fundamental program of economic justice," they hoped. Tactically, they recommended two days of direct action and lobbying: on the first, "a mass descent" onto the floor of Congress by "labor, church, civil rights delegations" would occur; on the second, a "mass protest rally" would gather to hear their reports and demand a second Emancipation Proclamation. Nowhere did they mention mass civil disobedience.[41]

In March, the NALC endorsed Randolph's plans for a "Jobs Rights March and Mobilization in Washington for Negroes." Randolph invited all the civil rights groups, suggesting a Lincoln Memorial rally, a march down Pennsylvania Avenue, an address by Kennedy, and visits to the House and Senate. "A million and one half of the black laboring masses are jobless!" Randolph wrote in a labor appeal. Thousands must join in a "mighty thrust of revulsion, resentment, rejection and resistance to this blight of black second-class economic citizenship." "Negro laborers" would lead a march on Washington "for their own liberation." Rustin won SNCC and CORE to the idea in April, and on May 6 King signed on. By the end of May, only the National Urban League and the NAACP held out.[42]

Excited, King was ready to throw "real force" against Kennedy and Congress, telling Levison looked forward to seeing "Negroes sitting all over them in Washington." Perhaps he might also call for a national "work stoppage." Levison refused to endorse King's militancy. Mass pressure might force Kennedy to change policy but only if he could be guaranteed a "controlled situation" that would not humiliate him on the international stage. King cared little for Kennedy's image. Moderates would have to join the march as "pressure builds from the bottom." Looking for allies, he was thrilled that the National Council of Churches had openly endorsed "direct action."[43]

Kennedy's announcement of his bill changed their calculations. Levison, King, Abernathy, Andrew Young, and King's new advisor, New York attorney Clarence Jones, hashed out the options on the phone. King did not try to blunt the jobs thrust or moderate the tactics to serve the Kennedy administration, as has been argued. King wanted a broad agenda, and he expected Randolph not to object. The FBI recorded King's priorities: "1. desegregation of public facilities, 2. jobs, and 3. to vote." Advisors agreed to drop plans for "work stoppages" and "passive civil disturbances, etc." Pull in all the civil rights organizations and mobilize white churches, they recommended. King had little to do with Rustin and Randolph's formal definition of goals or with the recruitment of most marchers, who were predominantly northerners mobilized by the March on Washington Committee, the NAACP, CORE, churches, and unions. This was a show directed from New York, which King ended up stealing.[44]

Talk of militant civil disobedience persisted, and King did nothing to discourage it. On June 9, King had announced a possible mass march on Washington, including congressional sit-ins to "help the President" redeem his "miserable" civil rights record. On June 11, Rev. George Lawrence of SCLC's New York office and King's new aide and attorney Clarence Jones announced "massive, militant, monumental sit-ins on Congress" if the Senate filibustered the civil rights bill. Lawrence and Jones left vague the relationship between a filibuster (whose date could not be predicted) and the impending March on Washington (whose date must be set). Levison rebuked them for using King's name to "shoot their mouths off" about civil disobedience. But even after Kennedy's speech, King included himself among those willing to present "our bare bodies in a nonviolent creative protest in case of a filibuster." On the floor of the Senate, Virginia Senator Wills Robertson warned his colleagues about the coming Negro invasion of demonstrators "whipped into a frenzy by Martin Luther King."[45]

Rustin used militant talk to recruit Howard University SNCC activists long after the official March on Washington coalition disavowed civil disobedience. SNCC's John Lewis recorded the buzz in militant circles: "A protest rather than a plea. Stage sit-ins all across Washington. Tie up traffic. Have 'lie-ins' in local airport runways. Invade the offices of southern congressmen and senators. Camp on the White House lawn. Cause mass arrests. Paralyze the city." Lewis's subsequent disillusionment was deep.[46]

The bigger the coalition, the more moderate the tactics. By the end of June, the White House, NAACP, NUL, and UAW had effectively quashed any hopes for more than a one-day rally with speeches. On June 19 ninety-six foundation and corporate leaders in New York pledged $1.5 million to the civil rights organizations. "Prevention of mayhem" seemed their highest priority, journalist Reese Cleghorn wrote. A Taconic Foundation official confided that "Bull Connor and the police dogs" helped open the capitalists' wallets. The new Council on United Civil Rights Leadership (CUCRL) met concurrently with the "Big Six" civil rights organizations—CORE, NAACP, NALC, NUL,

SCLC, and SNCC—to plan a moderate march. By then, most of the Big Six were not expecting militant protest anyway. On July 2, Rustin and Randolph assembled the Big Six in New York to plan the newly named March on Washington for Jobs and Freedom. The NAACP had the troops and the money to stage "a really mass demonstration," Norman Hill recalled, and Randolph preferred a broad coalition with the NAACP to a small militant march. King then joined Wilkins in disavowing any "civil disobedience" or congressional "sit-ins [even] in case of a filibuster." Rustin's "Organizing Manual No. 1" issued in mid-July did not mention direct action but promised state delegation visits to Capitol Hill and a "massive demonstration" at the White House. "Organizing Manual No. 2" in early August dropped both actions.[47]

King's hopes for strong support from white churches bore fruit in July when the Big Six became the Big Ten, expanding to include Reuther of the UAW, Matthew Ahmann of the National Catholic Conference for Interracial Justice, Eugene Carson Blake of the United Presbyterian Church, and Rabbi Joachim Prinz of the American Jewish Congress. Reuther and the UAW, fearing that militancy might feed the racist backlash, moved the rally to the Lincoln Memorial but paid for the sound system and brought thousands to Washington. King invited the masses to demonstrate the "propaganda value of numbers" in an appeal to *Amsterdam News* readers.[48]

As the date approached, organizers assured a nervous media, public, and Washington elite that a peaceful army was coming. South Carolina Senator Ohlin Johnston warned Rustin that "criminal, fanatical, and communistic elements, as well as crackpots, will move in to take every advantage of this mob." William Dawson, Chicago's senior black congressman, feared that just "one incident" involving "liquor" could annihilate all they had worked for. Walter Fauntroy of the D.C. Coordinating Committee promised to show "the Congress and the world that this is the true America, not what you have seen in Birmingham, Jackson and Cambridge." Rustin promised an "outspoken, but not raucous" March on Washington. Afterward, Whitney Young was thrilled the NUL helped make it a "dignified affair," relieved that militants had not chained themselves to senators' desks.[49]

An Agenda for Economic Rights

Throughout the spring and summer, civil rights leaders expressed aspirations for economic justice emergent in hundreds of local movements. The NAACP at its July annual convention warned that a "permanently unemployed mass of Negroes" could soon endanger "the American social order." Herbert Hill blasted discriminatory unions and demanded federal enforcement of fair labor practices. Former chair of the Council of Economic Advisors Leon Keyserling called for a high-consumption, full employment economy to meet the jobs crisis. The national CORE convention talked as much about unemployment and automation as it did about voting rights and nonviolence. Whitney Young received NUL board endorsement for a Domestic Marshall Plan, a massive ten-year "compensatory effort" for Negroes to prevent the formation of a "permanent underclass of dependents." Only then would "equality of opportunity" have "true meaning," he argued. It was time for some "shock treatment." The march must dramatize the general problems of Negro joblessness, poor housing, and malnutrition rather than simply tout Kennedy's "specific bill." The government and foundations must give generously to upgrade black employment, schooling, and social services, because getting a good job required a good education and a home near enough to the growing suburban labor markets, which required money. When whites objected to "quotas" and "reverse racism," they needed to be reminded they had already received three hundred years of "special consideration." There was nothing un-American about $12 billion for war-torn Europe, aid for Cuban refugees, or the GI Bill. To "destroy the racial ghetto and . . . [create] open housing opportunities" would indeed cost the nation something. The nation must choose between spending millions for prevention of poverty or "billions for crime, welfare, dependency and buying the loyalties of uncommitted nations whose minds we cannot win through example."[50]

Although many liberals, religious leaders, and reporters ignored the economic justice goals, the March on Washington Committee, under Rustin's deputy directorship, pushed the jobs agenda aggressively. Rustin's "Organizing Manual No. 1" fleshed out the specifics: a "massive Federal Public Works Program to provide jobs for all the unemployed"; a Federal Fair Employment Practices Act covering all employers; a $2 minimum wage; and the broadening of the minimum wage to include job categories such as domestic and agricultural labor, "where Negroes and other minorities work at slave wages." The March on Washington Committee's July 12 "Call to Americans" beckoned everyone to march against the "twin evils of discrimination and economic deprivation." Blacks still bore "the brunt of economic exploitation, the indignity of second-class citizenship, and the ignominy of slave wages."[51]

In a *New York Times Magazine* roundtable just before the march, King demanded federal help in establishing "untrammeled opportunity." Integrated housing and decent jobs were "most critical," he said. A man's earnings determined where "his family lives [and] whether his children will go to college." Appearing on National Education Television with Whitney Young and Wilkins, King called for an economic "crash program" to attack the root "conditions that produce so many social evils." Young plugged his "Marshall Plan" to general acclaim. Wilkins argued that the "real power and obstacle" in the ghetto was the nation's "property rights structure," whose agents cared little for slum overcrowding or "how many kids are bitten by rats." James Forman complained that Kennedy's voting rights provision granting the franchise to anyone with a sixth-grade education did not address the relationship between educational deprivation and powerlessness. Would the government ensure that poor black families would be able to earn more than $2.25 a day so that young children would not have to quit school to help feed the family?[52]

March organizers could count only on progressive unions. The AFL-CIO Executive Council voted overwhelmingly not to endorse the march, which was a great betrayal in King's eyes. President George Meany supported the FEPC but opposed mass marches and any hiring preferences for blacks that might undermine union seniority systems. Randolph, Rustin, and King appealed to progressive laborites for full and fair employment in a language of interracial social democracy. "Job competition in a shrinking labor market" would simply pit black and white workers against each other, Randolph argued. Automation threatened everyone, not just the unemployed. Randolph advocated creating millions of new jobs through federal investment in "new hospitals and schools, public health facilities," and decent housing.[53]

By August, the march committee had expanded the demands. "Organizing Manual No. 2" called for a comprehensive executive order banning discrimination in all federally subsidized housing, desegregation of all schools in 1963, and reduction of congressional representation in states where citizens were disfranchised. As long as southern Democrats kept blacks "voteless, exploited, and underpaid," white workers' low wages and poor working conditions would remain the same. Several white church officials wrote the committee to complain that a massive "witness" for civil rights should not even include economic demands. Rustin modified the wording of the minimum wage demand without altering its substance and told them to come anyway. A New York couple resisted marching that promoted "more socialism." Rustin responded that when millions were poor, "'free enterprise' and 'equal opportunity' are hollow platitudes." Thomas Kilgore of the March on Washington Church Committee made sure all the religious leaders knew that since "millions are deprived of the right to earn their bread, this will be a crusade also for jobs."[54]

The emphasis on jobs and freedom attracted diverse marchers to Washington. Working-class people came by the thousands. At least 250 unemployed workers came from Chicago, organized by the UPWA and the NUL. The

National Domestic and Migrant Workers Association brought two busloads of "domestic workers, unemployed and employed" people with banners reading "Freedom Now." White miners from Hazard, Kentucky, came "to petition President Kennedy for Jobs, their Hospitals," and local protection for "trade Union conditions."[55] Mobilization for Youth on New York City's Lower East Side, which was being red baited for organizing the poor to protest against the schools, the police, and the welfare department, reserved a train. "And the Lower East Side went to Washington," Frances Fox Piven recalled. Nine train cars carried five hundred black, white, and Latino people. Their "physical presence" had a "radical impact" on the march, raising poverty and civil rights policy to equal status on the national agenda, Piven commented.[56]

Despite the formal demands, the march included fewer unemployed and poor people than many had hoped for. Local groups had to raise money to pay for their passage after the Taconic Foundation turned down Randolph's request to subsidize transportation for the unemployed. Cleveland Robinson of District 65 criticized New York's middle-class black churches for sluggish organizing. SNCC activist Jane Stembridge wrote Tom Kahn that Mississippi's "sharecroppers and jobless Delta folk should really lead the parade!" But they were too poor to afford a ride on the "Freedom train." One NUL official shed no tears: "no one will know anyway, on TV at least, because people will all look pretty much alike on parade." But Whitney Young was glad to welcome thousands of the "most victimized" black Americans to Washington, "the residents from the south, the poor people, functional illiterates." The March on Washington Committee dropped plans for two unemployed workers to speak, however. Researchers revealed that the marchers were more educated and affluent than average blacks, disproportionately northern urbanites who paid their own way, and already members of civil rights organizations. Equal employment and school desegregation topped their list of goals. Asked specifically, they doubted whites would welcome them into their neighborhoods.[57]

Militants later criticized Rustin for tightly controlling the "approved" signs printed in bulk in uniform black letters by the UAW. Though others tried to moderate the slogans, Rustin stayed with jobs and freedom. Seven slogans dealt explicitly with jobs, housing, wages, the FEPC, police brutality, and federal funding. Seven more called for equal rights, voting rights, civil rights laws, integrated schools, an end to bias, and first-class citizenship. A final slogan incorporated the synthesis Rustin, Randolph, and King advocated: "CIVIL RIGHTS, PLUS FULL EMPLOYMENT EQUALS FREEDOM."[58]

The March on Washington was jubilant, tightly controlled, and far bigger than anything organizers expected. CBS broadcast the speeches live. Most speakers sounded the themes of jobs and freedom. Matthew Ahmann called for "civil rights legislation which will guarantee every man a job based on his talents and training." Rabbi Joachim Prinz chastised the "blindness of decent Americans" who failed to see or feel "the shame of millions of opportunities lost, millions of hopes denied, millions of lives wasted." Whitney Young declared Negroes "must march from the rat-infested, overcrowded ghettos to decent, wholesome, unrestricted residential areas dispersed throughout our cities." Wilkins called for FEPC legislation to secure the "responsibility and self-respect that goes with equal access to jobs."[59]

Randolph, Reuther, and James Farmer voiced more radical perspectives on civil rights and economic justice. Randolph defended Title II against businessmen's belief in the absolute "sanctity of property rights" over human rights, reminding the crowd that access to public accommodations meant "little to those who cannot afford to use them." The FEPC would also be useless if automation continued to "destroy the jobs of millions of workers." The Negro's enemies were also "the enemies of Medicare, of higher minimum wages, of Social Security, of Federal aid to education." Reuther doubted the nation would solve racial problems of "education or housing or public accommodations" as long as blacks remained "second-class economic citizens." "If we can have full employment and full production for the negative ends of war, then why can't we have a job for every American in the pursuit of peace?" he asked. CORE's Floyd McKissick read Farmer's letter from a Louisiana jail, which called for direct action "until we can work at a job befitting of our skills in any place in the land . . . until our kids have enough to eat and their minds can study."[60]

SNCC chairman John Lewis spoke militantly with vivid word pictures from the fields of Mississippi. Moderates successfully pressured Lewis to change his original text, but the speech retained most of its force and content. King helped mediate the dispute, simply commenting that it did not sound like Lewis to threaten to nonviolently "march through the heart of Dixie" like General Sherman. Lewis cut the reference. American politicians allied themselves "with open forms of political, economic and social exploitation," he charged. Lewis spoke for thousands who could not come to Washington because they earned "starvation wages" or "no wages at all." What would the Kennedy bill do for the "homeless and starving people of this nation?" Sharecroppers making less than $3 a day in the fields needed legal protection from economic reprisals. Where was Kennedy's legislation that would guarantee "the equality of a maid who earns five dollars a week in the home of the family whose income is $100,000 a year?" Only King received more cheers and applause than Lewis that day. The *Washington Post* called the speech the march's one "bitter, discordant note."[61] King had often denounced the poverty

Figure 6. Women marched down Independence Avenue, having failed to win a major voice in the march but "with our eyes open," remembered Dorothy Height. They, too, demanded "Equal Rights," "Decent Housing," and "Jobs for All at a Decent Pay." March demands also included extension of minimum wage protections to domestic workers. Copyright Wally McNamee/Corbis.

and low wages of the South and the need for radical change from below to overcome exploitation. But King would not alienate the coalition's moderates at the height of their support for southern desegregation. Within two years, King's disillusionment with liberals came to resemble Lewis's dissident spirit.

King's "I Have a Dream" speech was for many the climax of the day. He left out his customary call for a wide distribution of privilege and property and an end to class suppression of "the masses." King spoke of interracial brotherhood and the full citizenship rights due the Negro. But he also defended the movement's "whirlwinds of revolt," denouncing the "unspeakable horrors of police brutality" and the cruel confinement of Negroes to ghettos, demanding "the security of justice." After King, Rustin read the march demands to general acclaim. Michael Thelwell remembered how SNCC cynics who mocked the "bullshit and rhetoric" of the other speeches listened to King's "lyrical and rhythmic cadence" and his climactic repetition of "Let freedom ring!" Despite their "stubborn, intemperate hearts," they leapt to their feet, "laughing, shouting, slapping palms, and not an eye was dry."[62]

Dorothy Height of the National Council of Negro Women, Anna Arnold

Hedgeman of the National Council of Churches, and attorney and activist
Pauli Murray had all tried to persuade Randolph and the march leadership to
include young people, the unemployed, and women on the roster of speakers.
Murray even accused Randolph of sexual "tokenism." "We could not get
women's participation taken seriously," Height recalled. King was more sympathetic than others, but all the men gave them the "runaround." It was not
enough that Mahalia Jackson sang or that Daisy Bates was allowed to pledge
support to the male "fighters for civil liberties." The exclusion went deeper,
Height argued, symbolizing men's failure to understand black women's economic needs. Statistics showed the growing prevalence of mother-only families, but the leadership still believed that "if men were given enough, the
women would be better off." The march galvanized professional women to
fight sexism as well as racism, Height recalled. And at least one poor woman
who could not march nevertheless exercised her rights of petition. A Brooklyn
mother wrote John Kennedy about her struggles with gas bills, hungry children, evictions, and police and gang violence directed at her children. Worse
than any of these was the fact that "one pencil-pushing social investigator can
determine the plight of 10 helpless people." She saw no future for her children
other than "ghettoized" lives of poor housing and schooling, joblessness, and
welfare poverty. "How dare anyone tell me about the atrocities of Communism!" she wrote. Thousands like her would take to the streets with the welfare
rights movement by 1966.[63]

"Pass the Bill" was not the banner the Big Ten brought into their Oval
Office meeting with the president right after the march. Instead they gave Kennedy a seminar on his civil rights bill's economic shortcomings. Whitney
Young insisted the bill was pointed at the South, whereas the "big problems"
were northern. Randolph reiterated his arguments for job creation. Wilkins
and Reuther tried to persuade Kennedy to support the FEPC. "A job is really
basic," Reuther said, because it determined the housing, neighborhoods, and
schools Negroes could afford. JFK tried to deflect the heat by changing the
subject to black family values. Jews overcame discrimination and gave their
children discipline and education. Why couldn't black ministers preach similar strategies, even though black families were "split and all the rest"? McKissick responded that parents could not supervise children when they worked all
the time. Job discrimination killed black children's aspirations, and the many
injustices producing black poverty were "interrelated and interlocking."
Eugene Blake added that inner-city schools had the lowest budgets and the
worst paid, least qualified teachers. "If thirteen percent of the general population were unemployed like the Negro, you'd have a shooting revolution,"

Young interjected. The leaders relentlessly pressured Kennedy to heed black people's economic needs.[64]

Liberals packaged the march as an international advertisement for American democracy. Kennedy immediately lauded the "fervor and quiet dignity" of marchers who showed "faith and confidence in our democratic form of government." Hubert Humphrey wrote NALC president Troy Bailey, "Televised as it was around the world," it was "a turning point in American international relations [which] rest ultimately on morality, not power." The U.S. Information Agency commissioned a film to be shipped abroad that included dignified images of interracial marchers and little reference to what brought them to Washington. Kennedy offered no new civil rights or economic proposals, and he let Congress take its time. Only when Congressman Emanuel Cellers reported the civil rights bill to the full Senate with the FEPC attached to title VII did Kennedy accept it. Though he publicly endorsed full and fair employment and publicized his modest proposals for new job training programs, Kennedy ignored all the March's structural demands for an increase and extension of the minimum wage, public works employment, an executive order on home loan discrimination, and protection for civil rights workers. Militants saw a sellout by the middle class civil rights leadership and a public-relations victory for Kennedy. "This exploitation of so many angry and sincere people, whose indignation was misrepresented as some kind of testimonial for the system that had oppressed them, and against which they were protesting, must qualify as one of the greatest and most shameless manipulations of recent years," Thelwell wrote.[65]

The news media scarcely registered the economic issues. Journalists most consistently reported the violence that did *not* happen. "Police Precautions and Festive Spirit of Capital Keep Disorders at a Minimum" was the *New York Times* headline. A "gentle army" occupied the city, not "the emotional horde of angry militants that many had feared." The *Wall Street Journal* wondered whether a tactic "so laden with potential violence" had been worth the risk and answered, "This nation is based on representative Government, not on Government run by street mobs, disciplined or otherwise." The *Pittsburgh Courier* hailed the march as proof that Negro violence resulted from police repression, burying the myth that Negro crowds were violent by nature.[66]

Despite the invisibility of the economic demands in the press and Kennedy's transparent effort to "expropriate a revolution," Tom Kahn saw a widening recognition of Reconstruction's great lesson: "there can be no political or social freedom without economic security." All the major civil rights organizations united around a set of radical economic demands for "social reconstruction," and the crowd roared its approval, he reported in the socialist *New*

America.[67] In an exception that proves the rule, Reg Murphy of the *Atlanta Constitution* detailed the economic demands. Would the administration adopt an FEPC law, "the one thing that most speakers at this giant rally stressed the most"? There was real radicalism in the minimum wage demand and the demand for Title III protections, Murphy reported. But his editor, Eugene Patterson, praised Atlanta's hometown hero, who redeemed the whole day by preaching patriotism and the leavening influence of capitalist "plenty." King had preached to the middle class their duties to enlighten and uplift black folk who were still "not far enough from the cabin to comprehend the ways that are open to them." He spoke as if opportunity was dropping like peaches from New South trees. In Patterson's encomium, Malcolm X could find the "house Negro" he took King to be.[68]

King took pride in the fact that the March on Washington brought white America "closer into harmony with its Negro citizens than ever before." During a steamy July heat wave, *Newsweek* had sent out black and white survey researchers to gather reams of statistics on Negro and white attitudes. King celebrated their findings: "overwhelming majorities favored laws to guarantee Negroes voting rights, job opportunities, good housing and integrated travel facilities . . . exactly the changes that the nonviolent demonstrations present as their central demands." Yet *Newsweek* revealed schizoid splits in America's conscience over implementation, not principles, and over black people, not Negro citizens. A minority of southern whites and a bare majority of whites nationwide approved of federal fair employment practices legislation. Regarding stereotypes about Negroes, most whites agreed that "Negroes tend to have less ambition" and "Negroes want to live off the handout." Politicians exploited stereotypes of the work-shirking, welfare-cheating, tax-eating Negroes dependent on honest, working whites. King kept hearing from Americans seeking to persuade him that blacks needed to demonstrate themselves worthy of equality. A Cleveland citizen sent King some doggerel: "Po white folks must labor from sun to sun / to pay welfare taxes, while we has the fun. / Dey pay us to vote, dey reward us for sin / And the sweet Democrats keep the checks rollin in."[69]

Bombingham and the Contagion of Hate

The bombing of Birmingham's 16th Street Baptist Church on Sunday, September 15, 1963, which killed eleven-year-old Denise McNair and fourteen-year-olds Cynthia Wesley, Carole Rosamond Robertson, and Addie Mae Collins, shattered King's dream of interracial accord. Scores of armed blacks brandished their guns as Alabama state troopers invaded Birmingham. King called on Kennedy to send federal troops, and on September 19 King, Abernathy, Shuttlesworth, A. G. Gaston, and J. L. Ware met with the president. King predicted "the worst race rioting" in their lifetimes if the federal government failed to offer protection and open jobs to restore blacks' sorely tested faith in nonviolence. He considered calling a national work stoppage to force Kennedy's hand. On September 23 Kennedy met with Birmingham's elite, warning of imminent race war but assuring them they need yield only modest concessions. King was no "outside agitator," Kennedy insisted; if "nonviolent" King pulled out, "violent" SNCC would move in. Birmingham's businessmen must concede "some breakthroughs in employment," even if it amounted only to "public relations." Kennedy wanted black police and black clerks hired in stores. On December 9, three downtown stores hired black clerks. Not until 1966 did Birmingham hire its first black policeman.[70]

King called for a national Christmas boycott of Birmingham's industries. "Corporations which do America's business must be corporations of conscience," he told the SCLC convention on September 27. In the *Amsterdam News*, King praised organized labor's tradition of mass industrial disruption in pursuit of "economic democracy." Victor Hugo was right: there was "more misery in the lower classes" than "humanity in the upper classes." No longer would blacks trust the "goodwill and understanding of those who profit by exploiting us." Birmingham's "financial interests were interlocked" with the national power structure, King wrote in *Why We Can't Wait*. But U.S. Steel denied any corporate responsibility over "community policies on race relations." U.S. Steel was an "oligarchy of giant power" that would surely resist local tax hikes, but it left racial mores alone. "Profits were not affected by racial injustice," King wrote. In fact, racism boosted profits. "Only people were hurt, and the greatest single power in Birmingham turned its back." As Ed Clayton wrote in the October *SCLC Newsletter*, "the respected steel industry," an exemplar of American big business, "has kept racism alive with an abnormally fierce competition for its jobs."[71]

King learned similar lessons at home in Atlanta during the Action for Democracy movement, the last joint SNCC-SCLC campaign. King stood on the sidelines while the traditional Negro leadership undermined this militant desegregation campaign. Daddy King opposed the demonstrations, and King, Jr. limited himself to militant rhetoric. Violent clashes between police and protestors and over three hundred arrests shredded the city's moderate image. The local chair of SCLC resigned, fearing that SNCC-led demonstrations were "provoking violence," and the campaign petered out. But King articulated his evolving political economy at a December rally in Hurt Park. Atlanta had made no progress in schooling, health, housing, and jobs. This was the Old South "of oppression and exploitation," he argued. Out of 150 restaurants, only 30 were open to Negroes. Political and economic elites employed blacks as low-paid "menials and servants" while taxing them to support institutions privileging whites. Hospitals operated with public funds, but only 19 percent of hospital beds were available to Negroes. No Negro children attended elementary school with whites. Federal loans still underwrote whites-only housing development, despite Kennedy's executive order, and whites benefited from segregated public housing. Half of black Atlantans lived below the poverty line of $3,000, and the white median income was twice that. Why? Businessmen continually played "off Negroes against whites in order to secure the lowest possible labor cost," King explained. White political and economic power structured black poverty. Slowly accepting equal access to public accommodations, the southern oligarchy was only changing its stripes. The "City Too Busy to Hate" wasn't.[72]

SCLC debated serious strategic dilemmas, as King withdrew to reflect on Birmingham and the "Negro Revolution of 1963." Should they see Birmingham through, as Levison advocated, or move their forces to more fertile soil? Should they keep the heat on the federal government through direct action, or build political strength to counterbalance a looming white backlash? The press was reporting a "lull in the civil rights movement," raising fears of "battle weariness and financial problems," King told Clarence Jones. The movement needed some "dramatic push," but King was uncertain where or how to do it. Perhaps he should take up James Bevel's idea of a massive Alabama Freedom Army for the vote. But maybe "the only salvation is for the Democratic Party to regain losses in the South by gains in the North," he speculated with Jones. King conceded that Kennedy was "scared to death because of the civil rights issue." But the president finally took Lyndon Johnson's advice to travel south and make the case for desegregation in the national interest.[73]

John F. Kennedy's assassination in Dallas on November 22 threw the nation into a crisis of self-doubt that raised fundamental questions for the movement. Privately persuaded that a right-wing conspiracy was behind the assassination, King wrote that Kennedy was killed "by a morally inclement climate" of violence and racial hatred. He lashed out at America's unrestricted commerce in guns and its culture of gun-slinging heroes. Kennedy was a martyr, "a friend of civil rights and a stalwart advocate of peace." President Lyndon Johnson called King on November 23, and King said the only fitting memorial to Kennedy would be "to enact some of the great, progressive policies that he sought to initiate." On November 27, Johnson addressed a special session of Congress and a national television audience. "No memorial oration or eulogy could more eloquently honor President Kennedy's memory than the earliest possible passage of the civil rights bill for which he fought so long," he declared. Johnson risked "political suicide" with his "courageous and heroic" speech, King declared.[74] King was aware that the most powerful ally blacks could hope for within the established political order was the liberal wing of the Democratic Party, whose national leadership was already moving toward a more activist liberalism as a result of the civil rights movement, growing national awareness of poverty, and Kennedy's assassination.

Chapter 7
Malignant Kinship

In 1964, the movement's civil rights and economic justice agenda promised to converge with the federal government's policy priorities. The passage of the Civil Rights Act in July and the Economic Opportunity Act in August, Johnson's War on Poverty, promised cooperation between localities and the national state in service to civil rights, economic progress, and political realignment. But between the promise and the act fell the shadow of the New Deal racial state. From the local to the national level vested interests, old-line agencies, and racial "power structures" could be expected to defend the segregated and unequal status quo. The political moment was also fraught with danger: in this election year, whites' resistance to blacks' demands for desegregation, equality, and power escalated into a powerful political force. The movement had already drawn King's attention to poverty, the ghettos, and dilemmas of northern political and economic power. Summer rioting in New York only made these issues more urgent.

King wrestled with dilemmas of race and class. He sought to weave together and reconcile black mobilization, working-class solidarity, and moral persuasion directed at the white majority. Racial militancy risked alienating white allies. White workers in particular were anxious about black incursions into their employment niches and neighborhoods. Radicalism of any sort risked alienating the middle class and the religious latecomers to civil rights. But bland moralism and "reasonable restraint" risked losing the activist and grassroots vanguard, who became increasingly disillusioned with delay, "tokenism," and liberal compromise.

In January, *Time* named King "Man of the Year"; in December, he received the Nobel Peace Prize. *Time* praised King's capacity to inspire in his people "a Christian forbearance that nourishes hope and smothers injustice." Would King's leadership in the eyes of whites hinge on his ability to restrain violence among blacks? In *Why We Can't Wait*, published in June, King reaffirmed his utter dependence on the masses. In the 1963 "Negro Revolution," King explained, "organization" and "direct action" became "explosively, powerfully and socially transforming." He could not control the revolution, because it was "the people who moved the leaders, not the leaders who moved the people." Any leader seeking to "bottle up" this militancy would surely "be blown asunder in the ensuing explosion," King wrote.[1]

Over the course of the year, guided by Bayard Rustin and pressured by advisors such as L. D. Reddick, King moderated his calls for "special treatment" for blacks to make room for broader appeals to the white working class. Rustin again became King's principal advisor. Stanley Levison lay low, communicating through Clarence Jones. King shared Rustin's worries that racial resentments would fester unless the government relieved job competition at the bottom by expanding the pie for everyone. By the time King testified at the Democratic National Convention on August 19, he publicly advocated federal spending on public works and a guaranteed income for every American family. For Rustin, class-based alliances and broader progressive coalitions required a move "from protest to politics." But for King, political alliances with unions, churches, liberals, and the Johnson administration could never substitute for nonviolent protest; direct action necessarily complemented political alliances. With ghettos ready to explode and with intensifying winds of white reaction, strategies of moderation, compromise, and "tokenism" became unacceptable to King. At his furthest left, King envisioned a bottom-up coalition of poor people who could pressure the government to wage a real war on poverty if Lyndon Johnson's efforts faltered.

At the same time that he broadened his class perspective, King concluded that racism would be harder to uproot than he had previously thought. King resisted the liberal idea that civil rights policy was now "mopping up" the last vestiges of racism and that the next task was simply boosting economic opportunity through education, job training, or other strategies for "improving" poor people. Urban revolt led King to accent the racism at the base of black poverty and moved him to advocate policies that would specifically benefit the ghettos. By the end of 1964, civil rights and antipoverty legislation increasingly seemed incapable of addressing the real needs of unemployed, poor, and geographically segregated black people. "Power structures" everywhere were stacked against the black poor. When for the first time King faced the challenge of developing nonviolent alternatives to violent confrontations in the streets, King began to imagine massive disruption in the northern cities as a political tactic. But even liberal whites increasingly interpreted nonviolent protest as a prelude to violence, rather than its politically effective alternative.

Crossroads: Desegregation and Poverty

Organizationally, SCLC presented a picture of confusion and drift in early 1964. Andrew Young had replaced Wyatt Walker as executive director, and the staff inconclusively debated their next step. Dianne Nash and James Bevel proposed recruiting a nonviolent army of five thousand direct actionists to turn Alabama upside down. King promised he might die in a hunger strike or march on Washington again in the event of a southern filibuster against the strengthened civil rights bill.[2] Eventually SCLC decided to conduct a campaign in St. Augustine, Florida, a highly segregated tourist town then planning its four hundredth anniversary celebration—for whites only. The city was a stage made for nonviolent theater. St. Augustine had a staunchly segregationist city hall, a business elite vulnerable to negative publicity because it was dependent on northern tourist dollars, a police force with close ties to the Klan, and a reputation for brutal extralegal violence. The St. Augustine protests probably helped spur the Senate to break its filibuster and pass the Civil Rights Act, but locals paid a heavy price. King and Walker had learned from Birmingham that vivid images of confrontation, with black and white protesters putting their bodies on the line against white supremacists, moved the nation more effectively than inspired preaching or patient lobbying. In late March, SCLC sent sixty volunteers to join local black activists in demanding desegregation of all private and public accommodations. They also demanded an end to police brutality, new public and private hiring that included black policemen and firemen, and "a biracial committee to discuss the future." But since St. Augustine's black workers drew low wages from the seasonal tourism industry, they were less concerned with desegregation than with keeping bread on the table.

Dramatic desegregation protest and the passage of civil rights legislation only accentuated the realization that poverty, disempowerment, and dependency were the greatest obstacles to black freedom. In late May and early June, Andrew Young and C. T. Vivian led night marches to the historic downtown slave market as Klansmen poured into St. Augustine, shooting up black neighborhoods and beating protesters with lead pipes and bicycle chains. On June 9, King was arrested and jailed. He asked the city's political and business elite to negotiate and called on President Johnson to protect basic constitutional rights, but he was unsuccessful. Walker and King felt vindicated nonetheless. As the media publicized horrific violence and King remained in jail to maintain the pressure, on June 10 the Senate ended its filibuster and sent the civil rights bill back to the House, which passed it on July 2. King came out of jail on bond June 13. The city lost an estimated 122,000 tourists, and its economy lost perhaps $5 million. Local blacks also paid dearly. As protest leader Robert Hayling recalled, domestic servants, landscapers, and restaurant workers had "no contracts, no tenure, no seniority," and they "could be summarily dismissed, which they were, from their jobs." Klan attacks escalated through June, as northern clergy joined the protests. On June 25, after five hundred Klan members broke through police lines and savagely beat about two hundred marchers, King wanted out of St. Augustine. Governor C. Farris Bryant gave some political cover to the SCLC withdrawal by appointing an "emergency bi-racial committee," which never met. Judge Bryant Simpson oversaw a "special police force" that successfully suppressed Klan violence. Blacks gained no economic concessions on hiring, however. St. Augustine desegregated only after the Civil Rights Act passed. "Some communities, like this one, have to bear the cross," King remarked.[3]

King looked jubilant accepting a pen from Lyndon Johnson used to sign the Civil Rights Act in July. Someone wrote for King a speech he never gave, celebrating its "glittering rays of promise" in ending the poverty that was "endemic to the fetid, festering ghettos of the urban North." In contrast, King's first public response to the act appeared in July in the *Amsterdam News*. No legislation had yet grappled with the "extreme poverty" affecting Negroes and Puerto Ricans in New York, he wrote. Only a "massive public works program to employ the unemployed" could do that. The act could not address "the magnitude" of joblessness and substandard housing across the country.[4] Several days later, Harlem exploded in racial violence, giving new urgency to King's clarion call for black activists to join the War on Poverty.

Planning the Poverty Skirmish: 1964

"This administration, here and now, declares unconditional War on Poverty," Lyndon Johnson boldly announced in his State of the Union address on January 8. Johnson had something new, an unpublicized legacy of the Kennedy administration that Johnson could champion as his own. Bargaining with Congress for Kennedy's $11 billion tax cut, however, Johnson was forced to accept a total budget under $100 billion, and he earmarked less than $1 billion to the poverty program. Johnson's core convictions and political constraints made it likely that the program would remain fiscally conservative, paternalistic, focused on individual and community rehabilitation, and unlikely to tolerate any participation of poor or black people that might spur conflict. Johnson's commanding metaphor of war promised total victory, skillfully brooked no partisan dissent, summoned the whole nation to sacrifice, and helped Johnson persuade himself that mobilization would involve no conflict in his government or Democratic Party coalition. But a metaphor was not a war. And many black activists had come to see white welfare officials, social workers, educators, and politicians—the people who would be receiving most of the federal money—as enemies in what one Chicago black leader called "the ancient galling war against the poor."[5]

Martin Luther King and Michael Harrington fully expected that the weapons of civil rights protest would stock the War on Poverty's arsenal. After all, the civil rights movement opened the nation's eyes to pervasive poverty and spurred a poverty war likely to benefit more whites than blacks, they both argued. Black people's aspirations for integration and democratic participation should be the poverty war's central strategy, they hoped.[6]

But Johnson and the poverty planners hoped to appeal to middle-class idealism and placate the divided South. Scholars who stress Johnson's commitment to waging simultaneous war on poverty and racism capture his idealism and some of his expressed intentions, but not the full spectrum of his assumptions and political calculations, nor the constraints Congress and state and local officials placed on him. The president mentioned neither African Americans nor racial discrimination in his long message introducing the poverty legislation to Congress and the nation in March. As "President of all the people," Johnson charged middle-class Americans with a "special responsibility to the distressed and disinherited, the hungry and the hopeless of this abundant nation." Planners packaged the whole program to appeal to the voting majority—the "suburban, church-going housewife," as one planner put it—and to avoid tax increases. Poor people were guaranteed automatically to pass over a static "poverty line" as the nation's median income rose along with economic growth. The poverty war would not burden other classes.[7] There *was* a racial logic inherent in the program, but Johnson hoped it would support the politics of consensus. In the South, the War on Poverty was intended as more a *substitute for* than an *extension of* civil rights activism. A war on poverty would benefit the nation's poorest region and its large population of blacks without stirring up hornets' nests of racial conflict.[8] Johnson had no intention of mobilizing the poor for protest, much less leveling and unifying the terraced hills and valleys of the locally administered racial welfare state.

Johnson intended to uplift the welfare-dependent poor into the mainstream through established structures of local authority. His telephone tapes vividly reveal his deference to local elites and his paternalism. On January 4, Johnson touted the "prudence and frugality" of his poverty proposals to newspaper editor Walker Stone: "I'm going to try to teach these niggers, that don't know anything, how to work for themselves instead of just breeding, and I'm going to try to teach these Mexicans that can't talk English to learn it, so they can work for themselves, and I'm going to try to build a road in eastern Kentucky . . . so they can get down and go to school, get off our taxpayers' back." Johnson would provide a "hand up" to those stuck in ignorance, illiteracy, and welfare dependency. Local elites would define the "community," command the grunts, and attack poverty along conventional lines of education, social services, and vocational training. Johnson made a deal with Chicago's mayor Richard Daley in June: take the poverty war to "every ward," and Johnson would "drop a hunk" of money on Daley's city hall. "Get your planning and development people busy right now to see what you can do for the crummiest place in town—the lowest, the bottom," Johnson ordered. Would the poor share in strategic decisions, as the legislation promised? Would the poverty war be racially integrated from top to bottom? The logic of tight budgets pointed to helping the most seriously disadvantaged. But how would taxpayers, working- and middle-class whites and blacks, feel about throwing hunks of money at breeding Negroes in the nation's crummiest places? Liberal paternalism and pork barrel politics could backfire if enough people became convinced that Johnson's hand-ups were in fact handouts. Had Johnson listened more carefully to blacks, he might have created jobs for those who desperately needed them. He might have appreciated that blacks would accept nothing less than shared power. He might have offered neither a handout nor a hand up, but a hand extended in partnership.[9]

Johnson did listen—how much is unclear—for ninety minutes during an impromptu conference he called January 18 to discuss poverty with King, Wilkins, Whitney Young, and James Farmer. Randolph would have made the strongest case for jobs programs, but he was unable to attend. Young and King reportedly stressed the catastrophic dimensions of black unemployment and poverty. King said that poverty damaged "the whole Nation in general and the Negro in particular." It is unclear whether he stressed the need for full employment, but he reportedly argued that education, literacy, and job-training programs should be "inextricably tied" to desegregation. Farmer emerged confident that Johnson had promised them a simultaneous war on poverty, illiteracy, and racial discrimination. King praised Johnson's "realism" and "wisdom." Johnson had asked them all "to mobilize support" for his antipoverty program, King announced, hinting at Johnson's political as well as humanitarian logic. How they should do so was unclear, but Johnson had earlier emphatically urged King to cease demonstrations and push forward with voter registration. King already sounded some notes of skepticism about the War on Poverty. Nothing less than a "compensatory crash program" to integrate blacks into "the mainstream of life" would be effective, he told an interviewer. In June King published *Why We Can't Wait*, again praising Johnson, but urging him to fulfill his promises of a "battle against discrimination within the war against poverty." Would federal money challenge local vested interests and political elites? In a portent of the politics to come, King promised "outspoken agreement whenever proper and determined opposition whenever necessary."[10] That came sooner than expected.

Johnson's legislative proposal combined programs in early childhood education, social and legal service provision, and job training with the new idea of community action. Planners and social scientists converged on the idea of developing individual and communal "competency" to overcome "the culture of poverty" that purportedly prevented poor people from swimming into the "mainstream." (Many activists, including King, became increasingly convinced the mainstream itself pushed the poor under.) Though a minority of planners conceived of local Community Action Programs (CAPs) as arenas for confrontation and empowerment, most planners focused on education, job training, and other remedial services meant to uplift the poor. Johnson would not countenance more far-reaching proposals already on the policy table: targeted public spending to create jobs, a raise in the minimum wage, income redistribution through tax reform, or a family income policy covering all low-income people. Labor Secretary Willard Wirtz twice asked Johnson to spend up to $3 billion on new job creation programs but was met with stony silence; this sum was three times what Johnson had in mind for the whole War on Poverty. The Job Corps for the chronically unemployed, the Neighborhood Youth Corps for the unskilled and poorly educated, Head Start for preschool children and Upward Bound for college-bound teens, Volunteers in Service to America (VISTA) for idealistic middle-class youth, and even the Legal Services Program for the poor all fell within the educational, job training, and communal rehabilitation framework. And they could all be bought for less than $1 billion.[11]

Johnson had no idea that his War on Poverty would become so thoroughly entangled with the black quest for independent political power, however, as activists in a number of cities seized upon the legislation's promises of "maximum feasible participation" and won federal subsidies for black community organization, protest, voter registration, and even welfare rights organizing. Johnson decided to establish a new federal agency, the Office of Economic Opportunity (OEO), to coordinate most of the programs and approve grants. His thirst for "something big" elevated CAP to the program's center, soaking up half of the initial $800,000 appropriation. What had been small experimental programs supported by the Ford Foundation and Robert Kennedy's President's Committee on Juvenile Delinquency would now provide models for united community uplift in over a thousand cities by 1966. Johnson did not know that the foremost CAP, Mobilization for Youth (MFY) in New York City, had abandoned professional social services and academic research in favor of organizing the poor to confront welfare, education, and housing authorities. MFY found its greatest success mobilizing poor women to win the welfare benefits to which they were legally entitled. Little did Johnson know that his war on handouts would stimulate demands for adequate income provision.[12] When he found out from the mayors and governors that his program was subsidizing challenges to their authority, he and Congress moved aggressively to limit them. King ended up joining fights for poor people's participation in even the most traditional of social service programs.

From the outset King shared a pervasive skepticism within left circles about the meager resources the government devoted to the antipoverty effort and its failure to fulfill promises of democracy. King sought to strengthen the linkages between the war against racism and the War on Poverty and to extend its scope into areas it had not ventured: income support, jobs creation, and poor people's political empowerment. King continued to stress the common afflictions of poverty in a way calculated to appeal to middle-class whites and to extend the activism of the black movement to poor and working-class whites. In practice, however, by 1965 King had decided his greatest levers of power lay in mobilizing poor black people in their communities against specific forms of concentrated poverty, institutional racism, and disempowerment.

Ferment on the Left

The movement's economic agenda, the limited resources of Johnson's poverty war, and the deepening economic crisis at the bottom inspired a remarkable ferment on the democratic left. Many hoped the "automation poor" might form a new revolutionary class of what Andrew Hacker called "the society of losers." If they grew rapidly and found articulate political leadership, perhaps then they would reign in corporate institutions. "For then power will meet power, the power of a mass movement confronting the power of machine," Hacker dreamed. Social democrats all pointed out that joblessness was a much deeper social problem than was officially registered. A. Philip Randolph had warned that even if all construction jobs were open to blacks, only about 40,000 jobs would become available. Gunnar Myrdal estimated the proportion of jobless employable workers at 9 percent, nearly double the official unemployment rate. In his influential pamphlet "The Economics of Equality," Tom

Kahn at the League for Industrial Democracy (LID) argued, "Neither 'equal opportunity' nor 'preferential treatment' can solve the problem of Negro unemployment within the framework of a private economy which has failed to generate jobs." A *New York Times* reporter even commented that the actual Negro jobless rate of 20 percent, "were it general, would be a national catastrophe."[13]

In February 1964, Rustin, Randolph, Harrington, Walter Reuther, Myrdal, and other leading lights of the democratic left joined the British economist Robert Theobald under the improbable name of the Ad Hoc Committee on the Triple Revolution. Their March 1964 report profoundly shaped King's public policy rhetoric. The revolution of automation produced mass unemployment, the revolution of global militarization threatened human annihilation, and the human rights revolution offered hope that the challenges of the other two revolutions might be resolved. "Cybernation"—the revolutionary application of computer technology and automated tools to manufacturing—dramatically increased industrial productivity, generating material abundance capable of sustaining "all citizens in comfort and economic security." But the corporate economy was throwing millions out of work. Industrial capitalism had solved the problem of production but not the problems of consumption or equal distribution. That required a public, rather than corporate, redefinition of socially useful work and financial reward. Automation was breaking "the traditional link between jobs and incomes." To build a humane society and rescue the future from chaos, the nation must subsidize work not traditionally considered "profitable." Personal incomes dependent so much on private profit were relics of an outmoded "scarcity" society. Playing by new rules of an affluent society, the nation might commit itself "to provide every individual and every family with an adequate income as a matter of right." Teaching and learning were already considered valuable but not strictly profitable work, the committee argued. The federal government could train 100,000 more teachers, and employ the poor in rebuilding the nation's infrastructure, especially low-income housing, urban transit systems, and rural electrical grids. "National planning" would be essential. Corporate taxes on excess profits would generate money for direct income redistribution. Aside from the question of who would receive income and who would be expected to work in new jobs, the weakest link in the committee's analysis was political. Here the worldwide human rights revolution offered hope. "The American Negro, in his rebellion, asserts the demands—and the rights—of all the disadvantaged." Would blacks carry the banner? Would poor whites join? The committee's moral vision was redolent of Marxist humanism, Edward Bellamy, Henry George, and the American social gospel: "the unshackling of men from the bonds of unfulfilling labor frees them to become citizens, to make themselves and to make their own history."[14]

When twenty-two CORE activists from Harlem gathered at a training institute organized by the LID in February 1964, one championed the idea of national planning to employ the black and white jobless. "The guys on the left are always talking about economics and getting together and we'll all walk into the valley of success," another responded. "I can't hear that noise anymore. There's something *more* than economics," namely the fight for racial empowerment. The group listened without expression to Rustin's dream of "an alliance of all the poor, and organized labor, as well as the civil rights groups." But when discussion leaders turned their attention to organizing "political power" for the minimum wage and other tangible gains, they perked up considerably. The "guys on the left" had as much to learn. When Michael Harrington accepted the chairmanship of the LID in the fall, he wrote that democratic socialists would have to educate what he called "intellectually impoverished" trade unionists, liberals, and young black activists alike about urban reconstruction, jobs, and "national economic planning." If they failed in their educational role, Harrington feared there would be "a war not against poverty but among the poor themselves, black against white, organized against unorganized." Later, Harrington admitted that politicized blacks did not turn out to be the "Social Force" he had expected but actual people with sharpened racial and local grievances. The beloved community had passed, and politics "wasn't a folk song."[15]

The Ad Hoc Committee's vision inspired white student radicals who had already written off the liberals and laborites, looking for a "third force" outside the Democratic Party to force structural reforms in the political economy. In 1964 and 1965, SDS's Economic Research and Action Project (ERAP) sent dozens of idealistic white students into northern cities to organize "an interracial alliance of the poor" among the unemployed. Baltimore and Chicago ERAP projects tried to organize jobless men in the streets and the bars of poor neighborhoods. Chicago's ERAP bequeathed King his last slogan, "Jobs or Income Now." But poor people changed the organizers more than the other way around. As Bob Ross wrote Tom Kahn in July 1964, "Chicago is hot," organizing was tedious, and "the morass of brutalizations that people live with day by day becomes part of our world view." Several male organizers were getting drunk and street fighting to prove their "authenticity." Women proved to be the most successful in organizing poor women under the banner of "Garbage Removal or Income Now." Cleveland activists Sharon Jeffrey and Carole McEldowney patiently helped organize an interracial coalition of mothers on welfare, Citizens United for Adequate Welfare. Other women organized to win day care, playgrounds, and streetlights. ERAP did not advance the national full employment and economic planning agenda, but the project's women coalesced around "a basic challenge to the whole system of the welfare state," Nanci Hollander remembered. By 1966, most in ERAP had abandoned community organizing to mobilize against the Vietnam War and the modern university. Those who remained knew that the "'interracial movement of the poor' was not materializing, at least not fast enough to outrun nationalism among blacks and George Wallace's popularity among whites," Todd Gitlin remembered. Harrington observed that the ranks of the unemployed shrank rather than grew, easing the pressure from below. This was because the Ad Hoc Committee's third revolution, the growth of high-technology militarism, revived the economy and offered a grisly solution to "underclass" joblessness. They "had not realized that the public works programs we talked of might take the form of killing Vietnamese," Harrington recalled.[16]

Why We Can't Wait: From "Special Treatment" to "Full Employment"

In June 1964, King published *Why We Can't Wait*, a radical interpretation of the 1963 "Negro Revolution." Begun after the Birmingham bombing, the book was a searing indictment of economic racism. Finished after Lyndon Johnson declared war on poverty, it embraced a structural analysis of race and class and advocated a full employment policy agenda beyond Kennedy-Johnson liberalism.[17] King's analysis reflected the militancy and collective learning of 1963, but he couched it in terms morally compelling to the white majority. Hundreds of black communities nationwide had insisted "upon the mass application of equality to jobs, housing, education and social mobility." Militant poor and working-class blacks were now the nonviolent vanguard, not the prosperous and confident middle class King had earlier identified. King developed new metaphors and rhetorical set pieces to describe political and economic disempowerment. In 1963, the black masses had been inspired by African liberation movements and angered by exclusion from America's high consumption society. They now demanded a share of power, economic equality, and "living conditions measured by American standards rather than by the standards of colonial impoverishment." Blacks knew how limited had been the gains of desegregation. They revolted against pervasive "tokenism" in education, "jobs, housing, voting rights, and political positions." Uplifting and honoring the few had become white "policy," designed to placate restive blacks and assuage white consciences. Liberals were as implicated as segregationists. Despite higher wages in the North, the "subtle, psychological" racism there was as damaging as "the outright terror and open brutality of the South." King looked to the outer edge of the desegregation strategy and asked, "What will the Negro gain by being permitted to move to an integrated neighborhood if he cannot afford to do so because he is unemployed or has a low-paying job with no future?"[18]

King began the book with heartstring-tugging portraits of black children, following traditions of sentimental social documentary and progressive child saving likely to appeal to middle-class readers. A Harlem boy attended a segregated school and lived in "a vermin-infested apartment" surrounded by uncollected garbage, drunks, junkies, and "the jobless." His father was unemployed, his mother a mostly absent "sleep-in domestic." A little girl lived in a dilapidated house in Birmingham. Her mother died one night waiting for an ambulance, because most were reserved for whites only. Her father was a porter and would "always be a porter." Children like these lived in "an airtight cage of poverty" that smothered black people. Affluent Americans showed only their "poverty of conscience."[19]

King was uncovering deep, intertwined roots of class and race inequality and concluding both were more intractable than he had hitherto realized. Racism was more than an anachronistic social system, more even than just an expression of material interest or privilege. "Strands of prejudice toward Negroes are tightly wound around the American character," King wrote. The nation had been "born in genocide" against Native Americans. King shared widening doubts about Myrdal's faith that the American conscience and political system could uproot structural racism and not simply change laws or customs. But he responded to the white backlash as a force to challenge rather than to fear or accommodate.[20]

King's last chapter included analyses and policy prescriptions from racial liberalism and social democracy, pointing to uncharted terrain beyond Johnson's War on Poverty. The chapter has been compared to an unsuccessful and rickety bridge between Whitney Young's Marshall Plan for the Negro and Johnson's nonracial promises of opportunity for everybody. Actually, King was paddling rapidly toward a convergence of policy streams, hoping to build levies at a wider point of synthesis that affirmed Johnson's universalism but transcended the training and service strategies advanced by both Johnson and Young. King took on cargo Johnson had rejected: guaranteed work and income for all. His policy synthesis aimed to shore up America's bulwarks against a social hurricane gaining strength and speed by rising black militancy and mounting white resistance.[21]

Levison and Clarence Jones had helped King draft sections on the racial economic agenda in the fall of 1963, drawing conspicuously on Young's Marshall Plan. Occasionally, King stressed that blacks were economically marginalized and geographically isolated, no longer even members of the working class. The "locomotive of history" had left "black masses standing forlornly at dismal terminals." Other times, he described blacks as exploited in industries that reserved their worst jobs for blacks. "Many white Americans of good will have never connected bigotry with economic exploitation," King wrote. But the Negro knew they had a "malignant kinship." Look no further than the dingy shop floors and hot loading docks where blacks worked exclusively "because the pay is below a living standard." King did not parse the relative advantages enjoyed by white bosses and workers in such contexts. But low southern wages were "not an accident of geography," he wrote. Historically confined to unskilled jobs, black workers were now vulnerable to structural unemployment, economically imprisoned in two "circles of segregation": one throwing up barriers of "color," the other corralling them into the "culture of poverty." Gone was King's lonely island of poverty from which blacks might be rescued. Blacks inhabited suffocating prison cells. "In that separate culture of poverty in which the half-educated Negro lives," King wrote, echoing the NAACP's Herbert Hill, "an economic depression rages today."[22] This was not simply a paradox of poverty amid plenty. American abundance *structured* black poverty.

King joined Hill in holding government, unions, and businesses responsible for "plain, hard, raw discrimination" in the construction industry. Government spending and federally insured home loans created jobs "for which the Negro paid taxes but could draw no pay check." The federal government had a compelling responsibility to redress historic injustices. Mainstream organized labor obviously was not going to lead the charge. AFL-CIO member unions' resistance to desegregation suggested labor lacked "statesmanship, vigor and modernity." Blacks had "a right to expect more from their old allies," King reiterated. He never mentioned extensive AFL-CIO lobbying on behalf of Title VII, but neither did he vigorously join the NAACP-led attack on the conservative craft unions. Like Randolph, King knew that desegregated building trades were not going to solve the mass unemployment crisis. He feared the forces of reaction would profit from "a schism between the Negro and organized labor."[23]

King's initial solutions followed the logic of racial atonement, but did not challenge the gendered contours of the welfare state. Born into poverty because of centuries of invidious "special treatment," the Negro struggled to escape but was blocked by white gatekeepers protecting privileged positions in education and employment. "When he seeks opportunity, he is told, in effect, to lift himself by his own bootstraps, advice which does not take into account the fact that he is barefoot." The Negro needed "something special" to help his "absorption into the economic system." He did not want to "languish on welfare rolls any more than the next man." Men's low wages meant "the average Negro woman has always had to work to keep her family in food and clothes." King thought black women's freedom from exploitation principally meant freedom to be full-time mothers. To whites opposed to "special treatment" as "reverse discrimination," he argued blacks only wanted fair and honorable compensation and aid "to compete on a just and equal basis." King faced an uphill battle: a poll taken in 1963 revealed that 97 percent of whites were opposed to employment "preferences" for blacks. King now argued that a crash program to lift Negro standards would save tax dollars by preventing "school dropouts, family breakups, crime rates, illegitimacy, [and] swollen relief rolls."[24]

In the middle of King's book project, Johnson's declaration of war on poverty opened floodgates for Rustin and Randolph's dreams of an interracial movement for full employment. Rustin had opposed Levison's and Young's whole line of thinking, arguing that white workers would resent black "preferential treatment." Levison persuaded King to keep the racial atonement argument in the book, so they merged it with the class agenda. SCLC was meeting in Black Mountain, North Carolina, in a mood so radical that King's new advisor, white lawyer Harry Wachtel, implored King to throw away the audiotapes, lest red-baiting enemies get a hold of them. Rustin was reportedly predicting "political revolt" from the automation crisis. Wachtel later told Taylor Branch that King argued that entire industries must be "socialized to rescue the chronically unemployed." Jones and King consulted on the book changes, and King instructed Hermine Popper to address the "economic and cultural backwardness" of poor whites who were "not too far removed" from blacks in poverty. Practically, whites would reject a "Negro Bill of Rights," King wrote Popper.[25] How could he make an equally compelling moral case for whites?

King's Bill of Rights for the Disadvantaged stretched over the disadvantages of both racism and poverty. Its core was public investment in full employment to heal the multiracial scourge of automation. Stretching the meaning of "the disadvantaged" to cover whites involved some sleight of hand, because King began with a moral argument for black reparations based on their specific "disadvantages." "No amount of gold could provide an adequate compensation for the exploitation and humiliation of the Negro in America." But a "massive program by the government" could compensate for unpaid wages. There were ample precedents for targeted policies: land grant colleges, child labor laws, categorical welfare legislation, the Wagner Act, and especially the 1944 GI Bill. "Negroes form the vast majority of America's disadvantaged," King wrote, with considerable demographic ambiguity, but there were "millions of white poor" who would also benefit. Whites had been "derivative victims" of the slave system that had created an isolated regional low-wage labor market; they suffered the "deprivation and the humiliation of poverty if not of color." A century later, a system built on discrimination still "corrupts their lives, frustrates their opportunities and withers their education." Racism so confused whites that they "supported their own oppressors."[26] *Why We Can't Wait* lacked the self-help rhetoric of *Stride Toward Freedom,* but the historical analysis was essentially an elaboration of Randolph's speech to the 1956 NAACP convention.

King's adoption of Randolph's and Rustin's proposals for restructuring the labor market transcended the War on Poverty and affirmative action. Job losses from automation had to be offset with greater public and private investment in jobs. "Negroes will not long permit themselves to be pitted against white workers for an ever-decreasing supply of jobs," King warned, portending greater conflict at the core of the liberal coalition if public action was not forthcoming. King also called for expanding the "social work apparatus" to provide skills training to poor people of every race and age, not just the young. King had much more in mind than manpower development, rehabilitation, and youth education, as he echoed the political praxis of Septima Clark. Adult literacy and training in "the rights of citizenship, including the right to vote," all came under the rubric. The Bill of Rights for the Disadvantaged would spend tax dollars for citizenship education and political mobilization.[27]

King was heartened that direct action had educated African Americans to their "political potentiality." Hoping to broaden and extend the March on Washington coalition of labor, church, civic, and civil rights groups, King declared that blacks had reached a "new stage" of political freedom. The movement was now strong enough to form alliances, make deals, and abandon coalitions that did not benefit them. "Strategically situated in large cities" and key states, black voters held the balance of power in national elections. Reflecting Rustin's emerging call for a move from "protest to politics," King concluded that political power could well be "the most effective new tool of the Negro's liberation." But federal legislation attacking national poverty had to be backed up by a political constituency much broader than that which had sustained southern protest. King hinted at a more versatile mix of political tactics than sit-ins, freedom rides, boycotts, marches, and demonstrations. But he would never abandon protest for politics. The black response to the "complex dilemma of fast-paced progress and persistent poverty" had already produced "a dissatisfied, vibrant and powerful" movement. If the liberal-labor political coalition proved weaker than hoped, perhaps the black revolution of 1963 would inspire people "of all races, who live in equally desperate circumstances," to join with blacks marching in more militant directions. Perhaps a "legion of the deprived, white and Negro," could then "restructure an old order based too long on injustice."[28] Rustin would judge this dream of a lower-class grand alliance insufficiently grand, even quixotic. But King shared it with the democratic left, and therein lay the kernel of the 1968 Poor People's March.

Money and Democracy: Mississippi and Atlantic City

By the time King testified before the Democratic National Convention in August 1964, he had put programmatic flesh on the Bill of Rights for the Disadvantaged. In May, Clarence Jones and Harry Wachtel organized a "research committee" to advise King on matters of policy and public relations. Uninvolved in SCLC's direct action campaigns, the group would influence King's rhetoric and recommendations in years to come. Rustin, Reddick, Ralph Helstein, and Cleveland Robinson of District 65 were also members. Immediately, several asked King to mute his rhetoric of racial atonement to appeal to labor, poor whites, and Democratic Party liberals.[29]

King remained sanguine about the white backlash until the political earth shook under the Democratic Party. Jones warned that militancy like that shown by Brooklyn's CORE in threatening "stall-ins" on highways leading to New York's World Fair would provoke a counterrevolutionary movement that would hurt progressive interracial alliances. King defended CORE's "revolutionary" tactics. If friendly white allies resisted radical protest or black demands for "basic structural changes in the architecture of American society," they "never were real friends," King wrote SCLC.[30] When Rustin organized the largest school boycotts in the nation's history, King had only praise for actions that "punctured the thin veneer of the North's racial self-righteousness." "There is no 'back-lash,'" King wrote in the *Amsterdam News*, after his advisors recommended he state publicly that the "white backlash was a creation of the newspapers." Churches still solidly supported civil rights, white student volunteers would soon flood Mississippi to register voters, and Harris polls showed that Americans' support for the civil rights bill rose four points to 72 percent between March and May. King wrote that there was nothing new about white reaction. Whites resisting new black demands usually later accepted their justice.[31] It was time to advance, not retreat.

But that was before George Wallace won a white majority and a 43 percent plurality in the May 19 Maryland Democratic primary. The backlash was no simple conspiracy of elites protecting their privileges and power. Wallace mobilized millions of white suburbanites, southerners, and working-class Democrats whose racial privileges in jobs and housing felt like hard-won achievements that were now under siege by civil rights liberals and African Americans looking for easy tickets uptown. Wallace's approach was simple: combine thinly veiled attacks on blacks with open attacks on the Civil Rights Act and the "'pinknik' social engineers in Washington" who would enforce it. *They* were going force "open housing" upon homeowners. *They* were going to tell employers whom to hire, trampling on workers' "seniority rights."[32]

Reddick wrote King urgently from Maryland on June 10. Wallace skillfully conjured specters of school busing and "invaded neighborhoods," and he frightened whites with lurid cartoons of "angry, impatient [and] rowdy Negroes" screaming for "job quotas and preferences." Stop publicly demanding "preferences or compensatory treatment," Reddick beseeched, and organize proposals around principles of "opportunity" and "to each according to his need." African Americans would still benefit disproportionately simply because their needs were greater. Reddick offered a seminal vision of the Rainbow Coalition in place of a seemingly narrow politics of affirmative action. The Negro must join "all the disadvantaged"—Appalachian whites, "the American Indian, the Puerto Rican, the Mexican and the Oriental"—demanding an end to poverty and discrimination.[33]

King adopted this rhetoric of opportunity in arguing for a radical black-white alliance before the NAACP Legal Defense Fund on May 28, 1964, and in several *Amsterdam News* columns. Drawing on Jones's draft, King maintained that the "recognition phase of human rights" must expand to demand "nondiscriminatory meaningful opportunities for the Negro." The Negro's "institutionalized position in the American economy" must be radically changed. Even if the Civil Rights Act eliminated all discrimination, black poverty, "the historic and institutionalized consequences of color," would continue to disadvantage Negroes until whites joined with them to attack "all the causes of poverty." Only a powerful alliance including labor unions and white churches could support "a massive assault upon slums, inferior education, inadequate medical care," and the color-blind scourge of automation.[34]

King's testimonies for the Republican and Democratic Platform Committees on July 7 and August 19 accurately presented the demographics of poverty in an argument for universal income protections. Everywhere, King changed the politically charged words "special treatment" to "opportunity," calling for a massive new antipoverty offensive. With the Democrats, he even put a price tag on the Bill of Rights for the Disadvantaged. His proposals made no news, however, as Republicans nominated conservative Barry Goldwater, and Democrats wrangled over who could legitimately represent Mississippi Democrats. Jones and Wachtel sent statistics on poverty and suggested King define "the disadvantaged" to include anyone in a family making less than $3,000 a year (the government's new "poverty line"). Wachtel wrote King that most poor people lived "wretchedly in the rural areas," not in the racial ghettos. Federal subsidies to wealthy farmers cost over $7 billion a year. Why not give 25 percent of that to poor families? Jones sent a list of policy recommendations: a $2 minimum wage for farm laborers and migrant workers; national health insurance; a thirty-five-hour workweek; and public works projects to clear slums and build mass transit. King cut through the details and advocated a guaranteed annual income.[35]

The poverty population, though unconscionably and disproportionately black, was in fact predominantly white, King testified. King still thought blacks were the most "disadvantaged" group, with the nation's highest rates of poverty and unemployment (in fact that distinction belonged to Native Americans). Blacks made up only 22 percent of America's 9 million poor families, King explained; but half of all black families qualified as poor (by decades end they would comprise fully a third of the poor). The majority of the poor who were white stood to benefit from guaranteeing an "annual minimum subsistence" income of $3,000 to every American family. Blacks still wanted jobs more than welfare, but all families should be covered, whether or not the head of the family earned wages. The minimum wage was still only $1.50 an hour, and half of all America's poor had employed heads of families. Closely following the statistics and recommendations of Senator Joseph Clark's "Manpower Revolution" report, King estimated the cost of the guaranteed income at $50 billion over ten years. That about equaled federal corporate subsidies for the previous six years, he claimed. Though it was five times the first annual appropriation for the Economic Opportunity Act, it paled next to billions spent to warehouse poor people "in their hovels." But where was the constituency for such a program? "The poor" were neither organized nor influential; many did not even identify themselves as poor.[36] Where was the "legion of the deprived"?

King looked no further than Mississippi, where activists and courageous local people like Fannie Lou Hamer and Unita Blackwell had organized the Mississippi Freedom Democratic Party (MFDP). Excluded from the Democratic Party primaries and general elections, MFDP voters nominated their own candidates, wrote their own platform, and held a mock election in 1963 that attracted 80,000 people. Annell Ponder wrote in the *SCLC Newsletter* about people's excitement the first time they voted. Candidates demanded economic preconditions of freedom: low-interest loans for small farmers; government aid to farming cooperatives; public works for the unemployed; and fair employment practices in hiring, with penalties for those not complying. Since black agricultural and service workers had no federal minimum wage protections, they called for "minimum wages of $1.25 an hour and a maximum work-week of 40 hours."[37]

King toured Mississippi in late July and supported the MFDP's bid to be certified and seated as the "authentic" Mississippi Democratic Party delegation at August's national convention. King was deeply moved by the poorest Mississippians who built the MFDP despite murders, death threats, and economic reprisals. He praised Bob Moses and SNCC's and CORE's program of voter registration as the most creative attempt he had ever seen "to radically change the oppressive life of the Negro." Poor black folk had "no money, no guns, [and] very few votes," King preached, "and yet they are the No. 1 power in the nation." (They surely had guns, but King wasn't advertising the fact.) King addressed a rally in Jackson, praising 1,000 white volunteers from northern colleges who served as voting rights canvassers and freedom school teachers that summer. They were "our domestic Peace Corps, working to rid democracy of its sores of injustice." Mississippi's white leadership hated the federal government when it came to race and poverty, he said, but welcomed federal subsidies for "roads, hospitals, projects of urban renewal [and] farm and business subsidies."[38]

King offered the volunteers his own prescient analysis of the racially coded, ostensibly "color-blind" conservative political discourse of the mid-1960s, as adapted by Mississippi Senator John Stennis. Without referring to segregation, Stennis painted pictures of "undeserving, shiftless, [and] criminally dangerous" black people. Morally corrupted by welfare dependency, they roamed the "streets nightly in a frenzy of violence." Stennis ascribed their poverty to their own lack of "ambition and industry," King explained, even though their ancestors had built the southern economy without compensation. Stennis denounced "big government, radicalism and bureaucracy," even though he loved agricultural subsidies and corporate welfare. King demanded that white politicians "stop playing the Negro against the poor white for a landlord who pays neither him, the poor white, nor the Negro." It was time to revive Reconstruction and form a grand alliance devoted to securing abundance, work, and education for everyone.[39]

Mississippi Freedom Summer volunteers staffed freedom schools that engaged children, adolescents, and adults in innovative, participatory forms of learning. The historian Howard Zinn helped design the curriculum, charging the schools with finding "solutions for poverty, for injustice, for race and national hatred." One lesson explored southern violations of freedom of assembly. Another examined the "power structure" and the effect of cybernation on jobs and human rights. "*Why* are people poor? . . . [B]ecause we are lazy, or stupid? . . . [B]ecause we are Negro? . . . Are our jobs being taken away by machines?" Did the federal government care about poor people, white or black? Classrooms were overcrowded, exciting, unruly places where poor blacks spoke dangerous truths, engaging in open, impassioned debate. They loved to argue "anything from standards of Negro beauty to the Marxist view of private property," one volunteer remembered. Volunteers held classes in the evening for kids who chopped weeds all day in the cotton fields. Voting rights canvassers trod dusty roads in the daytime, meeting "tenant farmers too poor or too tired" or too intimidated to attend freedom school or church. They visited shacks filled with swarming flies and children with swollen bellies. They left wondering whether Mississippi's poor folk were any better off than the Vietnamese.[40]

When MFDP delegates arrived in Atlantic City, King implored the Credentials Committee charged with authorizing delegates to seat them and shine a "light of hope for all the disfranchised millions" in Mississippi, South Africa, and Fidel Castro's prisons. Fearing that nine white southern delegations would bolt the convention, Johnson told Senator Richard Russell he was sure King was against him, after hearing King on the radio say that blacks need not vote Democratic if the party rejected the MFDP. Feeding on a ready diet of slander served up by J. Edgar Hoover, Johnson complained to Hubert Humphrey that "the Communists have got hold of [King], and they're managing and directing him every day." The Johnson forces mounted a concerted campaign of FBI surveillance, political pressure, and economic intimidation to prevent the Credentials Committee from approving the challenge. They offered the MFDP two at-large convention delegates and promised reform in delegate selection in 1968. Walter Reuther thought the MFDP was "completely irrational" for not accepting the "victory." Certain that Negroes were bent on resurrecting the conflicts of "the Reconstruction period," Johnson was hearing reactionary cries from *northerners* that "the Negroes have taken over the country."[41]

Johnson's blatant power plays overwhelmed the MFDP's moral appeals. White allies deserted them, and black leaders urged capitulation. Rustin lectured that the MFDP should accept political compromise over the pure "morality" of protest. Reuther reminded King of "all this money" the UAW donated to SCLC over the years, calling in chips for Johnson. King responded he would not, indeed, could not, tell the MFDP to accept the compromise. Torn between expediency and justice, King told the MFDP delegation that as "a Negro leader" he might accept the compromise and work within the Democratic Party, but if he were "a Mississippi Negro," he would vote it down. Just "seriously think" about it, he said, Unita Blackwell recalled. King could have "stood up to the payoffs and buyouts" and more aggressively defended the MFDP, but Blackwell judged his heart to be in the right place. MFDP supporters received economic threats, the same techniques planter elites used to beat down poor sharecroppers. "Your husband is up for a judgeship, and if you don't shape up, he won't get it," a Johnson heavyweight threatened a committee member, according to SNCC's Courtland Cox. Though split between middle-class and poor people, most MFDP delegates rejected the offer. Bob Moses recalled widespread disillusionment with the "political system." "After Atlantic City, our struggle was not for civil rights, but for liberation," he said. Charles Sherrod stormed in anger, "We are not only demanding meat and bread and a job but we are also demanding power, a share in power!" Poor folk had again concluded "that the Federal Government is a white man." King stumped the cities that fall denouncing Republican candidate Barry Goldwater. But celebrating his Nobel Peace Prize in November, he named six Mississippi activists as the movement's "true heroes."[42]

The New York Riots and the Urban Racial Agenda

For four days in July 1964, blacks in Harlem and Rochester, New York, rebelled against ghetto conditions and police brutality. Though local leaders and youth gangs alike blamed disempowerment and police brutality, King stressed the need for socioeconomic change. New York City's violence broke out when a white policeman shot and killed a young black man. A broad coalition of black leaders called the Harlem Unity Council issued a nine-point proposal for police reform and community accountability. "This was a war between the citizens of Harlem and the police," CORE's James Farmer declared. King's friend Arthur Logan, active in Harlem's fledgling antipoverty agency, wrote him that longstanding community resentments had been sparked by poorly trained and violent police. Ghetto blacks were finally lashing out against "powerlessness." When King accepted Mayor Robert Wagner's invitation to mediate the conflict, Clarence Jones warned him Wagner might use him as "a buffer" against angry neighborhood activists. Local leaders in fact roundly criticized King for visiting Wagner on a "peace mission" before Wagner bothered to visit Harlem or King bothered to meet the Unity Council. Actors Ruby Dee and Ossie Davis privately protested that King had clumsily lent Wagner his "responsible" image to "downgrade and undercut" the Unity Council and "muffle the cries of an outraged community." King must demand police nonviolence as fervently as community nonviolence, they wrote. King got the message, pressing upon Wagner the Unity Council's program and urging the establishment of a civilian police review board to investigate brutality.[43]

But King resisted Jones's suggestion he call a national conference to discuss "unbridled police force" and the need to foster "Negro participation" in city government. King rhetorically shifted responsibility for violence from the black community onto ghetto conditions and policy neglect, following Rustin's advice. Nonviolence only worked where cities made progress "in housing, jobs and schools," King said. These remained Rustin's three principal issues through which to reconstruct the complex ghetto. White politicians could condemn "lawlessness," King wrote, but that was no substitute for "soul-searching analysis" and concrete concessions to black communities. Leaders needed "victories" they could show people. King promised to petition President Johnson for "millions of dollars *now* for full employment and for the elimination of slums." Again and again thereafter, he argued, "social peace must spring from economic justice." It was two years before King put police brutality and institutional racism in city housing and welfare agencies first on his agenda for preventing riots, as he came to see urban disempowerment as their principal cause.[44]

King unwittingly helped Wagner negotiate the mine field between the black community and his powerful police constituency. King thanked the mayor for promising to use federal money to put "the economically deprived back to work," and Wagner praised King's "great world stature." But Wagner held the cards. "Law and order" was a prerequisite for any progress, he declared, even though "individual police actions" were sometimes excessive. Shifting money from the city's $15 million antipoverty budget, Wagner promised 1,000 young people summer jobs cleaning up city parks. The Unity Council condemned the mayor's failure to appoint a police review board. Over the next four years, city officials across the country placated powerful police constituencies and drew on antipoverty budgets for "fire duty," throwing scarce poverty money at burning streets. No one intended the antipoverty program to be fire insurance, but OEO increasingly directed its limited resources toward pacifying troubled communities. One tragic consequence was that the public image of the War on Poverty became increasingly identified with urban blacks and violence.[45]

King had not mixed with Harlem's poor. But Andrew Young and Bevel led a team of southern organizers to Rochester with King's instructions to urge local black youth to turn their "energies and their work toward registration drives." Youth gang members laughed at the ministers' bib overalls, until the older men beat them at basketball. Young persuaded them to come to workshops where he argued that "votes were related to police brutality, housing, jobs and self respect." Young thought they were surprisingly articulate in drawing parallels between local police harassment and brutality in the South. They complained about Rochester's "crowded homes and schools, joblessness and the fact that they were ignored by *everybody*," he wrote. Hostile to the black middle class, black youth joined poor whites and Puerto Ricans in a commodity riot where "the poor seemed to rebel against the establishment."[46] In the end the youth did not warm to nonviolence and southern-style evangelical mobilizing, and the ministers did not return.

King hoped the socioeconomic appeal would be powerful with middle-class whites, and it became a permanent set piece in his repertoire. With a more acute sense of urban poverty and power, King wrote in fresh language on August 15.

America will be faced with the ever-present threat of violence, rioting and senseless crime as long as Negroes by the hundreds of thousands are packed into malodorous, rat-plagued ghettos, as long as Negroes remain smothered by poverty in the midst of an affluent society; as long as Negroes see their freedom endlessly delayed and diminished by the head winds of tokenism and small handouts from the white power structure.[47]

After Johnson's November landslide dampened worries over white backlash, King became more vocal about the racial economic power structures behind the riots. He drew attention to pervasive police-sanctioned white crime in black neighborhoods. "Rampant racketeering has a sanctuary in the slums and corrupts the ghetto's already miserable life," he informed readers of the *Saturday Evening Post.* The government must prevent riots, not just act as an "ambulance service" or a social science research mill substituting study for action. Revolts stemmed from "environmental conditions" rather than "racial" traits, he instructed *Playboy* readers. King denied any relation between violent "mobs" and the "disciplined, non-violent, direct-action demonstrators" he led. Conservative politicians cynically used rioting to divert public attention from degrading poverty to focus on "looting, and . . . the breakdown of law and order." King pointed out that 150 *whites* were arrested in Rochester, "including mothers stealing food [and] children's shoes." It was an interracial riot "against the establishment," the white leaders who neglected explosive problems of "slum housing, chronic poverty, woefully inadequate education and substandard schools."[48]

In some cities, mass disruption of urban institutions seemed the only way to get ghetto issues on the political agenda. In a speech to southern political scientists, King reiterated that only federal action could address manifold urban ills. Political science was politically impotent, he declared. Federal action would occur only when blacks demonstrated "in such massive numbers so as to threaten the stability of the present systems which deal with these issues." King's temporary agreement with Lyndon Johnson in the summer to suspend direct action was now clearly over.[49]

Class Coalitions and Wars on Poverty

As the dilemmas of race and class became acute, King continued to balance protest and racial mobilization with the dream of a class-based political alliance. The late September SCLC convention resounded with calls to political action and interracial alliances. "God is concerned about 'FEEDING THE HUNGRY,'" Andrew Young preached. "Our struggle must now rise above color, for there are poor, needy, jobless, and ill-trained persons of every color and nationality." Rev. Joseph Lowery followed: "Unemployment and underemployment . . . *These are the monsters*." King invited SCLC to "vigorously join the War against Poverty," extend its scope, press for more resources, and infuse it with the energy political elites lacked. Blacks should be skeptical of highly touted "Wars on Poverty" when space mission budgets vastly exceeded the recently passed antipoverty bill. Congress had recently appropriated $927 million for Johnson's program, just half the after-tax profits of the big three automakers. That was exactly "$23.67 for each of the 40 million of admitted poor!" King estimated. In August Congress had almost unanimously passed the Tonkin Gulf Resolution authorizing Johnson to repel any and all North Vietnamese aggression, King noted. "The aggression of the forces of poverty must be met with a full scale war, if the victims of this aggression, Negro and white alike, representing at least one fifth of this nation, are to feel they are partners in this land of opportunity."[50]

King did not have to look far to find reactionaries cooking up insidious myths that the War on Poverty was a program mainly to advantage the black poor, as they sought to keep working-class people divided. With the nomination of Barry Goldwater for president, the Republican Party joined hands with segregationists and embraced "racism, reaction and extremism," King told the SCLC convention. Whites must understand that the War on Poverty would benefit the 7.3 million white families who formed 78 percent of the poor. Hoping to revive the March on Washington coalition, King argued that Negroes must add their "political power to that of other groups (the religious communities, catholic, protestant, and Jewish, to Labor, to the liberals and intellectuals)." Watching the convention's proceedings, Anne Braden of the Southern Conference Educational Fund wrote with evident hope that it was "militant but not nationalist." The great challenge would be to convince all classes of white people to forge such a grand alliance.[51]

"Rightists have captured a major expression of power in our country," warned Charles Sherrod at a SNCC retreat after Goldwater won the Republican nomination: "Win or lose, the forces behind Goldwater will gain strength." Sherrod was prescient, but his warning was drowned out by the roar of Johnson's electoral landslide in November. Johnson won forty-four states with a margin of sixteen million votes and helped Democrats win thirty-eight more seats in the House and two more in the Senate. But Goldwater carried the Deep South states of Alabama, Georgia, Louisiana, Mississippi, and South Carolina and helped elect five new Republican representatives in Alabama. Johnson and King knew they would have to move fast to solidify southern biracial voting coalitions, but Johnson was not about to let King dictate the timing and methods.[52]

For the rest of the year, King rallied audiences he hoped would together "vigorously join the War on Poverty" to push for his $50 billion program of domestic reconstruction: the interracial unions, churches, urban ethnic Democrats at the core of the New Deal coalition, students, and anyone who cared about what his Nobel Peace Prize really meant. He started with the interracial unions who cared most about earning decent family wages. The expansion of unorganized, low-wage service industries undermined the economic security of all workers, but especially minority workers. In an October speech to the Drug and Hospital Employees Local 1199 in New Jersey, King praised their dedication to the nation's "underpaid, exploited and forgotten workers" as they crusaded to eliminate "poverty wages" and win decent working conditions. Returning to Atlanta after receiving his Nobel Prize, King called for a national boycott of Scripto pens in support of the company's seven hundred striking black workers who worked at "sub poverty wages." Scripto refused to give the same wage increase to blacks as to whites, assigning all the whites and only six blacks to skilled job categories. SCLC reportedly distributed two million flyers to 2,200 organizations. Southern African freedom fighters endorsed the strike. Four hundred fifty middle-class black ministers publicized the boycott through Operation Breadbasket. A black-labor alliance was King's highest priority, C. T. Vivian wrote affiliates, the inauguration of "our national economic drive." "The same system that exploits the Negro exploits the white man," King told a mass meeting of the strikers. Employers hollered " 'nigger, nigger, nigger' to keep them separated while they are exploiting both." "We must join the war against poverty and believe in the dignity of all work," he preached at Ebenezer Baptist Church. "I'm tired of this stuff about menial labor; what makes it menial is that we don't pay folk anything." After the strike was settled, however, workplace organizing did not become central to SCLC's national economic drive.[53]

King also worked to mobilize the white middle-class churches and Catholic parishes. In October, he addressed the Chicago Catholic Interracial Council, seeking support for a "gigantic Marshall Plan" for the poor. Pope Paul VI had invited Catholics to stand, as Jesus had, "with the people of the land." King invited the priests out of their sanctuaries to "take up our crosses in the streets [and] march with the unemployed . . . in quest of jobs and food." Catholics had their greatest strength in the big cities where the civil rights movement's next battles would be fought. "The great network of parishes can point the way to true integration," King preached. Then King dared urban whites to "live in racially integrated neighborhoods with the faith that America will be the richer when the walls of race and class are broken down." Liberal Catholic clergy who echoed King's integrationist messages were already meeting walls of resistance as white homeowners defended local turf in opposition to public housing and open housing legislation. Catholic attachments to geographically defined parish churches complicated whites' fears of losing both home and community.[54] Saul Alinsky had warned him about white resistance, but King believed housing was the key to the intersecting oppressions upholding concentrated and racialized poverty in the cities.

King again addressed the urban ethnics at the core of the New Deal coalition, working-class whites who might consider themselves middle class but whose security and identity rested on earlier interethnic coalitions of opposition to WASPs, Republicans, the KKK, and conservative bosses. King's post-election *Saturday Evening Post* article affirmed that racial harmony could be achieved through economic growth and a universal safety net built around the value of work. King again recalled their struggles for labor rights and Social Security in a strong and prosperous nation. A "grand alliance of Negro and white," consisting of "the vast majorities of each group," could realize the Popular Front dream of an integrated, full employment economy.[55]

Mobilizing college students, King focused on the ravages of economic racism, not the urgency of a workers' alliance. King tapped into the idealism of the student movement spreading rapidly to white campuses after Freedom Summer. Calling for a "Thanksgiving Fast for Freedom" to publicize hunger in Mississippi and the Deep South, King criticized white power, economic reprisals, and black poverty: "Sharecroppers are being thrown off their land, workers are being fired from their jobs, Negro children are being denied an adequate education; all are being cheated of their dream of a better life." Poverty oppressed most black people's lives, he insisted. "Deprivation—political, cultural, and most importantly, economic deprivation—has long been a way of life for millions of Negro citizens." This was the most radical of King's many fund-raising appeals to date.[56]

King saw his reception of the Nobel Peace Prize in December as an opportunity to address poverty in the United States and the world. America had much to learn from Scandinavian "democratic socialism," he announced on arrival in Norway. His Nobel lecture to the students of Oslo University revived long-running themes about mankind's "poverty of spirit," which lagged dangerously behind its "scientific and technological abundance." The largest problems growing out of this "ethical infantilism" remained racism, poverty, and war. "If man is to redeem his spiritual and moral 'lag' he must go all out to bridge the social and economic gulf between the 'haves' and the 'have-nots' of the world," King lectured. Lyndon Johnson invited him to the White House on his return, and King wasted no time telling the president that "Negroes wanted to be part of the antipoverty campaign [and] given roles of leadership." The day before, the City of New York awarded King its medallion of honor at city hall while Mayor Wagner and Vice President Humphrey looked on. King delivered a scathing indictment of America's economic inequality, military armament, and neglect of the poor. (The *New York Times* and *Herald Tribune* both ignored King's radical critique.) Scandinavian social democracies had "no unemployment and no slums," he preached. How could anyone consider the War on Poverty a step toward "economic justice" when forty million Americans remained poor? "The budget for the War on Poverty is less than one percent of the military budget," King lectured the liberals. Perhaps only "those at the bottom, [the] shirtless and barefoot people" of the nation, could lead the way.[57]

The Challenge of Black Nationalism: Jesse Gray and Malcolm X

King knew his effectiveness in the North depended on how well nonviolence and the promise of integration could deliver shoes, overcoats, and political clout to the urban masses. Clarence Jones agreed with Harlem housing activist Jesse Gray that "the movement will not get anywhere until they get political and economic power." Sharing with actor Ossie Davis his enthusiasm for Gray and Malcolm X, Jones sent King the text of Gray's speech, "The Black Revolution—A Struggle for Political Power," delivered to Harlem's Federation of Independent Political Action. A tenant organizer since 1952, Gray led Harlem's Community Council on Housing, which had publicized poor housing conditions with a series of rent strikes. The strikes achieved unprecedented unity, Gray recalled, a collective effort to "change the 350 year old concept of property first and people second." In his speech he insisted "breaking up the ghetto" was a white liberal scheme to "control the movement" and "scatter" blacks, diminishing their power. Whites and blacks both rejected housing integration, he said. Black pride, community organizing, community control of education and policing, and internal ghetto rehabilitation were his priorities. Gray agreed with King on most of the problems: "poor schools, bad housing, no jobs, no future for black youths." But Gray had a fuller appreciation of gender justice, calling for "nurseries for the many many mothers who wish to work." Gray also rejected direct action, all the fruitless "sit-ins, wade-ins, walk-ins, sleep-ins. . . . Real revolutionaries are out in the streets organizing people" through a "house-by-house, apartment-by-apartment organizing campaign centered on the needs of the masses." "Unified, organized black political power" alone could bring blacks into multiracial governing coalitions on terms of respect and equality. Middle-class dreams of integration and civil rights offered no hope to the poor. "Jim Crow is still the policy of the federal government," Gray concluded. Unlike King, Gray had no faith that northern white elites would push the federal government any further. Activists must develop new techniques of bringing "maximum pressure to bear upon government," he argued.[58]

Gray knew and worked with Malcolm X, whose revolutionary political economy evolved dramatically after he left the Nation of Islam in March 1964. Malcolm had called repeatedly for black economic independence through black ownership of land and businesses. Malcolm moderated this separatism in 1964, seeking rapprochement with civil rights organizations, advocating "better food, clothing, housing, education, and jobs *right now*" for twenty-two million blacks. The black community was not yet strong enough to join in coalitions, he insisted. "There can be no workers' solidarity until there is first some racial solidarity," Malcolm argued in May 1964. He thought the War on Poverty and more social welfare spending would probably exacerbate what he denounced as welfare dependency. The federal government was no ally, implicated as it was in black people's "oppression and exploitation and degradation." In the "human rights" phase of the struggle, American blacks would find international allies and indict the United States for genocide before the UN General Assembly, where the votes of poor nations could be more powerful than American dollars, he declared.[59]

Malcolm returned from his travels in Africa and the Middle East in 1964 appreciating the possibilities of multiracial humanism, sharply critical of capitalism and U.S. imperial "dollarism." To believe in capitalism was racist, he told a reporter. In December Malcolm called on Harlemites to embrace socialism and resist being "incorporated, or integrated, or disintegrated, into this capitalistic system." A capitalist was simply "a bloodsucker." Malcolm responded enthusiastically to King's speech praising Sweden's democratic socialism at Harlem's 369th Artillery Armory, during a community salute drawing 8,000 people coordinated by Cleveland Robinson. Malcolm reasoned that if poorer nations could eliminate unemployment, it was probably wiser to investigate socialist Sweden and Nigeria than to run "downtown picketing city hall." Malcolm defined black poverty as a product of wealth flowing out of the ghetto. Malcolm embraced neither Gray's strategy of local political empowerment nor Rustin's strategy of building progressive coalitions. "The only kind of power that can help you and me is international power," he argued, "not local power."[60] After his assassination in 1965, Malcolm influenced generations of black nationalists, and King selectively incorporated nationalist terms into his rhetoric. But he never thought a ghettoized economy controlled by blacks could ever employ enough people to be self-supporting.

Most of the terms of Martin Luther King's later radicalism were established by late 1964, however, before Johnson's escalation of the Vietnam War, the Watts riot, the rise of black power, and the 1966 Chicago Freedom Movement. True to his dialectical habit of mind, King recognized the need for both local black empowerment and national coalitions. At the time of Malcolm's death, he and King were converging on a socialist solution to poverty. Over the next two years, King came to share Malcolm's description of the American "nightmare," especially his disillusionment with the liberal state. Yet he never abandoned the commitment to class mobilization he articulated in 1964; he always returned to the need for jobs and income for all poor Americans as the essential precondition to full African American economic emancipation. And blacks might have to lead the way.

In his *Amsterdam News* column in the aftermath of the November election, King again warned that the civil rights and antipoverty legislation of 1964 would not address deeper structural issues of poverty and urban powerlessness. The Civil Rights Act gave weak protection for voting rights and proved irrelevant to northern segregation. "We have been promised a Great Society, but the promise of a war on poverty is not going to feed and clothe the hungry masses who are unemployed this winter," he wrote. For the first time in print, in a black newspaper where expressing such radical opinions was relatively safe, King directly challenged the government's and corporations' valuation of the profit system over human rights. Lyndon Johnson got support from Henry Ford and Walter Reuther, King wrote, but the president would soon have to decide whether automakers should "make high profits even at the expense of wholesale unemployment, or whether full employment must take precedence over unlimited profit." King still believed "people of goodwill" could make a truly Great Society. But as middle-class goodwill evaporated over the next three years, as urban politicians refused to implement "maximum feasible participation" of the poor in antipoverty programs, as cities were convulsed by violent protests, and as labor increasingly revealed itself to be an unreliable ally, King turned toward the "legion of the deprived" as the force for change. By 1966, King's posture of critical support for the War on Poverty developed into full-blown criticism, and in 1968 he summoned activists and poor people from all over the country to lay nonviolent siege to the nation's capital to demand jobs, income, and a share of power for the poor.[61]

Chapter 8
The Secret Heart of America

In 1965, the politics of civil and voting rights enforcement, the War on Poverty, the urban crisis, and the war in Vietnam became inextricably intertwined. The social democratic imperative—forging ties between civil rights groups and labor unions to organize unorganized and unemployed workers and bring them into a powerful new grand alliance—quickly became just one among several strategies, as King took upon himself and SCLC what properly would have been the work of a political party. The Selma voting rights campaign and its aftermath decisively demonstrated the interdependence of political rights and economic security, as activists and local people fought for their own economic survival, looking to the new War on Poverty for help. With so many proposals on the table to advance the economic agenda, King knew blacks had to secure the basic right to vote and accelerate southern realignment. Blacks could not even elect officials who would respect their civil liberties, much less translate the vote into substantive political power, equal opportunity, or access to the benefits of the welfare state. Federal support for independent black organizations promised a partial resolution of the dilemma of economic and political power. But if whites had a problem with the vote, so much more could they be expected to oppose an alliance between the federal government and the civil rights movement.

The president and Congress battled over the fiscal and programmatic dimensions of the War on Poverty, but the war was also fought in local trenches where struggles over implementation intersected the politics of black empowerment. Activists saw the War on Poverty as a resource, helping them challenge racialized poverty with time-tested tools of organization, mobilization, and direct action. In Alabama and Los Angeles, King saw how elite control and black mobilization from below politicized the War on Poverty. OEO found itself in the middle, but in such unequal contests the agency frequently sided with powerful vested interests. Mayors, governors, and congressmen moved to rein in radicals in OEO committed to maximum feasible participation. When indigenous black organizations did win resources, most often it was after long and costly battles and compromises that left activists feeling bitter toward local power structures and the federal government.

King made a fateful decision in the summer of 1965, as he pondered a dizzying set of strategic choices—a massive boycott of the state of Alabama, an effort to consolidate the southern black vote, civil rights–labor campaigns to organize the unorganized, and federally funded antipoverty projects that promised democratic involvement to the black and poor. For King, the urban crisis became the most pressing issue. He persuaded SCLC to pour talent and resources into a northern campaign even before the Watts riot underscored the need for demonstrating nonviolent alternatives to masses of black people who found little hope in southern desegregation or federal legislation. Sensitive to critiques that SCLC had not developed enduring organizations on the local level, King began his search for the keys that might unlock ghetto prisons. Stumping for Lyndon Johnson in Baltimore in October 1964, King had declared that to eliminate "slums, ghettos, poverty, unemployment, and segregation, we must recognize the power of the ballot." But his understanding of social change had been decisively shaped by Birmingham and Selma: when moments of decision presented themselves, King chose mobilizing tactics likely to win national media exposure and to advance national legislative agendas. "The social pathology of the Negro masses" was the same in the North and South, he wrote in June 1965. "Our forte is a nonviolent arsenal under the command of dedicated preachers of the gospel." SCLC needed a chart, compass, and "some North Star to guide us to a future shrouded with impenetrable uncertainties," King told the August convention. To combat injustice, they need look no further than SCLC's "time honored tactics and strategies . . . sit-ins, stand-ins, kneel-ins, boycotts, picket lines, marches, civil disobedience and any form of protest and demonstrations that are nonviolently conceived and executed."[1] These strategies had increasingly complemented the campaign for the ballot and had more effectively moved national elites to action.

Selma

In January 1965 King and SCLC decided to use mass protest to secure "Civil Right No. 1": the vote. In March, after months of nonviolent protest and brutal repression, King led the triumphal Selma to Montgomery voting rights march. After dramatic confrontations between local movements and state and local police, the federal courts and President Johnson intervened to protect the right to protest. King used the international media event to assemble a broad coalition of liberals, celebrities, and civil rights and church leaders to support voting rights. Congress and public opinion rallied in support. Johnson committed his administration to the Voting Rights Act in March, which Congress passed on August 5. Selma became part of the iconography of the 1960s: the brutal beatings of peaceful protesters on the Edmund Pettis Bridge; Johnson's public adoption of the movement anthem "We Shall Overcome"; triumphant integrated crowds marching the rural roads between Selma and Montgomery; and the tragic killings of Jimmie Lee Jackson, James Reeb, and Viola Liuzzo. SCLC's strategy is best characterized not as "provocation" but "nonviolent theater," Adam Fairclough persuasively argues. SCLC tried to publicize dramatic, not deadly, violence. In official discourse and press coverage, voting rights became a moral imperative, a fundamental badge of equal citizenship. In Johnson's words, it was an issue at "the secret heart of America . . . a challenge, not to our growth or abundance, our welfare or security, but to the values and purpose and meaning of our nation." Images of police violence gave way to pictures of interracial marchers, and black men with "VOTE" stenciled on their faces framed by billowing American flags. But in the movement itself, as well as the African American press, the vote was always intertwined with the rights of protest, the conquest of poverty, and the effective uses of political power. From the mountaintop of liberalism, the nation could believe it saw the promised land of racial equality. But African Americans had to pass through valleys of reprisal, poverty, and continued disempowerment. Poor black Americans had the vote, their marching feet, and little else, King believed. Most were "poor and untutored," he told the University of Oslo students back in December. Though they had crossed the Red Sea of segregationist repression, a "frustrating and bewildering wilderness" lay before them on the way to the promised land of "dignity, equality, jobs and citizenship." They had yet to defeat the "monstrous octopus" of global poverty.[2]

From January through March, King justified the Selma protests as essential to winning civil, political, and economic rights. The Civil Rights Act of 1964 had not protected voting rights. "Give us the vote, unconditionally," Andrew Young and James Bevel had demanded in 1964. Whites made black children "pick cotton six months of the year," crowding them "into shanties called schools." They had no right to require literacy or a sixth-grade education as a condition of voting for people they had oppressed. Nor, despite the Civil Rights Act, were black civil rights secure under Alabama's white supremacist regime. Dallas County sheriff Jim Clark had closed down the local movie theater after blacks sought integrated admittance, and he arrested Negroes for walking down the street in groups larger than three for unlawful assembly or breach of peace. King promised his *Amsterdam News* readers that black voting could not only rid Selma of Sheriff Clark, but also win blacks "jobs in some of the newly opening factories of the area." So too with the newly opening anti-poverty agencies. "Now 83% of the Negroes earn less than $2000 per family. The so-called war on poverty has little meaning for them, because they have no one to represent them where the decisions are made," King explained. Enforcing the Civil Rights Act, including its equal employment provisions, depended on electing local officials responsive to all of the voters. Winning an equal share of antipoverty money for the black community also depended on political power. Voting and power sharing were essential in democratizing the Jim Crow welfare state. The federal government had to help break the vicious cycle of powerlessness and poverty. Blacks seeking to vote faced relentless "harassment, economic intimidation and police brutality." The *Pittsburgh Courier* documented the massive denial of the vote in the Alabama black belt: in Dallas County, only 256 blacks, less than 1 percent of the 15,000 eligible Negroes, were registered, though they comprised 57 percent of the population. Blacks formed even greater majorities in the surrounding counties, with even fewer voters. While the national poverty rate was 21 percent, it was three times higher in these counties.[3]

Lyndon Johnson adamantly opposed King's strategies of protest. Just after the election, on the phone with A. Philip Randolph he described his intentions to use the poverty program to further a liberal, biracial New South coalition. Working-class blacks and whites would be voting in 1968, he said. The $1 billion antipoverty appropriation for fiscal 1965 would get "a lot bigger" and give these voters "a lot of economic hope." Johnson presented economic progress as flowing from Washington, D.C., but King knew that without local empowerment blacks would see neither civil rights, voting rights, nor the equal fruits of the War on Poverty. Johnson still saw demonstrations as a threat to his political consensus; King thought demonstrations were indispensable to achieving democracy. On January 15, Johnson asked King to cancel voting rights protests and instead publicize and lobby for his Great Society. Johnson was not publicizing it, but he thought it obvious what $8 billion in education, $1 billion in health care, and $1.5 billion in antipoverty spending would do for Americans earning less than $2,000 a year. "You know who earns less than two thousand, don't you?" he asked. But Johnson could not deny King's priorities, admitting that voting would solve 70 percent of Negro problems. Only after blacks achieved full political inclusion would politicians knock on King's door, instead of the other way around. King deftly reminded Johnson he had lost all of the Deep South states where black registration was under 40 percent. Johnson agreed, but implored King to stick to charismatic preaching for voting rights. King should imitate Hitler's propaganda techniques: relentless repetition of a simple message through radio, television, and the nation's pulpits. Do that for the vote, Johnson intimated. But for God's sake, stay off the streets.[4]

Anticommunism and the backlash had turned even more white Americans against protest. Johnson constantly looked to opinion polls. Sixty percent of Americans surveyed by the Gallup poll in June 1963 thought demonstrations "hurt the Negro's cause" more than they helped. By May 1964, it was 74 percent, and by October 1966, 85 percent. The accelerating FBI campaign of harassment and surveillance was already turning Johnson against King, with its "scurrilous" material on King's sex life. Relentless allegations by segregationists and anticommunists also took their toll on public opinion. When Gallup had asked in September 1964 how many agreed that most civil rights organizations were "infiltrated [and] now dominated by communist troublemakers," 46 percent agreed and 35 percent disagreed.[5]

Nevertheless, King insisted on street protests in Selma and its surrounding towns. On January 18, King and SNCC's John Lewis led four hundred voter registration applicants to the Dallas County Courthouse in Selma. Sheriff Jim Clark arrested over two hundred protesters for unlawful assembly and criminal provocation. Hundreds more arrests followed. In an extraordinary breakthrough on January 22, one hundred Selma teachers marched. With the support of Johnson's Justice Department, on January 21 a federal district judge issued a temporary restraining order against Clark, prohibiting harassment or intimidation of anyone trying to register. King kept protesting; Johnson fumed at this seeming ingratitude. On February 1, King violated a Selma parade ordinance limiting marchers to 100 people, leading 265 people to jail. Five hundred schoolchildren followed. By February 3, there were 2,600 people in jail in south Alabama. After a secret meeting with King on February 9, Johnson publicly promised he would submit a voting rights bill to Congress "very soon." But King was not about to give up any momentum in the "crisis" he thought necessary to galvanize public opinion and Congress behind voting rights legislation. Keep up the pressure through night marches, King wrote from jail to Andrew Young. "Get big-name celebrities in for moral support," involve federal officials, and call for a congressional investigation. "In a crisis we must have a sense of drama," he insisted. Then, on February 18, Marion police rioted against a night march, beating newsmen and marchers and mortally wounding Jimmie Lee Jackson as he tried to protect his mother. Mrs. Lucy Foster suggested an honorary mass march to Montgomery. King endorsed the idea and preached the eulogy at Jackson's funeral.[6]

High-level political maneuvering between King and Johnson continued until local militants took charge. On March 6, King called on blacks to march from Selma to Montgomery to present a petition of grievances to Governor Wallace. Wallace banned the march. King respectfully asked for federal marshals, Johnson refused, and King canceled the march. But on March 7, five hundred marchers led by John Lewis and Hosea Williams set off independently. They were tear-gassed, trampled, and beaten by state police on the Edmund Pettis Bridge leading to Montgomery in a horrifying spectacle captured by network television cameras, later called "Bloody Sunday." As David Garrow has demonstrated, the pictures more than anything else shocked the public and spurred Congress into unusually swift action. For millions, front-page photographs and evening news footage of helmeted state troopers clubbing demonstrators kneeling in prayer in a nightmarish fog of tear gas became permanent emblems of southern white brutality. Liberal groups responded to the images with demands for federal intervention. Assuming King was behind the "outrageous" television spectacle, Johnson told Bill Moyers that King "better get to behaving himself" because it looked like he was arrogantly trying to take "charge of the country."[7]

Neither local repression, judicial intervention, nor administration pressure could stop the momentum of nonviolent theater. King promised to lead a second march on Tuesday, March 9. Four hundred fifty white clergy flew to Selma, gathering at Brown Chapel with ordinary citizens outraged by racist violence. Stanley Levison hailed the emergence of new political "forces from all faiths and classes." That evening, three Unitarian ministers were beaten by whites in Selma; Rev. James Reeb of Boston died two days later. The Selma movement had one black and one white martyr, later to be joined by Viola Liuzzo, a thirty-nine-year-old white mother of five from Detroit murdered in her car on a rural Alabama road. Faced with Federal Judge Frank Johnson's injunction against a Selma to Montgomery march, under pressure from the administration, King on March 9 secretly agreed to stage a march, pray, and turn back from another confrontation at the Pettis Bridge. SNCC and local militants had prepared for a real march to Montgomery and felt King betrayed them again by making secret and unilateral decisions. But Bloody Sunday triggered a wave of sympathy demonstrations: 10,000 marched in Detroit behind King, Walter Reuther, the mayor, and the governor; 15,000 marched in Harlem, where 200 Catholic nuns stood out in a sea of black faces. The outpouring of clerical and union support was unprecedented. On March 15, the president announced his voting rights legislation on national television, identifying himself with the movement by proclaiming, "We shall overcome." The act would empower the attorney general to suspend literacy and other voting tests and authorize federal registrars to register voters in any state or county where less than half the voting-age population had been registered voters on November

1, 1964. Judge Johnson cleared the way for a march on March 21, and Lyndon Johnson federalized the Alabama National Guard to protect the marchers. Fruitlessly, Wallace begged Johnson to stop "street revolutionaries" from marching all over his capitol. "You can never satisfy them," he complained. "First it's a front seat on the bus. Next it's a takeover of parks. Then it's public schools. Then it's voting rights. Then it's jobs. Then it's distribution of wealth without work."[8] If the movement started an avalanche, how far down the slope would white supremacy slide?

Though universally framed as a voting rights march, the march to Montgomery was also a march against poverty. On March 21, as King led marchers across the Edmund Pettis Bridge, he repeated his rationale for demonstrations. "Negroes don't have much," because "the system" denied them education and cast them into "the long night of poverty." Negroes could only act with what they had: "our bodies, our feet, and our souls." Along the way, King came upon a broken-down church with holes in the roof and broken windows. "That's why we're marching!" he exclaimed. Over 300 people, including politicians, educators, and celebrities, completed the march. Over 30,000 people joined them at a rally at the capitol on March 25. Flanked by civil rights leaders and celebrities, King praised the outpouring of clerical and lay support, hailing Johnson's address as "one of the most passionate pleas for human rights ever made by a President." He chastised southern leaders who "segregated Southern money from the poor whites . . . segregated Southern mores from the rich whites . . . segregated Southern minds from honest thinking, [and] segregated the Negro from everything." In phrases he had penned the previous summer and often repeated, King summoned the nation to march for the American dream.

Let us march on segregated housing until every ghetto of social and economic oppression is dissolved and Negroes and whites live side by side in decent, safe and sanitary housing. Let us march on segregated schools until every vestige of segregated and inferior education becomes a thing of the past . . . let us march on poverty until no American parent has to skip a meal so that their children may eat . . . march on poverty, until no work-starved man walks the streets of our cities and towns in search of jobs that do not exist.[9]

King had part of his chart and his compass, but where was his north star?

Work remained to be done in the South, King wrote in March in his annual report to the *Nation.* Civil rights and antipoverty legislation fused "economic measures with civil rights needs." Title VI of the Civil Rights Act, which denied federal money to governments and corporations that discriminated against Negroes, was potentially "revolutionary." Working side by side with blacks, whites might discover that paltry advantages of racial status obscured their common economic exploitation. Businessmen valuing the good image of civic order more than segregation had hitherto been the movement's allies. Now there were millions of potential "white Southern allies among the rural and urban poor" who might join with blacks to topple all forms of exploitation. "To climb the economic ladder, Negro and white will have to steady it together, or both will fail." Would whites see the value in interracial political organizing or cling to their economic and status advantages?[10] King's prophetic vision of interracial emancipation hinged on the consciousness and actions of white workers, business elites, and the middle class of the new South. One thing was clear: without black voting, enforcement of any legislation would be seriously weakened. The movement had won one of its largest legislative victories. Could it be implemented?

The "State of the Race" and Strategies for Change

The debate over the future of the black movement had been roiling for months. In January 1965, announcing that the movement had reached a "crisis of victory," A. Philip Randolph convened a conference he called "The State of the Race," in New York City. A remarkable assembly of African American men and women debated whether black inclusion in American life would require revolutionary changes in American society, whether it was even desirable to "assimilate" into white middle-class norms and spaces, and what tactics were needed to realize black equality and freedom. Civil rights, Randolph argued, would never be secure without complete freedom from unemployment, poverty, ignorance, disease, fear, racial bias, religious bigotry, and war. To achieve all these together demanded "basic structural changes" in American society. But whites were abandoning the movement, thinking its goals achieved, admonishing blacks they must now earn their way into full equality. And movement energies were flagging, just like in the 1940s when big labor "lost its evangelism" and gave up the fight to organize the "Jim Crow, underclass black laboring masses." A gulf was widening between "the Negro masses and Negro classes." Underclass blacks were being seduced by "rabble rousers spitting fire and brimstone of Black nationalism." Mass Negro unemployment would not be alleviated simply by opening up trade union apprenticeship programs or even by full enforcement of Title VII of the Civil Rights Act against discriminating corporations. The black movement must hijack the War on Poverty, backed by a broad coalition of black and white workers, unemployed and poor people, and traditional civil rights, church, and labor forces. Only then could they forge a new consensus for federal housing, education, job, and income programs. Randolph endorsed "massive demonstrations" to supplement black voting.

The NAACP's Roy Wilkins objected to Randolph's call for basic structural change, arguing that enforcement of the Civil Rights Act presented real potential for economic change. Whitney Young touted his Marshall Plan for the Negro, calling for full employment through "extraordinary, emergency action" by business, labor, and government. Andrew Young criticized the goal of "assimilation into white society," supporting Randolph's strategy of mobilizing the masses where voter registration had failed. James Forman attacked the civil rights leadership for assuming that blacks should leave their communities and integrate into "middle-class American life." "The movement must now meet the black poor on their own terms," he argued. George Wiley, moving from CORE to found the Poverty Rights Action Center, advocated community organizing for political power. Cleveland Robinson of District 65 wanted to put massive pressure on the administration to raise the minimum wage and extend it to seventeen million uncovered workers.

Bayard Rustin was the most programmatically concrete as he elaborated on the Triple Revolution analysis and the Clark committee's proposals. Questioning what a war on poverty that spent only 27 cents per poor person per year could accomplish, he called for $5 billion a year for public works to employ the poor in building schools, hospitals, and community centers. He called for massive voter registration in the South, enforcement of Title VII, restraints on police brutality, and a new civil rights focus on "employment, housing, and education." He called for repealing the restrictive right to work section 14b of the Taft-Hartley Act, and for raising and extending the minimum wage. Rustin also voiced new demands: integration of the brand-new Medicare and Medicaid programs into "a national health plan," and involvement of black and white poor in the War on Poverty "decision–making process."

With so many issues on the table, no one debated at any depth the real political challenges of building a grand alliance that might realign the South and the nation. Rustin repeated his vision of "politics" that focused on building coalitions behind a full employment agenda. Most concretely, he spoke to the widening gulf between the social democrats and militant actionists in SNCC and CORE, whom he pejoratively labeled the "spontaneous left." Sharing their revolutionary goals, Rustin excoriated their presumed rejection of coalitions in favor of a fantasy politics of guerrilla warfare or the dream of a "revolutionary upsurge of the black and white poor against the whole society." He followed up in February with his famous essay in *Commentary*, "From Protest to Politics," arguing that the movement had entered a "revolutionary" phase requiring a "qualitative transformation of fundamental institutions" to realize "full employment, the abolition of slums, the reconstruction of our educational system, and new definitions of work and leisure." He did not propose how to reconcile the movement's divergent strategies or attract specific allies.[11]

Writing to King, Levison sharply disagreed with the idea that the civil rights coalition could be made "revolutionary." It was "militant only against shocking violence," revolutionary only in its dreams of ousting a reactionary southern agrarian elite. Any northern movement could only work through "reform," improving slum conditions and offering Negroes "security and opportunity." The freedom movement could not overthrow elites controlling the "mechanisms of power," Levison insisted. Americans simply would not "change their society in order to free the Negro." Levison implored King to be realistic about the organization's liberal funding base, accurately predicting steep declines in contributions "as SCLC bites deeper below the skin" of privileged whites. The FBI's presumed Communist puppet master was a moderating influence on King. Willing to risk losing influential "friends," King insisted on a more thorough revolution in values and social structure. Despite their emerging differences, however, King, Rustin, and Levison were convinced that the public sector must expand to carry the freedom struggle forward.[12]

White radical allies thought the moment ripe for forming revolutionary class-based coalitions. Harry G. Boyte, director of Operation Dialogue, a small SCLC program charged with opening interracial discussion in the South, caught well the post-Selma mood of expansive rights consciousness in one of his speeches: "Ladies and Gentlemen, I am preaching revolution! . . . There is a relationship between the well-stocked cupboards and the gleaming refrigerators, and the millions of kitchens offering only the emptiness of poverty. . . . The first function of government in this blindingly rich country is to see to it that everyone has a decent income. . . . The Civil Rights movement is becoming a Human Rights movement in this country." In Louisville, Anne Braden of the Southern Conference Educational Fund was thrilled that the freedom struggle she thought had begun with individualistic middle-class aspirations was now addressing poverty, low wages, "exploitation," and power. But Braden feared Johnson's War on Poverty might co-opt and localize an incipient socialist movement that might otherwise connect national agendas and local constituencies. Students could not expect to "start from scratch" and simply build local "pockets of power" along with grassroots people. Activists still lacked a socialist vision of national economic planning and a strategy that went beyond organizing local people for control over the vaguely defined "decisions that affect their lives." Many black activists in fact knew Johnson was sending them into an antipoverty battle "to fight an enemy army with a pea-shooter,"

Braden wrote. "Tutorial programs in the slums, day nurseries for working mothers, youth programs designed to combat juvenile delinquency" were all drawing activists' energies but would not be enough, she wrote. In February, Julian Bond ran in the Democratic primary to represent black Atlantans in the Georgia House of Representatives, discovering from local blacks "that their problems were largely economic." Bond's platform called for "a two dollar minimum wage, improved urban renewal programs, repeal of the right to work law, and an end to literacy tests for voters." He won the general election in June.[13] But Braden still worried about the future of southern socialism.

Whitney Young would have been happy with a democratic future, as he voiced his anxieties at the Institute for Policy Studies in April. Above all Young feared a regressive "alliance between the Midwest farm belt, the racist of the old South," and northern suburbanites. Young thought their defense of racially exclusive neighborhoods caused them to "cry violence in the streets" and to redouble their efforts to "segregate Negroes in hard-core cities." To avert this catastrophe, Young insisted Negroes must consolidate their political power and not allow political apathy or lack of education to replace the racist cops standing between them and full citizenship. But where should Negroes try to redraw the future electoral map of America?[14] Young did not specify.

In April, after debating its own direction, SCLC decided to continue its focus on southern voting rights and to make a massive new investment in northern protest and political organizing. Andrew Young advocated moving "very shortly into the North," where millions of ghetto blacks needed relief from "desperation and poverty." Rustin adamantly opposed the move north, arguing that SCLC should lobby for his national antipoverty proposals and commence a major voter registration effort in the South. L. D. Reddick recommended SCLC have a permanent representative in Washington to ensure black activists were "thoroughly integrated in decision making with regard to contracts for the war on poverty." Boston affiliate Virgil Wood added that "we want to go on record that the poor would have the main say-so on what will be done in the area of poverty." This became King's vital concern when Los Angeles exploded in violence that summer, just days after King had fruitlessly tried to uncork War on Poverty funding bottled up in the mayor's office. Wrestling with the dilemmas of local mobilization and national policy, King marched into a future shrouded in impenetrable uncertainties.[15]

The Elusive Promise of a Negro-Labor Alliance

After Selma, King might have followed up on C. T. Vivian's promise to strengthen the Negro-labor alliance through support for workplace organizing. King repeatedly invited labor to join the war against poverty, organize the unorganized, realign southern politics, and build a national constituency for social democracy. But workplace organizing yielded to more urgent commitments. King remained a mobilizer, hoping to use dramatic protest to shape the national policy agenda. Securing the vote, supporting southern relief and economic development, skirmishing within the War on Poverty, lobbying the president, desegregating education and housing, and developing northern action alternatives to rioting all presented more compelling challenges. FBI harassment and defamation took a toll, as King continued his traditional duties as SCLC fund-raiser. Soon, the Vietnam War became an urgent priority, drawing King into risky protest alliances.

Between the 1964 Scripto strike and the 1968 Memphis sanitation workers strike, King put little discernible time into workplace organizing and lobbying for the repeal of section 14b of the Taft-Hartley Act. Many labor unions, most egregiously the conservative AFL building trades, perpetuated the racial exclusions and structures of power against which black workers felt compelled to struggle. After a moment of comity and optimism in 1964, when George Meany rhetorically committed the AFL-CIO to an ambitious civil rights program, black rights organizations increasingly found AFL-CIO practices stubbornly resistant to change. The men who had battled the Communists in the 1940s continued to resist the demands of blacks and other minorities for access to jobs and representation in union hierarchies. In 1965, the NAACP criticized as "less than token" the AFL-CIO's progress toward inclusion of blacks. Unions still used qualifying tests to exclude blacks, who still climbed separate racial seniority ladders. In San Francisco, unionists even subverted a jobs agreement between civil rights activists and hotel employers. NALC president A. Philip Randolph grew sanguine, as the NAACP and EEOC increasingly charged AFL-CIO affiliate unions with stubbornly upholding white privilege. In 1966, the Civil Rights Commission discovered that Cleveland Local 38 of the International Brotherhood of Electrical Workers had a total membership of 1,258, and no Negro members. Randolph retired in June 1966 to lead the A. Philip Randolph Institute, which was funded by the AFL-CIO, and became less and less critical of racist labor practices. Randolph and Rustin increasingly turned their energies to formulating policy alternatives to the War on Poverty.[16]

With older industrial unions hemorrhaging members, public employee unionism surged as teachers, hospital workers, and municipal and state employees organized, many of whom were people of color. Even then, the proportion of American workers in unions declined from 30 percent in 1962 to 29 percent in 1973. Union political clout in the Democratic Party declined even faster. No longer were unionists the vanguard of social policy change. Unwilling to criticize the centrist economic and cold war foreign policies of Kennedy or Johnson, labor could not translate the increased worker militancy of 1964 into policy change or increased workplace power. The crucial missed opportunity and the measure of labor's declining political influence was their failure to repeal section 14b of Taft-Hartley in 1964, permitting states to outlaw the union shop. Repeal passed the House of Representatives, but neither Johnson nor Senate Democrats were willing to spend any political capital to challenge the inevitable southern filibuster.[17]

Cleveland Robinson continually reminded King of interracial unionism, and King always welcomed union support, especially in 1966 in Chicago. But King remained ambivalent toward labor and unwilling to spend time or resources supporting local union organizing. Robinson's efforts to focus King on the interracial populist strategy rarely succeeded beyond King's making speeches to labor gatherings and accepting their contributions. King spoke to the NALC convention in May 1965. "Call it democracy, or call it democratic socialism, but there must be a better distribution of wealth within this country for all God's children," King told the delegates. It was King's most open declaration of his democratic socialism to date. But King did not act upon the strategic vision shoulder to shoulder with labor until 1968, when a powerful alliance between sanitation workers and a united black community in Memphis drew King into their struggle.[18]

Robinson invited King to join in organizing 4,000 mostly black and Puerto Rican department store workers in New York that summer, but King was busy with his northern tour of ghettos. Neither did King join in the organizing efforts of the retail and department store workers in Alabama or the Deep South. By year's end, 3,000 new workers had won higher wages, vacations, and benefits. In Selma, 57 grocery store employees unionized, and 300 workers in Greensboro near Selma overwhelmingly voted to unionize a poultry plant. They staged their own voting rights marches, braved KKK terror tactics, and defied the company when management called in state troopers to intimidate organizers. But in Selma, RWDSU lost an election by one vote at a Coca-Cola bottling plant on August 18 after relentless company "intimidation." Robinson had asked for King's help, but King was putting out political fires in Watts, Los Angeles.[19]

In July, Robinson warned King that SCLC would need a stronger labor alliance when they confronted the "heart of the problem": "the stranglehold which the economic power structure has on the great masses of the people." If unions and civil rights forces were going to join the War on Poverty, they must fight employers who exploited and paid their workers poverty wages. The class coalition would need financial support from union war chests when

SCLC's funding dried up "from sources who must now be attacked" in the middle class, Robinson pointedly warned. King went so far as to write UAW president Walter Reuther later that month, calling for support in training southern organizers to "bring Unions into every sphere of labor activity here in the South." But that was where their collaboration ended. King got no news coverage organizing southern laundry workers, he once cryptically mentioned to Levison. More important, white workers made it an unpropitious time for a southern populist alliance. Southern white rank and file unionists increasingly embraced George Wallace in defiance of the AFL-CIO leadership, who almost alone remained loyal to Lyndon Johnson. Liberals on the Alabama AFL-CIO Committee on Public Education saw all but one of the Johnson loyalists they endorsed in the 1964 elections go down to defeat. Disaffiliations by local unions almost bankrupted the Alabama state AFL-CIO Council. Mainstream labor proved unyielding as the civil rights movement challenged white monopolies in northern employment and housing.[20]

King spoke often to the house of labor, soliciting support and urging a fuller commitment to desegregation of work and neighborhood. But as Cesar Chavez and the United Farm Workers organized thousands of migrant workers in California's Central Valley in 1965 and 1966, King only sent Chavez an inspiring telegram: "The fight for equality must be fought in the urban slums, in the sweat shops of the factories and fields. Our separate struggles are really one, a struggle for freedom, for dignity and for humanity." When 1,200 Mississippi sharecroppers from eight Delta counties formed the Mississippi Freedom Labor Union, they lost a bitter strike, unsupported by liberals, the AFL-CIO, or King.[21]

King increasingly criticized labor's lack of commitment to the War on Poverty. Labor boldly created the 1930s "anti-poverty fight," King told the Illinois AFL-CIO in October 1965, but now Washington ran the whole war. Labor was morally stagnant, privileged, complacent, and even regressive, King charged. Only the civil rights movement had dynamism and "profound moral appeal" as it pursued "basic democratic reforms." Labor's participation was essential if the War on Poverty were not to wither on the vine for lack of constituent support. With District 65 in New York in September, King charged that labor leaders had acted like Birmingham's white clergy, "moderates in a struggle for social justice." Church and middle-class support had actually been more reliable. With diminishing ranks, labor's very survival now depended on its ties to "a vibrant, dynamic social movement" composed of "the unemployed, the aged and elements of the church world." Appealing to class interests and resentments, King argued that massive public works did "more to abolish poverty than tax cuts that ultimately benefit the middle class and rich."[22]

After becoming NALC president in 1966, Robinson tried to enlist King in organizing workers "in the service and light manufacturing sectors" to raise their wages to $100 a week. He and King joined progressive unionists in opposing the war, but the war proved more divisive and destructive of a black-labor alliance. After King's assassination in Memphis, Robinson reflected, "In the past we looked to the labor movement for support; today we must see labor and labor must see us as partners and allies in the struggle to bring radical and immediate change, economically and socially to the millions in our nation who are living in abject poverty amidst unprecedented affluence." SCLC must finally be "an active partner wherever called upon by unions for the organization of the oppressed workers. . . . *Especially is this critical in the organization of Black workers in the South.*" King and labor won several signal victories together, but the Negro-labor coalition proved less solid than King's alliances across class lines, which he judged best pursued through strategies of protest, voting, and policy advocacy.[23]

Voting Rights, Poverty Politics, and Reprisals in the South

Voting rights activism and the implementation of the Voting Rights Act brought a dramatic expansion in black voter registration between 1965 and 1969 across the South, from 35.5 percent to 64.8 percent. Black registration lagged twenty points behind white, however, as the Justice Department sent far fewer federal registrars than were needed into southern counties. Southern elites resorted to stratagems to discourage or dilute black votes, especially the gerrymandering of districts.[24] Even after federal registrars arrived in Alabama, a rash of white reprisals proved that white economic power could still stifle black participation. It was a vicious circle. The vote was crucial to equal employment, civil rights protections, and full participation in the War on Poverty, but white economic power could be an insuperable obstacle to black voting. Black economic autonomy and access to federal antipoverty dollars proved essential to protecting the right to vote.

The Selma campaign left a wake of economic devastation that pushed SCLC into the politics of relief and the local implementation of the War on Poverty to bolster voting rights still under siege. Reprisals were worse after the Voting Rights Act as whites desperately tried to hold onto political power, Septima Clark informed King. Clark's project had registered 7,002 voters in advance of the arrival of federal registrars. The Citizen Education Project had

150 schools in and around Selma. But local people paid dearly. "In Selma, any-body who came to our meeting lost their job. Fifty or more did," Clark wrote. King sent money for groceries. "In addition to the usual expenses we have met such costs as hospital bills and emergency aid to people fired from their jobs," King reported in the *Amsterdam News.* The Selma Emergency Relief Fund Ser-vice appealed nationally in King's name for "immediate assistance" for victims of reprisals across the black belt. Unable to find alternative work, denied wel-fare and Social Security, people were besieging leaders of the Dallas County Voters League. Visits to poor people's homes uncovered widespread malnutri-tion, substandard housing, and arbitrary terminations of welfare for poor blacks who attempted to register.[25]

King and SCLC called on the public to boycott anything produced in Ala-bama, and on trade unions to refuse to transport or use Alabama products. If reprisals continued, *"the voting bill itself will be the great danger to the economic security of the Negro,"* he wrote, demanding recognition of voting rights and protection from police brutality. Already African Americans were being excluded from the "central structure" of the nation's "'nobly initiated' anti-poverty program." King demanded the federal government use its financial leverage under Title VI to stop manifold local rights violations. Over two hun-dred household heads in Selma had been fired and King charged the White Citizens' Council with coordinating an economic campaign "designed to drive Negroes out of the South and into the Northern ghetto." The boycott proposal met with widespread criticism however. Levison blamed it on strategically naive SNCC militants. King announced that Alabama Negroes were ready to suffer for justice, but a Birmingham organizer from the electrical workers declared that the economic losses would "crucify our own members." By the end of April, SCLC had abandoned the idea.[26]

Relief funds poured in from around the country, but Randolph Blackwell, SCLC's program director, found Selma's voluntary plan ineffective. Economic development and self-help employment, not simple relief, was this Ph.D. economist's principal concern, as he made clear to the middle-class Voters League. Blackwell advocated cooperatives supported by the poverty program, writing King that poverty and dependency could not be addressed until blacks voted, "and even then we would need real involvement of the federal govern-ment." Blackwell recommended that SCLC provide seed capital for a coopera-tive silk-screening business that would train and employ local poor blacks. Though his concerns were intensely local, Blackwell and SCLC staff in Ala-bama broke ground for economic development through housing and produc-ers cooperatives and fostered new black leaders in Alabama.[27]

In October 1964 the Office of Economic Opportunity opened for business, and skirmishing for the soul and control of the War on Poverty immediately began. In most locales, public officials initiated Community Action agencies and minimized the participation of the poor by centralizing control and stacking the governing poverty boards with political appointees. For several months OEO actually withheld funding from proposals that made inadequate provision for poor people's participation. But in early 1965, the U.S. Conference of Mayors pressured the administration to stop subsidizing experiments in independent local organizing. By the fall, major proponents of poor people's participation such as Richard Boone were forced out of OEO. Johnson acceded to a gubernatorial veto on local programs, and in 1967 Congress explicitly prohibited voter registration in federal antipoverty programs. The movement's time-tested tools for fighting racism would not be acceptable to combat racialized poverty under government auspices. Congress increasingly mandated the programs that local community action agencies could run, limiting local options to the "national emphasis programs," such as Head Start, that showed little taint of political mobilization. Community action in the War on Poverty settled back into traditional client-bureaucrat forms of service provision and was forced to accommodate to political and bureaucratic elites.[28]

King's early charges that the War on Poverty was being captured by the power structure in Alabama were soon echoed across the South. NAACP regional director Ruby Hurley complained in the spring that middle-class blacks had been appointed to Community Action Committees who did not represent the black community. As the historian Susan Ashmore has detailed, eventually SCLC "managed to bear some fruit" in Alabama, by the spring of 1966 working through OEO Title II programs in seven black belt counties: Dallas, Greene, Butler, Hale, Marengo, Perry, and Wilcox. But for every small victory there was a large defeat. In March 1965, the OEO Inspection Division reported that the CAPs in Alabama "produced tokenism: one or two safe Negroes on a board, or parallel Negro subcommittees that meet to approve the minutes of the main board." Selma's mayor simply appointed the CAP board. With the help of OEO, state officials merged majority black and majority white counties into white-controlled area committees, thwarting black-controlled initiatives at the county level. Area 11 was headed by White Citizens' Council leader Victor Poole. "If we let them [elect] their own representatives, they will pick the same ones who led those riots," explained Marion mayor R. Leigh Peagues, In April, the SCLC board protested that OEO had approved and funded southern antipoverty programs that "discriminate against Negroes and provide only token participation" of blacks and poor people's representatives on local boards. Congress must insist on nondiscrimination in local programs and remove or limit the "veto power of Governors" who were hostile to black-initiated poverty projects, they insisted. OEO director Sargent Shriver dashed off a note to King, citing statistics on black employment and representation on local CAP governing boards. But King knew that ethnic bodies sitting on boards controlled by whites did not translate into substantive representation. That took independent organizing.[29]

Flush with donations following the highly publicized Selma protests, SCLC initiated the Summer Community Organization and Political Education program (SCOPE). Under the direction of Hosea Williams, SCOPE put nearly five hundred student volunteers into almost fifty counties across the Deep South. SCOPE architects hoped to mobilize working-class and poor blacks through voter registration, community organization, and adult education, training them to win federal antipoverty money in defiance of the "white power structure." King publicized SCOPE's ambition to mount a "coordinated attack on the three basic problems of the South . . . disfranchisement, educational deprivation, and poverty." In Dallas, Butler, and Wilcox counties, where Negroes made up 70 percent of the voting-age population, black voting would mean black control of poverty programs, King explained.[30]

SCOPE's community-level organizing was short-lived, and the project became embroiled in controversy, as Blackwell charged Williams with corruption and ineffectiveness. Williams defended himself, reporting that SCLC activists had supported a union of maids and registered voters in four counties. But the deeper problem was that too many SCLC ministers preferred dramatic protest over organizing local democratic institutions. King lectured the field staff that they might be "shacking with the community" but would never marry it, James Orange recalled. Nevertheless, SCLC field staffers continued registering voters after the summer. Albert Turner led a team of fifteen organizers where SCOPE left off and reported steady progress: "285 registered in three days in Barbour County . . . 10,000 to date in Dallas County, and 1,277 for the month in Montgomery."[31]

The Citizenship Education Program organizers were more effective because they began with poor people's own experiences and aspirations and furnished them with the tools necessary to understand and change their situation. By late 1964, Dorothy Cotton, Andrew Young, Septima Clark, and Bernice Robinson were plotting "new directions" that would involve CEP students in "planning in the war on poverty." Political education, community organizing, training in direct action, and agitating for expanded government funding all formed part of a curriculum of "social change," Young informed the Field Foundation. Clark later estimated that between 1957 and 1970 the program had established 897 schools, trained 10,000 teachers, and played a key role in getting 700,000 black voters registered.[32]

Thousands of CEP students and their parents suffered economic reprisals, Clark reported, alleging that whites were consciously pushing blacks out
of the South. But blacks were determined to stay and fight "for their freedom
to share in the economic power structure." Literacy tests, "loss of jobs, fore-
closure of mortgages," and even bombings would not deter them. Alabama,
Louisiana, and Mississippi had the highest numbers of "destitute impoverished people" and not coincidentally the lowest rates of registration, she
explained. CEP programs expanded from reading and writing to encompass
"Implementation of the Civil Rights Bill, Negro History, Planned Parenthood
and Federally Assisted Programs." Students widely discussed the economics of
automation and unemployment, Clark reported. "New problems" called for
new policies and resources from foundations and the government.[33]

King involved himself in Blackwell's efforts to foster economic development for activists suffering reprisals in Crawfordville, Georgia. Whites fired
scores of blacks after voting rights and school desegregation protests rocked
the small town. White officials closed the Head Start center and threatened to
close the high school. King arrived after two weeks of demonstrations, promising that Crawfordville would be the "Birmingham and Selma of integrated
education." He praised local people who, despite the "hardship of the rural
south," joined the freedom struggle, and he promised support for those fired
from their "meager jobs." Federal judges issued a desegregation order and
demonstrations halted. CEP staff educated local blacks in how to apply for
antipoverty funds. Blackwell raised money from liberal and church groups to
launch a cooperative silk-screening business. When they ran into financial
problems the next spring, he demanded that SCLC not abandon local blacks
who were impoverished because they acted with SCLC's encouragement. Such
projects were vital in preventing "an exodus to urban ghettos" where blacks
became candidates for "welfare and massive unemployment," Blackwell passionately argued. King praised the enterprise, but SCLC's commitment faltered
as finances dried up.[34]

Crawfordville Enterprises failed after only six months, but Blackwell
revived it in September 1966 after he left SCLC to direct Southern Rural
Action, which was funded by the UAW, private foundations, and OEO. Begun
with $10,000 in capital, the enterprise employed 108 people by the end of 1968,
had a payroll of nearly $100,000, and had raised the weekly income of many
black women from only $15 to an average of $64. It also inspired other successful rural enterprises, Blackwell boasted.[35] SCLC had not stayed in Crawfordville. By July 1965 King had already turned his attention and the resources of
SCLC northward.

As with labor organizing, southern voting rights remained one of King's concerns. But it could not compete with the urban crisis, the War on Poverty, the black power controversy, or the Vietnam War. In print and before SCLC, King noted steady advances in southern voting, but criticized the Johnson administration's "restraint and caution." The Voting Rights Act applied to over 500 southern counties, but six months after its passage, "only 37 counties had received federal registrars," King protested in March 1966. King barely mentioned the Voting Rights Act in his 1967 book *Where Do We Go from Here?* criticizing the administration's "halfhearted implementation." The most thorough critique appeared posthumously under King's name in an essay otherwise preoccupied with war, riots, unemployment, and poverty. By 1968, 900 counties had become eligible for federal referees, but 842 remained "essentially just as they were before the March on Selma."[36] Many SCLC affiliates and the CEP continued to work on voting, but when King decided to "put power before programs," local voting programs gave way to planning for a massive march on Washington.

Poverty Politics and the Urban Crisis

During the summer of 1965, King scouted northern cities, searching for a key to the ghetto, an entry point into a multicelled prison of institutional and economic oppression. King reasoned back in March that street demonstrations that had revealed the "crude fascism" of the Southern social order would not work in the North. "However, rent strikes, school boycotts, electoral alliances summon substantial support from Negroes" and successfully dramatize local grievances, he wrote in the *Nation*. But failing to find effective levers of local and national power, King returned to strategies of street protest in August 1966. King's leadership and SCLC's movement culture and income depended on nonviolent demonstrations and national media exposure. For over a year they searched through cells of what Kenneth Clark called the "Dark Ghetto" before marching on white neighborhoods in Chicago. In the end, "marching feet" remained essential political weapons in the black poor's own war against poverty.[37]

King went on "people to people" tours of Boston, Chicago, Los Angeles, and Philadelphia that summer. Most of his advisors—Jones, Williams, Blackwell, and Rustin—opposed the move north, but King forged ahead with enthusiastic support from Andrew Young and James Bevel. The NAACP regarded King's northern expedition as a threat. Gloster Current warned local branches that the King "Juggernaut" might undermine the NAACP's working relationships with city and state officials. The "white heat of publicity" worked fine where southern activists confronted "an inflexible white power structure, a hostile local press, stupid police officials, and little or no Negro power." Not so the North, he argued. With resistance mounting, King searched for an appropriate urban stage. In August on *Face the Nation,* King threatened a "massive march on Washington" for D.C. home rule. He considered joining a Pittsburgh coalition challenging discriminatory building trades unions as part of an "economic freedom" campaign of picketing and protest. Congressman Adam Clayton Powell made it crystal clear that King was not welcome in Harlem. As Powell maintained an iron grip on Harlem's antipoverty program, his House Committee on Education and Labor exposed how political elites subverted "maximum feasible participation" across the country. Powell's committee and King converged in Los Angeles, where a battle was breaking out within the war against poverty.[38]

King in fact briefly considered Los Angeles as a site for a campaign supporting neighborhood activists in their fight for control of the local CAP. Mayor Sam Yorty had appointed a nineteen-member Youth Opportunities Board, which had not yet spent two-thirds of $29 million OEO had awarded a full year earlier. The independent Community Antipoverty Committee, a coalition of labor, African American, and Mexican American community groups, demanded a more democratic thirty-two-person board. Half must come from twelve designated poverty areas, they demanded, and the other half could represent the city, school board, and voluntary agencies. Democratic congressman Augustus Hawkins from south Los Angeles and OEO supported the coalition. Local people read the law and insisted on involvement, Hawkins recalled, then "public officials began to wake up" and decided community action was dangerous. At local hearings of Powell's committee, neighborhood activists accused downtown politicians of using federal patronage to build a political machine. Yorty's Youth Opportunities Board handpicked city officials and compliant ministers to serve on neighborhood poverty committees, treating Watts residents as "thoughtless, voiceless, irresponsible agitators," complained Shirley Taylor of the United Neighborhood Organization for Watts. Reverend Logan from Willowbrook testified to loud applause that jobless men were already "at war" and getting no help from the War on Poverty. Neither Head Start nor Youth Opportunities helped breadwinner fathers, whose own children looked down on them when they "don't bring in nothing." From Venice Beach, Bob Castile reported widespread disgust in his poor neighborhood with "school pushouts." Police arbitrarily arrested people, held them indeterminately without charges, and neglected real crime victims. Why couldn't the War on Poverty even provide streetlights?[39]

King arrived in Los Angeles on July 10, announcing on the radio that Yorty's poverty program would fail dismally if it excluded "the victims of poverty" from policymaking. Uneducated and poor people had "basic intelligence" and a competent understanding of what made them poor, King attested. Los Angeles blacks could organize around myriad issues, he thought: school segregation, job discrimination and unemployment, and housing discrimination, an issue that especially inflamed black resentments. Despite King's public criticism the year before, California's whites had overwhelmingly voted for Proposition 14, which repealed the state's fair housing law. But in Los Angeles, King said, the most urgent issue was poverty and the allocation of federal money. He hoped it would not become "a political football," but of course it already was.[40] King might have joined the War on Poverty in Los Angeles; instead, on August 11, a war broke out between the city and its poor.

The Watts rebellion quickly followed the passage of the Voting Rights Act. By the time the Los Angeles Police Department (LAPD) and National Guard suppressed the revolt, 34 people were dead, 900 had been injured, and 3,500 had been arrested. Now more than ever it was obvious to King that civil rights gains were irrelevant to the economic needs and racial resentments of big-city blacks. The chasm separating the black poor from the black middle class was almost as great as the chasm separating them from whites in the suburbs. This realization hardly constituted the revelation that Rustin imputed to King at this moment. But King felt even more urgently the need to redress the grievances of northern ghettos if the movement were to remain nonviolent.[41]

The Watts uprising was a class revolt, a commodity riot, and a racial rebellion against the "occupying forces" of the police. Angered by a drunk driving arrest by the notoriously violent LAPD, blacks started a looting spree, soon joined by whites and Latinos. Blacks attacked police and beat ordinary whites whom they dragged from their cars. As political elites and civil rights leaders assessed the riot's causes, antipoverty politics and backlash politics polarized the debate. Rioters called it "a chance to get even with the power structure." Many blacks and liberals blamed it on Yorty's indifference to the democratic voice of the poor, while Yorty blamed OEO and the activists. He denied his police had anything to do with provoking violence.[42] New York senator Robert Kennedy blamed ghetto conditions and middle-class black machine politicians who cynically traded black votes for patronage. For ghetto blacks, Kennedy stated, the "law was the enemy." California governor Edmund G. Brown denied that the uprising had anything in common with civil rights protests. "The riot took place in a scene of broken families and broken hearts, of lonely children and aimless adults, of frustration and poverty," he said, promising $1.7 million in antipoverty money to employ poor people in a cleanup operation. Brown did not mention the long history of police-community conflict. Congressman Hawkins fervently disagreed with Brown's separation of civil rights and ghetto grievances. The "root causes" of discontent in Selma and Los Angeles were nearly identical: police brutality, joblessness, segregated housing, and inferior education.[43]

King arrived and departed Los Angeles favoring the same socioeconomic reading of the violence he had the year before in Harlem. Watts underscored the urgency of addressing the gap between the "haves and the have-nots" and the need to listen to poor people themselves. King felt compelled to voice the grievances of the urban masses and channel their protest energies in nonviolent, integrationist directions before they embraced violence or nationalism. But the Watts riot and King's subsequent immersion in urban movements started a process of social learning about the realities of black powerlessness that moved him from Rustin's views toward those of Clarence Jones and Jesse Gray. King left Los Angeles with a deeper sense of the intransigence of city hall and the centrality of endemic police violence to African American community grievances. At the national level, however, he was not yet ready to confront police brutality as a primary issue in poor people's own war on poverty.

King arrived sounding ministerial, playing to a national middle-class constituency disposed to blame the rioters and vindicate the police. He promised to "redeem" the rioters to help them become useful citizens in a democracy of equals, urging officials to give them the chance to "repair the damage" they had wreaked upon the now smoldering city. Denying that civil rights protests had produced the violence, King nevertheless assigned collective responsibility, declaring that "none of us in this great country has done enough to remove injustice." Whites and Negroes committed to nonviolence were equally "dismayed, deeply hurt and bewildered." Dozens of whites wrote to King demanding he put an end to riots and guide his people toward constructive self-improvement. Many blamed him for the violence, citing a declining respect for law that King's methods encouraged. An angry woman wrote that blacks who for years heard King tell them "how mistreated they were [now] looted and burned their own businesses, stabbed their own neighbors and set their own homes ablaze." An avowed voting rights supporter from Texas was dismayed that King's incendiary promises to march on poverty had provoked violence. "Stop these stupid riots, marches, etc.," he wrote. King incited violence using divisive "communist's tactics in crying 'Police Brutalities,'" another accused.[44]

King's meetings with local blacks and city officials over the next two days constituted a marathon seminar on urban conflict. The *Los Angeles Times* covered his visit, but his more radical lessons did not make the national news. King preached before five hundred people at the Westminster Neighborhood

Association that "Negroes must join hands" from coast to coast. "And burn!" shouted a heckler. "Get out, psycho!" someone responded, defending King. "We don't need your dreams; we need jobs!" another militant shouted. King promised to persuade Yorty and Police Chief William Parker to visit the ghetto, but the crowd roared with laughter when King admonished them with mock gravity to "be courteous." King reassured Levison on the phone that the vast majority responded enthusiastically to his message of nonviolence. King advocated unity across class and regional lines. "Negro leaders—and I include myself—have failed to take the civil rights movement to the masses of the people," he admitted to reporters. King insisted on a "broadly based" and politically inclusive poverty program "to alleviate economic want." Hire and assign black police to black neighborhoods and promote them to "the precinct captain level," he demanded.[45]

Then King, Rustin, and local civil rights leaders met with Mayor Yorty and Police Chief Parker, demanding a civilian police review panel and conveying blacks' demands for Parker to resign. Yorty complained about "unfounded charges of police brutality" and criticized King for even associating his police with black "lawlessness, killing, looting and burning." Whites would not stand for Chief Parker's resignation. King shot back that Yorty was "insensitive to the social revolution," and demanded he unblock the antipoverty program. King interpreted the uprising as a desperate plea for attention from black youth who felt "alone in their struggle." All they wanted was dignity and work, he asserted. To ignore savage and humiliating police abuses or to portray the uprising as the "result of a criminal element" were dangerous delusions that might lead to an urban "Holocaust." These were among the strongest words King had ever directed toward a public official. Yorty retaliated by denying King access to Lincoln Heights jail. "I don't want to set off a prison riot," he explained. The view that nonviolent protest inevitably provoked violence was one of John Kennedy's core assumptions; now it was increasingly marshaled as a weapon against the War on Poverty itself.[46]

For the press, King chose to highlight the need for jobs; with Lyndon Johnson, he asked for a steadier flow of antipoverty money to the neighborhoods. Watts was a "class revolt of underprivileged against privileged," he asserted upon leaving Los Angeles. For poor blacks who had been "bypassed by the progress of the last decade . . . the main issue is economic." King and Johnson had a long conversation August 20, after which King reported he urged the president to vastly increase government efforts "toward obtaining full employment for both the Negro and white poor." In fact, Johnson did 80 percent of the talking, and King stayed focused on Los Angeles. Negroes there needed immediate "concessions to bring about a sense of hope," King told

Johnson, citing the danger of a "full-scale race war." When Johnson asked for specifics, King replied that Johnson had to get "this poverty program going." Johnson promised immediate action. After the conversation, he commanded Lee White to "move in with money, marbles and chalk," earmarking $25 million for the city's poverty program.

Watts came just after Johnson had narrowly pushed through a scaled-down antipoverty appropriations request in the Senate, he explained to King. "I'm having hell up here with this Congress," he moaned, explaining in addition that the poverty program was "raisin' the dickens in all of these states" where governors were as upset as the mayors with challenges to their authority. Yorty had earlier joined Chicago mayor Daley and the National Mayors Conference in protesting OEO funding for independent neighborhood organizing. Now conservatives were calling for law and order and blaming the violence on OEO and liberal permissiveness. "A man has no more right to destroy property with a Molotov cocktail in Los Angeles than the Ku Klux Klan has to go out and destroy a life," Johnson pontificated. King did not dispute the moral equivalency. Johnson mixed liberal sympathy with lurid pathology discourse: law and order was essential, but "it's no use giving lectures on the law as long as you got rats eating on people's children and the unemployed and no roof over their head and no job to go to and maybe with a dope needle in the one side and a cancer in the other." Johnson was genuinely worried, despairing that all of his reforms would come "to naught if you have a situation like war in the world or a situation in Los Angeles." For now, King was onboard. "The president is sensitive to this problem and is prepared to give us the kind of leadership and vision which we need," King announced. He would soon have harsher things to say about Johnson's leadership.[47]

OEO increasingly directed its disappointingly limited resources toward pacifying troubled urban communities. The War on Poverty became identified with urban blacks, violence, and rising welfare caseloads. Profound media distortions exaggerated the deviance of the urban poor and the amount of money militant urban blacks won from federal and local poverty officials. But conservative politicians like Yorty also made political hay, accusing OEO of inciting "the poor for political purposes" and staging a riot "to publicly strong-arm us into complete submission to federal whims." The War on Poverty raised expectations "beyond any possibility of fulfillment," making violence almost inevitable, he charged. Yorty may have had a point, given the discrepancy between Johnson's rhetoric and the scale of his appropriations. But Yorty's own role in dashing those expectations was widely denounced in the neighborhoods. Augustus Hawkins later drew a "direct connection" between Yorty's obstructionism and the riot. Local people responded enthusiastically to the promise of "maximum feasible participation," but young men grew frustrated with the dearth of "neighborhood youth" and "job training slots." Hawkins lamented how federal officials then turned the War on Poverty into cheap riot insurance. Federal involvement became reactive, seeking to get kids off the streets instead of anticipating problems and initiating "constructive programs, good quality programs, for their own sake."[48] Conservative politicians increasingly blamed urban mayhem on militants and their permissive government sponsors.

King spoke about the despair and alienation of ghetto youth and about their specific political grievances against poverty and the police, but the first riot commission of the 1960s minimized these grievances. Governor Brown appointed a commission headed by former CIA director John McCone to examine the causes of the Watts riot. They characterized rioters as marginal, irrational criminals lashing out in blind fury at the system. The commission concluded that a small minority of Los Angelinos had engaged "in an insensate rage of destruction." Rioters were "the permanent jobless, illiterates and untrained, unemployed and unemployable"—in Marxian terms, the *lumpen-proletariat*. They came from disintegrating families and were victims of militant and "brutal exhortations to violence." The McCone Commission barely mentioned issues of race or police violence. Conceding black grievances, they wrote that news "reports of controversy and bickering" over the poverty program had inflamed their anger, and that they felt "affronted by the passage of proposition 14." Further blaming the media, the commission believed that black people's self-discipline eroded as they watched press coverage of "unpunished violence and disobedience to law." Bayard Rustin later subjected these garbled findings to withering critique. Rioters responded with protest, rebellion, and looting caused by poverty and murderous police violence, which the commission whitewashed as "justifiable homicide," Rustin argued. African Americans were not "affronted" by Proposition 14 but justifiably infuriated that whites in California and Los Angeles "were rushing to reinforce the barriers" confining them to ghettos.[49] Like Lyndon Johnson, the McCone Commission spun its explanations around a wobbly center of gravity that only tilted rightward with continued violence. Official discourse that focused on dope addicts, fatherless families, and rat-bitten children in the "crummiest place in town" became even less politically marketable when those places were pictured as consumed by burning black rage.

Gun sales skyrocketed among California's whites after the uprising. King openly worried about it with Johnson. The day before his and Yorty's tense meeting, Sue Parker, a waitress and single mother living on the edge of Watts, fearing "riot violence," hid a loaded pistol in her kitchen. As she slept, her three-year-old son, Steven, discovered this new toy, peered down its barrel, and pulled the trigger. He was not listed among the thirty-four officially dead in the Watts riot.⁵⁰

King had long spoken of the human rights revolution sweeping the globe and its affinity with the civil rights movement. Watts lent urgency to King's plans for a northern crusade and injected new militancy into his analysis and rhetoric. It now felt like a revolutionary moment, when the movement had to respond to unprecedented challenges, and King spoke of a new phase of struggle. The northern struggle, he promised New York's District 65 and the Illinois AFL-CIO, would involve "fundamental human rights" beyond mere constitutional rights. "The human right to a decent house" was as morally absolute as the right to vote, he told a variety of audiences. "It is not a constitutional right that men have jobs, but it is a human right." King spoke a year later at Howard University. "Public accommodations did not cost the nation anything; the right to vote did not cost the nation anything," he told the students. "Now we are grappling with basic class issues between the privileged and the underprivileged. In order to solve this problem, not only will it mean the restructuring of the architecture of American society but it will cost the nation something. . . . If you want to call it the human rights struggle, that's all right with me."⁵¹

Chapter 9

The War on Poverty and the Democratic Socialist Dream

Money, marbles, and chalk were not what Lyndon Johnson had promised the black leadership and the nation at Howard University's commencement on June 4, 1965. Using soaring abstractions, Johnson tied black dreams of full equality to the administration's economic policy planning. "We seek not just freedom, but opportunity . . . not just legal equity but human ability, not just equality as a right and a theory but equality as a fact and equality as a result." Johnson's rhetoric left black leaders inspired but wondering what new policies could possibly match the promises. Johnson promised a huge White House conference in the fall, and his reasoning followed the movement's logic of historical atonement. Drafted by Undersecretary of Labor Daniel Patrick Moynihan and presidential speechwriter Richard Goodwin, Johnson's address made the case for special measures to rehabilitate blacks and prepare them to enter the mainstream economy. "You cannot take a person who, for years, has been hobbled by chains, and liberate him, bring him up to the starting line of a race and then say, 'You are free to compete with all the others,' and still justly believe that you have been completely fair." For whites to "open the gates of opportunity" was not enough. Blacks must be given "the ability to walk through those gates." In June, no one guessed what dynamite lay in one of the speech's central claims. The "most important" factor driving deteriorating economic and social conditions among the black poor, "its influence radiating to every part of life," Johnson intoned, was "the breakdown of the Negro family structure."[1] Nowhere in his address did Johnson acknowledge the policy dream of black leaders, which Moynihan ironically shared: jobs and income support.

King initially welcomed Johnson's speech as a declaration of war on black poverty. On the phone with Johnson, King called it the greatest civil rights speech ever delivered by a president. On *Face the Nation* in August, he praised Johnson's willingness to honestly talk about and repair the Negro community's "sagging, disintegrating family life." King expected the president to dramatically "expand our already existing programs."[2] In fact, Johnson's soaring rhetoric presaged a period of policy retrenchment, as promises of greater resources and democratic participation in the Great Society darkened under the smoke of domestic racial conflict and the Vietnam War. Despite Moynihan's intentions in using the issue of family security to address the crisis of joblessness and inadequate family income, blacks and whites on the left perceived either malevolence or confusion in Moynihan's and the administration's preoccupation with mending "broken families" as the key to liberating poor people. By 1966, they suspected that the conditions for full freedom and genuine equality—programs in jobs, housing, equal education, and the democratization of urban institutions—had been abandoned by an administration too timid to face the real causes of inequality and willing to use the rhetoric of family values to obscure that abandonment.

"Material Well-Being for Their Bodies"

King dared to dream otherwise, but he did not avert his eyes from the nation's nightmares of inequality on July 4, when he preached at Ebenezer Baptist Church about economic equality and multiracial democracy. King confessed that he had seen his dream of the 1963 March on Washington "shattered" by his witness to spreading poverty: in the nation's overcrowded Harlems, among low-paid cotton pickers in the Mississippi Delta, in the eyes of Chicago's hopeless unemployed men, and among his impoverished Appalachian "white brothers." "I still have a dream," his voice rose, "that one day all of God's children will have food and clothing and material well-being for their bodies, culture and education for their minds, and freedom for their spirits." His dream was shaped by multiracialism and a commitment to class equality as strong as his antiracism. "Sometimes a class system can be as vicious and evil as a system based on racial injustice," King preached. Poverty derived especially from the low wages "menial" workers were paid. The ground crew and the pilots, the janitors and the surgeons, slum dwellers and Henry Ford were all equally important to the national welfare. Celebrating Jamaica's cultural rainbow, King hoped Americans could celebrate their multiracial national identity as "one big family." But America was multiracial mostly at the bottom, where the scramble for jobs, decent housing, and public services would become fiercer if whites continued to arrogate privileges to themselves and perpetuate inequality. America's true mission to the world was not military but moral. America could still be a "city upon a hill," a beacon of multiracial democracy. Human history had never seen "so many racial groups and so many national backgrounds assembled together in one nation. And somehow if we can't solve the problem in America the world can't solve the problem, because America is the world in miniature and the world is America writ large." Indeed, it all came to naught if you had fire in the streets or war in the world.[3]

King tried to fill Johnson's gap between promise and program, advocating jobs, income support, and self-help. At Syracuse University in July 1965, King carefully distinguished between guaranteed work and guaranteed income. Rather than a handout, guaranteed work would be "dignifying" for poor people. For all those "physically able to work, useful employment must be found in private and public domains." For those unable to support themselves, the federal government should provide a "subsistence minimum without stigma." King had in mind "the unemployed . . . the aged, widowed heads of families . . . broken families with children [and] the disabled." These were simply ideals of the New Deal work relief and Social Security state, applied equally and fairly to all. King appealed to consensus values of self-help, the morality of work, and the undesirability of welfare dependency. Citing the rationale of the Employment Act of 1946, King called for "massive public works programs [to build] decent housing, schools, hospitals, mass transit, urban renewal, parks and recreation centers." Such a program would not constitute " 'make-work,' but the rebuilding of America." Education, training, and direct public investments would stimulate private investments and "lay the physical and moral foundations for the Great Society." Particularly for blacks, a big jobs program "would set the context in which self-help would be realistic and meaningful." King surely heeded mounting conservative arguments against the very programs he was criticizing as inadequate. Oppression was no "excuse for laziness and mediocrity," he told members of Atlanta's middle-class Hungry Club. Blacks must still "make full and constructive use of the opportunities" open to them, but he now included "all the new developments of the poverty program," including Head Start, adult education, and job training.[4] Negroes must rise to the public relations challenge and resist the trend to identify Johnson's opportunity programs as welfare programs. Whitney Young seconded the emotion: he wanted real jobs waiting for young people *and* adults at the end of training programs that taught real skills relevant to the labor force and paid trainees living wages in the process.[5]

Jobs and income were not just demands of the academic left or activist policy advocates. Robert L. Green joined SCLC as director of the CEP when Andrew Young became SCLC executive director in the summer of 1965. Fifty-four students came to an October workshop, mostly young working-class blacks from all over the South. Green handed out forms asking how Negroes could "become first-class American citizens." Nearly half of the student-teachers wrote first "a Guaranteed minimum wage by the government," Green summarized, concluding the working class clearly preferred work over welfare. For men, the second key to citizenship was adult literacy, and for women "economic aid to provide school children with clothes [and] spending money." What conditions bothered them most? The responses included "violence directed against Negroes, economic sanctions towards those who attempt to alter the social system, extreme poverty, and lack of unity among Negro leadership," Green summarized. Most of the students were working poor, not members of "the growing Negro middle class with a vested interest in the status quo." One student deplored the "degeneration of the poor, especially ghetto people, and the intimidation, economic sanctions and violence against rural Negroes with studied indifference on the part of the government." Others wrote, "Jobs. I may find one, but no money is in it"; "low wages"; "low income, poor housing conditions, poor schools"; and "police brutality."[6] Their emphasis on adult education for citizenship diverged from the priorities of federal poverty warriors, who focused resources on children and young adults to provide a way out of the "cycle of poverty." No one from the CEP sample mentioned the fragile black family.

Power and Pathology

The Moynihan report on the Negro family and the politics of Lyndon Johnson's White House conferences in November 1965 and June 1966 have drawn inordinate attention, but not to the ambitious economic freedom dreams of the movement. What energized the Moynihan controversy was its policy context as much as its victim-blaming discourse of black family pathology. The administration had seemingly endorsed then retreated from the freedom movement's emergent insights: the fundamental problems of racial inequality involved jobs, housing, education, and institutions that rendered blacks powerless in their segregated communities. Moynihan argued that Johnson's commitment to racial equality and the War on Poverty remained undiminished through 1965 and that black leaders sabotaged the Howard promises with "preposterous and fruitless controversy." But he overlooked the most eloquent indicator of an administration's policy priorities: the budget. In early 1965, Johnson decided to commit U.S. air and ground forces to Vietnam. Michael Harrington remembered that by July "domestic reconstruction was no longer central; Southeast Asia was." Harris Wofford read Johnson's dramatic about-face as going from championing the War on Poverty to abandoning OEO to fight alone for the "poverty program." "Within the administration, the President let the Budget Bureau cut the program for 1966–1967 from the expected $3.4 billion to $1.75 billion, and Congress cut another $138 million," Wofford accurately recalled. That summer, OEO's Office of Plans, Progress, and Evaluations called for a jobs program, more social services, and a negative income tax, projected to cost $10 billion a year. By the fall, Vietnam had imposed a permanent "reign of austerity." Thereafter, OEO could defend only its existing appropriations. Johnson compared himself to a prize bull dominating a pasture of "quivering" civil rights cows. But his own horns gored the War on Poverty, as irresolvable fiscal dilemmas that he and Congress created bled millions from domestic spending. Johnson's antipoverty policy fell back into a centrist Keynesianism governed by cold war military priorities. Together with the administration's continued insistence on top-down implementation and its paternalistic talk about pathological Negro communities and families, the move looked like retrenchment. Johnson's effort to cover policy retreat was evident in a sanguine August press release he sent King. Citing statistics that indicated declining overall adult and youth unemployment, but saying nothing about ghetto youth, Johnson boasted that America was "making progress toward equality of opportunity in a prosperous economy."[7]

"The progress of the nation has not carried the Negro with it; it has favored a few and by-passed the millions," King told the Illinois AFL-CIO convention in October, in sharp contrast to Johnson's scaled-back paean to the gradually improving society. At the August SCLC convention, King had expressed grave skepticism about growth economics. Acknowledging a "recent slight decline in unemployment," King indicated that black unemployment remained double that of whites, and black youth unemployment had reached 70 percent in some cities. Neither the private sector growth of the mid-1960s nor small antipoverty programs had sufficiently alleviated a deepening crisis generated by automation and a rapid expansion in the labor force. Even a raise in the minimum wage and a reduction of the workweek would still leave millions unemployed, King argued. "Public payrolls" accounted for much of the job growth of the past decade. This was increasingly true for blacks, as the middle class found employment niches in municipal bureaucracies serving poor cities and poor people. In the 1960s, blacks lost 50,000 private sector jobs in New York City and gained 94,000 public sector jobs. As King realized, most of these gains went to the nonpoor.[8]

King looked through aggregate statistics at the holes in the safety net and the rash of part-time and itinerant work at the bottom of the labor market. Progress was meaningless when hundreds of thousands had "no unemployment insurance, no social security, no medicare, no minimum wage." King described the vulnerabilities, not the incapacities, of the poor: of the working poor to layoffs, of older workers to competition from younger workers, and of minorities to competition from whites, whose seniority gave them advantages during downturns in the business cycle. "Negroes need the kind of employment that lasts the year through," King wrote in his March 1966 annual report to the *Nation*. "They need the opportunity to advance on the job; they need the type of employment that feeds, clothes, educates and stabilizes a family." Aggregate statistics measuring declining unemployment "veil the reality that Negro jobs are still substandard and evanescent."[9]

King's policy advocacy no longer drew on metaphors of poverty cycles or cultures. Only full employment would eliminate black poverty, stabilize family life, and stem migration into swollen ghettos, King told the Illinois AFL-CIO. With jobs, the Negro could chart his own path "freed from the smothering prison of poverty that stifles him generation after generation." Poverty was a prison whose inmates were unjustly incarcerated for the larger society's crimes. This was not a poverty cycle churning within communities or families. Rather, the iron feet of oppression trampled relentlessly over each generation. Poverty resulted from ongoing economic exploitation, low wages, and income inequality; it was the inevitable outcome of steps taken by privileged classes to sustain their privileges. By implication, political mobilization, protest, and conflict were the only effective resources of the poor. King never theorized about how thoroughgoing a transformation of capitalist society would be necessary to realize democratic socialism, or the degree to which it would accommodate markets, private ownership, and continued income inequality. But his political and structural explanations of poverty increasingly challenged liberal definitions that focused on something poor individuals lacked—skills, education, habits of work discipline, or "mainstream" norms they might pass on to their children. What if poverty resulted from each new generation's confrontation with changing but relentless forms of economic denial, as the anthropologist Elliot Liebow argued in his powerful 1967 portrait of Negro streetcorner men, *Tally's Corner*?[10] The island of poverty was larger than King had recognized, and millions of affluent Americans afloat on the vast ocean of material prosperity were dependent on the underpaid labor of its inhabitants.

Poverty was a form of social violence, King increasingly asserted, as cities continued to burn, crime rates rose, and middle-class fears of crime escalated dramatically. As King told the 1965 SCLC annual convention, the freedom movement was now confronting "the violence of poverty, which destroys the soul and bodies of people," as much as it was confronting segregation. In their ghetto prisons, young black men were "straitjacketed in the least skilled, most underpaid strata of our society." They had become "the legion of the damned in our economic army. Damned to hold the dirtiest jobs, the lowest paying jobs—and damned to be not only the last hired but also the first fired when reversals come to our economy." Fixation on black crime and violence only obscured the larger society's systemic violence.[11]

King's developing analysis of the labor market led him to portray poverty as a structural pillar of capitalist society. The civil rights movement had revealed by 1966 that the "content of freedom is security, opportunity, culture and equal participation in the political process." Social conflict was unavoidable, because achieving equality as a fact required changing the majority's "way of life."

Slums with hundreds of thousands of living units are not eradicated as easily as lunch counters or buses are integrated. Jobs are harder to create than voting rolls. . . . It is easy to conceive of a plan to raise the minimum wage and thus in a single stroke extract millions of people from poverty. But between the conception and the realization there lies a formidable wall. Someone has been profiting from the low wages of Negroes. Depressed living standards for Negroes are a structural part of the economy. Certain industries are based upon the supply of low-wage, underskilled and immobile non-white labor. Hand assembly factories, hospitals, service industries, housework, [and] agricultural operations using itinerant labor, would all suffer shock, if not disaster, if the minimum wage were significantly raised. A hardening of opposition to the satisfaction of Negro needs must be anticipated as the movement presses against financial privilege.[12]

Poverty was no longer simply a paradox in capitalist society. In the middle of the most sustained economic boom in American history, a rising tide did not lift all boats. It swamped some and pushed others into isolated backwaters. Some Americans would need to give up privileges and resources for others to live in decency. That took politics, but poor people's aspirations for participation were crashing against stone walls of local power just when policy debate seemed to throw responsibility for genuine equality back onto the doorsteps of black families.

As undersecretary of labor, Moynihan followed well-worn paths into "the tangle of pathology." "The Negro Family: The Case for National Action" was an internal policy document that was released to the public in August 1965 after being leaked to the press and widely distorted. Moynihan advocated an expansion of the War on Poverty, the demotion of welfare and community action, and the promotion of jobs programs and comprehensive European-style family allowances. But his report avoided policy prescriptions and framed the issue in terms of a family crisis. The editors of *Life* magazine would find such terms much more compelling than dry job statistics, he later admitted thinking. Moynihan was silent on what to do about the strong correlations he drew between thirty-five years of "catastrophic" black male joblessness and rising rates of "female-headed" families, "illegitimate" births, and Negro "welfare dependency." Rising rates of male joblessness correlated with widening ratios of black-to-white unemployment, a nonwhite "illegitimacy ratio" eight times that of whites, rising crime rates, a gradual rise in the proportion of female-headed black households to 25 percent, and a near doubling of the numbers of children on Aid to Families with Dependent Children (AFDC) between 1953 and 1963. Joblessness was behind this social catastrophe, but Moynihan also argued that a "matriarchy" rooted in slavery "reinforces itself over generations." Moynihan's moral case for "national action" focused on the most desperate blacks, pictured entirely as subjects and not agents of social change. So while much of Moynihan's causal analysis was structural, the key framing issue of family breakdown reinforced Lyndon Johnson's pathology discourse and his conviction that welfare dependency posed the principal obstacle to black mobility. "Welfare dependency" might have begun to "feed on itself," Moynihan warned. Between 1948 and 1962, AFDC cases rose and fell in tandem with nonwhite male unemployment rates. But in 1960, 1963, and 1964, when that rate fell, new AFDC cases rose. Moynihan did not recognize that the "welfare revolution" of the 1960s and 1970s had already begun: eligible mothers simply became increasingly willing to apply for benefits. After 1965, the welfare rights movement educated them to their entitlements, and judicial and bureaucratic reforms boosted the proportion of eligible mothers who actually received aid.[13]

Untethered to a program, released in pieces, the analysis was ripe for distortion. Bayard Rustin recognized that Moynihan's focus on the negatives of black community life played into conservative hands. The "tangle of pathology" could be easily exploited by those who argued that federal policy would have no effect whatsoever on matters of values and behavior. Journalists Rowland Evans and Robert Novak concluded just that: "the generations-old habits of the Northern Negro" could only be remedied by "self-improvement." After all, blacks' own culture, not the economy, kept them poor. Black leaders were looking for handouts or, in Rustin's case, advocating "class struggle," they argued. If "family breakdown" was to be the key to the ghetto, this could justify leaving the airtight cage locked and hapless ghetto prisoners to work their own redemption.

After black militants and moderates alike rose up in harsh criticism of the report, Johnson divorced his administration from Moynihan's thesis and disinvited Moynihan from the White House conferences. But the concept of the self-perpetuating cycle of poverty already lay at the core of the administra-

tion's rationales for the War on Poverty. The disproportionate number of children in poverty led OEO to explain the "crisis" in the following way:
"Condemned to deprivation, inadequate educational opportunity and cultural
alienation, far too many of these children will inherit poverty for their entire
lives and, in turn pass it on to their children." Elements of the poverty inheritance thesis had informed the sociology of E. Franklin Frazier and Kenneth
Clark, as each argued discrimination and joblessness robbed men of the
opportunity to be breadwinners. Clark published *Dark Ghetto* in early 1965,
explaining the ghetto's "self-perpetuating pathology." Male joblessness and
status loss led to family breakups, abnormal "matriarchal" families, youth
delinquency, pervasive despair, apathy, crime, and violence. But Clark posited
different causes and cures for these ills. Political powerlessness, unequal and
segregated education, and the sense of relative deprivation blacks felt watching
televised images of a white consumer utopia all exacerbated the employment
crisis. In *Youth in the Ghetto*, the 1964 program document for Harlem Youth
Opportunities Unlimited (HARYOU), Clark wrote, "Ghettoes are the conse-
quence of the imposition of external power and the institutionalization of
powerlessness. In this respect, they are in fact social, political, educational,
and—above all—economic colonies."[14]

Unlike Moynihan or Johnson, Clark dreamed that Harlem's "pathology"
could be overcome by a swelling tide of activism. Local movements had
already supplanted "antisocial and self-destructive" behavior with more
"effective personal and community action." During Montgomery's black
mobilization, *"the incidence of antisocial behavior and delinquency decreased
almost to a vanishing point,"* he hopefully pointed out. Further, reasoned militancy and resistance, rather than pathology, characterized several interviews
Clark's assistant, Willie Jones, collected on tape for the books. The interview-
ees criticized the cops, the courts, the hustling middle-class preachers, joblessness, and the only employment open to them, emasculating jobs pushing
mops. A teenager who directly challenged southern activists said, "all right,
you are accepted into Woolworth's; you fought and got your heads beat in.
But what your children think of you? Do you have any economic or political
power?" Charles Silberman caught similar sentiments in his popular book,
Crisis in Black and White. He reiterated the Frazier-Clark analysis of a self-
perpetuating black matriarchy. But Silberman endorsed a militant form of
"self-help" practiced by Chicago's Woodlawn Organization. The powerless
poor should wage their own war on "welfare colonialism" and the urban institutions oppressing them. Empowerment and struggle would do more to break
the purported cycle of poverty than paternalistic top-down federal policies.[15]

Several black critics argued that Moynihan portrayed poor black communities only through the lens of their dysfunctions, ignored the majority of stable two-parent black families, and failed to mention parallel trends among lower-class white families. Many objected to Moynihan's pseudo-ethnographic cartoon of the human male's propensity to "strut" like a rooster, and the black man's humiliation before "matriarchal" breadwinning women. Whitney Young had talked often enough about humiliated breadwinners and matriarchal women, but now he said Moynihan had "slandered" functioning black families. "Today's discrimination and prejudice prevent a man from getting a job, not the fact that his grandfather was a slave," Young asserted. James Farmer suspected an ideological cover for policy retrenchment, charging the administration with a "massive academic cop-out" that pictured blacks as incapable of positive action. Blacks would not be ready for freedom until they learned to behave themselves and "stop buying Cadillacs instead of bread." Anna Arnold Hedgeman of the National Council of Churches recalled her deep resentment at the victim-blaming idea that blacks were now perpetuating their own poverty. "There was no reason for singling out the families which they had helped wreck as special guinea pigs," she recalled thinking, "literally the basic problem was economic."[16] The Johnson administration abandoned Moynihan by the November planning conference but could not conceal its policy retrenchment, its undemocratic administration of the conferences, or its original intention to put family stability at the core of its agenda for black equality.

The report's most discerning critics protested its paternalism and the administration's drift away from its budgetary and democratic promises. The controversy reflected much more than a "new mood of self assertion and black pride"; critics analytically assailed what they took to be a rationalization for policy retreat. After making some initially intemperate remarks, Benjamin Payton of New York's Protestant Council wrote the most probing indictment. The family was not "the fundamental source of the weakness of the Negro community" when joblessness and powerlessness so powerfully determined the social problems of poor blacks and poor whites. Pathological blacks seemed incapable of mature political consciousness or social action. The administration was endorsing elite-administered social rehabilitation, forsaking the politics of black empowerment for the politics of white guilt and black moral rehabilitation. It was a "fragmented catalog of Negro disabilities," Tom Kahn concurred, tailor-made for casework by squads of social workers, not comprehensive policy planning. Moynihan had argued that the nation had moved "beyond civil rights," but the struggle against racism in urban social structures had just begun, Payton declared. The movement was indicting "the immaturity of the larger society," not asking whites to improve underdeveloped Negro communities. Payton called for annual expenditures of $32 billion "for housing and slum rehabilitation, education, job-training and job-creation programs, health and medical facilities." George Wiley, then at national CORE, advocated similar programs costing $25 billion a year. Certain that the administration had abandoned maximum feasible participation, Wiley described ghetto citizens with healthy democratic capacities and aspirations: "parents and students should be able to participate in the governing of the schools; clients of the welfare system in its operation; those affected by urban renewal in its plans and progress."[17]

King stepped into the fray in speeches in New York City in October and Chicago in January, deploying structural more than cultural explanations for black poverty, faulting failed urban institutions more than Negro families. He did find Moynihan's statistics "alarming" and acknowledged Moynihan's fear that future generations might even regress economically "by the dissolving of family structure." But King stressed the force of contemporary racism and the history of black family resilience. The basic causes of the crisis lay in America's guilty past and cruel present. Slavery assaulted families and facilitated "matriarchy." After emancipation, women worked in "domestic service at low wages"; they became principal breadwinners when men were absent from home, perpetuating "the matriarch." King did not acknowledge how many husband-wife family dyads held together despite rural poverty, migration, and the industrial city. Nor did he describe the complex networks of kin and fictive kin sustaining survival, community, and resistance, but he was not alone. King reiterated the longstanding logic of atonement: "No society can repress an ugly past when the ravages persist in to the present." America had only begun to pay its "debt to justice."

Ongoing discrimination and institutional racism assaulted families more than legacies of oppression, however. Changes in family structure grew out of "pervasive and persistent economic want" that demoralized white and black poor, King insisted. Deteriorating community services and failing institutions also undermined individual dignity and family cohesion. Black children faced "grades of schooling without learning" and walked home through "neglected filthy streets which abound in open crime." Women depended mainly on low-wage labor, not welfare, and struggled to find time to nurture their own children. The black mother spent days caring for white children to earn enough to sustain "her disintegrating family." The Negro man, facing discrimination and irregular, unskilled employment, felt "rage and torment." He "beat his wife and his children in order to protest a social injustice," King claimed, in a clumsy statement that came uncomfortably close to rationalizing family violence. Finally, King argued, white-organized crime syndicates, "numbers, prostitution and narcotics rackets" exploited ghetto colonies. They drained "wealth out of the community leaving a wealth of misery and corruption behind."

In King's view, black families had demonstrated resistance and resourcefulness through hundreds of years of oppression and were fully capable of collectively leading their own emancipation. Freed slaves "fought, stole, sacrificed and died for their families." Contemporary black families "marched together against clubs, guns, cattle prods and mobs." As important, the new Movement family could sustain and heal families and individuals suffering from oppression. "To grow from within the Negro needs only fair opportunity for jobs, education, housing and access to culture," King asserted. By tracing black family ills troubles to class inequality, persistent white racism, and the deterioration of urban community institutions, King pointed to collective political action as a way to transform black communities from within and win resources from without.[18]

King's address to the University of Chicago on January 27, 1966, was more radical, though the economic and identity needs of black men still dominated his analysis. King now spoke nearly exclusively of ongoing oppression. "Systematic economic exploitation" deprived blacks of opportunity that was essential to "the survival of our family units." "When you deprive a man of a job, you deprive him of his manhood, deprive him of the authority of fatherhood. Place him in a situation which controls his political life and denies his children an adequate education and health services while forcing his wife to live on welfare in a dilapidated dwelling and you have a systematic pattern of humiliation which is as immoral as slavery and a lot more crippling than southern segregation." Structural economic change was essential to the liberation of black communities, families, and personalities. King had become more sensitive to women's dilemmas, but most frequently he insisted that the ills of the Negro family could be easily cured by getting "some money in the pocket of a Negro man." Moynihan and King both assumed that breadwinner husbands earning decent incomes held the solution to ghetto ills. But Moynihan did not even refer to the widespread left faith in social action. Instead, he helped Secretary of Defense Robert McNamara engineer Project 100,000, a federal "opportunity" program that dramatically lowered military entrance requirements, channeling poor and poorly trained men into combat in Vietnam. The military, Moynihan commented, was the best patriarchy around, "a world away from women, a world run by strong men and unquestioned authority."[19]

Moynihan responded by blaming his black critics for Lyndon Johnson's policy failures. Conceding that Johnson "lacked the resources of time and political capital to force the issue" of equality, he nevertheless charged the black left with sabotaging authentic possibilities for reform by attacking his report and Johnson's administration. In reality, Johnson had imposed budgetary and political limitations on the War on Poverty even before his escalation of the U.S. war in Vietnam. By February 1967, however, Moynihan was preaching that blacks needed to overcome dependency through self-help. "Fatherless families" with strong networks of kin support might be adaptive and viable, he conceded. But "dependency" on "Welfare" was politically untenable, as was reliance on all of Johnson's opportunity programs meant to eliminate welfare: "Head Start, Upward Bound [and the] Job Corps." "This country is not fair to Negroes and will exploit any weaknesses they display," he argued. Black Americans could not afford "a large lower class that it is at once deviant *and* dependent. If they do not wish to bring it into line with the working class (*not* middle-class) world around them, they must devise ways to support it from within." Moynihan's new "realism" swiftly disposed of joblessness, pathology, matriarchy, and the idealistic case for national action. He claimed King alone had vindicated him with "balanced" statements about the "social catastrophe" of the suffering black family. Stanley Levison thought this "silly" and urged King to respond, but King declined. He would pick the terms and timing of his statements on "what it means to be a Negro in America."[20]

The Johnson administration's handling of the White House conferences did nothing to dispel criticism of its paternalism. King was appointed to the executive committee to draw up an agenda for the planning conference in November 1965, but he generally sent Ralph Abernathy or Walter Fauntroy, unwilling to associate himself with what increasingly looked like an exercise in talk substituting for action. King confessed to Clarence Jones in November that he doubted "anything concrete" would come of the conferences. Local activists whose names he submitted to the White House were not invited. At the June 1966 conference, grassroots activists like Septima Clark were overshadowed by business, labor, academic, and political elites. Johnson put Chicago businessman Ben Heineman in charge, and many of the panels looked to the private sector, not the government, for solutions. King was invited to speak at only one session. Anna Arnold Hedgeman thought the conference thoroughly rigged: "When we reached Washington, we found that no resolutions were going to be permitted, that they had structured it so that most of the experts were white experts. We were up against a power structure at its best and worst." SNCC boycotted the conference, opposed as it was to Johnson's Vietnam policy. Out of 2,500 invited guests only 150 represented grassroots organizers.[21]

A. Philip Randolph and Rustin used both conferences productively to galvanize broad support for their Freedom Budget for All Americans. Over the course of a year they built remarkable consensus among civil rights organizations and religious and labor groups on a detailed policy agenda, setting a standard against which the War on Poverty could be measured. The Freedom Budget called for outlays of $185 billion over ten years for full employment and a guaranteed income; new-home construction and public works to upgrade the nation's infrastructure; and expanded medical, education, and antipoverty programs to be centrally administered by OEO. Leon Keyserling, former chair of the Council of Economic Advisors, lent economic skills, as did Tom Kahn and Michael Harrington. Signatories of the budget proposal included most luminaries of the liberal left, including black power advocates Stokely Carmichael and Floyd McKissick, religious leaders Reinhold Niebuhr and Benjamin Mays, laborites Ralph Helstein, Cleveland Robinson, and Walter Reuther, King, L. D. Reddick, and dozens more. The economist Vivian Henderson also spoke eloquently at the White House conference about the need for jobs and income support. But White House officials dismissed all such proposals as "socialistic" and a desperate plea for "reparations." The conference did not move the policy agenda, which had stalled in the face of congressional opposition and Johnson's rapidly shifting fiscal priorities.[22]

Johnson launched a new program in January 1966, Model Cities, which was designed to make American cities "masterpieces of our civilization" by preserving, not demolishing, neighborhoods. Johnson stole rhetorical thunder from his left critics, but the underfunded program left King uninspired. The legislation backed away from "maximum feasible participation," relegated neighborhood representatives to advisory roles and restored power over redevelopment to private interests and municipal authorities. Johnson's message introducing the legislation mixed moral outrage with pathology discourse. Americans would "cripple each generation" of ghetto youth if they allowed "broken neighborhoods" to become hives of "deprivation, crime and hopelessness," while suburbs continued to devour the countryside. Johnson outlined the "special problem of the poor and the Negro," immobilized in ghettos, suffering "inadequate schools, streets of fear and sordid temptation, joblessness and the gray anxiety of the ill-prepared." Middle-class blacks might have "provided the leadership and the means for reversing this human decline," but they had fled the city, he lamented. Johnson avoided any critique of municipal power and institutions. "The size and scale of urban assistance has been too small, and too widely dispersed," he declared, not mentioning the fact that locally controlled urban renewal had become notorious as "Negro removal." In the spirit of his own critique, Johnson proposed to meet this national crisis with $2.3 billion over six years distributed to seventy cities as "seed" money for model rehabilitation programs. Chicago's Mayor Daley

joined New York's Mayor John Lindsay in criticizing the program's "inade-
quacy." Though King called the proposal "imaginative," he also wrote that the
Negro would be skeptical: "laws on paper, no matter how breath-taking their
terminology, will not guarantee that he will live in a 'masterpiece of civilization.'"[23]

By 1966, signs of a backlash against the racial politics of liberal pity and
exhortation for "the Negro" were clearly visible. Fewer people either identified
with or were willing to help poor people as conceived by the Johnson administration. The psychologist Robert Coles documented that racialized paternalism
resonated with neither black nor white working-class people. A black factory
worker testified to the frustration many working-class blacks felt with the discourse of racial pathology.

I'm thirty-seven years old. I am called a black man. The fact is, Mister, I work in a
factory, and I have a wife and three children and we live in an apartment. . . . But these
days I'm supposed to believe I am an oddball, a rare bird, you know. I'm supposed to
believe I live in a *ghetto,* and all around me are these *diseased* people, and they are
crazy, and they are *addicts,* and they are *prostitutes,* and they set *fires* . . . and they need
everything, man, everything—because the *racial tragedy* has gone to their heads. . . .
Hell, I work with white people, and I'd like my kids to go to school with them. But I
live where I do, and I'm happy living here, and there aren't rats eating up my kids or
cockroaches crawling on them. My kids eat good food, and brother, we're not rich,
either. I'm just a plain guy. . . . Why don't people talk about someone like me? Why
don't they call me an American citizen, not a black man or a Negro or all the other
words?[24]

Coles also interviewed a South Boston Irish woman who remembered her
father, a broken man too proud to ask for relief during the Depression until
his family nearly starved. Blacks "had it bad here," she conceded, but so did
everyone else, "except for the rich."

And it's the rich, out there in the suburbs, who keep on telling us what we should do.
They preached at us to take them [Negroes] here and let them live there, and act this
way to them . . . until you get sick hearing it all. Suddenly they're so kind, the suburban
crowd. They stepped all over us, and kept us out of everything, the Yankees and the
college people over there at Harvard did. Now they're so good. They're all excited and
worried about people, but only the Negroes get their sympathy, only them. Talking
about prejudice, that's what we face, prejudice against *us.* I think we should start suing
in all the courts, and marching down those streets, like the Negroes. Maybe if we had
done that a long time ago, we wouldn't be so up against it now.[25]

As long as the poor were conceived as racially isolated and behaviorally
maladapted people blocked from entering the "mainstream," the real class and

racial cleavages alienating working people from the poor and the "the limou-
sine liberals" remained clouded. As King pointed out, most poor people
worked every day. But working-class people had little reason to believe the
War on Poverty might benefit them. Fiscally conservative, limited in scope,
and paternalistic, Johnson's liberalism would have been a hard sell even without Vietnam. King got plenty of mail on the subject. "A very disgusted citizen"
wrote to King urging him to stop expecting handouts, and start doing "something constructive for your people!" "I do not expect to step from the ghetto
into the Statler Hilton; I do not expect to be constantly given to; like the Italians, Irish and Jews I will strive to improve my station in life by hard work,"
he wrote. Most Negroes sat around on their "dead duffs" expecting " someone
to hand them a welfare check," he charged. Without this enormous pauper
population, "we would not have a welfare or poverty program on the scale it
is today." In fact, then as now, African Americans earned higher percentages
of their total incomes than whites. It didn't matter. The war on poverty was
going to fail, King warned, "if it substitutes a 'welfare' approach for much-
needed economic reforms aimed at the creation of more jobs." Johnson's poverty program, meant to eradicate welfare dependency, was being increasingly
identified with welfare and the undeserving black poor.[26]

Skirmishing Within the War on Poverty

King's growing disillusionment with the War on Poverty became marked in
late 1965 and early 1966 as he deplored its inadequate funding and the administration's failure to support democratic organizations. King's 1966 report to the
Nation argued that though initially inspiring to black poor people, community
action had become a political football, "so embroiled in political turmoil that
its [financial] insufficiencies were magnified by paralyzing [political] manipulations." "Big-city machines felt threatened by it and small towns, particularly
in the South, directed it away from Negroes. Its good intentions and limited
objectives were frustrated by the skillful maneuvers of experienced politicians." King obliquely but unmistakably charged Johnson with "sabotage" by
launching an idealistic program and failing "to safeguard it from opportunists
and enemies." Antipoverty agencies practiced the same old tokenism. Whites
could neither share power with blacks nor allow them to wield independent
power in the small arenas the federal government helped them carve out for
themselves.[27] The compromises and defeats that led many militants to embrace
black nationalism radicalized King's commitments to democratic socialism
and nonviolent mass action.

Figure 7. King found himself increasingly at odds with Lyndon Johnson over Vietnam
and the president's tepid response to the urban crisis. King and Johnson in conference,
March 18, 1966, over the Civil Rights Act of 1966, whose open housing provisions
Congress gutted over the summer before the Chicago Freedom Movement marched
against ghetto walls. After Johnson won only small appropriations for the Model Cities
program and focused his legislative agenda on merely outlawing housing
discrimination, King increasingly wondered whether the administration would
sponsor social programs that might "cost the nation something." LBJ Library photo
by Yoichi R. Okamoto. A2133-10.

Though King tried to keep their divergent perspectives together, the
social democrats, with their focus on national planning and federal programs
through alliances with Democratic Party liberals, increasingly diverged from
militants who thought poor people themselves should control programs and
direct policy. These tensions came most visibly to the fore in April 1966 at a
policy conference organized by the Citizens Crusade Against Poverty (CCAP),
an umbrella organization bankrolled by Walter Reuther. CCAP put left
"experts" like Clark and Harrington around panel tables and relegated "grass-

roots voices" to the end of the conference. As Peter Marris and Martin Rein noted at the time, the early war on poverty had been a mass of contradictions. Planning, coordination, and research called for elaborate formal relationships among academics, administrators, representatives of business and labor, political leaders, and "representatives" of the poor. Democratic participation was local, messy, hotly contested, suffused with racial conflict and competition, and conducted on local streets as much as around citywide conference tables. When CCAP held its national meeting in Washington in April 1966, militant activists and low-income people organized by SDS radical Rennie Davis, fed up with their "exclusion" from conference planning, took over the rostrum from the keynote speaker, OEO director Sargent Shriver, and drove him from the building. The UAW's contribution to community action had stressed the need for "corporatist" alliances and coordination among business, labor, social service professionals, and citizens. But local activists committed to political independence, organization, militant protest, and community control saw "planning" in a radically different light.[28]

King became embroiled in conflicts between OEO and black activists at the national and state levels. James Farmer left CORE to organize the Center for Community Action Education, but OEO mysteriously withheld the promised funding through the winter of 1966. Farmer later insisted that his plan never went beyond literacy training, but Johnson was alarmed by press allegations that Farmer would be hiring civil rights activists seeking to "throw out the white power structure." King was unable to mediate the conflict or intercede with Adam Clayton Powell, chairman of the House Committee on Education and Labor, who complied with Johnson's directive to "axe" Farmer's program. "They want the rain without the thunder and lightning, the ocean without the terrible roar," Farmer lamented.[29]

King and his advisors shared widespread worries that poverty bureaucracies were deflecting activists from potentially more powerful action programs. Andrew Young warned the 1965 SCLC convention that the War on Poverty was taking activists off the streets and neutralizing them. "The enemies we now face will tempt us with comfort and pleasure that we might forget our brothers in the teeming ghettos of the nation while we languor in air-conditioned comfort." The enemy was no longer a brutal cop with a nightstick but the manager of a social welfare agency bribing activists with "high-paying jobs and positions of honor and prestige." King and Levison privately bemoaned the fact that talented activists with cushy jobs in the poverty program were "forgetting . . . about the need for militant action." They criticized Philadelphia's Leon Sullivan, who was receiving federal job-training money for his new Opportunities Industrialization Center (OIC) and no longer boycotting companies, which remained the strategy of Chicago's Operation Bread-basket under Rev. Jesse Jackson's leadership. Levison worried that the war in Vietnam and the War on Poverty were depleting movement energies. Liberal supporters moved from civil rights to antiwar work, while Negroes adopted a social work and "welfare approach" to poverty. Nor was Levison much impressed with Andrew Young's enthusiasm for the southern cooperative movement. Real planning for decent jobs would take a federal government commitment involving "billions" of dollars. On his own behalf, Sullivan spoke to Congress about his new cooperative relationships with businesses and about the effectiveness of the OIC in moving unskilled workers into skilled jobs, "new homes, nice automobiles." "I realized I had to zag, and the zag had to be production and training and preparation, because you frustrate a man more when you show him an open door and there are chains around his legs and he can't move," Sullivan testified.[30]

Levison and King did not mention Whitney Young, who raked in more millions from the War on Poverty and private foundations for the National Urban League than any other black organization. But even Young voiced a sharp critique of class and power. The NUL set up the National Skills Bank to find positions for blacks; On-the-Job-Training, which apprenticed blacks to private firms; tutoring and fellowship programs; and services such as family counseling. They helped thousands but inevitably left millions behind. Generally these and other job-training and job-referral programs offered hands up to those already on their way up. But Young was also a vocal defender of maximum feasible participation. In 1966, he admonished a group of social workers to become "catalytic agents of change," support protests and rent strikes, organize "marches on City Halls to protest ghetto conditions and Jim Crow schools," and proselytize "the unemployed that they have the right to work." "Paltry sums" appropriated for the poverty war were in no way equal to the challenge, he said. They should begin a real war on poverty by correcting the appalling exemption of agricultural workers from the $1.25 minimum wage. Then the government should "guarantee a decent wage and income" to everyone working for poverty wages in Florida bean fields or Detroit hospitals. "Poverty is big business in America," he said, and poverty warriors would have to fight powerful interests like California growers who howled when the Labor Department cut off the flow of Mexican braceros into the Southwest and wages rose. The War on Poverty needed more than summer soldier bureaucrats collecting checks from Job Corps administrative jobs. It needed real "poverty fighters."[31]

Poor people fight wars of position on ground not of their choosing, Antonio Gramsci has noted. In hundreds of locales, poor people and their nonpoor representatives successfully wrestled resources from government agencies and private foundations, who in turn tried to delimit their scope of action. In real ways, nevertheless, they got jobs and developed skills and political experience for themselves, and gained better housing, health care, legal representation, early childhood education, and income support for poor people. Frequently they broke the "rules" to politically activate their "clients," sometimes to confront antipoverty agencies. Especially where independent movements backed them up, they forced greater accountability on public institutions, such as hospitals or courts charged with enforcing housing codes. But resources never equaled the challenges, and social workers, administrators, educators, and doctors benefited disproportionately from the War on Poverty, as King recognized. Something was wrong with a government that spent an average of $500,000 to kill a Vietnamese soldier versus $53 to help a poor person, King charged in 1967. "And half of that is spent for the salaries for people who are not poor."[32]

In many places the programs reproduced a new class structure of relatively well-paid black social service professionals "serving" but not activating the poor on their own behalf. By 1968, Kenneth Clark and Jeannette Hopkins concluded, with thinly veiled scorn, "Politicians, social workers, social scientists, community actionists, and some indigenous workers have all benefited to one degree or another from anti-poverty programs. The poor seem to have benefited less." And even where the poor won small victories, poverty politics could become ghettoized when the "institutions" over which the poor exercised some control turned out not to be the most powerful institutions impinging upon their lives. George Lipsitz has shown how an extraordinary working-class organizer like Ivory Perry could leverage a half-time job as a local housing coordinator for the St. Louis Human Development Corporation into full-time activism organizing rent strikes and lead paint abatement campaigns that materially benefited his community. But two political scientists later concluded that the same politicized and underfunded CAP actually deflected attention from the city's most powerful white controlled institutions affecting economic mobility: schools, vocational institutes, employers, unions, and welfare departments. Moreover, local agencies could not address the largest dilemmas of metropolitan inequality: suburban privilege and corporate disinvestment. King looked to the nation to address these causes of the urban crisis.[33]

The struggle between community organizers, state and local power structures, and the OEO in Alabama reveals how political wrangling over federal grants inflated and then circumscribed black political expectations. In late 1965 and 1966, Randolph Blackwell helped the Anti-Poverty Coordinating Committee of Wilcox County apply for a grant from OEO to support a program of cooperative agricultural marketing, self-help housing, job training, and basic education for displaced sharecroppers. Blackwell envisioned "a radical program to break the cycle of destitution that has for generations plagued the rural South." Families had been evicted from their shacks and told by their bosses not to vote. One hundred farmers had lost their tenant farms, and they looked to OEO and the Farmers Home Administration for land, seeds, fertilizer, and equipment, hoping to "grow cucumbers, peas and okra on six hundred acres." Blackwell planned to reconstruct "Wilcox County as a socio-politico-economic unit." Educational programs would encompass "citizenship responsibility and rights, political organization . . . and community development." Local blacks needed federal voting registrars and federal antipoverty money, Blackwell insisted. People were eager to help themselves, but powerless blacks could not provide decent education for their children, develop health and welfare programs, or attain "vocational flexibility and financial security." To translate the promise of the Voting Rights Act into political power and to translate political power into economic power, local blacks needed assistance from the federal antipoverty program. But when their ally in the OEO Atlanta office resigned and Alabama governor George Wallace attacked the Wilcox County proposal in the summer, their grant fell through. So did a parallel grant in Lowndes County after Wallace charged that black power radicals were behind it.[34]

By December 1966, SCLC won another $302,000 grant from OEO for a smaller remedial education program in Wilcox County under a special OEO provision for migrant workers that governors could not veto. Sargent Shriver approved the grant in July, but withheld the money until after the November election so as not to give fuel to Wallace's anti-welfare backlash politics. Blackwell's soaring visions were reduced to adult basic education and "self-help plans" that gave displaced farm workers modest stipends while learning new skills. But local people celebrated a small victory. John Cook of Wilcox County SCLC wrote King on November 22 to thank him for his help in establishing a local black-controlled CAP: "If not for your Symbol and stand for the rights and freedoms for all men, Negroes would still be stumbling in the darkness of dispare [*sic*] . . . no man is too small or place too remote for you to venture out and help." King called the grant a "milestone," claiming it was the "first time that a civil rights organization in connection with a local community group" was funded by the federal government. By then Blackwell had left SCLC. King praised the "strong leadership of Mrs. Septima Clark and Mrs. Dorothy Cotton" in shepherding the grant.[35]

Many southern activists turned from interracial coalitions to black power politics, partly in response to OEO's unfulfilled promises of participation. The suspension of the Lowndes County OEO grant at Wallace's behest was the last straw that broke SNCC chairman Stokely Carmichael's belief in liberal anti-poverty politics. In the summer of 1965, Carmichael had helped found an all-black party, the Lowndes County Freedom Organization. Forming a makeshift tent city on donated land, scores of evicted sharecroppers organized them-selves and sought new forms of livelihood. Josephine Mayers recalled helping "black people to get jobs and learn how to do things for themselves." Her family bought land and built a house for the first time. Carmichael was furious at OEO's capitulation to Wallace's pressure, however, declaring on July 28, 1966:

We have to tell them that the only way anybody eliminates poverty in this country is to give poor people money. You don't have to headstart, uplift and upward-bound them into your culture. Just give us the money you stole from us, that's all. We have to say to people in this country, "We don't really care about you. For us to get better, we don't have to go to white things. We can do it in our own community, ourselves if you didn't steal the resources that belong there." We have to understand the Horatio Alger lie and that the individualist, profit-concept nonsense will never work for us. We have to form cooperatives and use the profits to benefit our community. We can't tol-erate their system.

Echoing Malcolm X, Carmichael concluded, "We have to control the econom-ics and politics of our community."[36]

Charles Sherrod in Albany came to a similar conclusion about how the poor could wage war on poverty, though his language was much less militant. Any community "composed of a large number of low-income Negro families will never be helped unless it helps itself," he wrote in 1966. With the help of Legal Services attorneys, VISTA volunteers, and religious and civil rights activ-ists, northern welfare rights activists had discovered that the poor could be effectively mobilized in demanding rights to income and other goods under the provisions of the Social Security Act that created AFDC. "Recipients must become familiar with the regulations so that they can acquire the power," Sherrod wrote, "and the accompanying self-respect and dignity, to constitute continuing opposition to and influence on the administration of Social Secur-ity."[37] King appreciated that income entitlements were effective organizing appeals, but he always included them with appeals on behalf of self-help, jobs, education, health, housing, and other social programs.

In Selma, Shirley Mesher, SCLC's Dallas County project director, galva-nized a grassroots movement aimed at winning control of Mayor Joseph Smitherman's poverty agency. Starting in the fall of 1965, Mesher organized a successful campaign that established a federal food commodity distribution center, set up a free school lunch program, challenged discrimination at local textile mills, and defended sharecroppers against eviction. They formed their own local agency, Self-Help Against Poverty with Everyone (SHAPE), and conducted what OEO later called "the most effective elections by the poor that have been held in the South, and perhaps in the nation." Mesher wrote to King in 1966 that conditions that made the vote necessary in Selma persisted: "the same shacks with the same leaks," the same low wages, the lack of municipal or private jobs, debt dependency among farmers, extortionate interest rates, and federal crop subsidies that made it profitable to evict black sharecroppers. Whites still manipulated welfare and surplus food programs to control blacks. Discrimination continued in federally assisted educational and welfare departments beyond the oversight of OEO. For whites, Mesher concluded, "their whole way of life . . . depends upon their controlling everything—and the Negroes with it."[38]

SHAPE collapsed when Mayor Smitherman successfully co-opted the middle-class black leaders of the Dallas County Voters League and convinced OEO officials that he had a biracial and representative poverty agency. Again King saw how whites stubbornly resisted integration or independent black leadership in such ventures. SHAPE's leaders charged federal officials with "high-pressure tactics, intimidation, threats and willful misstatement of facts" in ignoring the elected representatives of the majority-black poor running SHAPE. OEO accepted only token blacks handpicked by the segregationist "white power structure." Giving "complete control, planning and running of an Anti-Poverty program" to local elites effectively condemned the program to failure, Mesher protested.[39] With the demise of SHAPE, she, too, left SCLC.

The nation's most well-publicized Community Action controversy involved the Child Development Group of Mississippi (CDGM), a program initiated in 1965 by blacks involved in the MFDP, assisted by white volunteers and church groups. Though Head Start was the most moderate of the national emphasis programs, CDGM initially was radically empowering for local people, winning $1.5 million from OEO to employ 1,100 workers and serve 6,000 children in 84 centers. The staff, mostly drawn from the MFDP, exhibited all the enthusiasm and initiative of the 1964 freedom schools. King said he never saw anything like it, proclaiming it the nation's greatest program "in terms of grassroots participation." Children learned in crowded but nurturing classrooms, while adults found employment for the first time in occupations other than domestic service or farming. Many who drew income from CDGM later started businesses or went into politics. Ed Brown, a Mississippi SNCC activist, recalled that "by providing people with a financial base—all those hundreds

of jobs—it completely undermined the system of intimidation and violence—
'Don't vote, or I'll fire you and see that my friend cuts off your credit at his
store so you can't buy food or clothes.'" For the first time, "they didn't *need*
the white man's credit that kept them enslaved to him."[40]

No wonder Mississippi's senators John Stennis and James Eastland
attacked the program for financial corruption and "civil rights agitation," successfully eliminating CDGM's funding. Schools in over fifty communities
struggled through the winter to stay open. In February 1966, a "Romper
lobby" composed of Mississippi women and children descended on Congress.
After the publicity, OEO reinstated a grant of $5.6 million. But the victory was
tainted when the governor initiated Mississippi Action for Progress (MAP), a
competing Head Start program controlled by state officials and legitimized by
the participation of middle-class blacks. A report by the radical Protestant
Delta Ministry argued that MAP was controlled by political "forces that have
perpetuated the conditions maintaining poverty." MAP was part of the "'war
against the poor' . . . administered by bureaucrats insensitive to human need,
morality, and the politics of the South."[41]

On January 31, 1966, fifty Delta refugees from the Mississippi Freedom
Labor Union (MFLU) occupied an abandoned air base in Greenville, Mississippi. Thirty hours later, federal troops forcibly evicted them. Hoping to draw
attention to the plight of plantation people made homeless because of mechanization and political reprisals, activists testified to their deep disillusionment
with federal policy. Ida Mae Lawrence, chair of the MFLU Rosedale local,
declared, "You know, we ain't dumb, even if we are poor. We need jobs. We
need food. We need houses. But even with the poverty program we ain't got
nothin' but needs. . . . We is ignored by the government." The government
obviously cared more about its property than "poor people." Lawrence concluded there was "no way out but to begin your own beginning, whatever way
you can."[42]

King's hope in federal policy and an integrated War on Poverty are evident in SCLC's August 1966 appeal to President Johnson on behalf of those
evicted from the Greenville Air Base. Johnson should convert the base into "a
huge center for providing training, housing, and supportive programs" for the
poor. King and SCLC evinced an understanding of the political economy of
the South gained from years of movement experience: Johnson must "rectify
the tragic effects . . . of State-supported and perpetuated racial discrimination
in education, welfare administration, and employment and of mass Negro
unemployment." Displaced blacks only wanted equal participation and inclusion in productive society, SCLC claimed. Though Attorney General Nicholas

Katzenbach was sympathetic, Senator Stennis used his position on the Appropriations Committee to block any development on the base.[43]

King joined CCAP and a coalition of liberals and religious leaders again in October 1966 to save CDGM from complete replacement by MAP. They scored a partial victory when the program received another $5 million, and OEO evenly divided Mississippi's counties with MAP. But Fannie Lou Hamer fumed at the black middle class who joined with the white power structure in subverting citizen participation in the War on Poverty: "Sometimes I get so disgusted I feel like getting my gun after some of these schoolteachers and chicken-eatin' preachers." CDGM struggled on but eventually succumbed to the same racial and class power politics that doomed SHAPE in Alabama. King watched in bitterness the growing "cynicism" among Mississippi activists. He visited Quitman County, "the poorest county in the United States," where black children walked the streets shoeless. To survive, he told SCLC staff, poor people lived on trapped rabbits and berries. Local blacks had tried to wage their own war on poverty, despite the gaping racial holes in the local welfare state: "I saw their mothers and their fathers trying to carry on a little head start program, but they had no money. The federal government hadn't funded them but they were trying to carry on. . . . And I saw mothers and fathers who said to me not only were they unemployed, they didn't get any kind of income—no old age pension, no welfare check, no anything."[44]

Conditions worsened and hunger spread as evictions continued. Delta planters continued receiving enormous agricultural subsidies, responding to the passage of a $1 minimum wage law by evicting sharecroppers and firing day laborers. When counties replaced their surplus commodities programs with new food stamp programs, thousands of blacks who could not afford the minimum payments went hungry. When Robert Kennedy brought the Senate Subcommittee on Employment, Manpower and Poverty to Jackson in April 1967, NAACP lawyer Marian Wright, Fannie Lou Hamer, Unita Blackwell, and Amzie Moore conducted a seminar on economic oppression and disempowerment. Hamer doubted that landowners on the Sunflower County poverty board, "the people that have caused us to be in poverty, is going to get us out of it." In Blackwell's Issaquena County, black voters rejected the food stamp program, so county officials eliminated surplus commodities as well. "People who have participated in civil rights had been cut off from welfare," Wright reported, and voters continued to lose their jobs. "They are starving," said Wright. She advocated bringing Mississippi welfare payments up to national standards, outlawing reprisals, and funding public works to relieve unemployment. Mississippi needed more than Head Start, Unita Blackwell testified: all "Mississippi needs to go to school." But the plantation owners who evicted voters or proponents of school desegregation could not be trusted with adult education programs, she added. The poverty program had to "change the basic economic structure" and address the "root problem" of poverty, Wright explained. "Preserve the right of the people to participate," she implored. Before his publicized visit to desperately poor rural families, Robert Kennedy announced that since American "corporations are making profits greater than 70 of the countries of the world, you would think that all of us would be able to provide for some of our citizens."[45]

Jobs, Income, and Power

King shared local activists' disillusionment with elite control of the War on Poverty in 1965 and 1966. Yet, unlike Stokely Carmichael, King did not reject the poverty program and focus alone on self-help, reparations, or income entitlements. He renewed and intensified his calls for full employment and an end to slums through targeted federal spending. Vietnam occupied the energies of the left and the nation, and civil rights activism had to swim against a rising tide of white opposition, riots, official repression, and shrill ideological debate. Government inaction increasingly contributed to King's "shattered dreams," but government activism remained his key to wider economic freedom dreams.

An April SCLC board resolution reflected both the social democratic economic planning agenda and the priorities of local organizers. The board called for majority representation of poor people "on all local governing boards and executive committees" of antipoverty agencies. City halls must channel money into poor communities rather than into public bureaucracies. OEO must expeditiously fund civil rights organizations determined to fight poverty and disempowerment on their own terms. Educational and manpower programs must "destroy economic paternalism and rupture the master-servant relationship wherever it exists." The federal government must raise the minimum wage and extend it to poor and minority workers in "laundries, hotels and restaurants, farms, [and] hospitals." They called for "public service employment for those less able to compete in the labor market" and income guarantees for those unable to "participate in the job economy." Congress must repeal section 14b of the Taft-Hartley Act and unshackle free trade unions to fight for "an adequate share of the nation's wealth," they concluded. Democratic change from the bottom up and energizing reforms from the top down could harmonize and reinforce each other.[46]

For two years King had described the War on Poverty as inadequate and undemocratic. In speeches to SCLC and other groups in November 1966, in testimony before Congress in December, and in drafting his fourth book, *Where Do We Go from Here?*, King drew together several programmatic alternatives from the left and the black movement. His talk with activists became more explicitly anticorporate. Piecemeal approaches had to be replaced with a comprehensive and coordinated antipoverty policy, he argued. And domestic reconstruction was impossible as long as the United States was militarily involved in Vietnam.[47]

When SCLC gathered in Frogmore, South Carolina, on November 11, 1966, King again called for "Democratic Socialism," sharing his radicalism in a "quiet place" where he would not be red baited. Why did America still have forty million poor people nearly three years after Johnson declared war on poverty? SCLC activists must now ask what was fundamentally wrong with capitalism. Sweden had no slums, unemployment, or medical neglect, having successfully achieved an "equitable division of wealth." Southern desegregation had not cost capitalists anything, he declared, but abolishing slums entailed "messing with the captains of industry." "I believe that the gasoline that goes in my automobile is there because God made it," he preached. "I don't think it belongs to Mr. Rockefeller . . . I think the earth is the Lord's." Humans did not make wealth by themselves, so it was incumbent upon those who expropriated it to share it.[48]

Publicly, such direct challenges to corporate power and private ownership were rare in comparison to King's critique of policy failure and eroding working-class power. Testifying before hearings held by Senators Robert Kennedy and Abraham Ribicoff in mid-December 1966, widely called the "City Hearings," King criticized the "striking absurdity" of committing billions of dollars to reach the unpopulated moon "while the densely populated slums are allocated miniscule appropriations." Since the 1930s, minimum wages and Social Security benefits had lagged behind the economy's productivity growth. The weakening political power of labor and poor people accounted for this erosion of redistributive policies: "those at the lowest economic level, the poor white, the Negro, the aged, are traditionally unorganized" and unable to force increases in their wages and buying power, as industrial unions had earlier achieved. Jobs, income, and political power would be necessary for the poor to move out of poverty. King repeatedly pointed out that the crisis for black, poor, and unskilled workers was worsening, even as the black middle class prospered and the economy grew. A sharp rise in the 1966 nonwhite youth unemployment rate was particularly alarming, especially when inclusion of "discouraged" workers more than doubled the nonwhite rates.[49]

King no longer regarded poverty as the denial of minimal subsistence needs, an assumption built into the government's "absolute" poverty line. The 1964 line of $3,000 based on a fixed minimum subsistence food budget was too low to begin with, King said, but now it needed more than adjustment for inflation. Policy must "reduce the gap" between the poor and the majority by making the poverty line a percentage of median income, hence adjusting poverty standards to the rising "average standard of living of all America." "We are dealing with issues of inequality, of relative standing," King insisted. Such a redefinition would have raised the poverty line and drawn attention to the needs of millions of working poor people the War on Poverty ignored.[50]

Another new line of King's analysis criticized the War on Poverty as a piecemeal collection of uncoordinated measures. Levison and the sociologist S. M. Miller suggested King connect this critique with his advocacy of a guaranteed annual income to distinguish himself from others testifying before the City Hearings. King wanted material that was both "analytical and passionate," and Miller obliged with ghostwritten text. Since 1961, the government had chipped away at discrimination and poverty without abolishing either, King began. Reformers assumed that poverty stemmed from "multiple evils: lack of education restricting job opportunities; poor housing which stultified home life and suppressed initiative [and] fragile family relationships which distorted personality development." Housing and educational reforms have been bureaucratically lethargic, "piecemeal and pygmy." Poverty most fundamentally was a lack of income, he now asserted. A guaranteed annual income was the most revolutionary, complete, and direct approach to ending poverty. "Even Negroes, who have a double disability, will have a greater effect on discrimination when they have the additional weapon of cash to use in their fight." Economic security was the precondition as well as the result of civil and voting rights activism.[51]

Who was entitled to a job, who to income? How could American abundance, hitherto resting on structures of poverty, now be redirected to its abolition? King, Levison, and Miller followed the conceptual contours of the 1964 Triple Revolution analysis. King questioned the entire American structure of reward, especially the degree to which income and welfare state benefits were still tied to concepts of "work" no longer appropriate to an affluent society that had moved beyond scarcity. Incomes tied too closely to profits merely stuffed the "overfed mouths of the middle and upper classes." America's productive capacities now made poverty "as asocial, cruel and blind as . . . cannibalism." In an interdependent technological society, poverty was systemic, not the result of "personal defects." Unemployment, low and unequal wages, and an impoverished public sector were why the "richest fifth of the population is 10 times as rich as the poorest fifth," he said. Unemployment concentrated among minorities "and the failure of social security and welfare payments to keep up with the rising demands of society" were especially at fault for rising inequality.[52] The government and business must help people consume rather than merely put them to work.

Guaranteeing income would free Americans' creative energies to devise work that further "enriches the society" by improving its health and quality of life. King wanted a "radical redefinition" of remunerative work, quoting the nineteenth-century socialist Henry George: "work which extends knowledge and increases power and enriches literature and elevates thought is not done to secure a living." Americans had been traditionally rewarded for working "with land, with machines, with computers," but now self-fulfillment and public service were sufficient grounds for receiving income. Firemen worked when they were not putting out fires; artists and students received grants simply to travel and study. Why not reward a civil rights worker to spend a year reading, "meeting people and shaking hands, and talking with them about their problems?"[53]

How could a majority of Americans be persuaded to abandon the outmoded assumptions of the scarcity society and their deeply ingrained individualism? King adapted the Declaration of Independence to make room for new ideals of equality. In similar terms, nineteenth-century radical abolitionists such as Charles Reason had demanded freedmen's rights to land. For King, rights to "life, liberty and the pursuit of happiness" could be stretched beyond even what Franklin Roosevelt had promised in 1944. "A man also deserves an income because without a livable wage you do not have life in reality and in all of its dimensions," he told SCLC. A year later, in recruiting activists for the Poor People's March on Washington, King reiterated that fulfilling the rights of the Declaration depended upon having "a job or an income."[54]

The War on Poverty offered education and training to prepare workers for jobs presumed to exist in the private economy, but even with robust economic growth there were insufficient jobs at decent wages to eliminate poverty. King therefore called for guaranteed employment for all who were eligible for training. "Training has been a cruel hoax on the poor and Negroes, as the trained are not placed on jobs and are shifted to other training programs or allowed to drift in the limbo of the irregular marginal economy," he told the senators. Training provided opportunity for high-skilled Negroes already more likely to find work, so training should focus on "developing the low skilled" workers. Employment programs should follow the logic of "employment first—training later." Jobs could be redesigned for neglected workers "forced to the end of the employment line." King envisioned creating construction jobs for poor and black people and education, health, and welfare jobs for "nonprofessionals." Echoing the labor economist Frank Reissman's influential book, *New Careers for the Poor,* King called for upgrading of "paraprofessionals" to "avoid a new color line of black nonprofessionals and white professionals" in social services. To the objection that raising the minimum wage would destroy low-wage jobs, King responded that "the jobs that would disappear would be worth losing. . . . One decent job in the family might be more salutary than two or three marginal ones," he asserted.[55]

Although the guaranteed annual income would be a powerful equalizer, King continued to address specific policy arenas. A hotly contested report written for the Office of Education in 1966 by Dr. James S. Coleman concluded that family background, "home, neighborhood, and peer environment" were more important determinants of educational success than school expenditures. King reaffirmed his faith that education was indispensable to social mobility, a key assumption behind Title I of the 1965 Elementary and Secondary Education Act. As he wrote in *Where Do We Go from Here?*

The schools have been the historic routes of social mobility. But when Negroes and others of the underclass now ask that schools play the same function for them, many within and outside the school system answer that the schools cannot do the job. They would impose on the family the whole task of preparing and leading youngsters into educational advance. And this reluctance to engage with the great issue of our day—the full emancipation and equality of Negroes and the poor—comes at a time when education is more than ever the passport to decent economic positions.

King continued to call for compensatory spending for poor schoolchildren, for the construction of large, integrated educational "parks," and for schools to educate children "so well that family background is not an issue." "As a son of a tenant farmer, I know that education is the only valid passport from poverty," Lyndon Johnson announced as he signed the education act. King did not agree, but if Johnson really meant it, King meant to hold him to his promises.[56]

King recognized that without the political mobilization of the poor, no amount of policy analysis and advocacy would benefit them. In September 1966, Ralph Helstein had argued in this spirit to the board of the A. Philip Randolph Institute: "What do you do at the local level, in terms of organizing the communities? The Freedom Budget is not enough; there must be something more. Civil rights leaders need to look at themselves and ask themselves if they are doing the kind of job that needs to be done in mass movements."[57] The terms around which the unorganized urban poor would mobilize politically for metropolitan and national change were unclear to most civil rights leaders and liberal policymakers. Yet the escalating violence in America's racial ghettos and the political backlash against it made action increasingly urgent. Over the course of 1966, Chicago provided many of the lessons and terms of understanding poverty and the ghetto that fundamentally changed King's approaches to race, poverty, and power.

King's radicalism grew out of the interaction between the analytical perspectives and policy advice offered by his social democratic advisers with the lessons learned on the ground. His growing attention to poor people's powerlessness and the need for empowerment as a key to ending their poverty followed emergent ideas in the southern and northern black struggles. King's defense of maximum feasible participation of the poor in federal antipoverty programs and his demands for structural economic reforms were only part of the story. King's opposition to militarism and his observations of what the Vietnam War was doing to his hopes for national reconstruction, his experiences with local power structures and articulate black nationalists, and the intensity of the urban crisis itself all led King to search for leverage over structures of racial and class power.

Chapter 10
Egyptland

From 1965 to 1967, nonviolent movements and violent rebellions in the cities pushed King to deepen his analysis of political and economic power. Over time, he tested several keys that might open the largest cells of the ghetto prisons. Bayard Rustin had put jobs, housing, and education at the center of the urban agenda. For nearly two years in Chicago, King and SCLC experimented with various strategies, including educational desegregation, community-based tenant unions, voter registration, Operation Breadbasket, and mass protests against racially exclusive neighborhoods. As the Chicago Freedom Movement confronted the "slum colony," Mayor Richard Daley's political machine had enormous advantages, especially its control over municipal jobs and federal antipoverty resources. Though King was committed to testing community organizing in the North, SCLC's successes in Birmingham and Selma shaped their decision to stage mass marches against realty offices in Chicago's working-class inner suburbs in June 1966. Legislation then being debated in Congress would have extended nondiscrimination provisions to the real estate industry. Perhaps, again, national reform would follow publicized local confrontations.

When riots, demonstrations, and counterdemonstrations forced the city's political and business elites to the bargaining table, the ministers were unable to extract significant enforceable commitments. Reflecting on his Chicago experience, King came to define "powerlessness" as the central challenge of the urban ghetto, especially after police battled ghetto youth in July. Chicago hastened King's disillusionment with the federal government, the Democratic Party, liberals, and laborites who proved unwilling to support nonviolent challenges to segregated ghettos. Black people struggled for power in city hall, electoral politics, and bureaucracies that wielded authority over the poor. As King testified at the City Hearings, "To be poor and Negro in America is to be powerless . . . to be governed by police, housing authorities, welfare departments, without rights and redress." Ghetto bureaucracies staffed by whites proved as "oppressive as sweatshop employers or absentee landlords."[1] King tested his most radical ideas in the deprived places that still embody the nation's failure to resolve its contradictions of wealth and poverty, racism and equality, marginality and power. Ultimately, he concluded that neither community organizing nor local mobilization could solve the toughest dilemmas of metropolitan inequality. Attacking ghetto walls from within neither put masses in motion nor compelled concessions from those who benefited from urban segregation. Chicago, therefore, became a central prelude to King's decision to build a nationwide coalition capable of empowering all poor people and moving the nation toward democratic socialism.

King understood as early as 1961 how ghetto poverty reflected metropolitan racial apartheid, spatial and economic inequality historically engineered by government and private interests. Suburban wealth, power, and privilege formed an almost unassailable ghetto wall. "I can see no more dangerous development in our Nation than the constant building of predominantly Negro central cities, ringed by white suburbs," he told the City Hearings. As he wrote in *Where Do We Go from Here?* "The suburbs are white nooses around the black necks of the cities. Housing deteriorates in central cities; urban renewal has been Negro removal and has benefited big merchants and real estate interests; and suburbs expand with little regard for what happens to the rest of America." Black power activists responded with a radical politics of community control. King advocated empowerment within the black community but remained committed to desegregated housing across geographic lines of race and class. It was a national tragedy: "The poor and the discriminated huddle in the big cities—the poor houses of the welfare state—while affluent America displays its new gadgets in the crisp homes of suburbia." No federal policy has ever reversed this historic pattern of separation between poor and black inner cores and their white suburban rings. That comprehensive ambition was precisely what was so powerful, and so threatening, about King's strategies and dreams in Chicago. But King failed to fully grasp one strategic problem involving the class structure and dynamics of white suburbia. By confronting blue-collar defenders of homeowners "rights" in Chicago's inner suburban "bungalow belt," King hoped to dramatize the issue of housing and move legislators in Washington. Yet in between the bungalow belt and Washington lay the most powerful bastions of racial and class power, the truly affluent white-collar suburbanites living in outer rings beyond the reach of black homebuyers, black schoolchildren, and city taxes. These people could innocently consider themselves colorblind and join with King in deploring white working-class violence.[2]

The discourse of power and powerlessness that King adopted came from grassroots people who recognized leaders responsive to their grievances. In 1966, the U.S. Civil Rights Commission listened to their voices in open-ended

hearings in several cities. Ghetto residents' chief grievance was "the powerlessness of the Negro community," wrote a Massachusetts State Commissioner.
Whether discussing "housing, employment, welfare, the poverty program,
education, or municipal services, they inevitably made the point that no one
listens to them, no one consults them, no one considers their needs." Residents were especially bitter about urban renewal officials who refused to con-
sult them as bulldozers plowed through their communities. Cities practiced
blatant Jim Crow in delivering public services. People complained about police
harassment, the routine acceptance of vice and crime in slum areas, and slow
police responses to calls for help. Inferior schooling reinforced unequal
employment, they explained. Carrie McCall, who expected to graduate from a
black high school in Cleveland, knew that even with her diploma, "I'm not
going to be able to get a job anyway." Government-sponsored job training not
only failed to reach the hard-core unemployed but prepared people poorly for
the job market. Rev. Paul Younger announced that young Negroes "don't
believe you when you say training is the way to employment." David Major, a
black painting contractor, noted that in Boston developers met a labor short-
age in the construction industry by importing white workers from other states.
"The local unions are almost all-white and the imported labor is all-white. So
the Negro is either left unemployed or underemployed."

Women sharply resented the welfare system. "Man in the house" rules
barred AFDC payments to families with resident men. "A man doesn't want
to feel that he is going to take bread out of his child's mouth if he is really a
man," Mrs. King from Cleveland explained. "So he leaves." When Charlotte
Gordon of Gary, Indiana, went to work, social workers cut off her welfare
check a full month before payday, punishing her efforts at self-help. "Merchants raised prices when welfare checks were issued," welfare-reliant mothers
testified. Job training only taught them how to be "polite domestics," several
complained.[3]

Through the smoke of the urban rebellions and the sensationalized
"black power" controversy, urban activists offered eclectic, but coherent critiques of ghetto political economy, urban governance, and federal policy. At
the center of their analyses they placed powerlessness and institutional racism.
Rarely were their analyses legitimized by the commissions and public media
that defined mainstream public discourse during these years. In the end, the
politics of social justice was inundated by the politics of repression, police control, and riot prevention. Although liberals spoke of "feelings of powerlessness" without analyzing relations of power, these activists insisted that black
powerlessness was structured into the political economy. King became a
national voice for this widespread view in 1966.

Building the Chicago Coalition and Crystallizing the Issues

By mid-1965, a vibrant coalition of Chicago activists had emerged to challenge Mayor Daley and School Superintendent Benjamin Willis's perpetuation of educational segregation in school assignments. King linked this expression of institutional racism to larger patterns of labor market exploitation. The Coordinating Council of Community Organizations (CCCO) formed in opposition to Willis's policy of deliberately crowding black children into inferior schools, making them attend in double shifts while white schoolrooms had abundant vacancies. Even before he visited Chicago, King took up their issues. Education, he told the NAACP, held "the key to jobs, effective voting," and breaking the ugly "*de facto* segregation" that pervaded big cities. Public decisions had structured unequal educational and occupational opportunity in the North and South, he charged. Local officials purposefully made the Negro an expendable source of cheap labor, "the uneducated menial, the common laborer, the domestic worker." Having found one key to the ghetto prison, King envisioned its demolition and the construction of "soaring, integrated dwellings, rent controlled at the lowest levels." He had long portrayed unequal schools as symptoms of racial apartheid. Robert Penn Warren had challenged King in 1964 to find enough whites left in Washington, D.C., to integrate with the overwhelmingly black school population. "As long as there is residential segregation, and as long as the whites run to the suburbs," segregated schools remained, King confessed. The only answer was to plan "housing integration on a broad level." Short-term busing of children to integrated schools could forestall their developing "unconscious provincialism" and foster "a world perspective," but this was at best a stopgap measure.[4]

King dreamed of changing all of Chicago's structures of oppression, including Mayor Daley's power structure. In late July, King delivered twenty speeches over two days in support of CCCO and led an unprecedented 30,000 people to city hall. Decades of "indifference and exploitation" had left Chicago blacks "still protesting the social, economic, political, and educational shackles which have bound us just as surely as the leg irons of a Georgia chain gang." Chicago's "citizens and her social structures" cried out for "redemption and reform," he preached. Recognizing that SCLC had limited resources and staff, King envisioned first a spiritual transformation of the ghetto, a movement from hopelessness to hope, which became a consistent refrain in his speeches. Americans deserved "food and clothing," "culture and education," "freedom and human dignity."[5]

King met with Lyndon Johnson at the end of his northern tour. Outlining his jobs agenda, he requested the president cut off federal funds to segregated school systems and proposed legislation that would tax landlords' incomes, making ownership of slums unprofitable. "The ghetto is becoming more intensified than dispersed," King announced, recommending Johnson issue an executive order fighting discrimination by private mortgage lenders. Johnson instead handed a victory to Daley and Willis. Al Raby, chair of the CCCO, had appealed to Commissioner of Education Francis Keppel to suspend Chicago's federal aid until Willis reversed segregationist policies. On October 1, Keppel held up funds to Chicago under Title VI. King praised the move in a telegram to Johnson. But several days later, Keppel was compelled by the administration to restore the money and withdraw investigators from Chicago. Not for three more years would the federal government apply financial pressure on a northern school system. "Our work will be aimed at Washington," King announced in Chicago in January 1966.[6]

Andrew Young and James Bevel became key SCLC strategists for northern protest. Young was thrilled with the possibility of recruiting 100,000 soldiers into a nonviolent army capable of paralyzing the entire metropolitan area. SCLC could be a roving team of "social engineers" guiding local projects of "moral and spiritual urban renewal." Bevel read Kenneth Clark's *Dark Ghetto,* and in the summer of 1965 he "went down to work, to live, to be with them" in Egyptland, leading Chicago's interdenominational West Side Christian Parish. Late in October a SCLC-CCCO conference reached consensus on "abolishing" rather than improving the ghetto. Bevel argued for both building community institutions and staging demonstrations to dramatize slum conditions by targeting Chicago's realtors and developers "on television."[7] Would creation of local democratic structures be consistent with organizing Birmingham-style demonstrations?

SCLC was trying to solve a widely recognized dilemma of local empowerment and national politics aptly summarized by the activist sociologist Mike Miller: "We were all concerned about the temporariness of what we were doing in the movement. We had mobilized people for an event and it dissipated. There wasn't any continuing power that came out of it. How could you jump the gap between local problems and the omnibus economic and political issues that had to be treated on a national level?"[8] Could the inmates of the ghetto prison democratically organize themselves to control their own space and simultaneously join a powerful coalition capable of reengineering metropolitan economic landscapes?

SCLC was also attacking labor's and liberals' backyard. How could the movement both challenge labor and retain it as a powerful ally? In December 1965, the National Committee Against Discrimination in Housing sponsored a Chicago conference titled "1000 Harlems—How to Break up the Racial

Ghetto." Kenneth Clark accused Negro politicians of participating in a conspiracy "to exploit the ghetto economically." The ghetto was a prison "that
destroys and dehumanizes powerless people," he said. Only freedom from the
ghetto, not simply school desegregation, would transform black people's lives.
Clark was skeptical that organized labor would support open housing. "Most
unions are as reactionary on the housing issue as the National Association of
Manufacturers," he warned.[9] Perhaps Chicago would prove him wrong.

As with SCLC's previous southern campaigns, the ambitious political
goals of the Chicago Freedom Movement were broader than the compromises
contained in the open housing agreement with Mayor Daley and the Chicago
Real Estate Board (CREB) they secured at the moment of crisis. On January 7,
announcing the "Chicago Plan," King promised community organizing and
dramatic protest against all the "public and private institutions" that maintained slums. Northern injustice stemmed from "economic exploitation."
Adopting the vernacular of black nationalist radicals, King charged that the
slum was "a system of internal colonialism" as vicious as Belgium's exploitation of the Congo. Outsiders drained the community of "labor, money and
intellect." Chicago's 300,000 Negro workers found little beyond low-paying
service sector employment. Blacks comprised 23 percent of the population but
43 percent of the unemployed; the figure concealed thousands who avoided
employment offices, knowing "only a few dirty jobs were available." Whites-
only building trades unions locked out eager, qualified black workers. The
housing market was just as oppressive. Slumlords refused to maintain ghetto
buildings, bilking poor tenants of every dime. Black renters and home buyers
paid more for worse housing than their white counterparts, a vicious "color
tax" on their right to shelter. Realtors steered black clients back to the ghetto,
while banks and mortgage companies refused loans. Private institutions were
powerful, but the public sector played an integral role in oppression; hence it
could play the largest role in liberation. Blacks paid taxes but were cheated out
of quality education and city services. The courts and police were "enforcers"
of the ghetto colony, while city hall robbed "the community of its democratic
voice." The federal government had not addressed the urban crisis or the legacies of "slavery and segregation."[10]

The Chicago Plan meticulously outlined the political economy of the
ghetto but lacked a strategy to link specific tactics with broad objectives. King's
promise to "concentrate all of our forces and move in concert with a nonviolent army on each and every issue" reveals one of its strategic weaknesses: the
movement dispersed too few forces to bang on too many doors at once. They
planned to organize "unions to end slums" to develop black economic power
and recruit a base for mass direct action. Jesse Jackson would bring in minis-

ters through Chicago's Operation Breadbasket, which on a small scale was effectively winning jobs for blacks through community boycotts. The unemployed would organize to demand "meaningful employment and training." By March, King expected consensus on targets for "massive action." In the end they had no more success organizing unemployed black workers than had the Chicago SDS's Economic Research and Action Project.[11]

Big-city politics erected strong barriers. "The Negro IS the victim of 'economic exploitation,'" carped television commentator Len O'Connor, but "political exploitation" cemented the largest stones in the ghetto prison; blacks surrendered their only weapon, their vote, "to a precinct captain." King hoped to avoid a confrontation with Daley, whose resources and local power swelled with War on Poverty patronage dollars. King was "leading a campaign against the slums," not Daley, he explained disingenuously in March. Daley denied Chicago had any "slums," then bragged he had the largest rat eradication program in the nation. With over 30,000 jobs at their disposal and control over rent subsidies, housing code inspections, and welfare programs, Daley and his black clients constituted a formidable obstacle to independent action. The Daley machine used tactics of economic intimidation common in the South. Bob Lucas, president of Chicago CORE, recalled black precinct captains telling people, "If you don't vote for the Democratic ticket, you're going to be tossed off the welfare rolls [or] put out of the housing project." Community activist Clory Bryant ran against the Daley machine in the early 1960s. Public housing managers raised her rent from $61 to $178 a month, and neighbors and supporters stayed home, fearing reprisals from attentive aldermen.[12]

To dramatize the lack of decent, affordable housing, King moved into a third-floor walkup in Lawndale on Hamlin Avenue near "Bloody 16th Street," a neighborhood with eighty-two storefront churches and seventy bars. Businesses were closing as middle- and working-class people left the neighborhood, some of them benefiting from new poverty program jobs. SCLC assumed management of King's building, collecting rent for cleaning and repairs. Newspapers reported the owner was an elderly, bankrupt man too poor to correct the twenty-three code violations that Daley's building inspectors suddenly found. If absentee landlords were broke, the ghetto looked less like a product of exploitation than a place of economic marginality. Stanley Levison suggested that King keep moving addresses until Daley sent inspectors to every tenement in the city. King predicted "exciting days ahead." But Andrew Young complained to Levison that "Daley would not put them in jail" for illegally occupying the building. They had no other way to dramatize cold and unhealthy housing "for people with children in the winter." SCLC needed a radical action program that Daley could not co-opt or imitate, Young told Levison. "Daley is not in favor of rent strikes," Levison commented.[13]

Months of organizing did not recruit a nonviolent army, but the Chicago Freedom Movement assembled an impressive coalition with labor and Catholic support. The Chicago Freedom Festival on March 12 netted SCLC $80,000. King was especially eloquent. Black migrants had come north to encounter "not a land of plenty but a lot replete with poverty . . . not a Promised Land but rather another Egypt-land of denial, discrimination and dismay." King looked forward to a sea change in consciousness as ghetto blacks moved from passive subjects to active citizens, announcing that the ghetto's days were numbered. Labor remained schizoid, but King had reason for hope. The Chicago Federation of Labor and the Industrial Union Council, both in league with Daley and dominated by the lily-white building trades, spurned the movement. But in February, seventy-eight union leaders, under pressure from their black members, joined the freedom movement. Thousands of unionists showed up to rallies. SCLC cemented an alliance with the reliable United Packinghouse Workers of America (UPWA). Walter Reuther's AFL-CIO Industrial Union Department (IUD) supplied 125 organizers to help build the West Side Lawndale Community Union. They achieved unheralded but impressive results in tenant organizing. SCLC was organizing a movement to abolish "poverty of the spirit" so people could challenge "institutions which have relegated them to a life of economic and social deprivation," King told an interviewer. James Orange from Birmingham organized gang truces, threatening rival gangs with death if they strayed from nonviolence. "You think of West Side Story!" Levison exclaimed after the meeting.[14]

The ministers were no match for Daley's public relations and patronage machine, however, and neighborhood organizing failed to galvanize a broad visible constituency. In a story headlined "Dr. King Stirs Chicago But Still Lacks a Program," the *New York Times* reprinted official public relations materials meant to demonstrate that Daley's Urban Progress Centers made King's movement unnecessary: "29,000 apartments sealed and sprayed for rats . . . 23,000 poor children in Head Start kindergartens . . . 11,000 youths in the neighborhood youth corps." The *New York Times* quoted Bevel describing domestic colonialism. But next to Daley's concrete "achievements," the movement looked utopian even to Levison, who shortly thereafter told Clarence Jones that King was fruitlessly "trying to formulate a program for Chicago which they haven't got and need."[15]

In late June 1966, SCLC abruptly redirected its resources from community organizing to dramatic, media-focused demonstrations targeting realtors and white homeowners. King's March freedom festival speech ranged over several ills but gave primacy to the racially restrictive housing market responsible for segregated education and the "color tax" on ghetto housing. The walls of the "Dark Ghetto have arisen all around the Negro, with race prejudice and ghetto economics barring his escape into the community's better areas and suburbs," King proclaimed. Generation after generation of Negroes found themselves hung up by a "conspiratorial noose" tied by realtors, financial institutions, and white homeowners observing "restrictive covenants and (un)gentleman(ly) agreements." King primed his audience for dramatic protests. Northerners were wrong to insist that "legislation, welfare and anti-poverty programs now replaced demonstrations." Blacks had little strength except through protest and "creative tensions," King argued.[16]

SCLC and CCCO decided on demonstrations at a strategy session on June 29, but the decision revealed class and ideological strains within the movement. Bevel made a compelling case for organizing open housing marches in the suburbs concurrently with rent strikes in the slums. The Quaker activist William Moyer inspired them with reports of successful open housing marches on the North Shore. Most blacks could not buy houses in white neighborhoods, but marching offered the Negro the chance to "stand up and be a man," Bevel argued. Raising Chicago's visibility through an action program was his uppermost concern, as it was for King. "You can present bodies to bring about creative tension to expose the problem," King explained. "Economic and school problems are bound to this open city idea." King had a strong faith that Johnson and Congress would deliver on the open housing provisions of the 1966 civil rights bill. Jesse Jackson argued that community organizing could never "tackle the root causes of the slum." But a new Moses could lead a "*new Exodus . . .* into the broad land of decent houses, fresh air, and clean neighborhoods." Spiritual hope, marching feet, and television cameras might again educate the nation and transform a repressive social system. The decision remained controversial. CCCO administrator Al Pitcher thought SCLC's priorities were warped by the need to keep contributions rolling in by winning a publicized "national victory." Al Raby declared suburban marches had little appeal to ghetto blacks, who needed bread more than bungalows. But in late July, Andrew Young admitted to a reporter, "The trouble here is that there has been no confrontation . . . where they interrupted the network TV programs."[17] Mass protest was SCLC's métier, and demonstrations had won national legislation, resolving terrible southern dilemmas of local power. Why not galvanize a similar coalition of conscience around northern housing?

Nonviolence, Violence, and Power in Chicago

The "action phase" of the Chicago Freedom Movement commenced July 10, when King addressed an interracial crowd of 30,000 at Soldier Field on a blistering hot day. Organizers had assembled a broad coalition whose power might be amplified by national media events. The Chicago Urban League and local NAACP had joined the SCLC-CCCO bandwagon. Floyd McKissick of CORE agreed to speak. St. Clair Drake led the College Committee. The Spanish Speaking Committee reached out to Puerto Ricans, and the Welfare Committee assisted mothers in formulating demands on city government. Al Sampson organized the Freedom Army Committee, which was composed of gang members. The meatpackers, auto workers, steelworkers, and public employees marched with King. Organizers recruited clergy and rabbis. Catholic archbishop John Cody sent a message declaring housing discrimination sinful, instructing Catholics to join "the social revolution." Cody also urged unions to open up their apprenticeship ladders to blacks. Preaching self-help, National Baptist Convention president J. H. Jackson spurned the rally and denounced nonviolence as a Trojan horse for violence.[18]

At the rally, King indicted institutional racism in the most militant terms. Slums were "perpetuated by the huge real estate agencies, mortgage and banking institutions, and city, state and federal governments." He endorsed Bevel's dual strategy of mobilization at ghetto walls and organization within the black community. King quoted the Chicago Freedom Movement Program statement: "We are tired of living in rat-infested slums and in the Chicago Housing Authority's cement reservation. . . . We are tired of a welfare system which dehumanizes us and dispenses payments under procedures that are often ugly and paternalistic." He denounced inferior schools, job discrimination, the racial gap in incomes, and the "color tax." Aware of mounting white resistance, King exhorted his audience not to wait for Johnson, the Supreme Court, Congress, or Mayor Daley to free them.[19]

The Chicago Freedom Movement Program presented a detailed blueprint for reconstructing the ghetto. King marched to city hall and taped the lengthy document to the door, but few journalists or subsequent historians credited its detailed critique of urban political economy and institutional racism. Drafted by a CCCO committee, it called for "equality of opportunity and of results," integrated "housing, employment and education," and "power for the powerless." Open housing led the list of immediate action demands. Realtors, brokers, and banks must stop discriminating and support open occupancy legislation at the state and local levels. The Chicago Housing Authority must rehabilitate the public housing projects and build low-cost housing across Chicago. Ghettoized welfare recipients should receive subsidized housing in integrated projects. Congress must pass the civil rights bill, and Johnson must rectify Kennedy's failings by issuing an executive order covering all financial institutions.[20]

A laundry list of demands on government at all levels followed, incorporating the national agenda of the social democrats and the demands of local organizers for participation in powerful agencies. They aimed at the jugular of Daley's black patronage network, demanding "direct funding of Chicago community organizations by the Office of Economic Opportunity." Metropolitan-wide planning in housing and economic development would break down city-suburb divisions of power and privilege. The government should create "tens of thousands of new jobs" in urban reconstruction and hire equal numbers in "new sub-professional positions in health, education and welfare." They called for eliminating "welfare dependency by a guaranteed adequate annual income." Welfare Departments must recognize the right of "welfare unions" to bargain collectively, broaden eligibility requirements for poor families, and stop social workers from snooping in people's homes looking for men. They demanded equal "protection from police and the courts," and establishment of civilian police review boards. Precinct captains should be required to live in their districts. Job integration and promotion within government, business, and unions, and a $2 state minimum wage law would equalize economic opportunities.[21] The Chicago Freedom Movement had both a detailed blueprint of the ghetto prison and the key to unlocking one of its largest doors.

On July 14, blacks battled police on the West Side, creating sensational news that movement manifestos could not match. Police turned off a fire hydrant in ninety-eight-degree heat, triggering a confrontation with neighborhood youths and a three-day conflagration of looting, burning, and shooting. Two blacks died from police fire, and two police were wounded. Daley accused SCLC of inciting insurrection by showing a film about Watts. Aghast, King insisted they were educating black youth about the senseless destructiveness of violence. Mayor Daley had more power than anyone to prevent violence; by resisting the Chicago Freedom Movement Program, Daley was "inviting social disaster." King called for "structural changes," not sprinklers, and "massive programs" driven by moral urgency, not political expediency. Now directly challenging the machine, King promised a voter registration drive and threatened a mass obstruction of expressways to "fill the jails."[22]

On the last night of violence, Friday, July 15, gang members met with King and Andrew Young. Black youth "talked mainly about a desperate need for jobs," Young remembered, "but more than ever before about political power." King had plunged into the embattled night with about 100 ministers to preach nonviolence. They failed, as an estimated 5,000 citizens battled 1,000 police. National Guardsmen suppressed the riot. By early morning, gang leaders agreed to try nonviolence, though only "as a tactic." They called Daley's machine "oppressive," his Negro politicians "pawns." Their call for "power to the people" directly resulted from their wounded dignity at the hands of "police intimidation and harassment," Young announced. Immediately he called for a civilian review board. King announced violence was a response to "elected officials whose myopic racial vision has been further blurred by political expediency." Daley promised to put sprinklers on 244 fire hydrants and build several swimming pools in the ghetto. But playing to his white constituency, Daley attacked SCLC's support for youthful "colonial extortion empires," gangs that undermined black people's presumed high respect for the police. Daley appointed an internal police "panel." The police chief accused civil rights leaders of fomenting "tensions" and "animosities" with their overblown accusations of brutality.[23]

King was especially distressed by the nation's failure to understand nonviolent protest as anything other than a prelude to violent uprisings. "Publicity is not solving the problem," one woman wrote to him. King ran "from place to place starting little wars" with his calls for open housing and civil disobedience, she alleged. Again King struggled to maintain the blurring line in the press between disciplined demonstrators and rioters. "Nothing hurts me more than to see the television commentators refer to the chaotic outburst of an angry mob as a demonstration," he said. Distressingly but justifiably, ghetto blacks were concluding that violence was the only effective strategy for changing institutions. West Side blacks protested their "lily-white fire station" for ten years, but the city integrated it after one night of rioting, King announced. He was convinced that rioting eroded both white support and black faith in the possibility of nonviolent change. Starting a riot was becoming the surest way to get a summer jobs program.[24]

The Chicago riot was a turning point in King's radicalization. Police domination and institutional racism became key to understanding ghetto exploitation; they made empowerment the key to solving the urban crisis, King stated publicly and wrote in his column. The "power elite" could no longer control Negroes in open revolt; they could only decide whether black oppression would be overthrown violently or nonviolently. "Frustration generates aggression," King argued, reflecting prevailing sociological theories of collective behavior. Though a minority of residents had rioted, the grievances of the ghetto were widespread, the rioters enjoyed broad support, and the violence

Figure 8. After two days of pitched battles between police and residents of Chicago's West Side, African American Army National Guardsmen swept the streets searching young men for weapons, "restoring" order but not peace on July 16, 1966. Power became the central defining concept behind King's explanations for poverty and violence. "Police state conditions . . . are abhorrent to our Democratic traditions," he wrote. Copyright Bettmann/CORBIS.

was a response to "suppression" facing all classes of blacks. Millions of nonrioters "vicariously felt that they were striking out at the oppressor," especially police, King declared. Sociologists and social psychologists later reached the same conclusions after studying thousands of arrest records and surveying ghetto residents. One teenage Vice Lord confirmed, "It wasn't just the gangs. It was everybody. The people didn't want to riot. They wanted their rights." King reiterated that ghetto residents were "powerless" because their lives were "dominated by the welfare worker and the police man," while landlords and merchants took their profits to the suburbs. The whole slum system, not just schools, provided "cheap surplus labor in times of economic boom," he explained. Men could not be breadwinners, so manhood expressed itself in gang violence, which was deadlier than rioting but a matter of supreme indifference to whites. When they lashed out, ghetto residents were "blamed for their own victimization." Ironically, only when blacks attacked white property and police did white officials and reporters recognize their agency. "Law and order" rationalized history's most brutal forms of oppression. "Armed force cannot solve the underlying social problems," he asserted; "police state conditions . . . are abhorrent to our Democratic traditions."[25]

Powerlessness took primacy over social and economic deprivation in King's explanations of urban violence. Rustin's focus on jobs, housing, and education could no longer contain King's sense of the complex architecture of the ghetto prison. Police brutality invariably lit "the spark which ignites the flame of ghetto hostility," he told SCLC in August. The police department symbolized the "powerlessness and voicelessness of the ghetto." The limited scope and elite domination of the War on Poverty also had fatal consequences. A bureaucratic and "political maze" deflected good ideas and attacked symptoms, not causes. Chicago blacks expected a Marshall Plan, not Mayor Daley's "kindergarten projects." Antipoverty appropriations raised poor people's expectations for "dignity and opportunity," King charged, "while providing City Hall with additional patronage with which to further humiliate the poor, by making a mockery of the issue of maximum participation." Violence was almost inevitable, given the betrayal of liberal promises. "Petunia planting projects in Chicago's slums or rodent control units can only whet the appetite for real dignity and bring more fury at its denial," King told SCLC. Confronting "the giants of vested interest" required actual power.[26]

Empowerment through local organizing bore fruit but had little impact outside the ghetto. Buried in the pages of the *Pittsburgh Courier* in August was news of a signal victory, hardly visible outside Lawndale. The Federation of Tenant Unions, with the help of the AFL-CIO's IUD, had organized several thousand renters, held rent strikes, and negotiated new contracts for 3,000 tenants. A white real estate broker pronounced it "the beginning of a very serious revolution," and another cheered it as the beginning of much-needed ghetto revitalization. King celebrated a "landmark" federal court decision giving organized tenants the legal right to bargain collectively for rent and improvements.[27] But legal victories did little to diminish the sense of crisis and the urgency of attacking ghetto walls.

To the SCLC-CCCO coalition, the uprisings underscored the urgency of organized protest and the need for concrete concessions to lend credibility to nonviolence. No one in the Daley camp wanted to stage-manage nonviolent theater, especially when it was likely to provoke Daley's white working-class base in the bungalow belt to violence. Daley was bound to lose support in both black and white ethnic wards. The Chicago Freedom Movement's "action phase" escalated protests over the next three weeks until the mayor, a host of city agencies, local business leaders, and CREB were compelled to negotiate. Black and white couples "tested" realty offices and found them guilty of discrimination. Demonstrators staged interracial picnics and vigils in all-white neighborhoods and organized mass marches on realty offices. They were met by ever larger and more violent white crowds, most of them working-class Catholics in open revolt against the liberal church hierarchy. On August 5 in Gage Park, facing 4,000 angry whites, King took a blow to the temple from a flying rock. For the first time the Chicago Freedom Movement appeared on the front pages of national newspapers. Catholic reporter Karen Koko watched marchers' cars get firebombed, as youths screamed, "Burn them like Jews!" Sister Mary Angelica was felled by a flying paving stone in the parish where she taught first grade. Parishioners mobbed their own churches when priests held civil rights meetings, shutting them down. Mayor Daley increased police protection as demonstrations gained momentum and numbers. On August 8, Jesse Jackson announced plans to march on the town of Cicero, infamous for its 1952 riot against blacks trying to integrate an apartment complex. Key white allies began to defect. Archbishop Cody and Robert Johnson of the UAW met with Daley and called for a moratorium on demonstrations. Bevel acidly commented that if Cody lacked "the courage to speak up for Christ, let him join the devil." On August 14, Bevel led five hundred protesters through the downtown Loop, and the movement staged multiple marches on white neighborhoods. Daley, his police resources stretched dangerously thin, agreed to a "summit meeting" and dragged the bureaucrats, businessmen, and realtors in with him.[28]

Chicago Freedom Movement negotiators, CREB, the Conference on Religion and Race, and the Daley administration met on August 17. A chasm opened between the ministers' hortatory pulpit politics and city hall's politics of backroom horse trading. Daley's highest priority was to end demonstrations, so he formally agreed with all the movement's demands but remained evasive on measures for implementation. He deflected the pressure onto the quasi-public, quasi-private CREB, over which he disavowed any influence. CREB was adamant in denying its power over the private real estate market. King, Bevel, and Young demanded that Daley and CREB implement a comprehensive, enforceable "plan to aggressively desegregate the city." But the private, impersonal, and individualistic real estate market, Daley and CREB countered, was not amenable to public policy interventions. The summit meeting was punctuated by bitter exchanges about race. When Young said he feared Lawndale's "jammed-up, neurotic, psychotic Negroes" more than white mobs, Daley thought he was threatening further riots. Unless the ghetto was dispersed, Young retorted, the city would burn—with or without a movement. "The city didn't create this frustration or this situation," Daley responded. King interjected, "I hope we are here to discuss how to make Chicago a great city and not how to end marches. . . . We're trying to make justice a reality. . . . We want peace, but peace is the presence of justice."[29]

Daley's mixture of concessions and deflections of responsibility saved him from white recriminations and left a divided freedom movement holding what many saw as paper promises. The city promised to enforce its housing ordinance and pledged that welfare recipients and anyone displaced by urban renewal would find public housing all over the city. CREB promised to withdraw "all opposition to the philosophy of open housing" at the state level. Charles Hayes of UPWA thought this an absurd concession to show ghetto blacks. Daley obtained a court injunction restricting marches, and King threatened to defy the injunction and march on Cicero if the negotiations collapsed. But black negotiators had issued a preliminary list of demands that fell shy of the full range of their goals, and businessman Ben Heineman, who mediated the negotiations, held them to their original agenda. The final agreement issued on August 28 added up to little more than a series of nondiscrimination pledges to be monitored by the Conference on Religion and Race, a body with no legal enforcement authority. Bevel and Jackson felt outmaneuvered and wanted to march on Cicero. Unwilling to risk a bloodbath, King and Young shut down demonstrations and declared victory. Activists who charged King and the SCLC-CCCO negotiators with a "sell out" marched on Cicero anyway, and black demonstrators fought back this time.[30]

King admitted that SNCC-style grassroots organizing might have worked better than SCLC-style dramatic demonstrations. The Birmingham and Selma protests did not develop "permanent, seasoned and militant organizations," he wrote soon thereafter. "The tortuous job of organizing solidly and simultaneously in thousands of places was not a feature of our work." Instead they pursued a "crisis policy" that relied on "explosive events." Earlier, the media had projected images of nonviolent demonstrators suffering violent white repression. Now images of black rioters and of police protecting interracial demonstrators from white mobs filled the newspapers and television screens. As with all the southern campaigns, SCLC's penetrating analysis and ambitions far outstripped the concessions they won. The difference was that there was no Negro Revolution of 1966. No massive wave of protests spread across the contested terrain of northern cities. Instead, what followed was electoral backlash, more rioting, and policy reversals from Washington.[31]

King had hoped the demonstrations would galvanize Congress behind open housing legislation. Lyndon Johnson's proposed civil rights bill included prohibitions on discrimination by owners, developers, brokers, lenders, "and all others engaged in the sale, rental or financing of housing." In one sense it was Johnson's substitute for a costlier program of urban reconstruction widely demanded in the movement. The National Association of Real Estate Boards effectively lobbied against what they called threats "to property values and free enterprise." Johnson acceded to a series of House amendments that exempted 60 percent of the nation's housing from coverage, including small apartment buildings and homes sold by individuals through brokers. SCLC accused Johnson of "immoral, unprincipled surrender" to the real estate industry. When the bill died in the Senate on September 19, King openly doubted that Johnson did "battle for the bill." Ironically, tragically, when Johnson presented a stronger housing bill in 1968, it was not King's nonviolent activism but the rioting that followed his assassination that swayed the Senate to pass it.[32]

Though Congress and the realtors were as culpable, SCLC activists blamed city hall. "We saw the machine as the basis of the slums, of the poverty, of the exploitation of black folk," Young remembered. The failed Chicago agreement had as much to do with realtors, brokers, homeowners, renters, and financial institutions, not to mention the Catholics and laborites who jumped ship when the seas got rough. But the riots, protests, and negotiations revealed Daley's expertise at deflecting challenges to his power. As the Chicago movement turned from open housing back to the whole array of issues keeping Chicago blacks poor and powerless, the mayor appeared all too plainly as the prison warden. This realization propelled SCLC toward electoral strategies and a host of smaller, more local commitments. King celebrated all along the Chicago movement that preceded and followed his participation, praising the "community organizations, tenant unions, unions of unemployed, all united in a city wide movement." The interracial "coalition of conscience is rapidly emerging as a coalition of power," he announced just before negotiations.

Bevel commented on the broad and ongoing movement: "In Chicago, we had an open housing movement, and we organized rent strikes. We persuaded food stores to hire thousands of Negroes. We persuaded the Negroes to deposit their money in the black banks. We made the city hire Negroes to collect the garbage. We did a good job in Chicago."[33] King placed increasing emphasis on these local campaigns, but he knew they would not transform the economic geography of chocolate cities strangled by white nooses.

Black Power and White Backlash

Concurrently with the Chicago campaign, King managed the black power debate that threatened to split the March on Washington coalition apart. King thought the controversy destructive and overblown, as SNCC national leaders Stokely Carmichael and H. Rap Brown made news issuing inflammatory statements whites easily dismissed as "extremist." Whites treated even reasoned and articulate defenses of black power as a call to armed struggle, "black supremacy," and "reverse racism." King tried to mediate between black leadership separated by class, ideology, and generational experience. He tried to translate black power into terms understandable to whites. Few whites understood the common ground activists shared across the spectrum of black politics. Then the elections of 1966 registered the full force of white resistance and returned control of Congress to a centrist-conservative coalition with little interest in racial reconstruction. The white backlash was a response to rioting and to black demands for full equality, King was convinced, but he was concerned enough with sensationalized rhetoric to try to redefine black power.

Back in March, King had expected hardened opposition when the movement challenged "financial privilege," referring mainly to ghetto profiteers: slumlords, racist employers, and machine politicians resisting costly encroachments on their turf. Now white homeowners, many of them union members and Catholics, were reacting with an intensity of "hate" King had never seen in the South. Youths screamed "White Power!" in South Deering, jeering "Archbishop Cody and his Commie coons." King thought they suffered from "unfounded fears that Negroes create slums and constitute a threat to jobs," the *New York Times* reported. Marching brought to the surface "latent" hatreds among whites living in "low income enclaves," King said. King's class analysis did not cut very deeply into white society or fashion a political strategy to overcome the volatile mixture of economic insecurity and racial prejudice motivating white homeowners. In *Where Do We Go from Here?* King did not discuss how workers bore the burdens of integration while middle-class whites safely retreated to the suburbs. Whites were never committed to helping

Negroes "out of poverty, exploitation or all forms of discrimination," he wrote categorically. The rising "expectations of the Negro crashed into the stone walls of white resistance." King did not distinguish ghetto profiteers and rapacious realtors from working-class white ethnics who had barely escaped the inner city themselves. Reading King's statement that he had never "seen such hate," one woman from the bungalow belt wrote him that "these people are AFRAID!" The only Negroes her neighbors knew were those they saw on television, "Negroes who beat each other up, knife and shoot each other," Negroes in the streets, "rioting, looting, and burning." All whites wanted was "a safe neighborhood," so they kept running. "I haven't run—yet," she wrote. Explaining her neighbors' ignorance, however, she revealed her own when she asked why King couldn't work with youth to clean up the ghettos and become "plumbers and electricians." King did not write back to explain the monopoly building trades unions held on apprenticeships. Only black newspapers published the Chicago Plan.[34]

King stepped aggressively into "private" spaces, inflaming the backlash without strengthening the liberal "coalition of conscience," James Ralph argues. But from King's vantage point, advances had only come through struggle and confrontation. And there was nothing private about discriminatory banks, racist realtors, or Federal Housing Administration (FHA) mortgage appraisal policies that favored racially homogenous neighborhoods. Still, King's faith in executive leadership, legislation, and the mutability of custom may not have served him well. King confidently reiterated his southern argument that "morality cannot be legislated, but behavior can be regulated." If government enforced open occupancy, white toughs in Gage Park would soon be "playing basketball with Negroes," he told an August rally. The November elections certainly were a shock. "The crack of the white backlash reverberates across the nation, in Georgia, Alabama, California and Illinois," King commented. But this same reactionary force had undone Reconstruction and the movement would not "be intimidated," he resolved. In fact, race was not the only issue that drove white working-class people to defect from liberalism. The Vietnam War and war-induced inflation proved equally damaging, as blue-collar wages stagnated and workers expressed resentments of both Johnson's war and the middle-class antiwar movement. But in specific locales race proved powerful. Democrats lost forty-seven seats in the House, three seats in the Senate, and eight state houses. Illinois voters threw out of office liberal senator Paul Douglas, long a supporter of fair housing legislation and targeted jobs programs. Voters barely reelected Chicago's Democratic representative Roman Puchinsky, although he had supported the crippling House amendments to Johnson's bill. People in the Polish neighborhoods of his district were unconcerned with "Vietnam or rising prices or prosperity" but obsessed with "Martin Luther King and how they are moving in on us," he reported back in September. Puchinsky abandoned his support for open housing, which had long been one of the least popular civil rights goal with whites. In March 1967, only 24 percent of Americans polled by the Gallup organization wanted Congress to pass an "open housing bill."[35]

Observers saw what King never quite fully acknowledged: a revolt within the rank and file of Chicago unions and parishes. "Racist mobs . . . included not only many members of the building construction unions, but even white members of unions whose leaders were on the steering committee of the Chicago Freedom Movement," Philip Foner has noted. "Something tragic" happened to labor, King told a Louisville rally the next year, not mentioning these splits: "I have found in many instances businessmen more progressive."[36] King subsequently became more pessimistic about the liberalism of the white majority and looked instead to disfranchised groups and students to energize the progressive coalition.

The black power controversy was rooted in years of parallel praxis within the complex southern and northern movements, but it exploded in the mainstream press in early June after James Meredith was shot on a rural Mississippi road. King journeyed to Mississippi to join the Meredith March Against Fear, and stood fast when Whitney Young and Roy Wilkins backed out of the march after Stokely Carmichael demanded an all-black march with armed protection. Carmichael and Willie Ricks introduced the "Black Power!" slogan before a crowd in Canton, Mississippi, after suffering beatings and jailings. Internal contention, outrageous rhetoric, and threats of violence all proved extremely newsworthy; journalists shunted aside issues of poverty and urban segregation, which King had sought to make the center of public debate. King expressed "immediate reservations," afraid the slogan's needlessly "hostile connotations" would split the movement and fuel white backlash. King lamented that the slogan had deflected attention from the poverty of Mississippi and the need for a civil rights act in 1966, which would also have more substantially protected southern organizers' right to protest and organize, as well as forbid discrimination in jury selection. King withdrew his support for a strongly negative and, he feared, divisive critique of black power issued by Rustin, A. Philip Randolph, Wilkins, and Young. Black power was a distracting side issue, King charged. White elites purposely seized upon it "to justify resistance to change." The real issue should be the existence of "35 million poor" in an affluent society. It was time to organize "the poor in a crusade to reform society in order to realize economic and social justice."[37]

Black power was both a response and a stimulus to the white backlash, King thought. Power was a political and economic imperative; only separatism and attacks on nonviolence he found objectionable. Unsuccessful at dissuading CORE and SNCC activists from using the phrase, King reinterpreted it. In Memphis on June 7, King explained power was simply a means "to bring about political and economic change." Mass nonviolent action was the highest expression of black power. "Anyone throwing bricks against state troopers and national guardsmen and people with machine guns is not only violent, but they're foolish," he added. In Grenada, Mississippi, King endorsed local efforts to develop a cooperative supermarket with Small Business Administration funding and he supported new public housing that blacks could own. As an "expression of the collective pooling of resources," King said, the supermarket exercised "concrete, real black power." On June 12, as they marched through Marks, Mississippi, King praised Fannie Lou Hamer for facing violence and job loss, implicitly praising her steadfast interracialism in the face of nationalist arguments and the expulsion of whites from SNCC. Fearing the divisiveness of black power, King called for organizational unity to assault white "political dynasties . . . principalities and powers." He wanted more power and less talk about power, but the shrill ideological debate and the celebrity it brought key SNCC leaders accelerated that organization's loss of contact with the grassroots in black communities.[38]

Journalists and political elites minimized the common ground between the "nonviolent integrationist" and "black power" wings of the movement. While King basked in senatorial adulation during the City Hearings, Robert Kennedy berated CORE chairman Floyd McKissick for advocating black power. Programmatically, McKissick and King shared more common ground than not. Violence, not the black power slogan, fed the backlash, McKissick testified, pointing proudly to nonviolent CORE organizers who helped prevent rioting in Baltimore. McKissick denounced the social violence of ghetto schooling, job discrimination, and "the humiliation of public welfare." He shared King's dreams of federally financed jobs programs and full political citizenship, and echoed King's call for "a shift in priorities and values" away from war toward a real war on poverty. Like King, he pointed out that funding for military intervention in Southeast Asia and subsidies for corporations far outstripped niggardly spending on "welfare for the undeserving." Blacks demanded quality schools and aggressive desegregation, better housing and job-creating investment in the ghetto. Expressing CORE's move toward bourgeois black nationalism, McKissick explained that the black man must believe "he can become a black capitalist, not an exploiter but a black capitalist."[39] In calling for private investment and black capitalism, McKissick was actually closer to Robert Kennedy's policy approach than was King, whose democratic socialism led him to see flaws in the black capitalist strategy.

In *Where Do We Go from Here?* King synthesized the truths of black power with his commitment to integration, which he positively redefined to include shared power and redistributive justice. Concepts of cultural and economic interdependence had always been central to King's sermonizing.

However much we may try to romanticize the slogan, there is no separate black path to power and fulfillment that does not intersect white paths, and there is no separate white path to power and fulfillment, short of social disaster, that does not share that power with black aspirations for freedom and human dignity. We are bound together in a single garment of destiny. . . . The American Negro is neither totally African nor totally Western. He is Afro-American, a true hybrid, a combination of two cultures.[40]

Salvation was found in sharing culture and political power within a just economic order, not "separatism." Nevertheless, King conceded that in places such as the Alabama black belt, black power was the only viable strategy: "In many places, there are no white liberals or moderates to cooperate with," he conceded. As Rev. William McKinley Branch, a newly elected black official in Greene County, Alabama, explained, "We wanted the government to be polka dot, but the whites wouldn't cooperate, so we had to make it all chocolate."[41]

In numerous speeches over the next year, King hammered away at the negatives and positives of black power. Violence or even its poses would be suicidal and only provoke a more violent backlash. He pointed out the absurdity of trying to imitate the Cuban revolution in the United States. Castro had wide popular support and faced a divided army; neither condition favored black American revolutionaries. Again and again King called for the "creative and constructive" development of "political and economic power." Black power brought pride in blackness and was a "powerful psychological call to manhood." But King insisted that there was a much greater "masculinity and strength in nonviolence."[42] Much of King's journey in the last year of his life became an attempt to demonstrate how blacks could build substantive black power while cultivating alliances and aiming for an integrated society where whites and blacks of different classes shared political and economic power. King thought through his own synthesis of black power, integration, and democratic socialism. King also tested various strategies for bringing community organizations to bear on complex relations of power.

Urban Politics and Community Empowerment

Martin Luther King drew important lessons from the Chicago marches and concurrent efforts at community empowerment. Chicago renewed his sense of social ministry to the poor, his empathy for their plight, and his appreciation of their capacities. He rededicated himself to evangelizing the black middle class and the larger society to support economic redistribution. On August 28, King delivered his "Good Samaritan" sermon to Ebenezer Baptist Church. "I choose to identify with the underprivileged," he preached. "I choose to identify with the poor. I choose to give my life for the hungry [and] those who have been left out of the sunlight of opportunity."⁴³ King was proud he had offered Chicago's gang members a "sense of belonging." Gang members became nonviolent parade marshals, walking through a hail of rocks without retaliating. The Blackstone Rangers later sang at concerts to raise money, winning foundation and OEO job-training grants. The ghetto poor were not completely isolated and demoralized by their colonial domination, King concluded. Resourceful and adaptable, they could build strong institutions if they were given adequate resources. Bars were not the only ghetto institutions, he told the senators at the City Hearings. Churches cultivated hope, not hopelessness. Perhaps only 10 percent of the people were so "scarred" and "pathological" that they might choose violence. Remarkably, the other 90 percent refused drugs, rioting, and self-destructive "activities that they are driven to because of hopeless circumstances." King concluded that swift action was necessary to rescue the majority of decent people and their institutions.⁴⁴

Middle-class Negroes had to reach down to the grassroots "to organize and gain identity with ghetto dwellers and young people," King said. No wonder the Negro masses felt alienated from both white society and the Negro middle class. Too many successful Negroes swam away from "the muddy waters into the fresh water" where they "quickly forgot the stench of the back waters." They callously forgot "that uneducated and poverty-stricken mothers and fathers often worked until their eyebrows were scorched and their hands bruised so that their children could get an education." Privileged people would never realize their full human potential until their underprivileged brothers and sisters could also become who they "ought to be."⁴⁵

Cross-class mutual aid among black people was not enough, however. The black poor also needed the empathy of white humanitarians and the resources of the federal government. The white majority's poverty of conscience found its mirror image in the ghetto's "despair," he told Robert Kennedy. Invisible to middle-class suburbanites speeding past on elevated superhighways, poor people's cries of frustration were "unheard" and "unfelt." Kennedy enthusiastically agreed.[46]

Chicago's metropolitan racial and class segregation proved much more intractable than segregated southern public accommodations. Daley, CREB, and all the city's agencies failed to implement their parts of the agreement, King announced in March 1967. Black and white couples again tested the housing market and found the same hard raw discrimination. Perhaps militant "apostles of social disorder" were right to declare the settlement "a sham." Having tested local protest mobilization and political theater, King had already moved on to projects inspired by the organizing tradition and black power.[47]

King reconciled desegregation with community development in principle. The goal, he explained to Senator Ribicoff, was to balance long-term integration with short-term improvement of city housing and schools. In *Where Do We Go from Here?* King called for the construction of temporary ghetto housing, which would be torn down within twenty years as society made progress toward residential desegregation.[48]

Chicago deepened King's sense of the role public and private institutions played in maintaining the malignant kinship between race and class. In November 1966, King argued that the movement was now "grappling with basic class issues between the privileged and the underprivileged." To restructure America's social architecture would "cost the nation something," he said repeatedly. He also concluded racism was even more entrenched in American culture and social structures than he had earlier believed. With SCLC in November, King explained that major institutions were "structured on the basis of racism." "Genocide" now described not simply the massacre of Native Americans at the nation's founding, as it had in *Why We Can't Wait*, but the slow death "of millions of Negroes in the teeming ghettos of the North." After Chicago, King denounced the "triple ghetto, a ghetto of poverty, a ghetto of race, and ghetto of human misery."[49]

The conviction that Mayor Daley was the prison warden led straight to the voting booth, where in Chicago Hosea Williams coordinated a small SCLC voter registration campaign. "Chicago is a political city," King told a December rally, appealing to civic-minded church groups, student groups, and community organizations to help educate "an alert and informed electorate" who could pull independent levers of power. Voter registration was central to the "drive against slumism." Blacks must elect "independent aldermen" accountable to the people.[50] Two independent blacks did win seats in the aldermanic elections, but Republicans mounted unprecedented challenges in previously solid Daley wards that had seen open housing marches. Daley won the April 1967 mayoral election after denouncing King throughout his reelection campaign. Over time, appealing to "law and order" and opposing public housing in white neighborhoods, Daley shifted his electoral base from low-income black and white wards in the inner city to the more conservative white ethnic working- and middle-class wards on the periphery.[51]

Voting and black officeholding remained key forms of "legitimate black power" that King sought to promote after Chicago. In *Where Do We Go from Here?* King wrote, "Most of us are too poor to have adequate economic power, and many of us are too rejected by the culture to be part of any tradition of power. Necessity will draw us toward the power inherent in the creative use of politics." Integration was no longer adequately defined by "genuine interpersonal intergroup living." Now he insisted integration must include "the mutual sharing of power." In response to nationalists who would argue that "integration comes after liberation," King insisted they be dialectically related.

I cannot see how the Negro will be totally liberated from the crushing weight of poor education, squalid housing and economic strangulation until he is integrated, with power, into every level of American life. . . . In the struggle for national independence one can talk about liberation now and integration later, but in the struggle for racial justice in a multiracial society where the oppressor and the oppressed are both "at home," liberation must come through integration.[52]

"Integration in its true dimensions is shared power," King asserted at a late May retreat. Without this dimension, Stokely Carmichael would be proven right: integration would simply become a recipe for weakness. Like SNCC's grassroots organizers and SCLC's own Septima Clark, King saw education as key to social transformation and dreamed of turning "the ghettos into a vast school." "How shall we make every houseworker and every laborer a demonstrator, a voter, a canvasser and a student?" he asked.[53] King's answers covered a range of empowerment strategies. Community organizing, welfare rights, tenant unions, electoral strategies, adult education, selective buying, and black business development were all aspects of organizers' search for urban black power. The next year King tested their limits and strengths.

King aggressively broadened the definition of political participation to include representation of the poor in city bureaucracies and the development of indigenous welfare, community, and tenant unions as the pioneers of a new democracy. In 1967, King lamented the fact that the public paid attention only to marches, demonstrations, crises, and the oratory of "prominent personalities," like himself and Carmichael. Why did "very constructive but quiet programs of progress go on with little attention" from the media? The movement was not "dying simply because there is no marching in the streets."[54] Henceforth, he tried to lend his celebrity and financial support to ongoing efforts at group empowerment that had not been well publicized.

Chicago's West Side tenant unions had won signal legal and collective bargaining victories, organizing 10,000 tenants over the summer of 1966. But by the fall they learned that owners would rather sell than upgrade their buildings, so tenants had to find financing for their own cooperatives. By mid-December, the CCCO had raised $100,000 in seed money, and the Department of Housing and Urban Development approved $4 million in low-interest FHA loans to renovate 500 housing units. Finally, King boasted, tenants would "determine their own destinies," in a concrete example of "human as well as structural renewal."[55] King called for a national "union of slum dwellers." Tenant ownership and management might break "the cycle of defeatism and psychological servitude that mark the mentality of slumism." Though he had not made workplace organizing a major commitment, King tried to support Chicago's unionizing hospital workers. Unfortunately he got caught in the middle of a jurisdictional fight between the Building Service Union and the Teamsters—neither of which had distinguished civil rights records—and moved on to other fights.[56]

King plunged into barely publicized fights over model cities and urban renewal projects, demanding they be administered "of, by, and for the people." In late 1965, he had supported Englewood activists who were protesting Chicago's plan to bulldoze occupied homes and apartments to make way for downtown parking lots. "Negro clearance for the benefit of commercial interests," they called it. In his congressional testimony, King deplored "using urban renewal as a tool for Negro removal." Model Cities, he told the Shaw neighborhood association in Washington, D.C., had held out the promise of slum rehabilitation in partial compensation for the nation's failure to integrate the suburbs. But the community must fight for a say in the planning process and ensure that poor urban dwellers, not just businesses, benefited from the plan.[57]

King still believed War on Poverty activists could become the vanguard of a wider democratic revolution. "Maximum feasible participation" in law and practice created a new kind of citizenship, transcending occasional voting or tenant management schemes to foster poor people's "participation in major decisions" affecting their lives. Community action and job-training centers were important sites of insurgent citizenship where people were "hacking out the rights of the citizen" for everyone. Poor people won rights to grievance procedures against "the arbitrary actions of police, welfare, and public housing officials." The welfare rights movement in particular was widening the scope of democracy, he said, as had the labor and civil rights movements. Many nonpoor Americans had begun challenging the power of "professional elites [and] political bureaucrats" who were rarely held accountable to the electorate. Academia and churches had negligible resources compared to the military, for example, so students and religious social actionists were fighting for resources and representation. The majority could follow the minority in marching for "power for the people in the face of generations of domination by a decadent Southern oligarchy, corrupt big city machines and a conscienceless Pentagon." King dreamed of the day when government would stop serving "immediate profit" and start funding human needs in accordance with communal values.[58] But would the federal government and local governments support independent, community-based antipoverty programs? The record was mixed so far, but King had not yet tried to implement these programs in the North.

In July 1966, King told Levison that SCLC wanted to pursue federal and private financial support for community-based programs in education and job training. SCLC won a $109,300 grant from the Office of Education in the Department of Health, Education, and Welfare (HEW) for a two-month Chicago Adult Education Project in July 1967. King celebrated "the first joint effort by the Federal Government and a grass-roots civil rights organization to combat poverty in the urban North." They planned to instruct poor adults in reading, math, and job application skills. Employers such as A&P that had been pressured by Operation Breadbasket to hire blacks would offer on-the-job training in tandem with the project. King predicted it would free blacks of all ages from "the same cycle of isolation, exploitation and poverty that has trapped their own parents in the ghetto." It might even develop into a new "urban WPA." But Mayor Daley demanded that HEW channel all funds "through the machine-controlled poverty program," King protested in August. SCLC's project had its funds cut and was terminated early. CEP director Robert Green saw a clear act of reprisal against King's antislum and antiwar activism. "The local political structure" again torpedoed an opportunity to build community unions of the unemployed to "exert some control" over the low-wage, low-skilled urban labor market. As with the southern CEP, adult education involved activist citizenship. But even if it was packaged as a job-training program, it was too much for the machine.[59]

King took heart from the successes of welfare rights organizers, who continued to receive support from VISTA volunteers and Legal Services attorneys. The National Welfare Rights Organization was formed in 1966 by a coalition of welfare rights groups centered in Boston, New York, and California and coordinated by George Wiley. Women such as Johnnie Tillmon and Beulah Sanders became national leaders after leading local campaigns for benefits due them, such as winter clothing allowances for their children, but which welfare caseworkers arbitrarily withheld. In *Where Do We Go from Here?* King described "heartrending" bureaucratic abuses, humiliations, and arbitrary denials of legal benefits to women by imperious social workers. The activist-scholars Richard Cloward and Frances Fox Piven had shown that social workers withheld fully half of the benefits to which people were legally entitled. They theorized that massive protests at welfare offices could disrupt and overload local systems and precipitate a national "crisis" that might lead the Democratic Party to pass a guaranteed annual income, just as Birmingham's disorder had produced the Civil Rights Act. King endorsed the Piven-Cloward strategy, supporting "welfare unions" through which recipients would agitate for "the maximum legal limit" and thereby force "deeper solutions to the problems of poverty." Welfare recipients should be legally entitled to collective bargaining, he asserted. "Welfare and tenant unions need legislation to protect members from reprisals and intimidation. Fear of the loss of welfare or eviction from apartments inhibits organization." Labor won the Wagner Act, and welfare recipients and tenants needed the same protections for "mass organization."[60] But corporations and Congress had also backlashed against the Wagner act after World War II. The dream that the government would sponsor poor people's activism for social and economic rights guaranteed by government was bound to encounter fierce resistance.

Black Capitalism, Radicalism, and the Metropolitan Dilemmas of Power

Few of these social programs addressed King's central concern: the unemployment and low wages that produced poverty. Operation Breadbasket won local jobs, and in 1967 it went national, but it was still too small to address the larger crisis of unemployment. Jesse Jackson had brought Breadbasket to Chicago and built an impressive network of ministers who took the original idea in the direction of black capitalism. Describing the slums as an American bantustan, an "underdeveloped nation" with abundant labor and insufficient capital, Jackson summoned the nation to "provide the bootless with boots" in the form of jobs, and to teach "those with boots to pull themselves up" through business development. Breadbasket won support from several Chicago trade unions as it challenged and boycotted Country Delight and High Low Foods, and waged a successful sixteen-week campaign against A&P with forty stores in the black community. In turn Breadbasket aided black hospital workers, teachers, and bus drivers in local strikes. King called Jackson "a great dreamer and a great implementer of dreams" for winning jobs in white firms and for "building the economic base through Negro businesses."[61]

But Jackson's drift toward black capitalism troubled King because he thought it failed to address black poverty, labor exploitation, and political exclusion. King told a March 1967 Chicago Breadbasket meeting that a white man who preached black capital accumulation to poor people reminded him of somebody "telling you to lift yourself up by your bootstraps" while he was standing on your foot. As the movement advocated guaranteed incomes, programs like Operation Breadbasket could provide a measure of self-help. But what King saw as Jackson's single-minded pursuit of black capitalism raised doubts about his commitment to King's democratic socialist agenda. King "was quite rough on Jesse," Andrew Young remembered, because he believed that adequate jobs would have to come through the public sector, while "Breadbasket was essentially a private sector program." King never championed the cause of minority small businesses, as did people as diverse as Floyd McKissick, Robert Kennedy, and Richard Nixon. In September he heard from the Chicago owner of a gift shop faced with bankruptcy, asking his help with the Small Business Administration to make up the shortfall of capital. She thanked him for his participation in the "fight for jobs," but insisted, "if we do not now begin the establishment of businesses, we may very well find that in another 100 years we will be no better off in our fight for economic power and human dignity."[62]

In July, Operation Breadbasket officially became a national SCLC program, winning signal victories in Cleveland against Sealtest Foods. King reminded 150 ministers at a July 9 conference that corporations might yield concessions under pressure, but they were still primary culprits in perpetuating urban poverty. In one of his most radical statements, made again before a black activist audience, King criticized corporate power and not just policy failure. Slum Negroes faced "economic exploitation." "American industry and business, as part of the broader power structure, is in a large part responsible for the economic malady which grips and crushes down people in the ghetto." At a July 12 Breadbasket meeting, King demanded that his audience rigorously question the capitalist economy, preaching that "the earth is the Lord's and the fullness thereof." A minister's first concern should be with the "least of these." So as they negotiated with businessmen for jobs, they should pressure corporate leaders to "set aside profit for the greater good" and advocate "restructuring of our whole society." King had always seen the need to work with black businessmen who professed a commitment to race advancement. Black unity and collective economic advancement still trumped any overt advocacy of class conflict. But privately, King agreed with Bill Rutherford, SCLC's new executive director: to replace "white bastards with black bastards" as exploiters of black workers would be a cruel joke.[63]

King and others in SCLC saw nationalist economic strategies as either partial solutions or dead ends. Addressing the August 1966 SCLC convention, Rev. Walter Fauntroy, SCLC's Washington lobbyist, mocked efforts to sell "black panther sweatshirts to black people in the ghetto." Black people needed pride, well-paying jobs, well-equipped schools, and affordable housing, he preached, but they did not need sweatshirts. "We need green, economic power in this country," he preached, citing Rustin and Randolph's Freedom Budget as a start. Achieving political and economic "ghettoes of black power" promised little more than what blacks already had. "Green power" meant accessing the "coffers of the Wealth of this Nation . . . built on the shoulders of 300 years of our unrequited sweat and blood." Without mentioning the case for reparations, Rustin also derided black power advocates for abetting congressional reactionaries, who would be happy to let "Negroes run their own slum tenants, dilapidated schools and tax-starved communities" as long as they did not demand "radical and massive programs" of urban reconstruction and full employment. In fact, McKissick, Carmichael, and the Black Panther Party all called for federal spending for full employment for all Americans as a form of reparations for black Americans.[64]

In *Where Do We Go from Here?* King was more restrained. Black power gave "priority to race" just when automation was threatening all manufacturing jobs, he wrote. "Power for Poor People" was a better slogan. To simply "pool our resources and 'buy black'" would never create enough jobs or build sufficient affordable housing to end "the economic depression caused by centuries of deprivation." That would take "billions of dollars which only an alliance of liberal-labor-civil rights forces can stimulate." Before the Negro could be economically free, all Americans must promote "economic justice."[65] That meant redistributing wealth and economic power across both racial and class lines, King repeatedly insisted. As liberals, laborites, and moderate civil rights leaders distanced themselves from his anti-imperialism and socialism, however, and as Congress and the president retreated from the grand expectations of 1964, King concluded that the liberal-labor-civil rights coalition needed an infusion of mass protest energy from below. Depressed and desperate for an alternative to violence and reaction, King sought to forge a national constituency capable of redirecting federal policy away from militarism, inequality, and urban chaos. He settled upon the only tactic he thought open to the powerless poor: nonviolent direct action focused on the seat of national government itself.

After Chicago, King's proposals for resolving the dilemma of metropolitan power all had a quixotic ring, but in the context of burning cities and imperial defeat, one person's Quixote was another's Jeremiah. King was groping for metropolitan solutions that directly challenged the historic alliance of class privilege, racial exclusion, and independent political power in the suburbs. In August 1967, he addressed a voter registration rally held after the defeat of a Louisville open housing ordinance. He did not believe in separatism, he affirmed, but whites clearly did not want to live next door to blacks. "They're pinning us in in central cities," he said, and they could not get out. Blacks could only gain control of their urban spaces, elect the mayor, and tax any suburbanites who commuted to work in the city. If black people could win "political power" and "straighten up" their communities, perhaps whites would realize their mistake and return. With policymakers and social scientists, he advocated planned construction of entirely new integrated towns. "Inspection, fair housing, even rehabilitation cannot solve the problems of housing for the segregated poor," he wrote in *Where Do We Go from Here?* The American "underclass" needed affordable housing, supported by spending on the scale of the new Medicare program The disproportionate benefits that middle-class suburban whites and urban business elites had reaped from postwar housing policies had to be corrected, he argued.[66]

With the nation's middle class and political elites, King tied the welfare of blacks to the very survival of the cities, the heart muscles of American society and prosperity. Urban decline affected everyone, although Negroes suffered most, he told the City Hearings. The argument lay beyond protecting America's cold war international credibility. Cities were the nation's vital pumping stations, so it "may well become the Negro's supreme duty to rescue himself by saving the sinking cities of the Nation. They will not do it alone, but they will not permit it to be done without them." Mass civil disobedience was the best alternative to rioting, he told a group of social scientists in September 1967. This drastic medicine might even "restore Negro-white unity." Why? White leaders otherwise callous to the black poor had to care about the cities. "The vast majority of production is created in cities; most white Americans live in them. The suburbs to which they flee cannot exist detached from cities. Hence powerful white elements have goals that merge with ours." Newer forms of suburban investment and development, population growth and political power made this claim less and less true after the 1960s, however.[67]

Flattery could motivate people as much as fear. King carefully crafted his language to appeal to the values and self-importance of particular audiences. In August he addressed a national convention of realtors: "Democracy in housing really means integration in housing; integration in housing means not only integration beyond racial lines, but it also means integration beyond class lines." With their huge influence over "the housing problem," the realtors held the keys to decent schools and jobs for everyone.[68] Each of them could help make a neighborhood a brotherhood.

Other audiences heard more radical messages. King addressed the National Conference for a New Politics in Chicago, a contentious assembly of radical New Leftists and black nationalists. The discourse of black power and revolutionary reparations came easily to his lips. "The problems of racial injustice and economic injustice cannot be solved without a radical redistribution of political and economic power," he exhorted. "The ghetto is a domestic colony. Black people must develop programs that will aid in the transfer of power and wealth into the hands of residents of the ghetto, so that they may, in reality, control their own destinies." Some in attendance booed, but King told an interviewer he understood the hecklers. Having supported liberals who betrayed them all, he was the fall guy.[69] King selectively adopted nationalist themes. But his expansive determination to end poverty and his agenda for distribution across racial and class lines were more radical than the rhetoric of most black power advocates.

King's radicalization can also be measured by his divergence from Bayard Rustin, whose political strategies and categories of analysis King found inadequate to the challenges the movement faced after 1966. Rustin opposed both the Chicago campaign and black power. In his view, high unemployment, wretched housing, low incomes, and dead-end jobs caused riots. Rustin would not talk about "powerlessness," identifying the term with fainthearted liberals, who allegedly asked, "Don't the causes of the riots go deeper than economics, than jobs, housing, schools? Aren't there profound moral, cultural, psychological and other factors involved—powerlessness, an identity crisis?" King knew powerlessness was real and its opposite was power, not alienation. His race and class analysis was also more dialectical than Rustin's. For Rustin, racial inequality now stemmed not from "prejudice and discrimination" but from the "class structure" and technological changes marginalizing unskilled workers. America was not "two Americas, one black and one white," he argued, but "two Americas, one rich and one poor." King insisted on ripping out the intertwined roots of race and class. And Rustin wanted to keep civil rights separate from antiwar activism to maintain influence with Lyndon Johnson. For King, these issues were inseparable. In October 1966, Rustin ghostwrote for King a speech on the movement's principles: nonviolence, integration, constitutionalism, and economic action to alleviate unemployment. "Has the nation forgotten that for every Negro youth who throws a brick, there are 100,000 suffering the same disadvantage who do not?" Rustin asked. "For every Negro who tosses a Molotov cocktail, there are 1000 fighting and dying on the battlefield of Viet Nam." King filed away the five-page typescript and never used a word.[70]

Chapter 11
The World House

The U.S. political and military commitment to the anti-Communist Republic of Vietnam (RVN) began with President Truman's support for
the French against the Vietminh insurgency in their Southeast Asian colony,
led by the charismatic Communist nationalist Ho Chi Minh. Eisenhower was
unwilling to rescue the French from shattering defeat at Dienbienphu in 1954.
But he supported a separate anti-Communist regime led by Catholic president
Ngo Dinh Diem in South Vietnam, contravening the international Geneva
Accords, which called for elections, national reunification, and the withdrawal
of foreign troops. An increasingly autocratic and repressive South Vietnamese
government failed to suppress the indigenous National Liberation Front
(NLF). These were Vietminh insurgents who turned to armed struggle in 1961,
and who were increasingly supported by the forces of the Democratic Republic
of Vietnam (DRV) in the north. An enthusiastic sponsor of Diem's Asian
nationalism in the 1950s, John F. Kennedy acceded to Diem's overthrow in
1963, after committing 17,000 American military personnel to the Republic of
Vietnam. In the Tonkin Gulf Resolution of August 1964, Lyndon Johnson won
nearly unanimous congressional support to pursue "all necessary measures"
to aid the RVN, which faced a strengthening NLF insurgency and mounting
dissent from students and Buddhists in the cities. Torn between his advisors'
conviction that the RVN could be stabilized and his own doubts about the
costs of another land war in Asia, Johnson began bombing North Vietnam in
February 1965 and made a major commitment of U.S. ground forces in July.
An American antiwar movement spread out from the college campuses, mar-
shaling arguments that Johnson had heard and considered but ultimately
rejected. They argued that the southern RVN did not enjoy popular support
and was not viable as a separate state; that the United States was intervening
in a civil war against determined nationalists, not against a DRV Communist
war of aggression threatening the free world; and that "neutralization" of the
southern conflict through negotiations with the NLF would not trigger a
regional "domino effect" damaging to American interests and cold war prestige. Johnson marched into Vietnam with a remarkable degree of doubt, even

hopelessness, bending to his national security advisors and his own domestic political fears of anticommunist opposition from the right. "That's just a rat-hole there," Johnson's mentor, Richard Russell, told him in May 1964. But despite numerous international diplomatic initiatives, Johnson saw no path to negotiations. He also feared Congress would "impeach a President [who] would run out" of South Vietnam. The costs of abandoning the regime seemed to be greater than the costs of muddling through. U.S. military hopes focused on wearing down the will of the NLF and North Vietnamese. "I don't believe they're *ever* going to quit," Johnson confided to Robert McNamara before he sent in ground forces in June 1965. "And I don't see . . . that we have any plan for a victory—militarily or diplomatically." U.S. military strategy devolved to a combination of bombing and "search and destroy" missions designed to erode North Vietnamese will through "attrition."[1]

Martin Luther King's public opposition to the Vietnam War was more continuous with his early internationalism and more radical than popular understanding admits. The conventional story runs that King suddenly called for unconditional negotiations with the DRV and NLF in August 1965 but backed down under a storm of criticism. He struggled with his conscience until the winter of 1967, when he could "remain silent" no longer. Then in a famous address to Riverside Church in New York in April, he boldly denounced U.S. "aggression" in Southeast Asia. These are the milestones of the story, but King's critiques of militarism and imperialism and his identification with anticolonial movements were longstanding, and King was hardly "silent" in 1966. Over the course of 1965, King increasingly had argued that U.S. intervention unacceptably risked nuclear war. He also argued that the United States was not exploiting diplomatic avenues for nonviolent resolution. War crippled civil liberties at home when dissenters were smeared with the red paint of disloyalty, he said. King had long maintained that it was hypocritical to ask black Americans to fight for freedom abroad when they were forced into second-class citizenship at home. During 1966, King gathered new arguments. He thought it immoral to draft black and working-class men when so many white middle-class men avoided combat through college deferments. His greatest objection was that the arms race and Vietnam siphoned resources and political capital away from civil rights and the War on Poverty. Increasingly, King also focused on the costs the Vietnamese were paying, as American air and ground forces wreaked gruesome atrocities on Vietnamese peasants. Over time King judged the RVN hopelessly corrupt and repressive. At his most radical, he denounced the war as only one expression of America's global drive for military and economic hegemony, the ultimate purpose of which was to protect foreign markets for American corporate interests. King backed off from broadcasting this critique widely, though he still maintained the United States was an empire, stressing the "arrogance" of Lyndon Johnson's self-appointed role of world policeman. Having joined many peace marches and burned his bridges to Johnson, King then turned to a strategy of mobilizing the working poor and the "underclass" to compel a federal redirection of resources away from militarism toward fighting a real American war on poverty.

Diplomacy and Peace in 1965

King approached the Vietnam War cautiously, but he was emboldened by his Nobel Prize to speak broadly about the importance of nonviolence to international war and poverty. In 1964, Bayard Rustin had joined prominent radical pacifists in drawing up a "Declaration of Conscience" encouraging civil disobedience in order "to stop the flow of American soldiers and munitions to Vietnam." John Lewis, James Bevel, Robert Moses, and A. Philip Randolph all signed it, but King did not. Shortly after the election, King reiterated his general call for a world war on poverty. "If the world is to survive in Peace, then some concern for the world's hungry masses must grow out of the great wealth of this nation," he wrote. Poverty was the same in Mississippi, Harlem, or the Congo. In Norway to receive his Nobel Peace Prize, King avoided specific reference to Vietnam, but warned that nations choosing war risked "spiraling down a militaristic stairway into [a] hell of thermonuclear destruction." In the nuclear age even "a so-called limited war will leave little more than a calamitous legacy of human suffering." Students at the University of Oslo cheered when King declared that international war and world poverty were crises that demanded nonviolent action and "direct participation of masses in protest." If Negroes were conscripted to fight a "death struggle to protect freedom in Southeast Asia," King then argued during the Selma protests, why would their own government not "protect democracy in Alabama and Mississippi, New York, Chicago and Philadelphia"?[2]

Rustin and King did not place their pacifism ahead of their civil rights alliance with Lyndon Johnson at first. When radical pacifist David Dellinger organized a demonstration in front of the White House on July 3, 1964, Rustin and King chose instead to accept presidential pens at Johnson's signing ceremony for the Civil Rights Act. "There was no way of stopping the Vietnam war," Rustin told Dellinger, rapidly distancing himself from the radical pacifists. Just before Johnson ordered the bombing of North Vietnam in February 1965, King informed Clarence Jones that he did not vote for Johnson expecting him to request a popular referendum on Vietnam. The "Bob Moses theory" of involving ordinary people in "great decisions" was not applicable to foreign policy, King confided; it was a logic he never argued publicly and soon abandoned. Stanley Levison, Jones and Coretta King urged him to speak up, while Rustin argued against a break with Johnson long into 1967, reasoning that Johnson needed more help implementing civil rights and antipoverty policy than he needed opposition to the war. Clarence Jones wrote Lyndon Johnson directly, challenging his "irrational, illegal and immoral" support for RVN dictatorships. King might want his "tax dollars to go to the Anti-Poverty Program," Jones advised him in May, but he should take advantage of tax loopholes, since most of his taxes supported "violent means of death and destruction."[3]

Throughout the spring and into the summer of 1965, King criticized the futility of the war and the dangers of escalation, favoring a negotiated settlement including the NLF. He discussed the issue mainly with students: at Howard University and Antioch College, on a tour of Alabama's black belt, and with SCOPE volunteers. After John Shaw, a McComb activist, was killed in Vietnam, the McComb chapter of the Mississippi Freedom Democratic Party (MFDP) issued a militant antiwar leaflet calling for draft resistance. "No Mississippi Negroes should be fighting in Vietnam for the White Man's freedom until all the Negro people are free in Mississippi," they declared. The ensuing debate strained the Mississippi movement, but by early 1966 SNCC was publicly and adamantly opposed to the war. In July 1965, King made news in Petersburg by insisting the war "must be stopped" through a negotiated settlement. The United States would not defeat "Communism by guns or bombs [but] by making democracy work." King promised he might join in "peace rallies" as well as "freedom rallies." This terrain became as risky as open housing in the North.[4]

Johnson worried about mounting opposition to his Vietnam policy. In July, he urged King to rekindle the voting rights fire and expressed his distress over media reports about King's call for negotiations with the NLF. "I don't want to pull down the flag and come home running with my tail between my legs. . . . On the other hand, I don't want to get us in a war with China and Russia," Johnson confided. "I can't stay there and do nothing. Unless I bomb, they'll run me out right quick."[5]

King made his boldest move on August 12 at the SCLC convention, denouncing American escalation as the policy of "Goldwater" and demanding the administration negotiate directly with the NLF. The true enemy was war itself, he declared. Johnson's April speech at Johns Hopkins University had rehearsed every possible argument for intervention, from stopping the spread of world communism to maintaining American honor and credibility with

U.S. allies. He had even promised to rebuild the Mekong Delta on the model of the New Deal's Tennessee Valley Authority. King urged him to stop the bombing and rebuild all destroyed villages as a form of international atonement. For balance, he called on the North Vietnamese to drop their demands for U.S. "unilateral withdrawal." The war was the fault of no single party, so all should be flexible, King insisted. Still, he urged Johnson to make "unconditional and unambiguous" statements supporting negotiations with the NLF.[6]

King was already out on a limb. The SCLC board refused to endorse his linkage of civil rights to peace. By the end of September, King backed off from his call for negotiations under pressure from almost every corner, especially the president. Johnson admonished King on August 20 during a phone call that congressmen hostile to the war on poverty "all got the impression that you're against me on Vietnam," implying that King risked undermining Johnson's domestic consensus in the wake of Watts. "You don't *leave* that impression," Johnson commanded. "Let's not get this country divided!" Seeking cover, King acknowledged Johnson's call for "unconditional talks" and denied ever advocating "unilateral withdrawal," which no one accused him of doing. Neither man mentioned the central irreconcilable issue separating them. King had called for negotiations with the NLF, but Johnson had made negotiations conditional on *excluding* the insurgents. To recognize the NLF would undermine the whole rationale for U.S. intervention, by conceding that the war might not centrally be an act of North Vietnamese aggression against a representative government, that in fact it might be a civil war. By implication, U.S. intervention might itself be an act of aggression, not the defense of the "self-determination of free peoples" that the Truman Doctrine demanded and Johnson claimed. On the terms set by Johnson, the dilemma was irresolvable.[7]

Though King drew back from a direct confrontation with the president, Johnson went after King anyway. When Senator Thomas Dodd said King had "absolutely no competence" in foreign affairs, King knew Johnson was behind the attack. The press was "stacked" against him, he told his New York advisors in a conference call. "They have all the news media and TV and I just don't have the strength to fight." Cleveland Robinson alone suggested that King lead a popular peace movement. King threw in the towel, claiming he needed "to withdraw temporarily" to "get on with the civil rights issue." On CBS's *Face the Nation,* King defended his right to take a moral stand in favor of negotiations but disavowed any intention "to enter into the peace struggle." He had neither "the resources nor the energy" to fight on two fronts. A reporter asked, was not King's position aiding "the enemy"? Don't "confuse dissent with disloyalty," King shot back. Most Americans already seemed confused. In October, a clear majority of Americans polled by Gallup thought communists were organizing antiwar demonstrations.[8]

Levison and Rustin now both recommended King adopt a broad pacifist stance. Rustin had failed to dissuade King from sharing a podium with the antiwar activist Staughton Lynd, because Lynd was "in favor of tearing up draft cards and you are not." Now King should stick to themes of world hunger and poverty, Rustin instructed. King moderated his rhetoric. Addressing the Women's International League for Peace and Freedom in October, King argued more generally that the world had to transcend nationalism. In an age of technology and abundance, "there is no excuse for the kind of blind craving for power and resources which provoked the wars of previous generations." King opposed spending more billions on "an already awesome army" and "more devastating weapons." All God's children were vulnerable to nuclear annihilation, "the black, the white, the red, the yellow, the rich, the poor, the high, the low . . . the Southern Congressman with the Congolese and the Viet Cong [slang for the NLF insurgents]." Coretta King, not Martin, spoke at a march of 20,000 people on the White House organized by the Committee for a Sane Nuclear Policy in November 1965. "Did you educate Mrs. King?" a reporter asked in December. King responded that probably "she educated me." Since Boston, they had shared a path toward peace and racial and economic justice, he explained. Since Oslo, Coretta had urged him to preach nonviolence on the international stage.[9]

From July to October 1965, the volume of King's mail surged in response to critical news coverage. Critics complained King was mixing peace and civil rights to the detriment of civil rights, that King's proper place was to stop Negro rioting, not the war, and that King was violating the Logan Act, which prohibited citizens from conducting diplomacy. One reverend fumed that Coretta King had participated in a march where protesters "carried the Viet Cong flag." Don't serve up "Southeast Asia on a silver platter" to "godless" communism, he admonished. "Nicey-nicey do-gooders" advocating spineless negotiations "should pack up and take a one-way trip to Moscow, Peking, or Hanoi." A Los Angeles woman charged King with eroding respect for law and order by violating the Logan Act: "if a Negro minister can defy the United States Government, then *anything* goes." Many contributors threatened to stop donations. One black GI in Vietnam thought King was damaging his "effectiveness" by endorsing "draft dodgers." "The beatniks can protest and break these GI's hearts. I say let's build some confidence in our young people." King scrawled "Important" on a letter from Rev. Paul Heany of Atlanta, a veteran who had long argued that Negroes willing "to fight and die for our country" were entitled to equal rights. He could always counter charges of communism by referencing the long record of Negro "patriotism." No longer, he lamented. King had "deprived me of that argument."[10]

King's supporters were slightly more numerous and anticipated his later arguments against the war. A Japanese survivor of U.S. firebombing in World War II wrote in racial solidarity, deploring America's "low class of poverty" and the "terrible war fire" the Americans were raining down on Vietnamese. Several people protested the unequal burden the war placed on black and poor people. They were the victims of reduced antipoverty spending as well as a disproportionate share of combat casualties. A "White Republican Friend" wrote that it was "the poor man's son who is fighting and dieing in this sinceless war. While the rich men's sons are hiding out in colleges and other political jobs." "A march on Washington is in order," he advised King. One supporter was sick of college deferments and the "inequity and discrimination . . . in the selection of draftees." The Defense Department targeted politically weak and economically vulnerable high school dropouts and relaxed qualification standards to admit the poorest Americans and extend "opportunity" to blacks. A Catholic woman wrote that the billions spent on war, "most going to profits," were needed to "clear up slums." A black man with a son in combat called on King "as peacemaker" to stop Lyndon Johnson from "using our boys as cannon fodder. . . . I'm an old man and my boy is my only life." In February 1966, a Harris poll revealed that 62 percent of Americans favored and 20 percent opposed "a settlement in Vietnam that established a neutralist government that was neither pro-American nor pro-Communist." This was precisely what King and many on the left envisioned. But if they took the movement to the streets, the public would label them communist with prodigious help from the FBI, as it turned out.[11]

King continued to call for international economic justice, especially in the context of the U.S. refusal to alter its trade policies with South Africa. Here King foreshadowed his full-blown analysis of American economic neo-imperialism. While rich nations wallowed in opulence "10,000 people die of hunger each and every day of the year in the undeveloped world," he told the American Committee on Africa. South Africa's ruling Nationalist Party hid behind anticommunism, torturing political prisoners, suppressing civil liberties, and engineering "medieval segregation" that kept the black majority "in grinding poverty." Official U.S. opposition to apartheid was "muted and peripheral," while American "trade and investments substantially stimulate their economy," King charged. Billions of U.S. investment dollars flowed into South African automobile manufacture and banking, and into gold and minerals mined by "black slave labor." The United States supported South Africa's nuclear weapons program, he charged. The American economy was not

dependent on South Africa, so morally the U.S. must follow the Soviets in boycotting South African goods. King again called on the African National Congress, then pursuing armed struggle, to explore the "international potential of
nonviolence." African American solidarity with African liberation called for
nothing less.[12]

Speaking Through the Silence in 1966

In 1966, King was absorbed in the Chicago campaign and the black power controversy and less vocal in opposing the war. But his rhetoric foreshadowed
elements of the radical position he took in 1967. In January, the Georgia legislature refused to seat Julian Bond after SNCC compared the murder of activist
Sammy Younge in Alabama to "the murder of people in Vietnam." They
called on black men to resist the draft and join the civil rights movement, at
risk of their lives. SNCC's rhetoric anticipated King's by a year: the "Vietnamese are murdered because the United States is pursuing an aggressive policy in
violation of international law." Supporting Bond, King wrote in the *Amsterdam News* that America was approaching totalitarianism in persecuting dissent.[13] In December 1966, Bond finally won his Supreme Court case and took
his seat in the legislature.

Long before he broke his "silence" on Vietnam, King raised objections to
American atrocities, calling for modern prophets to speak truth to power. "A
war in which children are incinerated by napalm, in which American soldiers
die in mounting numbers while other American soldiers, according to press
accounts, in unrestrained hatred shoot the wounded enemy as he lies upon the
ground, is a war that mutilates the conscience. Yet important leaders keep their
silence," King wrote in the *Amsterdam News* in February. He echoed these sentiments with his congregation. To denounce Viet Cong bombings as "terrorism" while praising American violence against Vietnamese civilians as
"heroism" was the height of hypocrisy. Rustin urged extreme caution as King
considered whether to take this message to broader audiences. Though he was
not opposed to peace protest, Rustin warned King and Levison to expect a
"vicious attack" from labor and liberals who had "a vested interest" in protecting Democrats. South Vietnamese repression and Johnson's continued
bombing campaign soon drove an irrevocable wedge in King's circle between
Johnson loyalists and antiwar advisors.[14]

In April, King persuaded SCLC to condemn the South Vietnamese regime
of Generals Nguyen Cao Ky and Nguyen Van Thieu and advocate U.S. withdrawal and free elections. After a series of coups, the U.S. government finally

had a regime that it was confident would not negotiate with the NLF. But in early April, dissident Buddhists launched a "Struggle Movement" with support from segments in the South Vietnamese military. Stop aiding the "oligarchy" and "military junta against the Buddhists, Catholics and students of Vietnam," King demanded. A front–page *New York Times* story pleased Levison, who was glad that finally "Martin is sticking his neck out" publicly on the war. "Mass murder can never lead to constructive and creative government," King said. Liberal contributions were down, Levison admitted, as liberals fought over Vietnam and assumed King's "magic" kept him awash in cash. But the atrocities justified taking any hits Johnson loyalists could deliver. In mid-May, Ky brutally crushed the opposition in Hue and Danang with the support of U.S. Marines. Jones and Levison were disgusted that Roy Wilkins and Whitney Young had "snuggled up to Johnson" on the war, and their respect for Rustin was "going down the drain" because he, too, advised against a rift. The SCLC board agreed to an even stronger resolution referring to Saigon as "a bankrupt government." The "intense expectations and hopes of the neglected poor in the United States" were more important than a "sordid military adventure," they wrote. By June, King was convinced that Vietnam was siphoning away billions of dollars necessary for the Freedom Budget. When Secretary of Defense Robert "McNamara says we are going to send 18,000 more troops, then there won't be enough money—its a matter of guns or butter," King told Levison. Jones and Levison also urged King to denounce the class biases in local draft boards, which granted academic deferments to upper- and middle-class men and indiscriminately conscripted "Negroes and underprivileged whites" into combat. In November, King publicly criticized poor blacks' "disproportionate" conscription rates. Four in ten combat troops in Vietnam were black, four times their share in the population, he charged: a "totally unfair" "system" denied Negroes both education and educational deferments, funneling them into the military.[15]

Fatal Rifts in 1967

King's opposition to war was like a layered orchestral piece with many instruments and voices. Its first movement was inspired by his internationalism and conviction that war had become obsolete in the nuclear era, when the choice before humanity was either "nonviolence or nonexistence." A dramatic second movement focused on Vietnam followed in 1965, with loud clashes in the percussion nearly overwhelming the measured and moderate theme. A third movement in 1966 sounded sporadic dissonant notes of morality and politics.

A stormy, complex, final movement climaxed between the winter and summer of 1967. After that came thematic repetition, as King subordinated antiwar themes to the trumpets of his antipoverty crusade.

King's break with Johnson and the moderate civil rights leadership over the Vietnam War generated most of the press coverage he received during this period. His radical indictment of the war in Vietnam paralleled his radical critique of the War on Poverty, but his political economy received scant press attention as controversy swirled around black power and foreign policy. King often spoke of the "havoc" that the Vietnam War wreaked on America's "domestic destinies." Now the United States unequivocally had revealed itself the aggressor nation, and America's poor as well as Vietnam's peasants were its main victims. King now judged the NLF to be the authentic voice of the South Vietnamese people, condemning the anticommunist RVN military junta. Attacked from every side, he denied he could possibly "segregate" his conscience and separate his activism into artificial categories of peace and freedom. Theoretically, the United States could afford both "guns and butter." But politically, the administration and Congress had their hearts set on war, King argued. Now, as during the 1950s, war was feeding the forces of political reaction. And like the British who had lorded over India, the United States was an imperial nation whose basic motives were counterrevolutionary, he now argued. The principal rationale for U.S. military action was to secure huge profits for American corporations by protecting foreign investments from revolutionary regimes.

Early in 1967, King reportedly had a Pauline conversion on the plane home from his winter vacation in Jamaica. Thumbing through January's *Ramparts* magazine, he was shocked to see grotesque pictures of maimed and dead Vietnamese children. He joined antiwar senators Eugene McCarthy, George McGovern, and Jacob Javits at a Los Angeles conference sponsored by the *Nation* in late February. King opened his address with a grim montage of the casualties, evoking television images of "grief stricken mothers with crying babies clutched in their arms."[16] He led his first peace march in Chicago on March 25 and delivered his most controversial antiwar address at Riverside Church in New York City on April 4. He addressed the Spring Mobilization Against the War in Vietnam at the UN on April 15, a march organized by James Bevel that included what Levison dismissed as the antiwar "fringe element." Levison fervently opposed any act that might associate King with the "New Left" rather than the "more influential" Democratic Party doves, such as Robert Kennedy and Walter Reuther. King's antiwar advocacy evoked a storm of criticism from civil rights moderates, the administration, and the press. He backed off from several statements labeled "extremist," but mounted a spirited

Figure 9. Marching against the Vietnam War. King talks to Al Raby of Chicago's Coordinating Council of Community Organizations (CCCO) as they lead the march down State Street. To King's right is Jack Spiegel of the United Shoeworkers Union, and to Raby's left is King assistant Bernard Lee. A minority of progressive unionists joined interracial antiwar marches. March 25, 1967, Chicago. Photo courtesy of Jo Freeman, http://www.jofreeman.com.

defense of his position on *Face the Nation* on April 16, in an address at the University of California–Berkeley in May, and in many speeches, interviews, and television appearances that followed.

King pledged "eternal hostility to poverty, racism and militarism" in his April 4 Riverside address, which in its radicalism went beyond anything he said before or would say again. Levison recommended that King highlight the domestic costs of the war and continue to associate with the liberal opposition. Most Americans were reformers, not revolutionaries, he still believed. But King embraced explicitly radical positions ghostwritten by theologians Vincent Harding and John Macguire, assisted by Andrew Young. Bevel and Cleveland Robinson were also pressing King to mobilize the grassroots against the war. But Levison warned that, like Bevel, King would "lose status" if he gained prominence in the peace movement. King found widespread discontent in the ghettos and on the black campuses, he replied, where students inevitably went "wild about the V-N issue." Even politically, it was no longer wise to separate peace and civil rights, because the peace forces were now available "to have a March on Washington around the cut backs in the poverty programs." That was overly optimistic: the fractured peace forces either narrowly focused on Vietnam or were concerned with multi-issue agendas, especially power in universities, in which the poverty program was not the highest priority.[17]

The damage Vietnam did to the Great Society was King's most frequent critique, and often his first point. "While the antipoverty program is cautiously initiated, zealously supervised, and evaluated for immediate results," King told the City Hearings, "billions are liberally expended for ill-considered warfare." The administration underestimated the cost of the war by $10 billion for 1967, five times the poverty budget, King asserted. That year the war cost $27 billion. "The security we profess to seek in foreign adventures, we will lose in our decaying cities. The bombs in Vietnam explode at home—they destroy the hopes and possibilities for a decent America." Ending the war would make the "elimination of all poverty" feasible. Frequently, King simply stated, "the Great Society has been shot down in the battlefields of Vietnam." At Riverside, he remembered the "shining moment" of hope in 1964 when Lyndon Johnson promised war on poverty. But the Vietnam escalation in late 1965 left the poverty program "broken and eviscerated as if it were some idle political plaything of a society gone mad on war."[18] In all his major antiwar speeches, King repeatedly contrasted the obscene discrepancies between what the U.S. government spent on killing Vietnamese and what it devoted to uplifting America's poor: $500,000 to kill each Vietnamese soldier and $53 per year on each poor person, he claimed. "A nation that continues year after year to spend more money on military defense than on programs of social uplift is approaching spiritual death," King told the Riverside congregation. The nation had the resources but not the will to change national priorities.[19]

To counter anyone who insisted that peace and civil rights were separate issues, King repeatedly underscored the disproportionate burdens that black and poor people bore in fighting the war, even as they suffered second-class citizenship in America. The Negro was "100% of a citizen in warfare [but] 50% of a citizen on American soil." Black income was half that of whites, black unemployment and infant mortality rates more than double those of whites. Blacks were sent into combat and died in action at twice the rate of whites: one in five African American soldiers was killed, he said again and again. He could not remain silent "in the face of such cruel manipulation of the poor," he said. "We were taking the black young men who had been crippled by our society and sending them eight thousand miles away to guarantee liberties in Southeast Asia which they had not found in southwest Georgia and East Harlem," he told the Riverside congregation. He saw black and white men "fighting in brutal solidarity, burning the huts of a poor village," but the nation could not seat them in the same schools or make it possible for them to "live on the same block in Detroit."[20]

Critics charged that peace was a divisive distraction, alienating the administration and liberal white allies. King responded that the war itself was a Trojan horse for reaction and repression, strengthening the right and dividing the left, inflaming "hatred among our people." Wilkins, Whitney Young, Rustin, and Randolph all made a strategic choice to support Johnson's promises of butter as well as guns. Just after conferring with federal officials over the terms of a $213,000 job-training grant for the National Urban League, in January, Young charged antiwar liberals with using Vietnam as an "excuse" to run away from tough challenges to white racial privileges in their own backyards. "We are insisting that this country fight a war on poverty, and had better fight a war on poverty, with the same tenacity as in Vietnam," he said. Young and King bitterly confronted each other at a fund-raiser on Long Island in March. Young's relationship with Johnson might get him a foundation grant, King snapped, but would never get him into the "Kingdom of Heaven." In May, Young again railed against antiwar liberals' "defection" from the fight for rent supplements, guaranteed incomes, and the minimum wage. King admitted on national television that the civil rights movement was indeed at a low ebb. But he insisted that "the war itself has diverted attention from civil rights." The extreme right wing seized "a weapon of spurious patriotism" to suppress civil liberties and bolster their power and privilege at the expense of the poor, King said on *Face the Nation*. The war could only strengthen "the military industrial complex."[21] King likened anti–Vietnam War dissent to Abraham Lincoln's opposition to the Mexican-American War. Advocates of a bombing halt and negotiations were treated as "quasi-traitors." With domestic surveillance programs such as the new CIA Operation CHAOS, and with police savagely beating women at the October march on the Pentagon, King saw civil liberties as increasingly endangered. By November 1967, he was proudly comparing himself to socialist Eugene V. Debs, who was sent to prison during World War I for the seditious act of praising draft resisters.[22]

Imperial Interests and Presidential Arrogance

King repeatedly denied that Johnson bore primary responsibility for the debacle, but eventually he indicted the imperial presidency itself. The preceding four presidents, Congress, and indeed the nation bore "collective guilt." Still, King called on Johnson to "rectify the tragic mistakes" of the past. And King's assumption of societal guilt only went so far. As he put it bluntly, "the American public was duped into believing that the civil rebellion was being waged by puppets from Hanoi." Johnson and the hawks "brainwashed" Americans. Neither Russia nor China had troops in Vietnam, yet policymakers claimed U.S. troops had to fight a communist takeover.[23] By November, King echoed congressional doves in deploring the imperial presidency and national security state. Quoting Senator George McGovern, King questioned Johnson's arrogation to himself of "excessive executive powers." "Congress must never again surrender its power under our constitutional system by permitting an ill-advised undeclared war," he said. King saw the ascendancy of Ronald Reagan in the Republican Party as a menacing portent of reaction driven by militarism. "When a Hollywood performer, lacking distinction even as an actor, can become a leading war hawk candidate for the presidency, only the irrationalities induced by a war psychosis can explain such a melancholy turn of events," he declared to an antiwar labor conference in Chicago in November, after which he led an antiwar march with labor leaders.[24]

While King regarded the war's impact on domestic priorities as a tragedy, he increasingly saw the war itself as a crime against humanity. Gone were King's earlier concessions to Johnson's sincerity and his willingness to hold everyone responsible. It had always been a war of U.S. aggression, a war in violation of international law and the provisions of the Geneva Conference of 1954, King now asserted. The United States waged a war against an indigenous movement in South Vietnam that was more legitimate and popular than the succession of American sponsored military dictatorships. President Ngo Dinh Diem's war had really been a class war waged by "the wealthy and the secure" against peasants whose only dream was land reform. Relying on the judgment of journalist Bernard Fall, King claimed that only one-fourth of the NLF was communist. "Diem ruthlessly routed all opposition, supported extortionist landlords and refused even to discuss reunification with the north," King said. Hanoi was right to see the introduction of U.S. troops as the initial breach of Geneva. King painted a grisly picture of this intervention. Americans destroyed crops, poisoned wells, bulldozed villages, and herded families away from their ancestral communities into "concentration camps." This was not a northern war of aggression started by the DRV and supported by the Chinese, who, King accurately claimed, had no great love for Vietnamese. It was a bald attempt by the United States to recolonize Vietnam. How could the United States claim that national elections were legitimate when the junta suppressed the press, the Buddhists, and the NLF, "the only party in real touch with the peasants?" King urged the NLF to seek an alternative to a war that might end in nuclear annihilation. But the first step was for the U.S. to "stop the bomb-ings in the North and in the South."[25]

As a Baptist and a Gandhian, King was prepared to take lonely moral stands, acting as a modern Jeremiah castigating the sins of his own people, even inventing voices for those who were abused by America's leaders and ignored by its media. The good news was meant for "all men—for Communist and capitalist, for their children and ours," King preached. Appealing to "alle-giances and loyalties which are broader and deeper than nationalism," he spoke for the children whose pictures had shocked him into action, "for vic-tims of our nation and for those it calls enemy." Often he had melded his own dreams with the "dreams of the masses." "I speak for those whose land is being laid waste, whose homes are being destroyed, whose culture is being sub-verted. I speak for the poor in America who are paying the double price of smashed hopes at home and death and corruption in Vietnam. . . . The great initiative of the war is ours. The initiative to stop it must be ours."[26] The "voiceless" ghetto poor had found violent means of expression King under-stood but could not endorse. Few in the United States bothered to listen to the complex and contentious real voices of Vietnamese.

King traveled too far left for Levison at Riverside when King declared that he would not preach nonviolence in the ghettos while remaining silent about "the greatest purveyor of violence in the world today—my own government." Was not American use of untested weapons comparable to Nazi tests of "new tortures" on the Jews? When Levison called this "hard to accept," King replied that Americans were being brainwashed, just like Hitler had brainwashed the Germans. Levison insisted King not become "identified as a leader of a fringe movement." King retorted that he would not be kept in his "place" as a Negro leader of "Moderation." King's proposal to bring 6,000 people to North Viet-nam and stand near factories to stop the bombing was absurd, Levison said, and he thought it arrogant to speak "from the point of view of a Viet Cong peasant." King was surprised by the storm of public criticism and soon con-ceded to Levison that perhaps he should dissociate himself from the "fringe element." But perhaps someone would respect him for putting SCLC's "foun-dation grants" at risk because of his convictions. King saw a concerted attempt to "undermine me in the Negro community." This was plausible. Roy Wilkins had responded, "Is it wrong for people to be patriotic? Is it wrong for us to back up our boys in the field. . . . they're dying while we're knifing them in the back at home." At Levison's urging, King reemphasized his arguments about the impossibility of mixing guns and butter.[27]

Overlooked in the immediate storm of criticism and in most retrospective accounts, King's Riverside Church address was the first time he explicitly condemned American economic imperialism in Vietnam. The United States dominated a global political economy that subordinated third world welfare to first world corporate interests. "You launched into an attack on imperialism itself which is an attack on the system and not only the war," Levison objected. Domestically, King had identified poverty as functional to capitalism, and now his view of American foreign policy became more overtly Marxist. Much as America's domestic colonialists took profit out of slums, "individual capitalists of the West" invested huge amounts of money in developing nations, "only to take the profits out with no concern for the social betterment of the countries." U.S. counterrevolutionary interventions around the world—in Peru, Guatemala, Thailand, Cambodia, and Vietnam—emerged directly from political and business elites' need to maintain "social stability for our investments," he said. King had long spoken of South Africa in such terms, but now America was scarcely distinguishable from the British Empire, which was founded on racism and capitalist exploitation. America would not "solve the problem in South Africa" by boycotting gold, he told Berkeley students, because of its "huge investments" there. All over the world, America was "making peaceful revolution impossible by refusing to give up the privileges and the pleasures that come from the immense profits of overseas investment." America still had time to shuck off its "negative anticommunism" and align itself with nonviolent forces of social justice around the world. It was time to "get on the right side of the world revolution." "When profit motives and property rights are considered more important than people, the giant triplets of racism, materialism, and militarism are incapable of being conquered," he said.[28]

After Riverside, King mostly reserved talk of economic imperialism for his staff and sympathetic left audiences. At the August National Conference for a New Politics, he said that "capitalism was built on the exploitation and suffering of black slaves and continues to thrive on the exploitation of the poor, both black and white, both here and abroad." "A nation that will keep people in slavery for 244 years will 'thingify' them, make them things," King told SCLC activists earlier that month. America still protected its exploitation of the domestic poor and the security of its exploitative foreign investments with force.[29] Publicly, however, King more frequently echoed Senator J. William Fulbright in charging that the United States acted out of a nationalistic "arrogance of power." As King put it again and again, "We arrogantly feel that we have some divine messianic mission to police the whole world." American leaders betrayed evidence of a righteous "demonic delusion," believing that U.S. military might was inherently good and self-justifying. As he had after the Bay of Pigs invasion, he accused America's leaders of an "obsessive anticommunism" that denied other nations the right to go through the same growing pains that had characterized America's early revolutionary history. Framed as an explanation, this was as close as King ever came to endorsing revolutionary armed struggle.[30]

King had a shifting but consistent list of concrete demands. First, halt the bombing. If the United States stopped bombing in the south and north, "Hanoi would negotiate," he insisted. Second, declare "a unilateral cease-fire" to encourage talks. Third, stop militarizing the region, including Thailand and Laos. Fourth, recognize that the NLF commanded loyalties in the south and must be included in negotiations. Set a date for U.S. withdrawal in accordance with Geneva. Then offer asylum for pro-American refugees and reparations for the Vietnamese to rebuild their country. The first step was the most urgent. As he told the Spring Mobilization rally, "Let us take a single instantaneous step to the peace table—stop the bombing. Let our voices ring out across the land to say the American people are not vainglorious conquerors—stop the bombing."[31]

The national media found King's antiwar departure more newsworthy than any domestic policy critiques he had hitherto offered. King detailed his antiwar critique wherever he could, but most of the news focused on King's rhetorically provocative sound bites, his associations with the left wing of the antiwar movement, and the possibility he might countenance civil disobedience and open draft "resistance," which meant refusing in any way to deal with the selective service system. The *New York Times* featured a story about Jewish war veterans and their outrage over King's comparison between American and Nazi weapons experiments. On *Face the Nation* in April, reporters associated King with protesters at the April 15 UN demonstration who carried Viet Cong flags and burned their draft cards. Stokely Carmichael had called Secretary of Defense McNamara "a racist" and President Johnson "a buffoon." King had no problem appearing with Carmichael, he explained, though he preferred "dealing with issues rather than personalities." At Riverside, King encouraged mass legal conscientious objection for students and ministers, not student deferments, flight, or draft card burnings. "Our lives must be placed on the line," he declared. He admired Muhammad Ali and others who declared themselves "conscientious objectors on religious grounds" and went to prison when the status was denied to them.. By January 1968, when he visited Joan Baez in prison for civil disobedience in California, King was publicly praising those resisters, like David Harris, who turned in their draft cards, refused their college deferments, and went to prison without first seeking conscientious objector status.[32]

Riverside and the Spring Mobilization provoked a storm of criticism and put King on the defensive. Alfred Baker Lewis, an NAACP board member, claimed antipoverty spending could increase without pulling back from "Vietnam, where we are protecting some dark skinned people." The NAACP board soon voted unanimously not to "merge" the two movements. Ralph Bunche charged that King's move would "alienate many friends" and weaken the movement. The editors of the *New York Times* wrote that it was "facile" to link the War on Poverty and Vietnam. Fighting poverty was a generation's work involving confrontation with hostile "local political machines," stubborn "conservatives in Congress and the intractability of slum mores and habits." Ending the war would not automatically boost funding for domestic reconstruction, they wrote.[33] King's response was consistent with his traditional defense. He was not fusing the movements, he said, but seeking to link their "*fervor.*" He was not comparing Americans and Nazis in general, he said, just some of their military actions: "We are using napalm. Everybody knows it." King had few defenders in the mainstream press, but Paul Good in the *Nation* attacked the *New York Times.* Was indiscriminate killing in Vietnam nobler than "selective" Nazi genocide? Great Society programs crumbled in the face of $2 billion spent monthly for Vietnam, so poverty and the war were hardly "separate and distinct." Reinhold Niebuhr praised King's stand as "a real contribution to our civil, moral and political life," calling the war "an example of the 'illusion of American omnipotence.'"[34]

The black columnist Carl Rowan joined the attack, printing a series of unattributed charges questioning King's loyalty while denying it was a "guilt by association smear." King damaged civil rights and aroused suspicions of Negro disloyalty; he was now "persona non grata" with Johnson. Was King's speech an ego driven "publicity stunt"? Radio Moscow praised it, Rowan noted. "Others revived a more sinister speculation" of communist manipulation, he insinuated, giving credence to widespread FBI disinformation. King was besmirching his own moral authority, which after all could "make the difference between poverty and well-being for millions of Negroes," Rowan charged. Black people would never "break the vicious circle of poverty and unpreparedness that imprisons them unless the President provides leadership and Congress provides the circle-breaking programs and laws." King did not respond to Rowan's litany of innuendo or his claim that loyalty to Johnson in Vietnam was a precondition for black equality. Andrew Young called Rowan a "red-baiting, snide" character assassin. When Rowan and other reporters cited polls that King was supported by only a minority of African Americans, King praised the virtues of creative maladjustment; he was not a "consensus leader" but a "molder of consensus" and a voice of conscience.[35]

The Human Rights Revolution and the International War on Poverty

In opposing the war in Vietnam, King's main defense had been that consistency demanded nonviolence be applied equally to domestic and international conflict. King then joined Stokely Carmichael and other SNCC and CORE radicals in perceiving a commonality between America's oppressed minorities and the peasants of South Vietnam. King increasingly saw the U.S. military in terms similar to which he came to see the ghetto police: as enforcers of colonial economic interests. Carmichael recalled his deep admiration for King's "love for the people and consequently his honesty" in breaking his "silence" in Vietnam. At the root of war was the whole West's refusal to outgrow its inherent racism and dependence on global economic inequality, King wrote in *Where Do We Go from Here?* King reiterated the lessons of Gandhi and Nkrumah that he had absorbed in the 1950s: "Racism and its perennial ally—economic exploitation—provide the key to understanding most of the international complications of this generation."[36]

King's painful decision to risk splitting the civil rights coalition by opposing the war led him to return to an early conviction: the domestic struggle against poverty and racism was part of a worldwide human rights movement. King renewed his call for an "all out world war on poverty" as a necessary extension of America's commitment to eliminating domestic poverty. "Two-thirds of the peoples of the world go to bed hungry at night. They are under-nourished, ill-housed and shabbily clad. Many of them have no houses or beds to sleep in. Their only beds are the sidewalks of the cities and the dusty roads of the villages," he wrote.[37] Third world economic development posed a challenge that political independence alone could not meet. Decolonization brought unity of purpose, much like the southern civil rights struggle. "But as soon as independence emerges, all the grim problems of life confront [the new states] with stark realism: the lack of capital, the strangulating poverty, the uncontrollable birth rates and, above all, the high aspirational level of their own people. The postcolonial period is more difficult and precarious than the colonial struggle itself," he wrote.[38]

As he had done in the early 1960s, King wrote that the West must provide foreign aid with compassion, free of paternalistic control. Westerners should make the world's poor visible in a way that would create a "passionate commitment" to eliminating world poverty. Reflecting his era's faith in rising productivity and material abundance, especially in the "green revolution" in agriculture, King insisted that the West had the resources and technology for such a war. "The deficit is in human will," he wrote. "Even deserts can be irrigated and topsoil can be replaced." King called for the wealthy nations to create "a massive, sustained Marshall Plan for Asia, Africa and South America." Diverting just 2 percent of the first world's GNP for ten or twenty years might conquer poverty. King knew that the world population explosion could be the greatest enemy. An advocate of progressive birth control policies in the United States, he argued that the most effective population policy was one that promoted social justice. "When people see more opportunities for better education and greater economic security, they begin to consider whether a smaller family might not be better for themselves and for their children. In other words, I doubt that there can be a stabilization of the population without a prior stabilization of economic resources," he wrote.[39] Economic needs for jobs and security formed the context in which behavior shaped human destiny. Without economic change, no cultural change for the better would be possible.

Along with Vietnam and South Africa, conflict in the Middle East drew King's attention. In September 1967, after the Six-Day War, King brought his dialectical thinking and concern for international poverty to this crisis. King straddled a widening division among American liberals and leftists over the future of the occupied territories and the Palestinians. Denouncing American anti-Semitism, King insisted that Arabs respect Israel's security, territorial integrity, and right to exist. While expressing admiration for Israel's transformation of "a desert land into an oasis," he called on Israel to return all the occupied territories and not "deepen the bitterness of the Arabs." Industrial nations and the UN must recognize the crisis "of poverty and illiteracy and disease" besetting the Palestinians and much of the Arab Middle East. They deserved their own Marshall Plan. Western oil companies invested billions in the region, but the United States supported "Arab feudal rulers [who] neglect the plight of their own peoples." Poverty and powerlessness everywhere engendered violent conflict, and the West must address the immediate and long-term causes of war and underdevelopment.[40]

Ultimately King reiterated his faith that America could be a beacon for the world's oppressed. America was conservative because it had "something to conserve," King told SCLC at a May 1967 retreat. "People in Asia and Africa and South America are radical precisely because nobody wants to conserve poverty, disease and illiteracy." They must keep "the tension alive" between American conservatism and third world radicalism. As a multiethnic and affluent society, America could shine as a beacon of racial and economic justice to the world. After learning of the probable defeat of a new OEO appropriations bill in August, King spoke passionately in Louisville of the need "to get America straight . . . to get New York straight . . . to get Atlanta straight." "Why?" he asked.

Because if we don't get this thing straightened out here in America, I'm worried about the world. God has allowed more people of different races and national backgrounds to live in this nation than any nation on the face of the earth. So America is the world in miniature, and the world is America writ large. And if we can't get it straight here, the world is in trouble.[41]

King long spoke of America as a world house of international peoples. But now, amid collapsing domestic dreams, King thought it all the more important to put America's house in order and shift resources from militarism to the domestic and global conquest of poverty. What had once been a rationale for winning over the world's "uncommitted peoples" from the allure of communism was now simply an appeal to return to the City on the Hill, to heal domestic divisions as an example to the world.

By the summer and fall of 1967, King became convinced that Vietnam and urban chaos were fueling right-wing reaction and shredding the sense of national community that had given hope to his dreams at the 1963 March on Washington. The antiwar left increasingly reflected rather than overcame the nation's pervasive racial divisions. The National Conference for a New Politics, held in Chicago on August 31, 1967, brought black and white antiwar radicals into a stormy and brief coalition. Some wanted King to run for president, but King sided with the majority, who believed local organizing against the war was a superior strategy. A minority of black radicals demanded and won equal representation and control, but they remained suspicious of the "political paternalism" and countercultural style of middle-class whites who dominated much of the antiwar movement. As Simon Hall has detailed, the multi-issue agendas of black radicals and white radicals diverged in significant ways. Both opposed imperialism, but whites challenged authority on campuses while blacks challenged oppression in the cities. "Will you fight and die for your black brothers?" James Forman challenged an antiwar rally at Berkeley. At the October March on the Pentagon to Confront the Warmakers, whites and blacks held parallel and separate marches. Blacks marched under the banner "Self-determination for Black America and Vietnam," while whites marched under the banner "Support Our GIs, Bring Them Home Now!" The antiwar movement was fractured between radical and moderate wings, and black and white parallel movements. In this context King turned to the dream of a domestic "legion of the deprived," a multiracial working-class movement that might force the government to adopt the politics of community instead of chaos.[42]

Chapter 12

Power to Poor People

From the Detroit riot of July 1967 to his assassination in April 1968, Martin Luther King, Jr., labored to build support for the Poor People's March on Washington. King dreamed of replacing the faltering "coalition of conscience" with a powerful, multiracial coalition of poor people to compel Congress to enact an economic bill of rights under the slogan "Jobs or Income Now." SCLC had tried many keys during the previous three years: open housing, voting, adult literacy, boycotts, and community organizing. They won some local victories and learned important lessons. But SCLC had not been able to re-create the nonviolent theater of Birmingham and Selma, nor had it succeeded in organizing the power base of which the nationalists dreamed. In the face of intensifying white resistance, King concluded that only militant forms of civil disobedience could provide alternatives to the urban rioting that was accelerating racial polarization. Especially after the coercive response of the president and Congress to the Newark and Detroit rebellions, King refocused his attention on the levers of power in Washington, D.C. He increasingly had to respond to the same criticism that he aimed at the black power advocates—that he had no concrete alternative economic program to the Johnson administration's stalled and compromised antipoverty agenda. There was no dearth of imaginative policy proposals, he argued, simply lack of political will. "We have to put the horse (power) before the cart (programs)," he wrote in *Where Do We Go from Here?*[1] How could he help assemble and hold together a progressive coalition that could build power locally and orchestrate pressure for change at the national level?

King dreamed of widening the 1963 March on Washington coalition, appealing to the white middle class across lines of race; appealing for black unity across class lines; and appealing for a complex alliance across race and class lines between labor, unorganized workers, the unemployed, and poor people reliant on public assistance. King's political analysis of these various constituencies was shot through with ambivalence. King continued to evangelize the black bourgeoisie, urging them to replace smug individualism with the recognition of human interdependence and a commitment to service. Rich fools still argued that "most other Negroes are lazy"; complacent and individ-ualistic, they needed to understand systemic injustice. King continued praising students who "threw off their middle-class values" and replaced suits with overalls, embracing honored vocations as "jailbirds and trouble-makers."[2] He framed a vision of social change that white churchgoers could still find com-pelling in *Where Do We Go from Here?* Material poverty spoke volumes about the spiritual poverty and moral infantilism of the mainstream culture, which exalted values of military and technological progress over human decency, peace, and equality. A "revolution of values" was necessary to wipe poverty from the earth. Religious believers must make a commitment to eliminate hunger, ill health, and poverty for all God's children. "The agony of the poor impoverishes the rich; the betterment of the poor enriches the rich," he exhorted.[3] The broad liberal-church-civil rights coalition that had animated the first March on Washington might be revived. But crucial constituencies had defected or become divided.

Labor unions' compromises with militarism, racism, and privilege did not diminish King's faith that a progressive minority of laborites would join a new coalition. "Today Negroes want above all else, to abolish poverty in their lives and in the lives of the white poor," King told the shop stewards of New York's Teamsters Union in May 1967. Organized labor had pioneered in fight-ing poverty and should regard itself as a powerful ally rather than a competitor of the black and poor. King voiced hope in Walter Reuther's Citizens Crusade Against Poverty "for organizing the poor, Negro and White, in the South and the North." George Wiley had worked briefly for the crusade, and judged its commitment to action inadequate. Though listed on the letterhead, King had little discernible contact with the group. King was looking beyond the bound-aries of the Reutherite tradition: "The coalition of an energized section of labor, Negroes, unemployed and welfare recipients may be the source of power [behind] profound structural changes in society," he wrote.[4]

In 1963 the unemployed had not "led the parade" as A. Philip Randolph had dreamed it would. But now they and welfare recipients were central coali-tion players. King was clearly disillusioned with weak white middle- and working-class commitments to racial and economic justice. Taking up L. D. Reddick's prophetic insight from 1964, he affirmed that as they fought eco-nomic racism, "we must not overlook the fact that millions of Puerto Ricans, Mexican Americans, Indians and Appalachian whites are also poverty stricken. Any serious war against poverty must of necessity include them." Though most SCLC activists still regarded themselves as organizers for black equality and self-determination, King reached out to organize a multiracial coalition of poor people.

King was not going to moderate his radicalism anymore in the interest of constituencies that proved unreliable. His disillusionment with racial liberalism was evident everywhere. Racial liberals had been wrong to think that America's "dominant ideology" remained "freedom and equality," while racism was the aberration of "a few bigoted extremists," he argued in *Where Do We Go from Here?* After six years of liberalism, "the daily life of the Negro is still lived in the basement of the Great Society." Blacks took "equality" at its full meaning, but even whites of goodwill believed it to be "a loose expression for improvement." Though he still preached about mutual aid, not since 1964 had he referenced contented Negro street sweepers or called for individual Negro bootstrapping.[5]

King increasingly shared his democratic socialism with mainstream audiences, though he still reserved his frankest socialist expressions for SCLC staff. At a May 1967 retreat, echoing James Baldwin's refusal "to be integrated into a burning house," King questioned the structure of "the house itself." "Racism, economic exploitation and militarism are all tied together," he preached. All must be eliminated if any were to be conquered. Technocratic arrogance and bourgeois values sustained these "evil triplets." Appearing on the *Arlene Francis Show* in June, King explained that eradicating slums and creating jobs necessarily involved a "radical redistribution of political and economic power." He repeated these phrases on television and with university audiences. The whole country must place "democratic principles and justice above privilege."[6]

King's public statements still mainly centered on the promises and obligations of the national state. But with activists, he continued criticizing private ownership and control of the means of production. America still had forty million poor people because of the unequal distribution of wealth, he told the August 1967 SCLC convention. That was hardly new. But now King insisted that confronting poverty raised questions about the whole "capitalistic economy." "Who owns the oil? . . . Who owns the iron ore? . . . Why is it that people have to pay water bills in a world that is two-thirds water?" The society that had turned people into commodities continued to exploit the poor and protect its foreign investments with "military might."[7]

King's critique of "business control" of the state became more concrete as he contrasted subsidies to business, agriculture, and military production with the meager funds devoted to social welfare. President Truman had openly championed "the welfare state" as the institutional fulfillment of social and economic rights for all Americans: to education, health care, housing, and Social Security. Now middle-class Americans narrowly disdained "welfare" handouts to the poor, blind to the public infrastructure undergirding their individual achievements. And corporate welfare had flourished under the cold war state. Andrew Young helped illustrate these contradictions when in February he called the American system "socialism for the rich and free enterprise for the poor." King repeatedly used this wording in his speeches and press releases. Everyone knew the government spent billions on the space program and Vietnam, Young declared, but private aircraft producers received $160 million per year in subsidies. "Basic industries such as steel, transportation and oil are subsidized." People "cried against welfare handouts to the poor," King preached in August, but Congress breezily passed tax breaks and depreciation allowances to "make the rich richer." "Six Mississippi plantations receive more than six million dollars a year not to plant cotton, but no provision is made to feed the tenant farmer who is put out of work by the government subsidy." "Everyone is on welfare in this country," King told the press in January 1968; but when white or rich people receive welfare "we call it subsidies." Half of the War on Poverty's budget paid salaries to people who weren't even poor, he often repeated. Openly critical of state capitalism, King also strengthened his critiques of communist states that built oppressive class structures with the goal of abolishing class. King's disillusionment with the fragmented and unequal welfare state had led him to reemphasize individual rights, but it also strengthened his democratic socialism.[8]

Urban Violence and the Genesis of a National Crusade

The urban rebellions of the "long hot summer" of 1967 convinced King that the slow processes of community organizing and coalition building could not stave off racial war and "national suicide." Hundreds of people were killed in scores of cities across America. The ghetto violence left King marginalized in the media and ignored by the Johnson administration. Congress turned to red baiting and repression, shifting some of King's attention from the executive branch and galvanizing his determination to find a political alternative to violence. King committed himself to organizing a mass march and civil disobedience in the nation's capital in August, but the origins lay earlier than most realize. In October 1966, five hundred poor people, mostly welfare-reliant mothers, staged the first Poor People's March on Washington. In the middle of the black power controversy, King called for organizing "the poor in a crusade to reform society in order to realize economic and social justice." Tom Offenburger, SCLC's public relations director, recalled King's determination to dramatize working poor people's struggles that same month. Following a chilly reception by a group of Atlanta businessmen, King pointed to the maids and bellhops working in the hotel where they met. By paying people less than

$1 per hour, King said, businessmen were "keeping people in poverty." The poor should come to Washington "in mule carts" block traffic in the busy streets, and declare, "We are poor . . . you keep us down this way; and we've come to stay until you do something about it." Levison had talked to King over the winter about leading a new "bonus army," like the tattered and hungry World War I veterans in 1932 who had come to D.C. seeking their pensions and been brutally routed by General Douglas MacArthur. In March 1967, King envisioned marching on Washington with peace forces to protest "cut backs in the poverty programs." Then, in early August, after their hearings on poverty in Mississippi, Marian Wright relayed Robert Kennedy's suggestion that King bring the poor to Washington. King "treated me as if I was an emissary of grace," she recalled. Ideas for the Poor People's March had been ripening for some time. Now, grasping for hope, King pulled the strategy from the tree and told Coretta how elated he felt.[9]

Congress was not merely neglectful but positively repressive. Newark burned on July 12, and twenty-four people died. On July 19, the House passed a bill to criminalize the act of crossing state lines to incite or participate in a riot. The next day, southern Democrats and Republicans voted against even debating Johnson's proposed $40 million Rat Extermination Act. Opponents satirically speculated about a powerful "rat bureaucracy" and called for deploying an army of cats as a less budget-busting alternative. Representative Martha Griffiths, familiar with the gruesome problem from her years in Detroit, detailed the scourge of rat bites and the diseases they carried, but to no avail. Lyndon Johnson was furious. The federal government already spent millions killing rats that bit livestock, he stormed. Why not kids? King also lashed out at Congress. However many "anti-riot" bills "penned in the ink of personal vengeance" Congress passed would not end violence. "Moralizing about hard work and study" would not eliminate unemployment. Talk of family values would not save children growing up "in a crowded, rat-infested neighborhood." The poor did not need "anti-riot" bills, but rat control bills, rent-supplement programs, and more funding for the Model Cities program.[10]

Rioting stoked the conservative congressional attack on liberalism. In August, southern Democratic senators spearheaded a Judiciary Committee investigation into federal employment of alleged riot-inciting SNCC militants. A parade of police experts testified in support of Senator Strom Thurmond's assertion that "human rights can only be protected by safeguarding property." Looting and arson portended the collapse of "civilized society." Senator Sam Ervin grilled Nashville officials as to whether "SNCC, which is promoting revolution, riots, and bloodshed, is getting OEO grants." The Senate Subcommittee on Investigations began hearings that ran through August 1970. John

McClellan of Arkansas set the tone, announcing that riotous "civil disorders, sit-ins, unruly protest marches, disorderly demonstrations," and wanton law breaking were out of control. "Willful civil disobedience" leads inevitably to "criminal force and violence." The FBI and local police reaped a financial windfall from McClellan's Omnibus Crime Control Act in 1968.[11]

The Detroit rebellion, the worst civil uprising in a century, claimed forty-three lives over four days in late July, mostly African Americans who were shot by police and National Guardsmen, before President Johnson sent in army paratroopers, a move King supported. But King was deeply troubled by the administration's callous policy response, a mixture of repression and the appointment of a liberal-moderate riot commission. "Pillaging and looting and arson have nothing to do with civil rights," Johnson said, commanding troops into Detroit on July 24. The government would not "tolerate lawlessness." King dashed off a telegram to Johnson and held a press conference to discuss the political and economic causes of the riot, which principally lay in the Great Society's failure to provide employment for the urban poor. But King and Levison agreed that Johnson might warm to their proposals for jobs programs, since he had administered the National Youth Administration in Texas during the New Deal. So Congress took the brunt of King's criticism. Suicidal urban violence mirrored the "suicidal debate and delay in Congress," King argued. Every outbreak of unrest could be ascribed to "gross unemployment," so it was time to revive the Depression-era Works Progress Administration (WPA), guaranteeing "jobs first, training later." King spoke ominously for the urban masses newly aware of racial and economic oppression. "There cannot be social peace when a people have awakened to their rights and dignity, and to the wretchedness of their lives simultaneously. If our government cannot create jobs, it cannot govern." Political indignity and economic wretchedness must be uprooted together. It was senseless "to maintain a balanced budget with an unbalanced society." King knew the unemployed would flock to guaranteed work. After the riot, when General Motors announced a program to train 7,000 workers on the job in Detroit, 14,000 people showed up, he told the staff.[12]

Riots were a disorganized, even suicidal form of protest against the Great Society's failures, King insisted. "Most of them break out spontaneously," almost invariably triggered by "inept police action." Blacks responded with lawlessness because their lives were consumed by lawless "police brutality [and] the brutality of slum conditions." Further, by dispensing antipoverty funds in response to unrest, white officials had convinced millions of blacks that rioting was an effective way to get resources. Yet King insisted that violence brought more destruction than resources to black communities and heightened "the fears of the white majority while relieving the guilt."[13]

King felt alternately powerless, depressed, and essential to a nonviolent solution to the urban crisis. Lyndon Johnson did not respond to King's telegram. He prevented Labor Secretary Willard Wirtz from meeting with the nonviolent leadership to explain federal jobs programs. On July 25, Levison suggested that riots might have "a positive side" as national alarm bells for social change. King did not see it that way. America "is headed the way of the Roman Empire," he responded, citing rioting, the war, and rampant consumerism. Coretta recalled that Martin was "very depressed." He did not have the answers and felt nonviolence was failing, but whites either blamed him or expected him to control the riotous masses.[14]

King found his answer in tactics of mass disruption he had endorsed and then rejected in 1963. They had to escalate nonviolence into a force "greater than violence," King told his New York advisors. Appearing on *Meet the Press,* he promised to "disrupt" northern cities, "militantly and nonviolently, without destroying life and property." By the August 15 SCLC convention, King was searching for ways to "cripple the operations of an oppressive society [and] dislocate the functions of a city." Harris Wofford recalled King ruminating that a mass evacuation and burning of "a slum that was unsafe and beyond repair" might have the necessary impact. "Quite a symbolic action!" Wofford exclaimed. King finally decided with Levison on August 22 to target Washington, D.C., with civil disobedience. King said Mississippi had the worst poverty, but the problem was "national." Levison argued that a program to rebuild the ghettos employing "indigent Negroes" was more concrete than "the guaranteed annual wage" or the slogan "End Slums." Johnson and Congress were ignoring strong public support for domestic reconstruction. Indeed, Harris polls showed that 69 percent of Americans favored big federal projects "to give jobs to all the unemployed," while 65 percent agreed that "racial outbreaks" could be prevented by a "federal program to tear down ghettos." King's spirits lifted when he heard this, and he frequently referred to the polls as evidence for popular support for his programs. Strong support for guaranteed work in fact ran back to the 1930s but was never translated into policy. Unfortunately, after the long hot summer cooled, popular support for slum reconstruction slipped considerably by December. In January 1968, Americans ranked fighting the Vietnam War a higher priority than rebuilding urban ghettos.[15]

King's analysis of the causes of and cures for urban riots shifted as he reframed them broadly as political revolts against relative black deprivation, reactionary white politics, and Vietnam. King's policy recommendations centered on public works programs, the guaranteed income, and the rebuilding of slum housing. But in speeches to SCLC, social scientists, and the National Advisory Commission on Civil Disorders—known as the Kerner Commission after its chairman, Governor Otto Kerner of Illinois—King brought together causal explanations reaching into every corner of the political economy. King again put the government at the center of a web of public and private interests sustaining the ghetto. "The policy makers of the white society have caused the darkness: they create discrimination; they structured slums; and they perpetuate unemployment, ignorance and poverty," he testified. Black crimes were small and "derivative" compared to white official violations of welfare laws, building codes, fair employment laws, school desegregation orders, and standards of police conduct. "The slums are the handiwork of a vicious system of the white society; Negroes live in them but do not make them any more than a prisoner makes a prison." Rioters had neither "voice nor power," usually reacting to single incidents of police brutality. But the underlying causes that turned ghettos into tinderboxes derived from national trends exacerbating urban inequality, disempowerment, and dislocation. In several speeches, King listed five causes closely linked to the political dilemmas of 1967: "1. The white back-lash; 2. Pervasive discriminatory practices; 3. Unemployment; 4. The War in Vietnam; 5. Urban problems, crime and extensive migration." Lining up his arguments to persuade national elites, King was now less concerned with confronting municipal power than he was with bringing the resources of the nation to bear on the crisis of the city.[16]

Governor Kerner presided over a liberal-moderate commission comprising eight public officials, a corporate leader, a labor leader, and a civil rights leader. Only two commissioners, the NAACP's Roy Wilkins and Massachusetts Senator Edward W. Brooke, were black, both moderates. On the phone with his New York advisors, King knew African Americans would dismiss it because there were not "enough Negroes on it and No Negro Militants." Wilkins would be "hopeless" and would not understand that southern police violence also provoked urban blacks and southern reprisals spurred massive migration to the cities, worsening the crisis.[17]

Political reaction and Vietnam had fueled war in the cities, King thought. Across the country, the white backlash shattered black dreams of equality. Whites were still murdering southern civil rights workers and attacking nonviolent Chicago protesters. Blacks could only conclude that whites wanted them to stay "permanently unequal and permanently poor." Liberals proved more dedicated to domestic tranquility and gradual improvement than to genuine equality. Young black men bore double burdens of unemployment and Vietnam combat fatalities. The "insane pursuit of conquest" in Vietnam only increased their contempt for the U.S. government. "To war against your own people while warring against another nation is the ultimate in political and social bankruptcy," King charged. "The Negro who runs wild in a riot has been given the example of his own government running wild in the world," he told SCLC staff. The commission did not test King's hypothesis, because Johnson loyalists among commission administrators weeded out antiwar dissenters from the consultative staff of social scientists, effectively barring questions about Vietnam from the survey research designs.[18]

Unemployment and discrimination remained galling provocations, King continued. "Negro youth waste their barren lives standing on street corners," knocking on doors that slammed in their faces and responding with "rage and rebellion." With conditions worse than twenty-five years earlier, Negroes daily faced a "tragic depression," he told the commissioners and every audience that would listen. Wilkins challenged King's hyperbole, but King claimed that "the vast majority of Negroes in our country are still poverty-stricken and the middle class is still very small." The "lower class or the underclass" comprised 80 or 90 percent of black America. Wilkins probed King's association of violence and unemployment: Why did black Detroit riot, when more poverty money had been spent there than anywhere else, and where 35 percent of arrested rioters were employed? King had a ready answer: no program had been "massive enough" to address the enormity of the urban crisis.[19]

King's speeches also focused on dislocation, migration, and crime. The McCone Commission had blamed the migrant, marginal criminal poor, and King now too made them central actors. Black migrants who fled the collapsing southern farm economy were shuttled without national planning or economic relief into what E. Franklin Frazier called "the city of destruction," King testified. Then organized crime produced "an underclass of great numbers," while rootless migrants mixed with the "declassed and dispossessed" to form "a large antisocial force." Drafting this testimony with his advisors, King had insisted on highlighting "underclass" desperation, especially the fact that "Mississippi has driven Negroes out and starved them." King did not attempt to reconcile this focus on criminals and disoriented migrants with views he had expressed the year before in Chicago. But social scientists and the commission confirmed the accuracy of his earlier focus on broadly shared urban grievances expressed by fairly typical long-term residents of ghettoes.[20]

King's freewheeling exchanges with the commissioners in fact yielded more trenchant insights than his prepared texts, as he synthesized the "complex of causes" leading to violence, especially black youths' sense of injustice at their relative deprivation. King denied that nonviolent civil disobedience caused riots, because nonviolence had not been "practiced yet on any major scale." He would no longer speak of "law and order" but of "Law and Justice," because no order could prevail without justice. People devoid of hope did not riot he pointed out, and rebellions often occurred when conditions were improving because "progress tends to whet the appetite for more progress." But people whose own lives are dramatically improving did not riot, either. Urban black youth experienced "hope and despair." Witnessing national prosperity and civil rights progress in the South, they realized that they had been left behind. Atlanta had a widening economic "gulf" in housing and employment between the races and within black class structures. "Gaps within the society" stimulated rioting, he stressed. And, as King told a Canadian radio audience, blacks avoided attacking persons, not because they feared retribution, but because "property represented the white power structure." While blacks attacked property, they suffered 85 percent of the lethal violence inflicted by the forces of "order."[21]

Television brought these gulfs sharply into focus for the ghetto poor, King argued in *Where Do We Go from Here?* Dramatic images of southern confrontations and victories had raised their expectations. But they were also daily bombarded with images of white affluence, reminding them that little had changed in their opportunities. "From behind the ghetto walls they see glistening towers of glass and steel," he added, but young black men knew that "well-paying construction jobs" building skyscrapers were denied them. After years of protest, blacks were still "hopelessly locked out" of the building trades, King told the commission. With a history of building "the steady docks and the stout mansions" of the South, they were furious at the backsliding.[22]

King's overestimate of the size of the "lower class" nevertheless captured a dimension of what even the Labor Department described as a social catastrophe comparable to the Depression. Millions benefited from the 1960s economic boom, and the black-white income ratio narrowed from .48 in 1960 to .61 in 1970. But black Americans remained appallingly unequal, and in crucial respects the position of black youth and the material fortunes of the concentrated urban poor were indeed deteriorating. In 1959, 55 percent of blacks and 18 percent of whites were poor by the official definition adopted in 1963. By 1969, black poverty declined dramatically to 33 percent, though not far as white poverty, which fell to 11 percent. Black unemployment rates consistently remained double those of whites. Blacks were one quarter of the poor population in 1959, and one-third a decade later. As the black economist Andrew Brimmer noted, economic growth and policy neglect produced "a deepening schism in the black community between those enjoying expanding prosperity and those caught in a widening web of poverty." Clarence Jones had explained to King in 1964 that young black "discouraged" workers—those who had stopped looking for work and no longer showed up in unemployment statistics—grew dramatically between 1949 and 1963. In fact, the problem only worsened. In the 1960s, the labor force absorbed 12 million new workers, 1.5 million of whom were black. But there were 55,000 more unemployed black youths in the prosperous year of 1969 than in the recession year of 1959. In 1965, 60 percent of black men aged sixteen to twenty-four were employed; by 1980, just 40 percent. The origins of the urban crisis were political, cultural, and institutional as well as economic, rooted in the discrepancy between what a generation of black youth had been led to expect and the political backlash, police hostility, and economic retrogression they experienced. Theirs was no simple reaction to "grand expectations" that the economic boom, the "rights revolution," and the Great Society puffed up but could not fulfill. Their revolt was a new act in the ongoing national tragedy of race, space, and economic inequality.[23]

The Kerner Commission report, issued in March 1968, and written by a team of lawyers, presented less a coherent analysis than it did a compilation of ghetto grievances and possible reforms. The commission attributed riots to discrimination, migration, manufacturing decline, low black self-esteem, and—rarely mentioned, despite its prominence among expressed grievances—"indiscriminate and excessive" police violence. "Rioters" as measured by arrest logs or social surveys were fairly typical young black men. They were better educated than nonrioters and politically aware, but frustrated by unemployment and job discrimination. They were certainly not predominantly destitute migrants or career criminals. The commission aggregated their most frequently expressed grievances. "Police practices" and unemployment topped the list. Seven of the ten grievances that followed involved racist and undemocratic exercise of public authority. But the commission stopped short of adopting powerlessness as its overarching theme. "White racism" became the culprit, though any but the shallowest of readers would have to conclude that white institutions as much as attitudes were at fault. "White society is deeply implicated in the ghetto. White institutions created it, white institutions maintain it, and white society condones it" was the hard-hitting conclusion that Mayor John Lindsay of New York insisted should be inserted in the introduction. America was becoming "two societies, one white, one black—separate and unequal." It was both hard hitting and simplistic. Where in the scheme were the white poor or the black middle class, not to mention the rural poor, Mexican Americans. or Native Americans? As did most "experts," the commission also pushed the meaning of powerlessness in the direction of social psychology: "*The frustrations of powerlessness* have led some Negroes to the conviction that there is no effective alternative to violence as a means of achieving redress of grievances," they wrote.[24]

Despite the report's avoidance of class and power, King welcomed its antiracist analysis and called for implementation of its wide-ranging reforms. He telegraphed Wilkins, thanking him for mustering the courage to state "that white racism is the root cause of today's urban disorders." On the other hand, Bayard Rustin said he would "rather have a job program for blacks than a psychoanalysis of whites."[25]

The commission recommended reforms in employment, housing, and welfare but stepped gingerly around the central concern of ghetto activists: the structure of urban power. The *Report* called for extending and funding local antipoverty agencies and encouraging citizen participation. Blacks indeed had few ways to bring their "grievances against the agencies of local and state government, including but not limited to the police," the commission conceded. But "the existing distribution of political power within city governments" lay outside their purview. The *Report* recommendations did not even mention the nonviolent community organizations and protest groups that their own evidence suggested played vital roles in preventing riots. A Detroit survey found more self-reported counterrioters (14 percent) than rioters (10 percent). The former were "young men, ministers, community action agency and other antipoverty workers and well-known ghetto residents." Nonviolent groups effectively kept violence out of certain neighborhoods. On Detroit's northeast side, 21,000 people formed the Positive Neighborhood Action Committee, which organized quickly through block clubs after the riot broke out. "Youngsters, agreeing to stay in the neighborhood, participated in detouring traffic. While many persons reportedly sympathized with the idea of a rebellion against the 'system', only two small fires were set—one in an empty building." But the commission overlooked the need to support these people and their groups. In July, Andrew Young asked King to inform them "about the People of the Poverty program keeping the People quiet" and nonviolent in the cities, since Young had been listening to their stories and knew they needed support. Unfortunately, King lost the point in his larger analysis and policy recommendations.[26]

King's rhetoric was more morally charged and politically specific than the commission's, his analysis too complex to reduce to slogans about "two societies" or denunciations of "white racism." Violence at home and abroad, actual power and powerlessness, relative deprivation, and violations of law and justice lay at the core of the ongoing urban crisis.

Forging Race, Class, and Gender Alliances

King's principal challenge in planning the Poor People's March was persuading supporters that civil disobedience directed at the national government would actually benefit poor people and not drain local movements' energies. First, King came up with a protest strategy that combined a visible encampment of poor people in Washington with dramatic acts of civil disobedience. Then he developed a rhetorical synthesis for organizers and the poor that wove together a vision of black power and multiracial economic justice. King could eloquently frame the issue of poverty in terms of race and class and paint vivid word pictures of the social contradictions of capitalism. He was less adept at formulating program objectives or convincing committed organizers to abandon local efforts and take up a risky protest strategy in coalition with other ethnic groups. Organizers and supporters voiced myriad objections, unsure a national strategy would bear local fruit and skeptical about what a diversion to Washington on the issue of poverty would mean for their particular goals.

Marching and civil disobedience around poverty were all King had to offer organizers at the beginning, and almost everyone opposed him. But the vicious circle of rioting and white backlash had to be broken. Gandhi had made lonely decisions, and Baptist preachers had to be strong leaders of their flocks, he reaffirmed. King passionately argued that the possibility of further popular and congressional backlash was no reason to avoid civil disobedience. He felt vindicated by Harris and *Fortune* polls in which 90 percent of black Americans said King had the "best approach" to racial change and that they "trusted" him more than any other black leader. Civil disobedience was the only "alternative to riots," which fueled the backlash and could burn up the last remnants of white sympathy. And, as King told a national television audience, blacks had never made "a single gain without the confrontation of power with power." King reassured financial supporters that community organizing could turn the angriest ghetto militants into "disciplined legions for sound goals." In Cleveland, "the nation's ripest city for rioting," SCLC had averted violence "without quelling militant protest" through grassroots organizing, Operation Breadbasket, and voter registration.[27]

"Massive, organized civil disobedience is probably the best negative alternative to the burning and looting," L. D. Reddick wrote in August. But where was King's "constructive program for our urban ghettos"? SCLC's new executive director Bill Rutherford observed wide skepticism about protesting something "as vast and amorphous as poverty." James Bevel wanted to focus on cities and the war, Hosea Williams on voter registration, Andrew Young on southern field operations, and Jesse Jackson on Operation Breadbasket. Arthur Logan's wife, Marian, an SCLC board member, feared massive government repression. L. Howard DeWolf feared civil disobedience would provoke violence and risk a "Fascist-type revolution . . . ending civil liberties and civil rights and precipitating World War III." But King shared Young's conviction that if rioting continued and they failed to develop nonviolent alternatives, the riots themselves would "bring a right-wing takeover." Rustin categorically opposed any nonviolent disruption. King was naive if he thought "real working class responsible groups" would join the unemployed in an interracial alliance, knowing that so many unions had failed to do so in the past. Michael Harrington urged King to formulate achievable goals and win concrete victories to reverse the demoralization in movement circles. "You have to deliver," Harrington told him.[28]

King's rhetoric focused on national domestic policy and the social and economic contradictions of state capitalism and was not explicitly anticorporate. With SCLC staff or ministers of Operation Breadbasket, King advocated "messing with the captains of industry." But since most Americans supported jobs and the rebuilding of slums, King's official announcement on December 4 stated that the nation needed "a new kind of Selma or Birmingham to dramatize the economic plight of the Negro, and compel the government to act." King outlined the contradictions he sought to dramatize.

Consider . . . the spectacle of cities burning while the national government speaks of repression instead of rehabilitation. Or think of children starving in Mississippi while prosperous farmers are rewarded for not producing food. Or Negro mothers leaving children in tenements to work in neighborhoods where people of color cannot live. Or the awesome bombardment [of Vietnam] while political brokers de-escalate and very nearly disarm a timid action against poverty. Or a nation gorged on money while millions of its citizens are denied a good education, adequate health services, decent housing, meaningful employment, and even respect, and are then told to be responsible.[29]

The whole society was culpable, but "responsibility for removing the injustices can be laid directly at the door of the federal government," he insisted. King had analyzed and dramatized the role of private businesses, banks, homeowners associations, redevelopment authorities, and state and local governments in sustaining racial and class privilege. Yet the federal government was the most powerful agent of social change. It was the guarantor of civil and political rights in the South, and a powerful postwar engine of economic redistribution—although usually not in a way beneficial to the poorest Americans. "The President and the Congress," King contended, "have a primary responsibility for low minimum wages, for a degrading system of inadequate welfare, for subsidies to the rich and unemployment and underemployment of the poor, for a war mentality, for slums and starvation, and racism." For all these reasons, King promised, SCLC would lead "waves of the nation's poor and disinherited" to Washington, D.C.[30]

Not until February 1968 did they have a specific program, but King had a clear idea of what would appeal to black nationalists and social democrats. "Jobs or Income Now" had floated around the movement since 1964, and King introduced it to a staff meeting on November 28. "We're talking about the right to eat, the right to live," a basic right of social citizenship, he said. They were also demanding the rights of the "powerless poor in an economically oriented power structure" to get jobs and "control their own lives." King's exasperation with the staff was evident, however: "You see, I don't care if we don't name the demand—just go to Washington!" He continued lobbying the staff through the winter. "Let's find something that is so possible, so achievable, so pure, so simple that even the backlash can't do much to deny it," King told the staff in mid-January, "and yet something so non-token and so basic to life that even the black nationalists can't disagree with it." That was jobs or income. The staff could be "custodians of a creative black power," King promised. Groups from the National Urban League to the Black Panthers had endorsed full employment and the Freedom Budget, and perhaps they could move masses of people behind the idea.[31]

In January, SCLC formulated an action plan, and then issued demands in early February. The first phase of the march would imitate the 1932 Bonus March, by building shanties on the Washington Mall next to the Lincoln Memorial in full sight of the world. This march would have to be "sufficiently crisis packed," as Young put it. They planned to employ civil disobedience quickly, after lawful protests met with expected congressional stonewalling. Make no mistake, King told the staff on January 15, they would be confronting the "very federal machinery that has often come to our aid." On February 2, King announced tentative goals: a $30 billion annual appropriation for a real war on poverty; congressional passage of full employment and guaranteed income legislation; and construction of 500,000 low-cost housing units per year until slums were eliminated. This was $12 billion a year more than the Freedom Budget, and $25 billion a year more than Senator Clark's Manpower hearings recommended in 1964. It approximated what the United States spent that year in Vietnam.[32]

King revived the "bad check" metaphor from the 1963 march to build the case for national guarantees of economic rights. The promissory note issued African Americans at the nation's founding had been fraudulent, but now its guarantees of freedom and equality were to be extended to all Americans: "if one does not have a job or an income, he's deprived of life; he['s] deprived of liberty; and he's deprived of the pursuit of happiness." Human rights were not written into the Constitution, King argued, but civil rights could not be protected without economic power. "Washington has a debt. And they gave us a bad check the last time. But the resources are in the treasury of this nation. And we are going to collect what is justly ours."[33]

Field organizers objected that King was asking the nation's most vulnerable people to leave home and risk everything. Al Sampson in Newark remarked that poor people would be leaving their shacks and tenements and likely would have no place to return to. "What are they going to come back with?" he asked. Mississippi project director R. B. Cottonreader wrote Hosea Williams that the middle class was uncooperative and poor people's freedom of movement was limited by the very poverty they sought to protest. Many were "near starvation and out of work." Where should the dislocated and evicted poor people of Quitman County go? "I know they should go to Washington," he sniped, "but where will they go until the campaign goes to Washington?" He nonetheless promised to recruit between 150 and 200 local blacks. Herbert Coulton wrote from Petersburg that the Virginia SCLC chapter was broke and local people were resisting the D.C. campaign. They hadn't seen money from Atlanta for two years, but they had helped local blacks win political office. "These are victories that people could see," Coulton wrote. Why should they drop everything and go to Washington?[34]

Many SCLC activists were also in a nationalist mood, seeking racial unity, identity, and black economic development rather than multiracial coalitions. On February 2, Albert Turner and Hosea Williams wrote the Alabama staff that King would soon lead to Washington "thousands of Black people that can't eat, sleep, dress and learn in decency." Williams invited activists to voting rights meetings without even mentioning the Poor People's March, writing, "a united Black vote will bring the bacon home, and we don't mean just in the pocket of crooked politicians; we do mean on the breakfast table of the masses as well as the classes." Nationalist rhetoric dominated the SCLC Ministers Leadership Training Program in February, which was funded by the Ford Foundation.[35] Curricular materials invited ministers to fight "the violence, war-making and poverty which breeds on and feeds racism." But Bevel preached about seizing control of black communities. "The day of the interracial council is over," declared Dr. Archie Hargraves of Chicago's Urban Training Center. "The city is black cat's land now." "A kind of genocide has been perpetrated against the black people," King told the ministers, not physical, but "psychological and spiritual genocide." King reiterated familiar themes supporting his case for a new coalition of black poor and white poor. Daniel Patrick Moynihan, there to speak at the request of a Ford representative, complained King would not stand up for him against "near demented Black militants." King spent most of the time in his hotel room. He had become "weary and wounded," Roger Wilkins commented, "sad and depressed," Ralph Abernathy remembered.[36]

King did what he could to keep organizers' eyes broadly on poverty. In announcing the campaign, King said, "Naturally, it will be predominantly Negro," since blacks were "the poorest of the poor." Actually it was that way because so many black poor people were ready to move, as the most politicized group among the poor. Creating a genuinely multiracial coalition would be an uphill struggle. "I do not think I am at the point where a Mexican can sit in and call strategy on a steering committee," one SCLC staff member admitted. In an effort to broaden activists' appreciation of poverty as an issue that cut across racial lines, King circulated copies of Michael Harrington's *Other America* among the staff. Asked by King to write the first draft of the Poor People's Manifesto in December, Harrington wondered, given nationalist pressures, whether a white person should do so. Showing his commitment to interracialism and his preference for expertise over the "Bob Moses" approach, King urged Harrington to proceed.[37]

The Poor People's Campaign had to draw on the membership and organizational resources of mobilized groups, and the welfare rights movement had mobilized the greatest numbers of poor people. King explained to reporters in January that they would recruit AFDC mothers, who were the "real poverty stricken people." But in a crowded Chicago meeting with leaders of the National Welfare Rights Organization (NWRO) in February, King discovered that AFDC mothers would not just fall into line like Gandhi's salt marchers. "They jumped on Martin like no one ever had before," recalled Andrew Young. They grilled him, and then tutored him on the "Anti-welfare" law, "P.L. 90–248," signed by Lyndon Johnson on January 2. The law froze federal welfare expenditures and required work and training for women and their children over sixteen who were not in school. Robert Kennedy had introduced amendments on October 27 eliminating these provisions, but the NWRO lobbying effort had failed. King had not joined their protest. Why should they drop their welfare rights organizing to support a broad-based symbolic protest they couldn't lead? They agreed on an alliance, because they shared common ground, and King expanded his agenda to include theirs. NWRO called for a guaranteed annual income of $4,000 per family, incentives to allow working women to keep portions of their welfare grants as they earned their way out of poverty, and ambitious jobs programs for men. "There is a desperate need for jobs in the ghettos for men to permit them to assume normal roles as breadwinners and heads of families," read a NWRO pamphlet. King pressed the SCLC board to incorporate the Kennedy amendments into the Poor People's Campaign agenda. SCLC's ministers resisted him, Young recalled, because they wanted to make demands that "southern whites might accept, and they might accept hunger as an issue but certainly not welfare." But King won them over. Septima Clark's respect and admiration grew: "up to the time that Dr. King was nearing the end he really felt that black women had a place in the movement and in the whole world," unlike the other SCLC ministers, she recalled.[38]

Two weeks later, King was in Edwards, Mississippi, denouncing P.L. 90–248 as "one of the most vicious bills" ever passed, victimizing thousands of children. He blamed the "anti-welfare" middle class again for calling their own government benefits "subsidies" while disparaging "welfare" for undeserving Negroes. "Suburbia was built with federally subsidized credits," he explained, "and the highways and the roads that take white people out to the suburbs were built with federally subsidized funds to the tune of ninety percent." America had "socialism for the rich, and rugged free-enterprise capitalism for the poor."[39]

Previously, King's poverty discourse centrally asserted black men's employment needs, though he often professed his love for "the maids" and their search for dignified work. By 1967, with a mobilized constituency educating activists about the feminization of poverty and the abuses of power by social workers, King's imagery shifted. King frequently told a story about a New York City family of eight enduring "the agonies of real poverty." The mother became so distraught over a delayed welfare check that she committed suicide the evening before the check came. "Wait for the next morning," King beseeched his audiences. The "check that we all need as a people" had not arrived. "But morning will surely come." In Greenwood, Mississippi, Eutaw, Alabama, and Albany, Georgia, he denounced the punitive welfare law and prophesied the coming of economic, racial, and gender justice. "Now we are going to get the right for our wives and our mothers not to have to get up early in the morning, and run over to the white ladies' kitchen and clean and wash their clothes . . . but to be able to stay at home and raise their children." Black people were tired of "our fathers and our men not being able to be men, not being able to support their families."[40]

King's Deep South recruiting speeches in March also aimed to foster poor people's consciousness of shared poverty. "Poverty is here because white people in Mississippi are still determined to keep black people at the bottom," he told a crowd in Clarksdale, Mississippi. But by keeping "black people down, white folk have kept themselves down. They are poverty stricken too." King translated abstractions and policy prescriptions into compelling images and promises of tangible benefits. He told a mass meeting in Waycross, Georgia, on March 22.

And you know why we aren't free? Because we are poor. . . . Poverty is not having enough money to make ends meet. Poverty is being unemployed. Poverty is being underemployed. Poverty is working on a full-time job, getting only part-time income. Poverty means living in a run-down, dilapidated house. Poverty means, in many instances, not having hot water on a regular basis. Poverty means having rats and roaches all around the depressing housing situation in which you live. . . . We are tired of being on the bottom. We are tired of being exploited. We are tired of not being able to get adequate jobs. We are tired of not getting promotions after we get those jobs.[41]

Poverty afflicted diverse Americans, southern and northern, rural and urban, low-wage workers and the unemployed. "We have an underclass, that is a reality," he told SCLC activists in January. "An underclass is not a working class," he said, but immediately added, "thousands and thousands of Negroes work on full time jobs, with part time income." There was no moral or cultural difference between the unemployed underclass and the working poor. In Eutaw he summoned everyone to Washington, promising food and housing. "All ye who are heavy laden, come unto us. All ye who are unemployed, come unto us. All ye who are tired of segregation and discrimination . . . tired of being overworked and underpaid, come unto us. . . . And we will give you the rest of freedom and economic security." All poor people could fight together for decent jobs and income. Recruiting among Mississippi's poor, King echoed Randolph Blackwell and Septima Clark, promising they would make it possible to "stay in Mississippi and make it livable," thereby relieving Chicago's joblessness and poverty. And King appealed to the deepest aspirations of rural African Americans: "We want some land. We're going to demand our forty acres and a mule."[42]

Volunteers for the Poor People's March responded to King's encompassing call. About three hundred registration forms from Mississippi reveal some of the expectations of those who sojourned to Washington. Most registrants were women. Many had been arrested in civil rights protests and were affiliated with the Mississippi Freedom Democratic Party or the Child Development Group of Mississippi (CDGM). Their language of economic rights mixed class- and racial consciousness, personal needs and collective dreams. Virginia Mary Genes of Vaughan, Mississippi, wrote, "i have 6 children no one to suport them But me and i dont have a job and they wont give me one. and i need a job Bad." Mrs. Louella Wright wanted "mony, better housing and more jobs and better streets and I want land." Vonell Jamison, a young Head Start trainee from Marks, wrote simply, "So I can get what belong to me and my right to." James Kegler, Jr., a Job Corps graduate, wrote that he joined "to help the poor people and myself and other people and my state Mississippi."[43]

Racial grievances were acute, but many people spoke of the poverty they shared with whites. Mrs. Mary Hampton of Hattiesburg, an elderly CDGM volunteer, wrote "there are poor white as well as colored, we dont have enough food to eat. children need medicene. and this is the reason I want to go to Washington, D.C. to help better poor people's condition." Mrs. Bertha Johnson, a mother of six who brought all of them on the Mule Train to Washington, wanted "a good paying job, so I can take care of my family. The factories won't hire too many Black people. We can't get a chance to show our talent." An old man without work wanted "to see a good doc. and be able to receive my rights and Social Security benefits." Mrs. S. C. Rose Kendricks, age fifty-five, of Marks, an employee of the Associated Poverty Action Program, quoted the campaign recruitment literature, then wrote, "My house is falling in. Congressmen you have the job and you have the money. I want some of it so i can live too."[44] In 1963, Mississippi's poorest citizens had awakened to their rights and dignity, expecting equal opportunity, and a fair share of public services and the nation's affluence. They created their own political organization as a base to challenge the Democratic Party and national government. Now three hundred of them, having tested the Democratic Party and the War on Poverty and found them wanting, were on their way to Washington to protest—and collect.

Prospects for a multiethnic coalition of poor people received a boost in mid-March when activists from over fifty nonblack organizations gathered in Atlanta to join the campaign. They represented a rainbow of community organizers from around the country: Tom Hayden, from the Newark Community Union; Reies Tijerina from the Federal Alliance of New Mexico; John Lewis at the Southern Regional Council; Myles Horton of Highlander Center; a handful from Appalachian Volunteers in Kentucky; welfare rights activists; California farm workers; organized tenants; and the American Friends Service Committee and other church groups. King hailed "a new cooperation, understanding, and a determination by poor people of all colors" to win their rights. Delegates agreed that the "established powers of rich America have deliberately exploited poor people by isolating them in ethnic, nationality, religious and racial groups," read a press release. One poor white commented, "It is not really the poor people who are responsible for hatred in our country, but the powerful economic and political managers who want to keep us down. We will no longer permit them to divide us." Myles Horton was exultant, writing Andrew Young that they all had seen "a glimpse of the future . . . the making of a bottom-up coalition." The *Pittsburgh Courier* reprinted much of the press release under the heading "All Minorities Supporting MLK." The *New York Times* ignored it, focusing instead on King's hints in speeches that he, like Randolph in 1941, might cancel the March on Washington if Johnson made enough concessions.[45]

King was well aware of how the press treated violence, leadership conflicts, and protest tactics as more newsworthy than social analysis, community organizing, or coalition building. Media fascination with outrageous rhetoric and the potential for violence muted substantive discussion of King's top issues. On February 7, King told reporter Daniel Schorr that the media consistently drove nonviolent activists toward rhetorical militancy, because otherwise activists would not "get on the evening news." The press elevated and legitimated militants like Stokely Carmichael and put "a premium on violence." Reporters repeatedly asked whether King could maintain nonviolent discipline in competition with violent militants. "You media people are going to have to decide that this is your America too," Whitney Young had told a conference of journalists the previous May. Episodic "spot-news reporting" had utterly crowded out discussion of his Domestic Marshall Plan, and "'ghettoized' news coverage" had sensationalized rioting, obscuring real issues of urban inequality and serious interracial efforts to address them.[46]

In February 1968, Carmichael met with King and promised to support his nonviolent march. Whites wrote to Lyndon Johnson alleging King was the puppet of Carmichael, that nonviolence was a cover for "Communist" violence, and that "jobs or income" was a clarion call to armies of dependent Negro paupers. Would Johnson let "King get away with causing all these riots?" one wondered. Johnson should send "the military to clean them out," just as President Hoover had routed the bonus marchers, another wrote. One man wondered "how many of these people would really work if they were given jobs to take care of themselves and not live on welfare." King was an "arrogant demagogue," said another. "Not satisfied with political equality . . . he now demands economic equality, to be provided by government," under threat of violence. Poor people wanted an "elevated" form of equality built on individual opportunity and self-discipline.[47] The Negro should strive toward respectability before striding toward economic justice. In response to accusations like this, King was determined to show the nation the dignity of the jobless and working poor—and to powerfully assert their rights.

Samaritan in Memphis

On March 5, 1968, James Lawson invited King to Memphis, Tennessee, to support a black sanitation workers' strike against the city. The workers had been joined by a powerful cross-class black coalition, Community on the Move for

Equality (COME), which Lawson led. King recognized a compelling arena in which to dramatize the plight of the working poor, whose low wages and dangerous working conditions left them precariously close to the "underclass" he was recruiting in the black belt and the ghettos. "These are poor folks," King told reluctant staff members in mid-March. "If we don't stop for them, then we don't need to go to Washington." Here, at last, King found a concrete expression of a militant, insurgent, black-labor alliance, organizing unorganized workers to win collective bargaining rights, dignity, and higher wages. Memphis revived the civil rights unionism of the 1940s. William Lucy, an organizer for the American Federation of State, County, and Municipal Employees (AFSCME) and president of the Coalition of Black Trade Unionists, recalled King's excitement at the strength of a community-union alliance for economic justice. King knew the struggle was about "people who worked forty hours a week and still lived in poverty." King had championed the plight of low-paid workers ever since black and Puerto Rican hospital workers in Local 1199 struck in 1959. He seldom picketed factory gates, but here was a whole city on the march.[48]

Michael Honey's remarkable oral history collection, *Black Workers Remember,* documents the arbitrary firings, filthy and dangerous working conditions, low wages, and negligible job mobility that Memphis's black sanitation workers endured and resisted. Memphis and many other cities and states kept wages low by banning public employee unions. The workers struck in 1966, but the city suppressed the strike and fired thirty-three men. They had a keen sense of deprivation. More than half of the black population lived below the poverty line. James Robinson migrated to the city from a sharecropper's cabin and started as a sanitation worker at 96 cents an hour, working twelve-hour days for eight hours' pay. All the supervisors and skilled heavy equipment operators were white. Full-time workers made so little they were eligible for county relief, Robinson recalled. "We didn't have no benefits, no safety," Taylor Rogers remembered. They transferred dripping, maggot-filled garbage into tubs and carried it to trucks on their shoulders. Two black workers had recently been accidentally "mashed up" in a truck's garbage compactor and killed, Robinson told Honey, a gruesome symbol of how the city treated them like trash. "We had complained about faulty equipment," strike leader T. O. Jones recalled, to no avail. The two workers had no workmen's compensation or life insurance; the city paid their families a month's extra salary and $500 for burial expenses. Republican segregationist mayor Henry Loeb explained the compensation was out of compassion, not obligation.[49] One day supervisors sent black workers home during a rainstorm without pay while whites stayed on the job. Thirteen hundred workers spontaneously walked off the job.

The strike became a massive confrontation between the black community and the city. Workers demanded wages starting at $2.35 an hour, overtime pay, safety programs, and union recognition. They called upon AFSCME, which sent money and organizers. Mayor Loeb refused to negotiate on collective bargaining rights. When workers marched on city hall, police clubbed and maced them, along with several prominent ministers. The next day, February 24, seventy-five ministers formed COME. "The churches supported everybody," Rogers recalled, providing food, clothing, rent, mortgage money, and shelter for evicted workers. Teachers, community activists, and factory workers joined in, especially the United Rubber Workers, who lent them their union hall. When terrorists bombed the hall, the local NAACP joined the struggle. Trade unionists, Catholic activists, Roy Wilkins, and Rustin came from out of town. "Don't give an inch," Wilkins told a crowd of 7,000. AME minister H. Ralph Jackson coordinated community boycotts to pressure the merchants, making downtown "a ghost town." The city's two conservative newspapers demeaned the strikers and imposed a news blackout. The *Commercial Appeal* printed a cartoon showing an obese worker on top of a garbage can, with fumes forming the words "Threat of Anarchy." The *Press-Scimitar* praised police use of mace against protesters. Blacks boycotted the newspapers. People dumped garbage in the middle of streets to publicize the issue and pressure the city.[50]

COME voted to invite King because of his crowd appeal and power to bring in the national press. King's March 18 speech to 15,000 people at the Masonic Temple praised their amazing unity in a struggle crossing "class lines." "You are going beyond purely civil rights to questions of human rights," he told a crowd that clogged the aisles and spilled out of the church. "Now our struggle is for genuine equality, which means economic equality." King revisited familiar themes: all labor had dignity; an affluent nation was criminal in paying "starvation wages" to poor people who worked "every day." Garbage collectors were as important to the public health as doctors, he argued. If Loeb continued to refuse to recognize their union or provide for a dues checkoff, King advised they stage a "general work stoppage" to paralyze the city and compel concessions. Taylor Rogers remembered King's inspiring speech, which "brought people out, brought poor people together." The workers' slogan, "I *Am* a Man," contained a bundle of meanings connoting their racial struggle for personhood and the gendered aspirations for economic citizenship shared by black men and women. King's speech to the sanitation workers captured it well: "We are tired of our men being emasculated so that our wives and daughters have to go out and work in the white lady's kitchen."[51]

The next day was a disaster for King, Memphis, and potentially for the

Poor People's March. As King began his first Memphis march, several black youth started breaking windows and looting stores in the rear. Riot police removed their badges and indiscriminately beat looters and marchers. Police shot five people, killing one, and arrested three hundred. A hundred fires burned. A deluge of bad press and public criticism obscured the issues of the strike. The *New York Times* called it a "mini-riot" that showed how easily non-violence could "be used as a cover by rowdy elements bent on violence." King should imitate "his mentor" Gandhi by calling off marches and fasting in atonement for his people's sins. Wilkins saw violence as almost inevitable and refused NAACP support for the Poor People's March. The FBI covertly planted op-ed pieces claiming the militants were setting King up to stage the largest riot yet in Washington. The *St. Louis Globe Democrat* published one of these, claiming "Rev. King is more dangerous than Stokely Carmichael because of his non-violent masquerade. . . . Memphis could be only the prelude to a massive bloodbath in the nation's capital."[52] "Our Washington campaign is doomed," King told Levison. Unless he could stage a "powerful act" capable of refuting press allegations, the Memphis violence would weaken "the symbol" of nonviolence. Tom Offenburger wrote to the staff on April : "WE CANNOT AND WILL NOT BE INTIMIDATED BY THE VIOLENCE. . . . The issue at stake is not violence vs. nonviolence but POVERTY AND RACISM." The plans for Washington would not be changed. "We are going to correct economic racism," King promised.[53]

King vowed to return to Memphis to lead a nonviolent march. In his last, famous "mountaintop" speech, King spoke of their shared struggles to keep the media and the nation focused on the real issues. "The issue is injustice . . . the refusal of Memphis to be fair and honest in its dealings with its public servants," King insisted, not "a little violence" or "window-breaking." King bitterly remarked that the news articles he read barely mentioned the strike or the mayor's stubborn bigotry. So they had to march again to publicize the fact that 1,300 workers, God's children, were enduring "dark and dreary nights" in fear and insecurity. Memphis was not simply Memphis, he proclaimed. All over the world, "the masses of people are rising up . . . whether in Johannesburg, South Africa; Nairobi, Kenya; Accra, Ghana; New York City; Atlanta, Georgia; Jackson, Mississippi; or Memphis, Tennessee—the cry is always the same—'We want to be free.' "[54]

The next day, James Earl Ray murdered King with a single fatal shot as King stood on the balcony of the Lorraine Motel. Charles Cabbage, a local gang leader, was shocked that "white America could stoop this low." There "came a man talking love and nonviolence and walking hand in hand with white people, and they took his head off." "It ain't no such thing as no middle of the road no more," Cabbage vowed. Washington and Baltimore were among 125 cities that burned in the national convulsion of rage and fear that followed. At least thirty-nine people died as police, National Guardsmen, and army troops suppressed the uprisings. They arrested 21,000 black people. Troops protected the White House with machine guns, and Mayor Daley ordered his cops to "shoot to maim" looters. The violence brought concessions in Memphis and in Washington that nonviolence had not been able to win. The Civil Rights Act of 1968, with strong open housing provisions and protections for the civil rights of southern organizers, was passed by the Senate and signed by President Johnson. Federal mediators helped settle the strike, recognizing AFSCME as the sanitation workers' legitimate representative. In coming years, the union spread to the hospitals and the fire and police departments. Workers like Taylor Rogers and James Robinson got wage increases and health benefits. Memphis even elected a black mayor.[55]

"Economic justice, or equality for poor people and all people . . . [King] carried those themes with him all throughout his life," recalled Bernard Lee, who had met King during the sit-ins and become a close aide. With increasing strategic urgency, King pursued his dream. "It was just a matter of putting each piece in its perspective at the right moment. And economic justice, economic emancipation for poor people was the last phase."[56]

King chose identity with the poor, practicing the Good Samaritan's "dangerous altruism" on America's Jericho Roads, almost certain his death would be a violent one. He bequeathed his radical vision to a nation that increasingly spurned him while alive and was all too eager to canonize him in death. Moses was gone. Would a Joshua take his place?

Stones of Hope

Devastated by grief, SCLC organizers carried King's last dream to Washington, wrestling with dilemmas inherent in a black-led multiracial march for radical policy change staged in an increasingly reactionary political climate. Small but costly victories are discernible in the Poor People's March, despite abundant negative assessments by journalists and historians. Congress and the Johnson administration all but ignored the marchers. The FBI spread rumors of impending violence and scared off recruits by telling them they would lose welfare benefits if they joined the march. Tangled logistical, political, and public relations problems scuttled most plans for massive civil disobedience. "Very few people know how radical Dr. King was," Tom Offenburger commented. "He was a revolutionary," a leader capable of action far more radical than what the campaign achieved. Activists came to especially regret the decision to build an encampment housing several thousand poor people on one of the most sacred of American civic spaces, between the Washington Monument and the Lincoln Memorial. Resurrection City was an expensive logistical nightmare—construction, sanitation, communications, and security, all invented from scratch. It made the poor "visible" in a way activists could not control. "The wild side was from Washington, coming into the camp starting trouble," organizer James Orange recalled. In May, after several episodes in which news crews were excluded from the tent city and someone assaulted a white photographer, press coverage turned sharply negative. The average reporter entered Resurrection City, Hosea Williams charged, "like an underground assassin, looking for dirt and filth." Jesse Jackson recalled that "the press examined minutely the personal behavior of poor people and ignored the collective behavior of Congress."[57]

A scramble for leadership filled the vacuum left by King. "Like in any other city, everybody wanted to be the top politician," observed D.C. coordinator Kay Shannon. Marian Logan recoiled from their competition and the fact that they chose to sleep in motels rather than Resurrection City, indicative of values the movement was supposed to transcend. The multiracial coalition proved impossible to hold together. Reies Tijerina, leader of a few dozen Mexican Americans, complained of being ignored and refused to camp in the city. So did 100 Appalachian whites. Only about 300 nonblack poor people joined over 3,000 African Americans who camped out on the mall or participated in marches. Welfare rights organizers effectively staged several well-publicized demonstrations, beginning with a Capitol Hill vigil on April 22 before SCLC even arrived.[58]

High spirits and a sense of ownership pervaded Resurrection City despite its many problems, Shannon remembered. Poor people took "fierce pride" in the city they all built together. In late April, Bernard Lafayette tried to counterbalance the negative press with evidence of a spirit of cooperation among the marchers and volunteers in the D.C. black community. "Several women's groups have opened day care centers for the children," he reported. Taxi drivers took the marchers' children on free tours of D.C. Hundreds were now eating better than they ever had in Mississippi, Shannon noted.[59] Still, in the eyes of the white press and politicians, the community they made resembled the "slums" for which they were blamed instead of prefiguring their redemption.

A month and a half of sporadic demonstrations led to protracted, inconsequential negotiations with heads of executive agencies rather than a climactic

Figure 10. "Everybody's Got a Right to Work, Eat, Live." SCLC organized a "Mule Train," which traveled from Mississippi to Atlanta, then by train to Washington. Thousands of ordinary people turned out on rural back roads and city streets to honor the dream. Photo courtesy of Roland Freeman.

confrontation capable of riveting the nation. The Johnson administration vacillated, alternately ignoring the march, planning for widespread violence and repression, and engineering concessions so the marchers would go home. White House Aide James Gaither coordinated interagency responses, labeling all his folders "Riot Control—Poor People's March." Fear gripped official Washington in the wake of rioting. Harry McPherson recalled the controversy over restricting marchers in Lafayette Square. The White House police warned Johnson they might have to use lethal force against mobs "streaming into the lawn of the White House and headed for the House." Johnson refused to meet with marchers or leaders, delegating to agency officials all negotiations over concessions. In order to secure congressional approval of $10 billion to meet a Vietnam-generated budget shortfall, he accepted a $6 billion domestic spending cut. Johnson's stagnant War on Poverty embittered poor people and the left, while a widening foreign war he could not prosecute to victory strengthened the right and hobbled his plans for domestic reconstruction. On May 1, Johnson lectured his cabinet on the "remarkable gains" his administration had made in poverty, urban aid, education, "water pollution, school lunches, the

Indians, Appalachia, surplus foods." Don't talk to reporters unless they promise to report all the progress, he admonished. Listening to Ralph Abernathy, "you would think these times have seen no progress being made at all."[60]

Liberal allies in federal agencies delivered small victories to the poor people's army. Marian Wright ran shuttle diplomacy between Resurrection City, the Pitts Motel where the leadership stayed, and the executive departments, where she met with sympathetic officials crafting position papers. Discussions increasingly focused on hunger and food. Department of Agriculture (DOA) officials drafted major reforms in the commodity distribution and food stamp programs, which would have allowed people earning less than $30 a month not to have to pay for food stamps. Johnson's domestic advisor, Joseph Califano, gave tentative approval for the reforms in June. But, costing upward of $100 million, they were too much for Johnson. So the DOA scraped together $43 million to expand the distribution of surplus commodities in the poorest rural counties. The poor straggled out of Washington, "depressed that our government had been so niggardly," Wright remembered.[61]

Many of the poor made their way back home. Mississippi volunteer Bertha Johnson returned to Marks, and over the years she watched most of the volunteers leave Marks in search of jobs elsewhere. The main value was not in what she did in Resurrection City but in "what we learned and gained by sticking together." "You got to remember we were kind of naïve," Bertha Johnson Luster explained in 1997: "The SCLC leaders told us we were going to Washington to demand that our government give us forty acres and a mule. Now we weren't stupid. We knew that we weren't going to get forty acres and a mule, but we did believe the part about being able to get jobs and a better education for our children. . . . But most of us came back here to the same old same old. Over the years change has come, but it has been very slow."[62]

Activists took the concessions as small victories and learned valuable lessons. "Resurrection City was a success because it radicalized an awful lot of people," Shannon reflected. But Ernest Austin of Appalachian Volunteers recalled that radicals, white and black, received a healthy dose of pragmatism. Radicals who were committed to "restructuring the economic system of the United States because the system itself is corrupt" had to listen to black folk from "Mississippi who don't see this system as bad per se—they see themselves as locked out of it." In other words, "the poor were dictating to the more sophisticated in their thinking . . . 'immediate goals now, because those are what we need.'" Shannon thought they succeeded in dramatizing poverty to the media to "the degree that the middle-class was willing to see it." Future SCLC President Joseph Lowery agreed. Both the Chicago Freedom Movement and Poor People's March "were a tremendous success." Together they constituted "an exposure of the system." It was not SCLC's fault that "this country isn't ready yet to deal with the system."[63]

King wove his economic freedom dreams from skeins provided by the black movement and the democratic left. Progressives carried them forward. The political shortcomings of the march should not obscure its substantive critique of the American political economy or the dreams of economic equality and multiracial democracy embedded in its many demands. George Wiley of NWRO called for "a universal guaranteed annual income *above* the poverty level," including the creation of at least three million new jobs. Jesse Jackson called for repeal of "the freeze and compulsory work provisions" of P.L. 90-248. SCLC President Ralph Abernathy denounced rural malnutrition and hunger, demanding an end to crop subsidies to wealthy farmers, less niggardly food programs, and collective bargaining rights for farm workers. Victor Charles of the National Indian Youth Council spoke at OEO about poor antipoverty warriors "sold into bondage to local politicians and hostile governors." He called for poor people's participation at every level of administration and demanded that OEO centrally coordinate the "fragmented anti-poverty effort." SCLC's Bernard Lee implored the secretary of housing and urban development to "listen to us, the poor, as you have listened to the builder, the banker and the bureaucrat." Poor people must have access to affordable housing on a scale proportional to housing subsidized for the middle class, he demanded. SCLC's Bernard Lafayette demanded expanded health programs serving and employing the poor. Walter Fauntroy demanded that the class and racial privileges woven into the welfare state be unraveled. Stop affirmative action for white "high salaried administrators," overhaul "racist state departments of education," and make politicians accountable to the poor, not just middle class whites out in "the pampered schools of suburbia." Melvin Tom of the National Indian Youth Council gathered them all together: "guaranteed jobs, guaranteed income, housing, schools, economic development, but most important . . . these things on our own terms."[64] Without an outpouring of popular support, Congress and President Johnson felt free to ignore them. But they summarized years of experience within the democratic left and sustained hope in the possibility of a real war on racism and poverty.

Grief and exhaustion impaired SCLC's strategic and tactical decision making, but it did not diminish the power of the left's antipoverty tradition. On Mother's Day, Coretta Scott King and NWRO leaders led as many as 7,000 people down 14th Street toward the White House through burned-out streets of rubble, under banners calling for "Woman Power!" They argued for the fulfillment of the spirit of the original Social Security Act and the second New Deal: decent provision for mothers raising children, and secure work for breadwinning men. On Solidarity Day, June 19, the traditional "Juneteenth" celebration of the Emancipation Proclamation, she repeated her Mother's Day speech for a mass rally at the Washington Memorial. Mrs. King denounced the dominant culture's preoccupation with violence committed by oppressed people, and its neglect of economic violence committed by guardians of the status quo. "Poverty can produce a most deadly kind of violence," she said.

In this society violence against poor people and minority groups is routine. I remind you that starving a child is violence; suppressing a culture is violence; neglecting schoolchildren is violence; punishing a mother and her child is violence; discrimination against a workingman is violence; ghetto housing is violence; ignoring medical needs is violence; contempt for equality is violence; even a lack of will power to help humanity is a sick and sinister form of violence.[65]

More forcefully than her husband had articulated, Coretta King connected poverty and policy neglect to systemic social violence. Uprooting poverty and racism, not suppressing the poor, should be the nation's dominant priorities. Blacks were now mainly newsworthy when they looted and burned property, or when forces "restoring" order shot them in the streets. "We resolved to make America face itself," Abernathy said on Solidarity Day. Birmingham and Selma had successfully compelled dominant political forces to turn over America's most overtly racist rocks for the world to see. The "failure" of the Poor People's Campaign stemmed from the nation's unwillingness to pull larger stones of hope from strata of poverty and economic racism that were now visible to all, if they chose to look.[66]

Epilogue

After the Poor People's March, scores of activists who had worked to help King reconstruct his dream to address the needs of America's and the world's poor returned to their communities and continued their work in an increasingly conservative climate. Marian Wright Edelman founded the Children's Defense Fund, fighting poverty and racism under a new banner. Jesse Jackson shepherded Operation Breadbasket and ran for president after forming the multiracial Rainbow Coalition. Ralph Abernathy marshaled SCLC support for striking Charleston hospital workers of Local 1199 the next year. Andrew Young became U.N. ambassador under President Jimmy Carter, placing human rights on America's foreign policy agenda as it had not been before or has been since. Bayard Rustin advocated for Southeast Asian refugees during a time when most Americans would have preferred to forget them and the war that dislocated them. Michael Harrington wrote another book about poverty and helped form Democratic Socialists of America, sustaining the dream of a full-employment alternative to Reaganomics in the 1980s. Walter Fauntroy fashioned a legislative agenda for black America as the nonvoting representative of the District of Columbia to the Senate. Coretta Scott King worked tirelessly to define and preserve her husband's legacy, involving herself in struggles for gender justice and international peace.

Crown of Contention: The King Legacy

The culture wars over King's legacy began immediately after his assassination. The NWRO demanded that Congress pass a "living memorial" by repealing the 1967 public welfare amendments and guaranteeing jobs or income for every American family. Saks Fifth Avenue closed its doors for a day and printed excerpts from the "I Have a Dream" speech in the *New York Times*. White folks, setting aside their recent fear of King as a radical incendiary, froze King at a moment in 1963 as a moderate "civil rights" leader appealing to the nation's highest ideals to integrate Negroes into the mainstream. A few recalled more radical visions. "After Gandhi's death," Harris Wofford wrote, "the whole man seemed to have gone through a prism and come out divided into various beams: the pacifist Gandhi, the ascetic Gandhi . . . Gandhi the political artist."[1] King's prismatic diffusion has been even more dramatic, as a wide range of political figures have refracted beams of his legacy to colorize their own usable Kings.

Coretta Scott King and SCLC president Joseph Lowery, aided by musician Stevie Wonder and many congressional sponsors, lobbied for years to have King's birthday declared a national holiday. Conservatives mounted fierce resistance, remembering King only as a provocateur of violence, a champion of Ho Chi Minh, or an advocate of government "totalitarianism." The King holiday would give the nation an opportunity to celebrate its achievements in voting rights and desegregation, Mrs. King argued. African Americans could win some compensation for hundreds of years of slavery, and the nation had a rare opportunity to honor a man who "gave his life in a labor struggle." Generally, sponsors toned down King's radicalism in the interest of political consensus, however. As Lowery said during hearings in 1979, "Martin Luther King's leadership gave all Americans, white, black, yellow, red, and brown, a new sense of worth and purpose."[2]

When President Reagan finally signed the bill creating the King holiday, he wondered out loud whether FBI surveillance documents still closed under court order would reveal in 2027 whether King had been a Communist. On the holiday in January 1986, Reagan seized the opportunity to turn King into a color-blind opponent of racial "quotas" and affirmative action, an opponent of state power who would have endorsed Reaganomics had he been given the opportunity to take his freedom dream "a step further" into economic policy. A chorus of scholars and former King associates cried foul. Julian Bond lamented the commemoration of King the "dreamer," not "the antiwar activist," the "challenger of the economic order," or the "opponent of apartheid." Wyatt Walker called celebrations of the holiday "empty" without activism "against racism, poverty, and war." Newt Gingrich, who had recently been elected to Congress, responded, "King transcends all of us," like some mysterious deity knowable only through his malleable avatars of clay.[3]

Independently of the holiday, Coretta King and many movement veterans organized commemorations with a more radical edge. In August 1988, after Reaganism and the anti-apartheid movement had reenergized American antiracism and economic activism, Mrs. King called for direct action to force Congress to pass "stronger sanctions against apartheid" and new legislative agendas to fight "poverty, joblessness and homelessness." In January 1989, African American and Puerto Rican members of Local 1199 organized the multiracial New York City March for Racial, Economic and Social Justice to

demand reform of voter registration laws, full employment, affordable housing, and "a guaranteed and decent health-care system."⁴ Through the 1990s,
peace, civil rights, and labor activists repeatedly drew upon King's radical
vision. The Greensboro Kmart strike of 1996 represented a signal victory for
civil rights unionism, when fifty churches joined the Union of Needletrades,
Industrial and Textile Employees (UNITE) in organizing majority-black workers in the corporation's regional distribution facility. Workers won higher
wages, workplace protections, the right to organize, and a city council living-
wage resolution. As the strike wore on, Rev. William Wright, a leader of
Greensboro's Pulpit Forum, lamented, "If Martin were walking the streets of
Greensboro, he would be saddened to see that the dream has not come to full
fruition." The right to work at decent wages in a full employment economy
was a distant dream when corporations continued to "put profits over people," Wright explained.⁵

The plasticity of the King icon also proved useful to neoliberals. In
November 1993, after the defeat of his administration's $30 billion public
works "stimulus package," Bill Clinton invented a voice for King, as King had
for Saint Paul, but not to decry the moral corruptions of "capitalistic" selfishness. Addressing the Masonic Temple Church of God in Christ where King
gave his last speech, Clinton imagined King preaching communal and family
values to black folk. "I did not fight for the right of black people to murder
other black people with reckless abandon, nor for the freedom of children to
have children and fathers of the children to walk away." Having promised to
"end welfare as we know it," Clinton honored King's commitment to "the
right to work," explaining that "the ravages of crime and drugs and violence"
ultimately derived from "the breakdown of the family, the community, and
the disappearance of jobs." But stopping the violence was beyond the scope of
big government, Clinton preached.⁶

Progressives had a different answer. By 1994, dissatisfied with a popular
pattern of leisurely and lackluster King holiday commemoration, Senator Harris Wofford of Pennsylvania joined Representative John Lewis and Mrs. King
in proposing legislation that would turn what had become merely another day
off into a national day of service. They envisioned a day of cross-class, interracial volunteer work. "Imagine 10 or 30 million Americans helping friends and
strangers alike," Coretta King advocated, "to give blood, restore our parks,
tutor our children, rebuild our schools and recreational areas, improve the
environment, feed the hungry, house the homeless, help the elderly, assist
those with AIDS and other diseases, help the Special Olympics, stop the violence." She did not talk about social violence as she had in 1968. Bill Clinton
signed the bill into law on August 23. King's spirit of service would indeed be

honored if the nation were to hold an annual mass meeting of the Jericho Road Improvement Association. Radical restructuring of the Jericho Road that produces homeless beggars would not have found federal sponsorship. If those involved in Community Action in the 1960s learned anything, it was that federal, state, and local governments would not long tolerate or subsidize radical challenges to the political economy.[7]

Septima Clark's brief unpublished eulogy of King is perhaps the most moving and accurate of them all. "Racism, poverty, and warfare remain, yet our hearts retain the righteous dream of God's revolutionary kingdom," she wrote. King's religiously informed Christian socialism had considerably evolved in praxis, she recognized. "His peace was not in a cozy rally, but in a re-ordering of our national priorities from military power to that of human empowerment." Above all, King was someone who "spoke out against a war in Asia because its bombs took bread from the tables of the poor in America." Vietnam and the violent repression of domestic dissent radicalized Clark's rhetoric by the early 1970s far beyond King's, but her analytical linkages might again have become his, as happened before. Clark denounced "white America and its systems of domination," drawing linkages between educational deprivation, military conscription, criminal incarceration, and the murder of young black men by police and federal agents of repression. Around 1969, Clark drafted an address directed at black scholars and their obligations to identify "the enemy."

Educational systems which invariably spawn wretched schools and powerless officials in black communities are the enemy. Political systems which use code words like "busing," "welfare," "no quota systems," and "crime in the streets" to signal their fear of Black people and their willingness to hold us powerless as long as they can—these are the enemy. Economic systems which reject so many of the basic human needs of the poor and the weak in favor of the wealthy and their subalterns are the enemy. Health care systems which provide neither health nor care for the powerless and the poor are the enemy. Legal and penal systems which persistently place us in large overwhelming numbers behind bars and which place whites in almost all the seats of authority—these are the enemy. . . . A military system which serves as the only respectable alternative available to black youth who have been manacled and rejected by America's other systems, a military force which then is ironically guaranteed to be used in the future only against other nonwhite people—that is the enemy.[8]

Clark shared with many on the black left this move from a discourse of citizenship and equal rights to one of anticolonialism and liberation. King and Clark both embraced the discourse of liberation, transposing it into an ideal of integration as shared power at every level of American society, of shared living in every neighborhood and workplace. "The assassin's bullet killed the man—not the cause he stood for, nor his great name."[9]

A King for the Ages, or a King for Our Time?

Martin Luther King cannot be removed from the history and the cultures of opposition that shaped almost everything he said. We do King service not by lifting him up as a radical to the ages, but as a radical who emerged from and fed back into his own place and time. Only when we understand King with respect to his own resolved and unresolved dilemmas can we understand our own deepest difficulties in light of his legacy. "God gave him to this generation for this hour," Fred Shuttlesworth reflected, "but this generation either understood him not or mistook the words he spoke." Therein lies the supreme irony: the culture of celebrity compressed King into a narrow civil rights frame even before his death. The nation's and the media's obsession with violence versus nonviolence drowned out much of his rhetoric of opposition to racism, militarism, and poverty. King recognized and struggled against his own domestication during his final years. He had cooperated in his own symbolic construction as the American Gandhi; by 1968 it had become a straitjacket.[10]

The many biographies of King have caught important beams of his life and legacy, translating his prophecy, enriching this work even when I disagree. For Michael Eric Dyson, King is a Jeremiah for the ages and a scathing interlocutor to the Christian right. For Christopher Lasch, King is a model of the "spiritual discipline against resentment," affirming and redeeming the humanity of those we call enemy. For Stewart Burns, King is a moral prophet of racial brotherhood, never fully capable of making an equally compelling case for economic justice, but bequeathing "a life raft of nonviolence" to a world of terrorized and "disempowered consumers." For Taylor Branch, King is America's prophet of patriotic return to a faith in voting as the consummate exercise of nonviolence. For Cornel West, King speaks to us now as a prophetic preacher, a Protestant liberal, a nonviolent Gandhian, an American, a black folk Hegelian, and a Gramscian "organic intellectual." For Clayborne Carson, King was a conduit of collective ideas circulating from the bottom up as well as the top down. In that spirit, I conducted much of my inquiry.[11]

Understanding King's commitment to economic justice and human rights in the context of his movement can enrich our understanding of this watershed era of American history. First, King was part of an ongoing black freedom struggle which challenged racial and class inequalities in the economy and the New Deal state as much as it pursued civic equality and political citizenship. Second, King draws our attention to democratic socialist alternatives to economic and poverty policy in the postwar era. Though the Red Scare of the 1950s narrowed the focus of many civil rights organizations, McCarthyism did not destroy the American left nor its dreams of anti-imperialism, civil rights unionism, and economic justice. Third, King helps us understand the limitations of liberalism in achieving full equality and economic opportunity in the 1960s. Though the liberal moment of 1963–1964 offered a genuine missed opportunity to coordinate economic and civil rights policy, the weaknesses of the War on Poverty reflected a combination of inherited constraints and contingent failings of leadership. As King said, there was nothing new about the white backlash against desegregation and federal authority; it had weakened the New Deal, the Popular Front, and many determined efforts across the nation to desegregate schools, jobs, and housing. Even though local elites dominated the War on Poverty, racism and the related animus against welfare still undermined its limited efforts. But contingent events and decisions matter in history. Lyndon Johnson's leadership failings stemmed from his own failures of imagination, from constraints imposed by conservative local elites and congressional representatives, and above all from his disastrous decision to follow the logic of cold war liberalism into the jungles of Southeast Asia. King draws our attention to the devastation wreaked by the Vietnam War on progressive social movements, working-class Democratic constituencies, and domestic reform. He suggests that violent confrontations in the cities much more than black power rhetoric drove political reaction. And he asks us to reconsider the power of nonviolence in making social change, at a time when scholars are busy restoring the parallel black tradition of armed self-defense to history.[12]

King challenges the simplistic dichotomies governing our thinking about the 1960s, especially the distinction between an early phase of liberal achievement around individual civil rights and a later phase of radicalization, conflict, and failure, when African Americans allegedly demanded group entitlements that found little support with the majority. This view has some truth. But integration and black power, northern and southern movements, civil rights and human rights were never so much neat binaries defining phases of historical development than they were intertwined aspects of ongoing struggle. Though the rise of black nationalism in the 1960s is indisputable, King reminds us about an underlying consensus shared by diverse activists: that full employment for all Americans was an essential precondition for black freedom. Overwhelming majorities of Americans had supported the idea of a right to work since the 1930s. The nation's leadership might have galvanized a consensus behind more effective policies than the oversold and underfunded programs of the War on Poverty and what followed in the Nixon administration—job training, education, community services, welfare, and later, school busing and affirmative action in hiring and school admissions. (The greatest beneficiaries of expanding entitlements were of course elderly Americans who received more generous Social Security stipends and Medicare.) Gareth Davies argues that liberalism stumbled disastrously from a consensus philosophy of individual "opportunity" in 1964 to a self-defeating embrace of minority group "entitlement" by 1968. But the interracial left spoke loudly for a missed alternative: national action that would further racial equality in the context of human rights to decent housing, medical care, guaranteed work, wages, and family incomes for all Americans. King may have failed to understand class divisions within white society and how working-class whites would react to direct challenges in their neighborhoods. But this was even more true of elites who imposed the burdens of desegregation disproportionately on working-class whites and blacks (most famously in the Boston school busing crisis of the early 1970s). The financial, managerial, and racial limitations of Johnson's War on Poverty were discernible before the Vietnam escalation. But the tragic diversion of resources and political energies to Vietnam had as much to do the unraveling of liberalism as did the class revolt against policies of affirmative action, welfare reform, and school busing that rose from the rubble. Working-class Americans of all races saw little in the War on Poverty for themselves. They bore the brunt of fighting in Vietnam *and* the inflation triggered by war spending in 1966. They were profoundly disaffected, not just from the Democratic Party, but from the entire political process.[13]

For a time King excelled in forming interracial coalitions with middle-class and wealthy whites and blacks. He stayed at the top of the civil rights celebrity culture while remaining enormously popular among the poorest southern blacks. The cash and moral support of liberals and religious leaders proved indispensable to the civil rights victories of mid-decade. But many in the middle class eventually abandoned King because of his opposition to the war and because of officially sanctioned efforts to smear his radicalism with the paint of communism and insurrectionary violence. How much they rejected his larger project of metropolitan race and class integration and national wealth redistribution is unclear, so distorted were these positions by the press and especially the FBI.

Interracial coalitions among the working class proved the most promising, and the most disappointing of King's coalitions. The meatpackers, the hospital workers, the farm workers, and the public employees' unions all gave him hope. A stronger race-class alliance might have carried the war against poverty to a higher level, beyond growth economics and piecemeal reforms targeted at the most disadvantaged individuals and communities. But the progressive unions were never as strong as the dominant forces in the AFL-CIO, whose support for the war and resistance to the desegregation of jobs and neighborhoods made them unreliable allies. Many Americans came to see the War on Poverty as benefiting undeserving and riotous blacks, as conservative politicians loudly asserted it, as the media focused on urban violence and the racialized welfare-dependent poor, and as antipoverty dollars were in fact subverted for fire duty in the nation's burning cities. Though a minority of progressive trade unions supported King's strategies, the white poor and white workers did not heed the summons. King at the end was right, however: any class-based coalitions capable of moving levers of power must be multiracial and look to more flexible and inclusive institutions than the mainstream unions of the 1950s and 1960s.

In retrospect, we can give King and his generation more credit for changing the country than he could at the time. People who fight for democracy can make change. King's generation removed one cruel and historically specific form of white supremacy: the southern system of legalized Jim Crow and disfranchisement enforced by one-party rule, legal and extralegal violence. The freedom movement, the civil rights acts, and the war on poverty did not eradicate racism and poverty. But cumulatively they helped raise black incomes, improved the quality of life in many black communities, and provided training grounds for thousands of black elected officials who followed. "South African-style industrialization for whites only was certainly a possibility in the South" of the 1950s, writes Gavin Wright. But the freedom movement and the government forced open opportunities in southern industries and public employment, tangibly boosting black incomes. "Translating political gains into lasting economic improvement for the black population has proved to be much more difficult," Wright argues. This is true, but even here the movement yielded tangible results. James Button shows how in six southern cities over the 1970s black political power translated into improved police and fire protection, paved streets, and black employment in public works and recreation departments. Though far from achieving equality (especially as professionals and managers), blacks also made progress in private employment. Before 1960, only 12 percent of employers in the six cities had hired any blacks, but by the late 1970s the figure had jumped to 81 percent.[14]

King was right that aggregate statistics can mask glaring injustices. But mass activism, government antidiscrimination policies, and quickening economic growth in the 1960s dramatically raised incomes for middle- and working-class black families, as had happened in the early to mid-1940s when similar factors came into play. In the 1960s, black poverty declined from 55 percent to 33 percent, overall black unemployment dipped from 10 percent to 6.2 percent, and the ratio of black to white median income rose from 48 percent to 61 percent. Of course none of these gains eradicated inequality or segregation in housing markets and systems of education dependent on local taxes. By the 1980s and 1990s, economic growth no longer reduced poverty as effectively as the 1960s, as the fruits of growth accrued to wealthier Americans. Joblessness among young black men dramatically worsened in the 1970s and 1980s. The black middle class grew substantially. Yet as relative income inequality accelerated and the economy slowed, many factors combined to worsen the fortunes of the bottom third of black America: manufacturing loss in cities; persistent discrimination in employment and housing; urban fiscal crises and institutional decline; and growing proportions of poor people in mother-only families. A policy consensus emerged blaming "welfare dependency" rather than welfare insufficiency as a major cause of poverty, even though the average value of AFDC stipends declined after the mid-1970s. The real value of the minimum wage also declined by nearly a third in the 1980s, and recovered only a third of that loss in the 1990s. Cities became relatively poorer. The gap between family incomes in poorer cities and wealthier suburbs grew dramatically, up from 12 percent in 1959 to 21 percent in 1985. Indices of housing segregation nationwide declined only slightly. Cities such as Detroit and Philadelphia actually became more racially segregated. Residential segregation by race and class remains today a major factor in the enormous gap between black wealth and white wealth, the linchpin of school resegregation, the source of reactionary fears, stereotypes, and political divisions.[15]

Across the nation and its metropolitan landscapes, power has become increasingly suburban, and neither political party puts the needs of poor people or minorities at the top of its agenda. King dreamed of integration across racial and class lines, backed by a strong national state and a commitment to economic planning. But in the 1970s, despite the rise of urban black political power, cities lost tax revenues, employment, federal aid, and national electoral weight when power shifted to the Sunbelt and the suburbs. Reactionary populist politicians mobilized many working-class whites who lived between inner cities and affluent middle-class outer suburbs, where the beneficiaries of generous and exclusionary public policies wore sincere masks of colorblind individualism and racial innocence. Their political culture supported a politics of opposition to taxes, welfare, crime, drugs, and integrated public schooling, with profound racial consequences. King, Reddick, Whitney Young, and others saw this coming. Residents of poor and minority neighborhoods were and are held responsible for the legacies of neglect, disempowerment, and disinvestment they continue to bear.[16]

King's wave is inseparable from the ocean that was the movement and the democratic left. Examining King reveals a tradition of thinking about poverty that he popularized and refined, one that has become widely discredited, especially among those who do not need to think about poverty. King always regarded mass poverty as principally a reflection of unequal wealth and low-wage labor exploitation. Poverty was not reducible to poor people's cultural deficiencies or family pathologies. Racism was not mere prejudice, but foundational to a divided working class, to the institutional structure and political economy of the urban ghetto, and to larger landscapes of metropolitan apartheid.

King joined local activists in insisting that poverty would not be eliminated until poor people overcame their own political powerlessness through participation in institutions controlling their lives and shaping their prospects. In arguing for democratic empowerment as a social policy imperative, King and his circle challenged assumptions held by welfare reformers since the Progressive Era, that social change must proceed under the guidance of professional experts, that poor people are clients more than citizens. Only a movement that empowered people in the context of community could promise to reduce victimization and augment mutual aid and self-help among poor people, King held. Institutions matter. The urban uprisings were not simply responses to socioeconomic inequality but also violent protests against police violence and unresponsive institutions. Empowerment meant more than a healthy psychological determination to succeed. Yet King knew that local empowerment against communal impoverishment and the meeting of immediate needs were necessary but not sufficient conditions for economic freedom.

King hoped to pressure the national government to move in the direction of multiracial democratic socialism: a guaranteed income, full employment, and social revitalization planned in partnership *with* rather than *for* the poor. In our own era of government devolution and privatization, King reminds us that the national government has been the most consistent guarantor of equal rights in American history. It has been the most powerful single engine of economic distribution and, at least in name, is accountable to the people. But therein lies the paradox of invisible socialism for the rich and middle class, because government has in so many ways issued them checks backed by sufficient funds and underwritten their dreams. In this sense the greatest long-term threat to American democracy has been the continued demobilization of the electorate, especially the working class and poor, whose participation in voting has lagged further and further behind upper-income citizens. The whole economic and political calculus has also been skewed by America's role in the world. King warned of the power of the national state at home and abroad. America's claim to promote democracy and human rights is still undermined by imperial adventurism and contempt for diplomacy and international law. The cold war ended, but the concentration of power in the federal executive, the national security state, and its corporate partners continues unabated. Democratizing the imperial state remains as important as it was in the 1960s.

As King and SCLC pursued economic justice and northern desegregation after 1965, they relied on the tactical innovations of Birmingham and Selma, hoping to raise civil disobedience to powerful new levels. King had hoped to move in the direction of both community organization and coalition politics. Protest had worked best when it dramatized blatant injustices before powerful potential allies. The southern movement proved that when mobilizers worked in tandem with voting rights organizers, they could win allies and make simultaneous breakthroughs in access to public spaces and in local political representation. Since then, the political right has more effectively linked organized religious and suburban constituencies to electoral and Republican Party power. Protest is a powerful tool, as mass marches by Latinos and immigrants against punitive immigration reform in May 2006 attest. But protest cannot substitute for fostering grassroots institutions and ongoing efforts to link citizens to responsive electoral officials.[17]

Sharing his era's optimism about the limitless growth of America's productive capacities, King advocated a broader distribution of consumer goods and greater public investment in forms of work not traditionally defined as "productive" or profitable. He envisioned creating new jobs, principally in service to others and in forms of citizenship education that the government ultimately refused to sponsor. The Great Society had a rhetorical and real legislative legacy in championing nonpecuniary public goods: wilderness preservation, clean air and water, public media, the arts, public transportation. King drew on and radicalized the same cultural and spiritual critique of private enterprise and consumer capitalism that informed the spirit of the Great Society. Ultimately, King's "revolution of values" directly challenged the American middle class to heal their "sick society," fattened as they were on consumer goods and obsessed with technological gadgetry. A society of spiritually impoverished rich fools blind to their interdependence is not a truly rich society, he insisted. Smug individualism obscures the necessity and blessings of human interdependence, clouding our spiritual recognition that the greatest individual achievements are those of compassionate service and striving for social justice. King hoped this American tradition could prove as strong and enduring as acquisitive individualism. But King's central insight was that not merely middle-class benevolence but coalitions of working-class and multiracial power must compel higher syntheses of community and achievement, love and justice, civil and human rights.

Faced with great challenges born of serious dilemmas, King and his generation dreamed dreams but left dilemmas of inequality that remain unresolved in the twenty-first century. King did not foresee many of the challenges that followed hard on the heels of the 1960s. Mass immigration following the 1965 Immigration Act presented new versions of old challenges of interethnic competition and solidarity. The mass movement of married women into the workforce undermined older family-wage assumptions even as the number of mother-only families grew dramatically. The globalization of manufacturing and aggressive antilabor corporate and public policies accelerated a long-term slide in the strength of organized labor. King did not foresee the economic shocks and stagnant wages of much of the rest of the century, nor the problem of ecological sustainability inherent in the high-consumption society that underlay his egalitarian dreams. Dreams of a progressive executive still fill the sleep of the left, but exalting the valleys of poverty and powerlessness is the work of many nations, institutions, and communities. America's professions of equal economic opportunity still ring hollow for millions of Americans in the context of wildly unequal incomes and wealth, insecure jobs, and tattered safety nets that reflect the exaltation of market values over the rights of citizenship. Despite real advances in economic and social status, minorities remain isolated from potential allies, underrepresented in conventional politics, and subordinated in labor and housing markets. King knew poor folk could be violent and self-destructive, but the eclipse of the war on poverty by the successive wars on drugs, crime, and terrorism would have appalled him, though probably not surprised him. A country of radically unequal places, schools, and earning opportunities, a nation of prisons swollen with drug users serving punitive mandatory sentences, a society condoning widespread homelessness and single mothers shifting for themselves in low-wage labor markets—these are not features of a nation defined by "law and justice." But the dream of a public sphere in which all citizens equally pursue their happiness on a firm stage of economic security still has powerful allure. Democracy, community, a broad international vision of human rights, and compassion for the basic human dignity of all God's children remain powerful taproots for people determined to make history.

Notes

The following abbreviations appear in the notes. Numbers immediately following manuscript and repository information denote reel:frame or box:folder.

BR	Bayard T. Rustin Papers. Library of Congress, Manuscripts Division, Washington, D.C.
BU	Boston University, Mugar Memorial Library, Department of Special Collections, Boston
CD	*Chicago Defender*
CR	Cleveland Robinson Papers. Tamiment Institute Library and Robert F. Wagner Labor Archives, New York University
CUMD	Columbia University, Butler Library, Rare Book and Manuscript Division, New York
CUOH	Columbia University Oral History Collection, Butler Library, New York
FBI Jones Logs	Clarence B. Jones New York File—Surveillance Logs, David Garrow, FOIA Accession. Schomburg Center for Research in Black Culture, New York Public Library
FBI Levison Logs	Stanley Levison New York File—Surveillance Logs, David Garrow, FOIA Accession. Schomburg Center for Research in Black Culture, New York Public Library, New York
HL	Highlander Research and Education Center Papers. State Historical Society of Wisconsin, Social Action Collections, Madison
JFKL	John F. Kennedy Presidential Library, Boston
KC	Martin Luther King, Jr. Center for Nonviolent Social Change, Inc. King Library and Archives, Atlanta

KPBU	Martin Luther King, Jr. Papers. Mugar Memorial Library, Department of Special Collections, Boston University
KPKC	Papers of Dr. Martin Luther King, Jr. Martin Luther King, Jr. Center for Nonviolent Social Change, Inc., King Library and Archives, Atlanta
KPKC(3)	Papers of Dr. Martin Luther King, Jr., Series III. Speeches, Sermons, Articles, Statements. Martin Luther King, Jr. Center for Nonviolent Social Change, Inc., King Library and Archives, Atlanta
LAT	*Los Angeles Times*
LBJL	Lyndon B. Johnson Presidential Library, Austin, Texas
LBJT	LBJ Presidential Telephone Tapes. Miller Center for Public Affairs, University of Virginia, accessed via http://www.millercenter.org, 2003–5
LC	Library of Congress, Manuscripts Division, Washington, D.C.
LID	League for Industrial Democracy Records, 1920–70. Tamiment Institute Library and Robert F. Wagner Labor Archives, New York University
MLK-FBI File, ed. Friedly and Gallen	Michael Friedly and David Gallen, eds. *Martin Luther King, Jr.: The FBI File.* New York: Carroll and Graf, 1993.
MLK FBI Micro	*The Martin Luther King, Jr., FBI File [Microfilm].* Ed. David J. Garrow. Frederick, Md.: University Publications of America, 1984.
MLK-Levison FBI Micro	*The Martin Luther King, Jr., FBI File. Part 2. The King-Levison File [Microfilm].* Ed. David J. Garrow. Frederick, Md.: University Publications of America, 1984.
MSRC	Moorland-Spingarn Research Center, Manuscript Department, Howard University, Washington, D.C.
NAACP	National Association for the Advancement of Colored People Records. Library of Congress, Manuscripts Division, Washington, D.C.
NAACP Micro	*National Association for the Advancement of Colored People. August Meier, John H. Bracey, and L. Lee Yanike.* Papers of the NAACP [Microform]. Frederick, Md.: University Publications of America, 1987.

NUL	Records of the National Urban League, 1910–86. Library of Congress, Manuscripts Division, Washington, D.C.
NYAN	*New York Amsterdam News*
NYT	*New York Times*
NYU	New York University, Tamiment Institute Library and Robert F. Wagner Labor Archives
Papers 1	*The Papers of Martin Luther King, Jr.* Vol. 1., ed. Clayborne Carson, Ralph Luker, and Penny A. Russell. Berkeley: University of California Press, 1992.
Papers 2	*The Papers of Martin Luther King, Jr.* Vol. 2., ed. Clayborne Carson, Ralph E. Luker, Penny A. Russell, and Peter Holloran. Berkeley: University of California Press, 1994.
Papers 3	*The Papers of Martin Luther King, Jr.* Vol. 3., ed. Clayborne Carson, Stewart Burns, and Susan Carson. Berkeley: University of California Press, 1997.
Papers 4	*The Papers of Martin Luther King, Jr.* Vol. 4., ed. Clayborne Carson, Susan Carson, Adrienne Clay, Virginia Shadron, and Kiernan Taylor. Berkeley: University of California Press, 2000.
Papers 5	*The Papers of Martin Luther King, Jr.* Vol. 5., ed. Clayborne Carson, Tenisha Armstrong, Susan Carson, Adrienne Clay, and Kiernan Taylor. Berkeley: University of California Press, 2005.
PC	*Pittsburgh Courier*
POLL	Roper Center for Public Opinion Research. University of Connecticut, iPoll Data Base, accessed via Lexis-Nexis Academic Universe, 2003–5.
RJB	Ralph J. Bunche Oral History Collection. Moorland-Spingarn Research Center, Manuscript Department, Howard University, Washington, D.C.
Schomburg	Schomburg Center for Research in Black Culture, New York Public Library
SCLC	Records of the Southern Christian Leadership Conference. Martin Luther King, Jr. Center for Nonviolent Social Change, Inc., King Library and Archives, Atlanta
SCLC Micro	*Records of the Southern Christian Leadership Conference, 1954–1970 [Microfilm].* Part 1, Records of the

SHSW   President's Office. Ed. Randolph Boehm. Bethesda,
                 Md.: University Publications of America, 1995.
SHSW   State Historical Society of Wisconsin, Social Action
                 Collections, Madison
SOHP   Southern Oral History Program, Southern Histori-
                 cal Collection, University of North Carolina at
                 Chapel Hill. Library.
SPC   Septima Poinsette Clark Papers. Avery Institute for
                 Afro-American History and Culture, College of
                 Charleston, Charleston, South Carolina
WMY   Whitney M. Young, Jr. Papers. Columbia Univer-
                 sity. Butler Library, Rare Book and Manuscript
                 Division, Columbia University
WP   *Washington Post*

Introduction

1. King, "I Have a Dream," 28 Aug. 1963, in *A Call to Conscience,* ed. Carson and Shepard, 81–82.

2. King, "The American Dream," 4 July 1965, in *A Knock at Midnight,* ed. Carson and Holloran, 98–99; King, "Address to the Hungry Club," 15 Dec. 1965, KPKC(3), 12–13.

3. King, "The Birth of a New Age," 11 Aug. 1956, in *Papers* 3:346.

4. Harding, "Beyond Amnesia," 468–69; Garrow, *The FBI and Martin Luther King, Jr.,* 213; Garrow, *Bearing the Cross,* 214; David Garrow, "Martin Luther King Jr., and the Spirit of Leadership," in *We Shall Overcome,* ed. Albert and Hoffman, 29; Jose Yglesias, "Dr. King's March on Washington Part II," *NYT,* 21 Mar. 1967.

5. Ted Poston, "Negroes of Montgomery," *New York Post,* 15 and 19 June 1956, in *Reporting Civil Rights,* ed. Carson, 271. King, "The Non-Violence Of Dr. M. L. King," *NYAN,* 30 July 1966.

6. Fairclough, *To Redeem the Soul of America,* 197–99; Dyson, *I May Not Get There with You,* 37, 82; Lischer, *Preacher King,* 189; Cone, *Martin & Malcolm & America,* 282; Lewis Harlan, "Thoughts on the Leadership of Martin Luther King Jr.," in *We Shall Overcome,* ed. Albert and Hoffman, 67.

7. King modified one of his self-help set pieces in an address to high school students in 1964, adding "one extreme" to the recommendation: "And so if it falls your lot to be a street sweeper, *to carry it to one extreme,* set out to sweep streets like Michelangelo painted pictures." King, "Addison Jr. High School," 22 Oct. 1964, KPKC(3). In 1965, King had deleted this phrase originally taken from the sermons of Benjamin Mays, King, "A Great Challenge Derived from a Serious Dilemma," 15 Dec. 1965, KPKC(3).

8. Gerald Early, "Martin Luther King and the Middle Way," *Christian Century,* 113: 25 (28 Aug. 1996), 816, argues that King's sudden radicalization undermined his

moral authority. J. Mills Thornton argues that the movement abandoned its early "consensus" goals of liberty to embrace collectivism, which hastened its decline. William Chafe counters that there was a continuity and an organic development between economic goals in the early and later phases of an ongoing black freedom struggle, but he credits only King's later radicalism. Thornton, "Comment," and Chafe, "The End of One Struggle, the Beginning of Another," in *The Civil Rights Movement in America*, ed. Eagles, 136–37, 150–51. On white resistance, see Sugrue, *Origins of the Urban Crisis*, and Lassiter, *The Silent Majority*.

9. Biondi, *To Stand and Fight*; Ransby, *Ella Baker*; Self, *American Babylon*; Korstad and Lichtenstein, "Opportunities Found and Lost"; Hamilton and Hamilton, "Social Policies, Civil Rights and Poverty," 287.

10. Biographers perpetuated this left critique of King. Ling, *Martin Luther King Jr.*, 257, draws on white leftist Andrew Kopkind's critique to present King's last book; Lewis, *King*, 396–97, wrote in 1970 that King's own "bourgeois reflexes" limited his ability to formulate an "appropriate politics." But see Lewis review of Garrow, *Bearing the Cross*, in *Journal of American History* 74: 2 (Sept. 1987): 483–84.

11. See King, "NAACP Legal Defense," 28 May 1964, KPKC(3); King, "Illinois AFL-CIO," 7 Oct. 1965, insert b, KPKC(3).

12. Carson, *In Struggle*, and Lipsitz, *A Life in the Struggle*, discuss these concepts in depth.

13. Robert Moses, "Commentary," and Nathan Huggins, "Commentary," in *We Shall Overcome*, ed. Albert and Hoffman, 72–75, 87–89.

14. According to August Meier in 1965, King's most important function was "effectively communicating Negro aspirations to white people." Meier, "On the Role of Martin Luther King," *New Politics* 4 (Winter 1965): 52–59; Clayborne Carson, "Reconstructing the King Legacy," and Aldon Morris, "A Man Prepared for His Times," in *We Shall Overcome*, ed. Albert and Hoffman, 243–45, 35–58.

15. King, *Why We Can't Wait*, 135–36.

16. Smith and Zepp, *Search for the Beloved Community*, 114–18, note King's persistent Hegelianism, as have many others.

17. Watters and Cleghorn, *Climbing Jacob's Ladder*, 73.

18. King, "Facing the Challenge of a New Age," Dec. 1956, in *A Testament of Hope*, ed. Washington, 141–43.

19. King, *Stride Toward Freedom*, ch. 11.

20. Garrow, *Bearing the Cross*, 357, 289; Brink and Harris, *Black and White*, 54.

Chapter 1. Pilgrimage to Christian Socialism

1. King, *Stride Toward Freedom*, 90–91; King, "Autobiography of Religious Development," 22 Nov. 1950, in *Papers* 1:359; King, Sr., *Daddy King*, 89; King later recalled visiting Atlanta's impoverished Buttermilk Bottom neighborhood, where an old man sang "Been Down So Long That Down Don't Bother Me." Spiritual acquiescence to oppression troubled him, but he wrapped the memory in a communitarian imperative: "we are our brother's keeper." King, "Address Delivered at Rally," 21 June 1966, Yazoo City, Miss., KPKC(3).

2. Fluker, *They Looked for a City*, 5–19, 111–12, 238n19; H. Thurman, *With Head*

and Heart; Vincent Harding, introduction to *For the Inward Journey*, ed. A. Thurman, ix–xv; Baldwin, *Balm in Gilead*, 300; K. Miller, *Voice of Deliverance*, 120–21; Bennett, *What Manner of Man*, claims King "read or reread" *Jesus and the Disinherited* during the Montgomery bus boycott, but the words in King's 1950 essay "You—You Are Not Slaves" correspond exactly to Thurman's: compare King, "Six Talks Based on *Beliefs That Matter*," 29 Nov. 1949, in *Papers* 1:281, and A. Thurman, *For the Inward Journey*, 147, 125; King, "The Meaning of Hope," 10 Dec. 1967, KPKC(3).

3. King, *Stride Toward Freedom*, ch. 6; Clayborne Carson, "Introduction," in *Papers* 1:1–57.

4. King, *Stride Toward Freedom*, 22; King, Sr., *Daddy King*, 23–26, 37, 40–48 (King, Sr.'s emphasis is on racism, not capitalism, as the fundamental evil); King, "Testimony," 15 Dec. 1966, Senate Subcommittee on Executive Reorganization, *Federal Role in Urban Affairs*, 2996.

5. King, Sr., *Daddy King*, 25, 32, 51–53.

6. Ibid., 10, 57, 71, 82; Carson, "Introduction," in *Papers* 1:7–18; Meier and Lewis, "History of the Negro Upper Class in Atlanta," 128–33.

7. King, Sr., *Daddy King*, 94, 101, 104–5, 111–12, 125; Branch, *Parting the Waters*, 41–43; King, *Stride Toward Freedom*, 19, 22; Carson, "Introduction," in *Papers* 1:10.

8. Carson, "Introduction," in *Papers* 1:3, 31. King, "Autobiography of Religious Development," in *Papers* 1:360; C. King, *My Life*, 90.

9. Christine King Farris, "The Young Martin: From Childhood Through College," *Ebony*, January 1986, 58; C. King, *My Life*, 82–88; King, *Stride Toward Freedom*, 19; King, "Autobiography of Religious Development," 360. On Alberta Williams King, see Carson, "Introduction," in *Papers* 1:1, 29, 30; Garrow, *Bearing the Cross*, 464–65; King, "Address Delivered During 'A Salute to Dr. and Mrs. Martin Luther King,'" 31 Jan. 1960, in *Papers* 5:353; Alberta King quoted in Baldwin, *Balm in Gilead*, 122–23.

10. King, Sr. quoted in Carson, "Introduction," in *Papers* 1:34; King, "Drum Major Instinct," 4 Feb. 1968, in *A Testament of Hope*, ed. Washington, 267; King, "Application for Admission to Crozer Theological Seminary," Feb. 1948, in *Papers* 1:144.

11. King, "The Negro and the Constitution," May 1944, in *Papers* 1:109–10; Carson, "Introduction," in *Papers* 1:35; King, "Interview by John Freeman on 'Face to Face,'" 29 Oct. 1961, KPKC; King, "Autobiography of Religious Development," 362.

12. King, *Stride Toward Freedom*, 91, 145; Carson, "Introduction," in *Papers* 1:38; Benjamin Mays, *Born to Rebel* (New York: Scribner, 1971), 172; Stephen B. Oates, *Let the Trumpet Sound*, 8; K. Miller, *Voice of Deliverance*, 36–37; Branch, *Parting the Waters*, 54–55.

13. Garrow, *Bearing the Cross*, 46; King, "Kick up Dust," 6 Aug. 1946, in *Papers* 1:121; King, "The Purpose of Education," Jan.–Feb. 1947, in *Papers* 1:123–24.

14. A. Philip Randolph, "Address," June 1945, in *The Papers of A. Philip Randolph [Microfilm]*, ed. John H. Bracey and August Meier (Bethesda, Md.: University Publications of America, 1990), 28:197.

15. Bennett, *What Manner of Man*, 28; C. King, *My Life*, 84–85. Biographer L. D. Reddick, working from 1958 interviews, reported King learned that "the problems of workingmen were about the same, irrespective of superficial differences between them." Reddick, *Crusader Without Violence*, 74; King, *Stride Toward Freedom*, 90–91.

16. Charles V. Willie, "Walter R. Chivers—An Advocate of Situation Sociology,"

Phylon 9 (1982): 242–48; Bennett, *What Manner of Man*, 28; Walter Chivers, "Teaching Social Anthropology in a Negro College," *Phylon* 4 (1943): 354; Walter Chivers, "Negro Church Leadership," *Southern Frontier* 3, no. 12 (Dec. 1942): 1, and *Southern Frontier* 4, no. 1 (Jan. 1943): 4.

17. Walter Chivers, "Northward Migration and the Health of the Negro," *Journal of Negro Education* 8 (Jan. 1939): 41–42. O'Connor, *Poverty Knowledge*, 48–49, 64–65, 198–99. Chivers was writing in the tradition of E. Franklin Frazier and Kenneth B. Clark in blaming the "pathologies" of the "City of Destruction" on class and racial structures.

18. King, "The Significant Contributions of Jeremiah to Religious Thought," 24 Nov. 1948, in *Papers* 1:184–85, 194; King, "The Ethics of Late Judaism as Evidenced in the Testaments of the Twelve Patriarchs," 16 Feb. 1949, in *Papers* 1:201–5; King, "The Chief Characteristics and Doctrines of Mahayana Buddhism," 28 Apr. 1950, in *Papers* 1:322; King, "An Appraisal of the Great Awakening," 17 Nov. 1950, in *Papers* 1:342–53.

19. Reddick, *Crusader Without Violence*, 79; Smith and Zepp, *Search for the Beloved Community*, 24; King, "How Modern Christians Should Think of Man," 15 Feb. 1950, in *Papers* 1:274; King, "How to Use the Bible in Modern Theological Construction," 1949, in *Papers* 1:255; King, "A View of the Cross Possessing Biblical and Spiritual Justification," 1949–50, in *Papers* 1:267; King, "The Christian Pertinence of Eschatological Hope," 1949–50, in *Papers* 1:273.

20. King, "Examination Answers," 15 Feb. 1950, in *Papers* 1:290–94; King, "Religion's Answer to the Problem of Evil," 27 Apr. 1951, in *Papers* 1:428–30.

21. King, *Stride Toward Freedom*, 91. K. Miller, *Voice of Deliverance*, 46–47, 56–57, downplays Rauschenbusch's influence on King because he did not deal with racism. King, *Strength to Love*, 69, 80–81; Walter Rauschenbusch, *Christianity and the Social Crisis* (New York: Macmillan, 1907), 284, 350.

22. K. Miller, *Voice of Deliverance*; Fluker, *They Looked for a City*; Lischer, *Preacher King*, 6. Carson recognizes the false dichotomy between King's academic training and inherited values but claims the latter gave the former coherence. See Carson, "Introduction," in *Papers* 1:57.

23. King, "To Martin Luther King, Sr.," 15 June 1944, in *Papers* 1:112; The "colored patrons . . . while they admit that the gun was not pointed at them . . . seemed to think that it was a threat," the proprietor testified. W. Thomas McGann, "Statement on Behalf of Ernest Nichols," in *Papers* 1:328; Garrow, *Bearing the Cross*, 40.

24. For King even before Johnson's speech, Gandhi was one of four humans exhibiting the "spirit of God." King, "Six Talks in Outline," 24 Nov. 1949, in *Papers* 1:249; W. Miller, *Martin Luther King, Jr.*, 19–20; K. Miller, *Voice of Deliverance*, 53; Kapur, *Raising up a Prophet*, 11, 17, 38–39, 55–56, 64–66, 86; Mays, *Born to Rebel*, 156–57; H. Thurman, *With Head and Heart*, 133–34.

25. Johnson in P. Foner, *Organized Labor and the Black Worker*, 284; Mordecai Johnson, "A Pathway to World Peace," *Washington Afro American*, 9 June 1951, Mordecai Johnson Papers, MSRC.

26. In South Africa, Indian miners were taxed for simply working and their non-Christian marriages had been declared illegal. When masses of women went to prison and two died there, "strike followed strike as mine after mine joined the ranks." Fisher, *That Strange Little Brown Man Gandhi*, 15, 33, 26–27, 149–212; Smith and Zepp, *Search for the Beloved Community*, 48; Branch, *Parting the Waters*, 609. King often referred to

India's "little brown saint": see King, *Stride Toward Freedom*, 85. Indian author Ved Mehta commented profoundly on King and Gandhi's praxis in "Gandhism Is Not Easily Copied," *NYT*, 9 July 1961, SM8.

27. King, *Stride Toward Freedom*, 94; Barbour quoted in Garrow, *Bearing the Cross*, 43; King "To Alberta Williams King," October 1948, in *Papers* 1:161; King, "Notes on American Capitalism," 20 Feb.–4 May 1951, in *Papers* 1:435–36.

28. Lichtenstein, *State of the Union*; Marable, *Race, Reform and Rebellion*, 27–28; Von Eschen, *Race Against Empire*. After scoring his remarkable upset over Republican Thomas Dewey in 1948, Truman simply declared, "Labor did it." But labor and Truman sowed the seeds of their own destruction by joining the anticommunist crusade. Attacked from the right, Truman established the Federal Loyalty Security Program in 1947 and prevailed in the 1948 election by denouncing "Henry Wallace and his Communists" in the Progressive Party. See Schrecker, *Many Are the Crimes*.

29. Weir, *Politics and Jobs*, 41–58; Katznelson, "Was the Great Society a Lost Opportunity?" 189–92; On the FEPC, see P. Sullivan, *Days of Hope*, 224.

30. Niebuhr quoted in Brinkley, *Liberalism and Its Discontents*, 100; Wright, *Old South, New South*; Dudziak, *Cold War Civil Rights*; Sugrue, *Origins of the Urban Crisis*; on depredations of anticommunism in New York City, see Biondi, *To Stand and Fight*.

31. W. Jackson, *Gunnar Myrdal and America's Conscience*, 276, 258–60, 294.

32. Boyle, *The UAW and the Heyday of American Liberalism*, 24–25; James Carey, "Speech at the 45th NAACP Annual Convention," *NAACP Micro*, part 1, 10:583–88.

33. Eugene M. Austin, "The Peril of Conformity," *The Pulpit*, Oct. 1952, 13–15; King, "Transformed Nonconformist," in *Strength to Love*, 10–11; K. Miller, *Voice of Deliverance*, 107–8.

34. Coretta King in Garrow, *Bearing the Cross*, 46; C. King, *My Life*, 57–58; King to Coretta Scott, 18 July 1952, in *Autobiography of Martin Luther King, Jr.*, ed. Carson, 36; Edward Bellamy, *Looking Backward* (Boston: Houghton Mifflin, 1915), ch. 26.

35. King, "Jacques Maritain," 20 Feb. 1951, in *Papers* 1:437; K. Miller, *Voice of Deliverance*, 101–2; King, *Stride Toward Freedom*, 92–95; King, *Strength to Love*, 97–100; McCracken, *Questions People Ask*, 166–70.

36. King, *Stride Toward Freedom*, 94; King, "Paul's Letter to American Christians," 4 Nov. 1956, in *Papers* 3:414–20. Garrow quotes King as saying privately to friends late in the 1960s that "economically speaking he considered himself what he termed a Marxist." Garrow, *The FBI and Martin Luther King, Jr.*, 214.

37. "From Melvin Watson," 14 Aug. 1952, in *Papers* 2:157; McCracken, *Questions People Ask*, 165; K. Miller, *Voice of Deliverance*, 103.

38. Fox, *Reinhold Niebuhr*, 291. Scholars stress Niebuhr's theology and pacifism: see K. Miller, *Voice of Deliverance*, 53–59, 104; Carson, "Introduction," in *Papers* 1:55; Lasch, *True and Only Heaven*, 386–90; Branch, *Parting the Waters*, 80–87. Only Garrow, *Bearing the Cross*, 42, touches on political economy. King, "Reinhold Niebuhr's Ethical Dualism," 9 May 1952, in *Papers* 2:142–43, 150; King, *Stride Toward Freedom*, 97, 99.

39. Niebuhr, *Moral Man*, 252–53, 163, 201. King cited Niebuhr on the immorality of nations and social groups, and the efficacy of consumer boycotts for the black freedom struggle. King, *Why We Can't Wait*, 80; King, *Where Do We Go from Here?* 143.

40. King, *Stride Toward Freedom*, 93; King, "Reinhold Niebuhr's Ethical Dualism," in *Papers* 2:147.

41. Niebuhr, *Moral Man*, 206–7, 219.

42. Ibid., 221. King, *Strength to Love*, 87–92; King, "Unfulfilled Dreams," 3 Mar. 1968, in *A Knock at Midnight*, ed. Carson and Holloran, 192.

43. King, "The Theology of Reinhold Niebuhr," Apr. 1953–June 1954, in *Papers* 2:271–79.

44. Carson, "Introduction," in *Papers* 1:23; King, "A Comparison of the Conceptions of God in the Thinking of Paul Tillich and Henry Nelson Wieman," 5 Apr. 1955, in *Papers* 2:442, 508, 517.

45. "Paul Tillich," *Dictionary of American Biography*, 1981, reproduced in Biography Resource Center (Farmington Hills, Mich.: Thomson Gale, 2006); "Henry Nelson Wieman," *Encyclopedia of World Biography*, 1998, reproduced in *Biography Resource Center* (Farmington Hills, Mich.: Thomson Gale, 2006); King, "A Comparison of the Conceptions of God," in *Papers* 2:500, 487.

46. Sue Cronk, "She Feels Left Out—of Jail," *NYT*, 4 Nov. 1963, B3; C. King, *My Life*, 60, 90–91, 97, 102. Olson, *Freedom's Daughters*, chs. 20–22, and Honey, *Black Workers Remember*, ch. 11, present black women's antiracist valuation of masculinity. On King's "sexism" and purported belief in "separate spheres," see Cone, *Martin & Malcolm & America*, 274.

47. Transcriptions of audiotapes will be published in 2007 as volume 6 of the *Papers*. King, "The Three Dimensions of a Complete Life," 11 Dec. 1960, in *Papers* 5:574; Luke 10:29; King, *The Measure of a Man*, 27; King, *Strength to Love*, 27–30; King, "Address to the Hungry Club," 15 Dec. 1965, 6–7, KPKC(3); King, "Sermon at Ebenezer Baptist Church: Good Samaritan," 28 Aug. 1966, KPKC(3); King, "I See the Promised Land," 3 Apr. 1968, in *A Testament of Hope*, ed. Washington, 285; Lischer, *Preacher King*, 109.

48. King, "Rediscovering Lost Values," 28 Feb. 1954 in *Papers* 2:248–55. "Dives and Lazarus" will be published by the King Papers Project in volume 6 of the *Papers of King* in January 2007. The parable is in Luke 16:19–31. King, "Remaining Awake Through a Great Revolution," 31 Mar. 1968, in *A Testament of Hope*, ed. Washington, 274.

49. King, "A Knock at Midnight," in *Strength to Love*, 56–66.

50. William Gardner, "Rating Sheet for Martin Luther King, Jr.," 1 Dec. 1950, in *Papers* 1:380–81; Baldwin, *Balm in Gilead*, 39.

51. *Autobiography of Martin Luther King, Jr.*, ed. Carson, 46; King, "Recommendations to the Dexter Avenue Baptist Church," 5 Sept. 1954, in *Papers* 2:287–94. For positive responses, see *Papers* 2:307, 549; King, *Stride Toward Freedom*, 25. King, "To Dexter Avenue Church Members," 27 Oct. 1955, and "Annual Report, Dexter Avenue Baptist Church," 31 Oct. 1955, in *Papers* 2:577; "From J. Pious Barbour," 21 July 1955, in *Papers* 2:565.

Chapter 2. The Least of These

1. King, *Stride Toward Freedom*, 59–60.

2. King, "MIA Mass Meeting at Holt Street Baptist Church," 5 Dec. 1955, in *Papers* 3:71–79.

3. Kelley, *Race Rebels*, 55–61; Morris, *Origins of the Civil Rights Movement*, 18–25, 51–68.

4. Thornton, "Challenge and Response"; Braden, "The Southern Freedom Movement in Perspective," 18.

5. Reddick, *Crusader Without Violence*, 114; King, *Stride Toward Freedom*, 27–28; Thornton, "Challenge and Response," 325; Millner, "Montgomery Bus Boycott," 433; Yeakey, "Montgomery Bus Boycott," 11–13, 17–20.

6. "Testimony of Thelma Glass," March 1956, in *Daybreak of Freedom*, ed. Burns, 60–61; King in *PC*, 31 Mar. 1956, 2; "Interview with Store Maid," in *Daybreak of Freedom*, ed. Burns, 125.

7. Thornton, "Challenge and Response," 330; Branch, *Parting the Waters*, 131–32; Robinson, *Montgomery Bus Boycott*, xii–xiii, 23–25; Jo Ann Robinson to W. A. Gayle, 21 May 1954, in *Daybreak of Freedom*, ed. Burns, 58.

8. King, *Stride Toward Freedom*, 38–39; Branch, *Parting the Waters*, ch. 1; Yeakey, "Montgomery Bus Boycott," 100–111, 142–43.

9. White, "Nixon *Was* the One," 46–49; Yeakey, "Montgomery Bus Boycott," 115–30; Wofford quoted in *Children Coming On*, ed. Leventhal, 237.

10. Clyde Sellers, *Montgomery Advertiser*, 20 Mar. 1955, in *Daybreak of Freedom*, ed. Burns, 78-80.

11. McMillen, *The Citizens' Council*, 17–18, 43, 178, 198, 209; Thornton, "Challenge and Response," 343.

12. King, "Testimony in *State of Alabama v. M. L. King, Jr.*," 22 Mar. 1956, in *Papers* 3:186; King, *Stride Toward Freedom*, 35–37.

13. As a child, Parks read *Is the Negro a Beast?*, a pseudoscientific screed arguing blacks were animals "to be tamed and put to work for the white race." Determined to prove herself otherwise, she became a voracious reader of black history. Parks, *My Story*, 51–66; Yeakey, "Montgomery Bus Boycott," 253–54, 261; Robinson, *Montgomery Bus Boycott*, 20-21, 53–55; Leventhal, ed.*Children Coming On,*, 131.

14. Edgar N. French, "The Beginnings of a New Age," in *Walking City*, ed. Garrow, 177; Abernathy, *Walls Came Tumbling*, 140; King, *Stride Toward Freedom*, 54.

15. Abernathy, *Walls Came Tumbling*, 143–48; Ted Poston, "Fighting Pastor: MLK," *New York Post*, 14 Apr. 1957; Nixon quoted in *My Soul Is Rested*, ed. Raines, 48–49.

16. Robinson, *Montgomery Bus Boycott*, 53, 60–64; Yeakey, "Montgomery Bus Boycott," 345–47.

17. "To the National City Lines, Inc.," in *Papers* 3:80; Thornton, "Challenge and Response," 347, 366–67; "To the Citizens of Montgomery," 27 Jan. 1956, in *Papers* 3:107.

18. "Notes on MIA Executive Board Meeting," 23 Jan. 1956, in *Papers* 3:103; Gilliam, "Montgomery Bus Boycott," 239.

19. Gayle quoted in "Double Edged Blade in Montgomery," *Time*, 16 Jan. 1956, 20; King, *Stride Toward Freedom*, 113; see also *Daybreak of Freedom*, ed. Burns, 181.

20. King, *Stride Toward Freedom*, 134–35; King, "Interview by Martin Agronsky," 27 Oct. 1957, in *Papers* 4:298 (emphasis added); King, "Why Jesus Called a Man a Fool," 27 Aug. 1967, in *A Knock at Midnight*, ed. Carson and Holloran, 141-64. Various interpretations of King's "epiphany in the kitchen" stress its religious rather than social implications. See Garrow, *Bearing the Cross*, 57–58; West, "The Religious Foundations of the Thought of Martin Luther King Jr," in *We Shall Overcome*, ed. Albert and Hoffman, 118–19.

21. Notes of Donald T. Ferron, MIA Executive Board, 23 Jan. 1956, in *Daybreak*

of Freedom, ed. Burns, 121-23; "Notes on MIA Executive Board Meeting," 30 Jan. 1956, in *Papers* 3:110; "Notes on MIA Mass Meeting," 30 Jan. 1956, in *Papers* 3:113; King, *Strength to Love,* 125–26; King, *Stride Toward Freedom,* 135.

22. King, *Stride Toward Freedom,* 137; Reddick, "The Bus Boycott in Montgomery," 115; King and maid quoted in *Daybreak of Freedom,* ed. Burns, 127, 126, 134; King, interview by Donald T. Ferron, 4 Feb. 1956, in *Papers* 3:125.

23. J. Pious Barbour to King, 21 Dec. 1954, KPBU, 63:VIII; Barbour to King, March 1956, in *Papers* 3:171n; "From St. Clair Drake," 21 Mar. 1956, in *Papers* 3:181–82.

24. "Battle Against Tradition: Martin Luther King, Jr.," *NYT,* 21 Mar. 1956, 28; Wayne Phillips, "Negro Preachers Press Bus Boycott," *NYT,* 27 Feb. 1956; Lentz, *Symbols, the News Magazines, and Martin Luther King,* 26–33.

25. King, *Stride Toward Freedom,* 80; Robinson, *Montgomery Bus Boycott,* 68-71, 94; Bayard Rustin, "Montgomery Diary," in *Daybreak of Freedom,* ed. Burns, 166; "Report on MIA Mass Meeting, March 22, by Anna Holden," in *Daybreak of Freedom,* ed. Burns, 213.

26. "From Lillian Eugenia Smith," 10 Mar. 1956, in *Papers* 3:169–70; Smith to King, 3 Apr. 1956, KPBU, 64:VIII; "From Harris Wofford," 25 Apr. 1956, in *Papers* 3:226; King to Wofford, 10 May 1956, KPBU, 67:VIII, 33.

27. Rustin quoted in D'Emilio, *Lost Prophet,* 231, 237; Levine, *Bayard Rustin,* 78–81; see also Burns, *Daybreak of Freedom,* 20–22, 159, 165–70.

28. Smiley supported Rustin, writing FOR on February 29 that the "Red issue" tragically undermined Rustin's "good influence on King." Glenn Smiley to John Swomley, 29 Feb. 1956, BR, 46:5; Smiley to Neil Salinger, 29 Feb. 1956, in *Daybreak of Freedom,* ed. Burns, 163–64; Watters, *Down to Now,* 265. Abernathy quoted in Warren, *Who Speaks for the Negro?* 409.

29. King, "To Bayard Rustin," 20 Sept. 1956, in *Papers* 3:376–77; Rustin, "Notes of a Conference: How Outsiders Can Strengthen the Montgomery Nonviolent Protest," BR, 46:5.

30. George Barrett, "'Jim Crow, He's Real Tired,'" *New York Times Magazine,* 3 Mar. 1957, 67–69; Ted Poston, "Negroes of Montgomery," *New York Post,* 15 and 19 June 1956, in *Reporting Civil Rights,* ed. Carson et al., 271.

31. Hall quoted in Yeakey, "Montgomery Bus Boycott," 444–45; Hill Lindsay, "Negroes Look Around You," in *Daybreak of Freedom,* ed. Burns, 115; McMillan, *The Citizens' Council,* 44; Anna Holden, "Interview with a Prominent Local Attorney," 8 Feb. 1956, in *Daybreak of Freedom,* ed. Burns, 190–92.

32. *U.S. News & World Report,* 3 Aug. 1956, 84–86. See folders of general correspondence labeled "adverse" in president's papers, KPBU, SCLC, KC.

33. King, interview by Ferron, 4 Feb. 1956, in *Papers* 3:125; King, "Statement," 20 Dec. 1956, in *Papers* 3:486; King, *Stride Toward Freedom,* 50–51.

34. King, "Our Struggle," Mar. 1956, in *A Testament of Hope,* ed. Washington,, 77, 81; "From Bayard Rustin," 8 Mar. 1956, in *Papers* 3:164; King, "To William Peters," 25 Apr. 1956, in *Papers* 3:224–25.

35. King, *Stride Toward Freedom,* 76–84; Yeakey, "Montgomery Bus Boycott," 383, 389–98, 462–63; Reddick, *Crusader Without Violence,* 130; Leventhal, *Children Coming On,* 178; Robinson, *Montgomery Bus Boycott,* 97; Lewis quoted in *Daybreak of Freedom,* ed. Burns, 138; Mrs. Myron Lobman, *Montgomery Advertiser,* 2 Jan. 1956, in *Daybreak of Freedom,* ed. Burns, 112.

36. Poston, "Negroes of Montgomery," 270; Thornton, "Challenge and Response," 338–41, 360, 366. The bus company figures are from Gilliam, "Montgomery Bus Boycott," 254.

37. King, *Stride Toward Freedom*, 78; Poston, "Negroes of Montgomery," 266–69; "Interview with Maid by Willie M. Lee," 20 Jan. 1956, in *Daybreak of Freedom*, ed. Burns, 224; Robinson, *Montgomery Bus Boycott*, 102–3.

38. King, *Stride Toward Freedom*, 80; Robinson, *Montgomery Bus Boycott*, 71; Yeakey, "Montgomery Bus Boycott," 371–73; Cohen, *Consumer's Republic*, 189.

39. "Notes on MIA Executive Board Meeting," 30 Jan. 1956, in *Papers* 3:111.

40. Erna Dungee Allen, interview by Steven M. Milner, in *Walking City*, ed. Garrow, 524–25. On the Welfare Committee, see Yeakey, "Montgomery Bus Boycott," 379; Robinson, *Montgomery Bus Boycott*, 98; Virginia Durr to Myles Horton, 18 and 24 Feb. 1956, and Rosa Parks to Horton, 25 Feb. 1956, in *Daybreak of Freedom*, ed. Burns, 155–57; Parks, *My Story*, 142; King to Maxine Young, KPBU, 75:IX. On the Parks' hardships, see *Papers* 4:261, 5:389. Septima Clark remembered that Highlander supported Rosa Parks for a year, but the MIA only gave her $382 when she departed: "They didn't help her too much down in Montgomery," Clark recalled. Clark, interview by Jacquelyn Hall, 25 July 1976, p. 83, SOHP.

41. King, "To Arthur R. James," 1 June 1956, in *Papers* 3:287. See also *Papers* 3:370–71.

42. "From Ella J. Baker," 2 Feb. 1956, in *Papers* 3:139. Moore lost his postal service job in 1958, but he was among the first to welcome student organizers into Mississippi in 1960. See his correspondence with the NAACP and the National Sharecroppers Fund, Moore Papers, 1:1–3, SHSW; Ransby, *Ella Baker*, 176; Dittmer, *Local People*, 46–53.

43. King, "Testimony to the Democratic National Convention," 11 Aug. 1956, in *Papers* 3:335–38; King correspondence with Ernest Morgan, in *Papers* 3:345–46, 355; King, "To Ruth Bunche and Aminda Wilkins," 23 Nov. 1956, in *Papers* 3:437.

44. King, "To Rae Bradstein," 1 Aug. 1956, in *Papers* 3:332–33; King, "Desegregation and the Future," 15 Dec. 1956, in *Papers* 3:471–79; Stetson and Fleming in *Tearing down the Color Bar*, ed. Wilson, 285–86, 289–90.

45. "From Helen M. Hiller," 4 June 1956, and King, "To Helen M. Hiller," 6 July 1956, in *Papers* 3:293, 315; Yeakey, "Montgomery Bus Boycott," 512-13, 547, 550–66; King, *Stride Toward Freedom*, 154.

46. King, "To Archibald James Carey, Jr.," 27 Dec. 1955, in *Papers* 3:94; Horowitz, *Negro and White, Unite and Fight!* 207; "From Archibald James Carey, Jr.," 24 Feb. 1956, in *Papers* 3:139–40.

47. Gilliam, "Montgomery Bus Boycott," 230, estimates the boycott drew $225,000 in donations in 1956; King to Claude Sanders, 9 Mar. 1956, and ILGWU Local 10 to King, 19 Mar. 1956, KPBU, 1:I-5.

48. Warren, *Who Speaks for the Negro?* 213, 221.

49. "Notes on MIA Mass Meeting," 27 Feb. 1956, in *Papers* 3:144; Reddick, *Crusader Without Violence*, 22; Keith Brown to King, 23 Mar. 1956, KPBU, 91:XII; King, "To Homer Greene," 19 July 1956, in *Papers* 3:318.

50. "King Speaks at Big Rally in Brooklyn," *Montgomery Advertiser*, 26 Mar. 1956, in *Papers* 3:210; King, "The New Negro of the South," June 1956, in *Papers* 3:280–86; King, "Address to MIA Mass Meeting," 22 Mar. 1956, in *Papers* 3:200; Chester Bowles

to King, 28 Jan. 1957, KPBU, 89:IX; In 1961, an eighty-one-year-old black woman from Alaska sent King $1,000 and two bear hides, rejoicing at all the attention King and civil rights had received "since our Government has become so concerned about Russia getting ahead of us in Africa." Ada B. H. Murray to King, 6 Sept. 1961, KPBU, 55:VII-26.

51. "Notes on MIA Mass Meeting," 1 Mar. 1956, in *Papers* 3:151; King, "When Peace Becomes Obnoxious," 18 Mar. 1956, in *Papers* 3:207–8; King, "The Death of Evil upon the Seashore," 17 May 1956, in *Papers* 3:259; King, "Non-Aggression Procedures to Interracial Harmony," 23 July 1956, in *Papers* 3:321–28.

52. Robinson, *Montgomery Bus Boycott*, 60–64; Preston Valien, "The Montgomery Bus Protest as a Social Movement," Aug. 1957, in *Walking City*, ed. Garrow, 89; King, *Stride Toward Freedom*, 86, 187; C. King, *My Life*, 121; King, "Birth of a New Age," 11 Aug. 1956, in *Papers* 3:346; King, "The Montgomery Story," NAACP Convention, 27 June 1956, in *Papers* 3:309 (emphasis added).

53. King to J. A. Hanson, 27 Mar. 1957, KPBU, 60:VIII; King, "To Jewelle Taylor," May 1956, in *Papers* 3:242; Almena Lomax, "Mother's Day in Montgomery," 18 May 1956, in *Papers* 3:263–67; Vernon Johns to King, 8 May 1960, KPBU, 28A:IV.

54. "Notes on MIA Mass Meeting," 1 Jan. 1956, in *Papers* 3:113; King, "The New Negro of the South," June 1956, in *Papers* 3:280–86; King, "The Montgomery Story," 27 June 1956, in *Papers* 3:300, 308.

55. A. Philip Randolph, "Address at the 47th NAACP Annual Convention," *NAACP Micro*, supplement to part 1, 4:694–700.

56. King, "Paul's Letter to American Christians," 4 Nov. 1956, in *Papers* 3:414–20, is a later version of the NBC address.

57. "From Charles W. Kelly," 8 Sept. 1956, and J. Pious Barbour, *National Baptist Voice*, Sept. 1956, in *Papers* 3:365-66; John Hannum to King, 8 Apr. 1957, 6 July 1957, and King to Hannum, 30 Apr. 1957, KPBU, 60:VIII. Among over 1,000 news stories consulted for this study, I found one reference to this sermon, "King Warns Against Misuse of Capitalism," *Indianapolis News*, 5 Sept. 1960.

58. King, "Desegregation and the Future," 15 Dec. 1956, in *Papers* 3:474–77. On the social science "damage tradition," see Scott, *Contempt and Pity*, 122-29.

59. Gilliam, "Montgomery Bus Boycott," 274–76; King, "Address to MIA Mass Meeting," 14 Nov. 1956, in *Papers* 3:428–31.

60. King, "Statement on Ending the Bus Boycott," 20 Dec. 1956, in *Papers* 3:485–87.

61. "From Bayard Rustin," 23 Dec. 1956, in *Papers* 3:491–93; "New Fields Await Negroes, King Tells Mass Meeting," *Montgomery Advertiser*, 24 Dec. 1956, in *Papers* 3:494–95.

62. George Barrett, "Shot Hits Home of Bus Bias Foe," *NYT*, 24 Dec. 1956, 6; "From J. Pious Barbour," 11 Jan. 1957, in *Papers* 4:107.

Chapter 3. Seed Time in the Winter of Reaction

1. Fairclough, *To Redeem the Soul of America*, ch. 2; Eskew, *But for Birmingham* 27, 32. Morris, *Origins of the Civil Rights Movement*, 92, is more appreciative of King's inspirational leadership of local southern activists.

2. Benjamin Davis to King, 19 June 1960, KPBU, 23A:III-20; Carson, "Introduction," in *Papers* 4:19; Myles Horton to King, 20 Mar. 1959, KPBU, 28:IV-4; FBI Report, 22 May 1961, in *MLK-FBI File*, ed. Friedly and Gallen, 118.

3. Reddick, *Crusader Without Violence*, 211.

4. Rustin quoted in Carson, "Introduction," in *Papers* 4:2; Rustin to King, "Memo on the Montgomery Bus Boycott," 23 Dec. 1956, in *Daybreak of Freedom*, ed. Burns, 329–30; Southern Negro Leaders Conference on Transportation and Non-violent Integration, "Working Papers," Ebenezer Baptist Church, 10–11 Jan. 1957, SCLC, 71:IX.

5. Southern Negro Leaders Conference on Transportation and Non-violent Integration, "Statement to the South and the Nation," 10–11 Jan. 1957, KPBU, 2:I-11.For a different assessment of Rustin's capacities to shape the agenda through King, see Garrow, *Bearing the Cross*, 85–86.

6. Reddick, *Crusader Without Violence*, 183–85; Fairclough, *To Redeem the Soul of America*, 31–38, 47–48, 53; Morris, *Origins of the Civil Rights Movement*, 84–91, 117–19.

7. Branch, *Parting the Waters*, 208–9; Kotz, *Judgment Days*, 71; Stanley Levison to King, 19 Oct. 1957, 17 and 24 Jan. 1958, and 8 Jan. 1959, King to Levison, 15 Dec. 1958, KPBU, 2:I-10; Rustin quoted in Garrow, *Bearing the Cross*, 649n21; Bradford Laws to King, 11 Feb. 1958, King to Laws, 24 May 1958, KPBU, 29:A-IV; Levison to King, 8 Jan. 1959, KPBU, 2:I-10.

8. MIA Future Planning Committee, 14 Mar. 1957, KPBU, 2:I-11; King, "To Galal Kernahan," 29 Apr. 1957, in *Papers* 4:193. Reddick, *Crusader Without Violence*, 178–79; Garrow, *Bearing the Cross*, 88, 96, 101; Abel Plenn, "Report on Montgomery a Year After," *New York Times Magazine*, 29 Dec. 1957, 36.

9. Dr. Francis Townshend to King, 5 Dec. 1956, and King to Townshend, 9 Dec. 1956, KPBU, 66:VII-28T; King, "To Galal Kernahan."

10. King, "Address at Public Meeting of the Southern Christian Ministers Conference of Mississippi," 23 Sept. 1959, in *Papers* 5:285, 287. King's figures on comparable levels of black and Canadian income and the phrase "profit and loss," are traceable to the Southern Regional Council Report, "Negro Buying Power," KPBU, 68:IX.

11. King, "Advice for Living," in *Papers* 4:269, 280, 306, 326, 348–49, 392, 374; Reddick, *Crusader Without Violence*, 5.

12. Jessie Henry to King, 27 Dec. 1959, KPBU, 27a:IV; Barbara White to King, 5 Dec. 1960, and James Woods to White, 22 Dec. 1960, KPBU, 73A:IX; "Public Welfare Found Slighted," *NYT*, 21 May 1957, 30.

13. King, "The Birth of a New Nation," 7 Apr. 1957, in *Papers* 4:155–64; King, *Stride Toward Freedom*, 191; "Interview by Etta Moen Barnett," Accra, Ghana, 6 Mar. 1967, in *Papers* 4:145–47; C. King, *My Life*, 154–55.

14. Gold Coast Legislative Assembly Debates, 5 Mar. 1957, KPBU, 26A:VE; King, "Birth of a New Nation," 160–66.

15. James in Carson, "Rethinking African-American Political Thought," 115–16; C. L. R. James, *Nkrumah and the Ghana Revolution* (London: Allison and Busby, 1977), 58; Garrow, *Bearing the Cross*, 717n19; Stanley Levison to King, 28 Apr. 1958, KPBU, 2:I-10.

16. King, "A Realistic Look at the Question of Progress in the Area of Race Relations," St. Louis Freedom Rally, 10 Apr. 1957, in *Papers* 4:171–72; Carson, "Introduction," in *Papers* 4:10; James Pike and King to Chester Bowles, 8 Nov. 1957, in *Papers* 4:313.

17. King, "A Look to the Future," 2 Sept. 1957, in *Papers* 4:272; King, *The Measure of a Man*, 13–17, v.

18. King, "A Realistic Look," in *Papers* 4:172; King, "The Role of the Church in Facing the Nation's Chief Moral Dilemma," 25 Apr. 1957, in *Papers* 4:189; Fairclough, *Martin Luther King, Jr.*, 55.

19. King, "A Statement to the President of the United States," 23 June 1958, in *Papers* 4:427–29.

20. "Interview by Richard D. Heffner for *The Open Mind*," 10 Feb. 1957, in *Papers* 4:127; "Interview by Martin Agronsky for *Look Here*," 27 Oct. 1957, in *Papers* 4:292–99; see also *Papers* 4:119, 11; Wright, *Old South, New South*.

21. Garrow, *Bearing the Cross*, 29–30, 77; King, "Call to a Prayer Pilgrimage for Freedom," 5 Apr. 1957, in *Papers* 4:151; Bayard Rustin to King, 10 May 1957, KPBU, 34:IV.

22. King to Robert Wagner, 13 May 1957, KPBU, 73:IX; "Pilgrimage Girds for Rights Cause," *NYT*, 4 May 1957; King, "Address at the Prayer Pilgrimage for Freedom," 17 May 1957, in *A Testament of Hope*, ed. Washington, 199; Bayard Rustin to King, 19 June 1957, KPBU, 64A:VIII-22.

23. Eskew, *But for Birmingham*, 143–46. King joined the NAACP in praising the legislative compromise that sacrificed Title III in favor of the voting rights provisions, while Randolph denounced it. King, "To Richard Nixon," 30 Aug. 1957, in *Papers* 4:263–64; "From Richard M. Nixon," 17 Sept. 1957, in *Papers* 4:277; Sundquist, *Politics and Policy*, 226–38.

24. Fairclough, *To Redeem the Soul of America*, 44–45; Ella Baker, interview by John Britton, 19 June 1968, p. 18, RJB; King to J. H. Jackson, 17 Dec. 1957, KPBU, 61A:VIII-9; Horowitz, *Negro and White, Unite and Fight!* 207.

25. King, "Address Delivered at a Meeting Launching the SCLC Crusade for Citizenship," 12 Feb. 1958, in *Papers* 4:367–71, and King's directive to affiliates, 358–59.

26. Marshall quoted in Branch, *Parting the Waters*, 217; Morris, *Origins of the Civil Rights Movement*, 31, 33, 121–25; Ella Baker, interview by Eugene Walker, 4 Sept. 1974, p. 26, SOHP; Aaron Henry to King, 24 June 1958, and King to Henry, 29 May 1958, KPBU, 28:IV-4; "Mississippi Delegates Set Pace at Dixie Leadership Meeting," 29 May 1958, KPBU, 48:IV-154; Dittmer, *Local People*, 71–78.

27. Ella Baker to Stanley Levison and Bayard Rustin, 16 July 1958, BR, 46:1; Simpkins quoted in Morris, *Origins of the Civil Rights Movement*, 111; "Report of the Director," 15 May 1959, KPBU, 68:IX; King, "To Conrad J. Lynn," 9 Aug. 1957, in *Papers* 4:247; Moore to American Friends Service Committee, 23 May 1958, and Father John LaBauve to "Friends," 22 May 1959, Amzie Moore Papers, SHSW, 1:1–3; Dittmer, *Local People*, 72–73.

28. King, "Remarks . . . NAACP Convention," 28 June 1957, in *Papers* 4:233; King, "To Ramona Garrett," 16 July 1957, in *Papers* 4:235–36; King, interview by Mike Wallace, 25 June 1958, in *Papers* 4:433; SCLC, "Plan of Action," Feb. 1959, quoted in Morris, *Origins of the Civil Rights Movement*, 106.

29. Returning to New York, Baker insisted that racism and poverty were national problems, and she criticized the NAACP for ignoring Harlem's "poor children." Cantarow and O'Malley, "Ella Baker," 58–64, 70–72; Ella Baker, interview by Sue Thrasher and Casey Hayden, 19 Apr. 1977, pp. 19, 20, 35, 44–49, SOHP.

30. Baker interview by Walker, 14, 51, 65, 76–7, 91–95; Baker interview by

Thrasher and Hayden, 61; Baker interview by Britton, 37; Lerner, "Developing Community Leadership," 351; Cantarow and O'Malley, "Ella Baker," 53.

31. Alfred Duckett to King, 4 Apr. 1957, KPBU, 117:XVI-1; Carson, "Introduction," in *Papers* 4:32; King, "Draft, Chapter XI, *Where Do We Go from Here*, part 2, *Stride Toward Freedom*," KPBU, 94:17B; King, *Stride Toward Freedom*, 94–95; "From Melvin Arnold," 5 May 1958, in *Papers* 4:404–5.

32. King also tried to strike a balance between individual leadership and collective action. Rustin and Levison both criticized King's original "egocentric" narrative. King apologized for any self–preoccupation in his preface, crediting "poor and untutored" blacks for the Montgomery victory. In the end, only the middle chapters neglected Montgomery's collective leadership, but often King brought the story back to his own experience or influence. A woman "refused to retaliate" when a white man slapped her. She could have "broken that little fellow's neck," she said, but was "determined to do what Reverend King asked." King, *Stride Toward Freedom*, 9, 33–34, 102, 174, 191, 207, 213; Harris Wofford to King, 2 Apr. 1958, KPBU, 73:IX; Bayard Rustin's comments, n.d., KPBU, 71:IX; Stanley Levison to King, 1 Apr. 1958, KPBU, 29A:IV.

33. King, "Some Things We Must Do," 5 Dec. 1957, in *Papers* 4:334–40; Stanley Levison to King, 1 Apr. 1958, KPBU, 29A:IV-10; Levison to King, 5 Apr. 1958, KPBU, 2:I-10; E. G. Morris to King, 2 Mar. 1957, KPBU, 62:VIII-10; Theodore Shields to King, 24 Feb. 1957, KPBU, 68:IX.

34. King, *Stride Toward Freedom*, 37, 187, 194, 211, 222–24, 233–34; Scott, *Contempt and Pity*, chs. 6–7; King, "The Negro Is Part of That Huge Community," 2 Feb. 1959, in *Papers* 5:120.

35. Coverage of King and Curry: *NYT*, 22 Sept., 18 Oct., and 18 Nov. 1958; King, "Statement upon Return from Montgomery," 24 Oct. 1958, in *Papers* 4:513.

36. King, *Stride Toward Freedom*, 211, 218, 222–24; J. Pious Barbour wrote to King in October 1957 about a sermon in which he "gave the Bourgeoisie hell, especially the Negro Bourgeoisie and their Ranch homes." J. Pious Barbour to King, 3 Oct. 1957, in *Papers* 4:282–83.

37. King, *Stride Toward Freedom*, 28, 195–99, 202, 223–24. Eisenhower would never countenance any move toward "a structural change in the architecture of American society," King later wrote (*Why We Can't Wait*, 143).

38. King, *Stride Toward Freedom*, 106, 200–201; Beals quoted in *Voices of Freedom*, ed. Hampton and Fayer, 39.

39. King, *Stride Toward Freedom*, 192; Stanley Levison to King, 1 Apr. 1958, KPBU, 29-A:IV. King pulled his discussion of white economic anxieties from an earlier address to the Highlander Folk School. King, "A Look to the Future," 2 Sept. 1957, in *Papers* 4:272–73.

40. Lichtenstein, *State of the Union*, 103–5, 112–13; King, *Stride Toward Freedom*, 204; Lillian Smith to King, 14 Aug. 1958, KPBU, 84:XI.

41. King, *Stride Toward Freedom*, 203–4; Pfeffer, *A. Philip Randolph*; P. Foner, *Organized Labor and the Negro Worker*.

42. Morris, *Origins of the Civil Rights Movement*, 166–73, 141–57; Lichtenstein, *State of the Union*, 164.

43. Horowitz, *Negro and White, Unite and Fight!* 210, 223–26.

44. King to Cleveland Robinson, 15 Nov. 1958, KPBU, 68:IX-1; King to David Dubinski, 31 Dec. 1958, KPBU, 23:III-20; King, *Stride Toward Freedom*, 189, 199–200.

45. A. Philip Randolph to King, 19 Nov. 1958, and Reinhold Niebuhr to King, 6 Jan. 1959, KPBU, 2:I-7; Harris Wofford to King, 5 Sept. 1958, and Wofford to Stanley Levison, 5 Sept. 1958, KPBU, 73A:IX; Chief Justice Earl Warren to King, 27 Jan. 1959, KPBU, 73:IX; Robert B. Carter to King, 24 Sept. 1959, KPBU, 22a:2a.

46. Eugene Davidson to King, 10 Oct. 1958, *NAACP Micro,* 21:12; "Address at Youth March for Integrated Schools in Washington, D.C., Delivered by Coretta Scott King," 25 Oct. 1958, in *Papers* 4:514–15. "From Stanley Levison," 3 Nov. 1958, in *Papers* 4:525.

Chapter 4. The American Gandhi and Direct Action

1. Carson, "Introduction," in *Papers* 5:2–3; "Account of Press Conference in New Delhi on 10 February 1959 by Lawrence D. Reddick," in *Papers* 5:128.

2. "From R. S. Hukkerikar," 24 Feb. 1959, in *Papers* 5:133; C. King, *My Life,* 173; King, "My Trip to the Land of Gandhi," July 1959, in *Papers* 5:235; King, "Palm Sunday Sermon on Mohandas K. Gandhi," 22 Mar. 1959, in *Papers* 5:148.

3. W. Miller, *Martin Luther King, Jr.,* 85–93; C. King, *My Life,* 177; King, "My Trip to the Land of Gandhi," in *Papers* 5:237. For Quaker and Indian skepticism of Vinoba Bhave's capacity to dent Indian mass poverty, see Corrine Johnson to King, 26 Jan. 1959, and enclosed *Times of India* editorial, 8 Jan. 1959, KPBU, 19:III-9; King, "To Jayaprakash Narayan," 19 May 1959, in *Papers* 5:209–10; Durr quoted in Garrow, *Bearing the Cross,* 114.

4. King, "The American Dream," 4 July 1965, in *Call to Conscience,* ed. Carson and Shepard, 89; Reddick quoted in Carson, "Introduction," in *Papers* 5:11n54.

5. King, "My Trip to the Land of Gandhi," in Papers 5:236; King, "Statement upon Return from India," 20 Mar. 1959, in *Papers* 5:143; King, "Equality Now," 2 Feb. 1961, in *A Testament of Hope,* ed. Washington, 158; C. King, *My Life,* 176. King never mentioned the feminist Gandhi.

6. King, "Farewell Statement for All India Radio," 9 Mar. 1959, in *Papers* 5:135–36; editor's note in *Papers* 5:107n1.

7. King, "Palm Sunday Sermon on Mohandas K. Gandhi," in *Papers* 5:152–55.

8. C. King, *My Life,* 61–62, 161, 178–80; Levison quoted in *American Journey,* ed. Stein and Plimpton, eds., 108–9.

9. King, "A Walk Through the Holy Land," 29 Mar. 1959, in *Papers* 5:164–75.

10. King, "Remaining Awake Through a Great Revolution," 2 June 1959, in *Papers* 5:224–25; Clare Wofford and Harris Wofford, *India Afire* (New York: J. Day Co., 1951), 250–42, 333–34.

11. King, "Address at the Religious Leaders Conference," 11 May 1959, KPBU, 2:I-11; "Fight on Jobs Bias Spurred by Nixon," *NYT,* 12 May 1959, 19.

12. King, "The Negro Is Part of That Huge Community," 1 Feb. 1959, in *Papers* 5:116–20. On the Schactmanite circle, see Isserman, *The Other American,* 116–69.

13. Lichtenstein, *Most Dangerous Man in Detroit,* 349–54; Boyle, *The UAW and the Heyday of American Liberalism,* 134–35.

14. Ella Baker to Bayard Rustin and Stanley Levison, 16 July 1958, BR, 46:1; Levison to King, 28 Nov. 1958, KPBU, 2:I-10; King to President Eisenhower, 25 Jan. 1959, in *Papers* 5:111–12; "From Ella J. Baker," 26 Mar. 1959, in *Papers* 5:162–63.

15. King, "To Jesse Hill," 28 Jan. 1959, in *Papers* 5:114–15; Baker gave King "the devil" for accepting too many speaking invitations and neglecting SCLC. But preaching was his "art," King protested. Garrow, *Bearing the Cross*, 115–16; King, "Statement Adopted at Spring Session," 15 May 1959, in *Papers* 5:205–8; L. D. Reddick, "Notes on SCLC Administrative Committee Meetings," Apr. 1959, in *Papers* 5:177–79.

16. King, "Recommendations to the Board, Meeting of the SCLC," 1 Oct. 1959, KPBU, 48:VI; King, "Recommendations to Committee on Future Program," 27 Oct. 1959, in *Papers* 5:315–18; King, "To Paul Landis," 17 Nov. 1959, in *Papers* 5:322.

17. Walker quoted in Powledge, *Free at Last?* 108–9; Wyatt T. Walker to King, 16 Jan. 1959, in *Papers* 5:108–11; King, "Address at the Thirty-Sixth Annual Dinner of the War Resisters League," 2 Feb. 1959, in *Papers* 5:121; King, "To George Meany," 12 Jan. 1959, in *Papers* 5:106. On the Petersburg Improvement Association, see Morris, *Origins of the Civil Rights Movement, 183-88.*

18. SCLC Press Release, "Dr. King Leaves Montgomery for Atlanta," 1 Dec. 1959, in *Papers* 5:330–31; Garrow, *Bearing the Cross,* 122–24; King, "Address at the Fourth Annual Institute on Nonviolence and Social Change," 3 Dec. 1959, in *Papers* 5:333–43.

19. Tyson, *Radio Free Dixie*, 148–53; "NAACP Leader Urges 'Violence,'" *NYT, 7* May 1959, 22, 5; Reddick, "Notes on SCLC Administrative Committee Meetings," in *Papers* 5:178.

20. "NAACP Leader Urges 'Violence,'" *NYT*, 18 July 1959, 5; King, "Address at the Fiftieth Annual NAACP Convention," 17 July 1959, in *Papers* 5:245–50; Tyson, *Radio Free Dixie*, 162–64.

21. Tyson, *Radio Free Dixie*; Lipsitz, *A Life in the Struggle*, ch. 5; Dittmer, *Local People*; King, "The Social Organization of Nonviolence," Oct. 1959, in *Papers* 5:299–304; Braden quoted in Tyson, *Radio Free Dixie,* 216–17; see Forman, *Making of Black Revolutionaries,* 159, for his critique of Williams and defense of tactical nonviolence in 1959.

22. *The Crusader,* 11 July and 10 Oct. 1959, 5 Mar. 1960, in *The Black Power Movement, Part 2: Papers of Robert F. Williams*, ed. Timothy Tyson (Bethesda, Md.: University Publications of America, 2001), 10:263–68, 380–89, 581–90.

23. Ella Baker to Committee on Administration, 23 Oct. 1959, KPBU, 48:VI, and fragment, 68-IX; Baker, Report of Executive Director, 16 May–29 Sept. 1959, KPBU, 48:VI.

24. On black women's welfare work, see Gordon, *Pitied But Not Entitled;* S. Clark and Blythe, *Echo in My Soul,* 37–40, 52, 61, 83, 112–14, 117–18, 176; S. Clark and Brown, *Ready from Within,* 38–39, 105–10; "Septima" to "Biddie," 17 May 1955, and Clark to Myles Horton, 8 Mar. 1955, HL 9:12..

25. Septima Clark to Myles Horton, 8 Mar. 1955, HL, 9:12; S. Clark and Blythe, *Echo in My Soul,* 137, 140–41; Horton, *The Long Haul*, 87, 96–97, 99–103; Morris, *Origins of the Civil Rights Movement*, 141–53; S. Clark and Brown, *Ready from Within,* 32–33; Clark notes, "Extending Highlander," 3 Sept. 1955, HL, 9:12.

26. S. Clark and Blythe, *Echo in My Soul,* 142, 150; S. Clark and Brown, *Ready from Within*, 42–54; Bernice Robinson to Septima Clark, 20 Jan. 1957, quoted in Myles Horton to Carl Tjerandsen, 16 Feb. 1957, HL, 67:3; Horton, *The Long Haul,* 102–3; Wigginton, *Refuse to Stand,* 172, 179, 185–89, 244–51, 300–301.

27. Horton, *The Long Haul,* 100–105; S. Clark and Blythe, *Echo in My Soul,* 45–46, 162, 166; Septima Clark to Myles Horton, ca. Aug. 1956, HL, 9:12; Wigginton, *Refuse to*

Stand, 246; Septima Poinsette Clark, "The Movement . . . I Remember," n.d., SPC, 1:52. References to reprisals and economic survival saturate the detailed audiotape notes of the Highlander Workshops Inventory, pp. 65–70, 91–105, HL.

28. Septima Clark, "Report: Workshop on Social Needs and Social Resources," 27–28 Nov. 1959, HL, 9:12; King to Clark, 21 Dec. 1959, KPBU, 27a:IV-3; S. Clark and Blythe, *Echo in My Soul*, 134, 178; S. Clark and Brown, *Ready from Within*, 59; Wigginton, *Refuse to Stand*, 245.

29. McCain quoted in *My Soul Is Rested*, ed. Raines, 76–79; Chafe, *Civilities and Civil Rights*, 85–91.

30. Chafe, *Civilities and Civil Rights*, 93–97; Halberstam, *The Children*, 93; Oppenheimer, *The Sit-in Movement*, 40–44.

31. Laue, *Direct Action and Desegregation*, 71; Chafe, *Civilities and Civil Rights*, 79–81; Kelly Miller Smith, interview by John Britton, 22 Dec. 1967, p. 41, RJB.

32. William Gray to King, 24 Mar. 1960, and King to Gray, 6 Apr. 1960, KPBU, 27:IV-1; King to C. K. Steele, 19 Mar. 1960, in *Papers* 5:391n2; King, "Revolt Without Violence," *U.S. News & World Report*, 21 Mar. 1960, in *Papers* 5:392–94; "Integration: 'Full Scale Assault,'" *Newsweek*, 29 Feb. 1960, 24.

33. Claude Sitton, "Negro Sitdowns Stir Fear of Wider Unrest," *NYT*, 15 Feb. 1960, 1; Watters, *Down to Now*, 70–84, 110; King, "Debate with James J. Kilpatrick on *The Nation's Future*," 26 Nov. 1960, in *Papers* 5:556–64; James M. Lawson, Jr., "We Are Trying to Raise the 'Moral Issue,'" Apr. 1960, in *Negro Protest Thought in the Twentieth Century*, ed. Francis Broderick and August Meier (New York: Bobbs-Merrill, 1965), 273–81.

34. King, "Interview on *Meet the Press*," 17 Apr. 1960, in *Papers* 5:429; "Dr. King Sees Gain by Negro Sit-Ins," *NYT*, 18 Apr. 1960; "Truman Is Asked to Prove Charge," *NYT*, 20 Apr. 1960, 24; Harris Wofford to President Truman, and Wofford to King, 20 Apr. 1960, KPBU, 73A:IX; King to Truman, 19 Apr. 1960, KPBU, 90:XI.

35. Oppenheimer, *The Sit-in Movement*, 162–67; King, "To Dwight D. Eisenhower," 9 Mar. 1960, in *Papers* 5:386–87; "Alabama Forming Race-Riot Posses," *NYT*, 10 Apr. 1960; King, "To Patrick Murphy Malin, Roy Wilkins, and Carl L. Megel," 16 June 1960, in *Papers* 5:471–72. See also *Papers* 5:407, 425, 496; King, "Interview by Les Margolies," 22 Mar. 1961, KPKC, tape 88–5.

36. Oppenheimer, *The Sit-in Movement*, 134–36.

37. Bond quoted in *My Soul Is Rested*, ed. Raines, 85, and *Voices of Freedom*, ed. Hampton and Fayer, 63; Oppenheimer, *The Sit-in Movement*, 132–34; "An Appeal for Human Rights," *Atlanta Constitution*, 9 Mar. 1960; Weiss, *Whitney M. Young, Jr.*, 66–67.

38. King, "Keep Moving from This Mountain," *Spelman Messenger*, May 1960, 6–17.

39. King, "To Female Inmates," 24 Oct. 1960, in *Papers* 5:528; King, "Speech Re Influence of African Movements on U.S. Students," May 1962, KPKC(3); Thomas Patton to King, 7 Feb. 1961, and James Wood to Patton, 9 Mar. 1961, KPBU, 56:VII-35A. Wood promised to use the money for "Leadership Training."

40. "From Ella J. Baker," 23 Mar. 1960, in *Papers* 5:397; King, "Statement to the Press at the Beginning of the Youth Leadership Conference," 15 Apr. 1960, in *Papers* 5:427; Guy Munger, "Students Begin Strategy Talks," *Greensboro Daily News*, 16 Apr. 1960; Claude Sitton, "Dr. King Favors Buyer's Boycott," *NYT*, 16 Apr. 1960.

41. Lawson, "We Are Trying to Raise the 'Moral Issue,'" 273–81; Carson, "Introduction," in *Papers* 5:29–30.

42. Ella Baker, "Bigger Than a Hamburger," June 1960, in *Eyes on the Prize Civil Rights Reader,* ed. Carson, 87–88; Sitton, "Negro Sitdowns."

43. Carson, *In Struggle,* 10–17; Jane Stembridge quoted in Stoper, "The Student Nonviolent Coordinating Committee," 251; Lewis and D'Orso, *Walking with the Wind,* 40–43, 49, 56; Lewis quoted in *My Soul Is Rested,* ed. Raines, 71–73; Halberstam, *The Children,* 98–101.

44. Powledge, *Free at Last?* 110; Forman, *Making of Black Revolutionaries,* 12–13, 47, 107.

45. C. King, *My Life,* 161, 186; Garrow, *Bearing the Cross,* 129–30, 136–37; King, "Interview on Arrest Following Indictment," 17 Feb. 1960, in *Papers* 5:370–72; King to Benjamin Mays, 4 May 1960, KPBU, 31:IV-18A; "From Harris Wofford," 1 Apr. 1960, in *Papers* 5:403; King, "To Jackie Robinson," 19 June 1960, in *Papers* 5:476–78.

46. King, "To Friend of Freedom," 18 July 1960, in *Papers* 5:488; Bond in *My Soul Is Rested,* ed. Raines, 214; Forman, *Making of Black Revolutionaries,* 244–45; Branch, *Parting the Waters,* 578–79.

47. King, "Outline: The Philosophy of Nonviolence," 14 Oct. 1960, in *Papers* 5:520–21; Oppenheimer, *The Sit-in Movement,* 136; Carson, *In Struggle,* 26–29.

48. Oppenheimer, *The Sit-in Movement,* 136; Carson, "Introduction," in *Papers* 5:36–40; King, interview by Zena Sears on *For Your Information,* 6 Nov. 1960, in *Papers* 5:549–51; "550 Negro Convicts Go on Hunger Strike," *AC,* 6 Dec. 1960, 6.

49. *My Soul Is Rested,* ed. Raines, 90–92; Walker, "Protest and Negotiation,", 40–41.

50. "Statement Announcing the March on the Conventions Movement," 9 June 1960, in *Papers* 5:467–68; Norman Hill to King, 15 Jan. 1960, KPBU, 68:IX; Garrow, *Bearing the Cross,* 139–40; Harrington, *Fragments of the Century,* 110–16.

51. Wofford, *Of Kennedys and Kings,* 51–52; King and A. Philip Randolph, "Joint Platform Proposals to the 1960 Democratic Platform Committee," in *Papers* 5:482–85; "Text of the Democratic Rights Plank," *NYT,* 12 July 1960.

52. Lichtenstein, *State of the Union,* 166–200; Anthony Lewis, "The Civil Rights Plank," *NYT,* 13 July 1960, 20; Joseph Loftus, "Right to Work Is Major Target," *NYT,* 13 July 1960, 23.

53. Harrington, *Fragments of the Century,* 113–15; King, "Address at NAACP Mass Rally," 10 July 1960, in *Papers* 5:486.

54. King, "Three Dimensions," 11 Dec. 1960, in *Papers* 5:575; Willard E. Crawford to King, 20 Nov. 1960, and James Wood to Crawford, 6 Dec. 1960, KPBU, 22:III-16.

55. King to James F. Estes, Dec. 1960, in *Papers* 5:567; James Wood to Viola Knapton, 7 Nov. 1960, KPBU, 29:IV-8; Forman, *Making of Black Revolutionaries,* 127–33; Ransby, *Ella Baker,* 277–78.

Chapter 5. The Dreams of the Masses

1. Matusow, *Unraveling of America,* chs. 2–3.

2. Katznelson, *When Affirmative Action Was White;* for my own early synthesis, see T. Jackson, "The State, the Movement, and the Urban Poor"; Quadagno, *Color of*

Welfare, ch. 1; Patterson, *America's Struggle Against Poverty*; Branch, *Parting the Waters*, 383–84, 398.

3. King, "Interview by Les Margolies," 22 Mar. 1961, KPKC, tape 88–5; Sugrue, *Origins of the Urban Crisis*; Hirsch, *Making the Second Ghetto*; Irene Alexander to King, 17 Apr. 1961, KPBU, 7:I-43.

4. King, "Equality Now: The President Has the Power," *Nation*, 4 Feb. 1961, in *A Testament of Hope*, ed. Washington, 156. King copied paragraphs from a Southern Regional Council report written by law professor Daniel Pollitt. The SRC remains an Atlanta-based organization devoted to research and education on civil rights. Atlanta's Urban League director rebuked the plagiarism, but SRC director Howard Fleming informed King he was glad Pollitt's study "proved so useful." R. A. Thompson to King, 27 Feb. 1961, and Fleming to King, 17 Feb. 1961, KPBU, 58a:VII.

5. On the academic mystique of presidential power, see Wills, *Nixon Agonistes*, 210–11; King, "Appeal to the Honorable John F. Kennedy," 17 May 1962, 29–32, 10–13, BR, 46:2; King, "Equality Now," 153–55; Mike Wallace, "TV Interview with the Rev. Martin Luther King Jr.," *Afro Magazine (Baltimore Afro American)*, 11 Mar. 1961, 4.

6. Graham, *Civil Rights Era*, 34, 40–42; L. D. Reddick to King, 9 May 1961, KPBU, 56A; King, "The President's Record," *NYAN*, 17 Feb. 1962; Matusow, *Unraveling of America*, 64–65.

7. Oscar Hammerstein to King, 21 Apr. 1960, KPBU, 33:IV; Saul Alinsky to King, 3 Jan. 1961, KPBU, 7:I-43; John Wagner to King, 7 Dec. 1960, and King to Wagner, 15 Dec. 1960, KPBU, 73A:IX.

8. King, "Appeal," 14–17; King, "Equality Now," 156–57; Wallace, "TV Interview," 5; King, "The Future of Race Relations in the United States," 23 May 1962, Dartmouth College Library, Hanover, N.H. Self, *American Babylon*; Sugrue, *Origins of the Urban Crisis*.

9. P. L. Prattis to King, 17 Feb. 1961, and King to Prattis, 26 Apr. 1961, KPBU, 56:VII; Whitney Young to King, 24 Feb. 1961, KPBU, 59:VII; Whitney Young, "Address to the Negro American Labor Council," Nov. 1962, WMY.

10. King, "The President's Record"; King, "Appeal," 18; King, "Fumbling on the New Frontier," *Nation*, 3 Mar. 1962, 191–93.

11. Matusow, *Unraveling of America*, 68–69; King, "JFK's Executive Order," *NYAN*, 22 Dec. 1962; King, *Why We Can't Wait*, 20; P. L. Prattis editorial, *PC*, 1 Dec. 1962.

12. King, "The Negro and the American Dream," 25 Sept. 1960, KPKC(3); King, "My Talk with Ben Bella," *NYAN*, 27 Oct. 1962; King, "Question and Answer Period Following Address at National Press Club," 19 July 1962, KPKC(3); King, "Fumbling on the New Frontier," 190–91; Florence Luscomb to King, 31 Oct. 1960, KPBU, 29A:I; King, "The Future of Race Relations."

13. L. Howard DeWolf to King, 1 Apr. 1960, and King to DeWolf, 10 May 1960, KPBU, 23A:III-20; King, "Q & A," 119; In 1964 as a Nobel Laureate, King called on the world to "understand" ANC president Nelson Mandela's argument that nonviolent resistance was ineffective against a totalitarian regime. Fredrickson, "Non-Violent Resistance to White Supremacy," 216, 224–25; King, "Address to the American Negro Leadership Conference on Africa," 24 Nov. 1962, KPKC; King, "The Negro Looks at America," *NYAN*, 8 Dec. 1962.

14. King, *Strength to Love*, 32.

15. King quoted in Oates, *Let the Trumpet Sound,* 167.

16. King, "Reply to Communist Charges, Nashville *Tennessean,*" 14 Dec. 1961, KPKC(3); "Copy of Letter of W.E.B. Du Bois Applying for Membership in the Communist Party of the U.S.A.," 1 Oct. 1961, KPKC, 8:36. Du Bois's stark claim that "Capitalism cannot reform itself; it is doomed to self-destruction," recalled King's notes to himself on capitalism as a student.

17. FBI Memo, 18 Apr. 1960, in *MLK-FBI File,* ed. Friedly and Gallen, 114–16; Garrow, *The FBI and Martin Luther King, Jr.,* 22–26, 37–44, 49, 54, 59; King, "Question and Answer Period."

18. "Statement by MLK, June 11, 1959, HUAC hearings," KPBU, 29A:IV; Ralph Helstein to George Meany in "Report of Public Review Advisory Commission," 11 Feb. 1961, 42, KPBU, 56:VII-37. Levison saw the rhetorical connection: Levison and O'Dell, 2 June 1962, Levison Logs.

19. The sit-ins and King's tax trial in 1960 had elicited unprecedented labor support. Retail workers from District 65 and hospital workers from Local 1199 showed up to picket Woolworth's in Times Square. A May 17 New York benefit pulled in $85,000 to defend King and the students. Levison proclaimed it "a new stage of the struggle," because individuals ponied up thousands of dollars in addition to contributions from union treasuries. "Unions Here Support Dr. King," *NYT,* 12 May 1960, 28; Stanley Levison to King, Mar. 1960, KPBU, 2:I; Fink and Greenberg, *Upheaval in the Quiet Zone,* 78–79, 103, 113–14.

20. King, "Address to UAW Convention," 27 Apr. 1961, KPKC(3).

21. Pfeffer, *A. Philip Randolph,* 219–25; A. Philip Randolph to King, 27 Apr. 1960, KPBU, 64a:VIII; Bayard Rustin to King, 19 May 1960, KPBU, 71:IX; NALC Program, 17 Feb. 1961, KPBU, 44:VI-34.

22. King, "If the Negro Wins, Labor Wins," 11 Dec. 1961, in *A Testament of Hope,* ed. Washington, 203–5; George Meany to King, 22 Dec. 1961, KPBU 36:V; "SCLC's President: Report on AFL-CIO Convention," *SCLC Newsletter,* Feb. 1962.

23. King, "Address to UAW Convention"; King, *Strength to Love,* 21, 28.

24. King, *Trumpet of Conscience,* 12; Horowitz, *Negro and White, Unite and Fight,* 254–55; Stein, *Running Steel, Running America,* 117; Sugrue, *Origins of the Urban Crisis,* 143–44.

25. Charles Killingsworth, "Automation, Jobs and Manpower" (20 Sept. 1963), in *Poverty in America,* ed. Ferman, Kornbluh, and Haber, 139–52; Tom Kahn, "The Economics of Equality" (1964), in *Poverty in America,* ed. Ferman, Kornbluh, and Haber, 153–72.

26. King, "If the Negro Wins, Labor Wins," 203–6; King, "Address Prepared for Nat'l Convention, United Electrical Workers," Aug. 1962, KPKC(3).

27. King, "If the Negro Wins, Labor Wins," 201–3; King to Walter Reuther et al., 23 May 1962, SCLC, 4:24, including the steel, auto, electrical, maritime, transport, and packinghouse workers.

28. King, "Address Delivered at the Thirteenth Constitutional Convention of the United Packinghouse, Food and Allied Workers," 21 May 1962, UPWA Papers, Box 21, SHSW; King, "Address to the Transport Workers Union, AFL-CIO," 2–6 Oct. 1961, KPKC(3). Before the rise of the CIO, the NAACP pursued such an alliance in the 1920s, when first- and second-generation southern and eastern European immigrants—"inbetween" ethnics not yet treated or fully self-identified as "white"—battled the KKK

and WASP Republican political machines. For a vivid portrait of ethnic politics in the 1920s, see Boyle, *Arc of Justice.*

29. Horwitt, *Let Them Call Me Rebel,* 402–3; Sugrue, "Affirmative Action from Below," 149–59; Self, *American Babylon,* 175–91; on urban movements, see T. Jackson, "The State, the Movement, and the Urban Poor," 422–29.

30. Whitney Young, "Address Before the Sixth Annual Convention of the SCLC," 27 Sept. 1962, and Young, "Speech to Alpha Phi Alpha," 27 Dec. 1962, WMY, IV:122; Weiss, *Whitney M. Young, Jr.,* chs. 6–7.

31. L. Sullivan, *Build Brother Build,* 46, 64–68, 70–79; Leon H. Sullivan interview with John Britton, 25 Sept. 1967, pp. 6, 11, 13, RJB; Sugrue, "Affirmative Action from Below," 151–53.

32. King, invitation to Leon Sullivan, 24 Oct. 1962, and flyer for "The Philadelphia Story," SCLC, 172:41; "Negro Ministers Unfold 'Operation Breadbasket' in Atlanta," *SCLC Newsletter,* Dec. 1962; Garrow, *Bearing the Cross,* 223.

33. Branch, *Parting the Waters,* 335–39, 500–507; J. H. Jackson, *A Story of Christian Activism* (Nashville: Townshend Press, 1980), 445–46; J. H. Jackson, *Unholy Shadows and Freedom's Holy Light* (Nashville: Townshend Press, 1967), 195–96; Charles H. King, "Quest and Conflict," *Negro Digest,* May 1967, 7, 78–79.

34. Alfred Duckett to King, 13 Dec. 1959, KPBU, 23A:III-20; Duckett to Wyatt Walker, 5 Aug. 1962, and Duckett to King, 16 Sept. and 19 Dec. 1962, 9 Jan. and 7 Mar. 1963, KPKC, 8:37.

35. Harrington, *Fragments of the Century,* 93; O'Connor, *Poverty Knowledge,* 150–51; Isserman, *The Other American,* 180; Harrington, *The Other America,* 16–17, 21–25, 168–81.

36. Harrington, *The Other America,* 6, 11, 42, 75, 151, 155–56. See O'Connor, *Poverty Knowledge,* 134–36, for a critique of the Ford Foundation's assimilationist Chicago School assumptions.

37. King, "After the Bill Is Passed," *NYAN,* 20 June 1964; Harrington, *The Other America,* 75, 84, 177. Negroes found "pro-social" means of "self-assertion" in cities with sustained boycotts and protests. The study concluded that community organization and protest were effective antipoverty and anticrime tools, recommending their use in the War on Poverty. Fredric Solomon et al., "Civil Rights Activity and Reduction in Crime Among Negroes," *Archives of General Psychology* 12 (March 1965), 227–36.

38. Garrow, *Bearing the Cross,* 157–58; Lewis and D'Orso, *Walking with the Wind,* 166–67; Oates, *Let the Trumpet Sound,* 172.

39. "Excerpts of Dr. King's Address to Oslo Students," *NYT,* 12 Dec. 1964, 18; Watters and Cleghorn, *Climbing Jacob's Ladder,* 52–55, 69, 116–20; Powledge, *Free at Last?* 299, 301, 371; Lawson, *Running for Freedom,* 80–81.

40. Guyot quoted in Powledge, *Free at Last?* 305, 319; Watters and Cleghorn, *Climbing Jacob's Ladder,* 51.

41. Guyot quoted in Lawson, *Running for Freedom,* 82–83; Watters and Cleghorn, *Climbing Jacob's Ladder,* 54, 121–39; Annel Ponder, "Miss. Negroes Denied Vote Protest on Election Day," *SCLC Newsletter,* Aug. 1963, and "Citizenship Education in the 'Heart of the Iceberg,'" n.d., KPKC, 29:13.

42. Charles Cobb and Charles McLaurin, memo, 19 Nov. 1962, Amzie Moore Papers, SHSW, 7:1; Moses quoted in Watters and Cleghorn, *Climbing Jacob's Ladder,* 16, 131–33; Dittmer, *Local People,* 144–46; Mills, *This Little Light of Mine,* 45–52; A.

Young, *An Easy Burden,* 151–52; Cobb, "'Somebody Done Nailed Us on the Cross,'" 917.

43. Charles Sherrod, "From Sherrod," n.d., Charles Sherrod Papers, KC, 1:11; Tom Hayden to Al Haber, in Lyon, *Memories of the Southern Civil Rights Movement,* 21; J. Miller, *Democracy Is in the Streets,* 56–61.

44. King, "Draft, Address at 53rd Annual Convention of the NAACP," 5 July 1962, KPKC, 8:6; "King's People to People Tour Sweeps Delta," *SCLC Newsletter,* Mar. 1962.

45. King, "Virginia's Black Belt," *NYAN,* 14 Apr. 1962; King, "The Future of Race Relations," 5–6; King, "Literacy Bill Dies," *NYAN,* 26 May 1962; King, "Draft, Address at 53rd Annual Convention of the NAACP," 7.

46. James Wood to King, ca. Apr. 1961, KPBU, 58:VIII-44; Garrow, *Bearing the Cross,* 149, 151.

47. Andrew Young to King, 24 Mar. 1961, KPBU, 59:VII-56; A. Young, *An Easy Burden,* 8–9, 85–87, 131–44; R. Elizabeth Johns, "Refinement by Fire" (SCLC CEP, n.d.), HL, 9:12.

48. King, "Interview by Les Margolies"; King, "Unknown Heroes," *NYAN,* 12 May 1962; A. Young, *An Easy Burden,* 139; Septima Clark to King, 12 Dec. 1963, SPC, 3:122; Robnett, *How Long? How Long?* 90–94; Septima Clark, interview by Jacquelyn Hall, 25 July 1976, pp. 80–91, SOHP; Wigginton, *Refuse to Stand,* 312–13.

49. Wigginton, *Refuse to Stand,* 289; S. Clark and Brown, *Ready from Within,* 63–83, 143; "Citizenship Training Progresses," *SCLC Newsletter,* Feb. 1962. At Dorchester workshops, Jack O'Dell taught that under Reconstruction, blacks had held office and enjoyed civil and political rights: A. Young, *An Easy Burden,* 146–48. Morris, *Origins of the Civil Rights Movement,* 238; Septima Clark, "Success of SCLC Citizenship School Seen in 50,000 New Registered Voters," *SCLC Newsletter,* Sept. 1963, 11. See also McFadden, "Septima P. Clark," 91–92.

50. S. Clark and Blythe, *Echo in My Soul,* 201, 218–19, 235–38; King to Peggy Brooks, 22 July 1962, SPC, 3:122. Clark was a mother with a son who lived with his grandparents in Ohio, which may be why in praising her King described her activist role as "forced." Clark to Myles Horton, 24 Sept. 1963, HL, 9:12.

51. King, "Statement Re Wage and Hour Violations in Shrimp Industry," 15 Mar. 1962, KPKC(3); Andrew Young to Clarence Lundquist, Department of Labor, 2 Mar. 1962, KPKC, 15:54.

52. A. Young, *An Easy Burden,* 166; Claude Sitton, "Profile of Albany, Ga.," *NYT,* 22 July 1962, 117; Powledge, *Free at Last?* 340, 346, 360.

53. Forman, *Making of Black Revolutionaries,* 249–59; Watters, *Down to Now,* 152–56; Powledge, *Free at Last?* 347; Garrow, *Bearing the Cross,* 174–76, 181; Carson, *In Struggle,* 58; A. Young, *An Easy Burden,* 177.

54. Anderson quoted in, *Voices of Freedom,* ed. Hampton and Fayer, 114; Watters, *Down to Now,* 14–15, 147, 160; Hansen quoted in Fairclough, *To Redeem the Soul of America,* 101–2; Garrow, *Bearing the Cross,* 185–90; Claude Sitton, "Dr. King Among 265 Negroes Seized in March," *NYT,* 17 Dec. 1961, 1; Branch, *Parting the Waters,* 558; Claude Sitton, "Negro Groups Split on Georgia Protest," *NYT,* 18 Dec. 1961, 1; *Tribune* quoted in Lewis, *King,* 151.

55. Claude Sitton, "202 More Negroes Seized in Georgia," *NYT,* 14 Dec. 1961, 47; Sitton, "Guard Called out in Racial Unrest," *NYT,* 15 Dec. 1961, 29; Watters, *Down to Now,* 146, 78–85, 97, 109; Lentz, *Symbols, the News Magazines, and Martin Luther King,* 60-62.

56. "Letter from the Albany Movement to the Albany City Commission," 23 Jan. 1962, in *Eyes on the Prize Civil Rights Reader,* ed. Carson, 106–7.

57. Claude Sitton, "Negroes Defy Ban, March in Georgia," *NYT,* 22 Jan. 1962, 1; Watters, *Down to Now,* 174–75, 210–11, 214–18; Powledge, *Free at Last?* 380–86, 407–8; Garrow, *Bearing the Cross,* 208–9; Forman, *Making of Black Revolutionaries,* 273; Claude Sitton, "Dr. King Sets a Day of Penance," *NYT,* 26 July 1962, 1.

58. King, "Why It's Albany," *NYAN,* 18 Aug. 1962; Watters, *Down to Now,* 196–200.

59. Powledge, *Free at Last?* 382–84; Hedrick Smith, "Albany, Ga., Closes Parks and Libraries to Balk Integration," *NYT,* 12 Aug. 1962, 1; King, "Who Is Their God?" *Nation,* 13 Oct. 1962, 210.

60. Forman, *Making of Black Revolutionaries,* 276–77; Watters and Cleghorn, *Climbing Jacob's Ladder,* 3–4, 139, 164–68; King, "The Terrible Cost of the Ballot," *NYAN,* 1 Sept. 1962.

61. King quoted in Garrow, *Bearing the Cross,* 220; Abernathy, *Walls Came Tumbling,* 218–29; Wyatt Walker, "The Congo, U.S.A.: Albany, Georgia," *SCLC Newsletter,* Sept. 1962; "Interview with Bernice Reagon," in *Eyes on the Prize Civil Rights Reader,* ed. Carson, 143–45; King, *Why We Can't Wait,* 44–45; Sherrod quoted in Powledge, *Free at Last?* 417–19; Watters, *Down to Now,* 131.

62. King, "Why It's Albany"; Powledge, *Free at Last?* 416; Abernathy, *Walls Came Tumbling,* 225–26.

Chapter 6. Jobs and Freedom

1. King, "Negroes and Political Maturity," *NYAN,* 2 Mar. 1963; King, "Sit In, Stand In, Wade In, Kneel In," *NYAN,* 25 May 1963.

2. King cited approvingly Governor Terry Sanford's promise to eliminate employment discrimination in North Carolina. King, "Bold Design for a New South," *Nation,* 30 Mar. 1963.

3. King, *Why We Can't Wait,* 36, 39, 102–3; King, "Let Justice Roll Down," *Nation,* 15 Mar. 1965, 270.

4. Levison quoted in *American Journey,* ed. Stein and Plimpton, 114–15; Eskew, *But for Birmingham,* 91; Thornton, *Dividing Lines,* 140–54, 164–65; King, *Why We Can't Wait,* 49; Kelley, "The Black Poor and the Politics of Opposition," 311–13, 318.

5. Thornton, *Dividing Lines,* 162–260; Manis, *A Fire You Can't Put Out,* 85. Kelley, "The Black Poor and the Politics of Opposition," 317, criticizes Shuttlesworth's middle-class agenda, but Shuttlesworth spoke about how important the hiring of black policemen was to working-class blacks. "They Challenge Segregation at Its Core!" (SCEF, 1959), KPBU, 71A:IX; King, "Birmingham Part II Project 'C,'" *NYAN,* 17 Aug. 1963; "Business in Dixie," *Wall Street Journal,* 26 May 1961.

6. Eskew, *But for Birmingham,* 194–205; King, *Why We Can't Wait,* 50–53; "Negroes' Boycott Fought in South," *NYT,* 4 Apr. 1962; King, "Birmingham Part II Project 'C'"; Thornton, *Dividing Lines,* 268–69.

7. Morris, *Origins of the Civil Rights Movement,* 250–60; Eskew, *But for Birmingham,* 211, 216; King, *Why We Can't Wait,* 54; Walker recalled thinking Connor might do something rash to help the cause. He was clearly more ready for headline-

catching confrontation then King. Wyatt T. Walker, interview by John Britton 11 Oct. 1967, p. 54, RJB. Shuttlesworth recalled thinking if they could crack Birmingham, "we could crack any city": Shuttlesworth interview by James M. Mosby, Jr., Sept. 1968, p. 52, RJB. Thornton, *Dividing Lines,* 271–73.

8. Eskew, *But for Birmingham,* 288, 229–31, downplays King's achievement in recruiting these men, who purportedly co-opted King. Thornton, *Dividing Lines,* 297–302; Abernathy, *Walls Came Tumbling,* 238–40.

9. Eskew, *But for Birmingham,* 214–15, 222; Fred Shuttlesworth, "The Birmingham Manifesto," in *Documentary History of the Modern Civil Rights Movement,* ed. Peter Levy, (New York: Greenwood Press, 1992) 108–9; Abernathy, *Walls Came Tumbling,* 242–43.

10. On Greenwood, see Watters and Cleghorn, *Climbing Jacob's Ladder,* 59–63; A. Young, *An Easy Burden,* 112, 206–8; Foster Hailey, "15 Birmingham Negroes Seized," *NYT,* 18 Apr. 1963; "Birmingham Curb Asked in U.S. Suit," *NYT,* 20 Apr. 1963.

11. Walker interview by Britton, pp. 54, 62, RJB; "Alabama Riot Broken up by Police Dogs," *LAT,* 8 Apr. 1963; Thornton, *Dividing Lines,* 291; Foster Hailey, "Dr. King Arrested at Birmingham," *NYT,* 13 Apr. 1963, 1, 15; A. Young, *An Easy Burden,* 225; Foster Hailey, "Fighting Erupts at Birmingham," *NYT,* 15 May 1963, 1; Hailey, "New Birmingham Regime Sworn," *NYT,* 16 Apr. 1963, 1; King, "Civil Disobedience Should Be Employed" ("Letter from a Birmingham City Jail"), 16 Apr. 1963, in *Eyes on the Prize Civil Rights Reader,* ed. Carson, 153–58.

12. Eskew, *But for Birmingham,* 236–38; Natalie Jaffe, "9 Shops Picketed in Racial Protest," *NYT,* 21 Apr. 1963, 70; "4 Chain Stores Targets," *PC,* 27 Apr. 1963, 1; contribution letters in *SCLC Micro,* 5:43–48, 207, 262; "10-Year Racial Problem Seen by Bobby Kennedy," *LAT,* 22 Apr. 1963.

13. Garrow, *Bearing the Cross,* 247; Bevel in *Voices of Freedom,* ed. Hampton and Fayer, 131; Shuttlesworth interview with Mosby, 60–61, RJB; A. Young, *An Easy Burden,* 236; "Fire Hoses, Dogs Quell Alabama Racial Protest," *LAT,* 4 May 1963; Manis, *A Fire You Can't Put Out,* 368–70; King, *Why We Can't Wait,* 99.

14. McWhorter, *Carry Me Home,* 373–76; Eskew, *But for Birmingham,* 268; King, *Why We Can't Wait,* 100; A. Young, *An Easy Burden,* 240; "Bob Kennedy Warns City on Negro Rights," *LAT,* 4 May 1963; Garrow, *Bearing the Cross,* 250.

15. Foster Hailey, "U.S. Seeking a Truce in Birmingham," *NYT,* 5 May 1963; Thornton, *Dividing Lines,* 314; Foster Hailey, "Birmingham Talks Pushed; Negroes March Peacefully," *NYT,* 6 May 1963; Walker quoted in Powledge, *Free at Last?* 506; "Reminiscences of Bayard Rustin," 1987, p. 95, CUOH; Shuttlesworth interview by Mosby, p. 51, RJB.

16. *SCLC Micro:* Joan Blocker, 6 May 1963, 5:790; Anon., 3 May 1963, 5:694; Roselyn Greenleaf, 6 May 1963, 5:315; Robert Lowery, 5:476, 10 May 1963.

17. Manis, *A Fire You Can't Put Out,* 376–78; Claude Sitton, "Rioting Negroes Routed by Police at Birmingham," *NYT,* 8 May 1963, 1, 28; Kelley, "The Black Poor and the Politics of Opposition," 318; McWhorter, *Carry Me Home,* 414, 417. On Lingo's addictions and the undisciplined state police, see Birmingham police officer Ben Allen, quoted in *My Soul is Rested,* ed. Raines,175–77.

18. Manis, *A Fire You Can't Put Out,* 373–75, 380; Thornton, *Dividing Lines,* 315–17; King, *Why We Can't Wait,* 102–4; Smyer quoted in *My Soul Is Rested,* ed. Raines, 163; Philip Benjamin, "Negroes' Boycott in Birmingham Cuts Heavily into Retail Sales," *NYT,* 11 May 1963, 9.

19. Eskew, *But for Birmingham*, 288–89; Manis, *A Fire You Can't Put Out*, 386–90.

20. Thornton, *Dividing Lines*, 318–23; A. Young, *An Easy Burden*, 245–48.

21. Shuttlesworth interview by Mosby, pp. 39, 66, 88, RJB; Thornton, *Dividing Lines*, 322–25; Manis, *A Fire You Can't Put Out*, 380–88; A. Young, *An Easy Burden*, 247; King, *Why We Can't Wait*, 104; *My Soul Is Rested*, ed. Raines, 158–61.

22. Claude Sitton, "Birmingham Pact Sets Timetable for Integration," *NYT*, 11 May 1963, 1; "Negro Leaders' Statements on Birmingham Accord," *NYT*, 11 May 1963, 8; Stanley Levison and King, 10 May 1963, FBI Levison Logs; Thornton, *Dividing Lines*, 330; David Cort, "The Voices of Birmingham," *Nation*, 23 July 1963.

23. Manis, *A Fire You Can't Put Out*, 393; Claude Sitton, "50 Hurt in Negro Rioting After Birmingham Blasts," *NYT*, 13 May 1963, 1.

24. For Robert Kennedy's account of the riot, John F. Kennedy's tougher approach, and relevant Oval Office conversations of 12 and 21 May, see *Kennedy, Johnson, and the Quest for Justice*, ed. Rosenberg and Karabell, 96–99, 102–3, 109–10; Anthony Lewis, "U.S. Sends Troops to Alabama," *NYT*, 13 May 1963; Stanley Levison and Jack O'Dell, 14 May 1963, FBI Levison Logs; Philip Benjamin, "Dr. King Visits Pool Halls," *NYT*, 14 May 1963; A. Young, *An Easy Burden*, 250.

25. King, *Why We Can't Wait*, 112.

26. Bayard Rustin, "Birmingham Leads to New Stage of Struggle," *New America*, 18 June 1963.

27. King, "Address at Wrigley Field Freedom Rally," 26 May 1963, KPKC, tape T-33; King, "Address at the Freedom Rally at Cobo Hall," 23 June 1963, in *Call to Conscience*, ed. Carson and Shepard, 69–70.

28. Fairclough, *To Redeem the Soul of America*, 143–49.

29. Gloria Richardson, "Cambridge, Maryland, 'City of Progress' for Rich," *New America*, 31 Aug. 1963, 4; Robnett, *How Long? How Long?* 161–65.

30. Velma Hill, "Harlem Pickets Force City to Halt Project," *New America*, 10 July 1963, 8; Martin Oppenheimer, "Race Conflicts Stir City of Brotherly Love," *New America*, 10 Aug. 1963, 5; Gentile, *March on Washington*, 24–26, 95–98, 104; Kotz, *Passion for Equality*, 106–10; Lipsitz, *A Life in the Struggle*, 73–77.

31. John D. Pomfret, "President Voices Birmingham Hope," *NYT*, 8 May 1963; M. S. Handler, "Assertive Spirit Stirs Negroes," *NYT*, 23 Apr. 1963.

32. King, telegram to John F. Kennedy, 11 June 1963, White House Central File, Martin Luther King Letters JFKL, http://www.jfklibrary.org (accessed May 2006); "Transcript of the President's Address," *NYT*, 12 June 1963, 20; "Text of the President's Message to Congress Calling for Civil Rights Legislation," *NYT*, 20 June 1963, 16–17.

33. Oval Office Meetings, Presidential Recordings, 20 May 1963, tape 88.4, and 1 June 1963, tape 90.3, JFKL; *Kennedy, Johnson, and the Quest for Justice*, ed. Rosenberg and Karabell, 116–20. Title VI promised to cut off federal dollars to any government agency or contractor that practiced discrimination. Titles IV and V allowed the Community Relations Service to mediate disputes and extended the tenure of the Civil Rights Commission. Sundquist, *Politics and Policy*, 263.

34. Richard Russell, "The South States Its Case," *U.S. News & World Report*, 24 June 1963, 78; "Text of the President's Message to Congress"; meeting on Birmingham, 23 Sept. 1963, in *Kennedy, Johnson, and the Quest for Justice*, ed. Rosenberg and Karabell, 164–65.

35. Brink and Harris, *Negro Revolution in America*, 190; Sundquist, *Politics and Policy*, 263; "Text of the President's Message to Congress."

36. Labor economists, union representatives, and manpower and training experts testified about the challenges of expanding employment and incorporating the least skilled workers into a newly automated economy, but they almost never mentioned race. Charles Killingsworth, Leon Keyserling, and Gunnar Myrdal all testified. U.S. Senate, Committee on Labor and Public Welfare, *Nation's Manpower Revolution*, parts 1–10, Hearings, May 1963–June 1964 (Washington, D.C.: GPO, 1964); Stein, *Running Steel, Running America*, 69–88; Brown, *Race, Money, and the American Welfare State*, 210–13.

37. U.S. Senate, Committee on Labor and Public Welfare, *Equal Employment Opportunity* (Washington, D.C.: GPO, 1963): A. Philip Randolph and Roy Wilkins, 25 July 1963, 174–75, 199–200; Andrew Young, 26 July 1963, 178.

38. Pfeffer, *A. Philip Randolph*, 266–67; Garrow, *Bearing the Cross*, 265–81; Fairclough, *Martin Luther King*, 89.

39. King, *Why We Can't Wait*, 123–25; Malcolm X, "Message to the Grass Roots," Nov. 1963, in *Malcolm X Speaks*, ed. Breitman, 16; Forman, *Making of Black Revolutionaries*, 332–36.

40. "Reminiscences of Bayard Rustin," 190; Norman Hill interview by James M. Mosby, Jr., 12 Mar. 1970 , p. 28, RJB.

41. A. Philip Randolph to John F. Kennedy, 4 May 1962, JFKL, White House Central File, Martin Luther King Letters JFKL, http://www.jfklibrary.org (accessed May 2006); D'Emilio, *Lost Prophet*, 328; Pfeffer, *A. Philip Randolph*, 249–50.

42. A. Philip Randolph to CORE, SNCC, SCLC, NAACP, SNCC, and the National Council of Negro Women, 26 Mar. 1963 BR, 27:10; Randolph to Hobson Reynolds, 25 Apr. 1963, BR, 27:10; D'Emilio, *Lost Prophet*, 329–30; NALC Press Release, 22 May 1963, BR, 31:4.

43. Stanley Levison and Alice Loewi, 3 June 1963, FBI Levison Logs; New York FBI memo, 4 June 1963, in *MLK-FBI File*, ed. Friedly and Gallen, 161–63.

44. Conference call between Levison, Jones, King, Abernathy, and Andrew Young, *MLK-Levison FBI Micro*, 10 June 1963, 4:147–52. By stressing the resiliency of the economic agenda, I differ with Fairclough, *To Redeem the Soul of America*, 150–52, Pfeffer, *A. Philip Randolph*, 266–67, and D'Emilio, *Lost Prophet*.

45. "Dr. King Denounces President on Rights," *NYT*, 10 June 1963; Lawrence quoted in "Massive Protest in Capital Seen If Congress Fails to Aid Negroes," *NYT*, 12 June 1963; Levison quoted in Fairclough, *To Redeem the Soul of America*, 152; "Rights Plea Made at City College," *NYT*, 13 June 1963, 22; John Maffre, "Senator Cites the Rules against a Capitol Sit-in," *WP*, 14 June 1963, A9.

46. Sellers, *River of No Return*, 62–63; Lewis and D'Orso, *Walking with the Wind*, 202–3.

47. Reese Cleghorn, "The Angels Are White," *New Republic*, 17 Aug. 1963; D'Emilio, *Lost Prophet*, 337–39; Hill interview by Mosby; "7 Negro Groups Unite," *NYT*, 3 July 1963; Bayard Rustin, "Organizing Manual No. 1," "Organizing Manual No. 2," BR, 30:1. CUCRL became the major force behind strengthening the employment provisions of the Kennedy bill in the next year.

48. Gentile, *March on Washington*, 65–71, 259; Abner Willoughby to A. Philip Randolph, 28 June 1963, BR, 27:10; King, "March on Washington," *NYAN*, 24 Aug. 1963; The Justice Department insisted on a sound system large enough to keep the whole crowd drawn close around the Lincoln Memorial, where behind Lincoln's statue

sat Kennedy emissary Jerry Bruno holding "the cutoff switch in his hand," in case the crowd turned too militant. Lichtenstein, *Most Dangerous Man in Detroit*, 536n47.

49. Gentile, *March on Washington*, 138–39; Walter Fauntroy to "Fellow Citizen," 25 July 1963, BR, 27:11; "Rights Leaders Reaffirm Belief," *WP*, 26 Aug. 1963; Whitney Young, interview by Albert Gollin, 26 July 1967, WMY, I:9.

50. "NAACP Assails Rights Measures," *NYT*, 3 July 1963; "Kennedy Chided on Racial Crisis," *NYT*, 1 July 1963; Minutes, NUL National Board of Trustees, 16 May 1963, WMY, IV:12; Whitney Young, "National Conference on Religion and Race," 14 Jan. 1963, and "New Challenges in Today's Race Relations," 23 Sept. 1963, WMY, IV:127; Whitney Young, "Domestic Marshall Plan," *NYT*, 3 Aug. 1963.

51. Rustin, "Organizing Manual No. 1"; "The Time Is Now: A Call to Americans," n.d., NUL, Part II, series 1, box 26.

52. King et al., "What the Marchers Really Want," *New York Times Magazine*, 25 Aug. 1963; King et al., "Transcript of N.E.T. 'For Freedom Now,'" 23 July 1963, KPKC(3).

53. Pfeffer, *A. Philip Randolph*, 245; A. Philip Randolph to labor leaders, 18 July 1963, BR, 30:18.

54. Rustin, "Organizing Manual No. 2"; "Marchers Widen Rights Demands," *NYT*, 21 Aug. 1963; Barbara Moffett to A. Philip Randolph, 2 Aug. 1963, BR, 28:2; John Arnold to Cleveland Robinson, 4 Aug. 1963, and Bayard Rustin to Arnold, 7 Aug. 1963, BR, 28:4; Rustin to Andrew and Barbara Spadanuta, 15 Aug. 1963, BR, 28:8; Thomas Kilgore to Eugene Blake, 25 July 1963, BR, 31:1.

55. Stanley Aronowitz to A. Philip Randolph, 13 Aug. 1963, BR, 28:7, 29:2; Marion Jones to Cleveland Robinson, 26 Aug. 1963, Hamish Sinclair to Randolph, 22 July 1963, and Bayard Rustin to Sinclair, 1 Aug. 1963, BR 28:2.

56. Frances Fox Piven, interview by Noel Cazenave, War on Poverty Oral History Project, CUOH; Richard Cloward and Frances Fox Piven, personal communication with the author, 4 Apr. 2000.

57. A. Philip Randolph to Stephen Currier, 20 July 1963, BR, 27:11; Pfeffer, *A. Philip Randolph*, 254–60; Jane Stembridge to Tom Kahn, 16 Aug. 1963, BR, 28:10; Young, interview by Gollin; Gentile, *March on Washington*, 134.

58. Bayard Rustin to Jack Conway, 20 Aug. 1963, BR, 28:11.

59. "Excerpts from Addresses," *NYT*, 29 Aug. 1963, 21; "Address by Rabbi Joachim Prinz," 28 Aug. 1963, BR, 31:4; Gentile, *March on Washington*, 223–41.

60. A. Philip Randolph, Walter Reuther, and James Farmer (delivered by Floyd B. McKissick), "Excerpts from Addresses," *NYT*, 29 Aug. 1963, 21; Lichtenstein, *Most Dangerous Man in Detroit*, 386–87.

61. Lewis and D'Orso, *Walking with the Wind*, 216–23; text as delivered in Forman, *Making of Black Revolutionaries*, 336–37; "Original text of speech by John Lewis," 28 Aug. 1963, in *Eyes on the Prize Civil Rights Reader*, ed. Carson, 122–23; "Restrained Militancy," *WP*, 29 Aug. 1963.

62. King, "I Have a Dream," in *A Testament of Hope*, ed. Washington, 217; Thelwell, "The August 28th March on Washington," 73.

63. Height, "We Wanted the Voice of a Woman to Be Heard," 88–90; Olson, *Freedom's Daughters*, 285–89; Bernice Kelly to John F. Kennedy, 13 Oct. 1963, NUL, part II, series 1, box 24K; Anna Arnold Hedgeman interview by Katherine Shannon, 25 July 1967, RJB.

64. Meeting between Kennedy and civil rights leaders, 28 Aug. 1963, in *Kennedy, Johnson, and the Quest for Justice,* ed. Rosenberg and Karabell, 131–40.

65. Hubert Humphrey to Troy Bailey, 14 Apr. 1964, BR, 30:14; Dudziak, *Cold War Civil Rights,* 216–17; John F. Kennedy in NAACP press release, 31 Aug. 1963, BR, 31:4; Edward Folliard, "Kennedy Says March Advanced Negro Cause," *WP,* 29 Aug. 1963, A21; Thelwell, "The August 28th March on Washington," 72.

66. "Gentle Army," *NYT,* 29 Aug. 1963, 20; "Marcher from Alabama," *NYT,* 29 Aug. 1963, 17; Powledge, *Free at Last?* 539–40; "The Quiet Freedom," *WSJ,* 30 Aug. 1963, 6; Harold Keith, "Demonstration's Marchers Leave Legacy in Wake," *PC,* 7 Sept. 1963, 3.

67. Tom Kahn, "March's Radical Demands Point Way for Struggle," *New America,* 24 Sept. 1963, 1, 4.

68. Reg Murphy, "President Reassures 10 Leaders," *Atlanta Constitution,* 29 Aug. 1963; Eugene Patterson, "Long Way from the Slave Cabin," and "In the Shadow of Abe Lincoln," *Atlanta Constitution,* 29 Aug. 1963; Patterson, "I Have a Dream," *Atlanta Constitution,* 30 Aug. 1963.

69. King, *Why We Can't Wait,* 121–23; Brink and Harris, *Negro Revolution in America,* 140–42; Anon., 8 May 1963, SCLC Micro, 5:623.

70. Oval Office Meetings, 19 Sept. and 23 Sept. 1963, *Kennedy, Johnson, and the Quest for Justice,* ed., Rosenberg and Karabell, 144–48, 172–73; King and Clarence Jones, 16 Sept. 1963, and Jones and Bayard Rustin, 17 Sept. 1963, FBI Jones Logs; Thornton, *Dividing Lines,* 351–59.

71. King, "Address Delivered at the Seventh Annual Convention," 27 Sept. 1963, KPKC; King, "Sharing of Twin Needs," *NYAN,* 28 Sept. 1963; King, *Why We Can't Wait,* 113–14; Ed Clayton, "Birmingham Bombing Points Up a City with a Sick Soul," *SCLC Newsletter,* Oct. 1963.

72. King, "Demonstrating Our Unity," 15 Dec. 1963, KPKC, 3:20; King, "The Danger of a Little Progress," *NYAN,* 15 Feb. 1964; Fairclough, *To Redeem the Soul of America,* 175–77.

73. King and Clarence Jones, 29 Oct. 1963, and Stanley Levison and Jones, 4 Nov. 1963, FBI Jones Logs; see also *MLK-FBI File,* ed. Friedly and Gallen, 174.

74. King, "What Killed JFK?" *NYAN,* 21 Dec. 1963; King and Lyndon Johnson, 25 Nov. 1963, in *Kennedy, Johnson, and the Quest for Justice,* ed., Rosenberg and Karabell, 198, 204; conference call between King, Clarence Jones, and Ralph Abernathy, 22 Nov. 1963, FBI Jones Logs.

Chapter 7. Malignant Kinship

1. "Man of the Year," *Time,* 3 Jan. 1964, 14; King, *Why We Can't Wait,* 112, 132.

2. Fairclough, *To Redeem the Soul of America,* 178–79; Levison was furious at King's rambling speculations and "complete lack of leadership ability." King had become too obsessed with raising money from rich folks, Levison griped, to figure out his strategy and act consistently. Stanley Levison and Clarence Jones, 28 Feb. 1964, FBI Jones Logs.

3. Oates, *Let the Trumpet Sound,* 286–93; Garrow, *Bearing the Cross,* 324–27; Fair-

clough, *To Redeem the Soul of America,* 181–91; Robert Hayling interview by John Britton, 16 Aug. 1967, p. 26 RJB.

4. King, "A Plan for New York," *NYAN,* 18 July 1964.

5. Zarevsky, *President Johnson's War on Poverty,* 21–36. On the tax cut, see Lyndon Johnson and Ted Sorensen in *Taking Charge,* ed. Beschloss, 38–41; Rev. Lynwood Stevenson quoted in Matusow, *Unraveling of America,* 249.

6. King, "Annual Report to the SCLC," 11 Aug. 1965, KPKC(3); Harrington, *Fragments of the Century,* 94.

7. "President Johnson's Message on Poverty to the Congress," 16 Mar. 1964, in *Poverty in America,* ed. Ferman, Kornbluh, and Haber, 421–28; T. Jackson, "The State, the Movement, and the Urban Poor," 411–16. Though most planners and historians minimize the impact of black protest on the origins (not the implementation) of the program, at least one key architect of Community Action, Richard Boone, who is credited with keeping "maximum feasible participation" in the final draft of the Economic Opportunity Act, later acknowledged his own debt to black activism. SNCC and the Mississippi Freedom Democratic Party impressed upon Boone that poor people themselves "had a dramatic and deep understanding of their circumstances and very well knew what it would take for them to move out of poverty." "The Federal Government and Urban Poverty," transcript of a conference held 16–17 June 1973, Brandeis University, p. 352, JFKL.

8. Brauer, "Kennedy, Johnson, and the War on Poverty," 105–9.

9. Lyndon Johnson and Walker Stone, 6 Jan. 1964, WH640.06, LBJT; Nick Kotz regards the conversation as unreflective of Johnson's core beliefs, but I see it as revelatory. See Kotz, *Judgment Days,* 94; Richard Daley and Johnson, 20 Jan. 1964, in *Taking Charge,* ed. Beschloss, 168.

10. Robert Thompson, "Negro Leaders Agree to a Poverty Fight," *WP,* 19 Jan. 1964, A2; "Johnson Is Hopeful House Will Debate Rights This Month," *NYT,* 19 Jan. 1964, 1. In their first meeting, 3 Dec. 1963, Johnson and King reportedly agreed on the need for jobs and training, and Johnson thought he secured King's promise not to press on with demonstrations. He was perturbed to read in the press King's promise to continue "demonstrations until the injustices that have caused them are eliminated." Kotz, *Judgment Days,* 67, 92–93. King, *Why We Can't Wait,* 145–46; Garrow, *Bearing the Cross,* 310.

11. Matusow, *Unraveling of America,* 122–26; Brown, *Race, Money, and the American Welfare State,* 222–34.

12. Brauer, "Kennedy, Johnson, and the War on Poverty," 105, 108–13; Matusow, *Unraveling of America,* 110–11, 262–65.

13. Hacker quoted in Hentoff, *The New Equality,* 231; Kahn, "The Economics of Equality" (1964), in *Poverty in America,* ed. Ferman, Kornbluh, and Haber, 156–58, 164–66; John Pomfret, "Economic Factors Underlie Negro Discontent," *NYT,* 18 Aug. 1963, 154.

14. Ad Hoc Committee, "The Triple Revolution," in *Poverty in America,* ed. Ferman, Kornbluh, and Haber, 443–56.

15. Michael Harrington to Robert Pickus, 9 Dec. 1964, LID, 29; Harrington, *Fragments of the Century,* 198; Hentoff, *The New Equality,* 13–20.

16. J. Miller, *Democracy Is in the Streets,* 189–90; Harrington, *Fragments of the Century,* 154–56; Gitlin, *The Sixties,* 165, 226, 336; Evans, *Personal Politics,* 131, 140–45; Bob Ross to Tom Kahn, 27 July 1964, LID, 29.

17. Oates, *Let the Trumpet Sound,* 249, 263, 286; Stanley Levison, Bayard Rustin, Clarence Jones, and ghostwriters Nat Lamar, Hermine Popper, and Al Duckett assisted King over the fall and winter of 1963–64. King was anxious the team effort be kept secret lest it "hurt his national image," he confided to Levison. King and Levison, 13 Dec. 1963, FBI Levison Logs.

18. King, *Why We Can't Wait,* 22, 135–36, 117, 31, 23–28.

19. Ibid., ix–x, 81, 113.

20. Ibid., 119–20; History may have given King some hope, at least in 1963. Slavery's origins lay in "the economic factor," King preached in a sermon titled "Love in Action." Ideologies of white supremacy had grown out of the "tragic attempt to give moral sanction to an economically profitable system." But when slavery became less profitable, it grew more dependent on ideology and custom than economics, and was perpetuated by "sincere though spiritually ignorant persons." By implication, perhaps the ideological racism of whites might yet yield to moral appeals. King, *Strength to Love,* 40–43.

21. King, *Why We Can't Wait,* 119; Fairclough, *To Redeem the Soul of America,* 199–200.

22. King, *Why We Can't Wait,* 23–25, 48–49, 129–30.

23. Ibid., 24–25, 142.

24. Ibid., 132–38; Weiss, *Whitney M. Young, Jr.,* 152.

25. Stanley Levison and Alice Loewi, 2 Dec. 1963, and Popper and Stanley Levison, 27 Jan. 1964, FBI Levison Logs; King to Hermine Popper, 3 Feb. 1964, KPKC, 19:44; Garrow, *Bearing the Cross,* 311–12; Branch, *Pillar of Fire,* 211.

26. King, *Why We Can't Wait,* 137–38.

27. Ibid., 139.

28. Ibid., 147–51, 141–42.

29. Fairclough, *To Redeem the Soul of America,* 170–71.

30. Clarence Jones to King, 15 Apr. 1964, KPKC, 13:20; Garrow, *Bearing the Cross,* 322–23; King, "The Stall-In in Review," *NYAN,* 9 May 1964.

31. King, "The School Boycott Concept," *NYAN,* 11 Apr. 1964; King, "'White Backlash' A Myth—Dr. King," *NYAN,* 23 May 1964; conference call between King, Jones, Wachtel, Fauntroy, and Walker 10 May 1964, FBI Jones Logs.

32. D. T. Carter, *Politics of Rage,* 211–17.

33. L. D. Reddick to King, "Lessons from the Wallace 'Victory,'" 19 June 1964, KPKC, 20:5.

34. Clarence Jones to King, 15 May 1964, enclosing draft "Remarks," KPKC(3); King, "Remarks at the Convocation on Equal Justice Under Law of the NAACP Legal Defense Fund," 28 May 1964, p. 3, KPKC(3); King, "Recognition and Opportunity," *NYAN,* 6 June 1964; King, "After the Bill Is Passed," *NYAN,* 20 June 1964.

35. King and Clarence Jones, 14 May 1964, and Harry Wachtel and Jones, 21 May 1964, FBI Jones Logs; Wachtel to King, 14 Aug. 1964, KPKC, 25:26; Jones to King, 11 Aug. 1964, "Re: Draft Article Outline," KPKC, 13:22.

36. King, "Statement Before the Platform Committee," Republican National Committee, 7 July 1964, CR, 24; King, "Bill of Rights for the Disadvantaged," Democratic National Committee, 22 Aug. 1964, 5–6, 9–12, KPKC(3). the *Washington Post* mentioned only King's call for federal protection for southern civil rights workers: Robert Albright, "Kennedy Calls for Plank," *WP,* 20 Aug. 1964, A1.

37. Annell Ponder, "90,000 Negroes Vote in Mississippi Mock Election," *SCLC Newsletter*, Nov.–Dec. 1963.

38. King, "Ready in Mississippi," *NYAN*, 29 Aug. 1964; King, "Statement in Support of MFDP," 22 July 1964, KPKC, 16:3.

39. King, "Address Delivered to Mississippi Summer Project Participants," 25 July 1964, KPKC.

40. "Freedom School Curriculum," *SNCC Papers Microfilm*, 67:815, 68:0093, reprinted in http://www.educationanddemocracy.org; McAdam, *Freedom Summer*, 85; Alice Lake, "Last Summer in Mississippi," *Redbook* (Nov. 1964), in *Reporting Civil Rights*, ed. Carson et al., vol. 2, 244–45.

41. King, "Statement Re: Mississippi, Credentials Committee Democratic National Committee," 22 Aug. 1964, KPKC(3); Lyndon Johnson and Richard Russell, and Johnson and Walter Reuther, 24 Aug. 1964, in *Taking Charge*, ed. Beschloss, 524–27:Johnson and Hubert Humphrey, 14 Aug. 1964, quoted in Kotz, *Judgment Days*, 196.

42. Hampton and Fayer, *Voices of Freedom*, 199, 202–3; Dittmer, *Local People*, 285–302; Unita Blackwell, interview by Mike Garvey, Apr. and May. 1977, University of Southern Mississippi Oral History Program, Civil Rights in Mississippi Digital Archive, available at http://www.lib.usm.edu; Boyle, *The UAW and the Heyday of American Liberalism*, 195; Garrow, *Bearing the Cross*, 349; King, "Mighty Army of Love," *NYAN*, 7 Nov. 1964; Charles Sherrod, "Mississippi in Atlantic City," in *Reporting Civil Rights*, ed. Carson et al., vol. 2, 184–85.

43. "Position Papers for Use in Preparing Statements," 27 July 1964, KPKC(3); Garrow, *Bearing the Cross*, 342–44; King and Clarence Jones, 25 July 1964, FBI Jones Logs; Ruby Dee and Ossie Davis to King, 28 July 1964, BR, 46:1.

44. King and Clarence Jones, 25 July 1964, FBI Jones Logs; King, "Statement on NY Riots," 27 July 1964, KPKC(3).

45. "Wagner Rejects Demands for Civilian Police Board," and "Text of Wagner's Statement on Harlem," *NYT*, 1 Aug. 1964; Button, *Black Violence*, 29–37; see Gilens, *Why Americans Hate Welfare*, on the dramatic racialization of poverty images in the media starting in 1964.

46. Andrew Young, "SCLC Dispatches Anti-Riot Team North," *SCLC Newsletter*, July–Aug. 1964.

47. King, "Negros-Whites Together," *NYAN*, 15 Aug. 1964. See also King, "A Knock at Midnight," 9 Aug. 1964, KPKC(3).

48. King, "Negroes Are Not Moving Too Fast," *Saturday Evening Post*, 4 Nov. 1964, and "*Playboy* Interview" (January 1965), in *A Testament of Hope*, ed. Washington, 179, 359–60.

49. King, "Speech to Southern Assn. of Political Scientists," 13 Nov. 1964, KPKC(3).

50. Andrew Young, "Keynote Address," and Joseph Lowery, "Address," 30 Sept. 1964, KPKC, 31:8; King, "Annual Report, SCLC," 28 Sept. 1964, 10, KPKC(3).

51. King, "Annual Report, SCLC," 28 Sept. 1964, 8; Anne Braden, "SCLC Convention," *SCLC Newsletter*, Oct. 1964.

52. Charles Sherrod, "From Sherrod," n.d., Charles Sherrod Papers, KC; Graham, *Civil Rights Era*, 163.

53. King, "Annual Report, SCLC," 28 Sept. 1964, 9, 12; King, "1199 Rally," Oct.

1964, National Union of Hospital and Health Care Employees Records, Catherwood Library, Cornell University; Charles Levy, "Scripto on Strike," *Nation*, 11 Jan. 1965, 31; King, "The American Dream," 4 July 1965, in *A Knock at Midnight*, ed. Carson and Holloran, 94; C. T. Vivian to Affiliates, 10 Dec. 1964, SCLC, 172:39; P. Foner, *Organized Labor and the Black Worker*, 360–61.

54. King, "Address Delivered at the John F. Kennedy Annual Award Dinner of the Catholic Interracial Council of Chicago," 9 Oct. 1964, Catholic Interracial Council Papers, Chicago Historical Society, 95; McGreevy, *Parish Boundaries*.

55. King, "Negroes Are Not Moving Too Fast," 180–81.

56. King, "Statement on Relationship of Poverty and War," 6 Nov. 1964, KPKC(3).

57. "Excerpts of Dr. King's Address to Oslo Students," 12 Dec. 1964, *NYT*, 18; "Dr. King, Johnson Discuss Poverty," *NYT*, 19 Dec. 1964, 32; King, "Remarks on Accepting the NYC Medallion," 17 Dec. 1964, KPKC(3); "Dr. King Awarded a City Medallion," *NYT*, 18 Dec. 1964; "City Showers Honors," *New York Herald Tribune*, 18 Dec. 1964.

58. Clarence Jones and Jesse Gray, 30 Sept. 1964, and Jones and Ossie Davis, 13 June 1964, FBI Jones Logs; Jesse Gray, "The Black Revolution A Struggle for Political Power," 19 Dec. 1964, 1–3, 5, and Jones to King, 22 Dec. 1964, both in KPKC, 13:26; Jesse Gray, interview by Katherine Shannon, 26 July 1967, p. 12, RJB.

59. Malcolm X and Breitman, *Malcolm X Speaks*, 20–21, 31–35, 55, 38–39, 42, 128.

60. Ibid., 69, 74–77, 121–22, 129. Materials on the Armory salute are in "Salute to MLK," CR, box 24.

61. King, "A Choice and a Promise," *NYAN*, 5 Dec. 1964.

Chapter 8. The Secret Heart of America

1. King, "Northern Problems More Complex," *SCLC Newsletter*, June–July 1965; King, "Annual Report, SCLC," 11 Aug. 1965, 6–7, KPKC(3).

2. King, "Civil Right No. 1," *New York Times Magazine*, 27 Mar. 1965; Matusow, *Unraveling of America*, 181–87; Fairclough, *To Redeem the Soul of America*, 228; "Selma," *PC*, 27 Mar. 1965; "Excerpts of Dr. King's Address," *NYT*, 12 Dec. 1964, 18.

3. "One Man—One Vote," *SCLC Newsletter*, Mar. 1964; King, "Selma and Right to Vote," *NYAN*, 30 Jan. 1965; King, "More Negroes in Jail Than on Voting Rolls," *NYAN*, 27 Feb. 1965; "Mass Arrests Fail to Halt Selma Drive," *PC*, 13 Feb. 1965.

4. Lyndon Johnson and A. Philip Randolph, 5 Nov. 1964, WH6411.09, LBJT; Johnson and King, 15 Jan. 1965, in *Reaching for Glory*, ed. Beschloss, 119, 160–63.

5. USGALLUP.63–674, Q008, 21 June 1963; USGALLUP.64–691, R11, 22 May 1964; USHARRIS.101066, R3, Oct. 1966, all in POLL; Garrow, *The FBI and Martin Luther King, Jr.*, 168, 170; Lyndon Johnson and Cartha DeLoach, 20 Nov. 1964, in *Reaching for Glory*, ed. Beschloss, 149; USGALLUP.633POS, Q22, Sept. 1964, POLL.

6. Fairclough, *To Redeem the Soul of America*, 232–41; Beschloss, ed., *Reaching for Glory*, 172, 217.

7. Garrow, *Protest at Selma*, 163; Fairclough, *To Redeem the Soul of America*, 240; Lyndon Johnson and Bill Moyers, 8 Mar. 1965, in *Reaching for Glory*, ed. Beschloss, 221–23.

8. Fairclough, *To Redeem the Soul of America,* 241–50; Garrow, *Bearing the Cross,* 404; Wallace quoted in Branch, *At Canaan's Edge,* 96.

9. Oates, *Let the Trumpet Sound,* 345–49; King, "Annual Report, SCLC," 28 Sept. 1964, KPKC(3), 11; "Excerpts from Dr. King's Montgomery Address," *NYT,* 26 Mar. 1965, 22.

10. King, "Let Justice Roll Down," *Nation,* 15 Mar. 1965, 272–73.

11. A. Philip Randolph, "Opening Remarks," Whitney Young, "Help Wanted: New Jobs for Negroes," Bayard Rustin, "The Influence of the Right and Left in the Civil Rights Movement," and handwritten notes of George Wiley, all at the State of the Race Conference, National Council of Churches, New York, 30–31 Jan. 1965, George Wiley Papers, SHSW, 3:6; Kotz and Kotz, *Passion for Equality,* 136–37; "Statement to the Press," Conference of Negro Leaders, 31 Jan. 1965, BR, 17:7; Bayard Rustin, "From Protest to Politics," *Commentary,* Feb. 1965, 117–19.

12. Stanley Levison to King, 7 Apr. 1965, KPKC, 14:40; Levison to King, 27 June 1965, KPKC, 14:41.

13. Harry G. Boyte, "New Values—A National Imperative," 19 May 1965, SCLC 173:23; Braden, "The Southern Freedom Movement in Perspective," 86–91; Carson, *In Struggle,* 167–68.

14. Whitney Young, "The Negro and the Vote," Institute for Policy Studies, 14 Apr. 1965, WMY, IV:131.

15. "SCLC Board Meeting Minutes," 1–2 Apr. 1965, KPKC, 29:5.

16. P. Foner, *Organized Labor and the Black Worker,* 368–70.

17. Lichtenstein, *State of the Union,* 187–91.

18. Robinson asked him to talk about "economic freedom" as the culmination of the "civil rights revolution." Cleveland Robinson to King, 13 Apr. 1965, CR, box 24; Garrow, *Bearing the Cross,* 427; P. Foner, *Organized Labor and the Black Worker,* 361.

19. Max Greenberg, "Organizing in the South," *RWDSU Record,* 9 Jan. 1966; "New Freedom March in Selma, Alabama," *RWDSU Record,* 19 Sept. 1965, NYU.

20. Cleveland Robinson to King, 3 July 1965, CR, box 24; King to Walter Reuther, 19 July 1965, quoted in Honey, "Martin Luther King Jr., and the Memphis Sanitation Strike," 148–49; Stanley Levison and King, 14 Feb. 1966, FBI Levison Logs; Draper, *Conflict of Interests,* 115–21. Eighty-three percent of all white union members in Alabama voted for Wallace for president in 1968.

21. "Telegram to Cesar Chavez from Martin Luther King," n.d. [Sept. 1966], KPKC, 5:21; Levy, *The New Left and Labor in the 1960s,* 134–35.

22. King, "Illinois AFL-CIO," Oct. 1965, KPKC(3), 2–4; King, "Speech to District 65," 17 Sept. 1965, KPKC(3).

23. Cleveland Robinson to King, 14 July 1967, CR; Cleveland Robinson, "Southern Christian Leadership Conference and Labor," in Robinson to Dorothy Cotton, 16 July 1968, CR, box 24.

24. Lawson, *Black Ballots,* 329–34.

25. King, "The Nightmare of Violence," *NYAN,* 13 Mar. 1965; S. Clark and Brown, *Ready from Within,* 68–69; Elder Wm. Ezra Greer to participant in the Selma Freedom Movement, 18 Apr. 1965, and Greer to King, 14 Apr. 1965, SCLC, 148:13.

26. NBC, *Meet the Press,* 28 Mar. 1965, 2–4; Peter Khiss, "Dr. King Suggests Nation Boycott Alabama Goods," *NYT,* 29 Mar. 1965; "Of the Call to Boycott in Alabama," 1965, and King, "After the March: An Open Letter to the American People,"

n.d., SCLC, 123:2; Stanley Levison and Clarence Jones, 6 Apr. 1965, FBI Jones Logs; The black president of the Mobile longshoremen's local protested he had not been consulted. Thomas Buckley, "Dr. King to Press Plan for Boycott," *NYT*, 31 Mar. 1965, 17; King, "The Boycott Explained," *NYAN*, 10 Apr. 1965.

27. Randolph T. Blackwell, "A Report on Selma, Alabama," 10 May 1965, KPKC, 28:21. Although SCLC did not follow up on Blackwell's suggestions, Amelia Boynton wrote to Blackwell in November about her plans to start a garment factory to employ poor blacks. Boynton to King, c/o Blackwell, 13 Nov. 1965, SCLC, 146:12; Blackwell, "Summary Report," 10 June 1965, KPKC, 28:22.

28. Matusow, *Unraveling of America*, 245–64; Lawson, *Black Ballots*, 336; T. Jackson, "The State, the Movement, and the Urban Poor," 418–21.

29. Ashmore, "Carry It On," 152, 164, 169, 266–67; SCLC, "Resolution of SCLC Board of Directors," April–May 1965, SCLC, 122:27; Sargent Shriver to King, 6 May 1965, SCLC, 5:22.

30. Williams in *SCLC Newsletter*, Feb. 1964; At a training workshop, the historian C. Vann Woodward lectured on the nineteenth-century Readjuster and Populist movements, describing the challenges and achievements of insurgent biracial coalitions. SCOPE orientation materials, SCLC, 168:8–9; King, "Let My People Vote," *NYAN*, 19 June 1965. See also King, "Meaning of Georgia Elections," *NYAN*, 3 July 1965.

31. Randolph Blackwell, "Confidential Memorandum" to King, 28 Aug. 1965, KPKC, 28:23; Pierce Barker to King, 12 Sept. 1965, KPKC, 35:1, corroborates Blackwell; Hosea Williams, "Annual Report Voter Registration and Political Education," n.d., SCLC, 144:25; Orange quoted in Fairclough, *To Redeem the Soul of America*, 268–69; "There seems to be very little material improvement for Negroes despite the Movement's accomplishments," wrote a Georgia SCOPE volunteer, who recommended that SCLC start filling in potholes and teaching people how to care for children's infected sores. See John Kricker's and other SCOPE Student Questionnaires, KPKC, 35:3; Ashmore, "Carry It On," 263–64.

32. Andrew Young, "Annual Report to the Field Foundation, 1963–1964," KPKC, 29:13; S. Clark and Brown, *Ready from Within*, 69–70.

33. R. Elizabeth Johns, "Refinement by Fire" (SCLC CEP, n.d.), HL, 9:12; "Citizenship School Has Trained 1,400; Still Has Far to Go," *SCLC Newsletter*, June–July 1965.

34. King, "Address Delivered at Rally," 10 Oct. 1965, KPKC(3); King, press release, 10 Oct. 1965, SCLC, 28:9; Williams demanded the rehiring of all blacks fired during the crisis, an end to police brutality, and the implementation of OEO programs that might subsidize black people's economic autonomy. Hosea Williams statements, 23 Sept. and 8 Oct. 1965, SCLC, 121:15–16; Robert L. Green, "Quarterly Report to the Board," 8 Nov. 1965, KPKC, 29:14; Randolph Blackwell to King, KPKC, 28:23; Blackwell, "Press Release on Crawfordville Enterprises," Feb. 1966, SCLC, 122:2; "Georgia Negroes Launch Business," *SCLC Newsletter*, Jan.–Feb. 1966; Garrow, *Bearing the Cross*, 450.

35. A letter from Randolph Blackwell to King of 14 Feb. 1966 complained that SCLC was not meeting its obligations to Crawfordville (KPKC, 28:23). King to Blackwell, 16 Aug. 1966, KPKC, 28:23; Reese Cleghorn, "Unskilled Men Find Magic in Dedication," *Atlanta Journal*, 6 Mar. 1967; Randolph Blackwell, "Annual Report: Southern Rural Action Project," 25 Aug. 1967, KPKC, 6:13; "SRA Final Report Submitted to

OEO," 28 Aug. 1969, in folder titled "Southern Rural Action, Inc. Randy Blackwell," KC; Blackwell in "Minutes, Board of Directors Meeting, Urban Training Center," Chicago, 1 Nov. 1968, SCLC, 48:15.

36. King, "Freedom's Crisis," *Nation,* 14 Mar. 1966, 289; King, "A Testament of Hope" (Jan. 1969), in *A Testament of Hope,* ed. Washington, 320; Garrow, *Bearing the Cross,* 447, 459, 471, 478.

37. King, "Let Justice Roll Down," *Nation,* 15 Mar. 1965, 272.

38. Garrow, *Bearing the Cross,* 422; Fairclough, *To Redeem the Soul of America,* 274; Gloster Current to branch presidents, 15 Apr. 1965, NAACP, Part IV, box A58; King, "Interview on Face the Nation," 29 Aug. 1965, KPKC(3); "King, Powell Unit May Both Visit Pittsburgh," *PC,* 4 Sept. 1965.

39. U.S. Congress, House Committee on Education and Labor Subcommittee on the War on Poverty Program, *Antipoverty Program in New York City and Los Angeles,* 24 July and 7 Aug. 1965 (Washington, D.C.: GPO, 1965), 145–46, 163, 183, 179–80; Augustus Hawkins, interview by Robert Wright, 28 Feb. 1969, RJB.

40. King, "Transcript of Interview, KNXT-TV, Los Angeles," 10 July 1965, KPKC(3).

41. Lewis, *King,* 306–7; Garrow, *Bearing the Cross,* 439–40. Garrow quotes Rustin's bizarre claim that Watts was the "first time [King] really understood" the need for "more than a hamburger."

42. As Gerald Horne has argued, after the suppression of the interracial left in the 1950s, rebellious blacks expressed intense racial resentments, since no "class discourse was available to explain to the black masses what was happening." Horne, *Fire This Time,* 109–10.

43. "Eisenhower, Kennedy View Riot Differently," *LAT,* 18 Aug. 1965; "Leaders at Odds," *CD,* 27 Aug. 1965; "McCone Heads Panel," *NYT,* 20 Aug. 1965; for similar liberal statements disassociating civil rights from urban violence, see comments by former Community Relations Service director LeRoy Collins in Gladwin Hill, "Coast Riot Area Gets $1.7 Million," *NYT,* 19 Aug. 1965; "Hawkins Likens Riot in L.A. to Selma Marches," *LAT,* 19 Aug. 1965.

44. "Dr. King Arrives Here," *LAT,* 18 Aug. 1965; King, "Statement on Arrival in Los Angeles," 17 Aug. 1965, KPKC(3); "Curfew Lifted in Los Angeles," *NYT,* 18 Aug. 1965; Mrs. Fred Coory to King, 25 Aug. 1965, 16:25; James Redford to King, 13 Aug. 1965, 16:28; O. O. Raab to King, 21 Aug. 1965, 16:31, all in *SCLC Micro.*

45. "Dr. King Hears Watts Protests over Heckling," *LAT,* 19 Aug. 1965; Kotz, *Judgment Days,* 343; Horne, *Fire This Time,* 183.

46. "King Assailed by Yorty," *LAT,* 20 Aug. 1965; "L.A. Lacks Leadership on Rights," *LAT,* 21 Aug. 1965.

47. King in Garrow, *Bearing the Cross,* 440; King and Lyndon Johnson, 20 Aug. 1965, WH6508.07, LBJT; King, "Feeling Alone in the Struggle," *NYAN,* 28 Aug. 1965.

48. "Yorty Raps Shriver over Poverty Funds," *LAT,* 19 Aug. 1965; "The State," *LAT,* 22 Aug. 1965; Horne, *Fire This Time,* 290; Hawkins interview by Wright, 10–12.

49. Governor's Commission on the Los Angeles Riots, *Violence in the City,* in *The Politics of Riot Commissions,* ed. Platt, 264–68; Rustin, "The Watts 'Manifesto' and the McCone Report," *Commentary,* Mar. 1966, in Rustin, *Down the Line,* 140–47; Fogelson, *Violence as Protest,* ch. 1.

50. "Gun Loaded in Riot Kills Curious Boy," *LAT,* 20 Aug. 1965.

51. King, "Speech to District 65," 17 Sept. 1965, KPKC(3); King, "Illinois AFL-CIO," 7 Oct. 1965, KPKC(3). King, "Seventh Annual Gandhi Memorial Lecture, Howard University," 6 Nov. 1966, KPKC(3). See also King, *Where Do We Go from Here?* 130, and King, "Statement," 15 Dec. 1966, in U.S. Senate, *Federal Role in Urban Affairs*, 2981–82.

Chapter 9. The War on Poverty and the Democratic Socialist Dream

1. Lyndon Johnson, "To Fulfill These Rights," 4 June 1965, in *The Moynihan Report*, ed. Rainwater and Yancey, 125–31; Weiss, *Whitney M. Young, Jr.*, 152; Carter, "'Two Nations,'" 163–64.

2. King and Lyndon Johnson, 7 July 1965, in *Reaching for Glory*, ed. Beschloss, 389; Johnson and King, 20 Aug. 1965, WH6508.07, LBJT; King, *Interview on Face the Nation*, 29 Aug. 1965, KPKC (3).

3. King, "The American Dream," 4 July 1965, in *A Knock at Midnight*, ed. Carson and Holloran, 91–92.

4. King, "Address, Syracuse University," 15 July 1965, KPKC(3); King, "Annual Report, SCLC," 11 Aug. 1965, p. 9, KPKC(3); King, "A Great Challenge Derived from a Serious Dilemma," address delivered to the Hungry Club, Atlanta, 15 Dec. 1965, 4, KPKC(3).

5. Whitney Young, "White House Conference on Education," 21 July 1965, WMY, IV:134.

6. Robert L. Green, "Characteristics of Students at the Citizenship Education Program Workshop," 22 Nov. 1965, KPKC, 29:14; SCLC press release, 15 Dec. 1965, SCLC, 121:19.

7. Daniel Patrick Moynihan, "The President and the Negro: The Moment Lost," *Commentary*, Feb. 1967, 31–45; Harrington, *Fragments of the Century*, 204–5; Wofford, *Of Kennedys and Kings*, 319; Matusow, *Unraveling of America*, 250–51; Carter, "'Two Nations,'" 164; "Statement by the President on August Employment and Unemployment," KPKC, 26:8.

8. King, "Annual Report, SCLC," 11 Aug. 1965, 8–9; King, "Illinois AFL-CIO," 7 Oct. 1965, 4–5, KPKC(3); Brown and Erie, "Blacks and the Legacy of the Great Society," 319.

9. King, "Freedom's Crisis: The Last Steep Ascent," *Nation*, 14 Mar. 1966, 291.

10. King, "Illinois AFL-CIO," 5–6; Liebow, *Tally's Corner*, 222–24. See also Lipsitz, *A Life in the Struggle*, for similar conclusions reached by grassroots activist Ivory Perry.

11. King, "Annual Report, SCLC," 11 Aug. 1965, 9; King, "The Violence Of Poverty," *NYAN*, 1 Jan. 1966.

12. King, "Freedom's Crisis," 288–89.

13. Lee Rainwater and William Yancey, introduction, and Daniel Patrick Moynihan, "The Negro Family: The Case for National Action," Mar. 1965, in *The Moynihan Report*, ed. Rainwater and Yancey, 1–15, 47–94; Moynihan, "The President and the Negro," 41. See also Patterson, *America's Struggle Against Poverty*, chs. 7, 10, 11. Until 1962, the program was called Aid to Dependent Children,

14. Office of Economic Opportunity, "The American Poor," 1965, in *Social Sci-*

ence and Urban Crisis, ed. Victor B. Ficker and Herbert S. Graves (New York: Macmillan, 1971), 198; K. Clark and Harlem Youth Opportunities Unlimited, *Youth in the Ghetto,* 10–11; K. Clark, *Dark Ghetto.* Clark resigned before HARYOU was operational, claiming that it had been taken over, its purposes subverted, by Adam Clayton Powell's Harlem political machine. See Matusow, *Unraveling of America,* 257–58. Clark was chastened later by the lack of sophistication among the ghetto poor with whom he worked, concluding that they could be "easily bought" by political entrepreneurs.

15. K. Clark and Harlem Youth Opportunities Unlimited, *Youth in the Ghetto,* 19–20, 38–39; K. Clark, *Dark Ghetto,* 1–9; Silberman, *Crisis in Black and White,* 348.

16. See *The Moynihan Report,* ed. Rainwater and Yancey: Whitney Young, 415–16, James Farmer, 410, Bayard Rustin, 422; Anna Arnold Hedgeman, interview by Katherine Shannon, 25 July 1967, RJB; Whitney Young, "Address to North and South Jersey Chapters of the National Association of Social Workers," 29 Mar. 1966, WMY, IV:137. The historian Stanley Elkins had traveled to Washington to explain how slave families had been so damaged that a nearly permanent matriarchal adaptation formed like an oyster's shell around the humiliated and emasculated black father. Stanley Elkins, personal communication with the author, spring 1997.

17. Benjamin Payton, "A New Trend in Civil Rights," in *The Moynihan Report,* ed. Rainwater and Yancey, 395–402, and the editors' comments, 235–39. Allen Matusow argues that "thunderous denunciation" stemmed from wounded pride: Matusow, *Unraveling of America,* 197; George Wiley, "A CORE Challenge to the White House Conference," 18 Nov. 1965, George Wiley Papers, SHSW, 7:1; Tom Kahn to Irving Howe, 4 Aug. 1965, LID, folder 30.

18. King, "The Dignity of Family Life," 29 Oct. 1965, in *The Moynihan Report,* ed. Rainwater and Yancey, 402–9; see O'Connor, *Poverty Knowledge,* ch. 8, for a useful summary of "poverty's culture wars."

19. King, "The Negro Family: A Challenge to National Action," 27 Jan. 1966, SCLC, 28; King, "Freedom's Crisis," 291; King, "Sermon: Good Samaritan," 28 Aug. 1966, 6, KPKC(3); Appy, *Working-Class War,* 31.

20. Moynihan, "The President and the Negro," 41–43; King and Stanley Levison, 4 Feb. 1967, *MLK-Levison FBI Micro,* 6:699–702.

21. Carter, "'Two Nations,'" 172–78; Hedgeman interview; Clarence Jones and King, 13 Nov. 1965, FBI Jones Logs; Lawson, *In Pursuit of Power,* 45–47; Kotz, *Judgment Days,* 359.

22. Carter, "'Two Nations'"; D'Emilio, *Lost Prophet;* "A Freedom Budget for All Americans" and supporting testimony by Rustin and A. Philip Randolph can be found in U.S. Senate, *Federal Role in Urban Affairs,* 1853–2013. For King's marginal role in the White House conference, see Lewis, *King,* 308–12; Oates, *Let the Trumpet Sound,* 381. John Lewis, Ossie Davis, Ruby Dee, Whitney Young, Roy Wilkins, Pauli Murray, C. Vann Woodward, Kenneth Clark, Daniel Bell, Gunnar Myrdal, and I. W. Abel of the steelworkers all signed the Freedom Budget document.

23. "Text of President's Special Message to Congress," *NYT,* 27 Jan. 1966, 20; "Daley Says Johnson Will Need More Funds," *NYT,* 5 Mar. 1966, 9; King, "Freedom's Crisis," 290.

24. Robert Coles, *The South Goes North* (Boston: Little, Brown, 1967), 200–201.

25. Robert Coles, "The White Northerner: Pride and Prejudice," *Atlantic Monthly,* June 1966, 53–57.

26. "Disgusted citizen" to King, 10 Aug. 1966, *SCLC Micro,* 22:21; King, "Annual Report, SCLC," 11 Aug. 1965, p. 9. For a historical explanation of the correlation between hostility to welfare and racism, see Gilens, *Why Americans Hate Welfare.*

27. King, "Freedom's Crisis," 290.

28. Marris and Rein, *Dilemmas of Social Reform;* Boyle, *The UAW and the Heyday of American Liberalism.* See collected news clippings and policy papers in folders "Poverty: Citizens Crusade Against," Julius Bernstein Papers, NYU, and George Wiley Papers, SHSW, 3:1–2.

29. Farmer, *Lay Bare the Heart,* 203–5; "Policy Snags Literacy Project," *NYT,* 5 Mar. 1966, 10; Matusow, *Unraveling of America,* 253–54.

30. Andrew Young, "Keynote Address," 11 Aug. 1965, KPKC, 31:11; King and Stanley Levison, 1 July 1966, *MLK-Levison FBI Micro,* 6:1–6; Leon Sullivan, "Statement," in U.S. Senate, *Federal Role in Urban Affairs,* part 12, 2574–75, 2586–89.

31. Nancy J. Weiss, "Whitney M. Young, Jr.," in *Black Leaders of the Twentieth Century,* ed. John Hope Franklin and August Meier (Chicago: University of Illinois Press, 1982), 335–36; Young, "Address to North and South Jersey Chapters."

32. T. Jackson, "The State, the Movement, and the Urban Poor," 418–30, 430n49; King, "To Charter Our Course," Frogmore, S.C., 29 May 1967, KPKC(3).

33. Clark and Hopkins, *A Relevant War Against Poverty,* 252; Lipsitz, *A Life in the Struggle,* uses Gramsci to vividly illuminate Ivory Perry's career; Kerstein and Judd, "Achieving Less Influence with More Democracy"; Kelley, "The Black Poor and the Politics of Opposition," 325–27.

34. Leonard Mitchell to King, 24 Nov. 1965, KPKC, 28:5; Randolph Blackwell, "Wilcox County, New Structures Versus Old Problems—A Plea," 11 Mar. 1966, SCLC, 144:25; Ashmore, "Carry It On," 289–90.

35. "Program 'First' for SCLC," Staff News, Dec. 1966, SCLC, 123:18; John Cook to King, 22 Nov. 1966, KPKC, 28:7; King, "Annual Report, SCLC," 10 Aug. 1966, KPKC(3).

36. Mayers quoted in *Voices of Freedom,* ed. Hampton and Fayer, 272, 277; Stokely Carmichael, "We Are Going to Use the Term 'Black Power,'" 28 July 1966, in *Black Nationalism in America,* ed. Bracey, Meier, and Rudwick, 475–76.

37. Charles Sherrod, "Report on the Benefits of Social Security," 1966, Charles Sherrod Papers, KC, 3:7.

38. Shirley Mesher, "Selma—One Year Later—What?" SCLC, 144:25.

39. "Protest from the People of Dallas County Regarding the Community Action Program," n.d., SCLC, 144:25.

40. King, "Statement," 23 Oct. 1967, National Advisory Commission on Civil Disorders [Kerner Commission], in *Civil Rights During the Johnson Administration,* ed. LBJL, reels 4–5:2815; Greenberg, *The Devil Has Slippery Shoes,* 736–37.

41. Dittmer, *Local People,* 374; "Delta Ministry Commission Report," 1 Oct. 1965, Delta Ministry Papers, KC, 2:3.

42. "Press Conference," Feb. 1966, Delta Ministry Papers, KC, 3:16.

43. King and SCLC board of directors to Lyndon Johnson et al., 10 Aug. 1966, KPKC, 13:9.

44. Hamer quoted in Dittmer, *Local People,* 381–82; King, "Statement," 23 Oct. 1967, 2815; King, "Why We Must Go to Washington," 15 Jan. 1968, 2–3, KPKC(3).

45. U.S. Senate, Committee on Labor and Public Welfare, *Examination of the War*

on Poverty, Hearings, Jackson, Mississippi, 10 Apr. 1967 (Washington, D.C.: GPO, 1967), 580–95, 642–57.

46. SCLC Board of Directors, "Resolution of Meeting," 13 Apr. 1966, KPKC, 29:6.

47. See especially King, "Annual Report, SCLC," 28 Sept. 1964, KPKC(3); King, "Statement," 15 Dec. 1966, in U.S. Senate, *Federal Role in Urban Affairs;* King, "United Neighborhood Houses," 6 Dec. 1966, KPKC(3); King, "New Politics Convention," 31 Aug. 1967, KPKC(3); King, "Frogmore Retreat," 14 Nov. 1966, 16, KPKC(3); and King, *Where Do We Go from Here?* ch. 5.

48. King, "Frogmore Retreat," 21.

49. King, "Statement," in U.S. Senate, *Federal Role in Urban Affairs,* 2970–71; King, "United Neighborhood Houses," 6–7; King, "Frogmore Retreat," 16–18.

50. King, "Statement," in U.S. Senate, *Federal Role in Urban Affairs,* 2969; King, *Where Do We Go from Here?* 164.

51. King, "Statement," in U.S. Senate, *Federal Role in Urban Affairs,* 2792–93; King, "United Neighborhood Houses," 4–5, 9–10; King, "Frogmore Retreat," 21–22.

52. King, "United Neighborhood Houses," 11–13; King, "Statement," in U.S. Senate, *Federal Role in Urban Affairs,* 2968.

53. King, "United Neighborhood Houses," 6–8; King, "Frogmore Retreat," 23.

54. King, "Frogmore Retreat," 21; King, "Why We Must Go to Washington," 11; E. Foner, *Story of American Freedom,* 88.

55. King, "Statement," in U.S. Senate, *Federal Role in Urban Affairs,* 2971–72.

56. King, *Where Do We Go from Here?* 193. Johnson quoted in Kotz, *Judgment Days,* 332.

57. Helstein quoted in "Minutes of the Executive Board, A. Philip Randolph Institute," 19 Sept. 1966, SCLC, 42:1.

Chapter 10. Egyptland

1. King, "Statement," in U.S. Senate, *Federal Role in Urban Affairs,* 2974.

2. Ibid., 2968, 2983; King, *Where Do We Go from Here?* 201; Self, *American Babylon* is only one among a spate of recent studies to analyze these suburban structures. See especially Lassiter, *The Silent Majority.*

3. U.S. Commission on Civil Rights, *A Time to Listen, A Time to Act* (Washington, D.C.: GPO, 1967), 7, 21–26, 47–48, 52–53, 33–37.

4. King, "May 17—11 Years Later," *NYAN,* 22 May 1965; King, "Address, Syracuse University," 15 July 1965, KPKC(3); Warren, *Who Speaks for the Negro?* 215–16.

5. King, "July 1965 March on Chicago Speech," SCLC, 28:4; Oates, *Let the Trumpet Sound,* 358.

6. King then led a march of 1,000 on the White House in support of D.C. home rule legislation. "King Shifts Emphasis to 'Economic Freedom,'" *PC,* 14 Aug. 1965; Garrow, *Bearing the Cross,* 436, 448; Matusow, *Unraveling of America,* 201–3. King quoted in Fairclough, *To Redeem the Soul of America,* 286.

7. Young, "Political Power," n.d., SCLC, 28:14; James Bevel, "The Sickness in America Today," in *Urban America: Crisis and Opportunity,* ed. Jim Chard and Jon York (New York: Dickenson, 1969), 95; Bevel, "SCLC—Chicago Project," 26 Oct. 1965, KPKC, 5:26; King, "Annual Report, SCLC," 11 Aug. 1965, 6–7, KPKC(3).

8. Miller quoted in Kotz and Kotz, *Passion for Equality*, 166.

9. Clark quoted in Whitney M. Young, Jr., "White Status Symbol," *NYAN*, 4 Dec. 1965.

10. King, "The Chicago Plan," 7 Jan. 1966, 3–5, KPKC(3); King, "Why We Are in Chicago," *NYAN*, 5 Feb. and 12 Mar. 1966.

11. King, "The Chicago Plan," 5–7.

12. "Len O'Connor," 7 Jan. 1966, KPKC, 5:27; King quoted in Ralph, *Northern Protest*, ch. 2; Bryant quoted in *Voices of Freedom*, ed. Hampton and Fayer, 304–5; Anderson and Pickering, *Confronting the Color Line*, 170, 191.

13. "Dr. King Occupies a Flat in Slums," 27 Jan. 1966, 35; "Dr. King Is Sued," *NYT*, 5 Mar. 1966, 10; King, Bayard Rustin, and Stanley Levison, 1 Feb. 1966, Levison and Adelle Cantor, 14 Feb. 1966, and Levison and "Un," 1 Mar. 1966, FBI Levison Logs.

14. King, "Chicago Freedom Festival," 12 Mar. 1966, 1, KPKC(3); Garrow, *Bearing the Cross*, 466–67; Ralph, *Northern Protest*, 70–75; King, "Interview During Chicago Gathering with CCCO," 18 Mar. 1966, KPKC(3); P. Foner, *Organized Labor and the Black Worker*, 362–63.

15. "Dr. King Stirs Chicago But Still Lacks a Program," *NYT*, 24 Mar. 1966, 33; Stanley Levison and Clarence Jones, 23 Apr. 1966, FBI Levison Logs.

16. King, "Chicago Freedom Festival," 3; King, "Freedom's Crisis," *Nation*, 14 Mar. 1966, 291.

17. Bevel in Mary Lou Finley, "The Open Housing Marches" (Spring 1967), in *Chicago 1966*, ed. Garrow, 66–68; James Bevel, King, and Andrew Young in Anderson and Pickering, *Confronting the Color Line*, 200–201; Jesse L. Jackson, "A Strategy to End Slums," 31 May 1966, SCLC, 149:35; Alvin Pitcher, "The Chicago Freedom Movement: What Is It?" (November 1966), in *Chicago, 1966*, ed. Garrow, 176–77; Ralph, *Northern Protest*, 98–105.

18. "Leaders Climbing on Dr. King Bandwagon," *CD*, 17 June 1966, 1; "Rally Drawing Many City Segments," *CD*, 8 July 1966; "Ministers Miffed," *CD*, 17 July 1966; "Chicago Archbishop," *NYT*, 11 July 1966, 19; P. Foner, *Organized Labor and the Black Worker*, 364.

19. King, "Soldier Field Rally," 10 July 1966, 1–5, KPKC(3).

20. Harold Baron of the Chicago Urban League, George Riddick of the Chicago Church Federation, and Alvin Pitcher co-authored the "Program of the Chicago Freedom Movement, July 1966," pp. 1–5, SCLC, 150:13. Reprinted in *Chicago, 1966*, ed. Garrow, 97–109.

21. These demands included the equalization of school expenditures throughout the city, federal enforcement of Title VI against the Chicago Board of Education, and the hiring of minority teachers; better garbage collection, street cleaning, and building inspections in poor black neighborhoods; and democratic control of urban redevelopment projects. "Program of the Chicago Freedom Movement," 7–12.

22. King, "I Need Victories," address to rally, Chicago, 12 July 1966, KPKC(3); "Two Are Shot as Violence Erupts Again," *NYT*, 14 July 1966; "Troops Restoring Order," *NYT*, 16 July 1966.

23. "Chicago Calmer," *NYT*, 17 July 1966, 60; Privately with Levison, Young doubted that SCLC could stop hostile local people from "encouraging the riots," but Levison insisted that "it's Daley's riot, not your riot." SCLC must aggressively put the onus on Daley's "municipal apparatus" for ignoring "the whole body of grievances of

the people" before King got blamed for failing to stop the violence. Stanley Levison and Andrew Young, 15 July 1966, *MLK-FBI File*, ed. Friendly and Gallen, 484–85; "Chicago Officials Voice Concern over Apparent Gang Alliance," *NYT*, 20 July 1966, 23; "Chicago Names Police Panel," *NYT*, 26 July 1966.

24. Ruth Smyte to King, 11 Aug. 1966, *SCLC Micro 1*, 22:18; King, "Annual Report," 10 Aug. 1966, KPKC(3); King, "The Core of It," *NYAN*, 30 July 1966.

25. King, "The Non-Violence of Dr. M. L. King," *NYAN*, 30 July 1966; Fogelson, *Violence as Protest*, ch. 1; "Chicago Officials Voice Concern," *NYT*, 20 July 1966, 23.

26. "Rights Chiefs," *NYT*, 11 July 1966, 19; King, "Annual Report," 10 Aug. 1966, 19–20.

27. King, "Annual Report," 10 Aug. 1966, 5; "Chicago, Baltimore Marchers Mobbed," *PC*, 13 Aug. 1966.

28. "Rock Hits Dr. King," *NYT*, 8 Aug. 1966, 1; Karen Koko, "Chicago's Race March," *National Catholic Reporter*, 10 Aug. 1966; Garrow, *Bearing the Cross*, 495–503; Fairclough, *To Redeem the Soul of America*, 298–99; Finley, "Open Housing Marches," 22–23.

29. John McKnight, "The Summit Negotiations: Chicago," 17–26 Aug. 1966, in *Chicago, 1966*, ed. Garrow, 129–30.

30. McKnight, "The Summit Negotiations," 131; Garrow, *Bearing the Cross*, 503–25; "The 'Summit Agreement,'" 26 Aug. 1966, in *Chicago 1966*, ed. Garrow, 147–54.

31. King, *Where Do We Go from Here?* 158; Oates, *Let the Trumpet Sound*, 400–404; Garrow, *Protest at Selma*, 165.

32. Matusow, *Unraveling of America*, 206–7; Sundquist, *Politics and Policy*, 279–81; "LBJ Accused of Surrender," *CD*, 2 Sept. 1966, 36.

33. Young quoted in *Voices of Freedom*, ed. Hampton and Fayer, 302; King, "Annual Report," 10 Aug. 1966, 26; Bevel, "Sickness in America Today," 95.

34. King, "Freedom's Crisis," 288–89; Donald Janson, "Dr. King and 500 Jeered," *NYT*, 22 Aug. 1966, 1, 37; King, *Where Do We Go from Here?* 3–4; Mrs. Rich to King, 6 Aug. 1966, *SCLC Micro 1*, 22:18.

35. King, "Why I Must March: Address Delivered at Rally," 18 Aug. 1966, KPKC(3); King, "Statement on the Electoral Returns and White Backlash," Nov. 1966, KPKC(3); Califano, *Triumph and Tragedy of Lyndon Johnson*, 153; John Herbers, "Rights Backers Fear a Backlash," *NYT*, 21 Sept. 1966. Low- and middle-income ethnic voters on the northwest and southwest sides where open housing marches had occurred overwhelmingly voted for Republican Charles Percy. Ralph, *Northern Protest*, 222. On the war and inflation, see Hodgson, *America in Our Time*, and Appy, *Working-Class War*. Gallup gave 2,417 Americans three reasons for expected Republican gains in the House: equal numbers gave primacy to "the administration's handling of Vietnam, discontent over the high cost of living, [and] racial problems": USGALLUP.736, Q20, 21 Oct. 1966, and USGALLUP.742, Q14B, 9 Mar. 1967, POLL.

36. P. Foner, *Organized Labor and the Black Worker*, 364; King, "Which Way Its Soul Shall Go," voter registration rally, Louisville, 2 Aug. 1967, KPKC(3).

37. Garrow, *Bearing the Cross*, 484–96, 533–34; King, "Statement," 14 Oct. 1966, KPKC(3).

38. King, "Meredith March Rally Speech," Memphis, Tenn., 7 June 1966; King, "Transcripts of Speeches and Statements Along the Meredith March, Grenada, Miss.," 16 June 1966; King, "Address Delivered During the Meredith March," West Marks,

Miss., 12 June 1966; King, "Address Delivered at Rally," Yazoo City, Miss., 21 June 1966, all in KPKC(3); Carson, *In Struggle,* ch. 14.

39. "Kennedy Clashes with CORE Chief," *NYT,* 9 Dec. 1966, 1; Floyd McKissick, 11 Dec. 1966, in U.S. Senate, *Federal Role in Urban Affairs,* part 11, 2284–2315.

40. King, *Where Do We Go from Here?* 52–53.

41. Lawson, *In Pursuit of Power,* 92.

42. King, "Interview Following Address," University of California–Berkeley, 17 May 1967, audiotape, Pacifica Radio Archives, Los Angeles; King, "Address to Ministers Leadership Training Program," Miami, Fla., 19 Feb. 1968, SCLC, 26.

43. King, "Sermon at Ebenezer Baptist Church: Good Samaritan," 28 Aug. 1966, 8–9, KPKC(3).

44. King, "Judging Others," Ebenezer Baptist Church, 4 June 1967, KPKC; King, "Statement," in U.S. Senate, *Federal Role in Urban Affairs,* 2993.

45. King, "Statement," in U.S. Senate, *Federal Role in Urban Affairs,* 2989, 2992; King, "Sermon at Ebenezer Baptist Church: Good Samaritan," 7; King, *Where Do We Go from Here?* 131–32.

46. King, "Statement," in U.S. Senate, *Federal Role in Urban Affairs,* 2990–91.

47. Garrow, *Bearing the Cross,* 535; King, "Press Conference on Public Housing Agencies," 25 Mar. 1967, KPKC(3).

48. King, "Statement," in U.S. Senate, *Federal Role in Urban Affairs,* 2985; King, *Where Do We Go from Here?* 201–2.

49. King, "Seventh Annual Gandhi Memorial Lecture, Howard University," 6 Nov. 1966, KPKC(3); King, "Speech to Staff Retreat, Frogmore, South Carolina," 14 Nov. 1966, 6–7, KPKC(3); King, "Sermon at Ebenezer Baptist Church: Good Samaritan," 5.

50. King "Statement on Voter Registration Drive," 2 Dec. 1966, KPKC(3); King, "Press Conference at Liberty Baptist Church," Chicago, 24 Mar. 1967, KPKC(3); King, "Chicago, One Year Later," 1967, SCLC, 28:31.

51. Daley boosted his margin in the white ethnic wards from 52 percent in 1963 to 76 percent in 1967. Black voter turnout began a long-term slide that paralleled general declines in low-income voting, but Daley still held 70 percent of the black vote. Kleppner, *Chicago Divided,* 74–75; Ralph, *Northern Protest,* 223, 226.

52. King, *Where Do We Go from Here?* 154, 61–62. King and SCLC staff canvassed Cleveland neighborhoods for black mayoral candidate Carl Stokes that summer. (Stokes did not thank him, however, calculating that King and the city's militants lost him more white votes than they mobilized black votes in a city with a black minority.) Stokes in *Voices of Freedom,* ed. Hampton and Fayer, 417.

53. King, "To Charter Our Course for the Future," SCLC retreat, Frogmore, S.C., 29 May 1967, KPKC(3); King, *Where Do We Go from Here?* 155–56.

54. King, "Press Conference," 24 Mar. 1967, KPKC(3).

55. "Tenant Unions of the Union to End Slums to Coordinating Committee of the Chicago Freedom Movement," 30 Nov. 1966, KPKC, 46:17; King, "Statement on the Establishment of a Housing Redevelopment Project," 20 Dec. 1967, KPKC(3); King, "Interview by C. Johnson," Chicago, 28 July 1967, KPKC(3).

56. King, *Where Do We Go from Here?* 156; King, "Statement," in U.S. Senate, *Federal Role in Urban Affairs,* 2979, 2985, 2991–92; King, "Chicago, One Year Later";

King, "SCLC Convention," 16 Aug. 1967, KPKC(3); Anderson and Pickering, *Confronting the Color Line,* 292.

57. Helen Jones to King, 13 July 1965, KPKC, 5:24; King, "Speech to Englewood Community, Chicago, Ill.," 17 Nov. 1966, KPKC(3); King, "Statement," in U.S. Senate, *Federal Role in Urban Affairs,* 2977; King, "Shaw Urban Renewal Public Meeting," 27 Mar. 1967, KPKC(3).

58. King, *Where Do We Go from Here?* 157, 200; King, "Statement," in U.S. Senate, *Federal Role in Urban Affairs,* 2975; King, "Annual Report," 10 Aug. 1966.

59. King and Stanley Levison, 1 July 1966, *MLK-Levison FBI Micro,* 6:1–6; King quoted in SCLC press release, 17 July 1967, SCLC, 46:11; King, "Statement Re Chicago Adult Education Project," 26 July 1967, KPKC(3); King, "New Politics Convention," 31 Aug. 1967, 3–4, KPKC(3); Robert L. Green, "Progress Report, SCLC Chicago Adult Education Project," 12 Sept. 1967, SCLC, 151:6.

60. King, *Where Do We Go from Here?* 200; T. Jackson, "The State, the Movement, and the Urban Poor," 434–35; Kotz and Kotz, *Passion for Equality;* Francis Fox Piven and Richard Cloward, "Birth of a Movement" (1967), and "Dissensus Politics: A Strategy for Winning Economic Rights" (1968), in *Politics of Turmoil,* 127–40, 161–76. On Birmingham as a model, see "The Weight of the Poor: A Strategy to End Poverty," *Nation,* 2 May 1966; Piven, personal communication with the author, Nov. 2000.

61. SCLC press release, "'Green Power' for Negroes," 23 Nov. 1966, SCLC, 122:6; King, "Speech to Operation Breadbasket Meeting," 25 Mar. 1967, KPKC(3); Jesse Jackson, "Strategy to End Slums," 31 May 1966, SCLC, 139:45; P. Foner, *Organized Labor and the Black Worker,* 365.

62. King, "Speech to Operation Breadbasket Meeting," 5–6; Young quoted in Fairclough, *To Redeem the Soul of America,* 354; Fannie G. Perryman to King, 21 Sept. 1967, SCLC, 172:3.

63. King quoted in Garrow, *Bearing the Cross,* 585, 569; King, "The Crisis in Civil Rights," 12 July 1967, KPKC(3).

64. Walter Fauntroy, "Keynote Address," SCLC convention, 9 Aug. 1966, KPKC, 31:13; Bayard Rustin, "A Way Out of the Exploding Ghetto," *New York Times Magazine,* 13 Aug. 1967; "October 1966 Black Panther Party Platform and Program: What We Want, What We Believe," in Philip S. Foner, ed., *The Black Panthers Speak* (New York: Lippincott, 1970), 2.

65. King, *Where Do We Go from Here?* 49–50.

66. King, "Which Way Its Soul Shall Go"; King, *Where Do We Go from Here?* 201–2.

67. King, "Statement," in U.S. Senate, *Federal Role in Urban Affairs,* 2979; King, "The Role of the Behavioral Scientist in the Civil Rights Movement," 1 Sept. 1967, in *Journal of Social Issues* 25, no. 1 (1968), p. 7. Lassiter, *Silent Majority.*

68. King, "Transforming a Neighborhood," National Association of Real Estate Brokers, San Francisco, 10 Aug. 1967, KPKC(3).

69. King, "New Politics Convention," 31 Aug. 1967, 8, KPKC(3). King, "Interview on the *Arlene Francis Show,*" 19 June 1967, KPKC(3).

70. Rustin, "A Way Out of the Exploding Ghetto"; "Reminiscences of Bayard Rustin," 1987, p. 224, CUOH; Warren, *Who Speaks for the Negro?* 213; Bayard Rustin,

"Draft of Statement on Guiding Principles of the Civil Rights Movement," 12 Oct. 1966, KPKC(3).

Chapter 11. The World House

1. M. Young, *The Vietnam Wars*, chs. 1–10; Lyndon Johnson and Richard Russell, 27 May 1964, in *Taking Charge*, ed. Beschloss, 366–68; Johnson and Robert McNamara, 21 June 1965, in *Reaching for Glory*, ed. Beschloss, 365.

2. Shapiro, "The Vietnam War," 119; King, "Mighty Army of Love," *NYAN*, 7 Nov. 1964; King, "Nobel Prize Acceptance Speech," 10 Dec. 1964, in *A Testament of Hope*, ed. Washington, 226; King, "Nobel Lecture," 11 Dec. 1964, KPKC, 4:36; "Excerpts of Dr. King's Address," *NYT*, 12 Dec. 1964, 18; King, "Selma and Right to Vote," *NYAN*, 30 Jan. 1965.

3. Zaroulis and Sullivan, *Who Spoke Up?* 20, 26; Tracy, *Direct Action*, 128–33; King and Clarence Jones, 14 Feb. 1965, FBI Jones Logs; Jones to King, 7 May 1965, KPKC, 13:27.

4. Shapiro, "The Vietnam War," 122; Dittmer, *Local People*, 351–52; John Herbers, "Civil Rights and War," *NYT*, 5 July 1965, 4.

5. Lyndon Johnson and King, 7 July 1965, in *Reaching for Glory*, ed. Beschloss, 388–89.

6. "Text of the President's Address on U.S. Policies in Vietnam," *NYT*, 8 Apr. 1965, 16; "Dr. King to Send Appeal to Hanoi," *NYT*, 13 Aug. 1965; Shapiro, "The Vietnam War," 123.

7. King and Lyndon Johnson, 20 Aug. 1965, WH6508.07_8578, LBJT. I differ with Taylor Branch, *At Canaan's Edge*, 308, who interprets Johnson's command as a reassurance that King did not "leave that impression." M. Young, *The Vietnam Wars*, 151–60, 179.

8. Fairclough, *To Redeem the Soul of America*, 273; Garrow, *Bearing the Cross*, 445; Levison Log, 25 Aug. 1965, in *MLK-FBI File*, ed. Friedly and Gallen, 434, 435; King quoted in CBS News, *Face the Nation*, 29 Aug. 1965, v. 8, 206–11; Gallup poll, 29 Oct. 1965, USGALLUP.719, Q019C, POLL.

9. King still wanted to make a strong moral condemnation of the war, but Stanley Levison firmly declared, "you're not the person to do this." Conference call between Levison and King, 28 Sept. 1965, Levison Log, in *MLK-FBI File*, ed. Friedly and Gallen, 436–38; King, "Address Delivered at the Fiftieth Anniversary of the Women's International League for Peace and Freedom," 15 Oct. 1965, KPKC(3); King, "Interview by Arnold Michaelis," 1 Dec. 1965, Colgate-Rochester Divinity School, Rochester, New York; John Herbers, "Peace March Set in Capital Today," *NYT*, 27 Nov. 1965, 12; C. King, *My Life*, 293.

10. Letters in *SCLC Micro*: Fred Peters, 12 June 1966, 15:430–32; Mrs. Fred Coory, 23 Aug. 1965, 12:100–102; Frank Lee, 15 Jan. 1966, 14:224–27; Paul Heany, 12 Jan. 1966, 14:423–24.

11. Letters in *SCLC Micro*: Yasuharo Shima to King, 4 Aug. 1965, 12:2–4; Everett Patrick to King, 29 Jan. 1966, 14:404; Mrs. James W. Donahue to King, 24 Sept. 1965, *SCLC Micro*, 13:94; Ruth Rosenwald to King, 26 Jan. 1966, *SCLC Micro*, 14:466–68; Martin Degan to King, 22 Sept. 1965, 13:201. Harris obtained identical results the month

before with the wording slightly changed to a neutralist government "neither on our side nor on the side of the Communists." In October and November, the neutralist option scored low (5–6 percent), because Harris included it among four options, which included total victory and a UN supervised withdrawal (57 percent favored in November). USHARRIS.012466, R2, USHARRIS.66FEB1,R1, USHARRIS.102566,R1, USHARRIS.66NOV2, R1, POLL. Branch, *At Canaan's Edge*, 660.

12. King, "Address Delivered to the South Africa Benefit of the American Committee on Africa at Hunter College," 10 Dec. 1965, KPKC(3).

13. Shapiro, "The Vietnam War," 147; King, "Julian Bond and the Constitution," *NYAN*, 5 Feb. 1966; Carson, *In Struggle*, 188–89.

14. King, "My Jewish Brother!" *NYAN*, 26 Feb. 1966; King, "Who Are We?" 5 Feb. 1966, KPKC(3); Shapiro, "The Vietnam War," 129; King, Bayard Rustin, and Stanley Levison, 1 Feb. 1966, FBI Levison Logs.

15. Roy Reed, "Dr. King's Group Scores Ky Junta," *NYT*, 14 Apr. 1966; M. Young, *The Vietnam Wars*, 167–71; Stanley Levison and Clarence Jones, 23 Apr. 1966, FBI Levison Logs; Garrow, *Bearing the Cross*, 470; Shapiro, "The Vietnam War," 130; Levison, Bayard Rustin, and King conference call, 12 June 1966, FBI Levison Logs; "Dr. King Calls Draft Unfair," *NYT*, 3 Nov. 1966. African American combat fatalities remained disproportionate through 1967, but by the end of the war black and white fatalities had become comparable to their proportions in the population. See Appy, *Working-Class War*.

16. King, "The Casualties of the War in Vietnam: Address Delivered to the Nation Institute," 25 Feb. 1967, SCLC, 26.

17. King, "Beyond Vietnam," 4 Apr. 1967, in *A Call to Conscience*, ed. Carson and Shepard, 160; Kotz, *Judgment Days*, 373; Stanley Levison and McWilliams, 3 Jan. 1967, and conference calls, 18 Feb. and 27 Mar. 1967, FBI Levison Logs.

18. King, "Beyond Vietnam," 142, 159; King, "Statement," 15 Dec. 1966, in U.S. Senate, *Federal Role in Urban Affairs*, 2970; "Dr. King to Weigh Civil Disobedience If War Intensifies; Interview by John Herbers," *NYT*, 2 Apr. 1967.

19. King initially cited a figure of $322,000 per dead Vietnamese solider but revised it upward in April. King, "Casualties of the War in Vietnam," 6; "Dr. King Leads Chicago Peace Rally," *NYT*, 26 Mar. 1967, and excerpts in "Another Opinion," *NYT*, 2 Apr. 1967; King, "Press Conference on Position on Vietnam," 12 Apr. 1967, Los Angeles, KPKC(3); King, "The Domestic Impact of the War in Vietnam: Address Delivered at the National Labor Leadership Assembly for Peace," 11 Nov. 1967, KPKC(3); King, "The Other America," California Democratic Council, Los Angeles, 16 Mar. 1968, Pacifica Radio Archives, Los Angeles; King, "Why We Must Go to Washington," 5 Jan. 1968, KPKC(3); King, *Where Do We Go from Here?* 36, 86.

20. Gladwin Hill, "Dr. King Advocates Quitting Vietnam," *NYT*, 26 Feb. 1967, 1; King, "Beyond Vietnam," 143. See also King, "America's Chief Moral Dilemma," University of California–Berkeley, 17 May 1967, Pacifica Radio Archives, Los Angeles.

21. Whitney Young, "Search for Liberals," Fisk University, 6 July 1967, WMY, IV:155; "Vietnam Called 'Excuse' for Lag in Rights Fight," *WP*, 21 Jan. 1967, C5; King, "Press Conference on Position on Vietnam"; King quoted in CBS News, *Face the Nation*, 16 Apr. 1967, v. 10, 117; King, "The Other America." On Young's growing doubts about guns and butter, and his persistent support for Johnson, see Weiss, *Whitney M. Young Jr.*, 158–64.

22. King, "Casualties of the War in Vietnam," 8; King, "Domestic Impact of the War."

23. King quoted in *Face the Nation*, 16 Apr. 1967, v. 10, 116; King, "Interview on *Issues and Answers*," 18 June 1967, Washington, D.C., KPKC(3); King, "Casualties of the War in Vietnam"; King, "Transforming a Neighborhood into a Brotherhood," Annual Convention of the National Association of Radio Announcers, 11 Aug. 1967, KPKC(3).

24. King, "Domestic Impact of the War."

25. King, "Casualties of the War in Vietnam," stressed the violation of international law; King, "Beyond Vietnam," 146–54; King, "Press Conference on Position on Vietnam."

26. King, "Beyond Vietnam," 146, 153.

27. Ibid., 143, 149; Harry Wachtel and Stanley Levison, 6 Apr. 1967, King and Levison, 8 and 12 Apr. 1967, and Levison and Dora McDonald, 11 Apr. 1967, all in FBI Levison Logs; Wilkins quoted in Hall, *Peace and Freedom*, 102. King may have concluded the ghostwritten text was too radical when his recorded speech omitted from the printed version a speculation that the covert purpose of U.S. intervention was to goad "China into a war so that we may bomb her military installations." See King, "A Time to Break Silence," 4 Apr. 1967, in *A Testament of Hope*, ed. Washington, 242.

28. King, "Beyond Vietnam," 156–57; King, *Where Do We Go from Here?* 188; on Carmichael and the Panthers, see Hall, *Peace and Freedom*, 60; King, "America's Chief Moral Dilemma."

29. King, "SCLC Convention," 16 Aug. 1967, KPKC(3); King, "Three Evils of Society," National Conference for a New Politics, Chicago, 31 Aug. 1967, KPKC(3).

30. King, "Casualties of the War in Vietnam"; King, "Press Conference on Position in Vietnam"; King, "Transforming a Neighborhood into a Brotherhood," 11 Aug. 1967; King, "America's Chief Moral Dilemma." In *Where Do We Go from Here?* King made a general indictment of economic neo-imperialism but did not directly associate it with the Vietnam War, which he criticized on moral grounds. King, *Where Do We Go from Here?* 7, 35, 36, 133, 188.

31. King, "Beyond Vietnam," 154–55; King quoted in *Face the Nation*, 16 Apr. 1967, 116–17; "The People: Dilemma of Dissent," *Time*, 21 Apr. 1967.

32. King, "Beyond Vietnam," 155–56; Douglas Robinson, "Jewish War Veterans Attack," *NYT*, 6 Apr. 1967, 10; King quoted in *Face the Nation*, 16 Apr. 1967, 113; King, "Interview on *Issues and Answers*"; King, "Address at Santa Rita Rehabilitation Center," 14 Jan. 1968, Pacifica Radio Archives, Los Angeles; Burns, *To the Mountaintop*, 376–79.

33. Alfred Lewis, "Dr. King's Stand," *NYT*, 3 Apr. 1967, 32; John Sibley, "Bunche Disputes Dr. King," *NYT*, 13 Apr. 1967, 1, 32; "Dr. King's Error," *NYT*, 7 Apr. 1967, 36.

34. Lawrence Davies, "Dr. King's Response," *NYT*, 13 Apr. 1967, 32; Paul Good, "On the March Again," *Nation*, 1 May 1967, 551; Niebuhr quoted in Shapiro, "The Vietnam War," 133.

35. Carl Rowan, "Martin Luther King's Tragic Decision," *Readers Digest*, Sept. 1967, in C. Eric Lincoln, *Martin Luther King Jr.: A Profile* (New York, Hill and Wang, 1984), 212–18; Peter Kihss, "Rowan Terms Dr. King's Stand on War a Peril to Rights Gains," *NYT*, 28 Aug. 1967, 10; King, "America's Chief Moral Dilemma." On public opinion, see Kotz, *Judgment Days*, 378.

36. Kwame Ture (Stokely Carmichael), in *Voices of Freedom,* ed. Hampton and Fayer, 34–48; King, *Where Do We Go from Here?* 173–76.

37. King, *Where Do We Go from Here?* 176–77.

38. Ibid., 179.

39. Ibid., 177–78.

40. King, "Statement on the Southern Christian Leadership Conference's position on Israel and the Middle East," Sept. 1967, KPKC, 122.

41. King, "To Charter Our Course for the Future," 22 May 1967, KPKC(3); King, "Which Way Its Soul Shall Go," voter registration rally, Louisville, Kentucky, 2 Aug. 1967, KPKC(3).

42. Hall, *Peace and Freedom,* 108–26, 145.

Chapter 12. Power to Poor People

1. King, *Where Do We Go from Here?* 136–37.

2. King, "Ingratitude," Ebenezer Baptist Church, 18 June 1967, KPKC(3); King, "Address to Mass Meeting," 2 Feb. 1968, KPKC(3); King, "State of the Movement," Frogmore, S.C., 28 Nov. 1967, KPKC(3).

3. King, *Where Do We Go from Here?* 180–81.

4. Ibid., 142–43; King, "Civil Rights at the Crossroads," address to the New York Teamsters, 2 May 1967, KPKC(3).

5. King, *Where Do We Go from Here?* 6–8, 18–19, 69, 84–85, 132. King modified one of his self-help set pieces in an address to high school students in 1964, adding "one extreme" to the recommendation: "And so if it falls your lot to be a street sweeper, *to carry it to one extreme,* set out to sweep streets like Michelangelo painted pictures." King, "Addison Jr. High School," 22 Oct. 1964, KPKC(3). In 1965, King had completely deleted this reference to street sweepers originally taken from the sermons of Benjamin Mays; King, "A Great Challenge Derived from a Serious Dilemma," 15 Dec. 1965, KPKC(3).

6. King, "To Charter Our Course for the Future," Frogmore, S.C., 28 May 1967, KPKC(3); King, "Interview on the *Arlene Francis Show,*" 19 June 1967, KPKC(3); King, "The Other America," Stanford University, 14 Apr. 1967, KPKC, Tape 34; King, "America's Chief Moral Dilemma," University of California–Berkeley, 17 May 1967, Pacifica Radio Archives, Los Angeles.

7. King, "Where Do We Go from Here?" Eleventh Annual Convention of the SCLC, 16 Aug. 1967, in *A Call to Conscience,* ed. Carson and Shepard, 193–94.

8. Andrew Young, "Socialism for the Rich," SCLC press release, 1 Feb. 1967, SCLC, 122:1; King, "Three Evils of Society," National Conference for a New Politics, Chicago, 31 Aug. 1967, 4, KPKC(3); King, "Press Conference on the PPC," 5 Jan. 1968, 8, KPKC(3); King, *Where Do We Go from Here?* 186–87. See Katz and Thomas, "The Invention of 'Welfare' in America."

9. King, "Statement on Nonviolence," 14 Oct. 1966, KPKC(3); Tom Offenburger interview with Katherine Shannon, 2 July 1968, RJB; King and Stanley Levison, 27 Mar. 1967, FBI Levison Logs; Wright quoted in *Voices of Freedom,* ed. Hampton and Fayer, 454.

10. *Congressional Record,* 20 July 1967, pp. 19548–55; Califano, *Triumph and Tragedy,* 212–13; King, "Statement," 26 July 1967, KPKC(3).

11. U.S. Senate, Committee on the Judiciary, *Antiriot Bill, 1967,* Hearings (Washington, D.C.: GPO, 1967), 19, 163; U.S. Senate, Permanent Subcommittee on Investigations, *Riots, Civil and Criminal Disorders* (Washington, D.C.: GPO, 1967), part 1, p. 2.

12. "Johnson TV Talk on Troop Order," *NYT,* 25 July 1967, 20; King, "Telegram to the President, Press Conference," 24 July 1967, KPKC(3); Levison drafted much of the language of the telegram: Stanley Levison and Dora McDonald, 24 July 1967, and King and Levison, 29 July 1967, FBI Levison Logs; King, "Address Delivered at SCLC Staff Meeting," 17 Jan. 1968, KPKC(3).

13. King, "Telegram to the President."

14. Memo (unsigned), Harry McPherson to Lyndon Johnson, 28 July 1967, MLK Name File, White House Central Files, LBJL; "Rift Between King, LBJ Appears Beyond Repair," *PC,* 2 Sept. 1967; Stanley Levison, King, and Harry Wachtel, 25 July 1967, FBI Levison Logs; Garrow, *Bearing the Cross,* 571–74, 580.

15. NBC News, *Meet the Press,* 13 Aug. 1967, 7; King, "The Crisis in American Cities," 15 Aug. 1967, KPKC(3); Wofford, *Of Kennedys and Kings,* 231; King and Stanley Levison, 22 Aug. 1967, FBI Levison Logs; Weir, *Politics and* Jobs, 52; USHARRIS.081467, R1B, USHARRIS.112067, R1A, USHARRIS.012968.R3, all in POLL.

16. King, "The Crisis in America's Cities," address at the SCLC Convention, 15 Aug. 1967, in *Gandhi Marg* 12 (January 1968): 17; King, "Statement," National Advisory Commission on Civil Disorders (Kerner Commission), 23 Oct. 1967, in *Civil Rights During the Johnson Administration,* ed. LBJL, reels 4–5:2775, 2800; King, "Behavioral Scientist," 1 Sept. 1967, 4, KPKC(3).

17. King, Stanley Levison, Harry Wachtel, Andrew Young and Walter Fauntroy, 12 Aug. 1967, *MLK-Levison FBI Micro,* 7:510–18. Stanley Levison suggested the riots led to concessions, but Young and Walter Fauntroy doubted it.

18. King, "Crisis in America's Cities," 18–19; King, "Statement," Kerner Commission, 2776–78; King, "State of the Movement." Andrew Kopkind, "White on Black: The Riot Commission and the Rhetoric of Reform," in *Cities Under Siege,* ed. David Boesel and Peter Rossi (New York: Basic Books, 1971), 226–59.

19. King, "Statement," Kerner Commission, 2776–77, 2819–21; King, "Crisis in America's Cities," 18; King, "State of the Movement," 2–3; King, "The Other America."

20. Stanley Levison and King, 29 July 1967, *MLK-Levison FBI Micro,* 7:477–81; King, Levison, Harry Wachtel, Andrew Young, and Walter Fauntroy, 12 Aug. 1967, *MLK-Levison FBI Micro,* 7:510–18. See Bloom, *Class, Race, and the Civil Rights Movement,* 200–203, for a succinct summary of riot analysis.

21. King, "Statement," Kerner Commission, 2825, 2803, 2808, 2997–99; King, *Trumpet of Conscience,* 56–57; William Ryan, *Blaming the Victim* (New York: Vintage, 1971) ch. 9, discusses official carnage.

22. King, *Where Do We Go from Here?* 111–12; King, "Statement," Kerner Commission, 2812.

23. Graham, *Civil Rights Era,* 453; Andrew F. Brimmer, "Economic Developments in the Black Community," in *The Great Society: Lessons for the Future,* ed. Eli Ginzberg and Robert M. Solow (New York: Basic Books, 1974), 148, 150; Jaynes, Williams, and National Research Council Committee on the Status of Black Americans, *A Common Destiny,* 278, 302. King explained the statistical undercounts to the SCLC staff in "Why

We Must Go to Washington," 15 Jan. 1968, 4–6, KPKC(3). See Patterson, *Grand Expectations,* 637–39.

24. National Advisory Commission on Civil Disorders (Kerner Commission), *Report* (New York: New York Times Company, 1968), 143–44, 291–96.

25. Rustin quoted in McPherson, *A Political Education,* (Boston: Little, Brown, 1972), 376; King to Roy Wilkins, 4 Mar. 1968, NAACP, IV:A35.

26. Kerner Commission, *Report,* 127, 4–5; King, Andrew Young, and Stanley Levison, 12 Aug. 1967, *MLK-Levison FBI Micro,* 7:510–18.

27. When a minister complained that his congregation resisted his civil rights advocacy, King responded, "the members didn't anoint you to preach." King, "Guidelines for a Constructive Church," Ebenezer Baptist Church, 5 June 1966, in *A Knock at Midnight,* ed. Carson and Holloran, 110; King, "Address at Santa Rita Rehabilitation Center," 14 Jan. 1968, Pacifica Radio Archives, Los Angeles; King, "Interview on the *Arlene Francis Show*"; King, "Interview on *Issues and Answers,*" 18 June 1967, Washington, D.C., KPKC(3); King to "Friend," Nov. 1967, MLK Name File, LBJL.

28. Rutherford, Young, Harrington, and Logan in *Voices of Freedom,* ed. Hampton and Fayer, 454–59; L. Howard DeWolf to King, 11 Dec. 1967, KPKC, 8:24; "Dr. King Warns That Riots Might Bring Rightists' Rule," *NYT,* 18 Feb. 1968, 61; Fairclough, *To Redeem the Soul of America,* 361–62; Reddick in Garrow, *Bearing the Cross,* 575; "Reminiscences of Bayard Rustin," 1987, p. 270, CUOH.

29. King, "Statement at Press Conference Announcing the Poor People's Campaign," 4 Dec. 1967, SCLC, 179:25.

30. Ibid.

31. King, "Why a Movement?" 28 Nov. 1967, 3, KPKC(3); King in Garrow, *Bearing the Cross,* 591–93; King, "State of the Movement"; King, "Why We Must Go to Washington."

32. King, "Press Conference on the PPC," 5–6; Young in Garrow, *Bearing the Cross,* 583; King, "Why We Must Go to Washington." At a press conference the following day, King called for a massive program on the scale of the Freedom Budget or his Bill of Rights for the Disadvantaged. SCLC had "real experts" figuring out the details, he reassured skeptics. King, "Press Conference—Need to Go to Washington," Ebenezer Baptist Church, 16 Jan. 1968, KPKC(3); Garrow, *Bearing the Cross,* 595–96.

33. King, "Why We Must Go to Washington," 11, 16, 19.

34. Sampson quoted in Fairclough, *To Redeem the Soul of America,* 362–63; R. B. Cottonreader to Hosea Williams, 12 Feb. 1968, and Herbert Coulton to Williams, 20 and 24 Mar. 1968, SCLC, 178:19.

35. Albert Turner and Hosea Williams to Organizations in the State of Alabama, 2 Feb. 1968, SCLC, 177:43. Williams and Fred Bennette to Officers, Members, and Friends, 9 Mar. 1968, SCLC, 179:4. SCLC's proposal to the Ford Foundation reflected Kenneth Clark's assumption that "churches are the most pervasive social institutions in the Negro ghetto." The training program was intended to radicalize the black church and give ministers skills in community organizing. "A Proposal for Renewal of the Negro Ministry in America, Submitted to the Ford Foundation, Urban Training Center for Christian Mission," SCLC, 48:13; see materials in SCLC, 48:10, 50:16, 3:41.

36. Draft curricular materials, and James Bevel, "Address to Ministers Leadership Training Program," 20 Feb. 1968, SCLC, 48:11; Dr. Archie Hargraves, "The New Mythology," 21 Feb. 1968, SCLC, 50:16; King, "Address Delivered to Ministers Leader-

ship Training Program," 19 Feb. 1968, SCLC, box 26; Garrow, *Bearing the Cross,* 598–99.

37. King, "Press Conference," 1 Jan. 1968; Garrow, *Bearing the Cross,* 607; Harrington, *Fragments of the Century,* 129; Michael Harrington interview, Eyes on the Prize II research and development files, Blackside, Inc., Boston.

38. King, "Press Conference—Need to Go to Washington," 16 Jan. 1968; Kotz and Kotz, *Passion for Equality,* 248–53; "NWRO Demands for the Poor People's Campaign," n.d., George Wiley Papers, SHSW, 33:1; Clark quoted in McFadden, "Septima P. Clark," 93.

39. King, "Speech to Mass Meeting," Edwards, Miss., 15 Feb. 1968, KPKC(3).

40. King, "Why a Movement?" 10–11; King, "Address at SCLC Staff Meeting," 17 Jan. 1968, King, "Address at Poor People's Campaign Rally," Greenwood, Miss., 19 Mar. 1968, King, "Address," Eutaw, Ala., 20 Mar. 1968 and Albany, Ga., 23 Mar. 1968, all in KPKC(3).

41. King, "Address at Mass Meeting," Clarksdale, Miss., 19 Mar. 1968; King, "Address at Mass Meeting," Waycross, Ga., 22 Mar. 1968, both in KPKC(3).

42. King, "Why We Must Go to Washington," 7; King, "Address," Eutaw, Ala.; King, "Speech to Mass Meeting," Edwards, Miss.; King, "Address at Mass Meeting," Clarksdale, Miss.

43. Registration forms, SCLC, 181:7, 181;15, 181:4.

44. Ibid., 181:4, 181;6. See the brochure, *The Poor People's Campaign* (SCLC, n.d.), from which Mrs. Kendricks copied, "Poor people do not get decent jobs, decent incomes, decent housing, decent schools, decent health care, decent government, decent police. Poor people do not even get respect as human beings." Poor People's March Vertical file, folder 159–10, MSRC.

45. Poor People's Campaign News, "Black and White Together," 15 Mar. 1968, SCLC, 179:25; Eleanor Eaton, AFSC, to Andrew Young et al., 29 Feb. 1968, SCLC, 49:3; Horton quoted in Fairclough, *To Redeem the Soul of America,* 369; Ben Franklin, "Dr. King Hints He'd Cancel March If Aid Is Offered," *NYT,* 31 Mar. 1968; "All Minorities Supporting MLK," *PC,* 30 Mar. 1968.

46. Schorr quoted in Hampton and Fayer, *Voices of Freedom,* 457; Whitney Young, "Conference on the Role of the Press in a Period of Social Crisis," 6 May 1967, WMY, IV:154.

47. Letters to Lyndon Johnson from P. Case, 19 Feb. 1968, R. A. Cunningham, 30 Mar. 1968, E. L. Knox, 19 Feb. 1968, G. N. Boesinger, 14 Feb. 1968, G. Jacobson, 8 Feb. 1968, W. N. Powell, 23 Feb. 1968, and J. H. Nevins, 9 Feb. 1968, MLK Name File, White House Central Files, LBJL.

48. Oates, *Let the Trumpet Sound,* 452; Lucy quoted in *Voices of Freedom,* ed. Hampton and Fayer, 459–60.

49. Honey, *Black Workers Remember,* 290, 295, 304–5.

50. Beifuss, *At the River I Stand,* 38–40; Honey, *Black Workers Remember,* 287, 291, 300; H. Ralph Jackson interview by James Mosby, 10 July 1968, 10, RJB; Wilkins quoted in Fairclough, *To Redeem the Soul of America,* 370; J. Edwin Stanfield, "In Memphis: More Than a Garbage Strike," Southern Regional Council, 22 Mar. 1968, BR, 25:8.

51. King, "Address at Mason Temple Mass Meeting," Memphis, 18 Mar. 1968, KPKC(3); Honey, *Black Workers Remember,* 300, 314–18. See also King, "Why We Must Go to Washington"; Steve Estes, "I AM A MAN! Race, Masculinity, and the 1968 Memphis Sanitation Strike," *Labor History* 41, no. 2 (2000), 153–70.

52. Editorial, "Mini-Riot in Memphis," *NYT*, 31 Mar. 1968, 32; "Wilkins Sees Violence During D.C. March," *CD*, 4 Apr. 1968, 10; "The Real Martin Luther King," *St. Louis Globe Democrat*, 31 Mar. 1968, in McKnight, *The Last Crusade*, 62.

53. Tom Offenburger to SCLC staff, 1 Apr. 1968, SCLC, 122:10; Garrow, *Bearing the Cross*, 614–15.

54. King, "I See the Promised Land," 3 Apr. 1968, in *A Testament of Hope*, ed. Washington, 280–88.

55. Honey, *Black Workers Remember*, 300–301, 310, 316–17; Matusow, *Unraveling of America*, 207–8, 396; Fairclough, *To Redeem the Soul of America*, 382; Charles Cabbage, interview by James Mosby, 1968, p. 22, RJB. "He gave life to the strike and the strike gave him warmth and excitement and involvement, the two came together in a very beautiful way," Jerry Wurf, AFSCME International President, recalled in an interview by James Mosby, 21 Oct. 1968, RJB.

56. Bernard Lee interview by Paul Steckler, Eyes on the Prize II research and development files, Blackside Inc., Boston.

57. James Orange interview by Katherine Shannon, p. 31, RJB; Kotz, *Judgment Days*, 387; Offenburger interview, 66; Kotz, *Let Them Eat Promises*, 157. Uniformly negative accounts of the march can be found in Fairclough, *To Redeem the Soul of America*, chs. 14 and 15, and in Fager, *Uncertain Resurrection*.

58. Katherine Shannon interview by Claudia Rawles, 12 Aug. 1968 p. 9, RJB; Ernest Austin interview by Katherine Shannon, 9 July 1968, pp. 11, 20, RJB; Fairclough, *To Redeem the Soul of America*, 386–90; see Hampton and Fayer, *Voices of Freedom*, ch. 25.

59. Shannon interview; Lafayette quoted in "Poor Campaign Isn't in Trouble, Its Leaders Say," *PC*, 25 Apr. 1968.

60. Harry McPherson Oral History, LBJL; Cabinet minutes, 3 Apr. and 1 May 1968, Cabinet Papers, White House Central Files, LBJL; see also the James Gaither collection, White House Central Files, box 36, LBJL. For my assessment of the economic consequences of the civil rights movement, see T. Jackson, "The Civil Rights Movement."

61. See Marian Wright Edelman interview, 1988, Roger Wilkins interview, 1988, *Eyes on the Prize* II research and development files, Blackside, Inc., Boston; Kotz, *Let Them Eat Promises*, ch. 10, esp. 166–67. Califano blamed Abernathy for continuing to denounce the administration and Congress in equal terms for their "broken promises." That "did it for LBJ." Califano, *Triumph and Tragedy*, 287.

62. Bertha Johnson Luster, Oct. 1997, quoted in Freeman, *Mule Train*, 114.

63. Shannon interview, 20, 80; Austin interview, 19; Joseph Lowery interview by Robert Wright, 19 Oct. 1970, p. 40, RJB.

64. "Speech by Dr. George A. Wiley," 29 Apr. 1968, Wiley Papers, SHSW, 33:1; "Statements of Demands for Rights of the Poor Presented to Agencies of the U.S. Government by the Poor People's Campaign and Its Committee of 100, 29–30 April, 1 May 1968," 3–7, 14–16, 18, 27, 34–35, 36, 40–41, 45, SCLC, box 177.

65. Coretta King quoted in NWRO pamphlet "Woman Power," NWRO vertical file, MSRC; Fager, *Uncertain Resurrection*, 78.

66. Ralph David Abernathy, "Address," 19 June 1968, SCLC, 177:2; See also Andrew Young, "A Sermon," 19 June 1968, SCLC, 49:34.

Epilogue

1. Wofford, *Of Kennedys and Kings,* 117.

2. U.S. Senate, Committee on the Judiciary, *Martin Luther King Jr., National Holiday,* S. 25, Hearings, 27 Mar. and 21 June 1979 (Washington, D.C.: GPO, 1979), 20, 23, 27.

3. *Public Papers of the Presidents, Ronald Reagan: 1986,* vol. 1 (Washington, D.C.: GPO, 1988), 52–53, 60–61, 67; Robin Toner, "Saving a Dissenter from His Legend," *NYT,* 20 Jan. 1986, A24.

4. Flyers, 27 Oct. and 12 Dec. 1988 in CR, 38.

5. *Greensboro News and Record,* 16 Jan. 1996.

6. "Clinton Makes Emotional Appeal for Blacks to Help Stop Violence," *NYT,* 14 Nov. 1993.

7. U.S. Senate, Senate Committee on the Judiciary, *The King Holiday and Service Act of 1993* (Washington, D.C.: GPO, 1995), 19; "King Holiday Is Linked to a Day of Service," *NYT,* 24 Aug. 1994, B7.

8. Septima Clark, "The Occasion: Martin Luther King, Jr.," n.d., SPC, 1:61; Clark, "The Vocation of Black Scholarship: Identifying the Enemy," n.d., SPC, 1:74.

9. Septima Clark, "The Movement I Remember," n.d., SPC, 1:52.

10. Shuttlesworth quoted in Manis, *A Fire You Can't Put Out,* 441.

11. Dyson, *I May Not Get There with You;* Lasch, *True and Only Heaven;* Burns, *To the Mountaintop;* Branch, *At Canaan's Edge,* xi–xiii; Cornel West, "The Religious Foundations of the Thought of Martin Luther King Jr.," and Carson, "Reconstructing the King Legacy," both in *We Shall Overcome,* ed. Albert and Hoffman, 128, 123, 247.

12. Self, *American Babylon,* 328–34, offers an excellent historiographical review of some of these issues. On racism in the war on poverty, see Quadagno, *The Color of Welfare.* Katznelson, "Was the Great Society a Lost Opportunity?" Burns, *To the Mountaintop,* offers a spirited defense of nonviolence, though different from mine. Tyson, *Radio Free Dixie,* Lipsitz, *A Life in the Struggle,* and many local studies show how armed self-defense actually created spaces in which nonviolence could occur, from Monroe, North Carolina, to Bogalusa, Louisiana.

13. Davies, *From Opportunity to Entitlement.* Hodgson, *America in Our Time,* and Appy, *Working-Class War,* both stress the enormous effect Vietnam and Vietnam-induced inflation had on working-class disaffection, not only from liberalism, but the entire political process. Matusow, *Unraveling of America,* oddly ignores the political impact of Vietnam. Lassiter, *The Silent Majority,* presents the most comprehensive view of the southern and national politics of suburban sprawl.

14. Wright, "Economic Consequences," 177–81, 183; Button, *Blacks and Social Change,* 143, 148–51, 186–87; T. Jackson, "The Civil Rights Movement"; see also Graham, *Civil Rights Era,* 453. See John J. Donohue, III, and James Heckman, "Continuous Versus Episodic Change: The Impact of Civil Rights Policy on the Economic Status of Blacks," *Journal of Economic Literature* 29, no. 4 (Dec. 1991): 1641, 1629.

15. Cross, *The Black Power Imperative,* 431, 501; T. Jackson, "The Civil Rights Movement." Overall trends are covered in Patterson, *America's Struggle Against Poverty;* O'Connor, *Poverty Knowledge,* ch. 10; Katz, *Improving Poor People,* 77–98.

16. T. Jackson, "The State, the Movement, and the Urban Poor," 438–39. Lassiter, *The Silent Majority;* Self, *American Babylon.*

17. See the still relevant and remarkable William Grieder, *Who Will Tell the People?* (New York: Simon and Schuster, 1992).

Bibliography

Repositories

Avery Institute for Afro-American History and Culture. College of Charleston, Charleston, South Carolina

Butler Library, Rare Book and Manuscript Division, Columbia University

John F. Kennedy Presidential Library, Boston

Library of Congress, Manuscripts Division, Washington, D.C.

Lyndon B. Johnson Presidential Library, Austin, Texas

Martin Luther King, Jr. Center for Nonviolent Social Change, Inc. King Library and Archives, Atlanta

Moorland-Spingarn Research Center, Manuscript Department, Howard University, Washington, D.C.

Mugar Memorial Library, Department of Special Collections, Boston University

Schomburg Center for Research in Black Culture, New York Public Library

State Historical Society of Wisconsin, Social Action Collections, Madison

Tamiment Institute Library and Robert F. Wagner Labor Archives, New York University

Archive and Manuscript Collections

Clark, Septima Poinsette. Papers. Avery Institute for Afro-American History and Culture, College of Charleston, Charleston, South Carolina

Jones, Clarence B., New York File—Surveillance Logs, David Garrow, FOIA Accession. Schomburg Center for Research in Black Culture, New York Public Library

King, Dr. Martin Luther, Jr. Papers. Martin Luther King, Jr. Center for Nonviolent Social Change, Inc., King Library and Archives, Atlanta

King, Dr. Martin Luther, Jr. Papers. Series III. Speeches, Sermons, Articles, Statements. Martin Luther King, Jr. Center for Nonviolent Social Change, Inc., King Library and Archives, Atlanta

King, Martin Luther, Jr. Papers. Mugar Memorial Library, Department of Special Collections, Boston University

LBJ Presidential Telephone Tapes. Miller Center for Public Affairs, University of Virginia, accessed via http://www.millercenter.org, 2003–5

League for Industrial Democracy Records, 1920–70. Tamiment Institute Library and Robert F. Wagner Labor Archives, New York University

Levison, Stanley, New York File—Surveillance Logs, David Garrow, FOIA Accession. Schomburg Center for Research in Black Culture, New York Public Library

The Martin Luther King, Jr., FBI File [Microfilm]. Ed. David J. Garrow. Frederick, Md.: University Publications of America, 1984.

The Martin Luther King, Jr., FBI File. Part 2. The King-Levison File [Microfilm]. Ed. David J. Garrow. Frederick, Md.: University Publications of America, 1984.

National Association for the Advancement of Colored People. August Meier, John H. Bracey, and L. Lee Yanike. Papers of the NAACP [Microform]. Frederick, Md.: University Publications of America, 1987.

National Association for the Advancement of Colored People Records. Library of Congress, Manuscripts Division, Washington, D.C. Southern Oral History Program, Southern Historical Collection, University of North Carolina at Chapel Hill. Library.

Ralph J. Bunche Oral History Collection. Moorland-Spingarn Research Center, Manuscript Department, Howard University, Washington, D.C.

Records of the National Urban League, 1910–86. Library of Congress, Manuscripts Division, Washington, D.C.

Records of the Southern Christian Leadership Conference. Martin Luther King, Jr. Center for Nonviolent Social Change, Inc., King Library and Archives, Atlanta

Records of the Southern Christian Leadership Conference, 1954–1970 [Microfilm]. Part 1, Records of the President's Office. Ed. Randolph Boehm. Bethesda, Md.: University Publications of America, 1995.

Robinson, Cleveland. Papers. Tamiment Institute Library and Robert F. Wagner Labor Archives, New York University

Roper Center for Public Opinion Research. University of Connecticut, iPoll Data Base, accessed via Lexis-Nexis Academic Universe, 2003–5.

Rustin, Bayard T., Papers. Library of Congress, Manuscripts Division, Washington, D.C.

Young, Whitney M., Jr. Papers. Butler Library, Rare Book and Manuscript Division, Columbia University

Books and Collected Works by Martin Luther King, Jr.

The Autobiography of Martin Luther King, Jr., ed. Clayborne Carson. New York: Warner Books, 1998.

A Call to Conscience: The Landmark Speeches of Dr. Martin Luther King, Jr., ed. Clayborne Carson and Kris Shepard. New York: Warner Books, 2001.

A Knock at Midnight: Inspiration from the Great Sermons of Reverend Martin Luther King, Jr., ed. Clayborne Carson and Peter Holloran. New York: Warner Books, 1998.

The Measure of a Man. Philadelphia: Fortress Press, 1958.

The Papers of Martin Luther King, Jr. Vol. 1., ed. Clayborne Carson, Ralph Luker, and Penny A. Russell. Berkeley: University of California Press, 1992.

The Papers of Martin Luther King, Jr. Vol. 2., ed. Clayborne Carson, Ralph E. Luker, Penny A. Russell, and Peter Holloran. Berkeley: University of California Press, 1994.

The Papers of Martin Luther King, Jr. Vol. 3., ed. Clayborne Carson, Stewart Burns, and Susan Carson. Berkeley: University of California Press, 1997.

The Papers of Martin Luther King, Jr. Vol. 4., ed. Clayborne Carson, Susan Carson, Adrienne Clay, Virginia Shadron, and Kiernan Taylor. Berkeley: University of California Press, 2000.

The Papers of Martin Luther King, Jr. Vol. 5., ed. Clayborne Carson, Tenisha Armstrong, Susan Carson, Adrienne Clay, and Kiernan Taylor. Berkeley: University of California Press, 2005.

A Testament of Hope: The Essential Writings of Martin Luther King, Jr., ed. James Melvin Washington. San Francisco: Harper and Row, 1986.

Strength to Love. New York: Harper and Row, 1963.

Stride Toward Freedom. New York: Harper and Row, 1958.

The Trumpet of Conscience. New York: Harper and Row, 1967.

Where Do We Go from Here: Chaos or Community? New York: Harper and Row, 1967.

Why We Can't Wait. New York: Mentor, 1964, 1970.

Books, Articles, and Theses

Abernathy, Ralph David. *And the Walls Came Tumbling Down: An Autobiography*. New York: HarperPerennial, 1990.

Albert, Peter J., and Ronald Hoffman, eds. *We Shall Overcome: Martin Luther King, Jr., and the Black Freedom Struggle*. New York: Pantheon, 1990.

Anderson, Alan B., and George W. Pickering. *Confronting the Color Line: The Broken Promise of the Civil Rights Movement in Chicago*. Athens: University of Georgia Press, 1986.

Appy, Christian G. *Working-Class War: American Combat Soldiers and Vietnam*. Chapel Hill: University of North Carolina Press, 1993.

Ashmore, Susan Youngblood. "Carry It On: The War on Poverty and the Civil Rights Movement in Alabama, 1964–1970." Ph.D. diss., Auburn University, 1999.

Baldwin, Lewis V. *There Is a Balm in Gilead: The Cultural Roots of Martin Luther King, Jr.* Minneapolis: Fortress Press, 1991.

Barbour, Floyd B., ed. *The Black Power Revolt: A Collection of Essays*. New York: Collier, 1968.

Bennett, Jr., Lerone. *What Manner of Man: A Biography of Martin Luther King, Jr.* Chicago: Johnson, 1964.

Beschloss, Michael R., ed. *Reaching for Glory: Lyndon Johnson's Secret White House Tapes, 1964–1965*. New York: Simon and Schuster, 2001.

———. *Taking Charge: The Johnson White House Tapes, 1963–1964*. New York: Simon and Schuster, 1997.

Biondi, Martha. *To Stand and Fight: The Struggle for Civil Rights in Postwar New York City*. Cambridge, Mass.: Harvard University Press, 2003.

Bloom, Jack M. *Class, Race and the Civil Rights Movement*. Bloomington: Indiana University Press, 1987.

Boyle, Kevin. *Arc of Justice : A Saga of Race, Rights, and Murder in the Jazz Age.* New York: Holt, 2004.

———. *The UAW and the Heyday of American Liberalism, 1945–1968.* Ithaca, N.Y.: Cornell University Press, 1995.

Bracey, John H., August Meier, and Elliott M. Rudwick, ed. *Black Nationalism in America.* Indianapolis: Bobbs-Merrill, 1970.

Braden, Anne. "The Southern Freedom Movement in Perspective." *Monthly Review* 17, nos. 8–9 (1965): 1–91. Reprinted in *We Shall Overcome,* ed. David J. Garrow, 55–150. Brooklyn, N.Y.: Carlson, 1989. [Page citations are to the original].

Branch, Taylor. *At Canaan's Edge: America in the King Years, 1965–68.* New York: Simon and Schuster, 2006.

———. *Parting the Waters: America in the King Years, 1954–63.* New York: Simon and Schuster, 1988.

———. *Pillar of Fire: America in the King Years, 1963–65.* New York: Simon and Schuster, 1998.

Brauer, Carl M. "Kennedy, Johnson, and the War on Poverty." *Journal of American History* 69 (June 1982): 98–119.

Breines, Wini. *Community and Organization in the New Left: 1962–1968.* New York: Praeger, 1982.

Brink, William, and Louis Harris. *Black and White: A Study of U.S. Racial Attitudes Today.* New York: Simon and Schuster, 1966.

———. *The Negro Revolution in America.* New York: Simon and Schuster, 1964.

Brinkley, Alan. *Liberalism and Its Discontents.* Cambridge, Mass.: Harvard University Press, 1998.

Brown, Michael K. *Race, Money, and the American Welfare State.* Ithaca, N.Y.: Cornell University Press, 1999.

Brown, Michael K., and Steven P. Erie. "Blacks and the Legacy of the Great Society: The Economic and Political Impact of Federal Social Policy." *Public Policy* 29 (Summer 1981): 299–330.

Burns, Stewart, ed. *Daybreak of Freedom: The Montgomery Bus Boycott.* Chapel Hill: University of North Carolina Press, 1997.

———. *To the Mountaintop: Martin Luther King Jr.'s Sacred Mission to Save America, 1955–1968.* New York: HarperSanFrancisco, 2004.

Button, James W. *Blacks and Social Change: Impact of the Civil Rights Movement in Southern Communities.* Princeton, N.J.: Princeton University Press, 1989.

———. *Black Violence: The Political Impact of the 1960s Riots.* Princeton, N.J.: Princeton University Press, 1978.

Califano, Joseph A. *The Triumph and Tragedy of Lyndon Johnson: The White House Years.* New York: Simon and Schuster, 1991.

Cantarow, Ellen, and Susan Gushee O'Malley. "Ella Baker: Organizing for Civil Rights." In *Moving the Mountain,* ed. Ellen Cantarow. New York: Feminist Press, 1980.

Carson, Clayborne, ed. *The Eyes on the Prize Civil Rights Reader.* New York: Penguin, 1991.

———. *In Struggle: SNCC and the Black Awakening of the 1960s.* Cambridge, Mass.: Harvard University Press, 1981.

———. "Rethinking African-American Political Thought in the Post-Revolutionary

Era." In *The Making of Martin Luther King and the Civil Rights Movement*, ed. Brian Ward and Tony Badger. New York: New York University Press, 1996.

Carson, Clayborne, et al., eds. *Reporting Civil Rights, v. 1–2*. New York: Library of America, 2003.

Carter, Dan T. *The Politics of Rage: George Wallace, the Origins of the New Conservatism, and the Transformation of American Politics*. New York: Simon and Schuster, 1995.

Carter, David C. " 'Two Nations': Social Insurgency and National Civil Rights Policy-making in the Johnson Administration, 1965–1968." Ph.D. diss., Duke University, 2001.

CBS News. *Face the Nation*. New York: Holt Information Systems, 1972.

Chafe, William. *Civilities and Civil Rights: Greensboro, North Carolina and the Black Struggle for Freedom*. New York: Oxford University Press, 1980.

Clark, Kenneth. *Dark Ghetto: Dilemmas of Social Power*. New York: Harper and Row, 1965.

Clark, Kenneth, and Harlem Youth Opportunities Unlimited. *Youth in the Ghetto: A Study of the Consequences of Powerlessness and a Blueprint for Change*. New York: HARYOU, 1964.

Clark, Kenneth, and Jeanette Hopkins. *A Relevant War against Poverty: A Study of Community Action Programs and Observable Social Change*. New York: Metropolitan Applied Research Center, 1968.

Clark, Septima Poinsette, and LeGette Blythe. *Echo in My Soul*. New York: Dutton, 1962.

Clark, Septima Poinsette, and Cynthia Stokes Brown. *Ready from Within: Septima Clark and the Civil Rights Movement*. Navarro, Calif.: Wild Trees Press, 1986.

Cobb, James C. " 'Somebody Done Nailed Us on the Cross': Federal Farm and Welfare Policy and the Civil Rights Movement in the Mississippi Delta." *Journal of American History* 77, no. 3 (1990): 912–36.

Cohen, Lizabeth. *A Consumer's Republic: The Politics of Mass Consumption in Postwar America*. New York: Knopf, 2003.

Cone, James H. *Martin & Malcolm & America: A Dream Or a Nightmare*. Maryknoll, N.Y.: Orbis, 1992.

Cross, Theodore. *The Black Power Imperative*. New York: Faulkner, 1984.

Davies, Gareth. *From Opportunity to Entitlement: The Transformation and Decline of Great Society Liberalism*. Lawrence: University Press of Kansas, 1996.

D'Emilio, John. *Lost Prophet: The Life and Times of Bayard Rustin*. New York: Free Press, 2003.

Dittmer, John. *Local People: The Struggle for Civil Rights in Mississippi*. Urbana: University of Illinois Press, 1994.

Draper, Alan. *Conflict of Interests: Organized Labor and the Civil Rights Movement in the South, 1954–1968*. Ithaca, N.Y.: ILR Press, 1994.

Dudziak, Mary L. *Cold War Civil Rights: Race and the Image of American Democracy, Politics and Society in Twentieth-Century America*. Princeton, N.J.: Princeton University Press, 2000.

Dyson, Michael Eric. *I May Not Get There with You: The True Martin Luther King, Jr.* New York: Free Press, 2000.

Eagles, Charles W. *The Civil Rights Movement in America: Essays*. Jackson: University Press of Mississippi, 1986.

Eskew, Glen T. *But for Birmingham: The Local and National Movements in the Civil Rights Struggle.* Chapel Hill: University of North Carolina Press, 1997.

Fager, Charles. *Uncertain Resurrection: The Poor People's Washington Campaign.* Grand Rapids, Mich.: William B. Eerdmans, 1969.

Fairclough, Adam. *Martin Luther King, Jr.* Athens: University of Georgia Press, 1995.

———. *To Redeem the Soul of America: The Southern Christian Leadership Conference and Martin Luther King, Jr.* Athens: University of Georgia Press, 1987.

Farmer, James. *Lay Bare the Heart: An Autobiography of the Civil Rights Movement.* New York: Arbor House, 1985.

Ferman, Louis A., Joyce L. Kornbluh, and Alan Haber. *Poverty in America: A Book of Readings.* Ann Arbor: University of Michigan Press, 1965.

Fink, Leon, and Brian Greenberg. *Upheaval in the Quiet Zone: A History of Hospital Workers' Union, Local 1199.* Urbana: University of Illinois Press, 1989.

Fisher, Frederick B. *That Strange Little Brown Man Gandhi.* New York: Ray Long and Richard R. Smith, 1932.

Fluker, Walter E. *They Looked for a City: A Comparative Analysis of the Ideal of Community in the Thought of Howard Thurman and Martin Luther King, Jr.* New York: University Press of America, 1989.

Fogelson, Robert M. *Violence as Protest: A Study of Riots and Ghettos.* Garden City, N.Y.: Doubleday, 1971.

Foner, Eric. *The Story of American Freedom.* New York: Norton, 1998.

Foner, Philip Sheldon. *Organized Labor and the Black Worker, 1619–1981.* 2nd ed. New York: International Publishers, 1982.

Forman, James. *The Making of Black Revolutionaries.* Seattle: University of Washington Press, 1972, 1997.

Fox, Richard Wightman. *Reinhold Niebuhr.* New York: Pantheon, 1985.

Fredrickson, George. "Non-Violent Resistance to White Supremacy: A Comparison of the American Civil Rights Movement and the South African Defiance Campaigns of the 1950s." In *The Making of Martin Luther King and the Civil Rights Movement,* ed. Brian Ward and Tony Badger, 213–29. New York: New York University Press, 1996.

Freeman, Roland L. *The Mule Train: A Journey of Hope Remembered.* Nashville: Rutledge Hill Press, 1998.

Friedly, Michael, and David Gallen, eds. *Martin Luther King, Jr.: The FBI File.* New York: Carroll & Graf, 1993.

Garrow, David J. *Bearing the Cross: Martin Luther King, Jr., and the Southern Christian Leadership Conference.* New York: William Morrow, 1986.

———. *The FBI and Martin Luther King, Jr.: From "Solo" to Memphis.* New York: Norton, 1981.

———. *Protest at Selma: Martin Luther King, Jr. and the Voting Rights Act of 1965.* New Haven, Conn.: Yale University Press, 1979.

Garrow, David J., ed. *Chicago 1966: Open Housing Marches, Summit Negotiations, and Operation Breadbasket.* Brooklyn, N.Y.: Carlson, 1989.

———. *The Walking City: The Montgomery Bus Boycott, 1955–56.* Brooklyn, N.Y.: Carlson, 1989.

Gentile, Thomas. *March on Washington, August 28, 1963.* Washington, D.C.: New Day, 1983.

Gilens, Martin. *Why Americans Hate Welfare: Race, Media, and the Politics of Antipoverty Policy.* Chicago: University of Chicago Press, 1999.

Gilliam, Thomas J. "The Montgomery Bus Boycott of 1955–56." M.A. thesis, Auburn University, 1968.

Gordon, Linda. *Pitied But Not Entitled: Single Mothers and the History of Welfare, 1890–1935.* New York: Free Press, 1994.

Graham, Hugh Davis. *The Civil Rights Era: Origins and Development of National Policy.* New York: Oxford University Press, 1990.

Greenberg, Polly. *The Devil Has Slippery Shoes.* Washington, D.C.: Youth Policy Institute, 1990.

Halberstam, David. *The Children.* New York: Random House, 1998.

Hall, Simon. *Peace and Freedom: The Civil Rights and Antiwar Movements of the 1960s.* Philadelphia: University of Pennsylvania Press, 2005.

Hamilton, Charles V., and Dona C. Hamilton. "Social Policies, Civil Rights and Poverty." In *Fighting Poverty: What Works and What Doesn't,* ed. Sheldon H. Danziger and Daniel H. Weinberg, 286–311. Cambridge, Mass.: Harvard University Press, 1986.

Hamilton, Dona Cooper, and Charles V. Hamilton. *The Dual Agenda: Race and Social Welfare Policies of Civil Rights Organizations.* New York: Columbia University Press, 1997.

Hampton, Henry, and Steve Fayer, eds. *Voices of Freedom: An Oral History of the Civil Rights Movement from the 1950s Through the 1980s.* New York: Bantam, 1991.

Harding, Vincent. "Beyond Amnesia: Martin Luther King, Jr. and the Future of America." *Journal of American History* 74, no. 2 (1987): 468–76.

Harrington, Michael. *Fragments of the Century: A Social Autobiography.* New York: Saturday Review Press, 1973.

———. *The Long-Distance Runner: An Autobiography.* New York: Holt, 1988.

———. *The Other America: Poverty in the United States.* New York: Penguin, 1962, 1969.

Height, Dorothy I. "'We Wanted the Voice of a Woman to Be Heard': Black Women and the 1963 March on Washington." In *Sisters in the Struggle: African American Women in the Civil Rights-Black Power Movement,* ed. Bettye Collier-Thomas and V. P. Franklin, 83–92. New York: New York University Press, 2001.

Hentoff, Nat. *The New Equality.* New York: Viking, 1964, 1965.

Hirsch, Arnold R. *Making the Second Ghetto: Race and Housing in Chicago, 1940–1960.* New York: Cambridge University Press, 1983.

Hodgson, Godfrey. *America in Our Time.* Garden City, N.Y.: Doubleday, 1976.

Honey, Michael. *Black Workers Remember: An Oral History of Segregation, Unionism, and the Freedom Struggle.* Berkeley: University of California Press, 1999.

———. "Martin Luther King Jr., and the Memphis Sanitation Strike." In *Southern Labor in Transition, 1940–1995,* ed. Robert H. Zieger. Knoxville: University of Tennessee Press, 1997.

Horne, Gerald. *Fire This Time : The Watts Uprising and the 1960s.* Charlottesville: University Press of Virginia, 1995.

Horowitz, Roger. *Negro and White, Unite and Fight! A Social History of Industrial Unionism in Meatpacking, 1930–90.* Urbana: University of Illinois Press, 1997.

Horton, Myles. *The Long Haul: An Autobiography.* New York: Doubleday, 1990.

Horwitt, Sanford D. *Let Them Call Me Rebel: Saul Alinsky—His Life and Legacy.* New York: Knopf, 1989.

Isserman, Maurice. *The Other American: The Life of Michael Harrington.* New York: PublicAffairs, 2000.

Jackson, Thomas F. "The Civil Rights Movement." In *Poverty in the United States: An Encyclopedia of History, Politics, and Policy,* ed. Gwendolyn Mink and Alice O'Connor, vol. 1, 182–88. Santa Barbara, Calif.: ABC-CLIO, 2004.

———. "The State, the Movement, and the Urban Poor: The War on Poverty and Political Mobilization in the 1960s." In *The "Underclass" Debate: Views from History,* ed. Michael B. Katz, 403–39. Princeton, N.J.: Princeton University Press, 1993.

Jackson, Walter. *Gunnar Myrdal and America's Conscience: Social Engineering and Racial Liberalism, 1938–1987.* Chapel Hill: University of North Carolina Press, 1990.

Jaynes, Gerald, Robin M. Williams Jr., and National Research Council Committee on the Status of Black Americans, eds. *A Common Destiny: Blacks and American Society.* Washington, D.C.: National Academy Press, 1989.

Kapur, Sudarshan. *Raising up a Prophet: The African-American Encounter with Gandhi.* Boston: Beacon Press, 1992.

Katz, Michael B. *Improving Poor People.* Princeton N.J.: Princeton University Press, 1995.

Katz, Michael B., and Lorrin R. Thomas. "The Invention of 'Welfare' in America." *Journal of Policy History* 10, no. 4 (1998): 399–418.

Katznelson, Ira. "Was the Great Society a Lost Opportunity?" In *The Rise and Fall of the New Deal Order,* ed. Steve Fraser and Gary Gerstle, 185–211. Princeton, N.J.: Princeton University Press, 1989.

———. *When Affirmative Action Was White: An Untold History of Racial Inequality in Twentieth-Century America.* New York: Norton, 2005.

Kelley, Robin D. G. "The Black Poor and the Politics of Opposition in a New South City, 1929–1970." In *The "Underclass" Debate: Views from History,* ed. Michael B. Katz, 293–333. Princeton, N.J.: Princeton University Press, 1993.

———. *Race Rebels: Culture, Politics, and the Black Working Class.* New York: Free Press, 1994.

Kerstein, Robert J., and Dennis R. Judd. "Achieving Less Influence with More Democracy: The Permanent Legacy of the War on Poverty." *Social Science Quarterly* 61, no. 2 (1980): 208–20.

King, Coretta Scott. *My Life with Martin Luther King, Jr.* New York: Holt, 1969.

King, Martin Luther. *Daddy King: An Autobiography.* New York: William Morrow, 1980.

Kleppner, Paul. *Chicago Divided: The Making of a Black Mayor.* DeKalb: Northern Illinois University Press, 1985.

Korstad, Robert, and Nelson Lichtenstein. "Opportunities Found and Lost: Labor, Radicals and the Early Civil Rights Movement." *Journal of American History* 75, no. 3 (December 1988): 786–811.

Kotz, Nick. *Judgment Days: Lyndon Baines Johnson, Martin Luther King, Jr., and the Laws That Changed America.* Boston: Houghton Mifflin, 2005.

———. *Let Them Eat Promises: The Politics of Hunger in America.* New York: Anchor, 1971.

Kotz, Nick, and Mary Lynn Kotz. *A Passion for Equality: George A. Wiley and the Movement.* New York: Norton, 1977.

Lasch, Christopher. *The True and Only Heaven: Progress and Its Critics.* New York: Norton, 1991.

Lassiter, Matthew D. *The Silent Majority: Suburban Politics in the Sunbelt South.* Princeton, N.J.: Princeton University Press, 2006.

Laue, James H. *Direct Action and Desegregation, 1960–1962.* Brooklyn, N.Y.: Carlson, 1989.

Lawson, Steven F. *Black Ballots: Voting Rights in the South, 1944–1969.* New York: Columbia University Press, 1976.

———. *In Pursuit of Power: Southern Blacks and Electoral Politics, 1965–1982.* New York: Columbia University Press, 1985.

———. *Running for Freedom: Civil Rights and Black Politics in America Since 1941.* 2nd ed. New York: McGraw-Hill, 1997.

Lentz, Richard. *Symbols, the News Magazines, and Martin Luther King.* Baton Rouge: Louisiana State University Press, 1990.

Lerner, Gerda. "Developing Community Leadership." In *Black Women in White America.* New York: Pantheon, 1972.

Leventhal, Willy S., ed. *The Children Coming On . . . A Retrospective of the Montgomery Bus Boycott.* Montgomery, Ala.: Black Belt Press, 1998.

Levine, Daniel. *Bayard Rustin and the Civil Rights Movement.* New Brunswick, N.J.: Rutgers University Press, 2000.

Levy, Peter B. *The New Left and Labor in the 1960s.* Urbana: University of Illinois Press, 1994.

Lewis, David L. *King: A Biography.* 2nd ed. Urbana: University of Illinois Press, 1970, 1978 .

Lewis, John, and Michael D'Orso. *Walking with the Wind: A Memoir of the Movement.* New York: Simon and Schuster, 1998.

Lichtenstein, Nelson. *The Most Dangerous Man in Detroit: Walter Reuther and the Fate of American Labor.* New York: Basic Books, 1995.

———. *State of the Union: A Century of American Labor, Politics and Society in Twentieth-Century America.* Princeton, N.J.: Princeton University Press, 2002.

Liebow, Elliot. *Tally's Corner: A Study of Negro Streetcorner Men.* Boston: Little, Brown, 1967.

Ling, Peter. *Martin Luther King Jr.* New York: Routledge, 2002.

Lipsitz, George. *A Life in the Struggle: Ivory Perry and the Culture of Opposition.* Philadelphia: Temple University Press, 1988.

Lischer, Richard. *The Preacher King: Martin Luther King, Jr. and the Word That Moved America.* New York: Oxford University Press, 1995.

Lyon, Danny. *Memories of the Southern Civil Rights Movement.* Chapel Hill: University of North Carolina Press, 1992.

Manis, Andrew Michael. *A Fire You Can't Put Out: The Civil Rights Life of Birmingham's Reverend Fred Shuttlesworth.* Tuscaloosa: University of Alabama Press, 1999.

Marable, Manning. *Race, Reform and Rebellion: The Second Reconstruction in Black America, 1945–1990.* 2nd ed. Jackson: University Press of Mississippi, 1991.

Marris, Peter, and Martin Rein. *Dilemmas of Social Reform: Poverty and Community Action in the United States.* Rev. ed. Chicago: Aldine, 1977.

Matusow, Allen J. *The Unraveling of America: A History of Liberalism in the 1960s*. New York: Harper and Row, 1984.

McCracken, Robert. *Questions People Ask*. New York: Harper and Brothers, 1951.

McFadden, Grace Jordan. "Septima P. Clark and the Struggle for Human Rights." In *Women in the Civil Rights Movement: Trailblazers and Torchbearers, 1941–1965*, ed. Vicki L. Crawford, Jacqueline Anne Rouse, and Barbara Woods, 85–97. Bloomington: Indiana University Press, 1993.

McGreevy, John T. *Parish Boundaries: The Catholic Encounter with Race in the Twentieth-Century Urban North*. Chicago: University of Chicago Press, 1996.

McKnight, Gerald. *The Last Crusade: Martin Luther King, Jr., the FBI, and the Poor People's Campaign*. Boulder, Colo.: Westview Press, 1997.

McMillen, Neil R. *The Citizens' Council: Organized Resistance to the Second Reconstruction, 1954–64*. Urbana: University of Illinois Press, 1971.

McWhorter, Diane. *Carry Me Home: Birmingham, Alabama: The Climactic Battle of the Civil Rights Revolution*. New York: Simon and Schuster, 2001.

Meier, August, and David Lewis. "History of the Negro Upper Class in Atlanta, Georgia, 1890–1958." *Journal of Negro Education* (Spring 1959): 128–39.

Miller, Jim. *Democracy Is in the Streets: From Port Huron to the Siege of Chicago*. Cambridge, Mass.: Harvard University Press, 1994.

Miller, Keith D. *Voice of Deliverance: The Language of Martin Luther King, Jr. and Its Sources*. New York: Free Press, 1992.

Miller, William Robert. *Martin Luther King, Jr.: His Life, Martyrdom and Meaning for the World*. New York: Weybright and Talley, 1968.

Millner, Steven. "The Montgomery Bus Boycott: A Case Study in the Emergence and Career of a Social Movement in *Walking City*, Ed. Garrow, 381–573." Ph.D. diss., University of California, 1981.

Mills, Kay. *This Little Light of Mine: The Life of Fannie Lou Hamer*. New York: Dutton, 1993.

Morris, Aldon D. *The Origins of the Civil Rights Movement: Black Communities Organizing for Change*. New York: Free Press, 1984.

NBC. *Meet the Press: America's Press Conference of the Air*. Millwood, N.Y.: Kraus Reprint.

Niebuhr, Reinhold. *Moral Man and Immoral Society: A Study in Ethics and Politics*. New York: C. Scribner's, 1932.

Oates, Stephen B. *Let the Trumpet Sound: The Life of Martin Luther King, Jr*. New York: New American Library, 1982.

O'Connor, Alice. *Poverty Knowledge: Social Science, Social Policy, and the Poor in Twentieth-Century U.S. History*. Princeton, N.J.: Princeton University Press, 2001.

Olson, Lynne. *Freedom's Daughters: The Unsung Heroines of the Civil Rights Movement from 1830 to 1970*. New York: Scribner, 2001.

Oppenheimer, Martin. *The Sit-in Movement of 1960*. Brooklyn, N.Y.: Carlson, 1989.

Parks, Rosa. *My Story*. New York: Dial, 1992.

Patterson, James T. *America's Struggle Against Poverty, 1900–1985*. Cambridge, Mass.: Harvard University Press, 1986.

———. *Grand Expectations: The United States, 1945–1974*. New York: Oxford University Press, 1996.

Pfeffer, Paula. *A. Philip Randolph: Pioneer of the Civil Rights Movement*. Baton Rouge: Louisiana State University Press, 1990.

Platt, Anthony M., ed. *The Politics of Riot Commissions, 1917–1970: A Collection of Official Reports and Critical Essays.* New York: Collier, 1971.

Powledge, Fred. *Free at Last? The Civil Rights Movement and the People Who Made It.* New York: HarperPerennial, 1991.

Quadagno, Jill S. *The Color of Welfare: How Racism Undermined the War on Poverty.* New York: Oxford University Press, 1994.

Raines, Howell, ed. *My Soul Is Rested: Movement Days in the Deep South Remembered.* New York: G. P. Putnam's Sons, 1977.

Rainwater, Lee, and William L. Yancey, ed. *The Moynihan Report and the Politics of Controversy.* Cambridge, Mass.: MIT Press, 1967.

Ralph, James R. *Northern Protest: Martin Luther King, Jr., Chicago, and the Civil Rights Movement.* Cambridge, Mass.: Harvard University Press, 1993.

Ransby, Barbara. *Ella Baker and the Black Freedom Movement: A Radical Democratic Vision.* Chapel Hill: University of North Carolina Press, 2003.

Reddick, L. D. *Crusader Without Violence: A Biography of Martin Luther King, Jr.* New York: Harper and Brothers, 1959.

Robinson, Jo Ann Gibson. *The Montgomery Bus Boycott and the Women Who Started It: The Memoir of Jo Ann Gibson Robinson.* Knoxville: University of Tennessee Press, 1987.

Robnett, Belinda. *How Long? How Long? African-American Women and the Struggle for Civil Rights.* New York: Oxford University Press, 1997.

Rosenberg, Jonathan, and Zachary Karabell, eds. *Kennedy, Johnson, and the Quest for Justice: The Civil Rights Tapes.* New York: Norton, 2003.

Rustin, Bayard. *Down the Line.* Chicago: Quadrangle, 1971.

Schrecker, Ellen. *Many Are the Crimes: McCarthyism in America.* Boston: Little, Brown, 1998.

Scott, Daryl Michael. *Contempt and Pity: Social Policy and the Image of the Damaged Black Psyche, 1880–1996.* Chapel Hill: University of North Carolina Press, 1997.

Self, Robert O. *American Babylon: Race and the Struggle for Postwar Oakland.* Princeton, N.J.: Princeton University Press, 2003.

Sellers, Cleveland, with Robert Terrell. *The River of No Return: The Autobiography of a Black Militant and the Life and Death of SNCC.* Jackson: University Press of Mississippi, 1973, 1990.

Shapiro, Herbert. "The Vietnam War and the American Civil Rights Movement." *Journal of Ethnic Studies* 16, no. 4 (1989): 117–41.

Silberman, Charles E. *Crisis in Black and White.* New York: Random House, 1964.

Smith, Kenneth L., and Ira G. Zepp. *Search for the Beloved Community: The Thinking of Martin Luther King, Jr.* Valley Forge, Pa.: Judson Press, 1974.

Stein, Jean, and George Plimpton, eds. *American Journey: The Times of Robert Kennedy.* New York: Harcourt Brace Jovanovich, 1970.

Stein, Judith. *Running Steel, Running America: Race, Economic Policy and the Decline of Liberalism.* Chapel Hill: University of North Carolina Press, 1998.

Stoper, Emily. "The Student Nonviolent Coordinating Committee: Rise and Fall of a Redemptive Organization." In *We Shall Overcome*, ed. David J. Garrow, 141–62. Brooklyn, N.Y.: Carlson, 1989.

Sugrue, Thomas J. "Affirmative Action from Below: Civil Rights, the Building Trades, and the Politics of Racial Equality in the Urban North, 1945–1969." *Journal of American History* 91 (June 2004): 145–73.

———. *The Origins of the Urban Crisis: Race and Inequality in Postwar Detroit.* Princeton, N.J.: Princeton University Press, 1996.

Sullivan, Leon. *Build Brother Build: From Poverty to Economic Power.* Philadelphia: Macrae Smith, 1969.

Sullivan, Patricia. *Days of Hope: Race and Democracy in the New Deal Era.* Chapel Hill: University of North Carolina Press, 1996.

Sundquist, James L. *Politics and Policy: The Eisenhower, Kennedy, and Johnson Years.* Washington, D.C.: Brookings Institution, 1968.

Thelwell, Michael. "The August 28th March on Washington: The Castrated Giant." In *Duties, Pleasures and Conflicts: Essays in Struggle*, ed. Michael Thelwell, 57–73. Amherst: University of Massachusetts Press, 1987.

Thornton, J. Mills. "Challenge and Response in the Montgomery Bus Boycott of 1955–1956." *Alabama Review* 33 (July 1980), reprinted in Garrow, ed. *The Walking City*, 323–79.

———. *Dividing Lines: Municipal Politics and the Struggle for Civil Rights in Montgomery, Birmingham, and Selma.* Tuscaloosa: University of Alabama Press, 2002.

Thurman, Anne Spencer, ed. *For the Inward Journey: The Writings of Howard Thurman.* New York: Harcourt Brace Jovanovich, 1984.

Thurman, Howard. *With Head and Heart: The Autobiography of Howard Thurman.* New York: Harcourt Brace Jovanovich, 1979.

Tracy, James. *Direct Action: Radical Pacifism from the Union Eight to the Chicago Seven.* Chicago: University of Chicago Press, 1996.

Tyson, Timothy B. *Radio Free Dixie: Robert F. Williams and the Roots of Black Power.* Chapel Hill: University of North Carolina Press, 1999.

U.S. Congress. Senate. Subcommittee on Executive Reorganization. Committee on Government Operations. *Federal Role in Urban Affairs*, 89th Congress, 2nd session. Washington, D.C.: GPO, 1966.

Von Eschen, Penny M. *Race Against Empire: Black Americans and Anticolonialism, 1937–1957.* Ithaca, N.Y.: Cornell University Press, 1997.

Walker, Jack L. "Protest and Negotiation: A Case Study of Negro Leadership in Atlanta." In *Atlanta, Georgia, 1960–1961: Sit-Ins and Student Activism*, ed. David J. Garrow. New York: Carlson, 1989.

Warren, Robert Penn. *Who Speaks for the Negro?* New York: Random House, 1965.

Watters, Pat. *Down to Now: Reflections on the Southern Civil Rights Movement.* New York: Pantheon, 1971.

Watters, Pat, and Reese Cleghorn. *Climbing Jacob's Ladder: The Arrival of Negroes in Southern Politics.* New York: Harcourt Brace and World, 1967.

Weir, Margaret. *Politics and Jobs: The Boundaries of Employment Policy in the United States.* Princeton, N.J.: Princeton University Press, 1992.

Weiss, Nancy J. *Whitney M. Young, Jr. and the Struggle for Civil Rights.* Princeton, N.J.: Princeton University Press, 1989.

White, John. "Nixon *Was* the One: Edgar Daniel Nixon, the MIA and the Montgomery Bus Boycott." In *The Making of Martin Luther King and the Civil Rights Movement*, ed. Brian Ward and Tony Badger, 45–63. New York: New York University Press, 1996.

Wigginton, Eliot. *Refuse to Stand Silently By: An Oral History of Grass Roots Social Activism in America, 1921–1964.* New York: Doubleday, 1992.

Wills, Garry. *Nixon Agonistes: The Crisis of the Self-Made Man.* Boston: Houghton Mifflin, 1970.

Wilson, Joseph F., ed. *Tearing Down the Color Bar: A Documentary History and Analysis of the Brotherhood of Sleeping Car Porters.* New York: Columbia University Press, 1989.

Wofford, Harris. *Of Kennedys and Kings: Making Sense of the Sixties.* Pittsburgh: University of Pittsburgh Press, 1992.

Wright, Gavin. "Economic Consequences of the Southern Protest Movement." In *New Directions in Civil Rights Studies*, ed. Armstead L. Robinson and Patricia Sullivan, 175–83. Charlottesville: University of Virginia Press, 1991.

———. *Old South, New South: Revolutions in the Southern Economy Since the Civil War.* New York: Basic Books, 1986.

X, Malcolm. *Malcolm X Speaks: Selected Speeches and Statements.* Ed. George Breitman. New York: Grove Weidenfeld, 1990.

Yeakey, Lamont H. "The Montgomery, Alabama Bus Boycott, 1955–56." Ph.D. diss., Columbia University, 1979.

Young, Andrew. *An Easy Burden: The Civil Rights Movement and the Transformation of America.* New York: HarperCollins, 1996.

Young, Marilyn Blatt. *The Vietnam Wars, 1945–1990.* New York: HarperCollins, 1991.

Zarefsky, David. *President Johnson's War on Poverty: Rhetoric and History.* University: University of Alabama Press, 1986.

Zaroulis, Nancy L., and Gerald Sullivan. *Who Spoke Up? American Protest Against the War in Vietnam, 1963–1975.* Garden City, N.Y.: Doubleday, 1984.

Index

Schorr, Daniel, 349
SCLC Newsletter, 145, 185, 205
Scott, Obie, 47
Scripto strike (1964), 212–13, 229
Sea Pak Shrimp Factories (Georgia), 147–48
Seay, Rev. S. S., 78
Seeger, Pete, 76
self-help, 3, 12, 70, 92, 137, 253, 257
Self-Help Against Poverty with Everyone
  (SHAPE), 267, 269
Sellars, Clyde C., 55
Selma campaign (1965), 219–25; arrests, 222;
  Bloody Sunday, 223; and Johnson, 221–23; as
  march against poverty, 224; and the media,
  220; national sympathy demonstrations, 223;
  night marches, 222; economic reprisals for,
  232–33; and strategy of nonviolent theater, 6,
  220, 223
Selma Emergency Relief Fund Service, 233
Senate Subcommittee on Employment, Manpower and Poverty, 269
Senate Subcommittee on Investigations, 333–34
Senate Subcommittee on Labor and Public
  Welfare, 170
Senior Citizens Committee (Birmingham),
  162–63, 165
sermons and speeches: "The Challenge of
  Communism to Christianity," 42; "Dives
  and Lazarus," 48; early sermons on economic equality, 47–49; Easter sermon
  (1959), 101; "Good Samaritan," 298; "I Have
  a Dream," 1, 181, 359; "A Knock at Midnight," 48–49; "mountaintop" speech, 352;
  Palm Sunday sermon (1959), 100–101; Riverside Church address (1967), 309, 317–18, 319–
  20, 322–23, 324–25; "Three Dimensions of a
  Complete Life," 48; "Transformed Nonconformist," 41
Shannon, Kay, 354, 356
sharecropping system in rural South, 143–44
Shaw, John, 311
Sherrod, Charles, 208, 212; and Albany Movement, 149, 152–53, 154; and anti-poverty politics, 266; and SNCC, 118, 144
Shriver, Sargent, 235, 262
Shuttlesworth, Fred: and Birmingham, 18, 85,
  155–56, 157–59, 160, 161; and Birmingham
  bombings, 185; and King legacy, 363; on
  nonviolence, 106; and SCLC, 76, 104
Silberman, Charles, 253
Simms, Rev. B. J., 57
Simpkins, S. O., 88

Simpson, Judge Bryant, 191
Sitton, Claude, 116, 117, 150, 162, 165
situationist sociology, 32–33
Six-Day War (1967), 325
Small Business Administration, 304
Smiley, Rev. Glenn, 61–62, 73, 116
Smith, Bertha, 65
Smith, Rev. Kelly Miller, 76, 112
Smith, Kenneth, 37
Smith, Lillian, 61, 94
Smitherman, Joseph, 266–67
Smyer, Sidney, 162, 163
social gospel tradition, 25–26, 30–31, 33–36, 71
Socialist Party, 61, 71, 103, 120
Social Security Act, 124, 266
Solidarity Day (Poor People's March on Wash-
  ington, June 19, 1968), 358
South Africa, 12, 83, 129, 314–15, 323
Southern Christian Leadership Conference
  (SCLC), 6, 10, 13; and Albany Movement,
  148, 150, 154; and Birmingham protests, 155–
  56, 158–60, 163–65; Chicago Freedom Movement and urban activism, 280–82, 284, 285,
  290, 302, 304–5; economic programs, 304–5;
  and international movements, 78; and
  King's antiwar activism, 312, 315–16; and
  King's fund-raising, 78; leaders, personalities, and goals, 76–79; leadership and new
  campaigns (1964), 190–91; and Levison, 77,
  78–79, 86, 104; and March on Washington,
  171, 176; and militant direct action tactics, 13,
  77, 105–6, 219; Ministers Leadership Training Program, 344–45; and Negro-labor alliance, 85, 87, 280–81; northern protests and
  political organizing (1965), 228; OEO grants,
  265; Operation Breadbasket, 304; organizational structure, 75, 78; and Poor People's
  March, 341, 342–43, 344; SCLC-CCCO coalition, 280, 284, 285, 290; and sexism, 146; St.
  Augustine protests, 190–91; voting rights
  campaigns, 77–78, 85–90, 104–5, 145, 219–25,
  235. *See also* Chicago Freedom Movement
  (1966); Citizenship Education Programs
  (CEPs)
Southern Conference Educational Fund, 95,
  130, 211, 227
Southern Negro Leaders Conference on Transportation and Non-violent Integration
  (1957), 77–78
Southern Regional Council, 125
Southern Rural Action, 236

Acknowledgments

Nothing better exemplifies Martin Luther King's conviction about our fundamental interdependence than the writing of this book. First, thank you to the thousands of people, acknowledged and unacknowledged in these pages, who made and interpreted this movement for human rights and economic justice. I owe an equally great debt to all my interlocutors and readers who sharpened my interpretations and lent me their wisdom. The skilled librarians and archivists I met were invariably gracious and interested in this project, especially Dianne Ware, Charles Niles, and Gail Malmgreen. At Stanford University's History Department, Clayborne Carson, George Fredrickson, David Kennedy, John McGreevy, Jim Tracy, and Stewart Burns all helped me sharpen my questions at early stages of research. Clay Carson's scholarship, criticism, friendship, and stewardship of the King Papers Project has been invaluable. So has David Garrow's pioneering work and the body of research materials he has gathered. Vincent Harding encouraged this effort and modeled the activist scholar, and Henry Hampton showed what a life of dedicated public education could be. So did three scholars and teachers without whose inspiration I would never have followed this path: Leona Fisher, Michael Foley, and Dorothy Brown.

This study would have been impossible without generous institutions willing to invest in my curiosity. I owe a special debt to the Social Science Research Council for financial support and for bringing me in contact with the luminaries of historical poverty research, especially Michael Katz, Tom Sugrue, Robin Kelley, and Alice O'Connor, inspirations and discerning critics all. Northwestern University's Center for Urban Affairs and Policy Research provided financial support and sage advice from Christopher Jencks, Rebecca Blank, and William Julius Wilson. Doug McAdam and all the participants in the NEH summer seminar on the 1960s championed my interest in media criticism and popular culture. At Smith College and the University of Massachusetts, my work benefited from the companionship and criticism of Carl Nightingale, Kevin Boyle, Leo Malley, Victoria Gettis, Jack Wilson, and Dan Horowitz.

Thanks to the University of Pennsylvania's History Department, the Mellon Foundation, and the Russell Sage Foundation for supporting this and related projects. The International Center for Advanced Study at New York University under Tom Bender's extraordinary leadership assembled a talented group of researchers interested in exploring spaces of insurgent citizenship. The ICAS seminars enriched this book and my urban knowledge immeasurably. All these institutions exposed me to wonderful colleagues, readers, and interlocutors: Dana Barron, Carole Browner, Michael Jones-Correa, Julian Wolpert, Rob Lieberman, Mary Lewis, Jordana Dym, Wendell Pritchett, Sumner Rosen, Frances Fox Piven, Richard Cloward, and Martha Biondi. Allen Hunter's feedback surpasses all.

Here in North Carolina, I have found the most generous of readers in Walter Jackson, Bill Link, and Felicia Kornbluh, whose greenhouse of economic justice research has complemented my own. The Virginia Foundation for the Humanities provided an essential semester for writing in the stimulating and supportive company of Bill Freehling, Gordon Hylton, Roberta Culbertson, and Victoria Sanford. A million thanks to Kent Germany and Guian McKee at the University of Virginia's Miller Center, who opened my ears to the rich and bizarre world of presidential audiotapes. Recently, Michael Honey, Alice O'Connor, Kevin Boyle, Charles Payne, Jacqueline Rouse, and Robert Korstad all lent this project their invaluable eyes, ears, and constructive commentary.

I have been blessed with generous support for research assistants at Smith College and University of North Carolina at Greensboro. Their energy and enthusiasm for discovery continually freshened the well of this project: Kate Steinbeck, Stephanie Kendall, Gina Rourke, Sarah Burnett, Todd Pfeffer, Adam Arney, and Seth King. "Do I find you in good study?"

I am deeply grateful to the team at Penn Press for helping bring this ship into port. Peter Agree has been an ideal editor, patiently tutoring me in the intricacies of publishing. And I mean patiently. Series editors Thomas Sugrue and Michael Kazin each generously lent their time and prodigious insights. Jennifer Backer as copyeditor and Noreen O'Connor-Abel as project editor are exemplars of editorial precision and good humor. Finally, I cannot adequately express my gratitude to Grey Osterud. Grey knows better than anyone how to guide an author through mental storms to the calm eye, where we chisel away "all that is not elephant."

Friends and family have sustained me by balancing the scholarly enterprise with their warmth, laughter, travails, and support. Thanks especially to my mother, Dorothy Jackson, who always knew I had found my "calling"; to my siblings Martha, Anne, Johnny, Joe, and Mary and their families; and to Kay and Thor Krogh. Finally thanks to those friends and stalwarts whose encouragement, music, and love of adventure made this project a joy to escape from and to come back to: Anne Dykers, Tracy Erwin, Bob and Stephanie Mignon, Ellen Bruno, Dean McComb, Mike Fleming, the Martin and Guild guitar companies, Sabrina Odessa, Laurie Ruth, Jose Mestre, Janet Benton, Maureen Gillespie, Shari and Otto Fineman, Clara Sumpf, Andrew Light, Kathy Franz, Rick Barton, Jamie Anderson, Sallie Reid, Steve Berman, Elizabeth Gosch, Etty Cohen, Andrew Krystal, and Doug Waldruff. A million thanks to you all.